THEGREENGUIDE
South Korea

Decoration on the eaves, Sinheungsa, Seoraksan National Park, Gangwon-do
© Christophe Boisvieux/age fotostock

MICHELIN

THEGREENGUIDE **SOUTH KOREA**

Special thanks goes to the Korea Tourism Organization (KTO) and the **Korean Food Foundation (KFF)** for their help in the creation of this guide. Thank you to all the team at Michelin Korea: Arnaud Montigny, Anne-France Mattlet, Younseo Rhee, Chloé Tassel, Didier Broussard, Maria Gasper

Editorial Manager	Jonathan Gilbert
Editors	Nicole Jordan, JMS Books
Contributing Writers	Benjamin Joinau, Élisabeth Chabanol, Colonel Alain Nass, Patrick Beaudouin, Philippe Pataud-Célérier, Patrick Maurus, Nicolas Piccato, Xavier Liaudet, Oliver Duke
Production Manager	Natasha G. George
Cartography	Stéphane Anton, Michèle Cana, Thierry Lemasson, ©2010 Cartography data YeongJin/Michelin
Photo Editor	Yoshimi Kanazawa
Photo Researcher	Nicole D. Jordan
Proofreader	Margaret Browning
Interior Design	Chris Bell
Cover Design	Chris Bell, Christelle Le Déan
Layout	Michelin Apa Publications Ltd., Nicole D. Jordan
Cover Layout	Michelin Apa Publications Ltd.
Contact Us	The Green Guide Michelin Travel and Lifestyle One Parkway South Greenville, SC 29615 USA www.michelintravel.com Michelin TravelPartner Hannay House 39 Clarendon Road Watford, Herts WD17 1JA UK ℘01923 205240 www.ViaMichelin.com travelpubsales@uk.michelin.com
Special Sales	For information regarding bulk sales, customized editions and premium sales, please contact our Customer Service Departments: USA 1-800-432-6277 UK 01923 205240 Canada 1-800-361-8236

PLANNING YOUR TRIP

The blue-tabbed PLANNING YOUR TRIP section gives you **ideas for your trip** and **practical information** to help you organize it. You'll find tours, practical information, a host of outdoor activities, a calendar of events, information on shopping, sightseeing, kids' activities and more.

INTRODUCTION

The orange-tabbed INTRODUCTION section explores **South Korea**'s **Nature** and geology. The **History** section spans from the prehistoric period to the three kingdoms and through the Korean War. The **Art and Culture** section covers architecture, art, literature and music, while **South Korea Today** delves into the modern region.

DISCOVERING

The green-tabbed DISCOVERING section features Principal Sights by province, featuring the most interesting local **Sights**, **Walking Tours**, nearby **Excursions** and detailed **Driving Tours**. Admission prices shown are normally for a single adult.

ADDRESSES

We've selected the best hotels, restaurants, cafes, shops, nightlife and entertainment to fit all budgets. See the Legend on the cover flap for an explanation of the price categories. See the back of the guide for an index of hotels and restaurants.

Sidebars

Throughout the guide you will find blue, orange and green-colored text boxes with lively anecdotes, detailed history and background information.

☺ A Bit of Advice ☺

Green advice boxes found in this guide contain practical tips and handy information relevant to your visit or to a sight in the Discovering section.

STAR RATINGS★★★

Michelin has given star ratings for more than 100 years. If you're pressed for time, we recommend you visit the ★★★ or ★★ sights first:

★★★ **Highly recommended**
★★ **Recommended**
★ **Interesting**

MAPS

- ☺ Princpal Sights map.
- ☺ Region maps.
- ☺ Maps for major cities and villages.
- ☺ Local tour maps.

All maps in this guide are oriented north, unless otherwise indicated by a directional arrow. The term "Local Map" refers to a map within the chapter or Tourism Region. A complete list of the maps found in the guide appears at the back of this book.

© KTO

PLANNING YOUR TRIP

INTRODUCTION TO SOUTH KOREA

CONTENTS

Hwaeseong Fortress, Suwon

©KTO

DISCOVERING SOUTH KOREA

N Seoul Tower, Seoul

©Esther Arnet/Michelin

Welcome to South Korea

A journey through South Korea is a journey of discovery. Explore remote Buddhist temples hidden among the lush forests of the national parks, walk the walls of ancient fortresses and palaces, wander national museums and art galleries of every kind or introduce your taste buds to a unique culinary style. From the big cities to the small rural villages, the Korean people are welcoming and their culture is rich with tradition, history and spirituality.

SEOUL (pp98-215)

Located in the northwest corner of the country and as the capital of South Korea, Seoul has quickly grown into a megacity with slightly less than half of the country's entire population living in the greater Seoul area. Despite the rapid growth of this industrialized city, Seoul has maintained its individual character and has worked hard to protect and embrace its history. Temples, *Hanok* villages (with traditional Korean houses) and five major palaces dot the city landscape and vie for space alongside skyscrapers and high-speed transit lines. Traditional markets are a treasure-trove for bargain hunters and browsers, while name-brand shops and fashion boutiques appeal to those looking for more runway fashion and less flea-market finds.

With Bukhansan National Park located at the outskirts of the city, a hike toward the granite peaks or an overnight stay in one of the park's shelters enables travelers to explore some of the peninsula's natural bounties.

GYEONGGI-DO (pp216-231)

Surrounding the capital city, Gyeonggi-do is the most populous province in South Korea. The region offers a variety of daytrips for those basing their visit in Seoul. The walls of Hwaseong Fortress, a UNESCO World Heritage site, can transport you back in time to the late 18C, when the fortress and accompanying palace were first built. A little farther to the north lies the DMZ (demilitarized zone), which separates North and South Korea and is the most heavily militarized border in the world. Special tours are arranged for visiting the area.

GANGWON-DO (pp232-257)

Gangwon-do beaches are a summer hot spot for those escaping the busy urban areas and trying the local seafood is a must. But the province also shines during the winter. The snow falls first in Gangwon-do and stays here longer than in any other region in the country, which is a delight to skiers.

Nature reigns supreme in this province; the lovely Seoraksan National Park offers hikes for those wanting just a pleasant wooded stroll or those looking for a true mountain climb. Listed as a biosphere reserve with UNESCO, the park has more than 1,500 animal species and a diversity of rare flora living here.

GYEONGSANG-DO (pp258-315)

This province is rich in history, having seen the rise and fall of royal power over the centuries. Among the larger cities, such as Daegu (famed for textiles, traditional medicine and baseball) and Busan (South Korea's second-largest city), Buddhist temples and Confucian academies are pleasant spots for reflection and often offer amazing views of the nearby scenery. Gyeongju, a smaller but incredibly influential city in the province, is steeped in history and could almost be considered a museum in itself. From the Daereung-won Tumuli Park (royal tombs) at the center of the city to outstanding exhibits at the Gyeongju National Museum and the nearby Bulguk Temple and Seokguram Grotto, this ancient royal capital is a destination all its own.

JEOLLA-DO *(pp316-355)*

South Korea's southernmost region is a delight for the senses. Along with the well-preserved Seonamsa and Songgwangsa temples, a museum dedicated to the regions 2,000 dolmens and the area's national and provincial parks, the World Kimchi Culture Festival also takes place in Gwangju each year. Visitors can get back to nature in the protected wetlands of Suncheon Bay by participating in an ecotour of the area.

JEJU-DO *(pp356-373)*

As South Korea's largest island, situated southwest of Jeolla-do, Jeju-do is a province quite literally set apart. The volcanic island has long been touted as the "Hawaii" of South Korea, and although it has lost a bit of popularity with its countrymen in recent years, the island is as beautiful as ever. Strewn about with curious-looking dol hareubang (stone grandfathers), Jeju-do has a subtropical climate that keeps it warmer than the rest of the country, but four distinct seasons are still evident. Natural wonders abound and visitors may explore caves, the extinct volcano Seongsan Ilchulbong,

Suncheon Bay, Jeolla-do ©KTO

waterfalls, or Hallasan National Park, which encompasses the country's highest peak.

CHUNGCHEONG-DO *(pp374-405)*

Located in the middle, western part of the peninsula, Chungcheong-do is actually split into two halves— Chungcheongnam-do and Chungcheongbuk-do (the only landlocked province in the country). The region is mainly mountains, but offers a wonderful beach along the coast at Daecheon.

Although also known as South Korea's transportation hub, the city of Daejeon, the country's fifth largest city, has a rich cultural heritage, a lovely national park and is home to Ungno Lee Museum of Art, an exceptional art museum.

Explore the royal tombs at Gongju and make time to stop at the Gongju National Museum to view some of the spectacular exhibits. Not to be outdone, the Buyeo National Museum also has remarkable items on display.

Cheonggyecheon Stream, Seoul
© KTO

What to See and Do

TRADITIONAL DANCE AND OPERA

DANCE

Samulnori

Meaning "four instruments," *samulnori* is played by a group of four musicians. Each plays a different percussion instrument and dances while the long white ribbons on their hats swirl around them.

Salpuri

Originally, *salpuri* was a shamanist dance for chasing away evil spirits. The solo dancer improvises, and the rhythm gets gradually faster until a trance-like state is reached, the climax of the performance (see also p81).

Talchum

This masked dance began as a show performed by groups of traveling dancers. *Talchum* combines comedy, song and recitation in a satirical show, often targeting the nobility.
The masks represent traditional stock characters: the aristocrat, the grandmother, the monk, the monkey, the concubine, the servant and the shaman.

Buchaechum

This traditional ceremonial dance usually features a group of female dancers dressed in *hanbok*, a colorful traditional Korean costume. Dancers perform complex steps and manipulate fans to represent flowers, waves and butterflies.

OPERA

Pansori

Also known as Korean folk opera, *pansori* involves just two people—a singer and a drummer. Together, they perform ancient songs telling a story, which were originally handed down orally, and were particularly popular in the 19C (see also Music and Dance p81 and p329).

Changgeuk

The *changgeuk* is a more recent variant of *pansori* but is performed like a play. The performance might involve as many as 30 actors accompanied by an orchestra of around 50 musicians.

SPORTS AND ACTIVITIES

TAEKWONDO

This Korean martial art, practiced worldwide, is a source of national pride and is now recognized as an Olympic sport. Today, young Koreans learn and practice it during their 21 months of military service (see also p94).

SSIREUM

The national ancestral sport of wrestling, *ssireum* is practiced within a ring covered in fine sand, where adversaries grab each other's *satba*, a belted undergarment, and try to bring each other down. A match ends when one of the wrestlers makes contact with the ground with any part of his body, other than his feet. In the past, the winner of a *ssireum* tournament was given an ox as a prize, symbolizing his strength. Tournaments still take place today, especially during the lunar New Year and *Chuseok*, the harvest festival.

KARAOKE

There's no escaping karaoke; it is literally everywhere, but if the thought of crooning along to your favorite tune in front of an unknown public is too intimidating, hire a *noraebang*. This is a private room, normally hired by small groups of people, equipped with a microphone and a screen for the lyrics. (A *dallanjujeom* is another variation that usually features hostesses.) Alcohol is not normally served in a *noraebang*.

HIKING

The national parks are ideal for hiking. Clearly marked and well laid out (with rope supports for tricky areas), the parks are the green lungs of South Korea and are assiduously protected by the state. There are around 20 designated national parks, and the best seasons to explore them are, of course, fall, when the leaves are a glorious mix of golden-brown and red, and spring, when the azalea, forsythia and cherry trees are in bloom. *More information*: http://english.knps. or.kr.

SPAS

If it's within your budget, the best way to enjoy a spa in South Korea for the first time is to visit one of the luxurious thermal baths situated in the grand hotels (⏱ *see also Introduction to South Korea p87*). Here is a selection:

Asan – in Chungcheongnam-do, in the Onyang district of Asan, these "historic" baths are at the **Onyang Hot Spring Hotel** – ☎(041)-545-2141, www.onyanghotel.co.kr.
Asan Spavis (about 1hr from Seoul), a water park with outdoor pools – ☎(041)-539-2000, www.spavis.co.kr (in Korean); or **Asan Oncheon Hotel** – ☎(041)-541-5526, www.asanonchon. co.kr (in Korean).

Bugok – A vast spa resort not far from Daegu, Gyeongsangnam-do, **BugokHawaii** – ☎(055)-536-6331, www.bugokhawaii.co.kr.

Busan – There are several spas in the town. **Haesurak** on Songjeong Beach for thalassotherapy – ☎(051)-702-1995, www.haesurak.com (in Korean).
On **Haeundae Beach**, baths with a sea view at **Paradise Hotel** – ☎(051)-742-2121, www.paradise.co.kr. In the hot springs district of Dongnae, the Heoshimcheong baths at **Nongshim Hotel** – ☎(051)-550-2100, www.hotelnongshim.com.

Deoksan – Hot springs and saunas at **Deoksan Spa Castle**, Chungcheongnam-do – ☎(041)-330-8000, www.resom.co.kr/eng/index.html.

Icheon – The closest spa to Seoul, **Spa Plus**, is in **Hotel Miranda** in

Gyeonggi-do – ☎(031)-639-5000, www.mirandahotel.com.

Namhae – In Jeolla, in the south of the country, an attractive luxury resort combining a spa and golf course facing the sea, **Hilton Namhae** – ☎(055)-860-0100, www.hiltonnamhae.com.

Osaek – A beautiful valley in a mountain location combining hot and bubbling springs, **Green Yard Hotel** – ☎(033)-670-1000, www.greenyardhotel.com (in Korean).

Seoraksan – In Gangwon-do, two large resorts with waterparks: **Daemyung Resort Hotel** – ☎(82)-1588-4888, www.daemyung resort.com; and Seorak Waterpia at **Hanhwa Resort** – ☎(033)-635-7700, www.seorakwaterpia.co.kr.

Seoul – Yongsan Dragon Hill Spa – *40-713 Hangangno 3-ga, Yongsan-gu.* Ⓜ *Yongsan, line 1, exit 1.* ☎(02)-792-0001; www.dragonhillspa.co.kr. ⏱*Open daily 24hr, ₩10,000 5am–8pm; ₩12,000 8pm–5am.* A vast complex with hot baths and saunas on several levels. There's also a rooftop swimming pool, a golf driving range, numerous treatment rooms and even an icy-cold igloo-style area.

Central City – Central Spa – *Central City, 118 Banpo-dong, Seocho-gu.* Ⓜ *Express Bus Terminal, lines 7/3, exits 4/7.* ☎(02)-6282-3400. www.centralspa.co.kr (in Korean). ⏱*Open daily 24hr, ₩10,000 5am–9pm; ₩13,000 9pm–5am.* Classic Korean spa in the Central City mall adjoining the Marriott Hotel, on the first floor. Enjoy all the benefits of the *jjimjilbang* (bathhouse) in this traditional complex comprising baths, saunas, massages and relaxation rooms.

Yuseong – Traditional baths near Daejeon at **Hotel Spapia** – ☎ (042)-600-6006/6007, www.hotelspapia.com.

SHOPPING
OPENING TIMES

Department stores are generally open 10:30am–7:30pm/8pm, while other shops stay open until 10pm. Local mini-marts never close. Traditional markets, such as those at Dongdaemun and Namdaemun in Seoul, are also open all night.

SALES

Sales take place in department stores in January, April, July, October and December.

TAX

VAT is deducted when you buy articles in stores displaying the "tax free shopping" logo.

WHAT TO BUY
Liquor and Tea

Among the traditional liquors, there is the ubiquitous *makgeolli* (Korean rice wine). You will also find the millet wine *munbaeju*, which is considered one of the best Korean spirits.

As for tea, there are plenty of choices: everyday teas, ginseng tea (*insamcha*), green tea (*nokcha*)—in particular from Boseong (▶ *see p341*), citron (*yuzu*) tea (*yujacha),* cinnamon tea (*saenggangcha*), Job's Tears tea (*yulmucha)* made from the grain of this tropical plant, corn tea (*oksusucha*), jujube tea (*daechucha*), and the envigorating tea tonic *ssanghwacha*.

Antiques

It is prohibited to take objects, such as ceramics and pieces of calligraphy, that are more than 50 years old out of the country. If in doubt, check with the *Art and Antique Assessment Office –* ☎*(032)-740-2921.* Be suspicious of items purporting to be antiques that are cheap or relatively so since they could be fakes. However, you should be able to buy good copies at a reasonable price.

Handicrafts

South Korea's handicrafts have been protected thanks, in part, to its **Living National Treasures**—people who embody the perceived attributes of the nation. In this case they are the skilled artisans who practice traditional crafts. Selected by a committee of experts from the Korean Cultural Office, these talented men and women are responsible for maintaining and teaching such traditional skills as embroidery, woodwork, ceramics, papermaking, mother-of-pearl and lacquer work, and kite- and fan-making. ▶*See also Introduction to South Korea p95.*

Contemporary Art

Eclipsed by the art of China and Japan, Korea's contemporary art remains little known internationally, yet not only does Korean art decipher and portray Korean society brilliantly, but also its forms of artistic expression are unique and of a fine quality. Contemporary Korean photography can be a good investment. Although some photographers have moved abroad, following in the footsteps of Kim Atta or Koo Bohnchang, others whose work is likely to be of interest to collectors have remained.

Kim Jae Kyeongone has been compassionately documenting Seoul's rapid urbanization for some 20 years; while Kim Young-Sung has been uncovering South Korea's history through his photography. Other names to look out for are: Chung Chuha, Lee Gap Chul, Lee Sanghyun, Lee Sungeun, In Hyojin, Noh Suntag, Park Area and Won Seoung Won.

Contemporary Art Galleries
Photography

Gallery K.o.n.g – 157-78 Samcheong-dong, Jongno-gu, Seoul. ☎(02)-738-7776, www.gallerykong.com.

Gallery Now – 3F Seongji Bldg, 192-13 Gwanhun-dong, Jongno-gu, Seoul. ☎(02)-725-2930, www.gallery-now.com.

Korea
Be Inspired

Where can you find the best shopping at 2 a.m?

In Korea, anything is possible. Tomorrow's trends and fashion come out today. Where else can you get designer clothes custom tailored at 2 a.m. and pick them up the next day?

*For more information about South
Korean contemporary art* ⓒ*see Seoul
pp 129–130.*

Food

A globally recognized Korean specialty
kimchi (ⓒ *see p90*) is a side dish based
on fermented vegetables seasoned
with paprika. Today there are more
than 160 varieties of kimchi. Also good
to take home are: dried and roasted
seaweed; seafood in brine; the well-
known red pepper paste (*gochujang*);
and, for those with a sweet tooth,
attractive boxes of *hangwa*, a
traditional honey-based confection.

Ginseng

Ginseng, or *insam* in Korean (ⓒ *see
box p385*), is a medicinal plant.
Among other benefits, it is said to
calm the mind and strengthen the
vital organs. As with the mandrake,
with slender roots growing from a
central fleshy part, the root of the
ginseng plant can often look like
a human body, which apparently
increases its healing powers.
Ginseng root is available in various
forms—in its natural state, dried,
peeled or even steamed.

Ceramics

First produced in about 6,000 BC,
Korean ceramics are still renowned
for their finesse and elegance, and
they are widely admired around Asia.
Ceramics have undergone something
of a revival in recent years (ⓒ *see
Seoul Addresses, pp132, 148, 170, 180
and 186*).

SHOPPING PROGRAM

"First Premium Shopping" is a title
of authorization that is given by the
government to shops providing
goods and service of superior quality.
The aim of the program is to help
travelers have a safe and secure
shopping experience.
A pink panel certificate at the entrance
of shops will help you recognize them.
*For more information, visit the "shopping"
section at www.visitkorea.or.kr*

FAKE BRANDS

The counterfeiting of luxury brands is
a considerable problem.
Beware of buying "fake" items. You
may be fined or have the items
confiscated by customs officials on
your return.

BOOKS

*Eating Korean: From Barbeque to
Kimchi, Recipes from My Kitchen*
by Cecilia Hae-Jin (Wiley &
Sons, 2005)
*Seoultown Food: Korean–American
Recipes to Share with Family
and Friends* by Debbie Lee
(Kyle Books, 2011)
Mastering Korean (Barron's Educational
Series, 2008)
20th Century Korean Art by Kim
Youngnu (Laurence King, 2005)
Korea Style by Marcia Iwatate and Kim
Unsoo (Tuttle, 2006)
The Korean War by Max Hastings
(Simon and Schuster, 1998)
Fire and Ice: The Korean War 1950–1953,
by Michael Varhola
(Da Capo Press, 2000)
*Meeting Mr Kim: How I Went to Korea
and Learned to Love Kimchi*
by Jennifer Barclay
(Wakefield Press, 2008)
*Everlasting Flower: A History of
Korea* by Keith Pratt (Reaktion
Books, 2007)
Korea and Her Neighbours by Isabella
Bird (republished by BiblioBazaar,
2010)
*Korea: A Walk Through the Land of
Miracles* by Simon Winchester
(Harper Perennial, 2005)
*The Northern Region of Korea: History,
Identity and Culture* edited by Sun Joo
Kim (University of Washington
Press, 2010)
*The Columbia Anthology of Modern
Korean Poetry* (Columbia University
Press, 2004)

FICTION

*Land of Exile: Contemporary Korean
Fiction* by various authors (East
Gate Books, 2007). A collection of

short stories written after
the Korean War.

One Thousand Chestnut Trees by Mira
Stout (Riverhead Trade, 1999).
A woman in search of her past in
an enigmatic country—a mix of
memoir and fiction.

Please Look After Mom by Kyung-Sook
Shin (Knopf, 2011). A mother
disappears in the crowds at a train
station and her selfish family is
consumed with guilt.

The Curse of Kim's Daughters by Park
Kyong-ni (Homa & Sekey, 2005).
A fascinating insight into how
Korean society evolved during the
first part of the 20C.

The Living Reed by Pearl S Buck.
(Reissue by Moyer Bell, 2004).
Four generations of an aristocratic
family live through events from
the end of the 19C to World War II.

When My Name was Keoko by Linda
Sue Park (Yearling, 2004).
A brother and sister battle to
retain their identities in Japanese-
occupied Korea.

MAGAZINES

Koreana is a quarterly magazine on
Korean art and culture, published
by the Korea Foundation –
www.koreana.or.kr.

FILMS

Most of the films listed below are
available on DVD.

BONG Joon-ho, *Memories of Murder*,
2003. Based on a true story, this
detective film launched both
Bong Joon-ho and actor Song
Kang-ho. It describes the pursuit
of a serial killer in a Korea in full
economic boom. In *The Host*, 2006,
a monster is born in the huge river
that crosses Seoul due to an error
by the US military—a hilarious
veiled criticism of Korean society
and a big box-office success.

IM Kwon-taek, one of the great
Korean directors: *Chunhyang*,
2000; and *Drunk on Women
and Poetry*, 2002, a masterpiece
(director's prize at Cannes) that
retraces the life of Jang Seung-
eup, a quixotic 19C Korean artist.

IM Sang-soo, *The President's Last
Bang*, 2005. Detective film telling
the story, through a rose-tinted
lens, of the assassination of
President Park Chung-hee.

JEON Soo-il, *With the Girl of Black
Soil*, 2007. A prizewinner at Venice
and typical of Korean realism and
the work of director Soo-il Jeon,
a rite-of-passage film following a
young girl growing up in a hostile
environment.

JO Beom-jin, *Aachi & Ssipak*, 2006.
A crazy 2D animation and a
scatological parody of Korean
society that has become a
standard of "underground" Korean
culture. Not suitable for children.

KANG Je-gyu, *Brotherhood*, 2004.
The Korean War seen through the
destinies of two brothers.

KIM Jee-woon, *A Bittersweet Life*,
2004. A detective movie with
many influences, from Melville to
Tarantino, representative of the
Korean new wave. *The Good, the
Bad, the Weird*, 2008, a "kimchi
Western": a spectacular Korean
homage to Sergio Leone, with
several famous Korean wave
actors, retelling an Asian epic in
Mongolia.

KIM Ki-duk, *3-Iron*, 2004. Korean
cinema's biggest international hit
is a story of love and solitude in
an eerily silent 21C Seoul. *Spring,
Summer, Fall, Winter... and Spring*,
2003, is a poetic Buddhist film
centred on the redemption of a
man living in a Korea that fulfills
the Western fantasy of Asia.

KWAK Kyung-taek, *Friend*, 2001.
Four friends who grew up in the
Korea of the 1970s meet again at
the dawn of the new century and
realise what different paths their
lives have taken.

LEE Chang-dong, *Poetry*, 2010,
a grandmother is afflicted by
Alzheimer's disease while taking
poetry classes. Screenplay prize
at Cannes 2010.

LEE Jeong-hyang, *The Way Home*,
2002. The charming tale of a small-
town boy sent to stay with his
grandmother in the countryside,
and he doesn't understand her,
but he learns to. This film has
made audiences across the world
reach for their handkerchiefs.

LEE Myung-se, *Duelist*, 2005. In the
Korea of the 17C, Namsoon, a
young female investigator who
belongs to a unit of women
charged with looking after the
nobility and resolving delicate
problems, hunts down a rebel who
is a virtuoso swordsman. A martial
arts film, with impressive visuals,
that flies in the face of criticism of
the genre.

PARK Chan-wook, *JSA*, 2000.
A seminal film of the Korean
new wave on the male bonding
between soldiers from South and
North Korea guarding the border,
known as the Joint Security Area
(see p234).

ACTIVITIES FOR KIDS

In South Korea, children under 4 years
old travel free by train, and those aged
4–13 travel half-price. Children under
7 travel free on the subway and the
bus. See also the "Kids" pictogram
(👥) in the *Discovering* section.

SIGHTS AND ACTIVITES FOR FAMILIES

Chapter	Outdoor	Outings	Relaxing
Gyeongbokgung Bukchon (Seoul)		Watch the changing of the guard	Gyeongbok Palace, National Folk Museum
Gwanghwamun-Jongno (Seoul)	Changgyeong Palace's large park	Changgyeong Palace	*Jump*, show featuring martial arts. Ice-skating or splashing in the water in Gwanghwamun Square
Cheonggyecheon-City Hall (Seoul)	Green pedestrian area along Cheonggye Stream		The show *Nanta*
Jung-gu (Seoul)			Namsangol Hanok Village
Itaewon (Seoul)		Shop for video games at Yongsan Electronic Market; take in the view from N Seoul Tower	Traditional baths at Dragon Hill Spa
Teheran-no (Seoul)		Aquarium	
Mapo (Seoul)	Cruise on the Hangang; walk in parks	Panorama from top of the 63 Building	
Seodaemun (Seoul)		Agriculture Museum	

Southwest of Hangang (Seoul)			Swimming pools beside the Hangang
Songpa-gu-Jamsil (Seoul)		Lotte World Folk Museum	Lotte World amusement park
Suwon (Gyeonggi-do)		Hwaseong Fortress	Korean Folk Village; Everland amusement park
Seoraksan (Gangwon-do)	Cable car to Gwongeum		
Sokcho (Gangwon-do)	Sokcho and Naksan beaches	The US warshhip in Unification Park	
Gyeongju (Gyeongsang-do)	Good cycle rides		Bomun Lake Resort amusement parks
Busan (Gyeongsang-do)	Beaches, Dongnae cable car	Busan Aquarium; Jagalchi Market	
Jinju (Gyeongsang-do)	Hallyeo Maritime National Park; cable car to top of Mt. Mireuk		
Gwangju (Jeolla-do)		Gochang Dolmen Museum	
Mokpo (Jeolla-do)	Dadohae Haesang National Park	Boseong green tea plantations	
Mokpo to Yeosu (Jeolla-do)	Wolchulsan National Park; Yulpo Beach		
Yeosu (Jeolla-do)		Walk to Hyangiram hermitage; Yeosu Fish Market	
Suncheon (Jeolla-do)	Suncheon Bay		Suncheon Open Film Set
Jeonju (Jeolla-do)	Maisan Provincial Park	Nagan Folk Village	
Jeju-do	Water sports and activities		Amusement parks
Daejeon (Chungcheong-do)	Gyeryongsan National Park		Yuseong Spa hot springs
Buyeo (Chungcheong-do)	Daecheon Beach		Boryeong Mud Festival
Gongju (Chungcheong-do)	Watch changing of the guard beside the fortress		See a *pansori* performance; Baekje Cultural Festival

Calendar of Events

♿ For national public holidays, *see pp32–33.*

APRIL

Butterfly Festival – Hampyeong (Jeolla-do), late April to early May.
Jeonju International Film Festival – Jeonju (♿ *see p357*).
Kumdori Science Festival – Daejeon (♿ *see p392*).
Traditional Rice Cake and Drink Festival – Gyeongju (♿ *see p296*).

MAY

Damyang Bamboo Festival – Damyang (♿ *see p328*).
Herb Medicine Festival – Daegu (♿ *see p272*).
Jeonju Hanji Culture Festival – Jeonju, early May (♿ *see p357*).
Lotus Lantern Festival – Seoul (♿ *see p105*).

JULY

Boryeong Mud Festival – Boryeong (♿ *see p98 and p399*).

AUGUST

Gangjin Celadon Festival – Gangjin (♿ *see p341*).

SEPTEMBER

Geumsan Insam Festival – Geumsan (♿ *see p392*).
Gwangju Design Biennale – Gwangju, Sept–Nov. Next biennale in 2012 (♿ *see p333*).
International Mask Dance Festival – Andong (♿ *see p279*).
Moyang Fortress Festival – Gochang, around 9 Sept (♿ *see p333*).

OCTOBER

Baekje Cultural Festival – Buyeo and Gongju (♿ *see p407*).
Bibimbap Festival – Jeonju (♿ *see p357*).
Chilshimni Festival – Seogwipo (♿ *see p375*).
Daejeon International Balloon Fiesta– Daejeon (♿ *see p392*).
Jagalchi Festival – Busan (♿ *see p310*).
Reed Festival – Suncheon Bay (♿ *see p350*).
Southern Province Food Cultural Festival – Near Suncheon (♿ *see p350*).
World Kimchi Culture Festival – Gwangju (♿ *see p333*).

International Mask Dance Festival, Andong

©KTO

Know Before You Go

COUNTRY ID
Official name: Republic of Korea
Capital: Seoul
Area: 38,570sq mi/99,897sq km
Population: 50.5 million
Currency: won
Official language: Korean (*Hangeul*)

CLIMATE
Fall and spring are the ideal seasons to visit. The temperature varies between 51.8 and 78.8°F (11 and 26°C) during the day, so it is advisable to bring warm clothing for the evenings.
In **spring** (March–May), when azalea, forsythia and cherry trees are in bloom, there are numerous festivals, and it's an ideal time to discover South Korea's national parks.
The **summer** (June–August) is very hot and humid and includes the **rainy season** (beginning of July to the end of August). Storms and typhoons are fairly commonplace, so it is best to avoid this time.
Make the most of the dry weather and lovely blue skies of **fall** (September–November), when the trees put on a glorious golden-brown display—a perfect time for walks and excursions. By the time **winter** arrives, icy winds from Siberia sweep across the country and can cause the temperature to fall well below zero. This is the season when the *ondol* (underfloor heating), found in traditional-style accommodations, comes into its own and people take refuge from the cold in *oncheon* (thermal baths). Winter weather brings magical snowy landscapes.

USEFUL ADDRESSES
TOURIST OFFICES
The Korea Tourism Organization (KTO) has 27 offices abroad, in America, Europe, Oceania and Asia.
℘(82) 2-7299-497, www.visitkorea. or.kr/ (in English).

New York – KTO, 2 Executive Drive, Suite 750, Fort Lee, New Jersey, 07024, USA. ℘1-(201)-585-0909. Toll-free 1-800-TOUR-KOR(EA).
Canada – 700 Bay St, Suite 1903, Toronto. ℘1-(416)-348-9056.
London – KTO, 3rd Floor, New Zealand House, Haymarket, London SW1Y 4TE, UK. ℘(44)-207-321-2535.
Sydney – KTO, Level 18, Australia Square Tower, 264 George St, Sydney, NSW 2000, Australia. ℘(61)-2-9252-4147.
There are also branches of the KTO (Korea Tourism Organization) across South Korea. The KTO has a comprehensive website in English: http://english.visitkorea.or.kr. Tourist office details are given at the beginning of each sight in the *Discovering* section of this guide.

ENTRY REQUIREMENTS
ID AND VISAS
A **passport** that is valid for at least six months after the entry date is compulsory to visit South Korea. Holders of US passports and British Citizen passports can enter South Korea for tourism purposes for up to 90 days without a visa. You must also have an onward or round-trip ticket. Canadian tourists can stay for up to six months.

CUSTOMS REGULATIONS
You can import tax-free 2 US pints /1 liter of alcohol (if aged over 19); 200 cigarettes, 50 cigars or 8.8oz/250g of tobacco (if aged over 19); and goods purchased outside South Korea (including souvenirs) to a maximum value of USD$400 (£245).

VACCINATION
No vaccination certificate required.

INTERNATIONAL VISITORS
FOREIGN EMBASSIES AND CONSULATES IN SOUTH KOREA
Australia
Australian Embassy Seoul – 19th floor, Kyobo Building, 1 Jongno 1-Ga, Jongno-Gu, Seoul. Ⓜ Gwanghwamun

line 5, exit 4. ℘(82)-2-2003-0100.
www.southkorea.embassy.gov.au.

Canada
Canadian Embassy Seoul –
21 Jeong-dong, Jung-gu, Seoul 100-
120. Ⓜ Seodaemun line 5, exit 5 and
City Hall lines 1/2, exits 1/2. ℘(82)-2-
3783-6000. www.korea.gc.ca.

New Zealand
NZ Embassy Seoul – 8th floor, Jeong
Dong Building, Jeong-dong, Jung-gu,
Seoul 100-784. Ⓜ Seodaemun line 5,
exit 5 and City Hall lines, 1/2, exit 2.
℘(82)-2-3701-7700.
www.nzembassy.com/korea.

South Africa
South African Embassy Seoul – 1-37
Hannam-dong, Yongsan-gu, Seoul
140-884. Ⓜ Hannam line 1, exit 1, and
Oksu lines 1/3, exits 4/5. ℘(82)-2-792-
4855. www.southafrica-embassy.or.kr.

United States
US Embassy Seoul – 188 Sejong-
daero, Jongno-gu, Seoul 110-710.
Ⓜ Gwanghwamun line 5, exit 2.
℘(82)-2-397-4114.
http://seoul.usembassy.gov.

United Kingdom
British Embassy Seoul – Sejong-
daero 19-gil 24, Jung-gu,
Seoul 100-120. Ⓜ City Hall lines 1/2,
exit 2. ℘(82)-2-3210-5500.
http://ukinkorea.fco.gov.uk/en.

HEALTH
DISEASES
The good standard of hygiene in
South Korea means that the risk of
catching a disease is low. However, it
is advisable to pack some medicine for
possible stomach upsets, which affect
up to 20 percent of visitors (often due
to eating spicy food), as well as a few
other basic medicines, since it can be
hard to find their equivalent in South
Korea. Be aware, English is rarely
spoken in drugstores. Also, bring any
relevant prescriptions with you in case
of customs checks at the airport.

MEDICAL SERVICES
Hospitals are of a good standard
(in large towns, at least), but they
are expensive, so you are strongly
advised to obtain insurance covering
medical treatment abroad in case
of any problem. English is not
always spoken.

EMERGENCIES
English-speaking doctor hotline
(24hr) – ℘1339 from a land line; or
area code + 1339 from a cell phone.
This service provides English-
speaking doctors and help in health
emergencies.
**Translation bureau for police
and emergency services** –
℘1566-0112, Mon–Fri 8am–11pm,
Sat–Sun 9am–6pm. This service puts
you in contact with a police officer or
a translator in English so that you can
get help quickly.
*See also www.korea.net/detail.do?
guid=28303 for a list of police stations in
Seoul with English-speaking officers.*

Emergency Numbers
℘119 for fire and ambulance services;
℘112 for the police.

DRINKING WATER
Although tap water is safe to drink,
it is advisable to drink mineral water,
which is available everywhere.

SECURITY
South Korea is one of the safest
countries in the world, although this
does not always extend to the roads.
Korean drivers often accelerate well
over the speed limit and beep at
anyone driving within the speed limit.
Take care on the roads, particularly
outside built-up areas where there are
fewer restraints to curb speeders.

DRUGS
Possessing, using or trafficking drugs
is strictly prohibited in South Korea,
and the punishment for doing so
is very severe. The law applies to
everyone, including foreigners.

Getting There and Getting Around

BY PLANE

Until fairly recently just two companies, Korean Air and Asiana Airlines, operated domestic flights. The introduction of the high-speed train (the KTX) led to the airlines concentrating on major internal and international destinations, but today there is a much wider choice of airlines serving domestic destinations. Although most flights last less than an hour, given the low frequency of flights, it is often more practical to take the train.

Air Busan – ℘(055)-1666-3060. http://flyairbusan.com; or http://en.airbusan.com/AB/airbusan/english/main.jsp. This low-cost company flies to Seoul (Gimpo Airport)–Busan (*15 flights per day*); Busan–Jeju (*10 flights per day*); and now also to Taiwan, Japan and China. Book online or by phone.

Asiana Airlines – ℘(02)-1588-8000. www.flyasiana.com. Flies between Busan and Yangyang.

Eastar Jet – ℘(02)-1544-0080. www.eastarjet.com. Flies Seoul (Gimpo Airport)–Jeju (*13 flights per day*) and Cheongju-Jeju (*2 flights per day*).

T'Way – ℘(011)-1688-8686. www.twayair.com. Previously Hansung Airways, South Korea's first budget airline. Flies Seoul (Gimpo Airport)–Jeju (*11 flights per day*) and Cheongju-Jeju (*4 flights per day*).

Jeju Air – ℘(02)-1599-1500. www.jejuair.net. Flies between Seoul (Incheon, Gimpo Airport) and Japanese airports (Kansai, Kitakyushu, Nagoya).

Korean Air – ℘(02)-1588-2001. www.koreanair.com.

Jin Air – ℘(02)-1600-6200. www.jinair.com. This budget company launched by Korean Air in 2008 flies from Seoul (Incheon) to Bangkok, Macau and Guam.

BY TRAIN

South Korea has a very good rail network, run by **KORAIL**. There are four types of trains: the **KTX**, which is the fastest (186mph/300km/h) and the equivalent of France's TGV, is based on French technology. The line runs from Seoul to Daejeon, where it splits in two. The main Gyeongbu line runs east to Busan (KTX to Daegu). The Honam line links Daejeon to Gwangju and Mokpo. The KTX2 (205mph/330km/h) is gradually being put into service in sections on the Seoul–Busan and Yongsan–Gwangju line. The extension to Mokpo is scheduled to be finished by 2017.

The "super express" **Saemaeul** trains are not as fast as the KTX, but are about 30 percent cheaper.

A little slower and cheaper than the Saemaeul, **Mugunghwa** trains serve more stations. Finally, **Tonggeun** trains are the cheapest and slowest. They operate infrequently on certain specific commuter lines only, make frequent stops, and foreign visitors are unlikely to use them.

In major towns and cities, there may be more than one station—the one you arrive at will depend on the type of train you take, so it is worth checking when you buy your tickets.

BOOKING

It is advisable to book your ticket in advance, especially for an evening or weekend departure. You can book up to two months ahead of departure at stations and at some travel agencies. For details, enquire at a tourist office or consult the **KORAIL website**: http://info.korail.com/2007/eng/eng_index.jsp.

KOREA RAIL (KR) PASS

Exclusively for the use of foreign visitors expecting to spend less than six months in South Korea, the KR Pass allows you to travel by train (excluding tour trains and subways) any distance nationwide (seats cannot be guaranteed during major public holidays). A pass for 1, 3, 5, 7 or 10

days costs ₩58,200–185,100 (children aged 4-12 years: ₩29,100–92,500). Discounts are available for groups of 2–5 people and for passengers with an International Student ID Card aged 13–25 years. An e-ticket for the KR Pass can be purchased on the KORAIL website (*see above*); or a KR Pass voucher can be purchased in advance from appointed travel agencies abroad and exchanged in South Korean stations (*see website*). *See also the KTO website: http:// english.visitkorea.or.kr/enu/TR/ TR_EN_5_7.jsp.*

BY COACH/BUS

Buses are remarkably reliable, frequent, punctual, comfortable and inexpensive. The only downside is the risk of being caught in heavy traffic when traveling at rush hour.
There are two types: **express buses**, which are more comfortable, and **intercity buses**, which are a little cheaper. **Long-distance express buses** are comfortable and fast, having their own lane on expressways, and serve every part of the country. Be aware, buses don't always depart from and arrive at the same place in the same town. On long journeys, buses make one or two 15-minute stops at service stations. If you decide to stretch your legs, take note of where your bus is parked so that you can find it again among the many other identical buses.
In Seoul there are three main bus stations, serving different destinations (*see Useful Information p112*). Nearly all towns also have their own local bus service. Buses are harder to negotiate than the train and subway for foreign visitors, since destinations are written in Korean and drivers are less likely to speak English. If possible, have your destination written in *Hangeul* to show the driver. Tickets should be purchased directly from the bus terminal counters. It is also advisable to buy them in advance if you are planning to travel at the weekend or during holidays.

The **KOBUS** website **www.kobus.co.kr** will help you to plan your journey.

BY SHIP

A sizeable network of ferries connects the many islands along the coast, as well as the more distant islands of Ulleung-do and Jeju-do, with the mainland. Ferry terminals are found at Incheon, Mokpo, Wando, Yeosu, Busan, Pohang, Donghae and Sokcho. Services may be canceled at short notice due to bad weather conditions, particularly during the monsoon season, which happens during the summer. See the *Discovering* chapter for more detailed information about each destination. *See also the KTO website www.visitkorea.or.kr/intro.html.*

BY CAR

Thanks to the efficiency of the public transport system, there is no need to hire a car to get around major towns, but for long journeys or on the island of Jeju-do, a car can be a good idea. However, bear in mind that Koreans drive at speed, particularly on out-of-town roads, and the accident rate is high. One option is to engage both a car and a Korean chauffeur, though this is more expensive.
Travel by train to the region you wish to visit and hire a car when you get there.

ROAD NETWORK

The expressway network linking cities is extensive but with few exits, so if you miss the correct one, you may have a long wait for the next. Remember to drive on the right and always wear a seatbelt. The **speed limit** is normally between 50 and 62mph (80 and 100km/h) on expressways and 19 and 37 mph (30 and 60km/h) on regular roads. Don't be tempted to speed, although you will be passed often—speed cameras are plentiful on expressways and the police will fine foreign drivers. You may not be stopped on the spot, but you will receive a fine in the post upon your return home. Bus lanes are designated by a blue line. Many road signs are given in *Hangeul* only.

DRIVING PERMIT (LICENSE)

To drive in South Korea, you need an International Driving Permit (License), and must be aged over 21, have a valid passport and have had your own country's driving permit for over a year (you may need to show this also to the rental agency).

CAR HIRE

There are car-hire companies in airports, around major railway stations and in towns. The two largest rental companies are **Kumho Rent-a-Car** (*1588-1230, www.kumhorent.com*) and **Avis Rent-a-Car** (*1544-1600, www.avis.co.kr/eng/index.jsp*). Insurance is extra and it is advisable to take out the most comprehensive insurance available. Expect to pay ₩55,000–65,000 per day, including insurance, for a top-of-the-line car. *See also the KTO website: www.visitkorea.or.kr.*

TAXIS

There are two types—regular and deluxe. Regular taxis are a cheap way of getting around town.
There are normally plenty about, although they can be harder to find late at night. The fares are metered according to distance but switch to a time basis if you get stuck in traffic. Taxis are available when the light on the roof is lit. The minimum fare in a regular taxi is ₩2,400 for 1.25mi/2km, then ₩100 every 157yds/144m (20 percent increase midnight–4am). Regular taxis are white, orange or silver. Deluxe taxis are black; they are more comfortable, and the driver is more likely to speak English, but they are also more expensive.
Since many drivers don't speak English, it is helpful to have your destination written in *Hangeul*, or ask to be dropped near a well-known place.

Where to Stay and Eat

WHERE TO STAY

A selection of accommodations is described in the *Address Book* of each chapter in the *Discovering* section. To make it easy to find these addresses on the town and district maps, each hotel and guesthouse is marked with a number. Accommodations are classified in four price categories to meet different requirements.
The categories are based on the average price for a **standard double** room in **high season**.

ACCOMMODATION TYPES

At establishments that don't take credit cards, you may have to pay on arrival. In such cases, you may ask to see the room before paying.

Hotels

Hotels are divided into five categories (using the *mugunghwa* or "rose of Sharon"—Korea's national flower—as a symbol of quality; 5 flowers is the top rating) based on quality, size, service and facilities: super deluxe and deluxe (5 star), first class (4 star), second class (3 star) and third class (2 star). Rooms are either Western-style or traditional, that is, with underfloor heating (*ondol*).
In towns popular with tourists, prices can vary according to the season, with high season being April–May, July–

PRICE CATEGORIES				
	🛏 STAY		🍽 EAT	
	Seoul	Outside Seoul	Seoul	Outside Seoul
⬭	under ₩90,000	₩30,000–70 000	under ₩15,000	under ₩8,000
⬭⬭	₩90,000–150,000	₩70,000–120,000	₩15,000–40,000	₩8,000–15,000
⬭⬭⬭	₩150,000–250,000	₩120,000–200,000	₩40,000–80,000	₩15,000–20,000
⬭⬭⬭⬭	over ₩250,000	over ₩200,000	over ₩80,000	over ₩20,000

August and winter, depending on the geographical location. Generally, for a double room, expect to pay ₩200,000–400,000 in a super deluxe accommodation; ₩150,000–250,000 for deluxe; ₩100,000–150,000 for first class; ₩50,000–100,000 for second class; and ₩30,000–100,000 for third class.

Expect to pay an extra 10 percent VAT, which is not always included in the booking price, and possibly extra service charges (around 10 percent) at luxury hotels. In general, breakfast is not included in the price.

Motels and love hotels

Motels usually offer the best value for the money (₩30,000–50,000 a night; ₩70,000–80,000 in Seoul). Many are in fact "love hotels," known for their unusual appearance (in the form of castles, baroque mansions, etc.), and rent rooms by the hour. However, they also represent a viable option for tourists. Generally well maintained and sometimes eccentrically furnished (with heart-shaped beds, for example), the rooms are also well equipped (computer with internet connection, widescreen TV, video/DVD rental). They offer great value for the money, with one downside: most managers don't speak English, so booking a room can be difficult.

The motels recommended herein are generally the more conservative kind, with all the necessary amenities to welcome foreign visitors, even if English is not generally spoken.

Yeogwan

Slightly dated and more old-fashioned than motels, although sometimes not greatly so, yeogwan, also called jang and yeoinsuk (Korean for "motel"), are cheaper and far less well equipped than motels (no internet connection, for example), and again the owners generally don't speak English. Expect to pay ₩25,000–50,000 per night, or even less for the more basic yeoinsuk. Be aware that prices can, however, rise for certain events (festivals, etc.).

Minbak

These B&B-style accommodations are traditionally found close to beaches and national parks, and their prices can rise considerably during high season. Staying in someone's home, rather than in a hotel, is ideal for learning about the Korean way of life. The accommodation itself may be in an apartment or a room adjoining a house, but, generally, there are no private bathrooms. Prices are similar to those of yeogwan.

♦ **Gwangju International Homestay** – ℂSee p331.
♦ **HomestayKorea** – ✆(02)-777-7412. www.homestaykorea.com.
♦ **LEX Youth Korea** – ✆(02)-582-9660. www.lex.or.kr.
♦ **Go Homestay** – www.gohomestay.com - info@gohomestay.com.

Korea Stay

The Korea Stay program, launched by the Korean Tourism Organization (KTO), is similar to a home stay

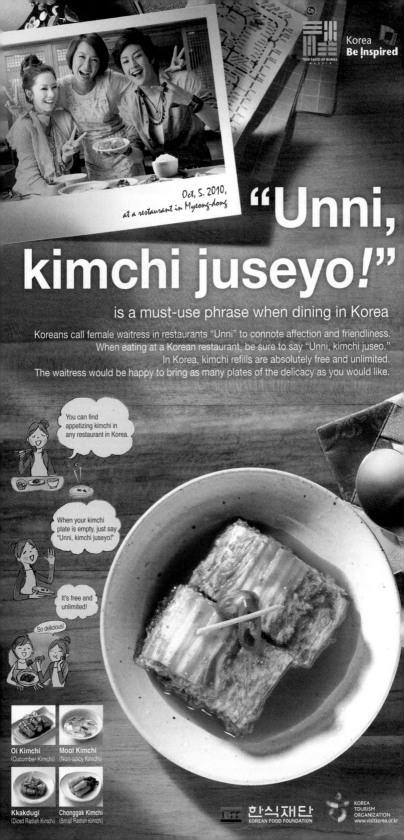

program and a bed and breakfast, offering visitors more opportunities to discover Korean family culture. Around 350 host families are participating in this program. Reservations can be made starting September 2011, on the internet or by telephone.

♦ **Korea Stay**– ✆ (02)-729-9460. www.visitkorea.or.kr; about ₩60,000 per night, breakfast provided

Hanok Stay

At least one night in a traditional house is recommended to experience a little of South Korea's lifestyle and culture. Rooms may be multipurpose when furnished accordingly, so a bedroom may be turned into a dining room, for example. They use a special underfloor heating system (ondol). Expect to pay ₩50,000–150,000 per night, sometimes including breakfast and the tea ceremony.

Selected addresses:

♦ **Seoul:** Bukchon Guest House, Seoul Guest House and Rak Ko Jae, in the Bukchon district (⏾see p131).
♦ **Jeonju:** Seunggwangjae, Yangsajae and Hakindang, in the village of Hanok (⏾see p357).
♦ **Andong:** Rak Ko Jae (⏾see p 279) and Jirye Artists' Colony (⏾see p 279); and also Suaedang. ✆ (054)-822-6661. www. suaedang.co.kr (in Korean).

Temple Stay

Buddhist orders welcome visitors to stay in their temples and share the daily life of the monks. The day begins between 3.30 and 4:30am with the dharma ceremony to calm the mind. Guests generally have the opportunity to learn Seon (Zen) meditation positions and techniques and to take part in the tea ceremony (dado). A day spent at a temple includes three vegetarian meals (barugongyang—the food is served in four wooden bowls and none must be wasted) and participation in daily tasks (usually cleaning). There may be

an architectural tour of the temple, and an English-speaking interpreter may also be available. Expect to pay ₩30,000–50,000 per person. www.engtemplestay.com.

Youth Hostels

Modern, well equipped and sometimes very well situated, the 52 hostels that are spread across the country are also a great source of information. The price per person is around ₩10,000 for a bed in a dormitory and ₩40,000–160,000 for a private room, depending on the number of beds and the facilities. Booking in advance is recommended. For a list of **hostels**, see www.hostels southkorea.com.

See also the Korean youth hostel association, **Hostelling International Korea**: Jeokseon Hyundai Building, room 409, Jeokseon-dong, Jongno-gu, Seoul. ✆ (02)-725-3031. www.kyha.or.kr/english.

Campsites

These are normally found in the vicinity of national parks. Drinking water is always available at campsites, but you are advised to bring your own food. ⏾See also the website: Korea National Park Service: http://english. knps.or.kr/ (click on "Experience" then "Campsites").

WHERE TO EAT

Most restaurants are open 10am– 10pm, but in larger towns fast-food chains and some snack bars are always open.

😊 Rice and soup are eaten with a spoon (sujeo); all other dishes are eaten with metal chopsticks.

😊 Note: it is very bad manners to eat from a bowl held in your hands (leave it on the table), as it is to blow your nose at the table. Also, don't be surprised if certain restaurants provide toilet paper instead of napkins. A selection of restaurants is described in the Addresses at the end of each chapter in the Discovering section.

Basic Information

COMMUNICATIONS
TELEPHONE
RENTAL

Cell phone companies have desks in most airports. If you land at Seoul's Incheon International Airport, you will find, for example, **SK Telecom** between gates 9 and 10 (6am–10pm) or 5 and 6 (6am–midnight) in the airport's passenger terminal; **KT**, between gates 6 and 7 or 10 and 11 (24hr) on the ground floor; **LG Telecom**, between gates 6 and 7, 10 and 11, or 13 and 14 (24hr) on the ground floor. Expect to pay about ₩3,000 rental per day. Phones can also be rented from **BBB Korea** (✆see Helplines below).

INTERNATIONAL CALLS TO/FROM SOUTH KOREA

The country code for South Korea is 82; to call South Korea from abroad, omit the initial 0 from the area code.

Calling Into South Korea
From **Australia** – ✆ 0011-82 + Korean area code + number.
From **South Africa** – ✆ 09-0-82 + Korean area code + number.
From the **UK** – ✆ 00-82 + Korean area code + number.
From **US/Canada** – ✆ -82 + Korean area code + number.

Calling From South Korea
To call Australia from **South Korea** – ✆ 001-61 + area code + number.
To call **South Africa** – ✆001-27 + area code + number.
To call the **UK** – ✆ 001-44 + area code + number.
To call the **US/Canada** – ✆ 001-1 + area code + number.

LOCAL CALLS WITHIN SOUTH KOREA

To telephone within the same zone or same town, dial the phone number without the area code. However, if calling from a cell (mobile) phone, the full area code should be dialed.
To call a different zone, dial the area code (including 0) and the phone number. The area code for **Seoul** is (02), for **Incheon** (032), for **Daejeon** (042), for **Busan** (051), for **Daegu** (053), for **Ulsan** (052).
South Korean cell phone carriers use **CDMA**, not the GSM system familar to many English-speaking users, who will therefore not be able to use their cell phones in South Korea. Cell phone rental is the best option (✆see Rental above). 3G phone users are advised to contact their network provider before they leave to check whether their phone will work in Korea and the resulting costs.

INTERNATIONAL PREPAID PHONE CARDS

A prepaid card of ₩30,000 gives you at least five hours of calls abroad, sometimes more, from any telephone. Cards are available from banks, convenience stores and kiosks.
To make a call, dial the access number provided, followed by your pin number, then the number you wish to call, including the country code if you are making an international call.

HELPLINES

Tourist Info Helpline – If you need tourist information in English, dial ✆**1330** for details of tourist sites, public transport, restaurants, etc.
In South Korea ✆**1330** from a land line (no area code necessary), 24hr; from a cell phone, dial the relevant area code + 1330.
If you want information about Seoul, dial 02 + 1330. This also links up with the South Korean emergency number, 119 (✆see Emergency Numbers).
From abroad ✆82 + area code + 1330, but drop the 0 from the area code (e.g., 82-2-1330 for Seoul).

BBB Korea – ✆1588-5644 (no area code necessary), 24hr, www.bbbkorea.org/eng/. The "Before Babel Brigade" is a pool of volunteer interpreters who will help with any language problems in any situation during your stay. An impressive 17 languages are spoken, including, of course, English. They also offer a cell phone rental service in cooperation with SK Telecom (see website).

120 Dasan – A useful call center offering advice on tourism in Seoul and life in Korea in general; questions can be texted too (see p112).

ELECTRICITY
The current supplied is 220V at 60Hz. Visitors from North America will need a voltage converter to use some appliances. Korean plugs have two round pins with no grounding pin, so an adaptor will mostly likely be needed even if the voltage is not an issue.

INTERNET
With South Korea being one of the world's most "connected" countries, internet cafés, or PC Bangs as they are sometimes called, are ubiquitous. Some offer free drinks, others sell instant noodle soups and other snacks. Motels nearly always have a computer and internet connection. Increasingly frequented by business visitors, hotels always have Wi-Fi and usually a business center equipped with computers.

MAIL
South Korea's postal network is very good. Post offices are open Mon–Fri 9am–6pm (5pm in winter) and Sat 9am–1pm. Delivery time to Europe, USA and Canada is between seven and ten days. Expect to pay ₩580 to send a postcard. International freight companies such as Federal Express, UPS and DHL can also be used for sending parcels.

MEDIA
NEWSPAPERS
The South Korean press is monopolized by the three main newspapers with the *Chosun Ilbo*, the *JoongAng Ilbo* and the *Dong-A Ilbo* having 70 percent of the market between them. Although sales are decreasing due to the popularity of free newspapers and online dailies, these three papers together sell

Newsstand
©KTO

almost seven million issues a day. Despite their reputation for being somewhat "conservative," they criticize government policy freely when they feel it is appropriate. The three English-language dailies are *The Korea Times (www.koreatimes.co.kr)*, *The Korea Herald (www.koreaherald. co.kr)*, and the *Korea JoongAng Daily (http://joongangdaily.joins.com/)*. They can be found at all the big hotels and in some large bookstores.

TELEVISION

The Korean TV channel *Arirang* is an English broadcasting station showing documentaries on Korea as well as a daily news bulletin. Many other channels, both terrestrial and cable (such as OCM), broadcast films either in the original version or with subtitles. English-speaking satellite news channels, such as CNN and BBC, are available in most of the major hotels.

HALLYU, THE "KOREAN WAVE"

President Kim Young-sam's policy of openness and South Korea's joining of the World Trade Organization in the 1990s enabled the country to spread its wings both commercially and creatively, exporting South Korea's culture to neighboring countries and beyond. Korean TV series have duly beaten audience records across Asia and have even reached Europe and the United States via the internet. This wave, or *hallyu*, has captured the interest of thousands of young people in Asia (and elsewhere), who have now become fans of South Korean mass culture (✆*see also p50*) to such an extent that, since 1999, the government has seen the *hallyu* as a major contributor to national economic growth.

MONEY
BUDGETING

The cost of living, compared to the West, is not too high. With the exception of Seoul, it is fairly easy to find a comfortable and well-appointed room for ₩40,000–50,000 (around $38 for 2 people—see the recommendations within our ⬭ and ⬭⬭ price categories), a good lunch for ₩10,000 ($10) and dinner for around ₩15,000–20,000 ($14–$19—see the recommendations in our ⬭⬭ and ⬭⬭⬭ price categories). However, coffee and cake remain very expensive, almost half the price of a meal. Public transport is inexpensive and taxis are cheap. It's not unusual to be able to cross an average-sized town for less than ₩10,000. When there is a charge to enter a museum, it is also usually reasonable. In total, excluding Seoul which is much more expensive, allow for a minimum budget per person, per day of ₩90,000–120,000 ($84–$112). For Seoul, allow for ₩187,500 per person per day, or $174.

CURRENCY

The Korean currency is the won. The coins currently in circulation are: ₩10, ₩50, ₩100, and ₩500; banknotes are: ₩1,000, ₩5,000, ₩10,000, and ₩50,000. At press time, $1 was equivalent to ₩1,079, but for the latest exchange rate, consult www.xe.com/ucc.

EXCHANGE AND BANKS

Currency can be exchanged easily at all major banks and at licensed agencies (in the Seoul districts of Itaewon and Namdaemun in particular). Banks are generally open Mon–Fri, 9:30am–4pm.

ATMs

With an international credit or debit card, cash in local currency can be withdrawn from some ATMs, although not all ATMs accept foreign cards. Look for the "Global" logo or the logo of your credit card company. ATMs are normally open between 7am/8am and 11pm/midnight (a few are open 24hr), and it is usually possible to select English for on-screen instructions. The commission charged is lower when cash is withdrawn during banking hours. **Note**: South Korean ATMs only accept 4-digit PIN numbers. If you have a 5- or 6-digit number, it will be necessary to change it to 4 digits. Some 24-hour mini-marts have ATMs displaying the "Global" logo.

Credit and Debit Cards

These are accepted at most hotels, restaurants and stores. However, you will need cash for shopping at traditional markets and in more basic restaurants and motels. In general, when venturing beyond the major towns, make sure you always carry some cash.

The Korea Pass Card

Launched in 2010 by the Korea Tourism Organization (KTO), this store-value card (available for ₩50,000, ₩100,000, ₩300,000 and ₩500,000), issued by the Korean government, is convenient for many purposes during your stay in Korea, such as accommodation, transporation, shopping and leisure activites. The card also gives access to special offers and discounts.

The "Transportion" option can be used nationwide and also on most subways, buses and taxis in Seoul. The pass can be purchased at airports, subway stations, convenience stores and also in 6,000 franchised discount stores located all over the country. Plus, the card is rechargeable, so you don't need to exchange your money.

See also ℘(082)-2-1330, *www.koreapass.or.kr/en.*

PUBLIC HOLIDAYS

On official public holidays, offices and banks are closed and, usually, only the museums remain open. It is advisable to avoid traveling around the time of the two major traditional celebrations – Seollal (Korean New Year) and *Chuseok* ("celebrating the harvest") – since you will be in the company of millions of Koreans. If you do travel at this time, it is certainly best to book ahead.

1 and 2 January – The New Year is celebrated on the first two days of the year, according to the Western calendar.

January or February – Seollal (also *Seolnal*, Lunar New Year). Named after the first day of the new lunar year (*Seol*), the festivities last three days. It is one of Korea's most important traditional celebrations, when *tteokguk* (rice cake soup) is served. *Seollal* is followed by **Daeboreum**, which celebrates the first full moon of the first month of the lunar year. Various rituals are performed to protect against misfortune and the evil eye. *Ogokbap* (boiled five-grain rice) is served and everyone wishes each other a year of good health and happiness.

1 March – Commemoration of the start of the independence movement against the Japanese occupation on 1 March 1919, when the Declaration of Independence was read out in Seoul's Tapgol Park.

April – Hansik, meaning "cold dishes" (not a public holiday), falls on the 105th day after the winter solstice. Now observed less than it used to be, the day is dedicated to the Dead. The graves of ancestors are tended carefully, and offerings are made, after which a cold meal is eaten.

May – The **Buddha's birthday** (eighth day of the fourth lunar month) is celebrated with wonderful lamplit processions and solemn rites in Buddhist temples. Don't miss the procession in Seoul.

5 May – Children's Day, with trips to the park, the zoo, the cinema….

8 May – Parents' Day (not a public holiday)

5 Jne – On the fifth day of the fifth month of the lunar year, **Dano** marks the seed-sowing season with festivals and major shamanist ceremonies (especially in Gangneung—⌖ *see box p253*).

6 June – **Memorial Day**, remembering those killed in military action. Ceremonies are held at Seoul National Cemetery.

17 July – **Constitution Day** (not a public holiday), the day the Korean Constitution was proclaimed in 1948.

15 August – **Liberation Day**, commemorating the end of the Japanese occupation in 1945 and the installation of the government of the Republic of Korea in 1948.

September/October – **Chuseok** or *Hangawi*, 15th day of the 8th lunar month, is harvest festival, when it is customary for Koreans to return to their birthplace or their ancestral home.

A big family festival with ceremonies dedicated to ancestors and graveside offerings, including *songpyeon*, a rice cake stuffed with beans, chestnuts, jujubes or sweetened sesame seeds steamed over pine needles.

3 October – **National Foundation Day**, marking the founding of Korea in 2333 BC by the legendary god-king Tangun.

9 October – **Hangeul Day**, commemorating the creation of the Korean alphabet, as recorded on 9 October 1446 in the **Hunminjeongeum** manuscript (not a public holiday).

25 December – **Christmas Day**, a national holiday celebrated as in the West.

Note: *The academic year, for both schools and universities, starts at the beginning of March*

TIME

South Korea is Greenwich Mean Time (GMT) + 9hr. Therefore it is 13hr ahead of New York, and 1hr behind Sydney. When it is 10am in South Korea, it is 9pm the previous day in New York, 1am the same day in London, and 11am the same day in Sydney. South Korea has been considering implementing Daylight Savings Time, but had not done so at press time.

TIPPING

Tipping is not usual in South Korea, athough there are signs that this may be slowly changing. Many major hotels now add a compulsory 10 percent service charge (on top of the 10 percent VAT) and some high-end restaurants do the same.

Taxi drivers don't expect a tip, however, unless they have performed an extra service, athough they may not hand back very small change.

TOILETS

All tourist sites and transport facilities have clean public toilets. There are two types: Korean, where you squat, and Western style. Always keep a supply of paper tissues with you, as few public conveniences have toilet paper. You can also use the toilets in shops, restaurants, hotels and office buildings.

WEIGHTS AND MEASUREMENTS

South Korea uses the international metric system.

Useful Words and Phrases

Ajumma	Middle-aged woman with children (sometimes used pejoratively)
Anchae	Building reserved for women in aristocratic houses, in which only men who are family members may enter. The *anbang* is the main room.
Bodhisattva	In Buddhism, those promised enlightenment but renouncing nirvana out of compassion for those living on Earth.
Bong	Peak (e.g. Ichulbong/ Ichul Peak)
Buk	North (e.g. Jeollabuk-do/ North Jeolla Province)
Cheon	Stream (e.g. Cheonggyecheon/ Cheonggye Stream)
Cheongja	Celadon, green-blue porcelain stoneware
Dang	Room in monasteries and palaces, less formal and less dignified than the *jeon*
Dancheong	Red and greenish-blue painted decoration on a building, using stylized, symbolic patterns and interlacing; it is ornamental but also protects the wood and rough surfaces at the edge of a roof. Inside, it covers the ceiling and frame of important buildings.
Do	Province (e.g. Jeolla-do); island (e.g. Namhaedo)
Dong	Smallest administrative unit of a town, village or city; district (e.g. Myeong-dong); east (e.g. Dongdaemun/ Great East Gate)
Donghak	"Eastern Learning," based on syncretism of Confucianism, Buddhism and shamanism against Westernization, founded in 1860
Ga	Section of a street (e.g. Euljiro-1 ga/Euljiro Street Section 1)
Gang	River (e.g. Hangang/Han River)
Gangdang	Lecture hall or auditorium
Geumdang	"Golden Hall," main hall of worship in a Buddhist monastery
Gidan	Foundations of a house
Gil	Small street (e.g. Garosul-gil)
Gisaeng	In traditional Korean culture, the *gisaeng* (pronounced "ki seng") are professional female entertainers (singers and dancers).
Gu	District (e.g. Jongno-gu)
Gul	Cave (e.g. Hwanseongul/ Hwanseon Cave)
Gun	County (e.g. Gijang-gun/ Gijang County)
Gung	Palace (e.g. Gyeongbokgung/ Gyeongbok Palace)
Gyo	Bridge (e.g. Janghwagyo/ Janghwa Bridge)
Haetae	Mythical creatures (unicorn-lions) that offer protection against the elements. They can judge right from wrong and good from bad.
Hallyu	The Korean "wave," the spread of South Korean popular culture overseas.
Hanbok	Traditional Korean costume
Hanok	Traditional Korean house
Ho	Lake (e.g. Bomunho/ Bomun Lake)
Hyanggyo	Local Confucian school which includes a temple dedicated to Confucius and his disciples
Iljumun	One of the three gates through which you pass when entering a Buddhist temple. Its columns

are aligned in a single row, so when viewed from the side, a single pillar is visible, and this should enlighten the viewer about the basis for the unity of soul.

Jangseung Wooden male or female totems supposedly intended to ward off evil spirits

Jeon Main hall (building, throne hall, or principal hall of worship) in temples and palaces

Jeongja Type of pavilion with an elevated wooden floor, commanding a fine view of the surrounding landscape

Jjimjilbang Korean sauna or bathhouse

Jingyeong Sansu "True scenery" or "true-view landscape," a Korean style of painting pioneered by Jeong Seon (1676–1759) with scenes of Geumgangsan (Diamond Mountains)

Kan (or gan) Distance between two pillars

Man Bay (e.g. Suncheonman/ Suncheon Bay)

Maru Floor made of thick raised boards, used mainly in summer. The wooden floor space was built high above ground in southern areas where the climate is hot and humid. Adopted in northern areas also.

Minbak Bed and breakfast accommodation

Mun Gate (e.g. Dongdaemun/ Dongdae Gate)

Myeon Administrative division (rural); township

Myo Shrine (e.g. Jongmyo/ Jong Shrine)

Nam South (e.g. Namsan/ South Mountain)

Oncheon Hot spring

Ondol A system of heating through direct heat transfer from the fireplace in the kitchen to the underside of a thick masonry floor. Stones covered with greased paper form the floor and distribute heat. This heating system dates back to Neolithic times.

Pansori A genre of dramatic narrative song or story-singing, sometimes called Korean folk opera

Pojangmacha Mobile food/drink stalls set up in the streets, operating during the day and at night

Pokpo Waterfall (e.g. Yukdam Pokpo/ Yukdam Waterfall)

Ri Village (e.g. Aewol-ri/ Aewol Village)

Sa Buddhist temple (e.g. Jikjisa/ Jikji Temple)

Samulnori Traditional Korean percussion quartet

San Mountain (e.g. Bukhansan/ Mt. Bukhan)

Sansin God of the mountain

Sarangchae Building reserved for men in aristocratic houses, sometimes with several *sarangbang* (rooms reserved specifically for men and used for leisure activities).

Sari Relics of Buddha or a monk

Seo West (e.g. Seodaemun/ Great West Gate)

Seodang Private village schools that provided elementary education during the Goryeo (918–1392) and Joseon dynasties (1392–1910). Led by the "*hunjang*" or headmaster.

Seohak Introduction of Catholicism, Western doctrines and ideas in the 18C

Seoktap Stone pagoda

Seong Fortress (e.g. Bukhansanseong/ Bukhansan Fortress)

Si/Shi City (e.g. Jeju-si/Jeju City)

Ssireum	Traditional Korean wrestling and national sport of Korea
Tap	Pagoda or stupa
Up/eup	Town
Yangban	High-ranking aristocratic official of the Joseon dynasty (1392–1910)
Yeogwan	Motel-style accommodation, usually cheaper than motels

Food and Drink

Banchan	Small plates or side dishes of vegetables, kimchi, noodles, etc. They are shared by diners and sometimes eaten prior to the main course.
Bap	Cooked rice or, in the broader sense, all food made by boiling grains in water
Bindaetteok	"Pauper's cake." A pancake made with ground mung beans.
Bokkeumbap	Fried rice (often with kimchi)
Bossam (suyuk)	Steamed pork served in thin slices in Chinese cabbage wraps
Bulgogi	Grilled marinated beef
Dakbokkeumtang	Spicy chicken stew with potatoes
Dakgalbi	Spicy grilled chicken with hot sauce, cabbage, sweet potatoes, onions, etc.
Doenjang	Fermented soybean paste used in casseroles or mixed with fresh mountain herbs.
Dolssambap	Stone pot rice served with lettuce and other leaves for wrapping.
Dolsot bibimbap	rice, vegetables, egg served in a sizzling hot bowl or pot
Dolsot jeongsik	Set menu served with rice cooked in a hot stone pot
Dotorimuk	Acorn jelly

Galbitang	Beef rib soup
Gamjatang	Pork backbone soup served with potatoes and vegetables
Galbi	Grilled beef
Galbijjim	Braised short ribs (beef or pork) with slightly sweet soy
Ganjang	Soy sauce
Gimbap	Rolls of rice, omelet, radishes, etc., wrapped in a sheet of seaweed and eaten as a snack
Gochujang	Red pepper paste
Gyeongju bbang	Local sweet filled with bean paste
Haejangguk	Soup eaten mostly as a hangover remedy, made of tripe and ox blood
Haemultang	Spicy seafood soup
Hangwa	Traditional confectionery made from honey
Hanjeongsik	Banquet table: a meal composed of countless small dishes
Hansik	Korean cuisine
Hoe	Raw fish
Hotteok	Small pancake stuffed with sugar syrup and crushed nuts
Injeolmi	Rice cakes
Insam	Ginseng
Jajangmyeon	Noodles with black bean sauce
Jang	Condiments
Jangajji	Pickled vegetables, roots, and fruits in fermented soy sauce, chili sauce or *doenjang*
Japchae	Glass noodles stir-fried with vegetables
Jeonbok-juk	Rice porridge with abalone
Jeotgal	Salted seafood
Jokbal	Glazed pig's feet
Kalguksu	Home-style noodle soup made of wheat flour noodles flattened, cut by hand and usually cooked in broth with clams/other seafood and zucchini

Romanization

The Korean Hangeul script was first romanized in the 1930s, making it easier for those accustomed to Western alphabets to read signs and find their way around. The system was revised by the government in 2000 to improve consistency, but the changes were met with some resistance, and the names of some towns, streets, hotels, restaurants, etc. are still commonly written using the old system. The result is a variation in spelling that can be very confusing for the visitor. The old system also used apostrophes and accents, which the new system has dispensed with.

Here is a list of the basic changes, which hopefully will explain some of the variation in spellings you will see.

ch – changed to *j*
(Cheju became Jeju)

ch' – changed to *ch*
(Ch'ungju became Chungju)

k – changed to *g*
(Kwangju became Gwangju)

p – changed to *b*
(Pusan became Busan)

p' – changed to *p*
(Kimp'o became Gimpo)

sh – changed to *s*

(*shi* became *si*, city)

t – changed to *d*
(Taegu became Daegu)

t' – changed to *t*
(T'aean became Taean)

ŏ – changed to *eo*
(Chōsun became Joseon)

ŭ – changed to *eu*

Kimchi	Pickled, fermented vegetables (often Korean white cabbage), salted and seasoned
Kimchi jjigae	Kimchi cabbage stew.
Kongnamulgukbap	Rice served in a broth with bean sprouts
Maeuntang	Spicy fish soup
Makgeolli	Lightly fizzy rice wine
Mandu	Dumplings
Naengmyeon	Chilled buckwheat noodle soup
Nakji bokkeum	Stir-fried baby octopus with various seasonings
Namul	Side dishes of vegetables or wild leafy greens
Pajeon	Green onion and seafood pancakes
Pondegi	Boiled silkworm larvae
Ramyeon	Instant noodles, the equivalent of Japanese ramen, popular eaten as a snack
Samgyetang	Chicken soup with ginseng
Seolleongtang	Milky soup made from a cow's bones and organs and beef shank, simmered over a long period
Sikhye	Cold sugary drink made of fermented rice
Ssambap	Rice with various leafy vegetables, cooked or fresh
Soondae	Korean blood sausage, often stuffed with clear rice noodles
Suyuk	Boiled meat cut into slices
Tteokbokki	Stir-fried rice cakes with vegetables in red pepper paste or soy sauce. A very popular street snack.
Twigim	Deep-fried food, including seafood, meat and vegetables

Seoraksan National Park
Chris Stowers/Apa Publications

Foreword

What springs to mind when you think of Korea? For a small peninsula which has punched well above its weight for over 2,000 years, it's remarkable how little the wider world knows about "The Land of the Morning Calm," an enchanting destination which marries the infectious energy of modern-day Asia with Buddhist temples, dynastic palaces, gentle mountains of pine, and a deliciously complex cuisine. Much of the blame can be apportioned to the noisy neighbor to the north, which tends to dominate global headlines—many visitors to South Korea are pleasantly surprised to find themselves in such a safe, friendly, prosperous and fascinating land.

Things haven't always been this way—while Korea has been friendly and fascinating since time immemorial, safety and prosperity arrived rather more recently. Its two-millennium-long line of kings and queens were choked off by 35 years of Japanese occupation, which only ended with World War II. Instead of being given the chance to recover from what amounted to a full-scale assault on its national identity, tremendous shifts in global politics saw Korea plunged headfirst into a catastrophic civil war, one that ripped the peninsula in half and left it among the world's most impoverished corners.

Just a couple of generations down the line, the recovery has been nothing short of mind-blowing. Central Seoul of the late 1950s was a desolate, treeless landscape dotted with shantytowns and riddled with bullet holes, the streets almost audibly creaking with broken buildings, broken friendships, broken families. Standing in the same place and witnessing the manic fast-forward to the present day, the difference is simply staggering—gleaming high-rise towers of chrome and glass sprout from pristine, neon-soaked stretches of tarmac, each one ringing with commerce and inhabited by immaculately dressed urbanites, all racing between offices, restaurants, bars, karaoke dens, university halls and more—as if to make up for time so cruelly lost to their grandparents and great-grandparents.

Much, of course, happened inbetween times in order to effect these seismic changes. The national economy was fired into overdrive during the autocratic days of the 1970s and 1980s, when the ubiquitous "Made in Korea" slogan adorned toys and cheap electronic goods exported around the world.

Autumn at Gyeongbokgung, Seoul
©KTO

These days are now long gone, with the military dictatorship pushed aside by a freely-elected democratic government, and basic consumer goods displaced by the technological wizardry of Samsung, LG (Lucky Goldstar), Hyundai and other gigantic Korean conglomerates.

The world sat up and paid attention, granting Korea some of its largest events—Seoul hosted the Summer Olympics in 1988, in 2002 Korea co-hosted the FIFA World Cup with Japan, and the World Championships in Athletics were held in Daegu in 2011. Going forward, the Winter Olympics will be held in the alpine resort of Pyeongchang in 2018, by which time the country will have hoped to cement its status as a winter sports powerhouse, its stars joining the ranks of world-famous Korean footballers and baseball players.

Yongpyong ski resort, Pyeongchang

©KTO

To these can be added movie stars, directors, painters and sculptors—Korea's quick-fire journey to the developed world saw far greater emphasis being placed on commercial production than artistic creativity, but since the turn of the millennium this imbalance has been addressed. Much of East Asia (as well as parts of Europe and Central America) fell head over heels for Korea's sugary TV dramas, while directors such as Kim Ki-duk and Park Chan-wook have been wowing global filmgoers at the cinematic edge of the spectrum.

After decades of rampant westernization, there has also been a noticeable swing back towards Korean tradition—you'll see more and more local styles on locally made clothing and furniture, and many of these are being adopted internationally. However, perhaps the biggest potential soft sell is Korea's famously spicy national cuisine, which is so much more than mere kimchi (which has filled many books on its own). Though it's taking time to catch on, wait a few years and you may well see mung-bean pancakes, super-spicy squid on rice, soy-bean broths or milky-white rice wine on restaurant menus in your own land—why not spend the intervening years trying out these delectable dishes, and many more, in their land of origin?

Then, of course, there's the sightseeing. Korea is a small land, and by making use of one of the world's best-developed public transport systems you'll find that there's no more than a day's travel between A and B—a fact that can make the country's myriad contrasts all the more striking. The capital city, Seoul, is a place of undeniable energy and fascinating historical interest, and this is where most travelers spend most, if not all, of their time. However, to truly grasp the real Korea you simply have to venture outside—you'll be rewarded with a succession of secluded temples, gorgeous hiking trails, remote islands and hidden beaches. You'll be able to ski and go hot-spring bathing in the same day, and have the opportunity to stumble across dinosaur footprints, scale extinct volcanoes, meditate in centuries-old temples, or stay in small villages seemingly caught in an eternal freeze-frame. Each corner of the land has its own dialect and culinary specialty, but even if sticking to the same area you'll be able to appreciate the intricate cobweb of religious and cultural overlays that makes Korea one of Asia's most beguiling corners.

The Country Today

The "Miracle on the Han River," as South Korea's incredible economic and commercial rise since the 1970s has become known, still fascinates the West, even though said miracle demolished entire industries as far afield as America and Europe. The growing success, underlined by the Korean Wave—the inundation of cultural products sweeping over Asia since the 2000s—is based on a winning formula that can only be understood in context with the peculiarities of Korean society. The complexities of a culture shaped by neo-Confucianist ideology and strict governance advocating an attitude of "dynamism" and excellence should not be overlooked.

The country is both triumphant and subject to doubts about its demographic future, among other things. As with any country that has undergone such dramatic political, economic and social shifts, debate about its future is lively. However, South Korea is a land of spiritual as well as material contrasts, as is demonstrated by the ubiquity of religion. If the country's incredible success derives from these contradictions, perhaps here too it will find the key to facing up to the challenges of the future.

KOREAN SOCIETY

Caught between its ancient cultural heritage and its new-found prosperity and embrace with modernity, Korean society is fascinating to observe. Both its heritage and history—recent as well as ancient—must be taken into account if the forces that shape it are to be fully understood.

THE NEO-CONFUCIANIST LEGACY

If there is one aspect of Korea you will find impossible to ignore, it is the legacy of neo-Confucianism. Originating in China in the 12C, the doctrine was first adopted during the Joseon dynasty (1392–1910), although not without considerable resistance. Many centuries were to pass before Korean society could be regarded as "Confucian." It could be argued that the decline of the monarchy and the ancient aristocracy, colonization by Japan and progressive Westernization have accelerated the spread of the values and practices that are thought of as Confucian. The 20C may in fact turn out to have been the most systematically neo-Confucian period in Korea's history, not least with the military regimes that ruled in succession from the 1960s to the 1980s.

In effect, neo-Confucianism incorporates ethical precepts intended to guide relationships between individuals and promote the smooth running of society, with a view to consolidating established authority in particular. The goal was a dynamic harmony between opposites. As far as customs and formalities were concerned, rites were intended to reinforce the links between humans and heaven or between the living and the dead. On a human level, some of these basic precepts still form the basis of the country's Confucian outlook on life.

A Hierarchical Society

The basic relationships to be respected are summed up as *samgang oryun* (three principles and five rules): the allegiance of the subject to the sovereign, the respect of children for their parents and that of a wife for her husband, a relationship of justice and loyalty towards the king, filial devotion and care towards one's parents, a division of labor between men and women, the relationship between the young and the old, and trust between friends.

The patriarchal figure dominates—king, president, father, elder, boss, and so on—and the individual is constantly defined through relationships of subordination and respect. Only with "friends" (people of the same age and, in general, of the same social standing) is equality in relationships really achieved. Age is key in such a hierarchy, not mere function or social standing, and the whole system serves to reinforce authority.

The negative aspect of the hierarchical society is evident in a certain willingness to promote people in the workplace according to age rather than ability, a lack of communication between generations and societal challenges which sometimes inhibit creativity.

The Separation of Male and Female

Men and women, like the Asian philosophical concept of yin and yang, complement each other but are essentially different: Korean texts recommend that the two sexes be kept "apart." Indeed, this is still happening today: of all the countries in the OECD (Organization for Economic Cooperation and Development), Korea holds the record for having the largest salary gap between the sexes, with women earning on average 38 percent less than their male counterparts. Men help women with the housework for 30 minutes a week on average, while in Europe the figure is 2 hours 30 minutes. The proportion of women in employment is around 50 percent while the average across the OECD varies between 60 and 70 percent. This separation creates two distinct worlds which have yet to be reconciled. However, changes are taking place in this macho society—in fact, Korean men have recently become rather popular in other Asian countries for their perceived gentle nature.

Relations and Occupations

The persistent hierarchical nature of Korean society may explain something that seems odd to Westerners: the practice of calling a person by a name that describes their relationship with a person or their social status—uncle (*ajeossi*), aunt (*ajumma*), elder or younger brother, student, teacher, etc. Given first names are seldom used except when dealing with inferiors (parents speaking to children or younger people) or with one's peers (friends of the same age). This practice confirms the importance of hierarchy in Korean society. The Korean language itself requires the use of these terms, and it is difficult to address someone without knowing the proper vocabulary. Married couples, for example, never call one another by their first names; instead they say "darling" or refer to one another using formulas such as "father of X" followed by the name of the first child, demonstrating the extent to which social context is essential to individual identity and, also, providing an insight into the place of institutions such as marriage.

Wedding ceremony

© KTO

The Importance of Marriage

An institution dating back to ancient times, marriage has traditionally afforded women a place in society. Rather than being the union of two free agents who wish to create a home together, it has principally been a pact between two families. Even today it remains one of the necessary rites of passage on the journey to adulthood, and an unmarried individual can be stigmatized as a pariah or abnormal. Thanks to the influence of modern life, the age at which people are marrying has increased and the matrimony market has turned into a hot conversation topic for thirty-somethings. As a result, even if people dream of marriage for love, they turn to intermediaries, with "meetings," as matchmaker-style dates are called. Beyond the cities, the scarcity of potential partners can drive people to seek marriage with those from another country (often with women from Southeast Asia). The disjunct between social pressure and personal aspiration may explain in part why, as elsewhere, Korea's divorce rate continues to rise.

According to the prevalent traditional view, wives are seen principally as mothers; some husbands, once they have fulfilled their purpose, therefore resort to professional services for sex. If you can read Korean, you will see that some streets of Seoul are lined with discreet businesses that, although officially illegal, are nonetheless flourishing: massage parlors (*anma*), karaoke with hostesses (*dallanjujeom*) and business clubs (*room salons*). The situation is such that money linked with the sex industry now represents 4 percent of GDP, according to a survey carried out by the Korean Institute of Criminology in 2003.

DISQUIET IN THE LAND OF THE MORNING CALM

Strong and traditional social mores contribute to the cohesion of the Korean people, but are not without their critics. Given that Korean society is generally very safe, visitors to Seoul may be surprised by the elevated levels of security compared with other major cities.

However, it should not be forgotten that official statistics can give a misleading impression, and it also depends largely on how society views the "crime." So unlike many other parts of the world, Korea seeks to meet challenges that are predominantly not strictly criminal.

Unenviable Records

For some years, South Korea has been setting the kind of records that it could happily do without. Official figures in 2009 showed that 31 people per 100,000 took their own lives, leading suicide to become the fourth most prevalent cause of death after cancer, heart disease and diabetes. The reasons for the high rate of suicide are many and complex, and include social pressure in a highly competitive society where failure reflects on the whole family, the importance of the opinions of others, difficulty in speaking about personal issues, and shortcomings in social care and the medical treatment of psychological problems. In recent years, a number of high-profile actors, businessfolk and politicians have taken their own lives, most notably ex-president Roh Moo-hyun.

Koreans' willingness to accept an alcoholic drink is important in many social situations: it is dificult to imagine an evening without *soju*, a liquor downed in shot glasses. There is plenty of night life in Korean towns, even in the country, and a lot of time is spent in groups (of work colleagues, at business meetings, clubs, associations, and so on). The social cost resulting from this problem is undeniable and inescapable, although it is rarely diagnosed as such and (male) Koreans tend instead to be proud of their "drinking culture," and the activity is increasingly popular with females.

A "Holistic" Society Confronted With Individualism

Korean society is evolving faster than its attitudes. The values underlying social interaction in Korea have been inherited from a past in which they were entirely reasonable and practical, but today they now have to compete with the "globalized" impulses typical of post-industrial societies. Korean society can be seen as fundamentally "holistic": the value of the social whole is honored above the individual. However, set against the competition of Western models and a consumer society in which the individual is greatly valued, things are changing quickly.

The group is still important as a driving force—and is often cited as a virtue to motivate citizens and workers, especially on a national scale when placed under threat—but in daily and private life, especially for the indulged children of the last few generations, the cult of self and personal interest now prevails, as it does elsewhere. There is certainly a disquieting element of *nunchi* (essentially, an innate feeling about or sense of something) judging and regulating society.

A recent study conducted by Samsung showed that Koreans suffer more stress at work than any other nation in the OECD and are also the most dissatisfied (of those polled, 87.8 percent and 74.4 percent respectively gave these responses). One of the reasons cited was the tendency to believe that any conflict can be resolved over drinks with work colleagues in the evening. Yet more and more workers are shunning the drinking culture of the professional world, and women have been the first to raise their voices against it—the very same women who, along with their inequalities in sal-ary, are also the victims of a good deal of sexism.

Faced with an often restrictive and time-consuming professional life, people find that their personal lives shrink in proportion. The public sector and employees of large firms continue to work a five-day week, but the average Korean has no more than 6 hours 27 minutes of real free time available every weekend (a 2008 figure that is now rising, however) and Koreans sleep less (7 hours 49 minutes, on average) than any other population in the OECD.

The treadmill continues at home, as childrens' education must be attended to and private lessons paid for at often expensive *hagwon* crammer schools, so a second job is sometimes required to cover these expenses. Family, religious and other obligations also squeeze the time available for pleasure or leisure, especially in large, congested cities.

The "Hurry-Hurry" Mentality

One of the first clichés foreigners learn in Korea, and not without some justification, is to be found in the expression *bballi bballi*—"hurry hurry"—which the Koreans themselves use to make fun of their penchant for getting things done rapidly. On a first visit, such speed and "efficiency" and the availability of everything to everyone at all times can seem attractive, but "hurry hurry" has an undeniable social, human and

Busy street of Myeongdong, Seoul

©KTO

even economic price. This modern tendency comes as a surprise to observers, for whom the Korea of the past was a world of languor, sometimes caricatured as an Oriental *dolce vita*, or even with a hint of slothfulness, as writer Jack London noted when passing through as a reporter.

Things have certainly changed, and the Koreans have long been galloping at breakneck speed toward the future. This can be explained, in part, as a way of avoiding some pretty painful collective memories—the Japanese made systematic efforts to annihilate Korean culture in the first half of the 20C, and the peninsula remains divided by the civil war that began the second half. There's also the element of national shame that is rarely, if ever, expressed—it was, essentially, the Americans who "rescued" Korea from these two calamities, so the degree to which Korea has become Americanized is hardly surprising. One Korean author summed up the situation as "we are hurrying and hurrying, we just don't know where," but there is evidence that things are slowly starting to change—working hours are decreasing, domestic tourism is increasing, and there's even some newfound respect for local traditions.

ENTERING THE LEISURE SOCIETY

The profound changes that have affected society during the last 15 years should nonetheless be borne in mind. As with all developed countries, Korea is slowly becoming a leisure society and free time is a growing preoccupation, as demonstrated by the recent campaign for, and eventual adoption of, the five-day week. A study of pastimes is equally revealing.

While TV and radio are still top leisure activities (86 percent in 2008), they are declining in favor of exhibitions, museums and arts events. Weekends are increasingly an occasion for trips to the countryside, as demonstrated by the success of the small hotels that almost double up as second homes in a rural setting. Sports like cycling, rafting and skiing are on the rise. More and more Koreans are travelling abroad and, of late, not necessarily in organized groups. The attraction of other lifestyles more attuned to the individual and dedicated to comfort features in numerous media investigations of "well-being." Some date this transition to the end of the 1990s when Korea moved from a quantitative to a qualitative economic approach.

EDUCATION

In addition to neo-Confucianism's legacy, its influence is also noticeable in the high standards of education and training—with emphasis on research—that provide numerous incentives to an economy that is not just run by a conventional Ministry of Economy, but rather a Ministry of Knowledge Economy.

With 82 percent of high school graduates going on to university, 53 percent of the population aged between 25 and 34 have studied in higher education, a rate well above that of the other OECD countries, where the average lies at about 40 percent. What is more, 70 percent of those involved were taking part in further education courses. It is nonetheless apparent that the tremendously important role of education, magnified by a system which encourages particular courses in private schools, can lead families to great sacrifices. Expenditures in this area for 2008 amounted to USD 14 billion, around ₩1.12 million per household, or three times the figure for 2000.

Debt puts a strain on families, sometimes even restricting the size of the family, and fierce competition in schools has been linked with suicides and elevated stress levels. "Education fever" of this kind paradoxically hampers socioeconomic development, but while everyone complains, no one dares to rebel for fear that their children might suffer because of it.

POPULATION

South Korea had a population of 50.5 million in 2010, with a high population density of 1,275 inhabitants per

Danji (apartment blocks) in Suwon, Gyeonggi-do

square mile (492/sq km). Contrary to popular belief, the country owes its demographic growth entirely to the influx of foreigners. A low birth rate and an aging population are two of the greatest challenges to economic growth in the not-too-distant future.

THE DEMOGRAPHIC CHALLENGE

With the lowest birth rate in the OECD (1.08 in 2005, with the average standing at 2.1), Korea is a country whose population will shrink and age unless it finds a solution. If current trends continue, Korea's population will begin to contract in 2018, and the largest proportion of senior citizens in the OECD is forecast for 2050—a whopping 38.2 percent of the population! Looking ahead, this presages a considerable drop in consumption, a labor force deficit and decreasing employment (three babies fewer amounts to the disappearance of one job). Growth in the 2040s could thus drop to 1.53 percent, in comparison to the current figure of 5 percent. Modern South Korea is built on an ideology of ethnic unity and "pure blood," but this homogeneity, which is becoming less accurate, will have to be completely reexamined—South Korea is already opening up to immigration through the rise of mixed marriages.

Foreigners represent investment and an influx of other currencies and work-force, not to mention a future solution to the birth-rate problem. Estimations of population levels in 2009 benefited from an influx of foreigners that resulted in an observed relative growth. The birth rate needs to be brought back up and a plan has been implemented to help young parents who have been discouraged by factors such as the lack of childcare facilities and the high costs of education. Public policy has also been considered to address factors such as work-life balance, with a proposal by President Lee to establish operation "Closed Office" after 5pm on Friday evenings, as anxiety among couples is perceived to be hampering the birth rate. Korea also needs to invest in a family policy: it spends only 0.4 percent of its GDP on fostering the birth rate, as opposed to 3.8 percent in countries like France. Furthermore, although traditional patrilineal society favors boys, the problem of boy-girl imbalance has lessened somewhat thanks to progress in attitudes and the official prohibition of determining sex prior to birth. By 2010, 49.79 percent of the population was female. However, while the proportion of the sexes is now balanced for the first child, a strong disparity in favor of boys is still apparent for the second and third birth. It should also

Seoul and surrounding mountains

©T. Bognar/Photononstop

be remembered that life expectancy in 2008 was 83.3 years for women and 76.5 years for men. South Korea achieved an increase in life expectancy of 26.7 years between 1960 and 2006, the most spectacular rise in the OECD.

THE RURAL EXODUS AND REGIONALISM

From a sociological perspective, the high population density experienced by Koreans in heavily urbanized areas creates an environment that is acknowledged not to be conducive to a high birth rate. The area around the capital accommodates slightly less than half of the population on just 12 percent of the country's land mass—greater Seoul is one of the most densely populated places on the planet. This situation is a result of a continuing flight from rural areas, and the drop in population experienced by inner-city Seoul corresponds to the development of new towns in the suburbs.

There is also a striking number of cities of over a million inhabitants for a country of such small dimensions (70 percent of the land is mountainous, making settling there difficult) and this only compounds the problem of demographic distribution. Even though a slow rebirth of the provinces is discernible, Koreans continue to favor the cities where modernity rules. In the 1980s the under-60s made up 80 percent of

the rural population; however, they now amount to no more than 50 percent.

In addition, the outlying territories were developed unequally after the Korean War. Gyeongsang-do (province in the southeast) produced several influential presidents and was in favor for several decades. The accession of president Kim Dae-jung from Jeolla-do (in the southwest) redressed the balance, and the regions have subsequently competed against one another—especially after the decentralization carried out in 1995—to attract investors (with numerous Free Economic Zones, for example) as well as tourists. This has encouraged the promotion of local heritage, resulting in festivals, anniversary celebrations and all kinds of events that have enhanced the attraction of the regions in a society increasingly seduced by leisure and tourism.

DIASPORA/IMMIGRATION

It would be impossible to write about Korea without mentioning the great Korean diaspora in China, Japan, the US, ex-member states of the Soviet bloc, Europe and South America, among others—no less than 6.9 million Koreans have settled abroad. Some are constrained by poverty or political circumstances, but most retain a strong ethnic identity, forming communities, such as Korea Town in Los Angeles, where they live a relatively comfortable existence.

The desire to leave Korea is still current, as has been shown in recent polls. It is not uncommon for a wife to take her children and settle abroad, sometimes even to change her nationality, leaving her husband home alone to earn money for the children's education. These children—second- and third-generation Koreans—in addition to the thousands of adoptees who attempt to trace their roots, are often welcomed with open arms when they return from so-called developed countries because they bring with them foreign attitudes while still being of the "same blood." They return to Korea, swelling the ranks of the immigrants, even though immigrant workers of other nationalities are sought principally to do the jobs Koreans will no longer take on. A new kind of diaspora in another sense can now be contemplated too, created from the children of the growing number of mixed marriages in the provinces, where the lack of potential wives is leading more and more country dwellers to seek the services of marriage bureaus offering young women of Vietnamese, Filipina and Chinese extraction. In 2011, stories about the hundreds of half-Korean children in the Philippines filled the newspapers. All of this is of major importance in a nation that has long considered "race" as an essential element of its identity.

THE ECONOMY

Is the Korean "dragon" still flexing its muscles? The famous "Miracle on the Han River" saw, in the space of half a century, one of the poorest countries in the world, at the end of the Korean War of 1950–1953, transform to compete with the G8 powers. South Korean products are becoming more and more widespread, although there are still a number of challenges to be faced on the road to the future, notably those of energy and population.

THE 1970S— "MADE IN KOREA"

Korea rebuilt itself not only on the back of foreign investment (from the US in particular), but also thanks to strong governmental control. Between 1970 and 1980, the tag "Made in Korea" denoted products for mass consumption sold at highly competitive prices. However, over time the emphasis has moved toward the quality of products with strong added value, such as electronics and computer equipment. From its humble beginnings as a developing country, Korea is now an industrial nation and a recognized "challenger." In just 38 years, the country has increased its GDP 243-fold.

THE KEY TO SUCCESS

South Korea ranks highly in a number of fields: electronics (top global producer of integrated circuits and digital screens), telephony (third place), shipbuilding (second place), public works, automobile manufacture (fifth place), steel production, oil-refining and more.

Several giants, known as *jaebeol*, lurk behind this success: Samsung, Hyundai, LG, SK, Daewoo, POSCO and others are conglomerates controlled by powerful families. Even though its policy of diversification and delocalization had to be scaled back after the crisis of 1997, Korea is still a major player today and, in certain sectors of industry, remains all but ubiquitous. It is, for example, the leading provider of goods and services in the energy sector (offshore platforms, tankers, etc.). For the *chaebol* (state-owned conglomerates), the world has become not only a vast marketplace but also a prospecting field where arable land and energy sources can be acquired. The key to this success? First and foremost, strong political will, which provided the fiscal means through grants, research and development aid, tax breaks and more, and then the application of technical know-how imported from the US, Japan and Europe that was quickly integrated and Koreanized.

In addition, the domestic market provided the testing ground and a profitable launch pad for products before they were exported to the global market. Access to the international market was achieved by degrees, but once it had started, there was no stopping it;

by 2009, Korea was in business with 223 foreign countries. A further factor was the strong motivation to outdo their Japanese competitors and to take the number-one slot in all global industries. The country also set a record for foreign investment in 2009, with a total of US $30.4 billion. Also in 2009, "operational excellence" achieved through quicker and cheaper production allowed Korea to win the contract to build nuclear power stations in the United Arab Emirates from the established G8 consortia, a historic coup.

THE CHALLENGES OF GLOBALIZATION

While South Korea's GDP may hover between 11th and 15th place in the international rankings (its GDP per capita varies between 30th and 38th), leaving the country in 12th place as a commercial power, it is worth remembering that it occupies first place in a number of sectors.

South Korea recorded the steepest growth for the first two quarters of 2010 of all the OECD countries (+7.6 percent), even beating its own surplus trade balance record (+35 percent in comparison with 2008). This capacity for recovery after, for example, the Asian financial crisis of 1997 is proof of the robustness and adaptability of the economy. Glo-

balization, however, also means that the country will have to face ever increasing competition from giants such as China and India. For the moment, Korea continues to sell them both the value-added technological products it manufactures and a range of cultural exports in the form of television series (drama), films, pop singers, Korean cuisine and so on— the famous *hallyu* (◉ *see p80*) or Korean Wave. But where will the South Korea of the future stand?

Although less than three hours by plane from a market of 1.5 billion people, representing 20 percent of the world's GDP, will it retain its commercial appeal when China and India catch up to its lead in quality of goods? Korea will have to take its turn in confronting the classic problems faced by developed countries, and predictions have been made that it will never achieve the GDP per capita of US $30,000 once anticipated for 2015, by which time it may well have the highest inflation rate in the developed world.

The great Korean conglomerates are certainly leaders in their fields, but most other small and medium-sized companies are not on a level to compete with them, as Jean-Marie Hurtiger, the CEO and Representative Director of Renault-Samsung has pointed out: "Collectively, Korea still thinks of itself as a challenger."

Working in the port, Mokpo

By its very size, South Korea could not claim to dominate every sector, and one of the challenges of the future will be its ability to develop more selectively, carefully choosing the areas in which to excel. Originality and creativity are also at stake—thanks to an emphasis on research and development, Korea is in fourth place worldwide for patents filed, but there are constant reminders of a deficit in innovation and a tendency to copy designs and technologies that have been developed elsewhere. Technical excellence on a large scale is an asset, but Korea will have to be able to reinforce its qualitative growth and truly become a country of innovation. This is just one of the issues at stake for the future—the problems of energy and demographics are yet more pressing.

ENERGY AND THE GREEN NEW DEAL

In August 2008 President Lee Myung-bak launched the Green New Deal, a green growth project with the ambitious aim of reducing carbon emissions to the lowest possible levels (-4 percent by 2020), investing 2 percent of GDP until 2013. In this way he is hoping to make South Korea one of the top seven green powers by 2020. The wish to shine as a "green" country in the eyes of the international community is unmistakable, but behind this plan there is an objective assessment: seen from an environmental perspective, Korea has been a poor student (in 94th place, globally, according to the World Economic Forum) and rapid industrialization makes it a polluter; CO_2 emissions have risen by 99 percent in 15 years, some 25 percent more than most European countries. Industry is the main culprit, but some blame also lies with the *appateu* or "APT," the apartment blocks that are responsible for a quarter of the emissions. Efforts are certainly being made—indeed, there is a national obsession with recycling—but the real problems are to be found in the air and the water, where promotion of green issues is essential.

The greatest driving force, however, is the country's energy dependence. South Korea is the world's tenth-largest energy consumer, with 50% being used by industry, but 97 percent of its energy is imported. It is also the fifth-largest global importer of petroleum, and in second place for gas. This strong dependency on fossil fuels has driven the government to promote energy-saving measures and to search for new deposits abroad.

Funding is also being channeled into research and the development of renewable and ecological energy sources: solar, wind and wave power are just some of the future sources being studied. South Korea is also looking to gain a slice of the growing green market. Transforming green goods and services into hard cash is going to be the alchemy of the future. All told, the sector's national growth rate is estimated at 11 percent for the next few years, and the Green New Deal could create a million new jobs by 2020, as well as generating a vast amount in revenue. It should not be forgotten that this country, devoid of any energy sources of its own, is nonetheless the premier global provider of services and equipment in the energy sector. South Korea is ranked fifth globally in the oil-refining sector, and Lee Myung-bak is intending to export 80 nuclear reactors by 2030, raising Korea to third place worldwide, which is the second great Korean project after the Green New Deal.

PRESTIGIOUS UNIVERSITIES

South Korea has a formidable higher education system, of which the three most renowned universities are Seoul National University, Sungkyunkwan University and Yonsei University. Other respected academies include Hankuk University of Foreign Studies, Ewha Womans University and the universities of Hongik and Sogang. All of these institutions are based in Seoul, which has more than 30 schools of higher education. There are two large foundations outside Seoul, KAIST (Korean Advanced Institute for Science and Technology) and POSTECH (Pohang University of Science and Technology).

History

As a result of its geographical location, the Korean Peninsula has been at the mercy of political upheavals throughout its entire history, and has often been the subject of rivalries between neighboring powers. It has suffered frequent invasions, not least at the hands of Japan, who annexed the entire peninsula in 1910, closing the door on almost two thousand years of uninterrupted regal rule, spread over several dynasties—each with its own fascinating tale to tell. The events of the 1950s were even more horrific than the occupation, with North and South Korea ripped apart by civil war; the two countries remain in a technical state of war to this day.

THE PRINCIPAL STAGES
THE PREHISTORIC PERIOD

According to legend, Dangun, a mythical ancestor born from the union of the son of the Lord of Heaven and a bear-woman, founded the first Korean state in 2333 BC. North Korea claims to have found his remains, but to date has been unwilling to share evidence with the rest of the world. More prosaically, the first traces of Homo sapiens on the Korean peninsula date back to the Lower Paleolithic: two-sided tools, stone axes, picks and hatchets have been discovered in rock strata, and may date back to before 700,000 BC. Archaeological evidence suggests that they continued to be produced until 100,000 BC, at which point smaller artifacts begin to appear. The use of knapped tools such as flint was common during the Middle Paleolithic. The Upper Paleolithic and later, after 30,000 BC, was characterized by the use of slender flake tools (such as scrapers and lithic flakes for carving), the use of raw materials and the appearance of bone implements. It was probably during the Neolithic, about 3000 BC, that groups of Evenks migrating from Manchuria and Siberia more or less supplanted the paleo-Asiatic population of the Korean Peninsula. During the Neolithic, communities making pottery (first of a primitive kind, then featuring comb-tooth patterns after 4000 BC) lived in clans as hunter-gatherers or fisher people.

CITY-STATES AND ROYAL CONFEDERATION
The Use of Bronze and the Formation of the City-States

The Dongyi tribes, or "eastern barbarians" as they are known in Chinese accounts, occupied a territory that extended from the Huai River through Shandong Peninsula and southern Manchuria to the Bohai Gulf and the Korean Peninsula. Thanks to the influence of the Chinese and Scytho-Siberian civilizations, the Dongyi underwent their own Bronze Age.

During their migration east, they absorbed or displaced the local tribes, who fabricated comb-tooth pots, and established their own culture, which made plain pottery. Dongyi society was based on agriculture and they continued to use stone tools, reserving bronze for weapons, sacrificial vases and ornaments. Such practices suggest the existence of a parallel social structure in which the possessors of bronze weapons appropriated agricultural production from Neolithic communities. To distinguish themselves from their inferiors and to affirm their power, the members of one tribe proclaimed themselves the "Sons of Heaven" and constructed imposing dolmens and tombs with stone sarcophagi. This development was the dawn of a kind of political power on the Korean Peninsula.

The Gojoseon Kingdom and the Chinese Commanderies

Tribes reaching the basin of the Taedong River (the Taedonggang, which now flows through the North Korean capital of Pyongyang) integrated with the local inhabitants to form the Gojoseon kingdom, which ruled the territory lying between the Liao River in southern Manchuria and the Taedong from the 4C BC to the beginning of the 3C BC. During the Chinese Warring States period, Gojoseon was certainly the equal of some of these kingdoms. Iron technology spread through northern Asia during the 4C and 3C BC, eventually reaching the Korean Peninsula, and iron tools were introduced in the north along the Yalu, Ch'ongch'on and Taedong rivers. Iron rapidly replaced bronze in the Gojoseon kingdom, with the immigrant groups who introduced it integrating themselves into the local ruling class. This mixed culture of bronze and iron from the northwest of the peninsula was to spread south by land and sea.

Burial practices changed, with dolmens being replaced by two new types of tomb: pit graves and earthenware jar burials. The Qin dynasty (221–206 BC) was succeeded by the Han dynasty (206 BC–AD 220) in China, and the Han went on to suppress revolts in the northern states, the refugees from which spread into Gojoseon territory. One such refugee, Wiman, from the Chinese state of Yan, usurped the throne in 190 BC. In order to bring to heel the Xiongu, a collection of nomadic tribes from northern Asia, the Chinese Han emperor Wudi (186–140 BC) took control of the northern end of the peninsula before taking advantage of the conflict between the Gojoseon and the southern tribes to continue his invasion to the southern coast.

The Han organized the conquered territories into commanderies named Lelang (Nangnang), Zhenfan, Lintun and Xuantu. Lelang, which some historians site in the vicinity of modern-day Pyongyang, was the center of Chinese culture on the peninsula until AD 313, when it was conquered by the kingdom of Goguryeo.

THE FORMATION OF A ROYAL CONFEDERATION

Buyeo

The tribal **Buyeo kingdom**, which occupied the vast fertile plains along the Sungari (also known as the Songhua) River in northern Manchuria, was to become a significant power during the 1C AD, rivalling even Goguryeo to the south.

The Buyeo kingdom was protected by its Chinese neighbors until the fall of the Han dynasty but then gradually weakened under a barrage of attacks by the Xianbei tribes to the north; in 494 AD the ruling families emigrated voluntarily to Goguryeo, and Buyeo was subsumed as a political entity.

As it was in Gojoseon, the basic Buyeo social unit was the clan; these banded together in tribes of different sizes, eventually becoming—given the oppression from China and neighboring powers and making use of the benefits of the metalwork cultures—a tribal league. Where Gojoseon and other tribal groups were primarily agricultural, however, the Buyeo raised cattle.

The Founding of Goguryeo

The Goguryeo tribes lived in the hilly valleys of the Hun (Tung-chia or Tongga) to the north of the central stretch of the Yalu River (the Amnok in Korean), which was one of the principal routes by which first bronze and then iron culture was able to find its way into the peninsula. Chumong, the legendary founder of Goguryeo, was the chief of one of the Buyeo tribes which had arrived from the north.

Goguryeo was in constant conflict with the Chinese, and even the Han dynasty failed to quell or conquer its powerful army, which included substantial cohorts of cavalry. Due to the scarcity of vital food resources across Goguryeo's mountainous territory, it became partially dependent on the lands it conquered to supply its daily needs.

The Tribes of the East and South

The coast was ruled by two tribes with cultures similar to that of Goguryeo— the Okjeo to the north and, farther south, the Eastern Ye, both of which were absorbed by the kingdoms formed from the ancient tribal leagues. The tribes situated south of the Han River (known as the Hangang in Korean) were the last to be reached by the metalwork culture spreading fr-om the continent, and they constructed dolmens similar to those found in the south. Their popula-

One of the "turtle boats" used by Admiral Yi Sun-sin to repel the invading Japanese (late 16C)

©KNTO

tion was periodically boosted by arrivals from the north and after Wiman's seizing of the Gojoseon throne in 190 BC, King Jun fled south and declared himself "King of Han" (a term distinct from the Chinese Han dynasty, pronounced with a different tone in Mandarin and written with a different Chinese ideogram). Such migrations continued after the conquest of Gojoseon by the Chinese Han, as people attempted to escape Chinese rule. The tribes south of the Han River banded together between the 4C BC and the 3C AD in tribal leagues known as the Samhan or Three Hans: Mahan, lying along the west coast; Jinhan, east of the Nakdong River (Nakdonggang); and Byeonhan, west of the Nakdong.

THE THREE KINGDOMS ERA

According to existing ancient texts, the era known as the Three Kingdoms of Korea was thought to have begun around the formation of said kingdoms in 1C BC. Archaeological discoveries at the end of the 20C may have pushed back this date by several centuries, though some international observers dispute these results. It was at this time that the Korean Peninsula was occupied by not three but four distinct political entities: the kingdom of Goguryeo, beside the Yalu (Amok) River to the north; the kingdom of Baekje, in the Geum River (Geumgang) basin to the southwest; the kingdom of Silla to the southwest; and a confederation, Gaya, to the south.

Goguryeo (37 BC–AD 668)

Goguryeo's population comprised five clans. The chief of the royal clan built a temple dedicated to ancestor worship and paying homage to territorial guardian spirits and agricultural deities, but the history of Goguryeo is one of constant conflict between the chief and the aristocracy. The state adopted the Chinese royal title of *wang* for its leaders at the turn of the 1C AD, by which time Confucianism had made its mark in society. Buddhism was introduced in 372 by a Chinese monk called Sundo. It immediately found favor with the people; however, Taoism also began to spread. Aristocrats were interred beneath a vast tumulus of earth or in a tomb covered with a cairn of stones.

Baekje (18 BC–AD 660)

The formation of the Samhan tribal confederations seems to owe much to the stream of refugees from the north. Baekje, one of the Buyeo tribes, fled Goguryeo, settled in the Han basin and unified the Mahan tribes before extending its power base south to found the eponymous kingdom. Baekje established relations with the Chinese dynasties in order to check Goguryeo expansion after 372, but its capital Han-seong (south of modern-day Seoul) was nonetheless destroyed in 475 before being rebuilt farther south at Ungjin (now known as Gongju) in the province of South Chungcheong. In 538 it was to move again, this time to a more auspicious site in Sabi (now called Buyeo). Economic and cultural developments in the dynasties of southern China allowed Baekje to become a sophisticated civilization, relying on sea routes to maintain contact with China while the Goguryeo kingdom had the use of roads. In 384 Malanant'a, a Central Asian monk arriving from southern China, introduced Buddhism, which became more rapidly and firmly established in Baekje than in Goguryeo, where Taoism was more popular.

Silla (57 BC–AD 668)

The most powerful of the Jinhan tribes occupied part of the Gyeongju Plain and was known as Saro. Legend has it that after hatching from an egg laid by a divine horse, a leader named Hyeok-geose became its first sovereign; according to recorded history, he was merely a member of the Bak clan and the chief of one of its six constituent tribes. Saro developed federal alliances with the other fortified city-states and began to expand, gradually transforming itself into a kingdom as its territories grew.

Silla society was divided into a number of ranks, including the "sacred bones" (members of the royal clan throughout almost all of the Early Silla period) the "true bones" (aristocrats), the rest of the community and those who had been enslaved. Distinctions were made between each of these ranks through their dwellings, the right to use precious metals, their clothes and their tombs. The *Hwarang* ("flower knights") were chosen from among the children of the nobility and led separate lives, studying singing and music while being subject to strict military discipline and receiving an education with its roots in Confucianism, Buddhism and Taoism. Some of these went on to achieve greatness, such as general Kim Yu-sin (595–673),

who was instrumental in the unification of a large part of the peninsula under Silla in the mid-7C.

The kingdom represented one of the easternmost points of the Silk Road. Silla culture underwent radical transformations under Chinese influence in the 6C and 7C, although the practice of Buddhism, which had been introduced by Goguryeo monks (Mukhoja in the mid-400s and Ado towards the end of the century) was not officially adopted by the kingdom until 527. Ancestor worship was also prevalent.

The Gaya Confederacy (AD 42–532)

The region west of the Nakdong River was occupied by the six most powerful tribes of the Byeonhan. The Geumg-wan Gaya or Bon Gaya tribe (which had settled near Gimhae) and the Dae Gaya tribe (which lived in the Boryeong area) formed the backbone of this tribal confederacy, but before Gaya could transform itself into a true state in its own right, it was annexed by the neighboring kingdom of Silla in 562.

LATER SILLA (668–935) AND BALHAE (698–926)

Often known as Unified Silla, this kingdom did not in fact extend as far as the northern borders of the older kingdom of Goguryeo during the unification of the peninsula, although it occupied all the territory south of a line stretching from the Taedong River to Wonsan Bay. Refugees from Goguryeo had settled on the Manchurian remnants of the kingdom in the far north to establish Balhae. Silla and Balhae went to war several times, leading Silla to construct a defensive wall along its northern frontier. In 926, Balhae was eventually wiped out by the Khitans, a people from the extreme north of China.

Later Silla, which had to administer lands and a population far larger than in the past, reorganized its territorial governance between 678 and 687, laying out its capital along the lines of Chang'an (modern Xian), capital of the Sui (581–618), and the cities of the Tang.

Although contact between the Three Kingdoms and their Chinese neighbors existed, it was mainly on a war footing. Silla and Balhae later established diplomatic relations with the Tang dynasty (618–907) and economic and cultural exchanges, principally carried out by sea, were conducted within the constraints of the Tang tribute system. Silla also sent ambassadors to the Imperial Court, which bestowed the title of "king" on its rulers and gave gifts of ginseng, silks, sealskin, gold, silver and horses to its ambassadors.

Tea growing was introduced to Silla when a plant seeds were imported from China in 828. Diplomatic overtures were also made to Japan. Trouble stirred up by the aristocracy at the turn of the 10C was compounded by popular revolts over taxes and forced labor, which brought about the ruin of the kingdom after more than 10 centuries of existence.

In 918, Wang Geon (877–943), a member of the insurgent nobility, became king of Taebong, the kingdom that was to become Goryeo.

GORYEO (918–1392)

The kingdom of Goryeo is pronounced "Ko-ryo," from which the English name for the country "Korea" emerged. The capital, Songdo (now the North Korean city of Kaesong), was founded in 919 by Wang Geon, who by 936 had subjugated virtually the whole of the peninsula. To thank Buddha for his protection, he resolved to build Buddhist monasteries on favorable sites and adopt the customs of the Tang dynasty. After the Tang's fall in 907 and the subsequent incursions led by the Liao dynasty of the Khitan Empire (907–1125), the kingdom was ruled by the Mongols between 1231 and 1368, when the capital was relocated to Ganghwa Island.

The king of Goryeo officially swore fealty to Kublai Khan in 1270, and the Koreans went on to learn how to ferment wine, distil *soju* (strong alcohol), refine sugar, grow pepper, and make *mandu* dumplings and *dubu* soya paste. Some of the Japanese islands sent tributes to Goryeo after it ransacked the Japanese island of Kyushu. Although Buddhism played a fundamental role in this period, the administration of the country was based on Confucianism.

The people of Goryeo often married within their own social or ethnic group, and divorces and remarriages were common. By the end of the era it was usual for family goods to be shared equally between siblings. The accumulation of wealth by the nobility and the growth of their power, along with the excessive indulgence shown toward ambitious Buddhist monks and the favoring of certain groups above others, served to weaken royal power.

Precious Archives

With its strong Confucian influences, the House of Yi (1392–1910), also known as the Joseon dynasty, attached great importance to rites and ceremonies marking significant moments in the year and in court life. Protocols of royal occasions of this kind were assiduously recorded (sometimes with the addition of illustrations) in manuscripts which were deposited in the royal library at Oegyujanggak on Gangwha-do, the island in the Yellow Sea west of Seoul. The French looted 297 of these manuscripts during a raid led by Rear-Admiral Roze in 1866 and removed them to the Bibliothèque Nationale in Paris. The Koreans, who regard the documents as an essential record of their history (they are inscribed on UNESCO's Memory of the World Register), petitioned the French government for their return for years and finally, in November 2010, presidents Nicolas Sarkozy and Lee Myung-bak settled this long-standing dispute as part of the G20 summit at Seoul; France returned the manuscripts to Korea on the basis of a long-term loan to be automatically renewed every five years.

Exhibit, Seoul Museum of History ©KTO

The military succeeded in imposing a dictatorship, and in 1392, general **Yi Seong-gye** took power and the temple name Taejo and founded another dynasty.

JOSEON (1392–1910)

The **Yi dynasty** called its kingdom Joseon, meaning "morning calm." To reinforce his power, Yi Seong-gye appointed 55 vassals who held a majority on the royal council responsible for important decisions in civil and military affairs of state. He relocated the capital to Hanyang (now Seoul) in 1394, surrounding the city with a 10.5-mi/17-km fortress wall with eight gates, including Namdaemun, the great southern gate, and Dongdaemun, the equally imposing eastern gate. The city was divided into five districts of 52 quarters, and a palace and government buildings were constructed.

The Joseon kings wanted to promote an ideal Confucian society based on the Chinese neo-Confucian model, casting off the Buddhist influence which had predominated in Goryeo. The sons of the *yangban* (noblemen) were trained in accordance with Confucian ideology—and usually at great length—before taking up posts in government. The society of the time was rigorously hierarchical and the principal concern of the *yangban* was to maintain family bloodlines, even if this meant marrying within a branch of the family of common descent.

Daily life was ordered according to Confucian principles intended to maintain social order and was based on rituals and ceremonies marking the passage from childhood to adult life, marriage, funerals and ancestor worship. Women were obliged to obey their parents before marriage and then their husbands; after the latter's death they were then obliged to obey their sons. Wives did not even officially bear a surname until the turn of the 20C.

In 1443, the Confucians devised *Hangeul*, the Korean alphabet comprising 11 vowels and 17 consonants, to facilitate administration during the reign of King Sejong; it was set out in a document for the people in 1446, but its use was suppressed by the powerful aristocracy of the time, who were fearful of handing over relative knowledge, and therefore influence, to the commonalty. (*Hangeul* did not, in fact, truly take hold until the end of Japanese occupation in 1945.) In 1592, the Japanese shogun Toyotomi Hideyoshi (1536–1598) decided to invade China, and 150,000 Japanese troops landed at Busan. They first occupied Seoul and then Kaesong and Pyongyang. The Korean admiral of the fleet, Yi Sun-sin (1545–1598) (*see box p 336*), commanded the construction of boats armored with iron plates and festooned with spikes and cannons;

the Japanese navy lost 160 ships, China intervened and the Japanese finally gave up their campaign in 1598. The Japanese introduced firearms, the use of the saber, tobacco, pimentos and zucchini to Korea. Korean prisoners held in Japan improved their pottery-making techniques and learned printing, while the Chinese introduced European methods for cannon manufacture and military training to Korea.

Much to the surprise of the government, Korea then suffered two invasions from Manchuria and was obliged to surrender in 1637. As subjects of the Chinese, the Koreans learned of the existence of Europe via Peking (Beijing) at the end of the 16C. They also discovered Catholicism or *Seohak* ("Western learning"). Western nations attempted to make contact with Korea from the turn of the 19C onward, although massacres of Catholics in 1839 and again in 1866 by the Daewongun (regent) were met with a French naval attack on Ganghwa Island (Ganghwado) at the mouth of the Han River in 1866; the French subsequently carried off precious manuscripts describing the ceremonies of the Korean ruling dynasty (see box p56).

The Japanese were the first to establish a treaty with Korea (which was signed under duress in 1876), followed by the US in 1882 and various European powers, including Britain in 1883. A large number of foreign advisors were appointed to help Korea modernize its currency, mines, agriculture, legal system and architecture, and to introduce electricity. *Donghak*, or Eastern Learning, sprang from this push toward Westernization.

JAPANESE COLONIZATION (1910–1945) AND THE KOREAN WAR (1950–1953)

Control of Korea became the prize in the rivalry between Russia, China and Japan that led to the First Sino-Japanese War in 1894 and the Russo-Japanese War in 1904, from which Japan emerged victorious. Powerless to resist, the Joseon dynasty was progressively wiped out as the Japanese took over the country, which became a protectorate in 1905 and was fully annexed by 1910. Korea remained a Japanese province until 1945, with a governor-general embodying all legislative, executive and judicial powers. Growing resistance against the Japanese took on a number of forms: a secret mission to La Haye in 1907, cells of Korean resistance troops in Manchuria and the formation of a provisional government in exile in Shanghai. Initially hailed as "enlightened," Japan's rule

A Flag Rich in Symbols

The center of the distinctive South Korean flag features a *taegeuk*, a design inspired by the Chinese yin and yang symbol with red and blue intertwined as one. The blue represents yin (the feminine) and the red, yang (the masculine). Four different trigrams (*kwe*) are arranged in the four corners of the flag: three solid bars represent the sky (*geon*), opposite three broken bars representing the earth (*gon*); two broken bars and one solid represent water (*kam*), and lie opposite two solid bars and one broken denoting fire (*ri*). The white background symbolizes peace and purity and the *taegeuk* all things in the universe.

© Chris Stowers/Apa Publications

became increasingly repressive, to the point of appearing intent on the systematic annihilation of Korean culture.

LIBERATION AND PARTITION FROM 1945 TO THE PRESENT

After the Japanese surrender of 1945, two differing administrations were established, with the Americans controlling the south and the Soviets installing their own protégés in the north (the Provisional People's Committee for North Korea, headed by Kim Il-sung). The 38th parallel became the border between North and South Korea. When the Soviet north refused elections, they were held in the south alone on 10 May 1948, confirming partition. An elected assembly established a constitution and declared the formation of the **Republic of Korea**, whose first president was **Syngman Rhee** (Lee Sung-man, 1875–1965). The north answered in September 1949 by declaring the **Democratic People's Republic of Korea** (DPRK) under President **Kim Il-sung**.

Believing that it would be easy to seize power, the North Koreans launched a surprise attack at dawn on 25 June 1950, and the Korean War began.

For a more detailed description of the conflict, see p60.

The despotism of the Syngman Rhee government worsened after 1952, and a third reelection was engineered. Riots broke out in 1960, claiming a number of victims; despite the imposition of martial law, the president was obliged to stand down. The 2nd Republic came into being in July 1960 with the election of President Yun Bo-seon (1897–1990), although this was overturned a year later by a revolt led by an army officer named **Park Chung-hee** (1917–1979). The KCIA (Korean Central Intelligence Agency), a division of the secret police with considerable powers, was created and a new constitution extended the president's authority. Park Chung-hee contrived his election in December 1963 and, with the support of an authoritarian regime founded on virulent anti-Communism, sought to rebalance the

country's economy. He was reelected in 1965, 1971 and 1978, despite rioting thanks to his despotic rule in the face of growing opposition; he was assassinated in 1979, though even today some Koreans look back on his rule with affection. Little changed immediately after Park's death– he was eventually succeeded by fellow military leader Chun Doohwan, who was to lead the suppression of the Gwangju riots in 1980 (over 200 died in what amounted to a government-sponsored massacre). His authoritarian leadership, combined with a series of financial scandals, provoked violent demonstrations and Chun designated **Roh Tae-woo** as the official candidate to succeed him.

Roh acceded to the opposition's demand for universal suffrage and, once elected, was obliged to follow a policy of democratization accelerated by the organization of the Olympic Games in 1988, which enabled him to make overtures to the Soviet bloc countries. Commercial treaties were signed between South Korea and the USSR in 1990, and exchanges with China were broadened. The democratization of South Korea was reinforced by the elections of Presidents Kim Young-sam in 1992, Kim Dae-jung in 1997 and Roh Moo-hyun in 2002. The 1997 election heralded a sea-change— while almost all leaders before him came from Seoul or the southeast, Kim hailed from the rural southwest—the hub of the opposition, and as such largely starved of government funding. Kim was, in fact, sentenced to death for his role in the uprising that led to the 1980 Gwangju massacre; he not only survived, but found himself leader of the country, then the recipient of the Nobel Peace Prize for his efforts to stabilize the North Korean situation. A historic summit meeting was held between President Kim Dae-jung and North Korean leader Kim Jong-il at Pyongyang in June 2000, cementing the political overtures made by the South to the North under President Roh Moo-hyun and known as the Sunshine Policy; this ended with the election of **Lee Myung-bak** in December 2007.

The DPRK itself had, following the war, attempted to reconstruct its economy with aid from other socialist countries; President Kim Il-sung (1912–1994) also launched the *Juche* movement, promoting political autonomy, economic independence and self-defense of the state to advance his country along an independent socialist route.

Pyongyang sought rapprochement with Moscow and Beijing by turns, according to the political situation, before aligning itself with China, its most faithful ally, in the 1980s. A dynasty was instituted by degrees and **Kim Jong-il** succeeded to the leadership.

THE KOREAN WAR IN CONTEXT

After Japan's capitulation on **15 August 1945**, Korea was partitioned along the 38th parallel. The American authorities suggested that the Russian forces, which had just entered the war against Japan (on 9 August 1945), should occupy the northern part of the peninsula and accept the surrender of Japanese troops stationed as far as Manchuria. The Americans would take care of the area south of the 38th parallel. After 1945, the 38th parallel became a **de facto border** between the two Koreas.

This situation was reinforced in 1948 with the declaration of the Republic of Korea (south of the 38th parallel, and now usually referred to as South Korea) under American and Western influence, and the Democratic People's Republic of Korea (north of the 38th parallel, and similarly now called North Korea) under Soviet control.

This partition line was to become the scene of numerous skirmishes and incidents after 1945—as the **Cold War** set in and tensions rose between European power blocs, the Korean War was the first open conflict of the period and one of the first examples of multinational intervention after a United Nations mandate was made to a single country, the United States.

THE PRINCIPAL PHASES OF THE WAR

The war began on 25 June 1950 with no initial formal declaration of hostilities. The North Korean offensive into South Korean territory was concentrated on the transport arteries leading to Seoul, and the capital fell on 28 June. North Korean troops continued their advance towards the south of the peninsula, occupying almost the entire country and pushing back South Korean units to their last redoubts around the city of Pusan (now romanized as Busan) on the banks of the Nakdong River, which had been established as the last line of defense (the Pusan Perimeter) in mid-July 1950.

United Nations Involvement

Security Council resolutions 82 (25 June) and 84 (7 July), which are still currently in force, condemned the North Korean invasion, demanded a halt to the offensive and gave the United States the mandate to form and command a multinational force under the UN banner to reestablish the status quo. The United States committed an infantry unit (Task Force Smith) on 5 July. The United Nations Command was established in Japan under General MacArthur on 7 July and the president of South Korea placed his own troops under the UNC, joining a multinational ensemble of detachments (fighting units were deployed by 16 countries, with five others providing medical support).

General MacArthur launched a large-scale amphibious landing behind North Korean lines at Incheon (a large port to the west of Seoul) on 15 September, breaking the siege of Busan and permitting a counteroffensive by UNC troops toward Seoul, which was liberated on 28 September.

A further landing was undertaken on the east coast in October, allowing progress northward on two fronts. The UNC was authorized to cross the 38th parallel and continue operations in the north on 10 October, and the multinational force, with its South Korean allies, entered Pyongyang on 19 October, finally reach-

Monument to fallen soldiers,
UN Memorial Cemetery, Busan

©Pietro Scozzari/age fotostock

ing the Chinese frontier (the Yalu and Tumen rivers) on 24 October 1950.

The Chinese People's Volunteer Army mustered troops north of the frontier over a period of a few weeks, crossing the Yalu in mid-October and entering the fray en masse at two different points (31 October and 26 November).

The assembled UNC forces crumbled and a hurried withdrawal was made from the ground they had gained: Pyongyang was lost on 4 December and a large-scale evacuation of both military personnel and civilians was organized at Heungnam-Hamheung at Wonsan Bay on the east coast.

The Chinese and North Korean forces advanced south and crossed the 38th parallel on 31 December 1950. Seoul was retaken on 4 January 1951.

The American command of UN forces under General Ridgeway succeeded in halting the retreat south of Seoul on a line running east-west through Osan, Jecheon and Samcheok at the end of January and the beginning of February 1951, thanks in part to its success in decisive engagements at Chipyong-ni and Wonju.

UN forces were able to begin an advance north by March 1951, and Seoul changed hands again on 14 March. Anticipating negotiations and wanting to avoid any prolonging of the conflict, US President Truman dismissed General MacArthur shortly afterwards (11 April), following MacArthur's demands for the use of nuclear weapons and the intervention into the conflict of Nationalist China; General Ridgeway was announced as his replacement.

After substantial troop movements, the two sides battled one another to a standstill by mid-1951, with the front stabilizing along the 38th parallel—neither side had gained much territory, but

Three Years of War—Some Statistics

Of the 1,269,349 combatants mobilized by South Korea, no less than 137,800 were killed and in excess of 32,000 were taken prisoner or listed as missing.

The total commitment of the United Nations (the US and 20 other countries) over the three years amounted to 1,940,498 military personnel (1,798,000 from the US), of which 40,670 died in combat (36,940 US fatalities); more than 104,000 were seriously wounded and 5,815 soldiers, including 4,439 Americans, are still listed as missing in action. *Source: South Korean Ministry of Patriots' and Veterans' Affairs (MPVA)—2010 commemorative plaque. For more information, visit http://eng.koreanwar60.go.kr/.*

both had suffered substantial human losses.

Although the "border" had solidified, protracted and particularly bloody engagements were nonetheless fought at the Imjin River (Imjingang), Inje, Heartbreak Ridge, the Punchbowl, Arrowhead, T-Bone and elsewhere until July 1953, with UN troops gaining ground principally in the mountainous areas of the center and the east to the north of the 38th parallel.

The 1953 Armistice

Negotiations began at Kaesong in the neutral zone on 7 July 1951 and were continued at Panmunjom (now romanized Panmunjeon) until the treaty was signed. Bargaining continually broke down over the difficult question of the mutual repatriation, whether voluntary or forced, of the numerous prisoners of war.

The **armistice** signed by the military commanders of the opposing forces on **27 July 1953** at Panmunjeom and Munsan suspended hostilities along the front line, separating the two sides along a military demarcation line (MDL) and establishing the **demilitarized zone (DMZ)** that now runs across the entire peninsula. (👆 *see p229*).

The terms of the armistice also awarded South Korea five Northwest Islands in close proximity to North Korean territory. In addition, the armistice established a **surveillance and supervision system** under the aegis of the Military Armistice Commission (MAC), a body made up of North Koreans, Chinese volunteers (who no longer attend) and representatives of the United Nations (UNCMAC).

The Neutral Nations Supervisory Commission (NNSC) is responsible for making sure that the various terms of the armistice are adhered to. Initially formed with representatives from four nations (with each side choosing two), the Commission now includes delegates from Switzerland, Sweden and Poland.

In addition to the Armistice Agreement, a **maritime demarcation line** known as the Northern Limit Line (NLL) was set up by the United Nations Command in 1953, extending the MDL out into the sea to the west and to the east. North Korea refused to recognize the line and has made frequent sorties across it, and the waters in the west have seen four bloody naval engagements between the two Koreas since 1999.

The Geneva Conference—held in 1954 to find a political solution to the war—ultimately failed, and the armistice under military control continues to this day; the basic terms of the Armistice Agreement of 1953 still hold, as do the monitoring systems that were set up.

The War Memorial of Korea, Seoul

©A. Pistolesi/Tips/Photononstop

Art and Culture

Many elements of Korean culture have their roots in China, and this is particularly true of the peninsula's traditional art and architecture. Local variations to the latter were largely incremental as far as temples, palaces and other large structures were concerned, though the wooden, mud-walled abodes of the common man became highly distinctive over the centuries—although declining in number with each passing year, pockets still survive around the land, even in central Seoul. The local take on traditional art was, perhaps, more subtle, though defined by its vitality and spontaneity; renowned historian Ko Yu-seop (1905–1944) summed up Korean painting as "technique without technique," "sketching without sketching," "asymmetry" and "lack of pretension." During the Three Kingdoms period, Korea developed its own techniques in the fields of pottery, jewellery and furniture design, and exported artisans to Japan, a country now far more famous in said fields. Indeed, contemporary Korean fare remains hugely underrated outside East Asia—for visitors from farther afield, this is likely to add a touch of mystery to the country's many superb galleries.

BASIC PRINCIPLES

Traditional Korean architectural forms adhere largely to **Chinese traditions**, with a basically rectangular structure, open to the south, over a stone base (the *gidan*) beneath sturdy wooden posts on foundation stones. The roof is secured to the posts by a series of beams, while the spaces between the posts are filled with cob (mud) or wood to form non-loadbearing walls. Doors and windows consist of wooden latticework covered with opaque white paper. The eaves extend beyond the walls to cover a veranda which runs around the building. A system to support the weight of the eaves was developed in China and then adopted in Korea and Japan with slight variations. The posts support consoles that can be combined in different arrangements, with their complexity depending on their period of creation—these are, however, more for decoration than any functional purpose.

Traditional buildings have long been topped with tiles, rather than thatched roofs, though the latter still remain in evidence on the far-flung southern island of Jeju. This is the rainiest place in the land, making somewhat ironic the fact that buildings elsewhere largely switched to tiles to guard against rainwater—tiles can be either convex or concave, which respectively correspond to masculine and feminine in the grand Confucian scheme of things. The edge tiles are frequently decorated, particularly in temples, where their designs are, short of asking a resident monk, the best way of divining the particular Buddhist sect in question. In addition, the gable seams are often covered with a white coating and topped with an antefix.

Since the 15C, the ridge tiles of palaces have featured a line of mythical grotesques, sometimes human in appearance. In large buildings, the wood and cob at the edges of the roof and the interior frame and ceilings are covered with protective paintwork known as *dancheong* ("red and green"), which features stylized, interlacing motifs. Murals of the Buddhist pantheon often complete the decor on the exterior walls of Buddhist pavilions. Although Confucian buildings are almost entirely devoid of color, funeral monuments have some color and private houses are always neutral. The dimensions of buildings are based on the number of *kan*, a unit of length measured as the distance between two posts, but the use of wood also limits the size. In addition, the rooms (*dang* or *jeon*) in temples and palaces are essentially intended to house cult images and altars, or the throne and its accessories. In all complex architecture of any size, a series of pavilions is arranged along an

Haeinsa Buddhist monastery

©KTO

axis within a courtyard that is generally enclosed by covered walkways—Buddhist monasteries and palaces also tend to follow this pattern.

The fragility of these constructions means that, in the oldest buildings, only the stone bases and the stones that supported the wooden posts survive; in addition, repeated Japanese invasions and the civil war of the 1950s means that where this is not the case, the building is likely to have been reconstructed several times during its history. The only architectural structures to survive from the very oldest periods are stone or brick tombs, which are most prevalent on and around the Yellow Sea coast—the most accessible are on the island of Ganghwado, just west of Seoul.

FORTRESS ARCHITECTURE

The main forms of military architecture are mountain fortresses and the fortifications of provincial capitals – the Gongsanseong fortress in Gongju serves as an excellent example of a mountain fortress, though better known is Suwon's Hwaseong (⟲ see p222), originally designed to usurp Seoul's palaces as the royal capital and also to house and honor the remains of his father, Prince Sado. Originally built as earthworks, military fortifications were constructed using stone from the

15C onwards. Typically rectangular or round enclosures, four principal gates, consisting of a semi-circular vaulted passageway beneath a pavilion, provide access through the fortress walls. Just two of the original eight gates in Seoul's fortress wall have survived the city's recent development.

ROYAL ARCHITECTURE

The dawn of the Joseon period, during which the capital was relocated from Gaegyeong (Kaesong) to Hanyang (Seoul) saw the construction of grandiose palaces, including Gyeongbokgung, Changdeokgung and Gyeongungung. Gyeongbokgung was the first to be built, located to the north of Seoul, within the fortified city walls. Following the traditional feng shui lead of contemporary Chinese designs, it was surrounded by a curtain wall and arranged south-to-north. When the king convened large assemblies, civil servants and soldiers would assemble in front of the throne room building, each standing beside a stone marker engraved with his rank at court, facing toward the building where the king was seated. The palaces fell victim to fire, and were reconstructed and modified over the years as needs dictated before being subjected to further devastation in the 20C. Their restoration has been under way for several years.

ABC'S OF ARCHITECTURE

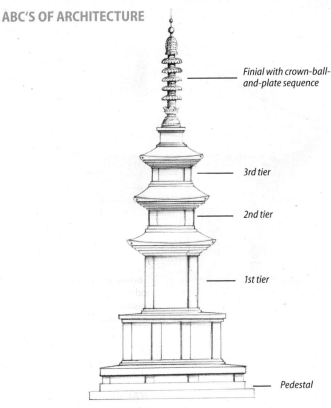

Finial with crown-ball-and-plate sequence

3rd tier

2nd tier

1st tier

Pedestal

Buddhist pagoda in stone

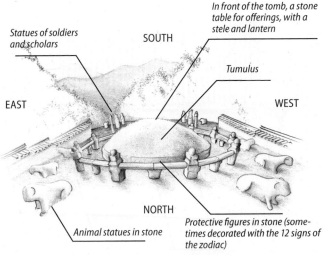

In front of the tomb, a stone table for offerings, with a stele and lantern

Statues of soldiers and scholars

SOUTH

Tumulus

EAST

WEST

NORTH

Animal statues in stone

Protective figures in stone (sometimes decorated with the 12 signs of the zodiac)

H. Choimet/MICHELIN

**Royal or aristocratic tomb from the Joseon dynasty
(from the north, looking south)**

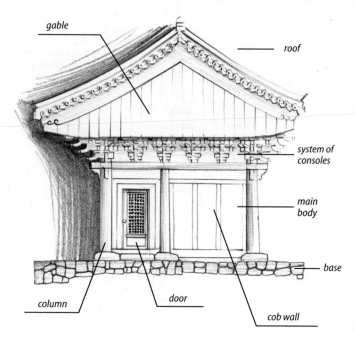

gable

roof

system of consoles

main body

base

column

door

cob wall

Side view of a pavilion in a Buddhist monastery

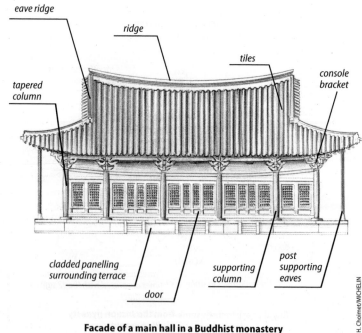

eave ridge

ridge

tiles

console bracket

tapered column

cladded panelling surrounding terrace

door

supporting column

post supporting eaves

H. Cholmet/MICHELIN

Facade of a main hall in a Buddhist monastery

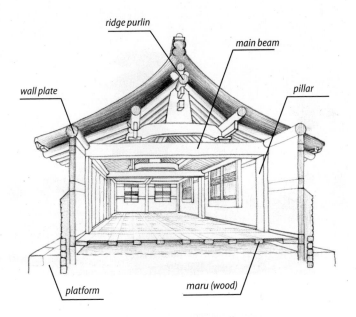

ridge purlin

main beam

wall plate

pillar

platform

maru (wood)

**Interior of a traditional Korean building
(with wing-style console)**

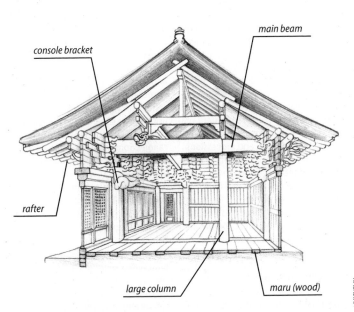

main beam

console bracket

rafter

large column

maru (wood)

**Interior of a traditional Korean building
(multiple-console style)**

Five-story stone pagoda, Jeongnimsa, Buyeo

©KTO

BUDDHIST ARCHITECTURE

The layout of Buddhist temple buildings (whose names all end with the suffix *sa*) in the Three Kingdoms was strictly controlled. Monastic layout was based on axes and symmetry: approaching from the south, there would be one or two gates, a pagoda, a main ceremonial room, and then a *gangdang*, or assembly room. The *tap*, or pagoda, determined the layout. In the Far East the *tap* took the form of a *stupa*, a large structure made of wood or stone, built to house relics known as *sari*, which were placed in the foundations or stored on one of the *stupa*'s tiers. The arrangement of buildings in a monastery was designed to venerate the relics, and processions were carried out around them in a clockwise direction. The pagoda stood in front of the main ceremonial building, the *geumdang*, which housed the most important religious images—some still remain today in the more important temples.

Mongol invasions in the 13C and the Japanese campaigns at the end of the 16C resulted in the destruction of many wooden pagodas. The base stones that supported the posts of the nine-tier wooden pagoda erected in 645 on the site of the Hwangnyong monastery at Gyeongju suggest that these first pagodas were similar to the pagoda of Horyu-ji, located in Nara, Japan. A number of stone pagodas (known as *seoktap*) have survived, with the oldest extant examples dating back to the 7C; pagodas from the Kingdom of Baekje can be found at the temples of Mireuksa (638) at Iksan and Jeongnimsa at Buyeo, while the rival Silla kingdom boasts its own survivors in Gyeongju, at the temples of Bunhwangsa (634) and Gameunsa (682). The pagodas at Gameunsa are examples of the classic style, with three stories of stone slabs rising from a square stone base or *gidan*. The pinnacle is topped with a parasol or canopy. Some stone pagodas are copies of Chinese brick buildings (such as those at Bunhwangsa), while others are more complex (the best examples being those at Bulguksa). During the Goryeo dynasty, pagodas became elaborately carved and boasted an extremely elegant heptagonal or octagonal section—this is often all that remains of monasteries that have long since disappeared.

No ancient Buddhist monasteries have survived in any South Korean city. This can be largely attributed to changes in the local Buddhist climate, which saw religious structures moving out of urban areas and into mountain valleys. The two most subscribed sects—the Jogye order and the Buddhist school of *Seon* meditation (introduced by Jinul and known as *Chan* in Chinese and *Zen* in Japanese)—both required the layout of their buildings to be dictated by the terrain, and as such the strict rules of the Three Kingdoms had to be abandoned. The monasteries were reached by several gates, usually three, with the third gate housing a reading room. This opened out onto a courtyard to the north, in the middle of which there stood a lantern-like stone pagoda in front of the main ceremonial chamber, often containing a representation of the Shakyamuni Buddha. Rooms for the monks and for secondary worship were arranged around all sides of the courtyard, and there may also have been either a room dedicated to prayers for the dead or, standing to one side, a small temple consecrated to *Sansin*, the mountain god. The musical instrument pavilion would house a bronze bell, a wooden fish, a bronze plaque shaped like a cloud and other instruments to be struck during worship. *Budo*, small *stupas* containing the remains of notable monks, would typically stand outside on a terrace.

CONFUCIAN BUILDINGS

Confucian buildings and complexes served both educational and cultural needs in honor of the philosophy's founder Confucius and other Confucian sages. Munmyo, South Korea's principal Confucian shrine, is in the grounds of the ancient educational institute Seonggyungwan (now Sungkyunkwan University in modern-day Seoul). *Hyanggyo* were government-run provincial schools, while the *seodang*, or "room of books," an elementary school without a temple (either public or private), was a feature of the Joseon era and resembled an ordinary house. The *hyanggyo* consisted of two rooms along a central axis, one of which was used for teaching and the other for the veneration and storage of tablets written by Confucian sages. Auxiliary buildings stood to either side of this axis. Numerous shrines were built to celebrate solemn rites for the protection of the Joseon (Yi) dynasty, including Jongmyo in Seoul, which conducted rites for the ancestors of the royal family.

THE HOMES OF THE NOBILITY

The strict separation of men and women ensured that space was also divided in family houses, with one building reserved for men (*sarangchae*) and

Ondol underfloor heating

©Chris Stowers/Apa Publications

one for women (*anchae*). Some rooms were heated with a hypocaust system (*ondol*), while others had a parquet floor (*maru*), as in more modest houses (⟳*see box p352*). Modern Korean apartments still utilise underfloor heating similar to the old *ondol* style, though these days floors are heated with gas, rather than burning wood.

TOMB ARCHITECTURE

Tombs were generally built in stone. Boulder-like burial tablets known as dolmen (and *goindol* in Korean) first appeared in the Bronze Age, followed by stone passage graves in the Goguryeo and Baekje kingdoms. Sarcophagi were either wooden or made of earthenware, though rare exceptions include several brick tombs in Gongju and, more pertinently, the great tumuli of the Gyeongju plains, which featured large wooden frames covered with stones and earth—these date back to between the 4C and 6C, and include Cheonmachong, "the tomb of the heavenly horse"—the sumptuous grave goods found inside included golden crowns with shamanist influences, and a belt and necklace in

gold, gilt bronze and silver. During the later Silla, Goryeo and Joseon periods, stone chambers were built according to *pungsu jiri* (Taoist-influenced feng shui) and covered with earth to form burial mounds.

SCULPTURE
BUDDHIST SCULPTURE

The Three Kingdoms of Korea Era (1C BC–668)

While Korea's Buddhist and funerary sculpture originated in China, it soon acquired distinctive local characteristics. Following the introduction of Buddhism (in 372 in Goguryeo, a little later in the other kingdoms), artistic quality reached great heights, though in the first stage of its growth, influences from China still played an important role—the oldest bronze statue from Goguryeo dates from 539, and still shows strong influences of Chinese sculpture (Northern and Western Wei) at the turn of the 6C, with a relatively large head and hands, draped garments, hands crossed across the chest and the back slightly bent in an attitude of meditation. In addition, the influence of the Chinese states of

Buddha triad carved in rock, Seosan, Chungcheong-do

©KTO

the Eastern Jin (317–420) and the Liang (907–923) are also perceptible in figures from Baekje.

Buddhist sculptures fulfilled a number of different functions, affecting their appearance, their materials and their iconography. Statuettes in bronze or pottery were typically placed on the house altars of great families (for household worship) or in pagodas as votive offerings. Larger statues made of stone, wood, ceramics, bronze and, from the 9C or 10C, iron, were located in temples, pavilions and grottos, where they were the focus of monastic and public worship.

Graceful statues in gilt-bronze of Mireuk Bosal (also known as Maitreya, or the future Buddha), seated thoughtfully with one leg across his knee like an enthroned bodhisattva, are clear examples of the kingdom's sophisticated culture. The gentleness and humanity emanating from the statues are the origins of the expression "Baekje smile." Vast engraved or sculpted images of the Buddha, found in mountainous regions far from cities and towns, is a feature which distinguishes Korean Buddhist sculpture from that of the Japanese. This tradition of sculpting living rock originated in India, crossing Central Asia to China before making the leap to Korea. The figures are often sculpted in the round from large blocks of stone (over which a pavilion is built) or carved into a rockface. Many such statues are scattered throughout Namsan (South Mountain) in southern Gyeongju, the capital of Silla. They have certain characteristics unique to Korea, including a clear preference for representing the lower body in two dimensions, and other tendencies toward abstraction, partly a result of working in granite (in Gyeongju, but also seen in the Seosan Buddha Triad, latter half of the 7C, Baekje).

Later Silla (668–935)

The period after unification saw Buddhist sculpture reach its apotheosis. The grotto at Seokguram, a shrine consecrated in the latter half of the 8C, was carved into the side of Tohamsan,

a mountain near Gyeongju (see p291). Facing the East Sea, it houses one of the masterpieces of Korean sculpture: a stone statue of the Buddha revealing distinct Tang dynasty influences. The seated Buddha is depicted wearing an expression of meditation and sitting on a lotus pedestal, surrounded by a pantheon of Buddhist deities. The monastery of Bulguksa, which dates back to the same period, stands at the foot of the same mountain (see p289).

The 8C kings Seongdeok (reigned 702–737) and Gyeongdeok (reigned 742–765) devoted themselves to the patronage of monasteries, resulting in the casting of great bells, such as the one in the monastery at Hwangnyong and the Emille bell of Bongdeok monastery, now in the Gyeongju National Museum (see p286).

Goryeo (918–1392)

The Buddha statues produced during the Goryeo era were usually very large in scale, but tended to lack vitality and expression. Their stiffness and formality became yet more pronounced during the Joseon period, which may be linked to the decline in intellectual creativity suffered by Buddhism under the increasing constraints of Confucianism. Although the influence of the art of the Chinese Song (960–1279), Liao (916–1125) and Jin (1115–1234) dynasties is unmistakeable, the Buddha's face, with its high cheekbones and half-closed, almost horizontal eyes, has been "Koreanized" and often tends towards the two-dimensional. This stylization became even more striking during the 10C and 11C. By the Mongol rule of the 13C and14C, Korea was experiencing an upsurge in the Lamaist art spreading out into China and Tibet.

Joseon (1392–1910)

The sculpture of later periods is of colossal proportions, but remained formal and expressionless. Many works that could be moved were seized by the Japanese during their invasions at the end of the 16C and taken to Japan. With the increasing influence of Confucianism, Buddhist sculpture was never to recover its past glories.

FUNERARY SCULPTURE

The second of the great sculptural arts in Korea is funerary sculpture. One of the first recorded statues is a winged pig with deer antlers and red lips, which guards the corridor leading to the tomb of King Muryeong of Baekje (523). Statues of civil servants and soldiers, as well as impressive animal sentinels (revealing Chinese influences), were produced during the later Silla period and lined the funeral paths leading to the tumuli of kings and nobles. The tumuli were also ringed by stone slabs carved with the 12 animals of the lunar zodiac, representing the 12 "double hours" of the day and the points of the compass (Gyeongju, Gwaereung, Gwaereung, *see p65*).

PAINTING
PREHISTORIC PERIOD

Several prehistoric **petroglyph** sites are to be found along the southern part of the Korean Peninsula's east coast. One of the most famous sites is at **Bangudae**, on the banks of a tributary of the Taehwa River (Taehwagang), which flows into the East Sea at the city of Ulsan (Daegokri, Ennyang-myeon, South Gyeongsang). Some 200 rock carvings depict whales, turtles, seals and other marine animals, as well as tigers, deer, cattle, goats, pigs and leopards, all etched into an area of rock approximately 6.5ft/2m high and 26ft/8m wide. There are also several images of people and tools, one showing a harpooned whale.

GOGURYEO
(37 BC–AD 668)

There has been a pictorial tradition on the Korean Peninsula since the time of the Lelang (Nangnang) commandery, founded in 108 BC. A lacquered basket discovered in a tomb in southern Pyongyang demonstrates the quality of some of the work, decorated as it is with characters associated with filial piety. After the fall of the Chinese commandery in AD 313, its traditions and artisans were absorbed by the Goguryeo kingdom,

which had a rich painting tradition during the Three Kingdoms period.

Tombs with painted murals can be seen near Donggu and Pyongyang (the latter, of course, now in North Korea, and as such a little hard to get to). Constructed between the 3C and the 7C, the walls and ceilings of the funerary chambers are decorated with scenes from the life of the deceased and include the animal guardians of the four cardinal points and heavenly bodies, all of Chinese origin. Later tombs reveal a change in subject matter, including country scenes, lotus flowers and decorative borders. This tradition of painting murals would eventually reach Japan.

BAEKJE
(18 BC–AD 660)

A number of tiles and bricks decorated with sophisticated designs and images have been discovered at Sabi (Buyeo), at one time the Baekje capital. Rural scenes with mountains, rivers, various species of trees, lotus flowers, phoenixes and monstrous faces are clearly visible on them, all demonstrating why the skills of Baekje craftsmen were vaunted across East Asia. They are the most beautiful representations of ancient landscapes to be found in this part of the continent, and offer at least a hint of what the paintings on more fragile surfaces, which now are lost forever, must have been like.

SILLA AND LATER SILLA
(57 BC–AD 935)

A number of paintings on birch wood depicting birds, heavenly horses and their riders have survived from the Silla period (reproductions are in the Gyeongju National Museum, *see p286*). A fragment of the illuminated Avatamsaka sutra, painted in gold and silver on violet paper dating from 754–755, is proof of the high quality of artistry achieved during the Later Silla period. This quality is confirmed by the wealth of richly decorated bricks and tiles and the figurative Buddhist plaques found at sites in the capital of Silla, such as Anapji—a pond on the grounds of an old Silla palace, and now part of Gyeongju National Park—as well as the monastery of Hwangnyong and the Gyeongju National Museum.

GORYEO (918–1392)

During the Goryeo period, thanks to the patronage of the king and the aristocracy, Buddhist monks were able to commission many paintings and other artworks. Richly colored, delicate pieces were used in ceremonial rituals and in the annual rites performed in remembrance of kings and queens. The generous use of gold and techniques achieving transparency lent the pieces a rare delicacy and luminosity, and the skill of the scribes and illustrators responsible for the sutras were praised as far away as China and Japan. Few examples of secular painting have survived from the period, although exceptional painters are specifically mentioned in historical texts, where it is also revealed that Koreans would travel to China to purchase works. Fans decorated with silver and gold were also produced during the period. Members of the Korean royal family living in Peking (Beijing) during the Mongol Yuan dynasty at the end of the Goryeo period often collected paintings that they took back to Gae-gyeong.

JOSEON (1392–1910)

Despite Buddhism's continuing popularity, the adoption of Confucianism as the official state belief during the Joseon period meant that Buddhist painting no longer enjoyed the same support, so commissions for elaborate and costly representations of the Mahayana pantheon became a thing of the past. Good relations between the Joseon and Ming courts favored cultural exchanges; Koreans had certainly been previously aware of Chinese painting, and court painting in the academic tradition of the Song from the south seems to have been better known than the work of the scholarly painters of the Wu school. Korean masters of the 16C went on to develop their own versions of classic landscape painting, retaining distant elements in their composition but limiting attention to the foreground, as in Ming painting. Korean artists also worked in the manner of the Chinese Zhe school, with thick washes of ink, vigorous brushwork and depictions of silhouetted cliffs and rocks (Kang Heui-an, 1419–1464; Yi Gyeong-yun, 1545–?). Shin Saimdang, 1501–1554, was a calligrapher and colorist of great delicacy specializing in floral art. As mother of the Confucian scholar Yi I (also known by his pen name Lee Yulgok), she also came to be regarded as a model mother of the time (☞see p255)—the main factor behind feminist protests when her face was put on the new ₩50,000 note.

During the 18C, when the creative spirit of Chinese painting was beginning to flag, an intellectual and cultural Renaissance in Korea resulted in departures of entirely Korean origin. The first of these was the appearance of "real landscape" (jingyeong sansu), pioneered by Jeong Seon (1676–1759), with his depictions of the Diamond mountain. He was followed by Gang Se-hwang (1713–1791), who produced an album of views of Songdo, the old capital of Goryeo. By the 18C typical Korean tastes had moved on to scenes of daily life, as typified by two artists: Sin Yun-bok (mid-18C) and Kim Hong-do (1745–c.1814). The works of Kim Du-ryang (1696–1763) are further examples of direct observation whose origins seem to draw on Silhak, a social reform movement promoting practical studies. Renowned for his landscapes, he also painted extremely realistic representations of animals in which a trace of Western influence (depicting foreigners, chiaroscuro) is unmistakable. In turn, the appearance of these new forms in the paintings of the 18C provided inspiration for later innovations in the 19C. Inspired by his encounters with Chinese scholars and calligraphers, Kim Jeong-heui (Chusa or Wandang, 1786–1857), took their work to new heights and created his own style of calligraphy; he became an important figure of the arts scene at the end of the Joseon period, both intellectually and aesthetically. Pupils such as Hong Se-seop continued

Kim Jeong-hui's tradition of innovation and invention (National Museum of Korea, Leeum Museum, Korea University Museum, Seoul).

CERAMICS

Pottery decorated with comb-tooth designs first began to appear during the Neolithic period (between approximately 4,000 and 1,000 BC). It was made using a technique that had originated in northeastern Manchuria and spread rapidly through the northwestern Korean peninsula. Pots with incised and imprinted geometric patterns had also begun to appear while the comb-tooth designs were making their way south (Amsa-dong on the Han River, not far from Seoul), and comb-tooth pottery was finally succeeded by plain earthenware.

Around the 10C BC Gaya later refined Baekje's eggshell-colored earthenware and also built the first tunnel, hill-climbing kilns, which could reach baking temperatures of 1,830°F (1,000°C) or more. Gaya was also the source of typical Silla pottery forms such as legged vases and horn-shaped glasses.

CELADON (CHEONGJA)

Korean ceramic-making reached its apotheosis during the Goryeo period. Besides making dark gray stoneware baked at high temperatures and destined for everyday use, Koreans began, at the end of the Later Silla period, to manufacture celadon (*cheongja*), ceramics with a blue-green glaze. This tradition, which had its roots in China, was adapted into a technique producing results that amazed even the Chinese; the most beautiful pieces date from the first half of the 12C. Celadon varies in color from olive green to blue jade, and the forms are equally diverse, ranging from household objects for the nobility to Buddhist liturgical pieces, including *meiping* vases (a wide-bodied container with a tapering neck), jars, cups, plates, pillows, perfume diffusers and *kundika* (a kind of water-bottle with a narrow neck). Engraved, molded, inlaid or painted using iron oxide or copper beneath a glaze, the designs on the ware depicted real and imaginary animals such as monkeys, turtles, cranes, lions, fish, rabbits, phoenixes and dragons, or plants such as grapes, lotuses, pomegranates, bamboo and melons. Figures of hermits or children sometimes also made an appearance; cranes flying across clouds or ducks beneath weeping willow trees were common Korean motifs.

BUNCHEONG WARE

The fascination of the Japanese masters and their pupils for Korean ceramics has its roots in the 15C, and was particularly inspired by *buncheong* stoneware. The Japanese captured hundreds of Korean potters during the invasions of the 1590s, and took them to their homeland. *Buncheong* was made in the 15C and 16C, during the earlier half of the Joseon period, and involved coating the pieces with a thin wash of engobe (diluted clay) before painting or decorating them with a *sgraffito* technique and finishing them with a glaze similar in consistency to that used for celadon.

WHITE PORCELAIN

Joseon ceramics reflect changes in tastes after the luxurious lifestyle of the Goryeo period. Although celadon manufacturing traditions were briefly retained in *buncheong* techniques, which produced bluish-green stoneware in the early Joseon period, Confucian ethics demanded simpler pottery and the preference during the era was for plain white porcelain. This had already begun to appear under Goryeo rule and was used in court ceremonies, as well as the daily life of all social classes. Cultural exchanges with the Ming court led to Korea's acquisition of "blue and white" porcelain, which it reproduced with cobalt purchased at great expense in China. Brown pigmentation under an iron oxide glaze was used from the 15C and the red glazed technique invented by the Korean potters of Goryeo experienced a renaissance in the 17C, but by the 18C, the production of quality white vases had been resumed.

Literature, Cinema and Television

Literature and cinema are among the most important keys to understanding Korea today. Korean cinema has become particularly popular, winning a number of major awards overseas. Original and profound, yet sometimes wacky or disconcerting, many films draw a great deal of inspiration from the literature that questions the war between North and South, the years spent under dictatorship and the country's rapid economic growth. Korean television series are less concerned with this critical dimension, but they have attracted record audiences in Asia since the early 2000s.

Mokpo Museum of Literature, Jeolla-do ©KTO

LITERATURE

For centuries Korean literature lacked its own alphabet and borrowed Chinese characters for its different writing systems—a classical system used by literary scholars for official documents, and a popular system for the vernacular. Only fragments of these texts remain, most having been lost as a result of censorship, rewriting and the ravages of war.

CLASSICAL LITERATURE

The First Texts

The first millennium AD relied partly on the Buddhist canon and partly on the Confucian classics, whose teaching was reinforced by a competitive system that established an aristocracy of scholars, who were both officials and authors. Most of what we know of this first millennium was not recorded until the Confucian **Kim Pushik** (1075–1151) wrote his *History of the Three Kingdoms (Samguk sagi)*, which consists mainly of a compilation of stories, now lost to us, according to the historiographical rules pioneered by Chinese historian Sima Qian. In the *Memorabilia of the Three Kingdoms (Samguk yusa)*, attributed to the Buddhist monk **Iryeon** (1206–89), we find the founding legends, historical sources and literary roots of Korea. The Buddhist monks **Wonhyo** (617–86) and **Uisang** (625–702) figure strongly in the formulation of the teachings of the Pure Land and the Flower Garland, helping to define a native, unified Buddhism. This movement resulted in journeys to "the west," as described in the *Memoir of a Pilgrimage to the Five Regions,* written by **Hyecho** in 719.

Literature in the more modern sense could be said to have begun with the Confucian poet **Choe Chiwon** (857–915). His works are steeped in a compelling lyricism and desolation in the face of the decline of the Silla dynasty.

With the arrival of the Goryeo dynasty (918–1392)—viewed by many as the golden age of Korean culture despite its turbulent events and foreign invasions—came a series of masterpieces. The wide-ranging intellect of **Yi Kyubo** (1168–1241) was to define the forms and vocabulary of Korean literature, both with his *Short Critical Essays* and his long narrative poems, such as *The Lay of King Tongmyong.*

The Joseon Dynasty

In 1392, the Joseon dynasty resolutely adopted Confucianism and Sinocentrism, and the key features of what we

Yi Munyol (born 1948)

Without doubt one of the best-known South Korean writers, his realist texts—provoking and cultivating ambiguity—have been consistently successful following publication of his first book, *Song Beneath a Fortress*. He deals with his difficult life after his father's defection to the North in *The Poet*, and frequently addresses the question of dictatorship and its effects, as revealed in *Our Twisted Hero*, and *Our Early Years*. Often prone to a tendency towards the "encyclopedic" (*The Son of Man*), he excels when using humor (*Hail to the Emperor*). His seminal work, *The Bird with Golden Wings*, is a stylistic gem described by André Veltman as "decisive and luminous, with infinite resonance." He now publishes epic novels and comic books, but with less success.

now consider to be the country of Korea were born. **King Sejong** (1418–50), one of the first monarchs, radically changed the intellectual landscape with the formal introduction of a native alphabet, the *Correct Sounds for the Instruction of the People*.

To demonstrate its effectiveness, the king wrote, or commissioned, a biography of Buddha and a collection of lyric poems under the title *Songs of the Moon Shining on a Thousand Rivers*, and then *The Song of the Dragons Flying to Heaven*, a poem justifying the new dynasty, which had arrived following a coup. Subsequently, despite the elite's contempt for this "people's alphabet," scholars hesitated between transcription in the official and respected Chinese, and support of the new alphabet, which was suppressed but used for anything non-official, such as private writings, songs or poems by courtesans.

Kim Shiseup (1435–93), a poet and courtier, is remembered for his five short stories entitled *New Stories from Kumo*, an ode to Taoist fiction and the supernatural. **Hwang Chini** (1522–65) was a courtesan (*gisaeng*) to whom were attributed some remarkable poems sung to music (*shijo*) before, in more recent years, she became a popular heroine of numerous novels and films.

The three verse *shijo* poems were illustrated by **Chong Cheol** (1536–93), a senior official who used his frequent exiles to compose *kasa*, a form of long narrative poem, such as *The Song of Kwandong*.

The Birth of Fiction

In the same period, **Heo Kyun** (1559–1618) wrote *The Tale of Hong Kiltong*, a local Robin Hood-style tale and the first novel to be written in Korean. His sister **Nanseol Heon** (1563–89) was a very gifted poet and could almost be described as a feminist.

Poetry reached lyrical heights with **Yun Seondo** (1587–1671), especially in his *Song of the Five Friends*. **Kim Manjung** (1637–92) formalized romantic fiction for subsequent centuries. *The Dream of Nine Clouds* and *Journey to the South* explore the areas between history and the imagination.

Pak Chiwon (1737–1805) remained attached to the "practical learning" movement known as *Sirhak* (reminiscent of the first encyclopedia compilers in 18C France) which was concerned with technique, innovations and the reconsidering of relations with China.

Kim Sakkat (1807–63) is a very special case. Hounded because of his grandfather's rebellious stance, this inspired poet traveled the country, taking his revenge upon society through poems laced with double meaning—they were either lyrical or obscene depending on whether read in Chinese or Korean.

The classical age ended with the popular shamanic-influenced *pansori*, a form of narrative (often a love story or satire) sung by one person, accompanied by a percussionist. A *pansori* performance is very long, often taking several hours from start to finish.

MODERN LITERATURE
The Turning Point

Modern literature was born when, with the arrival of Western powers, scholars and intellectuals began to consider the issue of national identity. **Yu Kiljun**, **Shin Chaeho** and **Yun Chiho**, among others, traveled and studied the culture and knowledge of the West, establishing schools and journals in Korea.

It was also a question of language. Founding figures included the poet **Choe Namseon** (1890–1957), the writer **Yi Kwangsu** (1892–1945) and the playwright **Yi Injik** (1862–1916).

Influenced by the social Darwinism disseminated throughout the Far East by China's Liang Qichao, the ideas of these three authors were supported almost universally, despite their collaboration with the Japanese.

It was around this time that schools were set up, publications and reviews were established, and women's rights became an issue, as had been the case in Japan a few decades earlier. The reviews featured the new Korean poetry, now finally a separate entity from music.

Kim Dongin (1900–51) represents the second branch of modern Korean writing, a strand that was realist but rejected moralism. His *Potatoes* is a masterpiece of naturalism. At the same time, *Azaleas* by the lyric poet **Kim Sowol** (1902–34) and *Your Silence* by the Buddhist monk **Han Yong-un** (1879–1944) brought new refinement to Korean writing, giving poetry the power to express the national spirit.

Yi Sanghwa (1910–43) was probably the first to describe the pain and resentment felt by many with his anti-colonial *Does the Spring Return to Stolen Fields?*

In the 1930s literature branched out, often embracing ideological conflicts. For the first time, albeit briefly, what we think of as a conventional novel took shape. **Hyun Jingeon** (1900–43) with *A Society that Drives You to Drink* and **Yom Sangseop** (1897–1963) with *Three Generations* managed to bring together the naturalistic trend, critical thought and modern techniques. The main figures belonged to **KAPF,** the Federation of Korean Proletarian Artists. Among them were **Kim Tong-hwan** (born 1901), author of the first modern long narrative poem, *The Night of the Border*, and **Kim Kirim** (born 1908), interested in bringing modernism to Korean poetry. **Jeong Jiyong** (born 1903) also deserves mention.

It was at this time that **Chae Mansik** (1904–50), with *A Ready-Made Life* and *Peace Under Heaven,* absorbed all these lessons and used them to paint a literary picture of the landscape of the colonial era with a humor rarely found in Korean literature.

Seo Jeongju (1915–2000) and before him **Yi Sang** (1910–37) are seen as exceptions, the former for an "historical" lyricism that led to collaboration with Japanese militarism, and the latter (*Wings*, etc.) for a modernist individualism that is remarkable even today.

TWO STYLES OF KOREAN LITERATURE

With the division of the country that resulted from Japanese colonial rule and the civil war (the Korean War, 1950–53), two opposing states emerged and with them two very different literary climates,

Yi Cheongjun (1939–2009)

A native of Jangheung, South Jeolla province (Jeollanam-do, a land steeped in shamanism and *pansori*), Yi Cheongjun devoted his life to literature and his roots. Author of a considerable body of prize-winning work, he stands apart from the realist and sentimental style characteristic of Korean literature. Many of his texts, such as *The People of the South*, are devoted to both his homeland and the mysteries of creation. Others are often allegorical, such as his masterpiece *Your Paradise*, a fable that takes place on a leper island whose residents try to escape by swimming, even when the island's new governor has authorized them to leave.

despite the fact that realism and moralism continued to prevail on both sides of the border.

South Korea

Hwang Sunwon (1915–2000) took on the role of social commentator, but from a unanimist point of view at odds with the political environment. **Yi Hocheol** (born 1932) hails from the north and writes about his homeland and the disasters of the political division, while **Pak Kyongni** (1926–2008), with her bestselling saga *The Land*, is acknowledged as a nationally important author acclaimed for her epic historical novels.

The Square by **Choe Inhun** (born 1936) caused a sensation in 1961. Taking advantage of what was a brief democratic interlude, he argued for a unified Korea, seeing the country's responsibilities as shared by North and South.

Kim Seongok (born 1941) is the first truly modern prose writer, adopting a tone and a humor that freed him from Korean novelistic traditions, particularly in *Seoul: Winter 1964*.

Yi Cheongjun (1939–2009) and **Hwang Jiu** (born 1952) are the writers who, through both prose and poetry, represent the martyred province of Jeolla, the former through a revival of traditional cultural forms, such as *pansori*, and the latter through his fight for democracy. **Kim Chiha** (born 1941) with *The Five Thieves*, **Ko Un** (born 1933) and **Shin Kyongnim** (born 1935) express themselves through poetry written in a very militant style, largely in response to the constant repression that Korean writers suffered between 1953 and 1987. They are the heirs of **Kim Suyoung** (1921–68), who, with *The New City and the Citizens' Chorus*, set the standard for socially engaged poetry.

A Little Ball Launched by a Dwarf by **Cho Seheui** (born 1942) is the most well-known bestseller of modern Korean literature. This collection of short stories pleads for the victims of industrial development, while **Pak Wanseo** (1931–2011) demonstrated the value of feminist literary insight. **Yi Munyol** (born 1948) had such success in the 1960s that there is now even "Yi Munyol syndrome," and **Choe Inho** (born 1945) shows that popular literature is as important as other forms.

A younger generation has since managed to establish itself with **Park Mingyu, Cheon Myong-gwan** and **Han Kang,** whose work has also appeared in film and song.

North Korea

The first modern writers belonging to **KAPF** were, of course, preoccupied with the issues of the prewar years. Some paid a heavy price when the country was divided. **Im Hwa** (1908–53), for example, the great poet and first literary historian, was one of the early victims of the purges, as was **Yi Taejun.**

Northern writers had to adhere to the state's policies. The expression of *Juche* (the spirit of self-reliance), Kim Il-sung's version of a political thesis first developed between 1910 and 1920, was compulsory, without fundamentally changing prewar sympathies. Kim Il-sung's influence consequently resulted in the re-emergence of the epic historical novel.

Han Sorya (1902–70?), also a member of KAPF, was the first prominent writer. His militant work follows his career. He was first approved by the government, then sent into internal exile, before finally being rehabilitated, mirroring the fate of scholars of the past. In 1946 he published *The Villagers*. *Anna* by **Li Chunjin** (1948) recounts Korea's links with the USSR; *An Old Friend of Mine*, by **Yun Sicheol** (1951), highlights the alliance with the Chinese; and *The Tuman River* by **Li Kiyong** (1954) revolves around the writer's role of remembering the past.

In the 1980s, literature featuring men and women involved in science and technology was given prominence. The general atmosphere and political context were both resolutely optimistic, with all "egoists" capable of being reformed.

Revolutionary opera offered both a literary and musical format, and *The Flower Girl* was the standard production.

Poster for the Jeonju International Film Festival

Hong Sok-jung, with *A Red Flower* and *Hwang Chini,* brought a surprisingly liberal tone to the literary scene, while the major work *Friends* by **Paek Nam-nyong** (1988) describes the grounds for divorce between a singer and her husband, whose status is too "modest" for her, justifying criticism of excess.

See also p13 for a selection of Korean litereature.

CINEMA AND TELEVISION

While South Korea's arthouse films export well and have received some prestigious awards, it is South Korea's television serials that are by far the most popular both at home and abroad.

EARLY DAYS

The first public screening of a film in Korea took place in 1903. The first real Korean film was produced in 1923, followed by others mostly based on traditional stories that continue to be popular today. The most famous is *Arirang* (1926), which denounces Japanese imperialism. After the release of this film, censorship laws became increasingly strict, finally resulting in 1942 in an outright ban by the Japanese occupiers on the use of the Korean language in the cinema.

In 1935, the original version of *The Legend of Chun Hyang* (portrayed by **Im Kwon-taek** for the 12th or 13th time in 2000 and selected for the official competition at Cannes) was the first Korean "talkie."

GOLDEN AGE

In 1953 movies took off again when President Syngman Rhee exempted the industry from tax, in so doing launching the golden age of Korean cinema.

One of the leading filmmakers of this period was **Yoo Hyun-mok,** whose best-known works are *Obaltan* (1961) and the surrealist masterpiece *Empty Dream* (1965). Other classics of the era are *Housemaid* (1960) by **Kim Ki-young,** the remake of which by **Im Sang-soo** was presented at Cannes in 2010, and *My Mother and Her Guest* (1961) by **Shin Sang-ok.**

The director **Im Kwon-taek,** who has more than a hundred films to his name, also began work during this period but did not gain fame until later with, among others, *Mandala* (1980).

DEVELOPMENT OF ARTHOUSE CINEMA

Europe, and France's New Wave in particular, greatly influenced Korean arthouse cinema, as can be seen from the work of directors **Hong Sang-soo** and **Park Chan-wook**. The French influence can also be seen in **Kim Jee-woon's** action film A *Bittersweet Life* (2005).

79

Top of the Bill

Look out for images of these well-known film and television actors and actresses during your stay in Korea:

Lee Byung-hun (born 1970), star of *JSA* (2000), *A Bittersweet Life* (2005), *GI Joe* (2009); he is currently the most famous actor in Korea and abroad, and received the French Arts and Letters award in 2006.

Jang Don-gun (born 1972), star of *Blood Brothers* (2005), is also widely known, particularly in the United States.

Won Bin (born 1977), star of *Blood Brothers* (2005) and *Mother* (2009).

Bae Yong-jun (born 1972), star of *Winter Sonata*, a soap opera popular throughout Asia, filmed in 2002.

Lee Yeong-ae (born 1971), star of *JSA* (2000), *The Jewel in the Palace* (2003)— the most popular Korean series of all time—and *Lady Vengeance* (2005).

Jun Ji-hyun (born 1981), star of *My Sassy Girl* (2001), now works in the United States under the name Gianna Jun.

Choi Ji-woo (born 1975), star of *Winter Sonata* (2002).

Song Hye-kyo (born 1981), actress and Dior model for Asia.

Kim Yun-jin (born 1973), star of the United States TV series *Lost*.

THE "KOREAN WAVE"

After a dark period of censorship at the hands of the various dictatorships, the arrival of democracy in the late 1980s gave rise, within the decade, to a revival of Korean cinema. The first film of note was **Kang Je-gyu's** *Shiri* (1999); after this, director **Park Chan-wook,** a box-office darling and symbol of the new Korean cinema, made *JSA* in 2000 (👆 *see box p234*) and *Old Boy* (2003), while **Kim Ki-duk's** films such as *Spring, Summer, Fall, Winter... and Spring* (2003) were the most exported.

At the beginning of the 2000s the "Korean Wave" or *Hallyu* began—both terms coined to describe the ultra-fast growth in the production and export of Korean films, TV programs and Korean popular culture in general. In the space of just a few years, most Asian countries (particularly Japan, where certain stars were lauded as demi-gods) and also South American and Eastern European countries had developed a passion for Korean films and television series in particular.

The best-known series include: *Autumn in My Heart* (2000), *Winter Sonata* (2002, 👆 *see box p242*), *The Jewel in the Palace* (2003), *All In* (2004), *Royal Palace* (2006) and *Boys Over Flowers* (*Kkotboda Namja*) (2009).

Several movies have attracted more than 10 million viewers in a country with just 50.5 million inhabitants: *Friends* by Kwak Kyung-taek (2001), *Silmido* by Kang Woo-suk (2003), *Blood Brothers* by Kang Je-gyu (2005), *The King and the Clown* by Lee Jun-ik (2005), *The Host* by Bong Joon-ho (2006) and *Haeundae* by Yun Jae-gyun (2009, 👆 *see p304*).

This increased global presence is accompanied by considerable growth in the industry itself. Around **140 films** are produced every year. The number of cinemas tripled between 2003 and 2006, and attendance has exploded (150 million tickets sold per year). Film festivals have also experienced a boom since the 2000s (👆 *see box p354*).

Since the *Hallyu,* the sets of Korean films and television series have become tourist attractions in their own right. Most are outside Seoul, such as HallyuWorld in Gyeonggi Province (Gyeonggi-do), Open Film Set in the city of Suncheon (👆 *see p350*) and the Andong Folk Village (👆 *see p274*). 👆 *See a selection of Korean films on p14.*

Music and Dance

The many traditional performing arts all share the common base of shamanism, which, over time, has absorbed numerous influences. Buddhism, Taoism and Confucianism have also shaped the arts in various ways, depending on where and for whom they were performed: in a slow, stately, precise manner in front of the court, or more freely and evoking the magical in front of ordinary people. Now, of course, these traditional forms have been pushed out of the mainstream by western styles of dance and music, as well as by K-pop, Korea's own take on popular music.

COMMON GROUND

Dance, theater, music, song: all of these traditional arts have their origins in **shamanism,** the Asian religion in which the shaman or *mudang*—a mixture of priest, sorcerer, magician and seer—serves as an intermediary between humans and spirits. So it is not surprising that the roots of these traditional performing arts lie in the *kut* (or *gut*) rituals that allow the shaman to enter the spirit world and intercede on the behalf of mortals.

Salpuri is an exorcism ritual performed at the beginning of each year to chase away evil spirits (*sal* in Korean). The dancer, dressed in white, moves very slowly in a circle to emphasize the almost inexpressible inner turmoil and feelings of sorrow *(han)* that are characteristic of Korean art. He attempts to soothe the souls of the deceased by guiding them to heaven with a long white scarf. The dancer's rhythm and breathing must be synchronized perfectly so that he is in complete harmony with heaven and earth and can act as a mediator. The dancer experiences ecstasy (*shinmyung*), the opposite of *han,* the yin and yang elements of the Taoist philosophy found in all Korean artistic expression.

Buddhist influences have also made their mark upon the arts and can be seen in popular dances such as *Seungmu*, demonstrating that the Korean arts are highly syncretic—that they have, in other words, absorbed the influences of several different belief systems.

DANCE

An intrinsic part of much religious expression, Korean dance is divided into several genres: **court dance, folk dance** and **masked dance**. The different natures of the dances are contained within the Korean word for dance (*muyong*): *mu* represents the

Traditional dance

©Chris Stowers/Apa Publications

spiritual, moral and refined, while *yong* suggests an entertaining, satirical, bawdy aspect. The first is performed mainly with the hands and the upper body, using restrained, stylized movements, synchronized with breathing and codified by Confucianism; the second is performed solely with the lower limbs, using spontaneous, extrovert movements, with roots in the earthy imagination of a community in search of a better future. In this way, the solemn majesty and artistic elegance of the court dances counterbalance the festive popular folk dances, which, though freer in form, are still ritualized according to the seasons and agricultural cycles. Many original royal court dances are still performed at the National Gugak Center, (formerly the National Center for Korean Traditional Performing Arts, 🍂*see p105*).

Included in the UNESCO Intangible Cultural Heritage List, *Cheoyongmu*, the only masked dance in which a human rather than a god or spirit is depicted, tells the story of Cheoyong who, through his song and dance, manages to drive out the evil spirits responsible for his wife's illness. In contrast, *Ganggangsullae* is a circular dance performed by young women, echoing, when performed, the cyclical nature of things that is so fundamental to Eastern philosophies. In the *talchum* mask dances (from *tal,* mask), behind the anonymity of the masks, the actors express the frustrations and irritations of everyday life.

The popular character of Malddugi, a modest servant who pokes fun at the hypocrisy of his masters (wealthy property owners and clergy), resurfaced on university campuses in the 1980s to denounce the dictators in power at the time. These masked dances combine comedy, song and recital, and are usually performed by traveling troupes. Finally, *Namsadang-nori* is an extraordinary combination of performing arts (with acrobatics, puppets, tightrope walking and juggling), all performed in a spirit typical of the Korean people, mocking the powerful while at the same time appeasing the spirits. It is a perfect socio-cosmic pressure-release valve.

MUSIC

Korean instruments are traditionally divided into eight sounds depending on the materials from which they are made: skin, silk, bamboo, metal, earth, gourd, stone and wood. Among the most popular are the *janggu* (leather hourglass-drum), *gayageum* (twelve-stringed zither), *haegeum* (two-stringed fiddle), *daegeum* (flute), *kkwaenggwari* (gong), *bak* (wooden clapper), *pyeongyeong* (stone chimes), and not forgetting of course the voice, a feature of the *pansori*, a major genre in Korean music (🍂*see box p329*) and designated an Intangible Cultural Heritage by UNESCO in 2003.

MUSIC AND DANCE TODAY

For all the intricacies of the traditional forms of music and dance, contemporary styles are far more relevant to—and popular in—the Korea of today. Local pop muisic, referred to as "K-pop" both at home and abroad, is simply inescapable across the land, and many artists have gone on to become household names in other Asian countries (as made clear by the legions of young Vietnamese men copying the hairstyles of Korean stars).

BoA has long been the biggest name in the K-pop scene, and has released albums in Japanese and Chinese. Unfortunately, while there has been a recent renaissance in the worlds of Korean art, design and cuisine, the musical scene remains characterized by a lack of depth—unlike in neighboring Japan, there are no contemporary styles indigenous to Korea, and those who choose to create music almost always fall back on international styles; punk, reggae, and bossa nova are among the genres to have dropped in and out of fashion, while nightclubs universally favor generic house and hip-hop.

The contemporary dance scene also revolves around international trends—swing dancing has become incredibly popular of late—though mention must be made of the B-Boy break-dance revolution, so popular that it now counts as a cultural export.

Religions and Schools of Thought

Korea has often been described as a land of spirits, and Koreans are thought of as a spiritual people. Even today, religions and other schools of wisdom still occupy an essential place in the past and present of Korean society. Although half the population is agnostic, the other half is extremely devout, and as the faithful are well able to follow several beliefs at once, or change from one to another, arriving at accurate statistics is rather difficult.

BUDDHISM

Buddhism arrived in China at the end of the 4C AD. First adopted by the royal court and the nobility, it was to become more widespread during the Silla dynasty under the influence of great Korean masters such as **Wonhyo** (617–686), who promoted a style of populist Buddhism. Having become the state religion, Buddhism acquired economic importance under the Goryeo dynasty with the rise of rich and influential monasteries, and it was during this period

that the famous Tripitaka Buddhist texts were written; they can still be seen in the temple at Haeinsa (see p270). The excesses of monastic power under the rule of the Joseon dynasty fed dissatisfaction among neo-Confucianists, who gradually rose to positions of authority and succeeded in imposing their beliefs as state-sanctioned ideology. Buddhists therefore became personae non grata at court and were even banished from Seoul. The monks sought refuge in the mountains and are still there today.

The 1900s saw a slight rebirth of influence, although Buddhism was to play no part in the great political upheavals of the 20C; there are just two Buddhists among the 33 signatories to the Declaration of Independence of 1 March 1919, for example. This trend began to reverse to an extent in the 1980s, although Buddhism still lagged behind Christianity in popularity. However, the numbers of the faithful have risen rather more sharply during this century: in 1962, there were 700,000 believers, but their number has grown constantly to compete with the number of Christians, reaching at least 10.7 million or more, according to some sources, in 2005.

This is, in a part, a result of the Christian practice of identifying with a religion, but for some, Buddhism is associated with the past and the backward rural regions. The great majority of Buddhist

Jikjisa, Buddhist temple, Daegu

©Chris Stowers/Apa Publications

temples are indeed in rural settings (933 temples in total, as opposed to only 58 in Seoul), and there are twice as many Christians as Buddhists in the capital, although the religions are evenly balanced in the countryside.

The growing importance of South Korea on the international stage has meant that Buddhists have less reason to hide away. A quarter of all Koreans now think of themselves as Buddhist, but this group, which tends to be less well-educated than the Christians and twice as likely to be country dwellers, is also much less likely to consist of practicing and active believers.

Korean **Mahayana** (Great Vehicle) Buddhism includes a number of different sects. The main Korean Buddhist order, known as **Jogye** and founded in the Goryeo period by the monk Jinul (1158–1210), favors a middle way between study and Zen (*Seon* in Korean), which arrived in Korea at the end of the Silla period and promotes meditation and "sudden illumination." *Won*, a local form of Buddhism that is more a fusion of beliefs, was first encountered in 1924 and by 2005 had won 6,800 followers.

CHRISTIANITY

Christianity has a short but unique history in Korea, which is the only country to have **self-evangelized**. The French missionaries who arrived at the turn of the 19C did so at the request of the first Korean converts, who had discovered the religion in China during the 18C. The associations with science, Western technology and "modernity" benefited Christianity, but these aspects were also the root of the great persecution perpetrated during the 19C by conservative factions who were unsettled by the threat of this foreign ideology. There are now 13.7 million Christians, some 29 percent of the Korean population, and most of these are active and practicing.

Catholicism

Catholicism reached Korea at the end of the 18C and many among the missionaries and the Koreans who converted paid the price (*see Jeoldusan in Seoul, p203*). Fleeing from persecution, Catholicism established itself principally in the rural areas, although the cathedral of Myeong-dong in the capital is testimony to the historic role Catholicism has played in the country's recent history. It was then somewhat overtaken by Protestantism, which had a far higher profile in urban areas and in the independence movement of the 1920s and 1930s, but Catholicism was able to regain its position during the struggle for democracy in the 1970s and 1980s. With some 5.1 million followers (10.7 percent of the total population), 4,100 priests (not to mention 14,600 monks and nuns) and a much stronger urban presence since the 1980s, Catholicism remains the fastest-growing religion in Korea. The 103 martyrs canonized in 1984 make South Korea the country with the largest number of Catholic saints outside Western Europe.

Protestantism and Its Variations

It is difficult to get a handle on all the Protestant sects in Korea. Arriving in 1884, well after Catholicism and only after the first trade treaties had been signed, the reformed religion was able to win over Koreans by associating itself closely with Western science and progress. Protestant ministers quickly built schools, universities, pharmacies and hospitals and achieved popularity principally among the urban middle classes. Due to its close involvement with politics and the independence movement (there are 16 Protestants among the 33 signatories of the declaration of 1 March 1919), the movement gained in influence, boasting 100,000 followers in 1910, 8.6 million in 2005 and 95,600 ministers by 2009, but as a group, Protestants remained extremely fragmented. In 1991, Presbyterians, who make up 60 percent of Korean Protestants, were divided between no less than 74 different denominations. Such competition is, however, part and parcel of the proselytizing zeal of the churches and the exponential growth of their flocks. Some have become mega-churches with

Yeouido Full Gospel Church, Seoul

©P. Deloche/Godong/Photononstop

congregations in the dozens of thousands, which subsequently have a strong influence on politics, education and economics . One such church is the Full Gospel Church at Yeouido (see photo above), whose congregation numbers 4.5 million, making it the largest parish in the world. The faiths of the Christian presidents of the Republic (such as Lee Myung-bak and Kim Dae-jung), and even of their wives, has also played a significant role in South Korea's history during the 20C.

LOCAL RELIGIONS
LOCAL BELIEFS

Korea also has its own forms of religion, including some that remain largely unknown in the Western world. A number of local beliefs and superstitions betray a trace of the **first animist religions** practiced on the peninsula, including rituals dedicated to various deities and spirits, principally house gods: ancestral gods, the gods of the site of the house, the gods of wealth, of the door, of the village and so on. These rituals were conducted in part by women and dedicated to village gods such as the deity of the *seonangdang*, which was often associated with a tree worshiped by the entire community. These religious practices have more or less disappeared with modernization, but in some rural locations, you may still see a piece of white paper hung on a beam or a jar filled with rice placed beside a bowl of water on a shelf, the remnants of these ancient rites.

Shamanism

Shamanism, which arrived in Korea with pastoral nomads from the steppes, is still an active belief and has many of the characteristics of the settled shamanism of agricultural societies. It has a similar form to **animism**, yet the charismatic figure of the **shaman** acts as an intermediary between humans and the spirit world in ceremonies known as *kut* (or *gut*) during which the shaman generally enters a trance. The shamanism found in the north of the country is more showy, typically involving music and chanting, the "descent" of the spirits, sacrifices, etc. It flourished in the wake of the Korean War and the population exodus that followed partition, supplanting the shamanism of the South, practiced in a sitting position without the North's chanting and ecstasy.

Nowadays many Koreans consult shamans (of either sex—in modern South Korea, this is a religion that is principally feminine), and in return for a fee, the *mudang* (female shaman) or *baksu* (male shaman) officiates at exorcisms intended to appease angered spirits, fulfill desires, bless new buildings or endeavors, protect a boat and its fishing crew as it sets out to sea, and much more. Most are also seers and some even practice *pungsu*

85

jiri, Taoist-influenced feng shui, which is still required for undertakings such as selecting farmland or constructing a building. Some mystics specializing in *pungsu jiri* operate from an office like any architect or real estate agent. There were about 600,000 active shamans during the 2000s. Shaman "temples" (to use terminology borrowed from Buddhism, a belief to which shamanism owes much and has also given much) are recognizable by the swastika (the cross widely used in Indian religions) on the signs and flags flying from their bamboo ridgepoles.

Cheondogyo

Also referred to as Cheondoism or Chondoism, Cheondogyo is an indigenous religion founded by Choe Je-u in 1860 and originally known as *Donghak* ("Eastern learning") to differentiate it from Western lore—Christianity, in other words. It is, however, a **syncretist religion**, mixing monotheistic Christianity with Buddhism, Confucian values and Taoist concepts. It has obvious social aims and was associated with both the peasants' revolt of the 1890s and the nationalist independence movement of the 20C. It ceased its political involvement after suffering harsh repression at the hands of the Japanese authorities, but its religious mission to 2,200 believers continues.

The Moonies

This famous sect, nicknamed for its charismatic founder, the Reverend Sun Myung Moon, is officially known as the Unification Church (Holy Spirit Association for the Unification of World Christianity). Established in 1954, the sect promotes the conservative and strongly anti-Communist values of its founder, who presents himself as the new Messiah with the stated goal to unite all religions and establish the rule of God in the struggle against Bolshevism. Mass weddings in soccer stadiums and the various scandals that have clung to this extremely wealthy sect are well known, although there are less than 180,000 believers worldwide. The Moonies are particularly well established in the US, where the Reverend Moon has lived since 1972.

PHILOSOPHIES
Confucianism

Conceived as a system of beliefs to regulate social interaction, this school of thought can also be seen as a means of social control for the self-regulation and justification of power. It is not a religion, although ceremonies are traditionally conducted to honor its wise founders. In modern Korea it exists only as an ideology prescribing behavior, values and rituals within a framework of ancestor worship, with great esteem is still shown toward older members of society.

Out of respect for tradition, however, regular ceremonies are held by the state and Confucian organizations at most large shrines—at Jongmyo, for example, where the shrine has been added to the UNESCO World Heritage List, at Munmyo on the campus of Sungkyunkwan University, at some Confucian academies or *seowon*, and local schools known as *hyanggyo*. For more on Confucianism, *see p42*.

Taoism

Taoism, too, is not an organized religion as such, although rituals are carried out at shrines dedicated to its gods throughout the Chinese-influenced world.

A school of thought drawing in essence on Chinese philosophy, Taoism's ethical guidelines are more than a little reminiscent of Buddhism in certain respects. Over time Taoism developed into a more popular form, incorporating elements of magic and superstition intended to ensure immortality in its most literal sense. In this form it influenced feng shui, medicine, the arts, Buddhism itself and large areas of Chinese culture, eventually reaching Korea.

Its influence is as profound as it is intangible in such differing areas as geomancy, the decorative arts, nutrition, gastronomy and others. In this respect at least, Taoism has achieved the Tao quality of being everywhere and nowhere at the same time.

Lifestyle

Korea may be a "young" country in terms of its economic development and Westernization, but beneath the hi-tech surface lies a country rich in ancient culture and traditions. Under the monarchy, the aristocratic elite, represented by two "noble" orders known as *yangban*, devoted themselves to public service (since trade was forbidden to them), to "studious leisure" comparable to the Roman "otium," and to literature and arts inspired by Chinese traditions. With the passing of time and the emergence of a newly wealthy urban bourgeoisie in the 18C, the lifestyle and customs of the elite were adopted by the comfortable middle classes, resulting in the mix of popular local traditions with the more refined customs of Chinese origin. Today, the Korean lifestyle is still based on the rustic and the aristocratic, which are constantly being rediscovered and reinvented to provide high-quality cuisine, crafts and entertainment.

BATHS
A PLEASURE SHARED

The pleasures of bathing in Korea should not be missed. In most districts you will still find public "bathhouses" known as *mogyoktang* and, until recently, these were an intrinsic part of social life. Since personal hygiene and a groomed appearance are very important in Korea, these public baths were a near-essential part of everyday life before the use of private bathrooms became widespread. However, the habit of going to the *mogyoktang* continues because it involves a lot more than simply washing. Women chat and exchange neighborhood gossip while enjoying their beauty treatment, while on the men's side (the baths are gender segregated), it is quieter, as they relax in the steaming waters after work.

In the changing rooms, you can pass the time playing "Go," watching television or having your hair done. Going to the bathhouse is also a family activity. The children, who may accompany either parent, are likely to be recruited to rub the backs of their elders with a small loofah-style towel that invigorates the skin. Bathtime therefore remains a special experience. Completely naked, you and your body reside in a soothing world of steam and water. Koreans have a very uninhibited and natural relationship with their bodies, and there is nothing unhealthy or ambiguous about the bathhouses.

These days the *mogyoktang* are slowly starting to disappear, although far more numerous now are large bathing and leisure centers called *jjimjilbang*.

jjimjilbang ©KTO

CATERING FOR ALL TASTES

The *jjimjilbang* have many more facilities than just baths and saunas—they can be gigantic affairs with several hot and cold pools (some infused with huge tea bags), snack bars, coffee vending machines, karaoke rooms, internet terminals and more. They have unisex areas in which people wear loose-fitting garments such as T-shirts and shorts (provided at the entrance, worn in common areas, and stowed away in a locker before entry to the pools). Rooms with clay walls, aptly named "ovens," can reach incredible temperatures and are often based on different themes: jade, amethyst, charcoal. The temperature plummets to the opposite end of the scale in the cold rooms. You can also enjoy a massage or facial, have a hair removal treatment or (last, but not least) lounge around lazily on the heated floor. This greater range of facilities makes it possible for couples or groups of people to go in the evening, or for the whole day, to relax and have fun without the sexes being separated, as in the traditional bathhouses. Most also have a dark room dotted with cushioned mats. These *jjimjilbang* are open all hours, and in a country with precious few single rooms or (outside Seoul) youth hostels, they usually make the cheapest places for solo travellers to spend the night. In Seoul there are several *jjimjilbang* in each district, and you'll be able to track one down in almost any urban area.

In the provinces, the **thermal spa** or *oncheon* is more common. The tradition became widespread during the occupation by the Japanese, who already used bathhouses in their own country. However, some hot springs have been used for their medicinal properties for centuries in Korea—the kings of Joseon bathed at Onyang, for example—and you can find such springs throughout the country, but the built-up nature of greater Seoul prohibits their development in the capital region. In the provinces, hot springs are often found near the sea, as at Haeundae or Busan, or in giant complexes such as Bugok. Some offer outdoor thermal baths and pools, as in Seorak Waterpia; others developed by hotel chains offer thalassotherapy treatments (Hilton Namhae, Jeju-do). *See p11 for a list of recommended hot springs and spas.*

A GUIDE TO BATHING

Whether you opt for a traditional bathhouse or a *jjimjilbang*, there's a certain procedure to be followed. After paying the entry fee (just a few thousand won for a simple *mogyoktang*), you remove your shoes and place them in a locker. You are usually given a second key for the changing room, where you remove all your clothes. Take a towel to dry

---

Intangible Cultural Heritage

Muhyeong munhwajae, meaning "intangible cultural property," is used to denote cultural heritage that is not material, like buildings or paintings, but rather arts and skills (such as dance and song) that are handed down over the generations. The original Korean expression *ingan munhwajae* or "human heritage" has sometimes led to *muhyeong munhwajae* being mistranslated as "living national treasure" but it describes essentially a technique, skill or art, rather than a person. These arts naturally have to be practiced by individuals who have received this heritage through apprenticeship or as a skill passed down within a family, and who preserve it, hence the misleading idea that they are themselves the "treasures." The heritage is widely varied, ranging from court dance (*see p81*) to the most humble crafts—by 2008 a total of 362 forms of intangible heritage had been recognized across the whole country. The broadest categories are music and crafts. With the exception of court cuisine, there is only one "holder" of the heritage per category; these individuals train disciples, the best of whom takes over on the holder's death.

yourself or one for exfoliation or "peel-ing" (usually red) and enter the shower area—you must shower before you pass through to the baths, which progress from the least hot to the hottest. Some are outside, which is wonderful in win-ter when snow adds to the experience. Finally, you can take a sauna or hit the steam room before diving into a bath of icy cold water – for brave souls only, but undeniably invigorating. Then, if you wish, you can go around again. There are areas where you can take a nap or have a body scrub (ttaemiri, usu-ally around ₩10,000), but be warned as it is quite a workout. On leaving, there are facilities for reapplying makeup, drying hair, and so on. If you have been to a hot spring, try to keep the water from the last bath on your skin without rinsing, so that you benefit from the minerals and other health-giving properties. In the jjimjilbang and in mixed areas, shorts and T-shirts are worn and are provided free of charge. If there is a pool, you have to wear a swimming costume; these can be expensive, so it is advisable to take your own. Some establishments also require bathing caps to be worn.

GASTRONOMY

Korean cuisine is not yet very well known in the West, but it is starting to gain in popularity. Low in fat and well-balanced, it is also rich in vegetable protein, fermented foods and fiber, so it would be a tremendous pity to leave Korea having only experienced its take on western food. Korean dishes can surprise with their combinations of **little-known flavors** that tend to be less popular in the West (bitter tastes are commonplace, for example) and with spices and unusual fragrances, but note that food is often very red in color rather than genuinely hot. It can take a while to get used to this cooking style, but it would be a shame to stop at the bulgogi and bibimbap that you will invariably be served, on the basis that, according to most locals, these are the only dishes that sensitive foreign palates can handle. We recommend that early on in your stay you try one of the "full"

traditional meals (hanjeongsik, baekban) where the table is covered with a large number of small dishes that will allow you to explore this culinary world of unique flavors, colors and textures. With such a wide selection, you are bound to find something to your taste!

CULINARY ORIGINS

The Korean mealtime today harkens back to the way it was served for cen-turies. Meals were eaten at low tables—they were served to the men on small, individual tables (soban), while women and children, and those lower down the social pecking order, usually ate at a communal table. The hansang charim, or single-service tray, formed the basis of the meal. There would always be rice, white (bap) if possible, sometimes mixed with barley (bori) when there was not enough white rice or, as is the case now, for dietary reasons. The rice may be replaced by another grain such as a dish of wheat or buckwheat noodles. Soup of some sort would always be served—these can be clear (guk), with vegetables (tang), or thick like a stew (jjigae). They very often had a base of fermented bean paste known as doenjang, which is the Korean equivalent of Japanese miso. Combined with vari-ous condiments and seasonings, along with the rice or noodles and soup, diners would create the range of banchan, or secondary dishes, that made up the rest of the meal.

THE INFINITE WORLD OF BANCHAN

An unwritten law based on the ancient Taoist theory of ohaeng, or "harmony of the five elements," ensures that the colors, ingredients, textures and fla-vors are varied in order to produce a dish that is balanced and as tasty as it is attractive. Vegetables are blanched, fried, pickled or simply seasoned raw as a salad to form the base: spinach, soy sprouts, garlic stems, shiso or aster leaves, zucchini—the list of namul (seasoned vegetable dishes) is long and enriched with wild plants that are gathered in season around the house

Condiments and Seasonings

An essential feature of Korean cuisine, *jang* are made with fermented soybeans (*doenjang*), and also with soy sauce (*ganjang*) or red pepper paste (*gochujang*) mixed with dried *doenjang* powder and malt. These three versions of *jang* are found everywhere. They form the basis of condiment sauces, pickles and preserves, and they are a major source of vegetable protein and antioxidants. Other common condiments and seasonings include garlic, Chinese chives, sesame seed oil and red chili powder.

or in the mountains. Dandelion, purslane, stonecrop, butterbur, shepherd's purse, wormwood and chard are used for their unique flavors. *Banchan* also include a number of roots and rhizomes, such as platycodon (*doraji*), codonopsis (*deodeok*), lotus and ginseng. But what would a meal be without at least one grilled or braised meat or fish dish? The possibilities are endless, and depend on both the season and the inventiveness of the mistress of the house: pancakes with scallions and seafood (*pajeon*) or mung beans (*bindaetteok*), vegetables dipped in egg and breadcrumbs (*jeon*), fried or steamed dumplings (*mandu*), or seaweed (*gim*). And don't forget *jangajji*: pickled vegetables and root or fruit fermented in soy sauce, chili sauce or doenjang. With kimchi, these form the *mitbanchan* or secondary dishes that will keep for a long time, ideal in the past for getting through difficult winters.

In order to cope with a climate that, in the center and north of the country, makes it impossible to grow crops during the cold season, these foodstuffs are harvested and processed during the spring and summer.

KIMCHI

King of the *banchan* and the basic Korean meal, kimchi is even more typical of the national cuisine than British toast or the American bagel. But just as bread on its own would not be regarded as a meal, kimchi is not a dish in itself, rather an accompaniment made of fermented vegetable. The traditional method of preparation softens the vegetable by soaking it in brine, which also begins the fermentation. The vegetable is then mixed with seasonings such as garlic, chili powder, scallions, onions, and, lastly, shrimp brine (*jeot* or *saeu-jeot*) or salted anchovy sauce (*myeolchi aekjeot*), two very strong sauces that start the second fermentation. Within a few weeks, the kimchi is ready. A complete food, rich in animal protein, calcium, vitamins and lactic acid, it can be stored for several months. In the past, pots of kimchi were buried (those buried in the winter were called *gimjang*) or stored in the courtyard of the house on an elevated stone platform or *jangdokdae*, with access to good ventilation and sunlight. These days kimchi tends to be stored in special refrigerators. Kimchi varies with the seasons, the availability of the ingredients and the region in which it is made: sometimes spicy and red according to different recipes, or "white" when prepared with more traditional ingredients (red peppers only arrived from South America via Japan in the early 17C). Sometimes it is more liquid, like *mulkimchi*. The vegetables most commonly used for its preparation are now Chinese cabbage (*baechu*), which has almost become synonymous with kimchi, *daikon* or giant white radish (in *kkakdugi* for example), and cucumber.

RESTAURANTS

Baekban, meaning "white rice," is the staple dish of conventional Korean cuisine, such as in a typical meal of rice, soup and *banchan*. *Hanjeongsik* is based upon the same formula but, consisting of a wide selection of *banchan* filling a huge communal table, is the modern version of a meal that came from the southern region of Jeollanam-

A traditional complete meal

©KTO

do, famous for its intricately prepared cuisine, which is also rich in seafood. *Hanjeongsik* also describes gargantuan meals with an endless succession of dishes, only to be followed by *siksa*, a meal in which rice is accompanied by soup and small *banchan*—it's a minor miracle that the average Korean remains so svelte.

Today, with the modernization and democratization of society, meals are eaten at a shared table and are only rarely served individually—many Kore-ans live their entire lives without ever once eating alone. It is even now the norm in many contemporary Korean restaurants to place the *banchan*, soup and single dishes (*ilpum yori*) in the center of the table so that it is impossible not to eat a meal in communal fashion. This is the case in the numerous establishments specializing in a main dish such as grilled meat, sautéed chicken, stewed octopus, mushroom ragout, or fish soup, which is designed to be cooked at the table and shared by the guests.

Dog Meat: A Bone of Contention

Western countries and defenders of animal rights condemn Korea's practice of eating dog meat. In this very old custom, which also exists in China and Vietnam, the meat is consumed mainly in the summer months during hot weather, to counteract lethargy. It dates back to the days when farmers could ill afford meat and needed animal protein and fats after the strenuous planting season. Only a specific breed is consumed, specially prepared by butchers, so there is no risk that you will be served dog meat as a substitute for another meat. However, note that *bosintang*, *yeongyangtang* and *sacheoltang* are all forms of dog soup. Despite the government's attempts to "gloss over" this tradition, it remains alive and the subject of often heated debate. Consumers would prefer a regulatory mechanism, rather than a head-in-the-sand approach; animal lovers condemn the conditions on farms and in abattoirs; while others maintain that it is simply a difference between cultures. It is a sensitive issue about which few people agree, although in the interest of balance it must be said that while many in the Western world do, indeed, consider dogs to be loyal family members, they munch away quite happily on animals that are sacred to other cultures.

Bibimbap

©Chris Stowers/Apa Publications

The changing habits of South Koreans have contributed to this: they eat out more frequently, with increasing numbers of hoesik or business lunches and dinners. One of the most famous dishes of these shared feasts is the so-called Korean barbecue: beef or pork ribs (*galbi*), seasoned or otherwise, or beef marinated in a slightly sweetened soy sauce (*bulgogi*). Diners grill small pieces of meat over embers or a griddle in the middle of the table and then eat them wrapped in a salad leaf with a little sauce and some onion or scallion. It is very convivial and practical for those with sensitive palates who might have trouble appreciating the local cuisine and find it difficult to eat a whole meal. It should be pointed out, however, that as with many local "traditions," this did not really start until after the Korean War, in the 1950s; previously, beef and pork were a privilege enjoyed only by the aristocratic classes.

NOT TO BE MISSED

Finally, it would be impossible to end without mentioning a few unique, well-known dishes that you should really try during your stay. The first of these, *bibimbap*, has almost become, like kimchi, a flagship dish for Korean cuisine, especially since it is often served on the Korean national airline. It consists of rice mixed with hot sauce, a little sesame oil and various seasoned *namul*: spinach, bean sprouts, zucchini, cucumber, platycodon root (a native bellflower)

©KTO

Pharmacopoeia and Medicinal Plants

Korea has developed a tradition of natural remedies based on roots, berries and mountain plants (and other more exotic ingredients such as stag's antlers, toads and centipedes). Medicinal plants (*yakcho*) are used to make various potions (*hanyak*) with unique flavors (and smells), and these are sometimes sold at exorbitant prices.

and some chopped meat, fried egg or raw beef for meat eaters. This full, balanced dish is of peasant, royal or religious origin, depending upon which expert you choose to believe—the Buddhists make a particularly charming case, claiming that the ingredients correspond to the temple colors of red for the pepper paste, yellow for the egg, green for the vegetables, blue for the meat, and white for the rice. Beef soup, such as *seolleongtang*, served clear and mixed with a bowl of rice, is more conclusively of royal origin. Invigorating, it is enjoyed as a stock rather than for the bony bits of meat it contains. You may prefer the delicious *samgyetang*, a soup made with a whole chicken stuffed with glutinous rice, ginseng, jujube and pine nuts and served with chopped spring onion (*see p385*). Very restorative, it is traditionally served during the hot summer; those with frazzled taste buds will be happy to note that it is also one of the few Korean dishes that can be described as bland in taste.

GASTRONOMY AND HEALTH

There is an old saying in Korea that "food is like medicine," but this concept has now progressed from eating healthily as a natural way to prevent illness to some extremes that turn the idea on its head, seeking a cure for all ills in food itself. It is supported by the fashion for organic products, "slow food" and a lifestyle that promotes wellbeing. Public opinion may have been too readily swayed by articles, often backed up with appropriate pseudo-science and spread around liberally by national newspapers, claiming that *doenjang* can cure cancer or that kimchi can prevent SARS. There's also the curious example of green tea, vaunted as a cure-all to the degree that some restaurants specialize in the pork of pigs raised on a tealeaf-based diet. However, this should not detract from the very real qualities of Korean food, so long as it is eaten sensibly. Like any cuisine, Korean food has its disadvantages when eaten in excess, due to its high fiber content and reliance upon fermented and pickled ingredients. It is therefore advisable to eat a variety of foods, and your body will no doubt benefit in some way from the many wild plants and prized medicinal herbs that are incorporated into the cuisine.
See also the gastronomic glossary pp36-37.

HEALTH
TRADITIONAL MEDICINE

The principles of traditional Korean medicine have their roots in classical China. They are based on a holistic view of the individual in which disease is seen as a symptom of a lack of overall balance and is not in itself the primary focus. The flow of energy along specific meridians within the body may be blocked or stimulated. This is the basis of acupuncture and moxibustion (similar to

Medical Tourism Information Center

©KTO

Taekwondo
©KTO

acupuncture but using a gentle source of heat instead of needles), which is also practiced in Korea, and acupressure (*jiap*), a variation of acupuncture using finger pressure, like massage. Another feature of Korean medicine is the recognition of "types," similar to the ancient Hippocratic humors. In Korea a person's type is their psycho-physiological profile, and in traditional clinics, some of which are extremely modern and boast high-tech equipment, the patient's type is established by taking the rate and feeling of the pulse. A treatment is then prescribed, usually consisting of sachets of bitter potions to be taken over a long period. Such treatments are not recommended for diabetics or people with liver conditions. If you intend to try one of these clinics, be aware that, unfortunately, there are a few charlatans around, so do select carefully – it's always best to get specific recommendations from a local.

GROWTH OF MEDICAL TOURISM

Medical tourism is increasing in Korea. It has no doubt been helped by the highly successful South Korean historical drama *Dae Jang-geum*, whose story revolves around an eponymous 16C royal physician who compiled the great *Donguibogam* book of medicine. However, it is Western rather than traditional medicine that attracts tourist-patients. With ultramodern equipment, the latest techniques and competitive prices, this new type of tourism is being actively promoted and developed, particularly in the field of plastic surgery, a practice in which South Korean doctors excel, thanks to the domestic market. However, studies reveal that, paradoxically, it is routine procedures, long-term treatments and internal surgery that are attracting most of the medical tourists. Figures show that in 2009, 60,201 people chose to be treated in Korea rather than in Thailand or Singapore, countries that are also popular for this service. While Korea is still a long way behind these two giants, which benefit from government sponsored marketing initiatives, it is seeing exponential growth with forecasts of increasing numbers (80,000 foreign patients in 2010) generating a significant cash income.

TAEKWONDO AND OTHER SPORTS

Taekwondo is the best-known Korean "national" sport and has been an Olympic event since 2000. Yet it is a relatively recent sport, having been developed in its present form in the 20C by General Choi Hong-hi. Formally established in 1955, taekwondo is based on traditional Korean martial arts such as *taekkyeon*, the origins of which date back to the Three Kingdoms. A beautiful but also violent martial art, taekwondo uses the legs to kick (*tae*), and the arms and fists to attack and above all to defend (*kwon*, to strike with the fist); completing the name of the art is *do*, a suffix of Chinese origin loosely corresponding to "the way" in English, and also prevalent in Japanese martial arts. Taekwondo is widely practiced in Korea by both sexes and is also very well established abroad. In fact, figures suggest that it is one of the most practiced martial arts in the world, with between 30 and 70 million participants. Demonstrations can be seen in Seoul (see p105).

Other traditional sports include *ssireum*, a type of wrestling somewhere between Mongolian wrestling and Japanese sumo (though very rarely seen nowadays outside traditional festivals), and **archery**, at which Koreans excel. They also proved themselves at football in 2002, when they co-hosted the World Cup, and at **figure skating** in 2010 with Kim Yu-na's stellar performance. Finally, baseball is very widely played, with **skiing** and **cycling** also making recent gains in popularity.

CRAFTS

Several of Korea's ancient craft traditions are admired well beyond its borders. However, with the frenzied industrialization of the 20C and the lack of interest in anything that recalls an "underdeveloped" Korea, many of these traditions have all but disappeared. Some have been saved at the eleventh hour, thanks to a few remaining practitioners, and now the **Living National Treasures** organization also protects artists and crafts people and their unique skills (see box p88). With self-confidence restored and the need to preserve a national identity in the face of globalization, these traditions are now not just being maintained, but also actively developed and constantly reinvented, taking them in directions that range from a slightly kitsch, artificial folklore style to an inspired renaissance. Since the liberation, the practice of adding the prefix "han," meaning (South) Korean, to these traditions has been adopted: *hanji, hanbok, hanok, hanjeongsik*, and so on.

PAPER

Korean paper or *hanji* was long appreciated in both Japan and China for its fineness, strength and absorptive qualities. However, the origins of Korean papermaking are unclear. It may have come from China in the 6C, or it may have existed in Korea as early as the 3C. *Hanji* is made from the bark of the native paper mulberry tree, which is crushed, macerated and then filtered. Other forms of paper exist, such as that made from wads of fabric, like felt; this

Traditional paper making

©Chris Stowers/Apa Publications

95

Hanbok, Korean traditional dress
©KTO

thick paper was then oiled and used to cover the floors of houses or to make waterproof clothing.

CERAMICS

This ancient art reached its zenith in the Goryeo dynasty (918–1392) with the famous celadon ware (&see box p339). The celadon craftsmen and their secret techniques suffered as a result of the Mongol invasions and were nearly wiped out, and again during the Japanese invasions of 1592. Some families of potters were forced to settle in Japan, where their descendants carried on their tradition and enriched Japanese ceramics. However, kilns have never stopped operating and modern potters and ceramists have tried, sometimes with great success, to recreate the perfection of the past both in terms of design and technique. Some pieces are more art than craft, and this will be reflected in their price.

HANBOK

Traditional Korean dress is rarely worn today except during festivals and international fashion shows. The traditional fabrics of colored silk or light ramie in pastel shades are rather beautiful, though it has to be said that unlike other Asian ware, they do not generally go well with the Western frame. Happily for locals and non-locals alike, a modernized form now also exists, with a wave of younger designers allying old styles and materials with those of the present day; Hillary Clinton is just one admirer of what may be termed neo-*hanbok*. Korean dress was also renowned for its embroidery and trimmings, such as the elaborate knots known as *maedeup*, which often feature even on the newer styles. Lastly there's *bojagi*, or traditional wrapping cloth, assembled from dozens of different pieces of fabric woven together like a quilt; it is used to wrap goods and is still made, if somewhat rarely, by hand.

OTHER CRAFTS

South Korea is known, too, for a range of other crafts. There's high-quality brass tableware such as soup bowls and chopsticks; many different string, wind and percussion instruments; a range of wooden masks (used by warriors, in shamanist ceremonies, plays and dances); and seals made of wood, jade, gold or ivory. To see a variety of Korean crafts visit the National Folk Museum or the shopping street of Insadong, both located- in Seoul.

Nature

For a relatively small and densely populated country, South Korea has a surprisingly high level of natural beauty. Part of this is due to the fact that over two-thirds of the peninsula is mountainous, while the dramatic seasonal changes also help—spring sees flowers popping up all over the place; summer is great for hiking or relaxing on beaches of white sand; and fall offers hillside foliage raging with reds, oranges and yellows. In fact, it could be said that you can return to the same place each season and have the impression that you are seeing it for the first time. And there are a lot of places to return to, including craggy mountain ranges, shimmering paddy fields, pristine beaches and contorted coastlines.

THE CHANGING SEASONS
SPRING – POM

Spring arrives at different times depending on the region: in early March in the south but not before mid-April in the northeast. One great place to head is Boseong, at the southern tip of the peninsula—although poorly suited to the farming of cereal crops, its green tea plantations receive nearly three million visitors every year. The hills are covered with tea flower blossoms, while cedar trees border the plantations, helping to break up the monotony of the long lines of tea bushes. As soon as the first leaves appear, so do clusters of women wearing white cloths on their heads, here to begin picking the leaves with which they hope to fill their wicker baskets.

A little farther south, on the island of Namhae, Korea's "Treasure Island," spring arrives just as early. Approaching the island, you can't miss the immense red suspension bridge—the largest in Asia—connecting it to the peninsula. The fields are covered with young garlic that, by April, is already 20in/50cm high. Near the village of Daraengi, terraces cling in spectacular fashion to the mountainside at an angle of 45 degrees; the village itself looks like a swallow's nest built in the hollow of a cliff. The gentle spring breeze and the waves lapping the shore add to the general feeling of great tranquility. It's a colorful scene, with bright yellow fields of rape, roads lined with trees covered in white cherry blossoms, soft green rice terraces and, in the background, the glittering azure blue of the sea.

In the northern part of Jeollanam-do (South Jeolla) is Damyang, known for its lush forest of bamboo. The Damyang Metasequoia Road, lined with dawn redwood trees, has been named one of the most beautiful in the country. By May the weather is already warm, and people

Spring, Tea plantation in Boseong, Jeolla-do

©KTO

flock to Damyang's Bamboo Festival to follow paths through the forest with poetic names like "the Path that Brings Good Luck" or "the Path of the Scholars."

SUMMER – YEOREUM

Summer starts in early June in most regions. This time of year is characterized by heavy, humid heat, followed by a rainy season that begins in late June and lasts until the end of July or early August. The heavy mugginess of August finally recedes in September, and the weather generally becomes very pleasant for the harvest festival (*Chuseok*).

To cope with the heat, Koreans flock to the beaches that line the peninsula. Haeundae in Busan is the best known, though the craggier west coast also has numerous beaches where you can swim safely. The very high tidal range of the Yellow Sea means that as well as being good for bathing, it is also a prime place for the collection of shellfish. The town of Boryeong, in South Chungcheong Province, began holding a **Mud Festival** in 1998 (*see p399*). It takes place in July on a sandy 2.5mi/4km beach where, at low tide, an expanse of mud appears. This is an opportunity to learn about cosmetics based on the mineral-rich mud—and generally to get very muddy if you join in the fun wholeheartedly.

Just offshore, a wide variety of shellfish, crabs, oysters, clams, octopus, conches and more are collected; many appear on the tables of the restaurants lining the sea road, making this one of the best places in Korea for a shellfish barbecue. The sea off the Korean Peninsula's east coast is azure blue in color, and much deeper and cooler than the Yellow Sea. Gyeongpo, near the town of Gangneung in the northeast, is the largest coastal resort.

The wide pine forest that borders the white sand beach provides a refreshing coolness. To the south of Gangneung lie the highlands of Taebaek. This region is known for vast expanses of wild flowers and also has deep caves that offer some respite from the sweltering summer heat

FALL – GAEUL

Fall is undoubtedly the season when Korea's nature is at its most dazzling, offering a range of glorious landscapes. Northeast of Seoul, the half-moon shaped island of Nami, or Namiseom, floats in the middle of Cheongpyeong Lake. At daybreak, the dawn mist disperses on the surface of the water to become lost in the tree-lined paths: majestic golden ginkgoes, dawn redwood, pine and Japanese cypress.

Autumn colours in Huwon Garden, Changdeokgung, Seoul

© Mauritius/Photononstop

©KTO

Winter, Naksansa, Sokcho

In Seoraksan, in the northeast, the fall colors create a magnificent palette. This is the country's third highest mountain after Hallasan (on Jeju-do) and Jirisan (in the southeast), and with each season it changes its hues. The rocks blend with the colors of the foliage of the *dangdanpung* trees, a variety of maple, creating a stunning landscape. Next to *Chilhyeongje* (Seven Brothers Peak) is Deungseondae, from where a panoramic view opens out over peaks and slopes dotted with splashes of red as the leaves of the trees become autumnal.

WINTER – GYEOUL

Winter arrives as suddenly as summer, but despite the cold,which lasts until mid-March, most daytime activity takes place under a clear blue sky. Snowfall may be occur in all areas except on the south coast and Jeju-do, the latter an island south of the Korean Peninsula, and one boasting a mild climate. The numerous winter resorts make the mainland a skier's paradise. However, it does get extremely cold despite the relatively low mountains (the average altitude is about 3,300ft/1,000m).

In Chuncheon, known as the "city of mist," you can take an atmospheric cruise on Soyang Lake and pierce the mist in the cold winter breeze. Covered with glittering snow, the willows and reeds swaying on the banks of the lake are a truly wonderful sight. Beyond the lake, the ancient Cheongpyeong Temple (Cheongpyeongsa), on the slopes of Mount Obong, looks like an apparition from another world in a coating of white. And what could be more majestic than a 160ft/50m frozen waterfall? Gugok Waterfall twists and turns through nine levels and is spectacular in winter when it appears to be frozen in time. The slippery surface provides a real challenge for ice climbers.

By following the steep roads that wind around Nae-Seorak in Seoraksan National Park, you may be surprised to see countless racks hung with pollack and whiting at this time of year. Preventing the mist from penetrating, a cold wind blows incessantly in the valley, whose average temperature falls to 14°F/-10°C for nearly two months.

The cold season is also the time for numerous festivals involving such antics as fishing with bare hands or through a hole in the 20in/50cm-thick ice.

Hundreds of fishing enthusiasts assemble to try their luck, and are overjoyed when joined by curious visitors from overseas.

Bulguksa Temple, Gyeongju
©KTO

Seoul means "capital" in Korean, but this ancient city has had many other names: Wiryeseong, Hanseong, Hanyang, Gyeongseong.... Much more than just the capital, Seoul is also Korea in microcosm. While we should not be quick to dismiss the provinces, which are rich in sights and regional cultural traditions that are less "globalized" than Seoul, this this intriguing and energetic city can easily gobble up your time, and will undoubtedly be a highlight of any trip to the country.

Highlights

1 Take a presidential tour of the **Blue House** (p130)
2 Participate in a **Temple Life Program** (p141)
3 Browse Korean and foreign contemporary art at **Seoul Museum of Art** (p156)
4 **Shop**, shop and shop some more (pp184–185)
5 Go for a mountain hike in **Bukhansan National Park** (p215)

A Bit of Geography

Hangang (the Han River) bisects the South Korean capital from east to west, dividing it into two completely different worlds. To the north, against the backdrop of the mountains Bugaksan, Bukhansan and Inwangsan, lies the administrative and historic town center, with palaces, blocks of traditional houses and the first buildings erected in Western style.

To the northeast are the popular markets of Dongdaemun; to the northwest, the student districts of Hongdae, Sinchon and Ewha. The centrally located Namsan Park, with its famous N Seoul Tower visible from far away, serves as a useful landmark. Traces of the southern boundary of the ancient wall can still be seen.

▶ **Population:** 11 million
⏱ **Michelin Map:** pp 106-107, pp108–109, pp110–111
🛈 **Info:** See Useful Information, p 112
▷ **Location:** South Korea's capital city is in the northwest corner of the country.
👪 **Kids:** Gyeongbokgung and the National Folk Museum, Namsangol Hanok Village, the Agriculture Museum, Bukchon (traditional houses and small museums). Lotte World amusement park and the COEX Aquarium. A cruise on the Hangang or a dip in the pool on the banks of the river in summer or the outdoor skating rink of Gwanghwamun Square in winter. A walk in Yeouido Park or Olympic Park. Shop for video games in Yongsan. The shows *Jump* and *Nanta* or a *samulnori* performance. Visit a bathhouse (*mogyoktang*), try some typical Korean food (*samgyetang*, *bibimbap*, *mandu* or a Korean barbecue).
🕐 **Timing: Three days** should be sufficient to explore the main sights of the capital and give you time to take in two or three palaces and museums (such as National Palace Museum of Korea or Leeum Samsung Museum of Art), not forgetting a Buddhist temple (Bongeunsa). Enjoy browsing Dongdaemun and Namdaemun markets and buying souvenirs in Insadong. Watch a sunset over the city from N Seoul Tower; see a traditional

performance of song and dance. Visit the fashionable areas in the south of the city, such as the tree-lined streets Garosugil and Cheongdam-dong; enjoy the student ambiance in Hongdae or the more international atmosphere in Itaewon. If you have **a full week** in Seoul, explore less well-known areas such as Seongbuk-dong, Inwangsan, Jeong-dong or Cheonggyecheon, all interesting places in which to walk and soak up the atmosphere. Or visit some markets a little farther out. Explore the art galleries of Apgujeong and Insadong, and discover some of the lesser-known palaces, fascinating museums like the Seoul Museum of History and the royal tombs of Seonjeongneung (UNESCO). Nature lovers will not want to miss the beautiful city parks or Bukhansan National Park.

Don't Miss: Changdeokgung and the Huwon Garden (UNESCO), Gyeongbokgung, the royal ancestral shrine Jongmyo (UNESCO), the National Museum of Korea and Leeum Samsung Museum of Art, the historic district of Bukchon.

Districts: The districts are listed in order of interest, from the historic center to the newest areas south of the city and finally Bukhansan with its national park—a beautiful, natural, get-away-from-it-all spot.

South of the river, the business districts of Teheranno in Yeouido have sprung up and revolve around areas combining trendy shops and businesses, as well as luxury homes, before melting into the sprawling lesser suburbs beyond the mountains of Gwanak district.

A Thriving City

In 2010 Seoul had some 11 million people out of a total country population of 50.5 million. Yet this figure represents a decline compared to 1990, when the city's core population probably reached 12 million. The relatively recent newcomers have not gone back home, or at least very few have done so. Instead many of Seoul's inhabitants have been attracted to the city's booming satellite towns, so the decline has only been relative. Hence it is impossible to understand the phenomenon of Seoul without also taking into account Gyeonggi-do, the province that surrounds it with an almost completed ring of conurbations like the petals around a flower.

The "Capital Region" occupies 12 percent of the country, yet 46 percent of the population are concentrated there, so it has a far higher population density than most other major global cities (between 1.7 and 3.5 times). The giant city of Seoul is almost like a living being, constantly renewing itself, but also able to re-create its ancient roots when the need arises. It is an increasingly cosmopolitan city and is the showcase of Korea. In 2010, nearly 8 million tourists visited, while there were 255,000 permanent foreign residents, amounting to 2.4 percent of the total population.

The location of the city is superb, on a plain crossed by the broad Hangang and protected by a ring of impressive mountains. At first glance Seoul is a complex mix of concrete and asphalt, but don't be swayed by first impressions—explore this little-known city with its beautiful parks, meet its people, and peel back the many layers of the history that have made Seoul such a fascinating city since ancient times.

ADDRESSES

🎭 ENTERTAINMENT

SHOWS

👥 Nanta 난타 – *Star Six Jeong Dong Art Hall* 스타식스 정동아트홀, *Jeong-dong, Jung-gu.* Ⓜ *Seodaemun, line 5, exit 5.* ☎(02)-739-8288. http://nanta.i-pmc.co.kr/en/index.asp. ♿ *Shows daily 2pm, 5pm and 8pm. ₩45,000–54,000.* A comic non-verbal show—a contemporary *samulnori*—set in a kitchen where utensils are used as percussion instruments. A sell-out at the Edinburgh Fringe Festival and a long-running Broadway show, *Nanta* has been seen by some 4 million people worldwide since 1997. *Nanta* is so popular that it is also on at other venues in Seoul and in Jeju (👁️*see website*).

👥 Jump 점프 – *Basement of Cine Core building, 33-1 Gwancheol-dong, Jongno-gu.* Ⓜ *Jongno 3-ga, lines 1/3/5, exit 15 and Jonggak, line 1, exit 4.* ☎(02)-722-3995. www.hijump.co.kr. *Shows Mon 8pm, Tue–Sat 4pm and 8pm, Sun and public holidays 3pm and 6pm. ₩40,000-50,000.* A popular non-verbal show that has also been on Broadway. Two burglars get more than they bargained for when they break into the home of a family of martial arts experts. Plenty of acrobatics and martial arts action with comedy.

Chong-dong Theater 정동극장 –
8-11 Jeong-dong, Jung-gu. Ⓜ *City Hall, line 1, exit 1 and line 2, exit 12.* ☎(02)-771-1550. www.mct.or.kr. *Shows Tue–Sun 4pm and 8pm. ₩30,000–50,000. Miso* tells the story of a young couple who meet and fall in love as the seasons of the year progress, featuring traditional Korean music, dance and song. Subtitles in English. The show has been running since 1997.

LG Arts Center LG 아트센터 –
679 Yeoksam 1-dong, Gangnam-gu. Ⓜ *Yeoksam, line 2, exit 7.* ☎(02)-2005-0114. www.lgart.com. A superb, well-designed cultural complex, with exceptional acoustics. Intended for contemporary productions, it also hosts leading international shows. 👁️*See the website for what's on.*

Dongsoong Arts Center
동숭아트센터 – *1-5 Dongsung-dong, Jongno-gu.* Ⓜ *Hyehwa, line 4, exit 1.* ☎(02)-766-3990. www.dsart center.co.kr. From theater to dance, via musical comedy, music, exhibitions and film, everything is revisited in an avante-garde spirit. This independent venue also has a small museum of *kokdu*, traditional Korean colorful wooden statues that accompany coffins at funerals. 👁️*See the website for what's on.*

Don't forget other venues in the capital, such as the **National Theater of Korea** close to Namsan and **Seoul Arts Center** south of Hangang (👁️*see also p 203*).

DINNER SHOWS

Korea House 한국의집 – *80-2 Pildong 2-ga, Jung-gu.* Ⓜ *Chungmuro, lines 3/4, exit 3.* ☎ (02)-2266-9101. www.koreahouse.or.kr. *Shows Mon–Sat 7pm–8pm and 8:50pm–9:50pm. Sun 8pm–9pm. ₩50,000. Restaurant. 12pm–2pm, 5:30pm–7pm, 7:20pm–8:50pm, Sun 6:30pm–8pm. ₩70,000-250,000.* Cultural center, restaurant and shop providing high-quality services. Enjoy royal cuisine from the Joseon dynasty. This venue showcases the best traditional Korean artists, some of whom are Living National Treasures (👁️*see box p88*), performing the traditional arts from court dance through percussion instruments and shaman music. There are also cultural activities including local cooking, martial arts and dance. *Reservations are required for the combined dinner and folk performance show.*

KARAOKE

Su Noraebang 수노래방 – *367-39 Seogyo-dong, Mapo-gu. Adjacent to the Sangsang Madang complex, on the street with the car park.* Ⓜ *Hongik, line 2, exit 5.* ☎(02)-322-3111. www.skysu.com. *Open 24hr. ₩10,000-38,000 for 1hr.* One of the best karaoke venues with glass-fronted booths on several floors visible from the street. The chain has branches in several districts of Seoul.

♟ BARS / CLUBS
♿ *See Addresses for each district.*

☈ SPORTS AND ACTIVITIES

TRADITIONAL ACTIVITIES

Yoo's Family 유스 패밀리 –
*156 Gwonnong-dong, Jongno-gu.
Not far from the royal ancestral shrine
Jongmyo.* ℘*(02)-3673-0323. www.yoos
family.com. Open Mon–Sat. ₩20,000–
70,000.* The Yoo family opens the doors
of its *hanok* to let you enjoy, for a few
hours, a Korean cultural experience. The
programs include cookery, calligraphy,
painting and traditional games.
Minimum two persons.

DAYTIME SHOWS

National Gugak Center – *2364
Nambusunhwanno, Seocho-gu, next
to the Seoul Arts Center.* Ⓜ *Nambu Bus
Terminal, line 3, exit 5.* ℘*580-3333.
www.gugak.go.kr.* ♿ *Shows Sat 4pm.
₩10,000.* This center for the traditional
performing arts includes a museum
(*open Tue–Sun 9am–5pm, no charge*),
two indoor stages and one outdoor.
As well as the shows every Saturday,
other events are held, including
workshops to help foreigners
understand Korean culture.

Seoul nori madang 서울놀이마당 –
Jamsil, Songpa-gu. Ⓜ *Jamsil, lines 2/8,
exits 1/2. Behind Lotte World.* ℘*(02)-
410-3168/9. Shows Apr–Oct, Sat–Sun
3pm. No charge.* Performances of the
traditional arts from music and dance
to demonstrations of martial arts on
an outdoor stage in the amphitheater
beside Lake Seokchonhosu.

Changing of the Guard –
At Gyeongbok Palace (♿*see p 121*).

RIVER CRUISES

A cruise (particularly good at sunset)
on the Hangang offers a different
perspective of the city, but watch out
for the rather irrelevant accompanying
music! *Yeouido Pier, Yeouido (the island
near Mapo district), near Wonhyo Bridge
(Wonhyogyo).* Ⓜ *Yeouinaru, line 5,
exit 3.* ℘*(02)-3271-6900.* Round-trip
cruises lasting 70min at 9pm and
11:30pm (₩11,000–15,000).
Approximately hourly departures on a
variety of routes. A ferry service at 11am,

Lotus Lantern Festival
©Lotus Lantern Festival

2:20pm, 5:40pm, 9:40pm (₩11,000–
13,000) provides a link with Ttukseom
(Ttukseom Hangang Park with outdoor
pool) and Jamsil (outdoor pool) piers.

☺ EVENTS / FESTIVALS

HI-Seoul Festival – *www.hiseoul
fest.org.* May (Festival of the Palaces),
August (Han River festival), October
(Arts Festival) and December/January
(Festival of Lights).

**Royal ancestral rite Jongmyo Daeje,
and accompanying music** – Jongmyo
Jeryeak, listed in UNESCO's World
Heritage Sites. First Sunday of May
at Jongmyo.

Lotus Lantern Festival – *www.llf.or.kr.*
May (Birthday of the Buddha).

Chungmuro Film Festival –
*http://english.seoul.go.kr/cav/ena/
ciff.php* August to September.

Seoul Fringe Festival – *http://english.
visitkorea.or.kr.* August.

**Sidance, Seoul International Dance
Festival** – *www.sidance.org.* October.

Seoul Performing Arts Festival –
www.spaf.or.kr/2010english. October
to November.

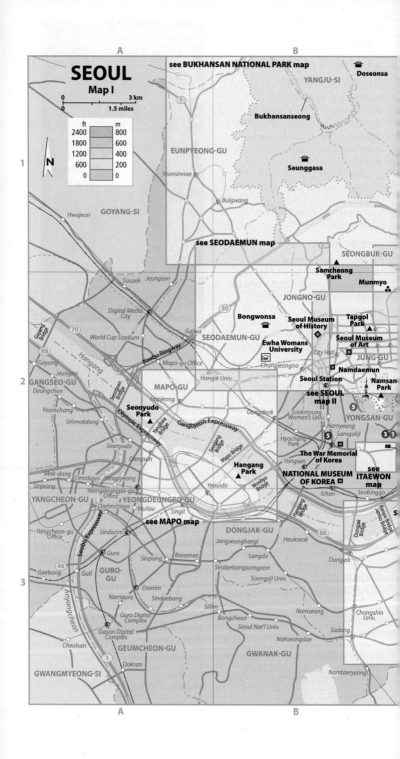

SEOUL
Map I

0 ——— 3 km
0 ——— 1.5 miles

ft	m
2400	800
1800	600
1200	400
600	200
0	0

N

A

B

see BUKHANSAN NATIONAL PARK map

Doseonsa

YANGJU-SI

Bukhansanseong

EUNPYEONG-GU

Seunggasa

1

Yeonsinnae

Bulgwang

Hwajeon

GOYANG-SI

see SEODAEMUN map

SEONGBUK-GU

Samcheong
Park

Munmyo

Susaek   Jeungsan

JONGNO-GU

Digital Media
City

Bongwonsa

Seoul Museum
of History

Tapgol
Park

Gayang
Bridge

World Cup Stadium

Gajwa

SEODAEMUN-GU

Seoul Museum
of Art

Naebu Ringway

Ewha Womans
University

City Hall

JUNG-GU

Gayang   Jeungmi

Mapo-gu Office

Chungjeongno

Namdaemun

2 GANGSEO-GU

Hongik Univ.

Seoul Station

Namsan
Park

Deungchon

MAPO-GU

see SEOUL
map II

Yeomchang   Sinmokdong

Hapjeong

Gongdeok

YONGSAN-GU

Sookmyung
Women's Univ.

Seonyudo
Park

Namyeong
Samgakji

Olympic Expressway

Gangbyeon Expressway

Seonyudo

Hyochang
Park

The War Memorial
of Korea

see
ITAEWON
map

Dangsan

Yongsan

Mok-dong   Omokgyo Yangpyeong

Hangang
Park

NATIONAL MUSEUM
OF KOREA

Sinjeong

Yeongdeungpo-gu
Office

Yeouido

Ichon

Seobinggo

YANGCHEON-GU   YEONGDEUNGPO-GU

Dorimcheon   Mullae

Singil

see MAPO map

DONGJAK-GU

Yangcheon-gu
Office

Sindorim

Jangseungbaegi   Sangdo

Heukseok

Dongjak

Gaebong   Guil

Guro   Sinpung   Boramae

Sindaebangsamgeori

3

GURO-
GU

Daerim   Sindaebang

Soongsil Univ.

Anyangcheon

Namguro

Sillim

Namseong

Chongshin
Univ.

Guro Digital
Complex

Bongcheon

Seoul Nat'l Univ.

Sadang

Gasan Digital
Complex

Cheolsan

GEUMCHEON-GU

Nakseongdae

Doksan

GWANAK-GU

GWANGMYEONG-SI

Namtaeryeong

A

B

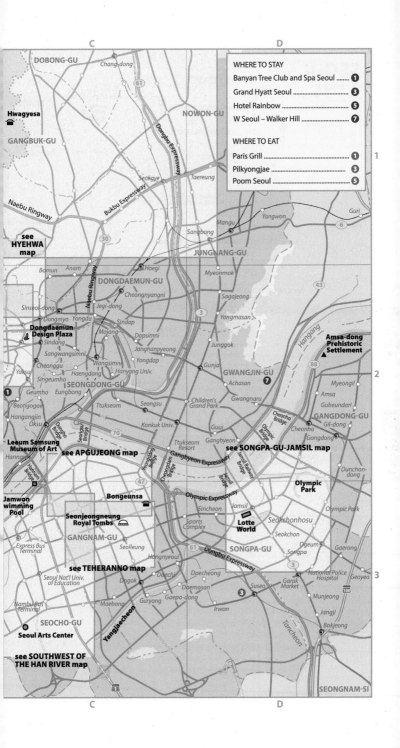

WHERE TO STAY

Banyan Tree Club and Spa Seoul .... ❶

Grand Hyatt Seoul .... ❸

Hotel Rainbow .... ❺

W Seoul – Walker Hill .... ❼

WHERE TO EAT

Paris Grill .... ❶

Pilkyongjae .... ❸

Poom Seoul .... ❺

DOBONG-GU

Chang-dong

NOWON-GU

Hwagyesa

GANGBUK-GU

Seokgye

Dongbu Expressway

Taereung

Naebu Ringway

Bukbu Expressway

Mangu

Yangwon

Guri

see
HYEHWA
map

Sangbong

JUNGNANG-GU

Bomun

Anam

Hoegi

Myeonmok

Sagajeong

DONGDAEMUN-GU

Cheongnyangni

Yongmasan

Sinseol-dong

Jegi-dong

Dongmyo

Yongdu

Sindap

Junggok

Dongdaemun
Design Plaza

Sindang

Majang

Depsimni

Hangang

Amsa-dong
Prehistoric
Settlement

Sangwangsimni

Janghanpyeong

Myeongil

Cheonggu

Singeumho

Haengdang

Yongdap

Gunja

GWANGJIN-GU

Amsa

Gubeundari

Yaksu

SEONGDONG-GU

Hanyang Univ.

Wangsimni

Achasan

❼

GANGDONG-GU

Geumho

Eungbong

Ttukseom

Seongsu

Children's
Grand Park

Gwangnaru

Cheonho

Gil-dong

Beotigogae

Hangangjin

Oksu

Konkuk Univ.

Guui

Gangbyeon

Cheonho
Bridge

Olympic
Bridge

Gangdong

Dunchon-
dong

Leeum Samsung
Museum of Art

Dongho
Bridge

Seongsu
Bridge

Ttukseom
Resort

Gangbyeon Expressway

see SONGPA-GU-JAMSIL map

❶

Hannam

Hannam
Bridge

Yeongdong
Bridge

Cheongdam
Bridge

Jamsu
Bridge

Jamsil Railway
Bridge

Olympic
Park

Olympic Park

Jamwon
Swimming
Pool

Bongeunsa

Olympic Expressway

Sincheon

Jamsil

Seokchonhosu

Seonjeongneung
Royal Tombs

Sports
Complex

Lotte
World

Seokchon

Express Bus
Terminal

GANGNAM-GU

Seolleung

SONGPA-GU

Ogeum

Songpa

Gaerong

Geoyeo

Hangnyeoul

Daecheong

National Police
Hospital

see TEHERANNO map

Dongbu Expressway

Seoul Nat'l Univ.
of Education

Daechi

Daemosan

Suseo

Garak
Market

Nambu Bus
Terminal

Dogok

Gaepo-dong

❸

Munjeong

Maebong

Guryong

Irwon

Jangji

SEOCHO-GU

Tancheon

Bokjeong

Seoul Arts Center

Yangjaecheon

see SOUTHWEST OF
THE HAN RIVER map

SEONGNAM-SI

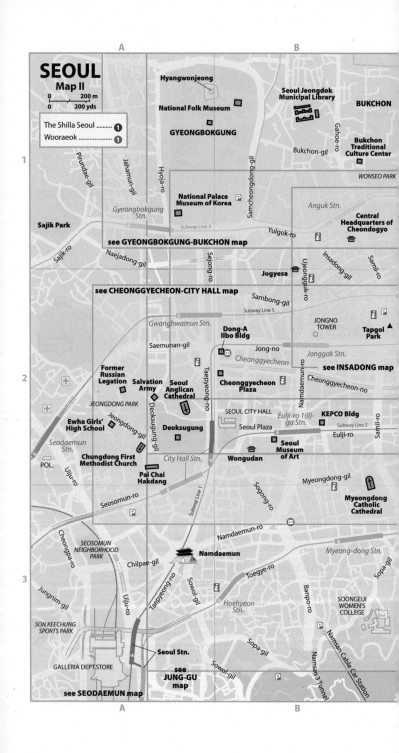

SEOUL
Map II

0   200 m
0   200 yds

The Shilla Seoul **1**
Wooraeok **1**

Hyangwonjeong

Seoul Jeongdok
Municipal Library

BUKCHON

National Folk Museum

GYEONGBOKGUNG

Bukchon-gil

**Bukchon
Traditional
Culture Center**

Pirundae-gil

Jahamun-gil

Hyoja-ro

Samcheongdong-gil

Gahoe-gil

WONSEO PARK

1

National Palace
Museum of Korea

*Gyeongbokgung
Stn.*

Subway Line 3

Anguk Stn.

**Central
Headquarters of
Cheondogyo**

Sajik Park

Sajik-ro

Naejadong-gil

Sejong-ro

see GYEONGBOKGUNG-BUKCHON map

Yulgok-ro

Jogyesa

Insadong-gil

Ujeongguk-ro

Samil-ro

see CHEONGGYECHEON-CITY HALL map

Sambong-gil

Subway Line 5

JONGNO
TOWER

Gwanghwamun Stn.

Dong-A
Ilbo Bldg

**Tapgol
Park**

Saemunan-gil

Jong-no

Jonggak Stn.

Cheonggyecheon

see INSADONG map

Cheonggyecheon-no

**Former
Russian
Legation**

**Salvation
Army**

**Seoul
Anglican
Cathedral**

**Cheonggyecheon
Plaza**

Namdaemun-ro

KEPCO Bldg

2

JEONGDONG PARK

Taepyeong-ro

SEOUL CITY HALL

*Eulji-ro 1(il)-
ga Stn.*

Subway Line 2

Eulji-ro

Samil-ro

**Ewha Girls'
High School**

Deoksugung

Seoul Plaza

*Seodaemun
Stn.*

Jeongdong-gil

Deoksugung-gil

**Seoul
Museum
of Art**

POL.

**Chungdong First
Methodist Church**

City Hall Stn.

Wongudan

Ulji-ro

**Pai Chai
Hakdang**

Myeongdong-gil

**Myeongdong
Catholic
Cathedral**

Seosomun-ro

Sogong-ro

*SEOSOMUN
NEIGHBORHOOD
PARK*

Subway Line 1

Namdaemun-ro

Cheongpa-ro

Chilpae-gil

Namdaemun

Myeong-dong Stn.

3

Jungnim-gil

Ulji-ro

Taepyeong-ro

Sowol-gil

Toegye-ro

Banpo-ro

**SOONGEUI
WOMEN'S
COLLEGE**

*SON KEECHUNG
SPORTS PARK*

*Hoehyeon
Stn.*

Sopa-ro

Namsan Cable Car Station

Seoul Stn.

**see
JUNG-GU
map**

Sopa-gil

Sowol-gil

Namsan 3 Tunnel

GALLERIA DEPT.STORE

see SEODAEMUN map

A   B

YEONGYEONGDANG

CHANGDEOKGUNG

INJEONGJEON

CHANGDEOKGUNG

HUWON GARDEN

Donhwamun-ro

Yulgok-ro

Jongmyo

Changgyeonggung-no

Former Daehan Hospital

SEOUL NATIONAL UNIVERSITY HOSPITAL

Hyehwa Stn.

MARRONNIER PARK

Former National Industry Institute

Daehang-no

KOREA UNIVERSITY

Naksan Park

see HYEHWA map

Jongno 3(sam)-ga Stn.

Jongno 3(sam)-ga Stn.

Changgyeonggung-no

Saeteo-gil

POL.

Jongno 5(o)-ga Stn.

Daehak-ro

Subway Line 1

Yulgok-ro

Jong-no

Wangsan-ro

Dongdaemun Stn.

see GWANGHWAMUN-JONGNO map

SEUN GREENWAY PARK

SEUN ARCADE

DAERIM ARCADE

Cheonggyecheon-no

HULLYEONWON PARK

Hullyeonwon-ro

Mabang-gil

Dongdaemun Shopping Center

Heunginmun-ro

Dongdaemun Design Plaza

Eulji-ro 4(sa)-ga Stn.

Eulji-ro

Eulji-ro 3(sam)-ga Stn.

Mareunnae-gil

Donhwamun-ro

Mareunnae-gil

Baeogae-gil

Dongdaemun History &Culture Park Stn.

Subway Line 5

see CHEONGGYECHEON-DONGDAEMUN map

SINSEONG ARCADE

Chungmu-ro Stn.

Subway Line 4

Toegye-ro

Hullyeonwon-ro

Geumhodong-gil

Namsangol Hanok Village

Subway Line 3

Jangchungdan-gil

Dongguk Univ. Stn.

Jangchungdan-gil

NAMSANGOL PARK

Samil-ro

N SEOUL TOWER

Namsan 1 Tunnel

DONGGUK UNIVERSITY

Namsan 2 Tunnel

Dongho-ro

Dasan-ro

Namsan Park

N

Yaksu Stn.

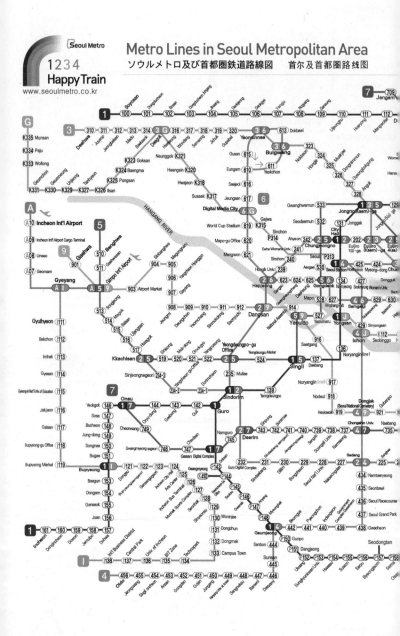

Metro Lines in Seoul Metropolitan Area
ソウルメトロ及び首都圏鉄道路線図　首尔及首都圏路线图

Seoul Metro
1234
Happy Train
www.seoulmetro.co.kr

Seoul Metro operates the Seoul subway line No. 1, 2, 3 and 4.
Produced on December, 2009 (For information on future opening stations or other questions,
please consult the offices in each stations or call 1577-1234)

USEFUL INFORMATION
Tourist Offices
Korea Tourism Organization (KTO)
한국관광공사
Tourist Information Center – Basement level, 40 Cheonggyecheon, Jung-gu. ☎(02)-7299-497/499 and 02-1330. http://english.visitkorea.or.kr. Open daily 9am–8pm. The main tourist office is in the basement of the KTO headquarters, but there are numerous others around the capital (☺ *see Addresses for each district)*, all are well stocked with brochures, plans and maps. Information is also available about guided visits, organized tours and train and airplane tickets. The main office contains a Medical Tourism Information Center, a fairly recent innovation catering to foreigners visiting Korea for medical treatment. Other Medical Tourism Information Centers can be found in Busan and at the Incheon airport.

Incheon International Airport
인천공항 관광안내소 *– Between gates 12-13 and 1-2 in Arrivals. ☎(032)-743-2600/03. Open daily 7am–10pm.*
☺ **Helpful hint —Goodwill Guide— Korea Tourism Organization** – The Goodwill Guide service offers the assistance of a friendly English-speaking guide during your trip. The guide is not a professional interpreter but will accompany you throughout your stay. You have to pay the guide's transport costs, admission charges, meals and, where appropriate, accommodation. Reservation is required 10–30 days in advance with the **Korea Tourist Organization** - *http://english.visitkorea.or.kr/,* under the section *Plan Your Trip/Traveler's Resources/Volunteer Tour Guides.*

Tourist information
iTourSeoul – *www.visitseoul.net.* Seoul Tourism Organization's useful website for tourists.
Hi Seoul – *http://english.seoul.go.kr.* A comprehensive and informative website on the city.

120 Dasan – *http://120.seoul.go.kr/foreign/english.html. Open daily 9am–10pm.* An English-speaking phone service offering information and help on virtually any kind of question relating to both tourism in Seoul and life in South Korea in general. **Call 120 in Seoul** (02-120 outside Seoul), then press 91. No charge apart from the cost of the call itself. You can also text questions from a Korean cell phone, text 01-120.
☺ **Helpful hint** – A **pass** giving unlimited access to the four main royal palaces (Changgyeonggung, Gyeongbokgung, Changdeokgung, Deoksugung) and Jongmyo is valid for one month *(Integrated Ticket of Palaces, ₩10,000)*. It is available from the ticket offices at each site.

Translation and Interpreting
Pan Trans Net 팬트랜스넷 – *☎(02)-778-2028. www.pantrans.net*
Ewha Graduate School of Translation and Interpretation 이화여대 통번역대학원– *☎(02)-963-5356*
Hanguk Graduate School of Translation and Interpretation 한국외대 통번역대학원– *☎(02)-2173-2435*

Banks and Exchange
Shinhan Bank Seoul Global Center 신한은행 글로벌 센터 *– 1F Seoul Finance Center, 84 Taepyungro 1-ga, Junggu.* Ⓜ *City Hall, lines 1/2, exit 4, and Gwanghwamun, line 5, exit 5. ☎(02)-773-3131. Open Mon–Fri 9am–4pm.* A banking service for foreign visitors.
Korea Exchange Bank, KEB 한국외환은행 *– 172-2 Itaewon, Yongsan-gu.* Ⓜ *Itaewon, line 6, exit 1. ☎(02)-792-3911. Open Mon–Fri 9:30am–4:30pm.* An agency specializing in transactions for foreigners. Service in English available.

Mail
Central Post Office 서울중앙우체국 *– 21-1 Chungmuro 1-ga, Jung-gu.* Ⓜ *Myeong-dong, line 4, exit 5. ☎(02)-6450-1114. www.koreapost.go.kr. Open Mon–Fri*

9am–6pm, Sat 9am–1pm.
The city's main post office. You can buy collectible stamps here too. Korea Stamp World is on the 2nd basement floor.

Health/Emergency

☎**119** for ambulance (and fire).

☎**112** for police. Some operators may speak English, although they may not be very fluent. (ℭ*see translation service below*).

Soonchunyang University Hospital
순천향병원 – *657 Hannam-dong, Yongsan-gu.* Ⓜ *Hannam, line 1, exit 1.* ☎*(02)-709-915 (9am–5pm). www.schch. co.kr/seoul/international/clinic/clinic.do.* A hospital with an International Clinic near Itaewon.

Samsung Medical Center
삼성서울병원 – *50 Irwon-dong, Gangnam-gu.* Ⓜ *Irwon, line 3, exit 1.* ☎*82-1599-3114 emergencies (02)-3410 -2060-1. www.samsunghospital.com.* A modern hospital providing international service.

Severance Yonsei Hospital
연세대학교 세브란스병원 – *134 Sinchon-dong, Seodaemun-gu.* Ⓜ *Sinchon, line 2, exit 3.* ☎*(02)-2228-5810, emergencies 010-9948-0982/3. www.severance.or.kr.* A large hospital providing international service.

English-speaking doctor – ☎*1339 from landline; (02)-1339 from a cell phone.*

Translation service for police and emergency services – ☎*1566-0112. Mon–Fri 8am–11pm, Sat–Sun 9am–6pm.* In the event of an accident, this service allows you to reach a police officer or a translator and get **immediate help in English.**

International SOS – ☎*(02)-3140-1700 (24 hr). www.internationalsos.com/ fr/asiapacificregion_korea.htm.* An emergency service (*fee*) for foreigners, providing medical advice over the phone, arranging hospital admissions and more.

Telephone
You can rent cell phones and buy prepaid international phone cards downtown, in Itaewon, for example. From Ⓜ Itaewon, line 6, cross the intersection, with your back to the Hamilton hotel, and in the first alley on the left, a number of shops offer cell phone rental and SIM cards. A counter near exit 1 sells prepaid phone cards. Alternatively, rent a phone upon arrival at Incheon International Airport (ℭ*see below*).

Consulates ℭ*See pp18-19*

GETTING THERE

BY PLANE – Incheon International Airport 인천국제공항 – ☎*(032)-1577-2600. www.airport.kr. Open 24hr.* Situated on Yeongjongdo Island, 32mi/52km west of central Seoul, the airport is connected to the mainland by the Incheon International Airport Expressway. There are also connections by bus and express train to Gimpo Airport, which mainly handles domestic flights.

☝ **Note**: *The airport takes its name from Incheon City, but the city itself is on the mainland.*

CALT – For the return journey, passengers flying with certain airlines (ℭ*see website*) may be able to check in and go through immigration and customs at CALT (City Airport, Logis & Travel) in Seoul's Gangnam district. Passengers then transfer to the airport in a limousine bus (*charge for bus, allow approx. 90min to Incheon, 1hr to Gimpo,* ☎*(2)-551-0077/8, www.calt. co.kr/eng/main.html*). Call or consult the website to check times and fare.

☝**Note:** *If you have goods to declare in carry-on bags, you must check in at the airport.*

City Center from Incheon International Airport

Airport Bus – *Buy tickets inside the arrivals hall near exits 4 and 9 and outside near exits 4, 6, 7, 8, 11, 13 and 9C.* Buses leave the airport between 5am and 11pm, every 10–30min. The journey takes 45min–1.5hr, depending on the destination. There are stops in different areas of the city, including at some of the luxury hotels (₩8,000–14,000). Details of the routes can be found on the airport website. The airport bus is the best way to get downtown.

KAL Limousine 칼리무진버스 – *Buy tickets from the KAL Limousine counter in the arrivals hall. www.kal limousine.com.* The Korean Air Limousine bus service serves major hotels and other destinations in the capital with several routes into the city (₩15,000).

Taxi – *Near exit 6 outside the arrivals hall.* Budget for ₩45,000–70,000 for Seoul, depending on traffic and destination, plus ₩7,100 toll for the Airport Expressway. Note that black taxis with yellow signs on the roof are luxury vehicles (₩70,000–₩100,000) and cost more than regular taxis. (🕭 *see also p 22*)

Train AREX 코레일 공항철도열차 – 🕿 *(032)-745-7788. http://english.arex. or.kr/jsp/eng/index.jsp.* An express train service between the airport and Seoul (*50min*). With regular departures, train service is also a good way of getting downtown. An AREX service also connects Incheon Airport with Gimpo Airport (*departures every 10min, journey time approx. 30min, ₩7,900*). Since Gimpo is served by the subway, you can also take the AREX to Gimpo, then the subway to Seoul, lines 1/9.

Gimpo International Airport 김포공항 – 🕿 *(02)-2660-2114. http://gimpo.airport.co.kr.* Closer to Seoul than Incheon International Airport, Gimpo is 11mi/18km west of the city center. It has two terminals: one for international flights (to China and Japan) and one for domestic flights. There are AREX express trains and airport buses connecting Gimpo with Incheon International Airport (*both take 30–40min, 🕭 see above*).

City Center From Gimpo International Airport

🅼 **Subway** – *Subway Gimpo International Airport, Seoul line 5, journey time 30–60min, depending on the destination.* The subway offers the most convenient and least expensive travel option into Seoul (₩700).

Train AREX – The express serves central Seoul from Incheon International Airport (🕭 *see above*).

Airport Bus – Buses serve all parts of Seoul, with frequent departures. Gimpo International Aiport offers standard limousine buses (₩4,500-12,000), KAL limousines that go straight to major hotels in Seoul (₩6,000), airport limousines (₩2,500-4,500), city coach buses (₩1,400), deluxe city express buses (₩1,300-3,600), city buses (₩700) Incheon ciy buses (₩700) and intercity buses (₩4,400-17,000). 🕭**Note:** normal city buses have very little room for luggage.

Taxi – Regular taxis are located at platform 1 with a minimum fare of ₩1,900. Deluxe taxis are located at platform 2 with a minimum fare of ₩4,500.

BY TRAIN – Seoul Station 서울역 – *122 Bongnae-dong 2-ga, Jung-gu.* 🅼 *Seoul Station, line 1/4, exit 2. Map I B2.* 🕿*(02)-392-1324.*

Cheongnyangni Station – *588-1 Jeonnong-dong, Dongdaemun-gu.* 🅼 *Cheongnyangni, line 1, exit 4. Map I C2.* 🕿*(02)-1544-7788.* Mainly serves the east of the country.

BY COACH/BUS – Seoul Express Bus Terminal 강남고속터미널 – *Gangnam Gosok Terminal, 19–4 Banpo-dong, Seocho-gu.* 🅼 *Express Bus Terminal, lines 3/7, exit 1. Map I C3.* 🕿*(02)-535-4151.* The main bus terminal, with a vast underground shopping mall, restaurants and cinemas, etc. Next to it is a second bus terminal **Central City Bus Terminal** – *19-5 Banpo-dong, Seocho-gu.* 🅼*Express Bus Terminal, lines 3/7, exit 4.* 🕿*(02)-6282-0600.* Departures to every major city in the country.

Dong-Seoul Bus Terminal 동서울 버스 터미널 – *546-1 Guui-dong, Gwangjin-gu.* 🅼 *Gangbyeon, line 2, exit 3. Map I D2.* 🕿*(02)-453-7710,*

(02)-455-3162. On two floors; it serves the entire country, especially the east, but with fewer departures than the Express Bus Terminal.

Sangbong Bus Terminal 상봉 버스터미널 – *83-1 Sangbong-dong, Jungnang-gu.* Ⓜ *Sangbong, line 7, exit 2. Map I D1.* ℘ *(02)-490-7751.* Buses for Cheongju, Chuncheon, Daejeon, Jeonju and Gwangju, primarily heading east and north.

Nambu Bus Terminal – *1446-1 Seocho-dong, Seocho-gu.* Ⓜ *Nambu Bus Terminal, line 3, exit 5. Map I C3.* ℘*(02)-521-8550.* Serves destinations south of Seoul.

BY SEA – Domestic Shipping Lines–Incheon Ferry Terminal 인천연안부두 여객터미널 국내선 – *Yeonan Budu.* Ⓜ *Dongincheon, line 1, then a 10–15 minute taxi ride.* ℘ *(032)-880-7530, (032)-888-0116.* Ferries to the islands near Seoul, such as Deokjeok-do with its beach, or those farther away, such as the popular Jeju-do.

International Shipping Lines–Incheon Ferry Terminal 1 인천연안부두 여객터미 널 국제선 – *Yeonan Budu.* Ⓜ *Dongincheon, line 1, then 10–15min taxi ride.* ℘ *(032)-891-2030.* Ferries to Dandong, Yingkou, Qinhuangdao, Yantai and Shidao in China. **Terminal 2** ℘*(032)-761-3068.* Ferries to Weihai, Qingdao and Tianjin in China.

GETTING AROUND SEOUL

Ⓜ **BY SUBWAY**– The subway system provides excellent coverage of the city and its outer suburbs (ⓒ*see map pp 110–111).* It is fast, clean, safe and very cheap (₩1,000 for short journeys/₩900 with a T-money card, free for children 6 and younger). It is easy to find your way around: area maps are available online and at each station, while stops and possible changes are announced on the train in Korean and English. The network is also equipped for disabled use. Tickets can be purchased from automatic ticket machines that give change. If you use a T-money or Seoul

City Pass card, remember to scan it by touching it against the card reader on the ticket gate both at the start and end of your journey. Visit www.smrt.co.kr for useful information; click on the subway map on the home page in English to plan your trip in advance. While trains can be crowded during rush hour, the subway is the best way to get around the capital, especially if you are in a hurry.

☺ **Helpful hint** – Subway stations have clean toilets and machines that generally accept international credit cards, although they don't always have instructions in English.

BY BUS – Buses provide extensive coverage of the city and are very economical; their tariff changes after a certain distance. There are five categories: **green buses** circulate within a restricted area, ideal for getting to a subway station (₩1,000); **larger green buses** crisscross the city's districts (₩1,000); **blue buses** connect outlying districts to the center (₩1,000); **red buses** allow easy travel to the larger outlying suburbs (₩1,800); and **yellow buses** run in specific central areas and provide a link to the business districts (₩800). Stops often provide route information in English and buses usually have their main destinations written in the Roman alphabet. If you want to make best use of bus services, consult the online interactive map http://english.seoul.go.kr/. There is also a very useful free interactive app for iPhone, in English, called **Seoul Bus** *(downloadable from iTunes).*

If you use a T-money or Seoul City Pass card, remember to scan it by touching it against a card reader at the start and end of your journeys.

☺**Helpful hint** – You cannot pay with notes larger than ₩1,000 on buses. With the **T-money card** (℘*(02)-1644-0088, www.t-money.co.kr)* you don't have to worry about having sufficient change to board a bus. It can also be used for taxis displaying the T-money logo, subways, in some convenience stores and to enter some cultural sites.

The card also gives you a reduction of ₩100 per trip and a free transfer from bus to subway, for example, if completed in 30min. It is available (₩2,500) at subway stations and convenience stores displaying the T-money sign, and can be recharged with credit. Unused credit can be refunded at some convenience stores; a refund fee of ₩500 will be deducted. The **Seoul City Pass** card *(www.seoul citypass.com,* ✆*(02)-1644-0088 – ₩15,000/1 day, ₩25,000/2 days, ₩35,000/ 3 days)* allows you to make up to 20 trips by bus (blue, green or yellow buses) or metropolitan subway per day in Seoul. The card holder cannot board the red bus or the Gyeonggi or Incheon buses. A discount for the **Seoul City Tour Bus** for sightseeing (⟲*see below)* is also avaialble. You can buy the card in some convenience stores at Incheon airport and from major Tourist Information Centers in the city center. ⊘**Note** that unused credit cannot be refunded.

The **Seoul City Pass+** card *(www.seoulcitypass.com)* combines T-money and tour card functions. The card itself costs ₩3,000, and you must charge it with credit. It can be bought at subway stations, convenience stores displaying the logo and some Tourist Information Centers. For transportation use, see the Seoul City Pass *(above)*. The Seoul City Pass+ covers admission to Gyeongbokgung, Changdeokgung, Changgyeonggung, Deoksugung, Jongmyo and the Seoul Museum of History, and offers discounts to other participating sights, some restaurants, PC bangs (a type of super Internet café), public telephones and convenience stores. The card can be recharged at subway stations (including some ATMs) and convenience stores. ⊘**Note** that this card can be refunded at some convenience stores; ₩500 is deducted as a refund fee.

Seoul City Bus Tour
Gwanghwamun, at the front of Donghwa Duty Free Shop. Ⓜ *Gwanghwamun line 5, exit 6.*
A good way to get an overview of the city and see the main sights. The single-decker City Course bus operates 9am–9pm (₩10,000), 2hr tour with departures every 30min; evening tour 8pm (₩5,000, 1.5hr). The double-decker Cheoggyecheon and Ancient Palaces Course bus operates 10am–5pm (₩12,000) 2hr tour with departures on the hour (but no

Seoul City Tour

©KTO

departure at 2pm); evening tour 8pm (₩10,000, 1.5hr). Tours do not operate Mondays, except the fourth week of July–15 August and public holidays. You can hop on and off during the day tours, but the evening tours are nonstop. Pay on the bus, at major hotels, or the ticket booth at the front of the Koreana Hotel. There is a 15 percent discount with KR Pass, and a 5 percent discount with the T-money card. ✆(02)-777-6090.

BY TAXI – There are several types of taxis in Seoul, and they are a good option for tourists because they are quite cheap and plentiful. All are metered, so there should be no need to haggle, although it is useful to check the price anyway before setting out. It is best to avoid taking taxis during the evening rush hour when traffic can be terrible, and you may have difficulty when the subway is closing and taxis are in short supply. Taxis are available for hire when the light on the roof is illuminated. Those accepting the T-money card display the logo. Some taxis also accept credit cards. There is normally no need to tip, unless you feel the driver has been particularly helpful.

Standard taxis 일반택시 – White and silver, but increasingly orange too (see also *International Taxis below*). ₩2,400 flat charge for 1.25mi/2km; ₩100 every 157yd/144m (or 35 seconds stationary). Between midnight and 4am, prices rise by 20 percent. Drivers do not often speak English, but most have the **Free Interpretation** service (7am–10pm, sticker on the right rear door or window). Call the number displayed and an interpreter will help you out.
To book a standard taxi, **Kind Call Taxi** – ✆(02)-1588-3382. **KT Powertel** – ✆(02)-1588-0082. ₩1,000 booking fee.
Luxury taxis 모범택시 – Black with a yellow sign on the roof. ✆(02)-558-8000. ₩4,500 flat charge for 1.86mi/3km, then ₩200 every 179yd/

164m or 39 seconds. More luxurious than the standard taxis, these vehicles offer a high-quality service and can be booked in advance.
Van taxis 택시정보 – ✆(02)-888-2000. The same price as luxury taxis. They are very spacious, can hold up to eight passengers and can be booked in advance.
International taxis 인터내셔널 택시 – *Orange.* ✆(02)-1644-2255. www.international taxi.co.kr. Standard cars ₩2,880 flat rate for 1.25mi/2km; ₩120 every 157yd/144m (or 35 seconds stationary); luxury cars, ₩4,500 for 1.86mi/3km then ₩200 every 179yd/164m or 39 seconds. Special taxi service for non-Korean speakers. Look for "International Taxi" on the side of the car. There are far fewer than the regular taxis, and they operate on a reservation basis. They carry four people; if your party is 5-8 people, ask for a van taxi. Fares increase by 20 percent midnight–4am.
Taxis for those with reduced mobility – ✆(02)-1588-4388.
BY WATER TAXI – **Water taxis** 수상관광콜택시 – ✆(02)-1588-3960. www.pleasantseoul.com. 9am–8pm. ₩58,000–72,500, depending on distance. A much calmer way of getting about away from the busy streets, you can hop on and off at any one of 15 embarkation points along the Hangang. The journey is quick, and it is an original way to cross the city from east to west. To avoid a long wait, it's a good idea to book in advance. The staff speak Korean, so go through your hotel or the tourist office to arrange the trip. The taxis can also be hired for customized tours (7–10 passengers per taxi, ₩50,000 for 20min tour, ₩70,000 30min, ₩90,000 40 min, ₩130,000 1hr. ✆(02)-1588-3960).

STAY / EAT
See Addresses for each district.

Gyeongbokgung – Bukchon★★★
경복궁 – 북촌

This is *the* historic district—where the court nobility lived—in the area between the two main royal palaces. Gyeongbokgung is sometimes compared with the Forbidden City in Beijing, although it is smaller in size, and with Changdeokgung is a UNESCO World Heritage Site. Bukchon includes several "dong" (neighborhoods) where small groups of very old houses still stand, some of which have been turned into small museums, restaurants, wine bars, cafés or shops. A stroll around the area is an absolute must in order to discover its beautiful traditional residences and the charms of a bygone era. Thanks to the maze of narrow alleyways, impenetrable to large vehicles, there is little heavy traffic.

VISIT

♣♣ Gyeongbokgung★★★ (Gyeongbok Palace) 경복궁
♿ *See Gyeongbok-Bukchon Map. 22 Sajikno, Jongno-gu.* Ⓜ *Gyeongbokgung, line 3, exit 5.* ✆*(02)-3700-3900. www.royalpalace. go.kr.* ♿☉*Open Wed–Mon, Mar–Oct 9am–6pm, Nov–Feb 9am–5pm.*

- ♿ **Michelin Map:** Map p119
- ℹ **Info:** Tourist Office 130-4 Gwanhoon-dong, Jongno-gu, to the north of Insadong-gil. Ⓜ Anguk, line 3, exit 6. ✆(02)-731-1621/734 0222. Open 10am–8pm.
- ▶ **Location:** Between the palaces Gyeongbokgung to the west and Changdeokgung to the east.
- ♣♣ **Kids:** Explore Gyeongbokgung and watch the changing of the guard; examine the models and reconstructions at the National Folk Museum
- ☉ **Timing:** If you visit all the galleries and museums and stop for lunch, the trip will take a full day, but it can be done in half a day by just visiting the main sites. The neighborhood is pleasant at any time of day and also in the evening for dinner or a drink. However, after around 10pm it is usually deserted.
- ⊘ **Don't Miss:** The superb Gyeongbokgung, the National Palace Museum of Korea and the traditional district of Bukchon.

Gyeongbokgung Palace

©KTO

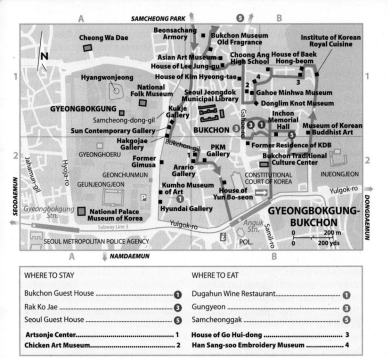

Closed Jan. (9am–7pm Sat–Sun and public holidays May–Aug.) Admission ₩3,000 adults, ₩1,500 ages 7-18. The **Integrated Ticket of Palaces** *pass allows access to the 4 main palaces and Jongymo for one month, ₩10,000.*

The history of the palace dates back to 1395, during the reign of Taejo, three years after the founding of the Joseon dynasty and following the relocation of the kingdom's capital (previously at Gaegyeong (Kaesong), North Korea) to its current site (see p172). With the peak of Bugaksan to the rear and Namsan (South Mountain) opposite, across the city, the location was deemed auspicious, and it was named Gyeongbokgung (Palace Greatly Blessed by Heaven). Along with the government district that surrounded it, the palace formed the heart of the capital and was the sovereign seat of the Joseon dynasty. The palace was destroyed during the Japanese invasions, led by Toyotomi Hideyoshi, that took place between 1592 and 1598; a fire was started by court slaves seeking to destroy records of their legal status. The king then moved to Changdeokgung (see p133), the royal palace just under a mile to the east, and Gyeongbokgung was abandoned for the next 250 years. The palace was finally rebuilt in 1868 by the Daewongun (regent), but was substantially different from the original construction, skillfully combining ancient Chinese architectural principles with the traditions of the Joseon court. At that time the palace complex consisted of some 330 buildings in an area of 0.15sq mi/40ha—a small city in itself. King Gojong and the royal family returned to Gyeongbokgung after its restoration, but they were to remain in residence for just 23 years. In 1895 the king was forced to take refuge in the Russian Legation following the murder of his wife, Queen Min, by the Japanese occupiers. About a year later, the king moved to Deoksugung, a third palace to the south (see p149).

The Japanese took control of Gyeongbokgung, moving or demolishing many of the buildings, and established the seat of their colonial government in this highly symbolic location. Having since demolished the buildings erected by the Japanese occupiers, the Korean government has been working hard to restore the palace to its former glory since the 1990s, and there are ongoing restorations.

The main entrance to the palace, **Gwanghwamun** ("may the light of enlightenment blanket the world") consists of a wooden structure with a double roof over a solid stone base pierced by three archways, the central and largest of which was reserved for the monarch. The side archways were for princes and senior officials, while those of lower rank had to use other gates. Gwanghwamun (Gwanghwa Gate) was moved by the Japanese occupiers to the eastern wall during the construction of the headquarters of their colonial government and then destroyed by bombing during the Korean War (1950–1953).

The gate was subsequently rebuilt on its original site in 1968, but was reconstructed yet again in 2010 and restored to its 19C form, using wood and stone. On either side of the entrance, two stone *haetae*, mythical animals, protect the palace. Three other gates provide access to the palace: **Geonchunmun** to the east, which is still in use, dates from 1865; **Yeongchumun** to the west was restored in 1975; and **Sinmumun** to the north was built in 1475 and restored in 1865. Of the two watchtowers that protected the south of the palace, only **Dongsibjagak** remains; formerly at the southwest corner, it is now located in the middle of a busy traffic intersection. **Seosibjagak**, its counterpart to the west, was demolished by the Japanese authorities in 1923.

Gyeongbok Palace is a maze of different buildings, courtyards, corridors, halls and pavilions, to which only certain people had access on the basis of rank or position. This enclosed group of buildings served to protect the privacy of the monarch, who remained virtually inaccessible to ordinary mortals, secluded in his private apartments at the back of the complex.

Once through the main entrance, the imposing gate **Heungnyemun** allows access to the first courtyard inside the palace area, across which flows Geumcheon Stream, from west to east.

During ceremonies held beneath the gate **Geunjeongmun**, which leads to the throne hall, second-ranking officials were positioned north of the bridge across the stream, closest to the monarch, while those in the third rank remained to the south. A second courtyard is then entered, containing the **Geunjeongjeon** (throne hall). The king held official audiences and received envoys from foreign powers here. The great courtyard has two rows of stone markers indicating where officials should stand, placed according to rank.

The magnificent stone staircase leading to the throne hall has interesting sculptures, including several Chinese phoenixes. Protective *haetae* guard both sides of the staircase, while the guardians of the four cardinal compass points and the twelve Chinese signs of the zodiac can be found carved into the stonework nearby. The building sits on two stone terraces. The throne itself is on a dais at the northern end of the throne hall, beneath a carved canopy. Behind it is a screen with a traditional representation of *Irwol-oakdo*—five mountains, the moon and the sun: symbols of hope and prosperity for the nation. The dragons on the ceiling are symbols of royal power.

The courtyard after the throne hall contains **Sajeongjeon**, the hall where the Royal Council was held. It was here that the monarch would discuss the everyday business of the kingdom with officials. Leave the courtyard by a door to the north and enter **Gangnyeongjeon**, which housed the royal apartments. The fine quality of the decorative ceilings is evident. In the next courtyard, behind **Gyotaejeon**, the queen's apartments, near the artificial mound *Amisan*, note the chimneys made of bricks and tiles, materials reserved for the aristocracy, which are decorated with interesting bas-reliefs.

East of this series of courtyards lie the apartments of the crown prince, **Jaesongdae** and, farther north, **Jagyeongjeon**, those of Queen Cho, the adoptive mother of King Gojong, with their richly decorated walls.

To the west, jutting out into a lake, is **Gyeonghoeru**, a large pavilion on stilts, which hosted parties and receptions held by the king for officials and foreign envoys.

Behind the apartments of the queen and queen mother, the palace complex opens out onto gardens. On the right is the **National Folk Museum**, a group of buildings constructed in the 1960s in the style of the temples at Bulguk and Geumsan that strike quite a different note. On the left, farther back, is the beautiful hexagonal pavillion **Hyang-wonjeong**, built on a small island in the middle of a lake and connected to the shore by a delightful small bridge.

To the north of this site is a separate royal residence, **Geoncheonggung**, built by King Gojong in the style of a scholar's house so that he could enjoy some quiet time with his wife, but it was here that Queen Min was assassinated by the Japanese occupiers in 1895.

To the left of Geoncheonggung is **Jibok-jae**, which served as an art gallery and library. The Chinese architectural influence is quite noticeable here. Farther west again are several sanctuaries, set apart from the palace. **Honjeon** housed the royal memorial tablets before they were relocated to Jongmyo Shrine. **Tae-wonjeon** contained the portrait of King Taejo, founder of the Joseon dynasty.

Gyeongbok Palace also holds reenactments of the **changing of the guard** ceremony, performed by around fifty soldiers in colorful costumes in what is said to be an accurate representation of the ceremony from the Joseon period. *Gwanghwamun and Heungnyemun, the main gates. 10am–4pm, on the hour. No charge.*

National Folk Museum
국립민속박물관

See Gyeongbok-Bukchon Map. 35 Samcheong-dong-gil, Jongno-gu. Located inside Gyeongbok Palace grounds. Gyeongbokgung, line 3, exit 5. *(02)-3704-3114. www.nfm.go.kr* *Open Wed–Mon Mar–Oct 9am–* *6pm Nov–Feb 9am–5pm. Closed Jan 1. (9am–7pm Sat–Sun, public holidays May–Aug) No charge. Guided tour in English, no charge between 10:30am and 2:30pm. Audio guide, ₩1,000.*

A museum of folklore and traditional Korean lifestyle, presented chronologically in three halls. The first covers prehistory to the time of the Three Kingdoms and Unified Silla. The second traces the history of the lifestyle of the ordinary people, particularly the farming communities who were governed by the seasons. The third focuses on the major events and ceremonies of the privileged classes of Korean society during the Joseon dynasty. The displays include models and reconstructions that children in particular will enjoy. There are also changing temporary exhibitions. Foreign tourists can take part in traditional craft workshops *(every Wed, see website or* *(02)-3704-3104)*, or performing arts workshops *(every Fri)*; a display of traditional music and dance takes place Saturdays at 3pm.

National Palace Museum of Korea★★ 국립고궁박물관

See Gyeongbok-Bukchon Map. 34 Sajikno, Jongno-gu. Gyeongbokgung, line 3, exit 5. *(02)-3701-7500. www.gogung.go.kr.* *Open Tue–Fri 9am–6pm; Sat–Sun and public holidays 9am–7pm. No charge. Guided tours in English (depending on the availability of a guide, check in advance), 3pm, no charge. Audio guide, ₩1,000.*

The museum is home to a collection of some 40,000 items relating to the lives of the monarchs and the court of the Joseon dynasty (1392–1910) exhibited on three floors. Displays cover objects belonging to the monarchy, such as royal seals, magnificent paintings by the renowned artists of the time, furniture (royal palanquins), and documents; also royal rituals, which were heavily influenced by Confucian philosophy. The refined life of the court is also explained along with its literary culture and the protocol surrounding the education of the princes.

121

National Palace Museum

©Chris Stowers/Apa Publications

🐾 WALKING TOUR

BUKCHON★★★ 북촌

▶ *Arrive at Ⓜ Anguk, line 3, exit 3. This is surely the prettiest walk though historic Seoul. The tour takes about 2hr without stopping to visit any of the countless museums and galleries (also of great interest if time is available); count on at least half or even a whole day if visits to museums are to be included.*

Bukchon means "North Village," as opposed to Namchon, "South Village," in Cheonghak-dong near Namsan (South Mountain). Sandwiched between two palaces, Bukchon housed the residences of the powerful court officials, while Namchon was home to scholars and artists. Bukchon consists of ten *dong* (administrative districts), including Gahoe-dong, Samcheong-dong, and Gye-dong. During the Joseon era, there were just 30 villas and their estates in Bukchon, but in the early 20C, these estates were gradually subdivided into smaller and smaller plots as a result of the increasing population, the democratization of society, the collapse of the old court aristocracy and unemployment during the Japanese occupation.
Today Bukchon contains 2,300 homes, of which 924 are *hanok*, traditional houses. Apart from some rare, very old *hanok*, most are in a transitional style typical

of the urban 1920s *hanok*, with a more compact layout, the various wings *(chae)* merging to become "rooms" *(bang)* arranged around a typically square courtyard. A precious 411 of these houses are listed as protected buildings, as the city of Seoul has a renewed interest in preserving its heritage.
In 2008, the city helped renovate 300 of these houses, acquiring 33 for various cultural programs (guesthouses, museums and such). Yet across Seoul the destruction continues: of a total of 20,000 *hanok* in 2005, there remained only 14,000 in 2009. In 2001 a restoration project was launched that could eventually transform Bukchon into a second Insadong (cafés, shops, a district almost exclusively for tourists).

▶ *The tour starts in earnest at the Ⓜ exit: walk straight ahead to the Hyundai building with the Gwansanggamgwancheondae stone tower in front; dating from the Joseon period (1434), it served as an astronomical observatory.*

▶ *Turn left immediately and walk up the street to Bukchon Traditional Culture Center.*

Bukchon Traditional Culture Center 북촌문화센터
♿ *See Gyeongbok-Bukchon Map.*
105 Gye-dong, Jongno-gu.

Ⓜ *Anguk, line 3, exit 3.* ✆ *(02)-3707-8388/8578. http://bukchon.seoul.go.kr.* 🕐 *Open Mon–Fri 9am–6pm, Sat–Sun 9am–5pm. No charge.*

The center is housed in a building dating from 1921. It was later bought by the city, opening as the Traditional Culture Center in 2002, and is a useful first stop for the walk. The architecture of the house is very well explained, and the wing converted into a museum offers an introduction to the history of the neighborhood. There is an excellent map/brochure in English to help you find your way around the district.

▷ *Go straight on; take the second lane on the left after the intersection. You will pass the Rak ko jae (Rakgojae) guesthouse in a beautiful old house (◔ see Addresses). Continue west toward a main street at the end of the lane. Heading back on the right, take the second lane on the right (cul-de-sac).*

Former Residence of KDB
한씨가옥

◔ *See Gyeongbok-Bukchon Map. 178 Gahoe-dong, Jongno-gu.* Ⓜ *Anguk, line 3, exit 3.* ✆ *(010)-8666-2182. By appointment only. No charge.*

This imposing building, also known as the **Han Family House**, was built in 1920 and has been completely renovated. The style is a combination of Korean *hanok* and a Japanese house, but it was built using Western materials and with Western-style doors and windows. The building belonged to the Han family before becoming property of the Korea Development Bank, which uses it for private functions and to accommodate special guests. At present, the residence is open only by appointment, but should be open to the public in 2011.

▷ *Return to the main street; take the lane beside the house on the right and head back east. When you are back on the street for the Bukchon Traditional Culture Center, turn left, then immediately right.*

Inchon Memorial Hall
인촌기념회

◔ *See Gyeongbok-Bukchon Map. 132 Gye-dong, Jongno-gu.* Ⓜ *Anguk, line 3, exit 3.* ✆ *(017)-310-0556. www.inchonmemorial.co.kr. By appointment only. No charge.*

This is another beautiful turn-of-the-century house that has plans to open to the public. It was bought in 1918 from Kim Sa-yong by **Kim Seong-su** (aka **Inchon** (1891–1955)), an important figure in 20C Korean history. Educator, entrepreneur and patriot, he founded the textile company Gyeongseung and in 1915 bought and developed Jungang High School (also Choong Ang High School (◔ *see below*), at the time in financial difficulties). In 1920 he founded the newspaper *Dong-A Ilbo* ("East Asia Daily"), and in 1932 he bought Bosung

Traditional houses, Bukchon

©KTO

College, which became Korea University in 1946, to educate the local elite.

He is also famous for his anti-Japanese activities during the colonial period. Protestants, Catholics and Buddhists gathered at this house on 1 March 1919 before the first of the demonstrations for independence from the Japanese. One of the rectangular buildings was the women and children's quarters. For a good view of the complex, go to the end of the lane and enter the courtyard of the **Daedong Taxation High School** (founded in 1925). From here there is a good view down to the house, and the districts Gye-dong and Gahoe-dong.

Leave through the gate on the right and walk straight ahead to a larger street (running west–east). Head left toward Changdeokgung. Take a left turn along the side of the palace to the next museum (omit if you want to do the circuit in 2hrs).

Museum of Korean Buddhist Art
한국불교 미술박물관
See Gyeongbok-Bukchon Map. 108-4 Wonseo-dong, Jongno-gu. Anguk, line 3, exit 3. *(02)-766-6000. www.buddhistmuseum.co.kr. Open Tue–Sun Mar–Sept 10am–6pm, Oct–Feb 10am–5pm. Closed public holidays. ₩5,000.*

This small museum has a fine collection of Korean Buddhist art, musical instruments, statues, and ritual objects and paintings, providing a very good introduction to the subject.

Note: *A pass (₩10,000) covers admission to the five well-stocked private museums in the area. It is valid for one month and represents good value if you have the time to spend a full day on the walking tour.*

Continue to the end of the lane.

In the passage on the right is the **Institute of Korean Royal Cuisine**, a research and teaching establishment owned by a Living National Treasure. At the end of the street, a stream runs

beneath the wall of the Secret Garden (**Huwon**); local women would come to wash clothes here. High on the left, built in a style that combines the modern with the traditional Korean, is the **House of Baek Hong-beom**. This *hanok* dating from 1910–20 was built on the site of the house of a courtesan, the mother of King Gyeongjong (1688–1724). It represents a transitional stage between the traditional *hanok* and the commercial *hanok* of the 1930s.

Retrace your steps and walk around a sharp bend to the **House of Go Hui-dong** *(currently undergoing renovation)*, the first Korean painter to work in the Western style (1886–1965).

Walk up the street on the right, go up the hill and enjoy the view of Gahoe-dong over a sea of traditional-style roofs. The street also leads to the entrance to Choong Ang High School, on your right. If you are restricted to 2hr, this and the subsequent museums can be skipped.

Choong Ang High School
중앙고등학교
See Gyeongbok-Bukchon Map. 1 Gye-dong, Jongno-gu. Anguk, line 3, exit 3. *(02)-742-1321-2. www.choongang.hs.kr. No charge.*

The school grounds are interesting for several reasons. To the left of the entrance, look out for the sacred 500-year-old ginkgo tree, which has long been the object of popular worship. You have to enter the grounds of the school in order to access the **Museum of Humanities** situated to the left *(use this as an excuse if the guard asks you where you are going)*. On its own, the museum is not overly interesting; however, the school and its grounds are quiet intriguing, but look around with discretion since this is a school and not a tourist attraction. Founded in 1908, the first high school was bought in 1915 by Kim Seong-Su (*see above, Inchon Memorial Hall*).

The main building dates from 1937 and was built by Korean architect Park Dong-geon in a Tudor Gothic style. The high school complex also contains a gray building on the site of a previous building dating from 1917, built by the Japanese occupiers but destroyed in 1934. The left wing was built in 1921 by Japanese architect Yoshikei Nakamura, who also designed the Bank of Korea and the Cheondogyo temple in Insadong (*see p140*). Its neo-Baroque style is typical of Japanese colonial rule. The building on the right dates from 1923 and was designed by the same architect. Behind all this, you will find a large sports field, and looking down to the right, you can just catch a glimpse of the Secret Garden (*Huwon*), which is rarely open to the public.

From behind the school sports field there is a good view of **Sinseonwonjeon** in the grounds of Changdeok Palace. It used to house the portraits of the Joseon kings, but the paintings were sadly destroyed by fire while they were being transported to Busan during the Korean War.

In addition to its old buildings in a style that is unusual for Seoul, Choong Ang High School was known as being a hotbed of insurgency against the occupying Japanese: it was from here that students set off on their demonstration for independence in 1926 at the funeral of King Sunjong.

Leave the school and take the lane diagonally on the right. Stroll through a beautiful neighborhood of old renovated houses to the Museum of Embroidery.

Han Sang-soo Embroidery Museum 한상수 자수박물관

See Gyeongbok-Bukchon Map. 11-32 Gahoe-dong, Jongno-gu. Anguk, line 3, exit 2. (02)-744-1545. www.hansangsoo.com. Open Tue–Sun 10am–5pm. Closed 1 Jan. ₩3,000 (included in the 5-museum pass).
This is a small private museum dedicated to embroidery and textile art, located in a lovely renovated Korean *hanok*, which makes a visit all the more worthwhile. The museum was founded by Han Sang-soo, a Living National Trea-

sure (the work was awarded the status of Intangible Cultural Heritage No. 80 by UNESCO). Enter the courtyard for a good view of the district's *hanok* (traditional houses), including the **House of Kim Hyeong-tae** (*see below*).

Keep traveling down the road to Gaho (Minhwa) Museum.

Gahoe (Minhwa) Museum 가회 민화박물관

See Gyeongbok-Bukchon Map. 11-103 Gahoe-dong, Jongno-gu. Anguk, line 3, exit 2. (02)-741-0466 www.gahoemuseum.org. Open Tue–Sun 10am–6pm. Adults ₩3,000 (included in the 5-museum pass).
This excellent, small private museum in a beautiful old house is dedicated to Joseon popular culture: amulets and talismans, books and many folk art paintings (*minhwa*) are on display. There are a total of some 1,500 items housed here.

Down the road and around the corner, you will see the small Donglim Knot Museum on the left.

Donglim Knot Museum 동림 매듭박물관

See Gyeongbok-Bukchon Map. 11-7 Gahoe-dong, Jongno-gu. Anguk, line 3, exit 2. (02)-3673-2778. www.shimyoungmi.com. Open Tue–Sun 10am–6pm. ₩2,000 (included in the 5-museum pass).
This small museum in an old building is dedicated to the art of braiding, macramé and decorative knots used in garments (*maedeup*), although it looks less like a museum and more like a shop giving demonstrations of work. Worth a visit if you have the 5-museum pass.

Return to the road and continue to the Chicken Art Museum on the right.

Chicken Art Museum 서울 닭 문화관

See Gyeongbok-Bukchon Map. 12 Gahoe-dong, Jongno-gu. Anguk, line 3, exit 2. (02)-763-9995.

www.kokodac.com. ◷ *Open Tue–Sun 10am–6pm. Closed 1 Jan and public holidays. Adults ₩3,000 (included in the 5-museum pass).*

This is a museum with an unusual theme. The exhibits on the ground floor are a little kitschy, with works related to poultry around the world, but much more interesting are the older Korean exhibits on the first floor. They show the symbolic importance of the hen and rooster in Korean culture through wonderful paintings and sculptures (*kokdu*, the wooden figurines that are used to accompany funerary processions), some of which are superb.

Across the street sits the **House of Kim Hyeong-tae**. This historical building—unfortunately not open to visitors—dates from the late Joseon era. It originally belonged to Yi Dal-yong (1883–?), a member of the royal family and head of the Jongchinbu (aka Jongbusa), the Office of Royal Family Affairs. Legend also has it that she was related to the family of Queen Min, the wife of King Gojong murdered by the Japanese occupiers. The traditional layout is unusual in *hanok* found in the northern part of the city; it has three separate wings (in C, L and I shapes) with beautiful, curved *cheoma* (the edge of a *Hanok's* curvy roof). However, the materials used are modern: brick, metal and glass. The current arrangement of the house and grounds dates back to 1938, when the grounds were divided up and only this small plot was left.

▷ *Walk over the pedestrian crossing at a dental practice housed in a hanok, head up the lane, turn left in the middle of a block of modern apartments, then take the tiny alley at the top of the hill on the right.*

You will be in the center of Bukchon Hanok Village. On your right is the **House of Lee Jung-gu**, another interesting building—sadly closed to the public—that you can view from the Asian Art Museum (◷*see below).* Built in 1938, the house displays Western architecture typical of the period, with walls of granite from Gaeseong and an interestingly shaped roof made with tiles from France, a luxury at the time. The building belonged to Min Dae-ik, a member of a powerful land-owning family. Min Dae-ik had other houses built in western Seoul, but apparently bought this one, already constructed, when the district was divided up.

▷ *Walk past the house and enjoy the picturesque view of the narrow streets lined with hanok with a view of Namsan (South Mountain) and the modern city center. On the right, a lane leads to another alley and into a cul-de-sac leading to the Asian Art Museum.*

Asian Art Museum
북촌 동양문화박물관
♿*See Gyeongbok-Bukchon Map. 35-91 Samcheong-dong, Jongno-gu.* Ⓜ *Anguk, line 3, exit 2.* ℘*(02)-486-0191. www.dymuseum.com.* ◷*Open 10am–7pm. Closed public holidays. ₩5,000.*

This eclectic and slightly kitschy museum is especially worth a visit for its pleasant garden with stunning views of Bugaksan (mountain), and to the rear, the House of Lee Jung-gu. There is also a small café with a delightfully tranquil terrace, worth the entrance fee alone if the weather is fine.

▷ *After the museum, continue straight ahead. When you reach the road in the hillside, turn right for the next small museum.*

Bukchon Museum Old Fragrance 북촌 생활사박물관
♿*See Gyeongbok-Bukchon Map. 35-177 Samcheong-dong, Jongno-gu.* Ⓜ *Anguk, line 3, exit 2.* ℘*(02)-736-3957/3968. www.bomulgun.com.* ◷*Open Tue–Sun, Mar–Oct 10am–7pm, Nov–Feb 10am–6pm. ₩5,000.*

This small private museum, also called the Everyday Life Museum, is very eclectic. The building in which it is housed is of little interest, unlike the exhibits on everyday objects of the late 19C and 20C, although they are arranged in a rather haphazard fashion.

▷ *Turn right, follow the lane to the end and walk around the top of the Korea Banking Institute and grounds, and join a wider road bordering parkland. Look for the entrance to Samcheong Park to the right.*

Samcheong Park 삼청공원

👣 *See Seoul Map I. Samcheong-dong, Jongno-gu.* Ⓜ *Anguk, line 3, exit 2.* ℘ *(02)-731-0395. No charge.*

This little known park on the slopes of **Bugaksan** is worth a detour. The hiking trails were closed to the public until recently for security reasons. North Korean agents infiltrated here in 1968 in an attempt to assassinate the president in the Blue House, the official presidential residence.

You can now take the ridge path as far as Buam-dong and Jahamun (also known as Changuimun), the small gate to the west, beyond Gyeongbokgung, along the Kim Shin-jo Route. Begin by getting your bearings at the Malbawi Information Center, where there are breathtaking views of the city. There are stopping points at the different pavilions along the Fortress Wall Trail. You will see Sukjeongmun, the least accessible of the four gates of Seoul. ⚠**Note:** *You must present your passport at the entrance (as it is a military area) and enter before 3pm.*

▷ *Continue descending while keeping left; at the intersection, turn left again. The Korea Banking Institute building and grounds will be on the left. To visit the Beonsachang Armory in the grounds, you must register with the gatekeeper.*

Beonsachang Armory 번사창

👣 *See Gyeongbok-Bukchon Map. 28-1 Samcheong-dong, Jongno-gu.* Ⓜ *Anguk, line 3, exit 1.* 🕐*Open Mon–Sat 10am–6pm. Closed public holidays. No charge. Go left at the bottom of the Korea Banking Institute complex, then turn right toward the old building.*

This building was erected in 1884 by Chinese engineers—hence the various Chinese architectural features: the use of brick, the shape of the windows, no canopies to the roofs, but a German ceiling!—to serve as an arsenal for the manufacture and storage of modern weapons; it could be regarded as the first "factory" in modern Korea. Beonsachang was one of four royal armories that existed at the time, but the other three have since disappeared. During the Japanese occupation, this building was used as a bacteriological laboratory and, after liberation, as a center for research on biological weapons by the US military.

▷ *Return to the main street and bear left.*

"Samcheong" literally means the "three blues" or the three pure elements—the mountains, the water and the people, according to the locals. In fact, the "three blues" are the three spirits that were worshiped here. This area offers many cafés, restaurants and galleries called Samcheong-dong-gil.

▷ *Continue straight on to rejoin Yulgok-ro, heading past Gyeongbokgung (the end of the walk if you are pressed for time) or take the lane on the left at the corner of the police station that leads directly to Jeongdok Library. Time permitting, keep straight on to visit the art galleries in the (suggested) following order: Kukje, Sun, Hakgojae, Former Gimusa, Kumho, (👣see map) and Hyundai (👣see below for details). After visiting the Hyundai Gallery, retrace your steps, turn right at the Hakgojae Gallery, and head straight on to Jeongdok Library (left) and the Artsonje Center (on the right corner).*

Seoul Jeongdok Municipal Library 정독도서관

👣 *See Gyeongbok-Bukchon Map. 19 Bukchon-gil, Jongno-gu.* Ⓜ *Anguk, line 3, exit 1.* ℘ *(02)-2011-5732.* 🕐*Open daily (except for 1st and 3rd Wed of the month and public holidays), Mar–Oct 7am–11pm (7am–10pm Sat–Sun), Nov–*

An Audience at the Palace in 1894

An invitation from the queen

"Hence it was with real pleasure that I received an invitation from the Queen to a private audience, to which I was accompanied by Mrs. Underwood, an American missionary and the Queen's physician and valued friend. Mr. Hillier sent me to the Kyeng-pok Palace in an eight-bearer official chair, escorted by the Korean Legation Guard. I have been altogether six times at this palace, and always with increased wonder at its intricacy, and admiration of its quaintness and beauty…."

Her Majesty, the King and the Crown Prince

"In a simple room hung with yellow silk we were entertained in courteous fashion with coffee and cake on arriving, and afterwards at dinner, the nurse, 'supported' by the Court interpreter, taking the head of the very prettily decorated table …. After this long delay we were ushered, accompanied only by the interpreter, into a small audience-room, upon the dais at one end of which stood the King, the Crown Prince, and the Queen, in front of three crimson velvet chairs, which, after Mrs. Underwood had presented me, they resumed, and asked us to be seated on two chairs which were provided.

"**Her Majesty**, who was then past forty, was a very nice-looking slender woman, with glossy raven-black hair and a very pale skin, the pallor enhanced by the use of pearl powder. The eyes were cold and keen, and the general expression one of brilliant intelligence. She wore a very handsome, very full, and very long skirt of mazarine blue brocade, heavily pleated, with the waist under the arms, and a full-sleeved bodice of crimson and blue brocade, clasped at the throat by a coral rosette, and girdled by six crimson blue cords, each one clasped with a coral rosette, with a crimson silk tassel hanging from it …. As soon as she began to speak, and especially when she became interested in conversation, her face lighted up into something very like beauty.

"**The King** is short and sallow, certainly a plain man, wearing a thin moustache and a tuft on the chin. He is nervous and twitches his hands, but his pose and manner are not without dignity. His face is pleasing, and his kindliness of nature is well known. In conversation the Queen prompted him a good deal. He and the Crown Prince were dressed alike in white leather shoes, wadded silk socks, and voluminous wadded white trousers ….

The Crown Prince is fat and flabby, and though unfortunately very near-sighted, etiquette forbids him to wear spectacles, and at that time he produced on every one, as on me, the impression of being completely an invalid. He was the only son and the idol of his mother, who lived in ceaseless anxiety about his health, and in dread lest the son of a concubine should be declared heir to the throne. To this cause must be attributed several of her unscrupulous acts, her invoking the continual aid of sorcerers, and her always-increasing benefactions to the Buddhist monks. During much of the audience mother and son sat with clasped hands."

Extracts from "Korea and Her Neighbours" (1898) by Isabella Bird Bishop, describing the atmosphere of intrigue at the palace during the reign of King Gojong, with Queen Min and the future King Sunjong.

Feb 8am–11pm (8am–10pm Sat–Sun).
No charge.
This library was formerly Kyunggi High School, the country's most exclusive school, which was moved to Gangnam in 1976 to encourage families to settle south of the river. The main building has an obvious modernist style. Dating back to 1938, it was the most modern school building for the time and even had central heating. The park is a good place for relaxing and picnicking. It also houses the Jongchinbu, one of three government offices from the Joseon era still standing, where the genealogical records of the royal family were kept. The building was moved to its current location in 1981. From the park with its ancient trees, behind Jongchinbu, you can also see several old *hanok* closed to the public.

▷ *Take the street opposite the library, then the first lane on the left. If you have time, stop off at the Arario and PKM galleries on the way. At the end of the lane, turn right.*

You will pass the **House of Yun Bo-seon** (8–1 Anguk-dong, Jongno-gu, Ⓜ Anguk, line 3, exit 1, closed to the public). A fine, large traditional black wooden house, this was the residence of the second President of the Republic, Yun Bo-seon (1960–62). Three entirely separate wings make up the residence. In the midst of a beautiful park, the *sarangchae* (men's wing) is an architectural gem, combining the aesthetics of the *hanok* with modern comfort (windows, electricity, etc.). This is another house that, unfortunately, is not open to visitors, except when occasional concerts or other special events are held.

▷ *At the end of the alley is the busy road Yulgok-ro and the Ⓜ Anguk.*

ADITIONAL SIGHTS
Art Galleries★
🚶*See Gyeongbok-Bukchon Map.*
Samcheong-dong has taken over from Insadong and Pyeongchang-dong as the

district for contemporary art. It is simply full of galleries, which are among the finest in Seoul. It is easy to spend at least half a day wandering from one to another, or just visit those suggested in the Bukchon walk.

Hyundai Gallery 갤러리현대
80 Sagan-dong, Jongno-gu.
Ⓜ *Gyeongbokgung, line 3, exit 5.* ✆*(02)-2287-3500. www.galleryhyundai.com.*
🕐*Open Tue–Sun 10am–6pm. Closed 1 Jan and public holidays. No charge.*
This is one of the best private galleries in Seoul, owned by the famous corporate group of the same name (*hyundai* means "modern" in Korean). Explore temporary exhibitions of contemporary art, mostly dedicated to young Korean talent.

Kumho Museum of Art 금호미술관
78 Sagan-dong, Jongno-gu. Ⓜ*Anguk, line 3, exit 1.* ✆*(02)-720-5114. www.kumhomuseum.com.* 🕐*Open Tue–Sun 10am–6pm. No charge.*
Walking up the street that runs alongside Gyeongbokgung, you'll find another gallery owned by a conglomerate. It has several floors, featuring exhibitions of contemporary art, mostly Korean, of variable quality.

Hakgojae Gallery 학고재 갤러리
70 Sogyeok-dong, Jongno-gu.
Ⓜ *Anguk, line 3, exit 1.* ✆*(02)-720-1524-6. www.hakgojae.com.* 🕐*Open Tue–Sat 10am–7pm (Sun 6pm). No charge.*
An excellent gallery in two parts showing traditional and contemporary art; one part is in a lovely renovated traditional house, where consistently good exhibitions are held.

Sun Contemporary Gallery
선갤러리
66 Sogyeok-dong, Jongno-gu.
Ⓜ *Anguk, line 3, exit 1.* ✆*(02)-720-5789. www.suncontemporary.com.*
🕐*Open Mon–Sat 10am–6:30pm. No charge.*
On the same street as the Hakgojae Gallery, this is the sister gallery of the Sun Gallery in Insadong and exhibits "young

talent" in contemporary art. Despite the limited size, this is one of the most interesting galleries in Seoul.

Kukje Gallery 국제 갤러리

59-1 Sogyeok-dong, Jongno-gu.
Ⓜ *Gyeongbokgung, line 3, exit 5.*
☎ *(02)-2735-8449. www.kukje.org.*
🕓 *Open Mon–Sat 10am–6pm (Sun and public holidays 5pm). No charge.*
Next door to the Sun Contemporary Gallery and exhibiting mainly big international names, Kukje Gallery is a must. It also includes a French/Italian restaurant modestly called "The Restaurant." It is nevertheless excellent, with a good café-bistro that sells delicious pastries and has a nice wine bar.

Artsonje Center 아트선제미술관

144-2 Sogyeok-dong, Jongno-gu.
Ⓜ *Anguk, line 3, exit 1.* ☎ *(02)-733-8945. www.artsonje.org.* 🕓*Open Tue–Sun 11am–7pm. Audio guide on entry. Guided tours 2pm and 4pm (also noon, Sat–Sun). ₩3,000.*
Opposite the Jeongdok Library, this complex includes a basement cinema, a coffee shop and Dal, an Indian restaurant, on the ground floor. The gallery presents a carefully chosen selection of young artists.

Arario Gallery 아라리오갤러리

149-2 Sogyeok-dong, Jongno-gu.
Ⓜ *Anguk, line 3, exit 1.* ☎ *(02)-723-6190. www.ararioseoul.com.* 🕓*Open Tue–Sun 10am–7pm. No charge.*
After the interesting **Artsonje Center** in the alley leading to the Insadong neighborhood, this is currently one of the most dynamic, innovative and fashionable galleries in the city. Its floor space may be limited, but its exhibitions get everyone talking. Additional gallery in Cheonan (👆*see p 405*).

PKM Gallery 갤러리

137-1 Hwa-dong, Jongno-gu.
Ⓜ *Anguk, line 3, exit 1.* ☎ *(02)-734-9467. www.pkmgallery.com.* 🕓*Open Mon–Fri 10:30am–6pm. No charge.*
This small gallery, situated in an alley at right angles to the previous one, is one of the galleries that sets the tone for Korean contemporary art, having exhibited some of the country's most remarkable artists over the past fifteen years.

Former Gimusa (Annex of the National Museum of Contemporary Art) 국립현대미술관 분관

👆*See Gyeongbok-Bukchon Map. Site of the former Defense Security Command and Armed Forces Seoul District Hospital, next to Gyeongbok Palace.*
The Gimusa (Defense Security Command) was built as a military hospital under Japanese rule and became a national security building, where people were interrogated during the dictatorship. It is being transformed into a central annex to hold exhibitions and part of the excellent collections of the National Museum of Contemporary Art, currently located outside Seoul in Gwacheon. *The National Museum of Contemporary Art Seoul branch is due to open in 2013.*

Cheong Wa Dae (Blue House) 청와대

👆*See Gyeongbok-Bukchon Map.*
1 Cheongwadae-ro, Jongno-gu. Organized tours (1hr) must be booked in advance. Meet at the information booth in the east car park of Gyeongbok Palace. Ⓜ *Gyeongbokgung, line 3, exit 5* ☎ *(02)-730-5800. www.cwd.go.kr.* 👆 🕓 *Open Tue–Sat. Guided tour 10am, 11am, 2pm and 3pm. Book at least 10 days in advance by email, giving the name, passport number, nationality and contact details in Seoul of the visitor(s), along with the proposed date and time of visit (tour@president.go.kr). No charge. Security is strict—you will be required to show your passport as ID. You might not catch a glimpse of the President or the First Lady, but it is a good opportunity to see the Republic of Korea's corridors of power.*
The tour includes: the garden Nokjiwon (the original site of the presidential palace), the central building of the Blue House (named for the color of its roof), Yeongbingwan (the banqueting

and reception hall for visiting state dignitaries) and Chilgung (the Pavilion of Seven Concubines, built in 1725, which contains the memorial tablets of seven royal concubines, who each bore a son who reigned as king).

🖐**Note:** *A new small museum gallery just in front of the Blue House is dedicated to the presidential residence and the policies of its distinguished occupants.*

Rak Ko Jae
©Rak Ko Jae

ADDRESSES

🛏 STAY

🛏🛏 **Bukchon Guest House**
북촌 게스트하우스 – *72 Gye-dong, Jongno-gu.* Ⓜ *Anguk, line 3, exit 3.* ℘*(02)-743-8530/010-8001-8321. www.bukchon72.com. 5 rm. ₩70,000/100,000* 🚇. This small guest-house in a lovely restored traditional building with modern comforts (heating, shared bathroom with hot water) is managed by the municipality. It is a good opportunity to sleep "Korean style" (on the floor) at an affordable price, in a charming neighborhood. Airport pickup available.

🛏🛏 **Seoul Guest House**
서울게스트 하우스 – *135-1 Gye-dong, Jongno-gu.* Ⓜ *Anguk, line 3, exit 3.* ℘*(02)-745-0057. www.seoul110.com. 10 rm. ₩40,000/220,000* 🚇. This traditional old house hidden away down a lane is a real find. On entering the courtyard, you are greeted by the friendly owners (and a big dog!), and it is as though you have been whisked away to the countryside, while still in the historic center of town. This is a guesthouse with real charm. The rooms range from basic (a futon on the floor and no bathroom) to comfortable (annex room). As the location is hard to find, it's a good idea to consult their website. English spoken.

🛏🛏🛏 **Rak Ko Jae** 락고재 – *98 Gye-dong, Jongno-gu.* Ⓜ *Anguk, line 3, exit 2.* ℘*(02)-742-3410/010-5286-1855. www.rkj.co.kr. 4 rm. ₩180,000/450,000* 🚇 ✗ *reservations required.* A superb traditional *hanok* (restored by a carpenter who is a Living National Treasure). A perfect place in which to discover the charm and elegance of Korean traditions, while enjoying the calm atmosphere of this unspoiled neighborhood. With its pleasant garden, this is as much a cultural center as a guesthouse, and it offers a range of activities (*Pansori* concerts, workshops, kimchi making and more.). Sauna and massage areas are also available, and the catering service has a good reputation.

🍴 EAT

🍴🍴🍴 **Dugahun Wine Restaurant**
두가헌와인 레스토랑– *109 Sagan-dong, Jongno-gu.* Ⓜ *Anguk, line 3, exit 1 or* Ⓜ *Gyeongbokgung, line 3, exit 5.* ℘*(02)-3210-2100. Open 11am–1am. A la carte ₩60,000/Fixed price menu ₩80,000.* A luxury Italian restaurant in a small renovated princely palace. The pleasant garden is also home to a Russian house dating from the early 1900s. Excellent food and a fabulous wine list *(₩65,000/₩7,700,000)*. Quite expensive but worth trying for the atmosphere, food and service.

🍴🍴🍴 **Gungyeon** 궁연 가회점– *170-3 Gahoe-dong, Jongno-gu.* Ⓜ *Anguk, line 3, exit 2.* ℘*(02)-3673-1104. www.goongyeon.com. Open daily noon–3pm, 5:30pm–9pm. Closed public holidays. Fixed price menus ₩65,000/₩155,000.* This restaurant serves elegant dishes in the "royal cuisine" style, prepared under the guidance of Han Bok-ryeo, a Living National Treasure, who learned the art of fine cuisine from Joseon Hwang Hye-seong, who had herself learned her trade from the last court chef, Han Hee-sun. The food is exceptional, although served in a rather impersonal atmosphere.

🍚🍴🍴 **Samcheonggak**
삼청각 한식당 – *330-115 Seongbuk-dong, Seongbuk-gu.* Ⓜ *Hansung Univ., line 4, exits 5/6 or* Ⓜ *Anguk, line 3, exit 1.* ☎*(02)-765-3700. www.samcheonggak.or.kr. Open daily noon–3pm, 6pm–10pm. Fixed price menus ₩59,000/₩130,000.*
As this restaurant is out of town, it's a good idea to take a taxi on leaving the subway. This large complex perched on the mountain above Bukchon was built for the inter-Korean talks organized by the Red Cross in 1972, before becoming one of the three most prominent restaurants in Seoul. Bought by the city of Seoul in 2000, it is now a cultural center with a tearoom (great views from the terrace) and a restaurant serving high quality Korean food.

🍜 TAKING A BREAK

Yeon 까페 연 – *63-20 Samcheong-dong, Jongno-gu.* Ⓜ *Gyeongbokgung, line 3, exit 5, or* Ⓜ *Anguk, line 3, exit 1.* ☎*(02)-734-3009. http://cafeyeon. cyworld.com. Open 1pm–11pm. ₩6,000.*
A small café in a carefully restored traditional house, providing an intimate setting for afternoon tea or an aperitif. The regulars, like the owners, are keen on travel.

🍸 BARS

Romanée Conti
로마네 꽁띠 와인바 – *62-6 Samcheong-dong, Jongno-gu.* Ⓜ *Gyeongbokgung, line 3, exit 5 or* Ⓜ *Anguk, line 3, exit 1.* ☎ *(02)-722-1633. Open noon–1am. Steak ₩31,000/₩41,000; wine starting from ₩55,000.* This lovely Korean building with bay windows in hilly Samcheong-dong also has a charming wine bar.

🛒 SHOPPING

Seoul Selection Bookshop
서울 셀렉션 북카페 – *105-2 Sagan-dong, Jongno-gu.* Ⓜ *Anguk, line 3, exit 1.* ☎*(02)-734-9565. www.seoul selection.com. Open Mon–Sat 9:30am–6:30pm.* A must for books and movies on Korea and Korean music, and for visitors who want to get to the bottom of the real Korea, its culture and traditions. The store publishes a monthly magazine, *Seoul & Dokkaebi, Maps and Guides,* and has a highly informative website.

Yido Pottery 이도 도예 갤러리 – *10-6 Gahoe-dong, Jongno-gu.* Ⓜ *Anguk, line 3, exit 2.* ☎*(02)-722-0756. www.yido.kr. Open daily 10am–7pm. Closed 3rd Sun of month.*
This lovely store has several floors with a café and a gallery selling pottery created by the owner Yoon Yi-shin, who is both artist and potter, as well as beautifully crafted items from the best Korean kilns. It's quite reasonably priced considering the high quality.

Minhwa – *31-40 Gahoe-dong, Jongno-gu.* Ⓜ *Anguk, line 3, exit 1.* ☎*(011)-9260-7296. www.galerie minhwa.com (French only). Reservations required.* Philippe Tirault, a connoisseur of Eastern art, sells his sumptuous selection of Korean and, more broadly, Asian antiques at attractive prices. This beautiful traditional house is an essential port of call for enthusiasts and collectors alike.

Gwanghwamun-Jongno★★★

광화문 – 종로

This area takes its name from Gwanghwamun, the main gate that opens on to Gyeonbokgung, at the end of Sejong-no (Sejong Avenue). It is the historic, political and symbolic center of Seoul. Formerly the main commercial thoroughfare, Jong-no ("Avenue of the Bell") heads east toward Dongdaemun, the Great East Gate. The presence of the city bell pavilion (Boshingak) on the avenue accounts for the road's name.

This part of Seoul's historic center contains royal palace complexes such as Changdeokgung and its sumptuous gardens and Jongmyo, an important shrine with superb Confucian architecture, to mention only those sites listed on the prestigious UNESCO World Heritage List. There are many other sights worth seeing and "minor" palaces that you may nevertheless find more peaceful and charming since they are less crowded.

VISIT

♣ Changdeokgung★★★ (Changdeok Palace) 창덕궁

♿See Gwanghwamun-Jongno Map. 99 Yulgok-ro, Jongno-gu. Ⓜ*Anguk, line 3, exit 3.* ☏*(02)-762-8261. www.cdg.go.kr.* ☉*Open Tue–Sun, Apr–Oct 9am–6:30pm, Nov 9am–5:30pm, Dec–Feb 9am–5pm, Mar 9am–5:30pm.*
Visit by guided tour only, tours in English 10:30am and 2:30pm, ₩3,000. Huwon Garden is within the palace grounds, but a separate ticket must be purchased. Changdeok and the Huwon Garden are included in the **Integrated Ticket of Palaces**. *Unescorted tours available some Thu, Apr–Nov.*

Changeokgung was built in 1405 by King Taejong as a secondary palace. The slopes of Bugaksan rise directly behind the building in a perfect example of the quest for harmony between

- ♿ **Michelin Map:** Map p134
- ℹ **Info:** 215 Sejongno, 1-80, Jongno-gu (in front of the Donghwa Duty Free building).
  Ⓜ Gwanghwamun, line 5, exit 6. ☏(02)-735-8688. Open 9am–10pm.
- ▶ **Location:** The historic center, between Gwanghwamun and Tapgol Park; Jongmyo, and farther north; the palaces Changdeokgung and Changgyeonggung.
- ♣ **Kids:** See the show *Jump* featuring martial arts (♿*see Seoul Addresses p104*), explore Changgyeonggung and its garden, go ice-skating in Gwanghwamun Square in winter or cool down in its fountains in summer.
- ◷ **Timing:** Since Changdeokgung is a must, plan your schedule around the times of the palace's guided tours. The other palaces are pleasant to stroll around, but will not take more than an hour if you just want to view the buildings.
- ✦ **Don't Miss:** Changdeokgung and the stunning Huwon Garden, the royal ancestral shrine of Jongmyo.

nature, geographical positioning and the manmade—in this instance, the palace and gardens. The marriage between nature and the work of man, so perfectly achieved at Changdeokgung, provokes the same emotions in the visitor today as it did in King Seongjong, who said:

"Although Gyeongbokgung is magnificent and splendid, the perfect location in this city is really Changdeokgung."

Richly decorated eaves and rafters of Changdeokgung

©KTO

The palace "of prosperous virtue" was destroyed by fire during the Japanese invasions of 1592–98, but it was rebuilt to become the principal royal residence in 1610. However, King Gojong chose to move the court once more to Gyeong-bokgung in 1868 (⟳ see p118).

In 1907 Changdeokgung became, for a brief time, the royal residence under King Sunjong, the last ruler of the Joseon dynasty, after the forced abdication of his father King Gojong. The court remained under house arrest until the death of Sunjong in 1926. The royal family returned to live at Changdeokgung on their return from Japan in 1963, but they only inhabited a small part of the complex.

The last queen, Yun, lived there until 1966, and Princess Deokhye remained in the palace with other family members until her death in 1989. Changdeokgung became a UNESCO World Heritage site in February 1997.

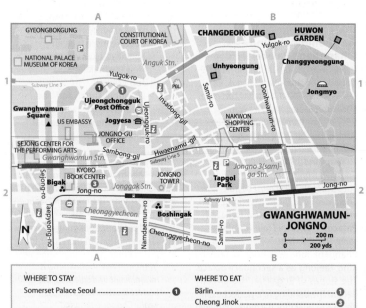

WHERE TO STAY	WHERE TO EAT
Somerset Palace Seoul .... ❶	Bärlin .... ❶
	Cheong Jinok .... ❸

The main gate, **Donhwamun** or "great virtues that comfort the hearts of men," was built in 1412 and restored in 1609; it remains the oldest of its kind in Korea. Built in 1411, the stone bridge **Geumcheongyo** (B1) provides access to the interior of the palace and bears many interesting carvings—turtles decorate the stone at the bottom of the central pillars on one side of the bridge and *haetae* (mythical animals) the other. These stone creatures represent the tutelary guardian gods of the palace. Similarly, above each of these animals, there are genies, also tasked with warding off evil spirits.

The entrance of the palace is through **Jinseonmun**, the gate that opens onto the first courtyard. Several coronation ceremonies have been held here, including King Gojong's. Royal protocol dictated that only kings could enter the main pavilion, hence they had to be crowned outside. On the left, **Injeongmun** opens onto the courtyard of the throne hall. This is where the king held his official audiences and received foreign envoys. It was the center of royal power. The throne hall was built in 1405, but later restored. The flooring is Western-style and the ceiling decorative. Stone markers on the courtyard across which the king would walk indicate where members of the court would stand: state officials on the eastern side, according to hierarchical rank, with the highest-ranking official standing closest to the throne, and the military on the western side.

To the east, **Seonjeongjeon** was the administrative hall and housed the apartments of the king. Farther on, **Heuijeongdang** housed the apartments of the king's family. This building was destroyed by fire in 1917 and rebuilt with material taken from Gyeongbok Palace, which had been partly dismantled by the Japanese occupiers. Note the reception room, which is furnished in Western style and is wired for electricity. Another result of the drive for modernization in Korea after it opened up to the outside world was that the main gate was designed so automobiles could pass through it. There is a building nearby that was formerly used by high-ranking royal officials but converted into the royal garage by the Japanese occupiers; it now houses cars and palanquins of the period.

Daejojeon housed the queen's rooms. Note also that the royal kitchen was reorganized in Western style at the end of the Joseon era.

Farther away, **Nakseonjae** is a complex of fine buildings constructed in 1847 to accommodate the royal concubines and, as such, these buildings were located at a distance from the apartments of the queen. This is where the king would come to escape the restrictions of protocol and to escape the marital bed. The descendants of the royal family lived here between 1963 and 1989, on their return from Japan. The youngest son of King Gojong died here. At **Sangnyangjeong** (pavilion), look out for the circular gate, depicting the sun on the east side and the moon on the west.

Huwon Garden★★★ 후원

🏛 *See Gwanghwamun-Jongno Map.*
🕐 *Visits by guided tour only, English tours at 11:30pm and 2:30pm. ₩5,000.*

The Secret Garden is the highlight of the palace and a rare example of a traditional Korean royal garden. Set discreetly among the beautiful woodland of this large unspoilt park, pavilions, water features and bridges are in complete harmony with nature. The sovereign's family came here to relax, paint, write poetry or hold banquets. The young princes were also educated here and learned the skills of horse riding and archery.

Beautiful pavilions are dotted around **Buyongji** (pond), where the princes used to study. The pond is square in shape, with a small circular island at its center. The design represents the earth (the square) and heaven (the circle) in accordance with Cheonwonjibang, the Taoist concept of the cosmos. Enjoy the tranquil atmosphere here, and look out for the stone carving of the fish jumping out of the water in the southeastern corner.

Huwon Garden

©Ch. Boisvieux/hemis.fr

The small pavilion **Buyeongjeong** (1792), jutting out over the water, is unusual for its polygonal shape. Opposite is the royal library **Guyanggak** (1777) where ten thousand books were kept. Note the pretty little Eosu gate that leads to it. On the right is the pavilion **Younghwadang** built in 1692 as a peaceful haven for the king to meditate and rest. It would later be used to host competitions for recruitment of senior officials.

Farther on, **Bulromun** (Bulro Gate) near **Aryeonji** (pond) is carved from a vast single block of stone. It wishes the king good health and long life.

The **Youngyeongdang** and **Seonhyangjae** building complex is quite interesting. Currently open to the public Tuesday and Wednesday only, the pavilions were built by Prince Hyomyeong in 1828 in the classic architectural style of a Korean noble house. It was built with 120 rooms and separate wings for the men, women and servants. This is where the king would see what life was like for his subjects. When staying here, he would adopt their habits and take part in study, just as the scholarly class did.

Pretty **Jondeokjeong**, a hexagonal pavilion built in 1644, can be seen on the special tour of the innermost part of the garden. It features a sumptuous two-story roof reflected in a pond of lotuses. Nearby is the strange fan-shaped pavilion Gwallamjeong.

Finally, in one of the farthest parts of the garden, the **Ongnyu** Stream flows into a circular fissure carved out of the rock in 1636. The king and his family would relax and enjoy themselves here in this beautiful landscape, drinking and composing poems.

Jongmyo★★ (Royal Ancestral Shrine) 종묘

♿ See Gwanghwamun-Jongno Map. 155 Jong-no, Jongno-gu. Ⓜ Jongno 3-ga, lines 1/3, exit 11. ℘(02)-765-0195. http://jm.cha.go.kr. ◷ Open Tue–Sun, Mar–Sep 9am–6pm, Oct–Feb 9am–5:30pm. Guided tours in English 10am, 11am, 2pm, and 3pm. ₩1,000.

The shrine was built in 1395 at the beginning of the Joseon dynasty, when the capital was moved to Hanyang, now Seoul. It then contained one hall with seven rooms, each designed to accommodate the memorial tablet of a king and one or more of his queens. The fourth king of the dynasty, Sejong, erected an additional building for the kings who would die subsequently. Rooms were then added on both east and west sides, making nineteen in total. The complex was destroyed by fire in 1592, during the Japanese invasions, and the current buildings date from the reconstruction of 1608. A fabulous example of Confucian architecture from the Joseon era, it was designated a World Heritage Site by UNESCO in 1995.

The Rites and Rituals of Jongmyo

Rituals play an important role in any society, frequently serving to maintain social order. Linked to the authority of the sovereign and the successful—or unsuccessful—reign, they are symbolic of a nation as a whole. Rituals and ceremonies were performed at Jongmyo for the dead kings, while in Sajik Park (ⓘ *see p199*), west of Gyeongbokgung, homage was paid to the gods of the earth and the harvest. Jongmyo, therefore, played a prominent role in the greatness of the kingdom. The rituals performed there were accompanied by *Jongmyo Jeryeak*, ancient court music that has been awarded the status of Masterpiece of the Oral and Intangible Heritage of Humanity by UNESCO. The music can still be enjoyed at Jongmyo today, once a year on the first Sunday in May, when the ceremony for the deceased kings *Jongmyo Daeje* still takes place. Descendants of the House of Yi (Joseon dynasty) attend the occasion.

At the entrance are **two lotus ponds**. In the Joseon era, the presence of a pond and a mountain were highly significant, symbolizing a harmonious and virtuous world. On the right, the first building complex includes the shrine housing the tomb of King Gongmin, the last monarch of the Goryeo dynasty, which preceded the Joseon. This served as a means of establishing the legitimacy of the new dynasty. The central **Hyangdaecheong** pavilion was used to store ritual objects. Beyond this, behind a raised paved courtyard is **Jeongjeon**, the long main hall. A feeling of solemnity pervades the whole place. The 19 shrines are carefully aligned. They contain the memorial tablets of the kings and queens of the Joseon dynasty, from Taejo (1335–1408) and his queens Han and Kang, to Sunjong (1874–1926) and his queens Min Tae-ho and Yun. Inside, the building takes the form of a long corridor, unobstructed by columns, where tables bearing offerings were set out. The limited decor is simple and sober. To the right of the entrance, in the courtyard, **Gongsindang** (Hall of Meritorious Subjects) contains the memorial tablets of 83 distinguished people, including many state ministers.

At the far end of the park, **Yeongnyeongjeon** (Hall of Eternal Peace) is a second, smaller sanctuary, originally built in 1421 but whose current buildings date from 1608. The central part houses the tablets of the ancestors of Taejo, the first king of the Joseon dynasty. Along the sides are the tablets of seven kings of secondary importance.

Royal Ancestral Rite and ritual music of Jongmyo Shrine

▷ *A footbridge connects Jongmyo to Changgyeong Palace.*

👤👤 Changgyeonggung★★ (Changgyeong Palace) 창경궁

🌿 *See Gwanghwamun-Jongno Map. 2-1 Waryongdong, Jongno-gu.* 🅜 *Hyehwa, line 4, exit 4.* 🖉 *(02)-762-4868. http://cgg.cha.go.kr.* 🕐 *Open Tue–Sun, Apr–Oct 9am–6:30pm, Nov 9am–5:30pm, Dec–Feb 9am–4pm, Mar 9am–5:30pm. Guided tour in English 11am and 4pm. ₩1000.Changgyeonggung is included in the* **Integrated Ticket of Palaces***. Additional ticket purchase required for Honghwa Gate.*

The palace was built in 1104 by King Suk-jong of the Goryeo dynasty, as the royal residence for the capital of the south. Hence Myeongjeongjeon (the palace's central building) and Honghwamun (Honghwa Gate) and Myeongjeong-mun (Myeongjeong Gate) face toward the east and not the south, as would be the case during the Joseon period. The palace was occupied by King Taejo, founder of the Joseon dynasty, while waiting for Gyeongbokgung to be built when Seoul was established as the kingdom's capital in 1394. King Sejong subsequently had a new palace built on the site in 1418 for his father King Taejo,

who had abdicated in Sejong's favor, although it was customary for former kings to live far from the palace of the reigning monarch. The buildings were expanded in 1484 to house the widows of King Sejo. Destroyed during the Japanese invasions of 1592–1598, the palace was rebuilt in 1616 and again in 1834 after a major fire. During the Joseon dynasty, Changgyeonggung served as a secondary palace to house the queens or the king's father. In 1907, the Japanese colonizers transformed the site into a zoo and botanical garden. The zoo was moved in 1983, and the Korean government has since been restoring the site to its former glory. All that remains of the Japanese park is the botanical garden, some beautiful walks and the cherry trees that were planted. The palace is entered through **Honghwamun,** a beautiful wooden gate with triple archways that dates from the 1616 reconstruction. In 1750 King Yeongjo met here with his subjects to discuss fiscal relief, a most unusual event that made a deep impression on the people. As you cross the arched stone bridge **Okcheongyo** (1484), keep an eye out for the sculptural detail of the balustrade and the pillars carved with fantastical animal heads that guard the bridge.

Detail, roofs of Changgyeonggung

©KTO

Unhyeongung

©KTO

Myeongjeongmun is the next gate, which gives access to a spacious courtyard where the throne room is situated. As in other royal palaces, the main pathway across the paved courtyard was reserved for the monarch alone. The stone markers on either side indicated where officials would stand, depending on their rank. The main hall **Myeongjeongjeon** dates from 1616. It is the oldest of its kind in Korea and is seated on a raised double-stone terrace. The steps mounting the terrace are less imposing than in other palaces, but no less finely worked. Look out for the carvings of phoenixes on clouds and the *haetae*, mythical animal protectors. The room itself has a finely crafted ceiling. At the rear, **Sungmundang** was used for study.

Continuing on, **Tongmyeongjeon** housed the apartments of the queen. Nearby is a delightful pond. Also in the palace grounds are two stone observatories dating from the Joseon era, one for the study of the heavens and the other, with a flag, to monitor the wind. To the north is **Chundangji**, a man-made pond built in 1909 during the Japanese occupation, on the site of a rice field cultivated by the king himself to ensure good omens for agriculture and crops in the kingdom.

Finally, a **small botanical garden,** also created by the Japanese, is still in place today.

Unhyeongung★ (Unhyeon Royal Residence) 운현궁

♿ *See Gwanghwamun-Jongno Map.*
114-10 Unnidong, Jongno-gu.
Ⓜ *Anguk, line 3, exit 4.* ☎ *(02)-766-9090. www.unhyeongung.or.kr.*
🕐 *Open Tue–Sun, Apr–Oct 9am–7pm, Nov–Mar 9am–6pm. ₩700. Audio guide 10am–5pm, ₩1,000.*

A building of relatively modest size, Unhyeongung was the private residence of the formidable conservative regent Heungseon Daewongun (Yi Ha-eung) who governed the kingdom between 1863 and 1873 during the minority of his son, the future King Gojong. The complex looks more like the traditional residence of a nobleman of high rank than a royal palace, but it is nonetheless a superb collection of wooden buildings, restored in 1996. King Gojong spent his childhood here until he took the throne at the age of 12.

A small exhibition traces the Daewongun's life. To get a feel for the atmosphere of the time, you can try on a traditional costume (🕐 *Nov–Mar 10am–5pm, Apr–Oct 10am–6pm, ₩3,000).*

The visit begins with **Noandang**, the men's apartments, and continues toward the central part of the complex, **Norakdang**, where many royal ceremonies took place, including the marriage of King Gojong and Queen Min. Finally, there is the magnificent women's pavilion and a beautiful gallery that overlooks an access gate to the rear of the site

Yanggwan, to the rear of the palace, was built in 1912 for the Daewongun's grandson and to welcome guests of the former Korean royal family. Built in the Western style, it is a fine example of the foreign influence that was prevalent during the period, which saw the end of the Korean monarchy *(access is via the school next to the palace)*. The forced abdication of Sunjong in 1910 marked the end of the dynasty.

👥👤 Gwanghwamun Square 광화문광장

🧭 *See Gwanghwamun-Jongno Map.*
Ⓜ *Gwanghwamun, line 5, exits 2/7.*

If the proposal to build a square in the middle of the widest avenue in Seoul had its detractors, the result has been a resounding success, with the gate itself (Ganghwamun) at one end of the square, leading to Gyeongbokgung and views to Bukhansan (Bukhan Mountain). The square is in fact a vast oblong-shaped plaza-style area. Children come here to have fun in the fountains in summer, and crowds flock to the skating rink in winter.

The statues of two key figures in Korean history, **King Sejong** and **Admiral Yi Sun-sin** (🧭 *see box p336*), look down from commanding positions.

Statue of Admiral Yi Sun-sin, Gwanghwamun Square

©KTO

Two interesting exhibition areas dedicated to these rulers lie below ground. Look for the entrance behind the statue of King Sejong (📞 *(02)-399-1114*, 🚹🕐 *open Tue–Sun 10:30am–10:30pm, audio guide in English, no charge*). The reign of the greatly revered King Sejong (1397–1450) marks the most important period of the Joseon dynasty in literary, scientific and artistic spheres, as well as in agricultural and military terms. He encouraged the invention of *Hangeul*, the Korean alphabet that ultimately allowed the people access to culture. Admiral Yi Sun-sin (1545–98), one of the greatest Korean heroes, invented the "turtle boat," a formidable warship with a metal shell. He confronted the Japanese military during Toyotomi Hideyoshi's invasions of 1592 and destroyed much of its fleet even though he was unable to repel the invader decisively. These exhibitions are interactive and ideal for very young children.

Jogyesa (Jogye Temple) 조계사

🧭 *See Gwanghwamun-Jongno Map.*
45 Gyeonji-dong, Jongno-gu. Ⓜ *Anguk, line 3, exit 6.* 📞 *(02)-732-2183.*
www.jogyesa.org.

Jogyesa is the center of the Jogye order of Korean Buddhism, the predominant form in Korea. Built in Suson Park in 1910 by Manhae Hanyongwun, it was initially named Gakhwangsa, but was renamed after the Korean War. The building of Buddhist temples in Seoul had been banned during the Joseon era. The visit takes in the main building, where rituals are still carried out much of the time. Entry to the temple is permitted providing visitors respect the religious nature of the building. Outside, note the **seven-tier stone pagoda** (encased in glass) and the traditional **bell pavilion**. This popular temple may not be particularly old (as opposed to Seoul's grand palaces), but as a building used by people on a daily basis, it is an interesting and enjoyable place to looking around. If your visit coincides with the Buddha's birthday (🧭 *see p32*), the setting will be particularly colorful.

The temple shop sells religious and non-religious items and gifts, and there is an information center for foreign visitors (🕐 *open daily 10:30pm–5pm*) close to the bell pavilion. Along with information about the temple, you can learn about Buddhism in general, and there are free guided tours by volunteers.

The temple also offers a **Temple Life Program**, which are activities open to foreigners to learn about Buddhism. *2nd and 4th Sat of the month: regular programs, 5–15 people, ₩2,000. 1st and 3rd Sat: non-regular programs (5-day advance reservation required), min 5 people.*

ADDITIONAL SIGHTS
Bigak 비각
🍵 *See Gwanghwamun-Jongno Map. Gwanghwamun, at the intersection, in front of the Kyobo Book Center.* 🅜 *Gwanghwamun, line 5, exit 4.*
A small pavilion built in 1904 to celebrate the 40th anniversary of the accession to the throne of King Gojong. The stele was engraved by Crown Prince Sunjong. The complex was restored after the Korean War in 1954 and again in 1979.

Boshingak 보신각
🍵 *See Gwanghwamun-Jongno Map.* 🅜 *Jonggak, line 1, exit 4. 33ft/10m to the right of the subway exit.*
This is the old city's **belfry**. The huge bell was rung in the morning and evening at the opening and closing of the gates, marking the rhythm of city life. The belfry is situated on the capital's main east–west road, Jong-no (Avenue of the Bell), linking Dongdaemun, the main eastern gate, with Sejong-no.
It was built in 1395 during the building of the Joseon dynasty's new capital, and restored in 1979. The original bell, cast in 1468, is kept at the National Museum, while the current one dates from 1985. Huge crowds gather at the first of the year to see (and hear) the bell rung by a dignitary to mark the solemn coming of the New Year.

Tapgol Park 탑골공원
🍵 *See Gwanghwamun-Jongno Map. Pagoda Park, 38–1 Jongno 2-ga, Jongno-gu.* 🅜 *Jongno 3-ga, lines 1/3, exit 1.* 🕐 *Open 9am–6pm. No charge.*
The park takes its name from its famous ten-tier stone pagoda, a masterpiece of Buddhist art 40ft (12m) high, carved with impressive sculptures. The pagoda dates from 1466 and is all that remains of Wongaksa, the temple built by King Sejo, which was the focal point of the Jogye order of Korean Buddhism. The temple was destroyed in the early 16C, at a time when Buddhism was opposed by the monarchy. Created at the instigation of John McLeavy Brown, the British adviser to King Gojong, Tapgol Park was the first Western-style park in Seoul. Opened in 1913, people come here to stroll and listen to concerts, but it is most known as being a symbol of resistance against the occupying Japanese. It was here on 1 March 1919, beneath the park's octagonal pavilion, that students and intellectuals drew up a declaration of independence, sparking a popular protest movement that was violently suppressed by the Japanese occupying forces. A memorial service is held every 1 March. The park may no longer be at the forefront of Korean political affairs, but it is still a meeting place for many, including Seoul's older citizens who come to chat or play "Go," an ancient board game.

Ujeongchongguk Post Office 우정총국
🍵 *See Gwanghwamun-Jongno Map. 397 Gyeonji-dong, Jongno-gu, next to Jogyesa.* 🅜 *Anguk, line 3, exit 6.*
A small pavilion close to Jogye Temple (Jogyesa), it housed the administration of the first Korean postal service. In 1884 King Gojong decided to provide the kingdom with a modern postal system, in keeping with the country's policy of opening up to the outside world, but the building caught fire ten days after its inauguration, which put a halt to the project for some years.

Somerset Palace Seoul

©Somerset Palace Seoul

ADDRESSES

🏨 STAY

🍴🛏🛁 **Somerset Palace Seoul** 서머셋 팰리스 호텔 – *85 Susong-dong, Jongno-gu.* Ⓜ *Anguk, line 3, exit 6.* ☎*(02)-6730-8888. www.somerset palaceseoul.com. 400 rm. ₩304,000/ ₩320,000, 3 nights minimum stay* 🛏 ✕. The location, quality of service and good facilities all combine to make this apartment hotel one of the best in Seoul. The rooms are equipped with kitchenettes that are cleaned every day. This is an ideal option for medium- and long-term stays. There is a large roof terrace for BBQs in the evening and a small swimming pool.

🍴 EAT

🍴🛏 **Cheong Jinok** 청진옥 – *Ground Floor, Room 123, Tower "Le Meilleur, Jongno Town," 24 Jongno 1-ga, Jongno-gu, at the rear of the building.* Ⓜ *Gwanghwamun, line 5, exit 4.* ☎*(02)-735-1690. Open daily 24 hr. ₩8,000.* Opened in 1937, the restaurant is famous for its *haejangguk*, a soup made of beef bones, blood and intestines. The standard version of this dish is perfect for dealing with the aftereffects of a festive night out. The premises are pleasant and simple, the decor is retro, and the restaurant has a following of loyal regulars.

🍴🛏🛁 **Baerlin** 베어린 레스토랑 – *Somerset Palace, Ground Floor, 85 Susong-dong, Jongno-gu, entrance via the hotel lobby.* Ⓜ *Anguk, line 3, exit 6.* ☎ *(02)-722-5622. www.baerlin. co.kr. Open Mon–Sat 11:30am–11:30pm. Closed public holidays. ₩19,900/₩69000.* A German tavern conveniently located in the Somerset Palace, offering hearty food in a pleasant and modern bistro overlooking a garden. Homemade sausages from ₩19,900, Wiener schnitzel from ₩26,000. Sauerkraut ₩69,000: order 24 hours in advance.

🍸 BARS

Top Cloud 탑 클라우드 – *33 Fl, Jongno Tower Bldg, 6 Jongno 2-ga, Jongno-gu.* Ⓜ *Jonggak, line 1, exit 3.* ☎*(02)-2230-3001. www.top cloud.co.kr. Open daily noon– midnight.* The bar is on the 33rd floor, ideal for a drink while enjoying breathtaking views over the city. There is also a restaurant and live music in the evening, but the main attraction is the view.

🛍 SHOPPING

Kyobo 교보 – *Basement of Kyobo Life Bldg. Jongno 1-ga, Jongno-gu.* Ⓜ *Gwanghwamun, line 5, exit 4 or direct access to the shop from the subway line.* ☎*(02)-3973-5100. Open 9:30am–10pm. Closed main public holidays.* Korea's leading bookstore, with a large foreign book section. Many books in English on the arts, traditions and culture of Korea. There's also a booth where you can buy tickets for the main shows in Seoul.

Insadong★★
인사동

This area is regarded as the bohemian quarter of Seoul and has long been the haunt of artists. Its charm lies in the narrow streets dotted with old shops selling brushes, paper, antiques, etc., and the area has now become a very popular tourist center. Although some of the galleries are not the best in town, there are still enough interesting ones to make a visit worthwhile and provide a good introduction to traditional Korean culture. Insadong is also a popular place to shop for souvenirs, such as in the Ssamziegil complex.

VISIT
Mokin Museum 목인박물관
See Insadong map. Cheongseok-gil, Insadong. Ⓜ *Anguk, line 3, exit 6.* ℘*(02)-722-5066. www.mokinmuseum.com.* Ⓞ*Open Tue–Sun 10am–7pm. ₩5,000.* A delightful small museum with a collection of 8,000 *mok-in* (or *kokdu*) wooden statues, dating from the Joseon period to the present day, used to decorate funeral biers. Carved and painted by local craftsmen in a naive and colorful

- **Michelin Map:** Map p144
- **Info:** Tourist Office 130-Gwanhoon-dong, Jongno-gu, north of Insadong-gil. Ⓜ Anguk, line 3, exit 6. ℘ (02)-731-1621 or (02)-734-0222. Open 10am–8pm. Second office 85-8 Ggyeonji-dong, Jongno-gu, in a traditional building toward the rear of Temple Stay Bldg. Ⓜ Anguk, line 3, exit 6. ℘ (02)-737-7890. Open 10am–8pm.
- **Location:** Insadong extends to the historic center, around the main street Insadong-gil, which runs from north (Ⓜ Anguk) to south (Tapgol Park and Jong-no).
- **Timing:** A half-day is quite sufficient. The area has good restaurants, but note that everything closes early (9:30pm–10pm).
- **Don't Miss:** Shopping for souvenirs and arts-and-crafts goods, a stroll through the traditional side streets.

Ssamziegil shopping complex ©KTO

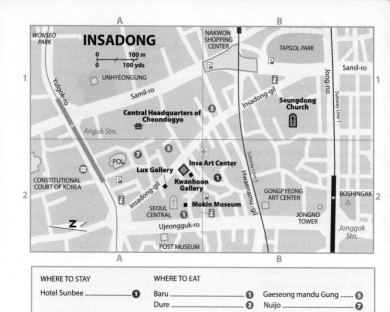

INSADONG

WONSEO PARK	NAKWON SHOPPING CENTER	TAPGOL PARK	Samil-ro

WHERE TO STAY
Hotel Sunbee **1**

WHERE TO EAT
Baru .... **1**   Gaeseong mandu Gung **5**
Dure .... **3**   Nuijo **7**

style, they have great charm and represent an integral part of Korean folklore, illustrating the special relationship of Koreans with death and the afterlife.

Central Headquarters of Cheondogyo 천도교 중앙총부

See Insadong map. 88 Gyeongun-dong, Jongno-gu. Ⓜ *Anguk, line 3, exit 6.* ℘*(02)-735-7579.* Ⓢ*9am–6pm. No charge.*

This building, the main temple of the Cheondogyo sect, was built between

Ssamziegil

38 Gwanhun-dong, Jongno-gu. Ⓜ *Anguk, line 3, exit 6.* ℘*(02)-736-0088.* Ⓢ *10am–8:30pm. No charge.* This extensive shopping complex houses more than 70 stores that sell a range of items from fashion and art to food, accessories and souvenirs. Spiral staircases connect the floors and take shoppers to a rooftop garden. The open courtyard on the first floor regularly has performances and exhibits. Art galleries and restaurants round out the offerings.

1918 and 1921 in German-inspired Baroque style architecture by a Japanese architect, and its height represents the ultimate symbol of Korean nationalism. At the time of its construction, the red-brick and granite building was one of the three highest in Seoul, along with the Catholic cathedral in Myeong-dong and the headquarters of the Japanese colonial government. Grand Master Su-un founded the Cheondogyo movement (*see p 86*) in 1860. Its philosophy, a syncretic combination of Buddhism and Christianity, was at the time opposed to the conservative ideas of the Joseon dynasty and those outlined by Westerners. With the central belief that God lies within us, Cheondoism proposed finding a modern path to reform, specific to Korea. The sect is known for its role in resisting the Japanese occupation, especially at the time of the people's Declaration of Independence on 1 March 1919.

Seungdong Church 승동교회

See Insadong map. 137 Insadong, Jongno-gu. Ⓜ *Jonggak, line 1, exit. 3.* ℘*(02)-732-2340/3. No charge.*

This temple is one of the oldest Protestant buildings in the country. The

Presbyterian Church was established in Korea in 1893, mainly as a result of the efforts of the Rev. Samuel Moore, an American missionary.

The redbrick building is a fine example of early 20C Western architecture in Seoul. The Protestant Church played an important role in the fight against the Japanese colonizers.

Students met here to distribute independence pamphlets. Most importantly, it was here that the Declaration of Independence was drawn up, which was proclaimed on 1 March 1919 in the nearby Tapgol Park (*see p 141*).

ART GALLERIES

Insadong has been a center for both ancient and modern art. You will also find antique shops here, which, although relatively expensive, are good for browsing.

Most of the contemporary art galleries have become greatly influenced by commercial considerations, leasing their space to artists who can afford them and lacking a proper program of exhibitions. This makes for an eclectic and sometimes unfocused overall experience, yet there are still some serious places to visit.

Lux Gallery 룩스갤러리

185 Gwanhun-dong, Jongno-gu. Anguk, line 3, exit 6. (02)-720-8488. www.gallerylux.net. Open daily 10am–7pm (Sun and public holidays 11am–7pm). No charge.

One of the best galleries for photography. Tiny but with a great reputation.

Insa Art Center 인사갤러리

188 Gwanhun-dong, Jongno-gu. Anguk, line 3, exit 6. (02)-736-1020. www.insaartcenter.com. Open daily 10am–7pm. No charge.

A large arts center in the heart of Insadong belonging to the Gana Arts Center which has its headquarters in Pyeongchang-dong. With no artistic policy as such, you'll find some of the best artists exhibited on the center's four levels, along with some unknown artists that just might catch your eye.

Kwanhoon Gallery 관훈갤러리

195 Gwanhun-dong, Jongno-gu. Anguk, line 3, exit 6. (02)-733-6469. www.kwanhoongallery.com. Open daily 10:30am–6:30pm (irregular closures). No charge.

A gallery with six exhibition spaces which opened in 1979, showing both Korean and international artists. The exhibition program may be only sporadic, but it remains one of the best private galleries in the neighborhood.

Art gallery, Insadong ©KTO

ADDRESSES

🏠 STAY

🛏 Hotel Sunbee 호텔 썬비 – *198-11 Gwanhun-dong, Jongno-gu.* Ⓜ *Anguk, line 3, exit 6 and* Ⓜ *Jonggak, line 1, exit 3.* ☎*(02)-730-3451. www.hotel sunbee.com. 42 rm. ₩77,000* 🛏.
Located in an alley in the heart of the traditional tourist district of Insadong, this hotel combines modest prices and a convenient location, quiet but still close to the busy streets. The rooms are a fairly standard design and lack charm, but are relatively large and have a computer with internet access and a jacuzzi. You can also choose a room with traditional bedding. A good solution for those on limited budgets.

🍴 EAT

🍲 Gaeseong mandu Gung 개성만두 궁 – *30-11 Gwanhun-dong, Jongno-gu.* Ⓜ *Anguk, line 3, exit 6.* ☎*(02)-733-9240. www.koong.co.kr. Open daily 11:30am–9:30pm (last orders 9pm). Closed public holidays. ₩8,000/10,000.* An old lady bustles about in the lobby preparing ravioli according to the popular recipe from Gaeseong, the town in North Korea where it originates. The *mandu* are eaten steamed or in soup. A very good place for lunch.

🍲🍲🍲 Baru 발우공양 사찰음식점 – *5F Temple Stay Bldg, 71 Gyeonji-dong, Jongno-gu.* Ⓜ *Anguk, line 3, exit 6.* ☎*(02)-733-2081. www.baru.or.kr. Open daily 11am–2:30pm, 5:30pm–9pm. A la carte ₩10,000/20,000, fixed price menus ₩25,000/53,000. Reservations recommended.* Baru serves temple cuisine—meals revealing subtle flavors made from ingredients grown by the temple monks, according to tried and tested recipes, and all vegetarian of course. Set menus of 10 to 15 dishes follow one after another. Located near the temple Jogyesa, on the fifth floor of the Temple Stay Building.

🍲🍲🍲 Nuijo 뉘조 레스토랑 – *84-13 Gwanhun-dong, Jongno-gu.* Ⓜ *Anguk, line 3, exit 6.* ☎*(02)-730-9301. www. nwijo.com. Open daily 11:30am–3pm, 5pm–10pm. Closed public holidays.*

Fixed price menus: ₩15,000 (lunch), ₩70,000 (dinner). A good place for both traditional and modern Korean food. The owner endeavors to provide dishes based on wild plants and unfamiliar flavors, a possible new path for Korean haute cuisine, while avoiding the pitfalls of fusion cooking. The menus, however, also include meat and fish.

🍲🍲🍲 Dure 두레 음식점 – *8-7 Insadong, Jongno-gu.* Ⓜ *Anguk, line 3, exit 6.* ☎*(02)-732-2919. www.edoore.co.kr. Open daily 12pm–4pm, 6pm–10pm. Closed public holidays. A la carte sharing platters for around ₩50,000, fixed price menus ₩60,000/120,000.* A classic venue for *hanjeongsik*, a Korean meal consisting of a vast array of dishes, popular with the neighborhood artists (you may be lucky enough to hear an improvised concert in the room next door) and foreign ambassadors. The high prices in this top-class restaurant are well justified, even though the service, perhaps as a result of its success, is sometimes a little curt.

🍵 TAKING A BREAK

Yetchatjip, Old Tea Shop 옛찻집 – *2F 196-5 Gwanhun-dong, Jongno-gu.* Ⓜ *Anguk, line 3, exit 6.* ☎ *(02)-722-5332. Open daily 10:30am–11pm. ₩6,000/10,000.* A famous tea-house in the Insadong district. Attractive decor and a warm atmosphere, with birds that are allowed to fly about freely. Delicious teas and hot or cold infusions. The perfect place to relax and take a break from shopping. Try the *mogwai-cha*, flavored with quince, or, in winter, *yuja-cha*, which contains lemon and vitamins.

Dawon 경인미술관다원 – *Kyungin Art Gallery, 30-1Gwanhun-dong, Jongno-gu.* Ⓜ *Jonggak, line 1, exit 3 or* Ⓜ *Anguk, line 3, exit 6.* ☎*(02)-730-6305. www.kyunginart.co.kr. Open daily 10am–10:50pm. Closed public holidays. ₩6,000/10,000.* This tea house in a traditional 19C L-shaped building is in the garden of a museum of fine art *(open Wed–Mon 10am–6pm, closed public holidays, no charge).* The complex is always full of people, but still a good place for tea or a traditional infusion.

Korean ceramics for sale

©Chris Stowers/Apa Publications

🍷 BARS

Kanpan opnen jumakjip
간판없는 주막집 – 130-21
Insadong, Jongno-gu, in the alley
behind the baseball pitch on Insadong.
Ⓜ Jonggak, line 1, exit 3. ☎(02)-723-
9046. Open 1:30pm–12:30am. A bar
with a difference serving *makgeolli*,
fermented rice alcohol, one of the
specialties of the district. Cheap
mismatched furniture, a bare floor,
inscriptions and plaques from floor
to ceiling—the lively, relaxed student
atmosphere is kept in check by the
grandmother who runs the place
with a rod of iron. A bowl of alcohol
accompanied by grilled fish costs
₩13,000. Since the menu is limited,
you won't need to spend hours
choosing! A fun experience.

Min's Club or Mingadaheon
민가다헌 – 66-7 Gyeongun-dong,
Jongno-gu. Ⓜ Jonggak, line 1, exit 3 or
Ⓜ Anguk, line 3, exit 6. ☎(02)-733-2966.
Open daily 12pm–2:30pm, 6pm–11pm
(last orders 9:30pm). Closed public
holidays. A la carte ₩40,000/50,000,
fixed price menus ₩21,000/90,000, wine
starting from ₩40,000. Min's Club is in a
house dating from the 1930s, built by a
relative of Queen Min. In a style typical
of the urban *hanok*, it has a traditional
design but with Western elements such
as the glass corridor and the size of the
rooms, designed for European furniture.
The fusion restaurant is not great,
but the wine bar is charming. Small
outside terrace.

🛒 SHOPPING

KOREAN CAKES
Nakwon tteok jip 낙원떡집 –
1 Nakwon-dong, Jongno-gu. Ⓜ Anguk,
line 3, exit 6. ☎ (02)-732-5579. Open
daily 7:30am–10:30pm. Dating from the
time when, at the end of the Joseon
dynasty, some female courtiers went
into business, this has been the place
for Korean cakes for the past 90 years.
Make sure you try one of their fine
range of traditionally steamed rice cakes
(tteok), which appear at all traditional
Korean festivities. They start at ₩3,000.

CALLIGRAPHY AND SEALS
Myung Sin Dang Brush Store
명신당필방 – 18 Gwanhun-dong,
Jongno-gu. Ⓜ Anguk, line 3, exit 6.
☎(02)-722-4846. Open daily 9am–8pm.
A store that has been specializing in
the sale of calligraphy materials for two
generations. You will find brushes of
different sizes and styles, as well as ink
and stones. It is also possible to have
a personalized seal produced in 30
minutes (₩30,000–2,000,000,
depending on the material chosen).

ARTS AND CRAFTS
Korean Craft and Design
Foundation 한국공예디자인문
진흥원– 182-2 Gwanhun-dong,
Jongno-gu. Ⓜ Anguk, line 3, exit 6.
☎(02)-733-9040/42. Open daily Mar–
Oct 10am–9pm; Nov–Feb 10am–8pm.
A foundation run by the Ministry of
Culture, Sports and Tourism for the
promotion of Korean crafts.

Korean wooden masks

©Tibor Bognar/age fotostock

From lacquerware and jewelry to ceramics, the ground floor shop sells many items made by Korean masters and Living National Treasures. Exhibitions are also held here.

Nabchung Brass 다원 – *Gwanhun-dong, Jongno-gu.* Ⓜ *Anguk, line 3, exit 6.* ☎ *(02)-736-5492. Open Mon–Sat 10am–7pm.* A superb selection of traditional crafts in copper and brass, both religious and everyday objects, produced by Lee Bong-joo, a Living National Treasure.

Talbang 탈방 – *71 Gwanhun-dong, Jongno-gu.* Ⓜ *Anguk, line 3, exit 6.* ☎ *(02)-734-9289. Open daily 10am–10pm. Closed main public holidays.* A small shop selling a fine assortment of handmade Korean wooden masks. Jung Sung-an, who has been carving masks of the great classical Korean figures for the past 20 years, is regarded as a master in the field.

Jang ji bang 장지방 – *81 Gyeonji-dong, Jongno-gu.* Ⓜ *Anguk, line 3, exit 6.* ☎ *(02)-26 3-7 8254. Open daily 10:15am–8pm. Closed main public holidays.* This family-run firm has been manufacturing *hanji*, traditional Korean paper, for four generations. The current head, an outstanding craftsman, has been declared a Living National Treasure.

Tong-In 통인 – *16 Gwanhun-dong, Jongno-gu.* Ⓜ *Anguk, line 3, exit 6.* ☎ *(02)-733-4867. www.tonginstore.com. Ground floor open daily 10am–7pm, other floors open Tue–Sun.* A five-story building selling gifts, souvenirs and handicrafts, with an unmissable antiques gallery on the 4th floor. Especially noted for its beautiful antique Korean furniture.

TEA

O'Sulloc Tea House 오설록 – *170 Gwanhun-dong, Jongno-gu.* Ⓜ *Anguk, line 3, exit 6.* ☎ *(02)-732-6427. www.osulloc.com. Open daily 9am–10pm (Fri–Sat 11pm).* The store's ground floor features an extensive selection of roasted, fermented and fragrant green and black teas. The one flavored with orchid is particularly popular. The tea room on the first floor and the VIP area are nicely designed and are good places to relax and take a break.

Cheonggyecheon City Hall★★
청계천 – 시청

This part of Seoul's historic center, around City Hall, includes underground shopping malls, hotels, offices, luxury department stores, numerous boutiques and important historic sites. It was to the west of this neighborhood that, in the late 19C, the first foreign institutions in Seoul were built (embassies, churches, schools, etc.). Since Lee Myung-bak, the former mayor of Seoul, made the decision to renovate the Cheonggye Stream (Cheonggyecheon) and its banks, restoring the river so that it once more flows along its original course, it has become a popular place for Seoulites to meet and walk.

VISIT
Deoksugung★★ 덕수궁 (Deoksu Palace)
See Cheonggyecheon – City Hall map. 5-1 Jeong-dong, Jung-gu. M City Hall, lines 1/2, exits 2/12. ℘(02)-771-9955. www.deoksugung.go.kr. Open Tue–Sun 9am–9pm (₩10,000). Guided tour in English (no charge) Tue–Fri 10:30am; odd months Sat 1:40pm; even months Sun 1:40pm.

- **Michelin Map:** Map p152
- **Info:** 3F Press Center, 25 Taepyeongno 1-ga, Jung-gu, same floor as the Seoul Global Center. M City Hall, lines 1/2, exit 4 ℘(02)-2075-4119. Open 9am–6pm. Second office 10-2 Gwancheol-dong, Jongno-gu, in front of the Samilgyo Bldg. M Euljiro 1-ga, lines 2/3, exit 1. ℘(02)-720-0872. Open 9am–10pm.
- **Location:** At the heart of the historic city around Deoksugung.
- **Kids:** Enjoy the stream and green areas around Cheonggye, have fun watching the show *Nanta* (*see Seoul Addresses p104*).
- **Timing:** While Deoksugung is not to be missed, how you spend your time depends on your interests. History buffs will want to spend a few hours walking in Jeong-dong, while fashion enthusiasts will be drawn to department stores like Lotte.
- **Don't Miss:** Deoksugung, a walk beside Cheonggyecheon.

Changing of the guard, Deosku Palace

©Chris Stowers/Apa Publications

149

Urban Development of the Capital

With a population of around 11 million, which has been growing steadily over the past six years, the city of Seoul alone accounts for roughly a quarter of South Korea's total population, yet comprises just 0.6 percent of the country's land mass. Taking into account the entire Capital Region, which includes Gyeonggi-do (the province that surrounds Seoul) and the neighboring city of Incheon, slightly less than half of the national population, or more than 24.7 million people, live here. These figures in themselves provide an initial overview of the demographic and economic importance of Seoul and the surrounding region and help shed light on the urban development of a city and region in a state of continual evolution.

Rows of Tower Blocks

Arriving from the airport by road, some of the first sights to greet you as you enter Seoul are its mountains and residential tower blocks beside the Hangang. Depending on when they were erected, these buildings usually have 5 floors (1960–1970), 15 floors (1980–1990), or as many as 30 in the case of the most recent buildings. Apartments of all kinds lurk behind their monotonous, often identical, facades. The names of the corporations that built them—Hansin, Hyundai, Samsung, etc.—are painted in huge letters on their external walls, making their mark on the urban landscape in no uncertain terms (see photo p47).

Called **danji** in Korean, over the past 50 years these tower blocks have become the most common type of residence in South Korea. Symbols of the country's modernization and economic development, they were readily taken up by Korean families seeking home ownership. The state initiated the process, organizing the first wave of construction as part of ambitious plans for national development, and provided financial incentives. The private sector soon took over, taking advantage of the process started by public agencies to build apartment buildings. Depending on the area, they often built for the middle and upper classes, as can be seen in the districts of Apgujeong and Socho, where smart new blocks stand alongside more traditional low-rise housing (two to three levels at most) which is usually much more densely packed and clustered around small winding streets, in contrast to the regular layout of the **danji** and the principal thoroughfares across the city.

Business Districts

While residential areas are spread throughout the capital, the business district is concentrated mainly in two places: **Gangbuk**, literally "north of the river," and **Gangnam**, "south of the river." The former is the historic center, where high-rise office buildings now tower over the former royal palaces, including along the two main avenues, Sejong-ro and Jong-no—the urban development of the latter in the 1980s contributed to Seoul being awarded the 1988 Olympics. The two business centers compete for the head offices of national and international companies; although, of the two, Gangnam stands out thanks to its contemporary construction, which have frequently replaced the previous generation of rather squat buildings. Several new service sectors are now emerging as part of Seoul's policy of multipolarity, and today groups of skyscrapers reach upward like huge granite columns. They include the Digital Media City district to the west, near the football stadium built for the 2002 World Cup, Yongsan-gu, specializing in electronic products, which has been completely redeveloped, and the Techno Mart area of Gwangjin-gu.

A Living City

Recent changes in the urban development of Seoul include work on public spaces and the development of major cultural and leisure activities. The economic affluence achieved in the 1990s had an impact on the habits of South Koreans and their cities, beginning with Seoul. In addition, a number of measures to attract foreign investment and tourists were implemented, following the Asian economic crisis of 1997, which was strongly felt in South Korea. There are four good examples of this: the development of the banks of the Hangang, the renovation of the Insadong district, the restoration of the Cheonggyecheon (Cheonggye Stream) and the construction of the Dongdaemun Design Plaza and Park (DDP).

In the 1990s it was decided to make the **riverbanks** accessible and turn them into recreational areas. On a section of the bank between the river and Route 88 (the Olympic Expressway), South Koreans can now relax, have a picnic, play sports, etc. More recently, the antiques district **Insadong** has undergone the inevitable pedestrianization that frequently occurs in large city centers. Cars are rare here and the elegant shops are full of customers, although the original charm of this part of the old center has been altered by the policy of urban beautification.

In the early 2000s, the then mayor Lee Myung-bak undertook the restoration of the Cheonggyecheon which had been covered over in the urban development of the 1950s for sanitation reasons (see p155) and to cope with traffic flow. At the end of this meandering green-blue stretch of water lies **Dongdaemun Design Plaza and Park**, covering an area of 101,660sq yd/85,000sq m and designed by Iraqi–British architect Zaha Hadid. The entire complex is dedicated to design (with a museum, shops, a design school, etc.) and there is a 3,588sq yd/3,000sq m park. Built to replace Dongdaemun's old baseball and soccer stadiums, it represents Seoul's flagship policy of positioning itself as the capital of Asian design. It demonstrates, once again, the inseparable link between economic and urban development that is so characteristic of town planning in Korea and can be seen throughout the Capital Region, with projects such as the new town of Songdo near Incheon and the International Center for Culture and Tourism at the city of Goyang, in Gyeonggi Province.

Today, Seoul is a contrasting blend of urban and rural landscapes, built as a result of both public projects and private initiatives. High-rise in more ways than one—the city's mountains compete with man-made skyscrapers—the monotony of the apartment complexes is partly offset by the (sometimes audacious) architecture of increasing numbers of buildings, some of which have been designed by internationally renowned architects. Bustling city districts are nevertheless crisscrossed by wide avenues that provide room to breathe and areas in which to relax—various squares, cycle paths, parks….

The result is a dynamic and active city, but also one that can be tough and at times unforgiving. To fully understand and appreciate Seoul, Western aesthetic terms of reference have to be set aside, but for visitors who are curious and eager to explore—once they have ventured beyond the concrete walls—Seoul will be generous in return.

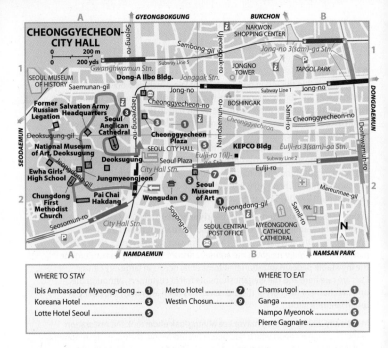

This palace was built in the 15C as a residence for Prince Wolsan, the son of King Sejo, who was removed from the throne in favor of his brother King Yejong. During the Japanese invasions led by Toyotomi Hideyoshi in 1592, the royal family was forced to flee to Uiju, on the Manchurian border. On his return in 1593, King Seonjo took up residence here, as the royal palaces in the capital had been devastated. Once Changdeokgung had been rebuilt (1615), King Kwanghaegun settled there and left Deoksugung.

Monarchs continued to live at Changdeokgung for some considerable time. It was not until 1897 that King Gojong returned to live at Deoksugung, after fleeing Gyeongbokgung following the assassination of Queen Min by the Japanese occupying forces and taking refuge for 13 months in the neighboring Russian Legation. Even after abdicating in favor of his son Sunjong, Gojong remained in the palace until his death in 1919.

The Japanese occupiers reduced the surface area of the palace complex by two-thirds and the buildings that can be seen today represent just one-tenth of what was originally here. The name of the palace has been changed many times, and it was King Sunjong, the last of the Joseon dynasty, who named it Deoksugung (Palace of Virtuous Longevity) after his father's abdication. The Korean kings only lived here for brief periods and the palace was always linked with misfortune.

The palace complex can be entered through the Daehan gate, **Daehanmun**, which faces eastward, unlike the gates of other royal palaces of the Joseon dynasty which traditionally faced south. Like most buildings in the palace, it dates from 1906, having been rebuilt after a fire that year. It was moved back from its original position to allow for the widening of the road in the 1960s. Once inside the palace grounds, you will see the small stream called Geumcheon (Golden Stream) and the bridge that crosses it, **Geumcheongyo**, two features that were typical of the royal palaces of Seoul: to purify the minds of the king's officials and public servants, and to mark a boundary between the dwelling place of the sovereign and those of mere mortals.

The Junghwa gate, **Junghwamun**, leads to the courtyard of the main building. The walls that once enclosed an inner courtyard have disappeared. Note the carvings on the stairs: the royal dragon insignia and the *haetae* (mythical creatures) surrounding it. The gate's central arch was reserved for the king only. The throne room, **Junghwajeon**, sits on a double stone terrace at the back of a courtyard which, just as in the other royal palaces, is crossed by a paved pathway into which markers have been set to indicate where officials should stand according to their rank.

The original throne room had two levels, which must have made it seem even more majestic. Inside, you can see all the trappings of royalty: the throne, the traditional representation of *Irwol-oakdo* with its five mountains, the moon and the sun of hope and prosperity for the nation, and the dragons decorating the ceiling.

To the rear is the magnificent two-story **Seogeodang**, the pavilion where King Seonjo lived until the reconstruction of the palaces that were destroyed during the Japanese invasions of the late 16C. As a sign of empathy with the difficulties experienced by his people, the king wished it to be very plain and unadorned, resulting in a building of particular beauty. On the right, King Gojong received foreign envoys at **Deokhongjeon** hall. The construction dates from 1911 and was even supplied with electricity. **Hamnyeongjeon** included King Gojong's sleeping quarters and is where he died in 1919. Behind this is **Jeonggwanheon**, the first Western-influenced building to be erected in a Korean royal palace. Built in 1900 and designed by a Russian architect, this building is where the king listened to music, held receptions and even took coffee—a beverage he had come to enjoy during his stay in the Russian Legation.

Returning to the rear of the throne room, the **Jeukjodang** pavilion was used by Gojong as an office and the site where he worshiped his ancestors. The king received distinguished guests at **Junmyeongdang**. To the left of these buildings sits the three-story **Seokjojeon**, which was King Gojong's little-used modern palace, built between 1900 and 1910 by British architect G.R. Harding in a Western Neoclassical style. The second floor contained the imperial apartments; the first floor, several reception halls; and the ground floor, the staff quarters. It was subsequently used at the end of the Korean War for Soviet–American summits and later became the National Museum and then the Royal Museum. The building now houses an annex of the National Museum of Art, Deoksugung (👜 *see below*).

Finally, on leaving, you will see a pavilion with a water clock that dates from 1536 and a bell from the Buddhist temple Heungcheon, cast in 1462.

Just as at the main royal palace, Gyeongbokgung, you can attend a **re-enactment of the changing of the guard under the Joseon dynasty** *Daehanmun (main gate), 15 Feb–31 Dec Tue–Sun 11am, 2pm and 3:30pm (except on wet days). No charge.*

National Museum of Art, Deoksugung
덕수궁 미술관

👜*See Cheonggyecheon – City Hall map. In the grounds of Deoksugung.* 📞*(02)-2022-0600.* 🕐 *Open Tue–Thu 9am–6pm, Fri–Sun 9am–8:30pm. Variable entrance charge.*

Holding temporary exhibitions, pending the opening of the new museum annex in the former Gimusa (👜 *see Bukchon p 130*), this is the museum's inner city annex, but will almost certainly change its function when the new building is open. The main museum building is in Gwacheon, a suburb of Seoul. *A new branch of the museum will open at Sogyeok-dong, Jongno-gu in 2013.*

🐾 WALKING TOUR

JEONG-DONG★ 정동

▶ *Tour along Jeong-Dong, Jongno-gu takes 1hr30min–2hrs. Start from the street on the left next to Deoksugung, facing the main gate.* M *City Hall, lines 1/2, exits 2/12.*

Jeong-Dong is the neighborhood where the majority of Westerners lived after Korea opened its doors to foreigners. Missionary churches, foreign embassies and modern schools were built here around the palace area by Europeans and Americans. King Gojong tried to save his dynasty by introducing reforms and opened the country up to the outside world, despite difficulties with the Japanese authorities. The late 19C and early 20C buildings, the first buildings of the modern era to be constructed on Korean soil, have a certain period charm.

Pai Chai Hakdang, East Building 배재학당

See Cheonggyecheon – City Hall map. 34-5 Jeong-dong, Jongno-gu. (070)-7506-0072.
Constructed in 1916, this brick building was part of the first modern Western-style school in Korea, established by the American Methodist missionary Henry Gerhard Appenzeller in 1885 and endorsed by King Gojong. It now houses a **small museum** (*open Tue–Sun 10am–5pm, no charge*), providing an overview of the first Western missionaries to come to Korea and of their work.

Chungdong First Methodist Church 정동제일교회

See Cheonggyecheon – City Hall map 34 Jeong-dong, Jongno-gu. (02)-753-0001.
This building, erected in 1897 by the American Methodists, is the first Korean Protestant church built in Western style. The use of redbrick and the church's tower are typical of the time when Catholic and Protestant missionaries came to spread Christianity in Korea. They were very successful, and Christianity is now well established in the country.

Ewha Girls' High School (Ewha Hakdang) 이화학당

See Cheonggyecheon – City Hall map. 32 Jeong-dong, Jongno-gu. (02)-3277-3152.

The first school for working-class Korean girls opened in 1886 and was founded by Methodist missionary Mary Scranton, who had decided that young Korean women had as much right to education as their male counterparts. Despite initial resistance, the idea of promoting secular education for women made progress, eventually leading to the founding of the famous Ewha Womans University (*see p 202*). Of the original structure, only Simpson Hall, built in 1905, remains; it now houses a small museum.

Former Russian Legation 구 러시아공사관

See Cheonggyecheon – City Hall map. 15 Jeong-dong, Jongno-gu.
The remains of the former Russian Legation overlook a small square. The three-story tower, which is still standing, was only part of the building constructed in Renaissance style in 1890 by the Russian Aleksey Seredin-Sabatin. The legation was destroyed during the Korean War and only partially rebuilt in 1973. It was here that King Gojong and his son, the crown prince, took refuge after fleeing Gyeongbok Palace in 1895, following the assassination of Queen Min by the Japanese occupiers. The king stayed here for just over a year. During the 1970s renovation, a secret room connecting the legation to Deoksu Palace was found in the basement of the tower. In the park below, there is a memorial in honor of the Sisters of St. Paul de Chartres. These French nuns were the first Catholic women missionaries in Korea in 1888; One of their houses originally stood on this site. The Pauline convent in Seoul is now in Myeong-dong, behind the cathedral.

Retrace your steps toward Deoksugung, and Jungmyeongjeon lies at the end of an alley on your left.

Jungmyeongjeon 중명전

See Cheonggyecheon – City Hall map. 1 Jeong-dong, Jongno-gu.
Home to Western missionaries, this Western-style, two-story brick building was built by Russian architect Aleksey

Seredin-Sabatin and was incorporated into the Deoksugung complex during its expansion in 1897. It housed the Royal Library. When the American Legation was established to the rear of Jungmyeongjeon, it became an annex cut off from the palace complex. This is where, in 1905, the Eulsa Treaty between Korea and Japan was signed, under the terms of which Korea became a protectorate of Japan. The building was restored to its original grandeur and reopened in 2010; it is now a museum with exhibits relating to King Gojong and his era.

▷ *Returning toward Deoksugung, take the street that runs beside the wall on your left for a picturesque walk between the ancient walls of the palace and the old American Legation, now the ambassador's residence.*

Salvation Army Headquarters 구세군 본관
&See Cheonggyecheon – City Hall map. 1-23 Jeong-dong, Jongno-gu. ☎ (02)-720-9432.

The Salvation Army building was completed in 1928 in the red brick commonly used in the West at the time. It was restored in 2003. The architect was inspired by the Clapton Congress Hall in London to construct the entire building in Neoclassical style. It was used to train Salvation Army officers and was the headquarters of their missionary activity, which began in Seoul in 1908. A small museum (*no charge*) presents the history of the Salvation Army organization in Korea.

▷ *Travel down the road, turn right and then right again to reach Korea's Anglican Cathedral, which is next to the British Embassy.*

Seoul Anglican Cathedral (Seonggonghoe) 서울 성공회성당
&See Cheonggyecheon – City Hall map. 3 Jeong-dong, Jongno-gu. ☎(02)-730-6611.

This granite neo-Romanesque cathedral was built in 1922 by Arthur Dixon, a British architect, under the supervision of Mark Trollope, the third Anglican bishop of Korea. Dedicated on 2 May 1926, it was erected during the Japanese occupation and the architect was not allowed to construct a cruciform design as originally planned. The transept was not completed until later, in 1926. On leaving the cathedral, look for the charming Anglican diocesan bishop's residence, which is in the traditional Korean style. There is also a detached building that is part of Deoksu Palace, the Yangijae, which dates from 1905.

▷ *The tour ends here. Walk along Sejong Ave to the City Hall subway station (lines 1/2) or cross the avenue and head north, toward Gwanghwamun, to Dong-A Ilbo Building.*

Dong-A Ilbo Building 동아일보빌딩
&See Cheonggyecheon – City Hall map. 139 Sejong-ro, Jongno-gu. ☎(02)-2020-2055.

This building was erected in 1926 to house the headquarters of the Korean newspaper *Dong-A Ilbo*. In the external walls, the architect included large windows that open out on to the avenue below. This design is typical of Western-style buildings in Korea from the 1920s. The newspaper having moved to a smart new building, the old Dong-A Ilbo Building is now home to the private **Ilmin Museum of Art** (*www.ilmin.org*, Øopen Tue–Sun 11am–7pm, no charge), exhibiting ceramics, paintings and calligraphy from the Goryeo and Joseon eras.

ADDITIONAL SIGHTS

♟♟ Cheonggyecheon Plaza★ 청계천광장
&See Cheonggyecheon – City Hall map. Cheonggyecheon, Jongno-gu. Ⓜ City Hall, lines 1/2, exit 4. ☎(02)-2290-7111. http://english.seoul.go.kr/.

Featuring a colorful contemporary artwork by Claes Oldenburg and Coosje van Bruggen called simply *Stream*, the plaza marks the entrance to the banks of the Cheonggyecheon, the stream that flows across downtown Seoul. By the mid-

1950s it had become little more than a stinking sewer and was covered over by a roadway in 1955. When he was mayor of Seoul, Korean president Lee Myung-bak, as part of his radical ecological town planning policy, launched a project to "restore" the original river. The result is impressive: a pleasant 3.6mi/5.84km walk bordered by trees and shrubs in the heart of the city; clean water (though pumped and filtered, as the original river had dried up); a decrease in air pollution, temperature and even noise; plus one hundred million visitors since its opening in 2005. From an ecological standpoint, the restored Cheonggye Stream does not quite match the success of Yangjaecheon, a stream in the southern part of the city flanked by similar green areas, but it does provide a different perspective from which to see the city, a peaceful place to walk and a natural exhibit space for fanciful sculpture and seasonal decorations.

Seoul Museum of Art (SeMA) 서울시립미술관

See Cheonggyecheon – City Hall map. 37 Seosomun-dong, Jung-gu. Ⓜ *City Hall, lines 1/2, exits 1/11/12.* *(02)-2124-8800. http://seoulmoa.seoul.go.kr.* Ⓞ*Open Tue–Sun 10am–9pm, Mar–Oct Sat and some public holidays 10am–7pm; Nov–Feb 10am–6pm. Closed 1 Jan. Charges vary, depending on the exhibition.*

This building once functioned as a courthouse, so the road beside the palace leading to it was often used by married couples about to be divorced. As a result a superstition grew up that young couples should avoid it. Now renovated (only the facade remains), it is not actually a museum but hosts temporary exhibitions of modern art, both Korean and foreign. These are often very good, and it is always worth checking the program. At the weekend it can become crowded.

Wongudan Temple of Heaven 원구단

See Cheonggyecheon – City Hall map. 87 Sogong-dong, Jung-gu. Ⓜ *City Hall, lines 1/2, exit 6 behind the Westin Chosun Hotel. No charge.*

A beautiful octagonal three-story shrine, built in 1899. King Gojong proclaimed himself emperor of Korea here on 2 November 1896, severing ties with the Chinese Qing dynasty tradition. The construction of an altar, with its Chinese-inspired architecture, meant that the Korean ruler could now offer sacrifices to heaven directly, just like his counterpart in Beijing.

Traditionally, the Joseon kings conducted their rituals at the Sajik altar (*see p199*), honoring the gods of the Earth and the Harvest and observing some secondary agricultural rites, but they were not able to honor heaven. The

Cheonggyecheon

©KTO

Seoul Museum of Art

© Seoul Museum of Art

Wongudan site contained other buildings which were destroyed by the Japanese occupiers in 1910 to make way for the Joseon Gyeongseong Railroad Hotel, the first luxury Western-style hotel in Korea, which originally stood on the site of today's Chosun Hotel.

ADDRESSES

🛏 STAY

Ibis Ambassador Myeong-dong – 이비스호텔 앰배서더명동 – 59-5 Myeong-dong 1-ga, Jung-gu. M Euljiro 1-ga, line 2, exit 6. ℘(02)-6361-8888. www.ambatel.com/myeongdong. 280 rm. ₩132,000/172,000. ₩17,000 ☐ ₩29,900 ✗.
A city center location, catering mainly for businessmen. Rooms on the upper floors, like the bar, have a good view over Namsan and the district of Myeong-dong. You can also enjoy the hot baths and gym in the business center.

Metro Hotel 메트로 호텔 – 199-33 Euljiro 2-ga, Jung-gu. M Euljiro 1-ga, line 2, exits 5/6. ℘(02)-752-1112. www.metrohotel.co.kr. 75 rm. ₩88,000/143,000 ☐. A business hotel in the city center, at affordable prices. Well presented, with design-oriented decor. The rooms are functional, clean and pleasant. If possible, try to stay on the upper floors as they have more light. Book online for a 5 percent discount.

Koreana Hotel 코리아나호텔 – 61-1 Taepyeong-ro 1-ga, Jung-gu. M Gwanghwamun, line 5, exit 6 or M City Hall, lines 1/2, exit 3. ℘(02)-2171-7000. www.koreanahotel.com. 337 rm. ₩196,000/350,000. ₩20,000 ☐. ₩18,000/₩43,000 ✗.
A mid-range hotel in a prime central location, close to Seoul City Hall and Gyeongbokgung and Deoksugung (royal palaces). The rooms are quite spacious, comfortable and well equipped. There are also several restaurants, a bar, shops, a business center, gym and sauna.

Lotte Hotel Seoul 롯데호텔서울 – 1 Sogong-dong, Jung-gu. M Euljiro 1-ga, line 2, exits 7/8 or M City Hall, lines 1/2, exits 5/6. ℘(02)-771-1000. www.lottehotelseoul.com. 1,120 rm. ₩350,000/440,000. ₩35,500 ✗. Right in the heart of the city center, this huge world-class hotel offers luxurious accommodation and a wide range of services including bars and restaurants, duty-free shops, a spa, a fitness center, a business center, and even one floor specifically reserved for women. Many foreign dignitaries have stayed here.

Westin Chosun 웨스틴 조선호텔 – 87 Sogong-dong, Jung-gu. M City Hall, lines 1/2, exit 6 or M Euljiro 1-ga, line 2, exit 8. ℘(02)-771-0500. www.westin.com/seoul. 453 rm starting at ₩245,000☐. ₩30,000 ✗. The oldest international hotel in Korea, founded in 1914, this luxury establishment is absolutely top of the range, with friendly, personal service, a relaxing atmosphere and comfortable rooms. The Wongudan Temple of Heaven is just behind the hotel.

⑨/EAT

Nampo Myeonok 남포면옥 – *125 Da-dong, Jung-gu.* Ⓜ *Euljiro 1-ga, line 2, exit 1.* ✆*(02)-777-3131. Open daily 11:30am–10pm (Sat–Sun 9pm). Closed public holidays. A la carte* ₩*8,000, fixed price menu* ₩*52,000.* A classic Seoul restaurant with over 40 years' experience of serving cold noodles (*naengmyeon*) in North Korean style. Presidents and celebrities have crowded in to eat here alongside the regulars in an old-fashioned but nice atmosphere.

Chamsutgol 참숯골 – *19 Mugyo-dong, Jung-gu.* Ⓜ *City Hall, lines 1/2, exits 4/5.* ✆*(02)-774-2100. Open daily 11am–9:30pm.* ₩*6,000/ 56,000.* This famous restaurant, on the corner of a street behind the Seoul Financial Center, serves the very best Korean beef, including fine, very tender, barbecued *hanu*. The decor is nothing special, but the key attraction is the food.

Ganga Seoul Financial Center 강가레스토랑 – *2nd Lower Ground Floor, 84 Taepyeongno 1-ga, Mugyo-dong, Jung-gu.* Ⓜ *City Hall, lines 1/2, exit 4.* ✆*(02)-3783-0610. Open daily 11:30am–3pm, 5:30pm– 10pm. Closed public holidays. Fixed price menus: lunch* ₩*30,000/50,000, dinner* ₩*35,000/60,000. Reservations suggested.* Ganga specializes in Indian cuisine, from tandoori to a wide variety of curries, as well as samosas. Everything is accompanied by delicious naan bread and washed down with the occasional *lassi*. The setting is elegant in shades of blue, complemented by Korean furnishings.

Pierre Gagnaire Lotte Hotel 피에르 가니에르레스토랑 – *30 Eulji-ro, Jung-gu* Ⓜ*City Hall, line 1* Ⓜ *Euljiro 1-ga, line 2, exits 7/8.* ✆*(02)-317-7181. www.pierregagnaire.co.kr. Open Mon– Sat noon–3pm, 6pm–10pm. Closed public holidays. Fixed price menus: lunch* ₩*50,000, dinner* ₩*300,000.* Seoul's leading restaurant, located in the highly kitschy Lotte complex. Well-known French chef Pierre Gagnaire brought haute cuisine and molecular gastronomy to Korea. This pioneering restaurant had a difficult start, but now seems to have found its niche. A completely unique experience, with prices that are among the highest in Seoul, but justifiably so, as it is very exclusive. It also offers "lighter" fixed price menus both in the evening and at lunchtime. Pierre's Bar in the same building is an excellent alternative with delicious early-evening light meals at a fixed price.

🛒 SHOPPING

Lotte Town 롯데타운 – *1 Sogong-dong, Jung-gu.* Ⓜ *Euljiro 1-ga, line 2, exit 7.* ✆ *(02)-771-2500. www.lotte town.com.* An enormous shopping complex with large stores and a hotel, run by the Lotte Group, one of the most powerful Korean conglomerates. **Lotte Main Department Store** *(open daily 10:30am–8pm)* is a classic 13-story building with a superb duty-free shop for tourists on the 10th floor. In addition to luxury boutiques, two floors of restaurants and event halls, convenience services such as mobile phone charging, interpretation and personal lockers are also available on-site. **Avenuel** *(open daily 10:30am –8pm)* includes luxury shops, in a VIP building. **Lotte Youth Plaza** *(open daily 11:30am–9:30pm)* is a mall catering to young people that sells clothes and fashion items.

Jung-gu★★
중구

From the day Seoul Station opened in 1900, everyone who traveled to the capital chose to do so by rail, arriving at this major terminus situated near Namdaemun, the Great South Gate and powerful symbol of the city. Taking advantage of the crowds who passed through in the early 20C, a lively central market grew up near the gate, selling just about everything. Today the area around Namdaemun is still primarily a place for shopping, notably in Myeong-dong, which became a prime fashion venue in the 1980s. To the east, however, is the folk village of Namsangol, in Cheonghak-dong, one of the most picturesque districts in Seoul under the Joseon dynasty, with streams crisscrossing the slopes of Namsan (South Mountain). Chungmuro (the street and the area immediately surrounding it) was the headquarters of the film industry, and while it is no longer the Korean Hollywood of yesteryear, it is still of interest to keen photographers looking for fresh material.

VISIT
👥 Namsangol Hanok Village★ 남산골한옥마을
👁 See Jung-gu map. 84-1 Pildong 2-ga, Jung-gu. Ⓜ Chungmuro, lines 3/4, exit 3. ☏(02)-2264-4412. www.hanokmaeul.org. 🕐 Open Wed–Mon, Apr–Oct 9am–9pm; Nov–Mar 9am–8pm. Guided tour in English available. Reservation required. No charge.

This village, built between 1993 and 1998, includes **five superb traditional Korean houses** from the late Joseon period, which were moved here following the formation of the park. All are interesting from an architectural point of view and have been renovated so they can be put on show for the public. Note particularly the residence of Prince Park Young-hyo, which is a typi-

🧭 **Michelin Map:** Map p162

ℹ️ **Info:** Tourist Office 49 Namchang-dong, Jung-gu, in Namdaemun Market. Ⓜ Hoehyeon, line 4, exit 5. ☏(02)-752-1913. Open Mon–Sat 9am–6pm. Second office 53-1 Myeong-dong 1-ga, Jung-gu. Ⓜ Euljiro 1-ga, lines 2/4, exit 6 on the street between the Lotte Department Store and Myeongdong Cathedral, in front of the Woori Bank. ☏ (02)-774-3238. Open daily 9am–10pm (Nov–Feb 9am–9pm).

▶ **Location:** To the northeast of Namsan Park, to the south of Dongdaemun Market.

👥 **Kids:** Namsangol Hanok Village.

🕐 **Timing:** It's a shoppers' paradise: allow a day to visit the district's markets and shops. If you prefer culture, set aside two hours to visit Namsangol Hanok Village.

😊 **Don't Miss:** A stroll around Namdaemun Market, the lively atmosphere of Myeong-dong shopping district, the charm of the traditional Namsangol Hanok Village.

cal nobleman's house with the men's apartments (sarangchae) separate from those of the women (anchae). The home of young Queen Yun, before her marriage to the last king of Korea, also has the charm and style associated with the houses of the ruling elite, like those of Yun Taek-yeong, her father, and General Kim Chun-yeong.

Yi Seung-up was a master carpenter who rebuilt Gyeongbok Palace under the Daewongun (regent); the style of his house is relatively sophisticated for that of a commoner in a hierarchi-

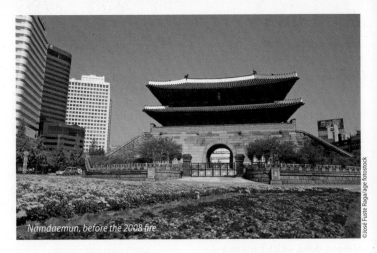

Namdaemun, before the 2008 fire

©José Fuste Raga/age fotostock

cal Confucian society. The village also stages cultural events and traditional games, and there is a pleasant park. It is situated in the Pil-dong area, formerly named Cheonghak-dong or "blue cranes district," after the birds that used to be seen here.

Members of the Korean nobility frequently came here in the summer to enjoy the beauty of the location and its refreshingly cool stream. The area (full of scholars and artists) was also known as Namchon, or South Village, as opposed to Bukchon (North Village), the area occupied by senior royal officials (&see p122).

Namdaemun★ 남대문 (Sungnyemun 숭례문)

&See Jung-gu map.
Namdaemun-ro 4-ga, Jung-gu.
Ⓜ *Seoul Station, lines 1/4, exits 3/4 or*
Ⓜ *Hoehyeon, line 4, exit 5.*

Seoul's National Treasure No. 1 was built in 1398 and is officially named Sungnyemun, although it is more commonly known as Namdaemun (Namdae Gate, or the Great South Gate). This was the largest of the nine gates providing access to the city in the 10.5mi/17km-long fortress wall. Rebuilt in 1448 under King Sejong, the ancient wooden structure was renovated in 1962, but was then destroyed by fire in 2008, much to the dismay of the entire nation. It is being rebuilt in the original style.

BUILDINGS FROM THE PERIOD OF JAPANESE OCCUPATION

In 1876, the Japanese empire imposed a treaty of friendship on the kingdom of Korea, followed by a protectorate in 1905 that ultimately led to its outright annexation between 1910 and 1945. The Japanese presence gradually intensified, and Jung-gu became the commercial and business district. Reminders of the period are still evident in the Colonial architecture of some of the buildings.

Seoul Station 서울역

Bongnae-dong 2-ga, Jung-gu.
Ⓜ *Seoul Station, lines 1/4, exit 2.*

The first station was built here at Namdaemun in 1900 and connected the capital to the port of Incheon, the main gateway to the country. The current building was completed in 1925 and was designed by Japanese architect Tsukamoto Yasushi. Using red brick, typical of Western-style construction of the time in Korea, it was modeled on the station of the German city of Paderborn. The whole structure, with its central dome, has a neo-Renaissance style dotted with elements of the Baroque. In 2004, the arrival of the KTX, Korea's high-speed train, saw the construction of an ultra-modern station adjacent to the old one. The old building has been restored to its original look and is now open as a large cultural complex.

Seoul Station

©Choi Jaejin/age fotostock

Bank of Korea Museum
한국은행화폐금융박물관
&See Jung-gu map.
106 Namdaemun-ro, Jung-gu. Ⓜ *City Hall, lines 1/2, exit 7 or* Ⓜ *Hoehyeon, line 4, exit 7.* ☎ *(02)-759-4881. http://museum.bok.or.kr.* Ⓞ*Open Tue–Sun 10am–5pm. No charge. Audio guides in English ₩500.*
Built between 1907 and 1912 by Japanese architect Kingo Tatsuno, this site was originally home to Dai-Ichi Ginko, the First National Bank of Japan. It eventually housed the Joseon Bank, founded in 1911, and became the headquarters of the Bank of Korea in 1950. This three-story neo-Renaissance building is typical of the Japanese colonial period. It has a symmetrical H-shaped structure with exterior walls made of granite blocks.

Note the circular towers topped with domes at the corners. Don't overlook the interior, which has retained its former splendor.

Shinsegae Old Building
구 신세계백화점본점
&See Jung-gu map.
52 Chungmuro 1-ga, Jung-gu. Ⓜ *Hoehyeon, line 4, exit 7.* ☎*(02)-1588-1234.* Ⓞ*Open daily 10:30am–8pm.*
Dating from 1930, this building housed the modern Japanese Mitsukoshi department store, the first of its kind in Korea. It was renamed Shinsegae ("New World") in 1963. Despite its recent radical restoration, the building has retained its architectural features from the Japanese colonial period.

Bank of Korea Museum

©KTO

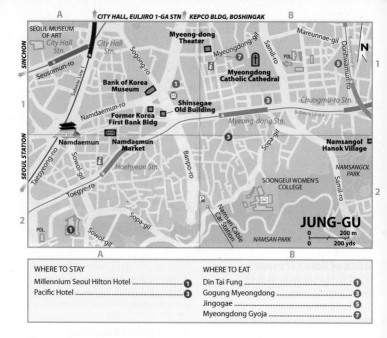

WHERE TO STAY		WHERE TO EAT	
Millennium Seoul Hilton Hotel	❶	Din Tai Fung	❶
Pacific Hotel	❸	Gogung Myeongdong	❸
		Jingogae	❺
		Myeongdong Gyoja	❼

Former Korea First Bank Building 구제일은행본점

🔊 See Jung-gu map. 53-1 Chungmuro 1-ga Jung-gu, next to the Shinsegae department store. Ⓜ Hoehyeon, line 4, exit 7.

Built in 1933 by the Japanese architect Kingko Hirabayashi, this was the first building design in Korea to be selected by the tender process. Typical of the Japanese occupation era, it first housed the Chosun Savings Bank and then became the headquarters of First Bank, today renamed Standard Chartered Bank. The neo-Baroque building has stately columns and five floors around a steel structure.

Myeong-dong Theater 명동예술극장

🔊 See Jung-gu map. 54 Myeong-dong 1-ga, Jung-gu. Ⓜ Euljiro 1-ga, line 2, exit 6. 𝄞(02)-1644-2003.

Myeong-dong Theater was originally a cinema. It was built in the Baroque style during the Japanese occupation. Dating from 1936, the building became the National Theater between 1957 and 1973, and its successful renovation, completed in May 2009, allowed it to reopen

its doors to a variety of artistic and theatrical works.

KEPCO Building 한국전력공사빌딩

🔊 See Cheonggyecheon – City Hall map 5 Namdaemun-ro 2-ga, Jung-gu. Ⓜ Euljiro 1-ga, line 2, exit 6, opposite the subway exit.

Built in 1928 to house the headquarters of the Keijo Electric Company, this concrete and metal structure, despite looking somewhat grim, is a good example of modern Japanese architecture.

It boasted an elevator and was supposed to be both fire and earthquake proof. The building still contains the offices of KEPCO, the Korea Electric Power Company.

ADDITIONAL SIGHTS
Myeongdong Catholic Cathedral 명동성당

🔊 See Jung-gu map. 1 Myeong-dong 2-ga, Jung-gu. Ⓜ Myeong-dong, line 4, exit 8. Ⓜ Euljiro Ipgu, line 2, exit 5. 𝄞(02)-774-1784. www.mdsd.or.kr. Mass in English Sun 9am.

Seoul Cathedral was built between 1892 and 1898 and was consecrated in May

162

1898. French priest Eugène Jean Coste drew up the plans for this beautiful neo-Gothic red and gray brick building 223ft/68m long, 95ft/29m wide and 75ft/23m high (151ft/46m including the spire). Chinese workers, who had constructed similar buildings in the past, were employed to carry out the project. Note the original depictions of saints, including 10 French missionaries of the Missions Étrangères de Paris order, martyred near Seoul during the Christian persecutions of 1839 and 1866. A crypt contains a chapel dedicated to the martyrs. Near the cathedral you will notice the old buildings where the archbishops used to live and the convent of the Sisters of St. Paul de Chartres. You can visit their **small museum** housed in a former convent chapel built in 1930 (*(02)-795-3706-3255, open Tue–Sun 10am–11am, 1:30pm–4:30pm)*. The Korean Church, and especially Myeongdong Cathedral, played a significant role in the struggle for democracy during the post Korean War period when a military government ruled the country, and the vast square in front of the cathedral is still the scene of rallies and popular protests.

ADDRESSES

STAY

Pacific Hotel 퍼시픽호텔 –
31-1 Namsan-dong 2-ga, Jung-gu. Myeong-dong, line 4, exit 3. *(02)-777-7811. www.thepacifichotel.co.kr. 139 rm. ₩160,000/220,000. ₩20,000* . Adjoining Namsan Park and close to the shopping areas of Myeong-dong and Namdaemun, this mid-range hotel is handy for both the city center and peaceful walks in the nearby park. Ask for a room overlooking this green space.

Millennium Seoul Hilton Hotel 밀레니엄서울힐튼호텔 –
395 Namdaemunno 5-ga, Jung-gu. Seoul Station, line 1, exit 8 or Hoehyeon, line 4, exit 4. *(02)-753-7788. www.hilton.co.kr. 681 rm. ₩356,000/396,000. ₩37,000* , . A luxury city-center hotel at the foot of Namsan and near Seoul railway station and Namdaemun Market. It has everything you would expect from this class of hotel, with very comfortable rooms, most of which have stunning views. Enjoy the swimming pool and spa, and try your luck in the casino.

EAT

Din Tai Fung 딘타이펑식당 –
104 Myeong-dong 2-ga, Jung-gu. Euljiro 1-ga, line 2, exit 6 or Myeong-dong, line 4, exit 5. *(02)-771-2778. www.dintaifung.co.kr. Open daily 11am–10pm. A la carte ₩8,500/24,000, fixed price menus ₩35,000 for two.*
A Taiwanese restaurant chain that is well established in Asia, specializing in a wide variety of dim sum, steamed Chinese dumplings. Also worth trying is the spicy *sanlatang* soup, with its unusual flavors. It has an open kitchen, a pleasant interior and moderate prices, all the ingredients needed to attract the crowds. You may have to wait a while to be seated, but table turnover is fairly rapid.

Myeongdong Gyoja 명동교자 식당 –
33 Myeong-dong 2-ga, Jung-gu. Myeong-dong, line 4, exit 8. *(02)-776-3424. www.mdkj.co.kr. Open daily 10:30am–9:30pm. Closed public holidays. ₩7,000.* A popular restaurant famous for its *kalguksu*, Korean noodles. The name literally means "pasta cut with a knife." The decor is simple and the service "rustic," but the food, which is very popular in summer, is plentiful and cheap. A second restaurant owned by the same proprietor has opened up in the neighborhood.

Gogung Myeongdong 고궁 명동 –
12-14 Chungmu 2-ga, Jung-gu, behind the Sejong Hotel. Myeong-dong, line 4, exit 10. www.gogung.co.kr. *Open daily 10:30am–10pm. Closed public holidays. A la carte ₩8,000/35,000, fixed price menus ₩37,000/39,000.* A popular chain restaurant that specializes in *bibimbap*, rice mixed with vegetables and condiments. Try *Jeonju bibimbap* for ₩11,000, which is very filling. Ideal for lunch after a morning's shopping.

Jingogae 진고개한식 –
30-16 Chungmuro 3-ga, Jung-gu.
Ⓜ *Chungmuro, line 4, exit 6.* ☎*(02)-
2267-0955. Open daily 11am–10pm.
Closed 1st & 3rd Sun of the month and
public holidays. ₩14,000/150,000.* This
has been a classic venue since 1963.
Clean but rather impersonal, the
interior does not look very special.
The regular clientele comes from
the neighborhood of printers and
photographers. The beef ribs stew
(*galbijjim* at ₩14,000), flavored with
cinnamon and jujube, is a delight,
as are the crab in soy sauce pickles
(*gejang* at ₩15,000) and the *bossam*
kimchi, fermented cabbage stuffed
with a wide range of ingredients.
Jingogae also serves excellent
Japanese bento and sushi.

Wooraeok 우래옥 – *118-1
Jugyo-dong, Jung-gu. 1st street on the
right after the subway exit.* Ⓜ *Euljiro
4-ga, lines 2/5, exit 4.* ☎*(02)-2265-0151.
Open Tue–Sun 11:30am–10pm (last
orders 9:20pm). Closed public holidays.
A la carte ₩10,000/46,000.* Classic North
Korean cuisine, specializing in grilled
meats. Opened in 1946, it has one
branch in Gangnam and two in the
United States. The decor is pleasantly
old-fashioned, clean and comfortable.
On the menu: grilled meat including
bulgogi, ₩28,000 per portion; rib of beef,
₩40,000; *naengmyeon* (cold noodles)
or *galbitang* (soup), ₩10,000. Quite
expensive but high quality.

🛒 SHOPPING

Shinsegae Main Department Store
신세계본점 – *2-5 Chungmuro 1-ga,
Jung-gu.* Ⓜ *Hoehyeon, line 4, exit 7.*
☎*(02)-1588-1234. http://department.
shinsegae.com. Open daily 10:30am–
8pm.* The oldest department store
in Korea, founded in 1930 and home
to luxurious boutiques featuring
international brands in a building dating
from the Japanese colonial period. The
annex, built in 2005, hosts a spacious,
more traditional department store.

**Myeong-dong Underground
Arcade** 명동 지하쇼핑센터 –
*On Namdaemunno Ave, which
separates Myeong-dong from the Lotte
Department Store.* Ⓜ *Euljiro 1-ga, line
2, exits 6/7.* This small shopping mall is
the place to come if you need glasses—
there are a number of opticians here.
The low cost of prescription glasses in
Korea makes a visit worthwhile, even
if only to purchase a back-up pair
(frame + lenses from ₩30,000, approx.
$30). Your sight will be checked free
of charge, and you can pick up your
glasses on the same or following day.

Namdaemun Market 남대문
시장 – *Namchang-dong, Jung-gu.*
Ⓜ *Hoehyeon, line 4, exits 6/7.
http://map.indm.net/map_eng.htm.
Open daily 24 hr some sections,
Mon–Sat 10am–8pm other sections.*
A major wholesale and retail market in
Seoul with over 10,000 stalls selling a
wide variety of products and organized
into themed sectors. These range
from clothes, shoes and household
linen, to dishes, sports equipment,
cameras, jewelry, souvenirs, and even
ginseng. The tourist office located
in the market will help you if you are
looking for specific items, or see the
online interactive map, address above.
The market is particularly popular with
tourists shopping for bargains or those
who just want to enjoy the atmosphere.
At night the main streets are packed
with thousands of open-air stalls selling
small snacks.

Namdaemun Market
© Chris Stowers/Apa Publications

Itaewon★
이태원

This legendary neighborhood has been welcoming strangers for years. During the 1960s the fields of pears that gave the place its name gave way to the nearby US military base and its thousands of GIs. The area became rather disreputable, with a slew of brothels and sleazy bars. Over time, however, Itaewon has rebuilt its image and become more genuinely cosmopolitan, embracing all the foreign communities in the city, as well as Koreans ready to slum it a little. Today there are bars and international restaurants, and the thriving nightlife attracts an especially interesting and colorful crowd on Saturday evenings. Situated below the southern slopes of Namsan and surrounded by several embassies and the homes of wealthy Koreans such as the Lee (Samsung) family on the one hand and, on the other, by the working-class neighborhood where immigrant workers from Asia and Africa live, Itaewon could almost be Seoul in microcosm. While exploring the area, be aware that pickpockets sometimes operate here, so be sure to stay alert and keep your belongings close by.

Michelin Map: Map p166

Info: Tourist Office 127 Itaewon-dong, Yongsan-gu. In the subway station in front of the ticket machines, Ⓜ Itaewon, line 6. ✆(02)-3785-2514. Open daily 9am–10pm.

Location: South of Namsan Park.

Kids: Shop for video games in Yongsan Electronic Market (see Addresses), try the hot spring water at Dragon Hill Spa (see p11), the view overlooking Seoul from the N Seoul Tower.

Don't Miss: The exceptional works in the National Museum of Korea and the Leeum Samsung Museum of Art.

VISIT
National Museum of Korea★★★ 국립중앙박물관
168-6 Yongsan-dong 6-ga, Yongsan-gu. Ⓜ Ichon, lines 1/4, exit 2. ✆(02)-2077-9000. www.museum.go.kr. Open Tue, Thu, Fri 9am–6pm, Wed and Sat 9am–9pm, Sun and public holidays 9am–7pm. No charge, except for special exhibitions. Guided tours in

National Museum of Korea ©KTO

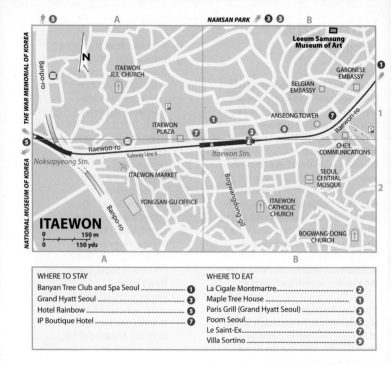

WHERE TO STAY	
Banyan Tree Club and Spa Seoul	❶
Grand Hyatt Seoul	❸
Hotel Rainbow	❺
IP Boutique Hotel	❼

WHERE TO EAT	
La Cigale Montmartre	❷
Maple Tree House	❶
Paris Grill (Grand Hyatt Seoul)	❸
Poom Seoul	❺
Le Saint-Ex	❼
Villa Sortino	❾

English (daily 10:30am–11:30am and 2:30pm–3:30pm); ℘*(02)-2077-9686. Audio guide ₩3,000.*

Housed since 2005 in an avant-garde building that aims to represent a modern interpretation of traditional Korean architecture but which is a very large solid affair, the spacious National Museum of Korea has a rich collection of 135,000 items, only a part of which can be displayed at any time in the museum's six galleries.

Two galleries trace Korea's history from the origins of Korean culture in the Paleolithic Era to modern times and the end of the Joseon dynasty. A third displays beautiful calligraphy and secular and religious paintings, while another houses Buddhist sculptures, lacquerware, works in wood and metal, and outstanding ceramics. The last two galleries cover the diversity of Asian cultures and contain donations made to the museum: some 800 Korean and foreign coins. Look out for the fine bronze Korean bodhisattva in meditative posture; a gold censer from the Baekje period; the unique, glitter-ing, golden crown of Silla; the exquisite celadon ware from the Goryeo period; and some remarkable paintings from the Joseon period.

🚶‍ The **Children's Museum** enables the very young to discover Korean arts and culture through play. The museum complex also includes a hall for temporary exhibitions.

Leeum Samsung Museum of Art★★ 리움삼성박물관

℘ *See Itaewon map. 747-18 Hannam-dong, Yongsan-gu.* Ⓜ *Hangangjin, line 6, exit 1.* ℘*(02)-2014-6900. www.leeum. org.* Ⓞ*Open Tue–Sun 10:30am–6pm. Closed 1 Jan and public holidays. Digital guide ₩2,000. ₩10,000.*

This is the most prestigious private museum in Korea. Its collections, including several National Treasures, are *(along with the Kansong Art Museum,* ℘*see p192)* among the richest in the country after those of the National Museum.

They come from the private collection of the founder of Samsung, Lee Byung-chul, hence the museum's name: Lee + (Muse)um: Leeum.

Opened in 2004, this museum replaced the old Hoam gallery in the city center. A completely original overall effect is achieved by the combination of three linked buildings, each designed by one of the world-famous architects Jean Nouvel, Mario Botta and Rem Koolhaas. One pavilion is dedicated to temporary exhibitions, the next to the superb collection of traditional Korean art and the final one to contemporary art.

There are displays on the history of modern Western art, but the real highlight is the Korean section containing many unique items. Start your visit on the top floor and the celadon gallery where the ceramics are beautifully displayed. Then walk down the Guggenheim-style spiral staircase to view the paintings, furniture, etc. The audio guides are very helpful.

Namsan Park★ 남산공원

See Seoul Map II. A city center park created around Namsan (South Mountain) accessible from several districts. The easiest way to climb the mountain is by cable car. San 1-19, Hoehyeon-dong 1-ga, Jung-gu. Myeong-dong, line 4, exit 4, 15min walk to Namsan Tunnel 3, left-hand sidewalk, then steps (or free elevator) up *to the cable car.* (02)-753-2403 (day)/ 757-1308 (night). www.cablecar.co.kr. *Open daily 10am–11pm. Round-trip ticket ₩7,500, single ticket ₩5,000. Or climb one of the many paths on foot, e.g. from the cable car entrance or behind the botanical garden near the Hyatt Hotel. Access routes are also at the National Theater and opposite the Hilton.*

Under the Joseon dynasty, Namsan marked the southern edge of the city and parts of the old fortress wall can still be seen on the mountain. As the metropolis grew, it crept around the mountain, which today stands in the urban center. The park has some fine views of Seoul and some lovely walks away from the hustle and bustle of the city. Climb to the top of Namsan to see **Bongsudae**, the stone beacons in which fires would be lit to send messages from mountain to mountain across the kingdom, warning of impending danger.

The ultimate goal of most walkers is the **N Seoul Tower**. (02)-3455-9277/88. www.nseoultower.co.kr. *Open daily 10am–11pm (Fri–Sat 10am–midnight).* ₩8,000. This **famous tower** was erected on the top of Namsan in 1969 for radio and TV transmissions. At a height

View of Seoul from Namsan Park

©Ch. Boisvieux/hemis.fr

Love locks (representing couples' undying love), N Seoul Tower

©Esther Arnett/Michelin

of 777ft/237m, it is visible from much of the city and is a useful landmark. An elevator takes you to the top. A popular place to dine or just have a drink, there is public access to several floors including observatories and the rotating restaurant **n GRILL**. The rooftop terrace is worth the trip for its magnificent view. It is a popular romantic spot for young couples who come here to make promises for the future. Finally, look out for the amazing Sky Restrooms on the second floor, with their panoramic view. The Botanical Garden at the southern end of the park has something of interest throughout the year.

The War Memorial of Korea
전쟁기념관

8 Yongsan-dong 1-ga, Yongsan-gu. Ⓜ *Samgakji, lines 4/6, exit 12.* ℰ*(02)-709-3139. www.warmemo.or.kr.* ◷*Open Tue–Sun 9am–6pm. No charge.* This large building incorporates a museum that explains the history of war in Korea and the role of the Korean Army and Korean expeditionary forces abroad, as well as offering detailed insights into the Korean War of the 1950s. On the grounds you can also view a wide range of military vehicles. A highly informative museum on a subject of great pertinence to a country that has endured so many conflicts.

ADDRESSES

🛏 STAY

🛏 **Hotel Rainbow** 레인보우호텔 – *98-2 Galwol-dong, Yongsan-gu.* Ⓜ *Namyeong, line 1, exit 1.* ℰ*(02)-792-9993. www.rainbowinseoul.com. 65 rm.* ₩*55,000/73,000.* ₩*6,000* ⊡ ✕. Although outside the tourist areas, this small hotel is in the center of the capital, close to a subway station. The chief attraction is the price of the rooms if you are on a tight budget.

🛏🛏🛏 **IP Boutique Hotel** 아이피 부띠끄 호텔 – *737-Hannam-dong, Yongsan-gu.* Ⓜ *Itaewon, line 6, exit 2.* ℰ*(02)-3702-8000. www.ipboutique hotel.com. 133 rm.* ₩*200,000/210,000.* ₩*18,000* ⊡ ✕. A new hotel with a fresh and original design in the central Itaewon district with its rich nightlife. Receive a 35 percent discount on accommodation for bookings by phone or online.

🛏🛏🛏🛏 **Banyan Tree Club and Spa Seoul** 반얀트리클럽스파 서울 – *San 5-5, Jangchung-dong 2-ga, Jung-gu.* Ⓜ *Dongguk University, line 3, exit 5 or* Ⓜ *Beotigogae, line 6, exit 1.* ℰ*(02)-2250-8000. www.banyantree.com/en/seoul. 50 rm, starting from* ₩*802,000* ✕. A luxurious hideaway, this hotel enjoys a superb view of Namsan and the

Hangang. Spacious rooms with sumptuous bathrooms, a design reflecting the four seasons and the five Asian elements: water, fire, metal, wood and earth. A fabulous pool, golf courses and tennis courts, and a superb spa.

⊖🛏🛏🛏 **Grand Hyatt Seoul** 그랜드 하얏트 서울 호텔 – *747-7 Hannam 2-dong, Yongsan-gu.* Ⓜ *Itaewon, line 6, exit 2 or* Ⓜ *Hangangjin, line 6, exit 1.* ✆ *(02)-797-1234. www.seoul.grand. hyatt.com. 600 rm. ₩200,000/320,000. ₩36,000* 🛌🍴🍸. A classic among the large Seoul hotels. The renovated rooms are preferable, as they are more stylish. The only downside is that it is a long way from any subway station.

Banyan Tree Spa
©Banyan Tree Club Seoul

🍴/EAT

⊖ **Maple Tree House** 단풍나무집 – *116-1 Itaewon-dong, Yongsan-gu. Just behind the Hamilton Hotel.* Ⓜ *Itaewon, line 6, exit 1.* ✆ *(02)-790-7977. Open daily 11:30am–10:30pm. Closed public holidays. ₩11,000/34,000.* The successful team led by Ho Lee Chow opened this small chain of Korean steakhouses that are especially popular with expatriates, serving good quality meat in a pleasant atmosphere.

⊖🛏🛏 **La Cigale Montmartre** 라 씨갈 몽마르트르 – *123-33 Itaewon-dong, Yongsan-gu.* Ⓜ *Itaewon, line 6, exit 2.* ✆ *(02)-796-1244. Open noon–1am. A la carte ₩10,000/30,000, fixed price menus ₩30,000/45,000.* The French chef in this restaurant offers Mediterranean and Parisian cuisine. The house specialty is mussels.

⊖🛏🛏 **Le Saint-Ex** 르 쌩떽스 – *119-28 Itaewon-dong, Yongsan-gu.* Ⓜ *Itaewon, line 6, exit 1.* ✆ *(02)-795-2465. Open noon–3pm, 6pm–midnight (last orders 9:30pm, Sat–Sun 10pm). ₩50,000, fixed price menus ₩16,000/24,000.* A French bistro, opened in 2000, with a French chef and staff. It has a friendly atmosphere and offers modern bistro cuisine with a specials board and a selection of French wines. Homemade desserts, French cheeses, brunch at weekends and vegetarian dishes. Good value for the money. There's a wine bar at night. Le Saint-Ex also hosts

exhibitions, and the owner is a real font of information on Korea.

⊖🛏🛏🛏 **Paris Grill** 파리스 그릴 – *Grand Hyatt Seoul Hotel, 747-7 Hannam 2-dong, Yongsan-gu.* Ⓜ *Itaewon, line 6, exit 2 or* Ⓜ *Hangangjin, line 6, exit 1.* ✆ *(02)-799-8161. www.seoul.grand. hyatt.com. Open daily noon–2:30pm, 6pm–10:30pm. ₩100,000, fixed price menus ₩90,000/₩110,000.* Classic European cuisine in a spacious and well-designed setting. The kitchen is open to the restaurant, from where there are especially beautiful views over the city. Reservation recommended. Ask for a table near the window.

⊖🛏🛏🛏 **Poom Seoul** 품 서울 – *Daewonjeongsa, 3rd floor, 358-17 Huam-dong, Yongsan-gu. Just in front of the Goethe Institute, on the Namsan coast road. Bus no. 402/405, Huam Spring stop (huamyaksuteo).* ✆ *(02)-777-9007. www.poomseoul.com. Open Mon–Sat noon–3pm, 6pm–10pm. Closed public holidays. Fixed price menus: lunch ₩50,000/70,000, dinner ₩100,000/250,000.* This Korean restaurant, opened by a renowned "food stylist," is one of the most sought-after for its setting, fine tableware and service, and also, obviously, for its food! It cannot claim to be the most innovative nor the most authentic, but the dishes are very tasty and appeal to Western palates. Reservations must be made at least 24hrs in advance.

Villa Sortino 빌라소르티노 –
12-12 Itaewon-dong, Yongsan-gu.
Ⓜ *Itaewon, line 6, exit 2.* ℘*(02)-553-9000. Open 11:30am–2:30am (Sun 10:30pm).* ₩*80,000/100,000.* Traditional Italian cuisine (and flavors) of a semi-gourmet standard. The atmosphere is friendly and the sommelier will guide you through his impressive selection of Italian wines (*from* ₩*60,000*).

🚋 TAKING A BREAK

Passion 5 패션파이브 –
729-74 Hannam-dong, Yongsan-gu.
Ⓜ *Hangangjin, line 6, exit 3.*
℘*(02)-2071-9505.* A luxurious, carefully designed tearoom. The building's architecture and dazzling array of pastries and sweets make it a good place for a mid-morning or afternoon break, even if prices are on the steep side.

🍸 BARS

B1 비원 – *119-7 Itaewon-dong, Yongsan-gu.* Ⓜ *Itaewon, line 6, exit 1.* ℘*(02)-749-6164. Open 6pm–3am (Fri and Sat 5am). Admission Thu–Sat after midnight* ₩*10,000. Cocktails* ₩*6,000/10,000.* The fashionable bar/loungé/club of recent years. Rather crowded at weekends, it is calmer and more pleasant for a drink during the week. An international clientele.

Macaroni Market 마카로니마켓 –
737-50 Hannam-dong, Yongsan-gu.
Ⓜ *Itaewon, line 6, exit 2.* ℘*(02)-749-9181. Restaurant opens 11am–1am, club 6pm–2am. Restaurant* ₩*13,500/55,000.* This Italian restaurant has a small club, **Function**, which is particularly popular with expatriates, and the restaurant also doubles as a bar. Expect a slightly more upmarket crowd than B1.

Naos Nova 나오스노바 – *448-120 Huam-dong, Yongsan-gu. On the Namsan coast road, 5min from the Hilton Hotel. Bus no. 401/604 and 7.* ℘*(02)-754-2202. www.naosnova.net. Open daily noon–1am. Closed public holidays. Fixed price menus: lunch* ₩*32,000/68000, dinner* ₩*90,000/130,000. Wine from* ₩*45,000, cocktails* ₩*23,000/27,000.* A good bar-restaurant serving 50 types of champagne, 40 wines and more.

🛒 SHOPPING

Eden Pottery 에덴포트리 –
168-17 Itaewon-dong, Yongsan-gu.
Ⓜ *Itaewon, line 6, exit 1.* ℘*(02)-793-0828. Open daily 9:30am–7:30pm. Closed 1st & 4th Wed of the month.* A good store selling Korean pottery, located in the building's basement. There's a wide choice of celadon ware and other pieces in the style of the Joseon dynasty, as well as more contemporary designs.

Hamilton Shirts 해밀턴셔츠 –
128-13 Itaewon-dong, Yongsan-gu.
Ⓜ *Itaewon, line 6, exit 4.* ℘*(02)-798-5693. www.hs76.com. Open daily 10am–7:30pm.* This shop is owned by a tailor with a longstanding reputation for design and made-to-measure clothes: shirts (*from* ₩*30,000*) and suits (*around* ₩*500,000*). There is a very good choice of fabrics and the clothes will be completed within a week.

Yongsan Electronic Market 용산전자상가 – *Behind Yongsan Station.* Ⓜ *Yongsan, line 1, exit 2. Open daily 10am–7:30pm, depending on the stores. Open in part on 1st & 3rd Sun of the month.* In an area full of shops selling electronic goods, you will find computers and other computer products, telephones, televisions, DVD players, stereos, etc. at the market, all at very good prices. See, for example, the shopping center **Etland** 용산전자랜드 (℘*(02)-707-4700, www.i-etland.co.kr*) close by.

Apgujeong★
압구정

This district, which remained fairly undeveloped until the 1970s, has since become the chic and expensive part of the city. Seoul's well-heeled citizens come here to shop in its luxury boutiques and dine in its smart restaurants and cafés, or pay a discreet visit to one of the numerous cosmetic surgery clinics. To the untrained eye, there's nothing special about the appearance of the apartments and other buildings to distinguish them from those in the rest of the city, but walking around Apgujeong's streets, especially at night, it's clear that Seoul's affluent, fashionable set, and perhaps even the odd Korean celebrity, are close at hand. Shoppers can enjoy browsing the luxury shops, before sampling some of the fine food on offer in one of the excellent local restaurants or a cocktail in a stylish bar. In recent years, several well-respected galleries have also opened here, adding a cultural dimension to the area.

VISIT
Garosu-gil★ 가로수길
See Apgujeong map.
Sinsa-dong, Gangnam-gu. Ⓜ *Sinsa, line 3, exit 8. Walk straight ahead on leaving the subway and turn left after 200yds.*

- **Michelin Map:** Map p173
- **Location:** Southeast of the Hangang and Seoul's historic center. Around Dosan Park.
- **Don't Miss:** Horim Art Center, the upmarket district of Cheongdam-dong, a stroll along fashionable Garosu-gil.

Garosu-gil ("tree-lined street") is Seoul's new fashionable area for the smart young crowd. It's a very pleasant neighborhood for a drink or a snack—try an afternoon coffee and pastry—before looking round the shops. However, the main show is on the street itself—this exclusive road is a great place for people-watching. If you have time, try exploring some of the adjacent streets too.

Art galleries in the Dosan Park neighborhood★
See Apgujeong map.
This small park is named after Ahn Chang-ho, a Korean patriot killed by the Japanese occupiers, and contains his tomb. The park may only be a pass-through to enjoy the surrounding streets, which are full of fusion restaurants, bars, cafés and galleries.

Dosan Park

Down the Centuries

A Great Location

In the center of the Korean Peninsula, on a wide navigable river, not far from the Yellow Sea, bordered by a fertile plain to the south and protected by a mountain range to the north, Seoul's geographical location was a major factor in its choice as the country's capital. The first communities founded settlements here notably in the Neolithic Era (after 8000–7000 BC) (&see *Amsa-dong p 212*), and around 1300 BC small city states began to establish themselves on the slopes of the mountains.

There are traces of one such city-state still to be found on the south bank of the Hangang (the modern-day district of Songpa), established at the time of the Three Kingdoms and thought to have been the first capital of the kingdom of Baekje (18 BC), originally called **Wiryeseong,** then renamed **Hanseong** when the Baekje were at their most powerful. However, under pressure from neighboring kingdoms, the Baekje moved to present-day Gongju (475) and then to Buyeo (538), abandoning Hanseong to invaders. The Hangang basin became a battlefield for several centuries; the Goguryeo and Silla tenuously occupied the area, particularly north of the Han, building forts to guard the hinterland.

Once the country was "unified," the ancient city was largely abandoned, but the region, which was of strategic importance, remained occupied. The Goryeo dynasty (918–1392) renamed Hanseong **Yangju** and then made it their capital of the South. In 1067 they changed the name again, to **Namgyeong** ("Southern Capital"). In 1308, it was demoted to the rank of "Prefecture" (*Hanyang-bu*), but it remained a royal city and hunting ground. From the 12C the Goryeo kings had considered moving their capital from Gaegyeong (Kaesong, North Korea) to the southern city, given that the site was deemed so auspicious. The proposed move continued to be an issue throughout the 14C and eventually became a contributing factor in the downfall of the Goryeo dynasty.

A Fresh Start

Wanting to give his new dynasty a fresh start, the natural choice of capital for the founder of the Joseon kingdom (1392–1910), Taejo Yi Seong-gye, was on the Hangang. The first buildings were constructed: Gyeongbokgung, the royal palace; **Sajikdan**, the altar where "soil and grain" ceremonies were performed; Seonggyungwan, the Confucian Academy; Jongmyo, the royal family's ancestral shrine; and the fortress wall. In late 1395 the court moved to the new city **Hanseong** (or **Seoul**, which means "capital" in Korean) and remained there for the next 515 years. Seoul's layout was inspired by the great cities of Tang China but was extensively adapted to the location. Four main gates and four ancillary gates gave access to the city that grew behind the fortress wall, around the four mountains that are in the center of modern-day Seoul.

In the early 20C, the Japanese occupiers renamed the city (**Gyeongseong** in Korean) but retained it as the capital. They changed its face radically, however, by constructing new buildings and completing the modernization that had begun in the late 19C. The arrival of a tram system, a railway station and new markets, and the swift development of the surrounding districts brought the city into the 20C rather abruptly, upsetting its former urban balance. The Korean War and the economic development from the 1970s onward have also had a major effect on the city (&see pp150–151).

| OKSU-DONG | A | B |

APGUJEONG

0   400 m
0   400 yds

WHERE TO STAY

Hotel Tea Tree and Co .... ❶
Imperial Palace Hotel .... ❸

WHERE TO EAT

Gorilla in the Kitchen .... ❶
Jung Sik Dang .... ❸
Palais de Gaumont .... ❺
Samwon Garden .... ❼
Wooriga .... ❾

Platoon Kunsthalle
플래툰쿤스트할레

97-22 Nonhyeon-dong, Gangnam-gu. Ⓜ *Hak-dong, line 7, exit 10. 10min walk to Dosan Park or take a taxi; or* Ⓜ *Apgujeong, line 3, exit 3, then bus no. 301/361/472, Youngdong High School stop.* ☎ *(02)-3447-1191/7. www.kunsthalle.com.* ◷ *Open Mon– Sat 11am–midnight.*

This unique cultural complex is the result of a collaboration between Germany and Korea. The building is made of 28 cargo containers, inside which a café, rooftop bar, art gallery, shop and the studios of resident artists all serve to create a hip cutting-edge buzz of the kind associated with street and contemporary art. The Kunsthalle regularly hosts evenings with excellent DJs (*Thu*

Platoon Kunsthalle

©Platoon Kunsthalle

and Fri), plus events such as flea markets with an auction on the first Saturday of the month (8pm–midnight), etc. Check the website or subscribe to their email newsletter for current happenings.

Atelier Hermès Maison Hermès★ 메종에르메스

630-22 Sinsa-dong, Gangnam-gu. On the left heading toward Dosan Park after the Hak-dong intersection. M Sinsa, line 3, exit 2, then bus no. 145/4212, Horim Art Center stop. ☏(02)-544-7722. ⏰Open Thu–Tue 11am–8pm. No charge.
A gallery exhibiting contemporary art is on the third floor of this branch of the famous luxury Parisian fashion house. Once a year it also holds an exhibition of the work of the three Korean artists nominated for the Missulsang Prize (awarded by the Fondation Hermès). There is a book café in the basement.

Horim Art Center 호림아트센터

135-897 Buk 33-gil 6, Dosandaero Gangnam-gu. M Sinsa, line 3, exit 2, then bus no. 145/4212, Horim Art Center stop. ☏(02)-541-3525. www.horimartcenter.org. ⏰Open Tue–Sun 10:30am–6pm (Wed 8pm). Closed public holidays. ₩8,000.
This cultural complex, in a building that is a work of contemporary art in itself, includes a café, **Artisée**, an art gallery, a restaurant and an excellent museum of Korean ceramics with permanent and temporary exhibitions, whose collections of celadon and pottery could justifiably claim to rival those of Leeum Museum. The exhibition room of Seoul Auction, the Pyeongchang-dong auction house, is located in the same complex.

313 Art Project 313아트프로젝트

313 Dosandaero, Sinsa-dong, Gangnam-gu. M Sinsa, line 3, exit 2, then bus no. 145/4212, Horim Art Center stop. ☏(02)-3446-3137. ⏰Open Mon 2pm–6pm, Tue–Sat 11am–6pm. Closed Sun and public holidays. No charge.
A beautiful contemporary art gallery opposite Horim Art Center, in a simple and elegant style.

ADDRESSES

🏨 STAY

🛏🛏 Hotel Tea Tree and Co 호텔 티트리앤코 – *535-12 Sinsa-dong, Gangnam-gu. M Sinsa, line 3, exit 8. ☏(02)-542-9954. www.teatreehotel.com. 38 rm. ₩100,000/150,000 🛏.* A small hotel combining an excellent value for the money with an interesting location, right next to Garosu-gil with its smart shops and cafés. The rooms are modern; ask for one with a terrace, as these have more light. This is one of the few "boutique hotels" in Seoul.

🛏🛏🛏🛏 Imperial Palace Hotel 임페리얼팰리스호텔 – *248-7 Nonhyeon-dong, Gangnam-gu. M Hak-dong, exit 1 or M Gangnam-gu Office, line 7, exit 2. ☏(02)-3440-8000. www.imperialpalace.co.kr. 405 rm. ₩300,000/360,000. ₩29,000 🛏 🍴.* An upmarket hotel with extravagant decor, defined as "the elegance of antique European style." The Imperial Palace Hotel's aim is to appeal to the "artistic feeling" of its guests, in addition to offering comfortable accommodations and excellent service. Try the spa rooms, which are ideal for rejuvenating the body after a long day of sightseeing.

🍴 EAT

🍽 Samwon Garden 삼원가든 – *623-5 Sinsa-dong, Gangnam-gu. M Apgujeong, line 3, exit 2. On leaving the subway, walk toward Cheongdam-dong, then turn into Seongsu Bridge Ave. Samwon Garden is approx. 500yds on the right. ☏(02)-548-3030. www.samwongarden.com. A la carte ₩7,000/59,000, fixed price menus ₩31,000/51,000.* The best-known restaurant for Korean-style grilled meat south of the river. A vast establishment (with space for 1,200 diners!) that has nonetheless managed to maintain its high quality selections. Meat portions per person ₩24,000/54,000. Reservations are recommended.

🍽🍽 Gorilla in the Kitchen 고릴라인더키친 – *650 Sinsa-dong, Gangnam-gu, close to Dosan Park. M Apgujeong, line 3, exit 3. ☏(02)-3442*

-1688/4688. www.gorillakitchen.co.kr. Open daily 11am–10pm, bar open 11am–midnight. A la carte ₩50,000, fixed price menus ₩45,000/120,000. High quality organic food is served at this fashionable health-food restaurant, whose motto is: "No cream, no fat, no worries." Located on a smart street beside Dosan Park, you can eat or have a drink on its pleasant terrace. It was opened by the famous actor Bae Yong-jun (⌚*see box p238*).

Jung Sik Dang 정식당 – *Acros Bldg, 3rd Floor, 649-7 Sinsa-dong, Gangnam-gu. Ⓜ Apgujeong, line 3, exit 2. ✆(02)-517-4654. www.jung sikdang.com. Open daily: Mon–Sat noon–3:30pm (last orders 2pm), 6pm–10:30pm (last orders 8:30pm); Sun noon–4pm (last orders 2pm). Closed public holidays. Fixed price menus: lunch ₩40,000, dinner ₩120,000.* Offering Korean nouvelle cuisine of a high standard, Jung Sik Dang has attracted a lot of attention since opening in 2009. With delicious food, very well presented, and excellent service, it's a good place for lunch, when the fixed price menu is a great value for the money.

Palais de Gaumont 118 팔레드 고몽 – *10 Cheongdam-dong, Gangnam-gu, in a street behind the Prada store, on the avenue leading from the Galleria Dept. Store. Ⓜ Apgujeong, line 3, exit 1. ✆(02)-546-8877. http://stomm79.maru.net/gaumont/. Open daily 6pm–10pm. Fixed price menus ₩115,000/150,000.* In its heyday this French restaurant was a pioneer of European haute cuisine and the best restaurant in Seoul. It remains a luxurious, elegant venue with food to match. Dinner only.

Wooriga 우리가 – *Hyoyeong Bldg, 2nd Floor, 631-3 Sinsa-dong, Gangnam-gu, in a street beside Dosan Park. Ⓜ Apgujeong, line 3, exit 3. ✆(02)-3442-2288. Open Mon–Sat noon–3pm, 5pm–10pm. Closed public holidays. Fixed price menus: lunch ₩30,000, dinner ₩150,000. Reservations suggested.* Wooriga serves traditional but sophisticated Korean food. Everything is delicious and beautifully produced, but the setting is unfortunately rather impersonal.

🍴 TAKING A BREAK

Coffee Smith 커피스미스 – *536-12 Sinsa-dong, Gangnam-gu. Ⓜ Sinsa, line 3, exit 8. ✆(02)-3445-3372. Open daily 9am–2am (Sat–Sun 3am). ₩5,000/10,000.* Large crowds flock to this smart café. Young people gather to share coffee and desserts and enjoy the relaxed atmosphere. It's a good place to stop and take in the neighborhood atmosphere.

Deux Crèmes 두 크렘 – *533-11 Sinsa-dong, Gangnam-gu. Ⓜ Sinsa, line 3, exit 8. ✆(02)-545-7931. Open daily 10am–midnight. ₩8,000/W10,000.* On the trendy street of Garosu-gil, this tearoom is comfortable and has a "designer" look with wooden-clad floor and walls and smart furniture. You can enjoy a piece of homemade cake here, accompanied by tea or coffee. The locaiton also doubles as a wine bar.

Deux Cremes
©KTO

🍸 BARS

Goshen 고센 – *88-23 Cheongdam-dong, Gangnam-gu. Ⓜ Gangnam-gu Office, line 7, exit 4. ✆(02)-515-1863. www.i-goshen.com. Open daily 11am–6am.* Whatever time of day you visit— the afternoon, evening or even first thing in the morning—this is a pleasant place to enjoy a drink, although the prices are a bit high thanks to the affluence of the clientele from Cheongdam-dong. The terrace is open in summer.

Soulsome 소울 썸 – *99-3 Cheongdam-dong, Gangnam-gu, in the basement. Ⓜ Gangnam-gu Office, line 7, exit 4.*

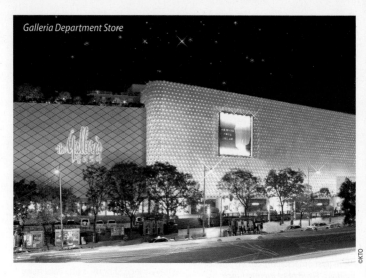

Galleria Department Store

©KTO

(02)-542-5667. Open daily 7pm–2am (later Sat–Sun). This fashionable lounge bar is the neighborhood's prime night-time venue. Opened by "party animal" DJ Jonwook, the music is hip, the setting trendy and the atmosphere guaranteed.

🛒 SHOPPING

Galleria Department Store
갤러리아백화점 *– 494 Apgujeong-dong, Gangnam-gu.* Ⓜ *Apgujeong, line 3, exit 1.* *(02)-3449-4114. Open daily 10:30am–8pm (Fri–Sun west bldg until 8:30pm).* There are two parts to this branch of the department store franchise: Luxury Hall East, which sells only premium brands, and Luxury Hall West, which is just a little less upscale. The facade, made up of 4,330 glass discs, is dazzling at night and reflects the natural light during the day. Both stores are popular with their well-heeled clientele.
⊙ **Note:** *They are some distance from the subway.*

Lee Young-hee 이영희 *– 665-5 Sinsa-dong, Gangnam-gu.* Ⓜ *Gangnam-gu Office, line 7, exit 4.* *(02)-547-0630. Open Mon–Sat 11am–6pm (Sat 3pm).* Lee Young-hee is the high priestess of *hanbok* haute couture. She sells tasteful, elegant "modern *hanbok*" adapted to contemporary tastes, with a hint of Western influence. To buy a customized garment, make an appointment in advance.

Seoul Auction (The Collection)
서울 옥션 *– 135-897 Buk 33-gil 6, Dosandaero, Gangnam-gu.* Ⓜ *Gangnam-gu Office, line7, exit 4.* *(02)-542-2412. www.seoulauction.com. Open daily 9:30am–9pm during exhibitions. No charge.* This auction room occupies the ground floor of the Horim Art Center. There is a room where you can view the items being offered for sale (generally a week later) at its Pyeongchang-dong headquarters (⏲*see website*). Depending on what is to go in the sale (Korean antiques and modern art regularly feature), viewing the lots is usually an interesting experience.

Teheranno
테헤란로

A brand-new neighborhood built from scratch by developers and planners in the 1970s, Teheranno is laid out on a grid system similar to many North American cities. As Seoul's financial and business district—there is a huge fair and convention center—the cost of real estate makes it one of the world's most expensive places per square inch. The only real attractions for the (non-business) traveler are the cultural park, the site of the royal tombs of Seonjeongneung and Bongeunsa, the temple that was originally located in open country, plus the huge underground COEX shopping mall.

VISIT

Samneung Park★ 삼릉공원 and Seonjeongneung Royal Tombs 선정릉

See Teheranno map. 47 Gil 5 Seonneungro-dong, Gangnam-gu. Ⓜ *Seolleung, line 2, exit 8.* ℘*(02)-568-1291. http://seonjeong.cha.go.kr.* Ⓒ*Open Tue–Sun, Mar–Oct 6am–9pm, Nov–Feb 6:30am–9pm.* ₩*1,000.*
The setting for the three royal tombs of the Joseon kings, known collectively as Seonjeongneung, is the peaceful, leafy

- Ⓑ **Michelin Map:** Map p178
- Ⓘ **Info:** Tourist Office 159 Samseong-dong, Gangnam-gu. East Gate out of the COEX Exhibition Center, opposite Shinhan Bank. Ⓜ Samseong, line 2, exits 5/6. ℘(02)-538-0264. Open daily, Mon–Sat 8:30am–6pm, Sun 9:30am–6pm.
- Ⓑ **Location:** South of the Hangang, around the COEX Tower and Teheran-ro.
- Ⓐ **Kids:** Visit the COEX Aquarium with its amazing stock of over 40,000 marine plants and animals.
- Ⓒ **Timing:** Exploring Samneung Park and Bongeunsa generally takes around one hour per site, but dedicated shoppers can soon find time slipping away if they get lost in the maze of the COEX Mall. Otherwise, Teheranno is essentially a business district.
- Ⓓ **Don't Miss:** The royal tombs of Seonjeongneung (listed by UNESCO), Bongeunsa, the COEX Mall shopping center.

Seonjeongneung royal tombs

©KTO

WHERE TO STAY		
Grand InterContinental Seoul		❶
Hotel Hawaii		❸
Ibis Ambassador Seoul		❺
Park Hyatt Seoul		❼

WHERE TO EAT		
Chaegeundam		❶
Cornerstone (Park Hyatt Seoul)		❸
Table 34 (Grand InterContinental Seoul)		❺

Samneung Park, which is in stark contrast to the surrounding urban jungle of concrete, asphalt and steel. After visiting the buildings where the funeral rites were conducted, head to the northwest part of the park to see **Seolleung**, the **tomb of King Seong-jong** (1457–94), who played a key role in establishing Confucianism in the kingdom. He sought to achieve a balance between the power of court officials and the educated elite, and supported the publication of numerous important works. His third queen, Jeonghyeon, is buried beside him on a hill to the northeast. Her tomb is a more humble affair. Their son, who became King **Jungjong** (1488–1544), also tried (unsuccessfully) to stabilize the system and mitigate the power of royal officials over the provincial scholars. He was initially buried in Gyeonggi-do, but his queen, Munjeong, decided to move his grave here in 1562 in the hope of being laid to rest alongside her husband. Unfortunately, it was not possible, and Jungjong is one of three Joseon kings buried apart from their wives. His tomb (Jeongneung) is similar in structure to those of his immediate ancestors, with large statues standing guard nearby. The 40 tombs of the Joseon dynasty (scattered over 18 locations) are collectively listed as a UNESCO World Heritage Site.

Bongeunsa★ 봉은사 (Bongeun Temple)

🕭See Teheranno map.
73 Samseong-dong, Gangnam-gu.
Ⓜ *Samseong, line 2, exit 6. On leaving the subway, walk straight ahead and take the next main road on the left (Bongeunsa-ro).* 📞*(02)-3218-4895. www.bongeun.org. No charge.*

This temple was founded by the monk Yeonhu in 794 during the Silla era, not far from its current location. It was moved to the slopes of Mount Sudo in 1562. Destroyed, rebuilt and restored many times, a number of its pavilions were added fairly recently.

The main center of the *Seon* (Zen) branch of Korean Buddhism between the 16C and 19C, it is a good example both of a traditional temple and of Buddhist culture within the confines of the capital. A service run by volunteers *(on the left as you enter)* explains about Buddhism and helps guide your visit around the site. The guides also provide information on the activities you can attend that offer a glimpse into temple life *(Thu 2pm–4pm, ₩10,000)*, including meditation, the tea ceremony and 24-hour retreats during which you can refocus, reflect and rejuvenate. You may also attend services at 4am, 10am and 6pm *(Oct–Feb)* or 7pm *(Mar–Sept)*.

Bangeunsa
©Chris Stowers/Apa Publications

👥 COEX Aquarium
근멕스아쿠아리움
♿ *See Teheranno map. In the COEX Mall, 159 Samseong-dong, Gangnam-gu.* Ⓜ *Samseong, line 2, exits 5/6.* ☎*(02)-6002-6200. www.coexaqua.co.kr.* 🕐*Open daily 10am–8pm. ₩17,500.*
Find out what lies below the surface of Korea's mountain streams, lakes and deepest oceans. This fabulous aquarium has 40,000 plants and 650 species of marine animals. Walk the length of the 236ft/72m tunnel, and feel as if you are in the middle of the ocean. It is not just children who will enjoy the visit—both young and old will find plenty of interesting sights.

ADDRESSES

🏨 STAY

🛏 **Hotel Hawaii** 하와이호텔 – *77-9 Samseong-dong, Gangnam-gu.* Ⓜ *Samseong, line 2, exit 6.* ☎*(02)-547-9663. www.hotelhawaii.co.kr. 36 rm. ₩70,000/120,000. ₩3,000* 🍴. A small hotel conveniently located next to the COEX Mall and Bongeun Temple. Simple but clean rooms. The subway is just 15min away. A good option for those on tight budgets.

🛏🍴 **Ibis Ambassador Seoul** 이비스 앰버서더서울 호텔 – *893-1 Daechi-dong, Gangnam-gu.* Ⓜ *Seolleung, line 2, exit 1 or* Ⓜ *Samseong, line 2, exit 4.* ☎*(02)-3454-1101. www.ibis.ambatel.com. 317 rm. ₩105,000/148,000. ₩17,500* 🍴 🍽. This business hotel offers moderate prices in an expensive part of the capital. The rooms are simple but functional, and there is a sauna with hot baths. Another good option for those on limited budgets. A free shuttle bus will take you to CALT, the city center airport bus terminal *(♿see Seoul Useful Information p 113)*.

🛏🍴🍽 **Grand InterContinental Seoul** 코엑스인터컨티넨탈 호텔 – *521 Teheran-no, Gangnam-gu.* Ⓜ *Samseong, line 2, exit 5.* ☎*(02)-555-5656. www.seoul.intercontinental.com. 518 rm, starting from ₩230,000. ₩30,000* 🍴 🍽. This is ideal accommodation for both business travelers and tourists, next to the Korean World Trade Center and two minutes from the vast COEX Mall. The hotel offers the full range of services that you would expect from a luxury establishment, with spacious, pleasant rooms and a spa center, the Metropolitan Fitness Club. The **InterContinental Seoul COEX**, which shares the same website, is located at the other end of the block. Clients can use the facilities of both establishments.

🛏🍴🍽🍽 **Park Hyatt Seoul** 파크 하얏트 호텔 – *995-14 Daechi 3-dong, Gangnam-gu.* Ⓜ *Samseong, line 2, exit 1.* ☎*(02)-2016-1234. www.seoul.park.hyatt.com. 185 rm. ₩255,000/380,000. ₩32,000* 🍴 🍽. A luxury hotel in the heart of the business district. The well-designed rooms have large picture windows, and the bathrooms have a view too. Enjoy the spa and 6,135sq ft/570sq m fitness center on the top floor. The pool offers more fabulous views over the city.

℉/EAT

😋😋 **Chaegeundam** 채근담 – *Basement of the Ildong Bldg, 983 Daechi-dong, Gangnam-gu.* Ⓜ *Samseong, line 2, exit 3. On leaving the subway walk straight ahead for about a third of a mile (600m), then take the 2nd right.* ✆*(02)-555-9173. www.chaegundaam.com. Open daily noon–2:30pm, 6pm–8:30pm (last orders). Fixed price menus: lunch* ₩*19,000, dinner* ₩*62,000.* An excellent restaurant with its roots in vegetarianism, although it has become famous for the barbecued meat that it also serves.

😋😋😋 **Table 34** 테이블 34 – *InterContinental Seoul COEX, 34th Floor, 521 Teheran-no, Gangnam-gu.* Ⓜ *Samseong, line 2, exit 5.* ✆*(02)-559-7631. www.seoul.intercontinental.com. Open Mon–Fri noon–2:30pm, 6pm–10pm. A la carte* ₩*80,000/100,000, fixed price menus: lunch* ₩*45,000/55,000, dinner* ₩*90,000/130,000.* Excellent French cuisine and impeccable service with stunning views of the surrounding neighborhoods. Thanks to a spacious layout, you won't feel crowded, while the private rooms make it a popular place for business meetings and romantic meals. A fine wine list.

😋😋😋😋 **Cornerstone** 파크 하얏트 코너스톤 – *Park Hyatt Seoul, 995-14 Daechi 3-dong, Gangnam-gu.* Ⓜ *Samseong, line 2, exit 1.* ✆*(02)-2016-1220. www.seoul.park.hyatt.com. Open daily for breakfast 6:30am–10:30am, lunch 11:30am–2:30pm, dinner 6pm–10pm, brunch (Sat–Sun and public holidays) 11am–3pm.* ₩*75,500/105,000.* The Park Hyatt has several international restaurants but brunch at the Cornerstone is especially popular at weekends, for those who can afford it! Plate service and buffet, central grill. Fixed price menu with champagne ₩105,000.

🛒 SHOPPING

Association for Preservation of Important Intangible Cultural Properties 중요무형문화재 보존회 – *112-2 Samsung-dong, Gangnam-gu.* Ⓜ *Samseong, line 2, exit 4.* ✆*(02)-3453-1685. Open Mon–Sat 9am–6pm. Closed public holidays.* Next to the Ramada Hotel, this store sells only the work of craftsmen who have been named Living National Treasures. The work is on display in two rooms on either side of the entrance; you'll find ceramics, wooden and metal items, musical instruments, furniture, seals, jewelry, etc.

COEX Mall 코엑스몰 – *159 Samseong-dong, Gangnam-gu.* Ⓜ *Samseong, line 2, exits 5/6.* ✆*(02)-6000-0114. www.coexmall.com. Open daily 10am–10pm.* This is the largest underground mall in Asia. An endless maze of shops awaits you, selling everything from clothing and fashion accessories to cosmetics and sporting goods. There are also restaurants and cinemas. A very popular place for young people to meet and shop.

AK Duty Free 에이케이면세점 – *524 Bongeunsaro, Gangnam-gu, 1st & 2nd Lower Ground Floors of the InterContinental COEX Hotel.* Ⓜ *Samseong, line 2, exits 5/6.* ✆*(02)-3484-9600. Open daily 10am–9pm (Fri 9:30pm).* You can buy duty-free luxury goods here, in this store laid out over two floors.

Cheonggyecheon Dongdaemun★
청계천-동대문

Gradually, the factories that fuelled the 1970s "Made in Korea" era began to close down when this working-class area slipped into recession. The industrial buildings were replaced by the various markets that now make up the vast Dongdaemun Market area, which extends along the newly restored Cheonggyecheon (Cheonggye Stream). Yet this lively district has held on to its unique character despite the rapid changes that modernization has brought about, and some cultural sites remain. There are plenty of places to eat and drink, and you can buy everything you could possibly want, if you know where to look. The stores and stalls are grouped according to their specialty, selling everything from electrical goods to toys, herbs and fabrics.

🐾 WALKING TOUR

DONGDAEMUN MARKET
동대문시장

▶ *Allow around 3hr, or 2hr if you end the tour at Dongdaemun. Start at* Ⓜ *Sindang, lines 2/6, exits 1/2.*

- 🚹 **Michelin Map:** p182
- 🚩 **Info:** Tourist Office 18-21 Euljiro 6-ga, Jongno-gu, opposite Dongdaemun History & Culture Park. Ⓜ Dongdaemun History & Culture Park, lines 2/4/5, exit 14. 📞 (02)-2236-9135. Open 9am–10pm.
- ▶ **Location:** Around Dongdaemun Market, to the east of the historic part of the city.
- 🕐 **Timing:** The antiques shops are generally closed on Sundays. Malls such as Migliore and the Doota stay open until the early hours.
- 😋 **Don't Miss:** The markets— a mix of old and new Korea—and a snack at an open-air food stall, the exotic herbs and plants at Gyeongdong Oriental Medicine Market, Janganpyeong Antiques Market and the flea markets, late-night shopping complexes such as Doota Mall.

Cultural stop-offs are at the Dongmyo religious shrine and Dongdaemun itself (one of the old city gates). The complete tour takes in several of the markets,

Dongdaemun

©KTO

181

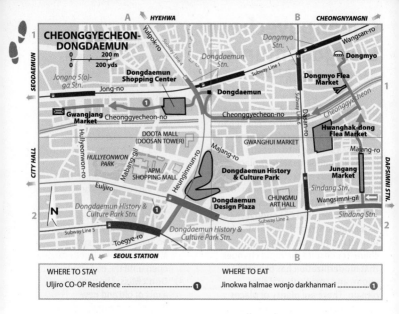

WHERE TO STAY	WHERE TO EAT
Uljiro CO-OP Residence .... ❶	Jinokwa halmae wonjo darkhanmari .... ❶

and you can mingle with the locals and enjoy a specialty snack or dinner, in a laid-back, down-to-earth atmosphere. Avoid Sundays when most shops and stalls are closed, except around Dongmyo where things are still usually quite lively.

If your shopping list is a long one, pop into a tourist office for a full run-down of the various markets and the goods they sell. For the covered flea market, head farther east in the direction of the antiques district and the outlying market selling traditional medicines. South of the Cheonggyecheon are large complexes such as the Doota Fashion Mall (Doosan Tower) and the cultural Dongdaemun Design Plaza and Park.

The walking tour begins with the **small food market of Jungang** (see *Cheonggyecheon – Dongdaemun map above*), where you instantly enter a world filled with all the colors, sounds and smells of Northeast Asia. Seasonal fruits and vegetables are sold here in a lively, down-to-earth atmosphere.

▷ *Leaving Jungang Market through the exit on the opposite side from the entrance, you will reach an intersection.*

At the end of the street in front of you, you will see the new Lotte Castle Tower residential buildings, but take the small alley running parallel, which veers off to the left in front of the entrance to some stairs leading underground.

This small alley is home to a street market where time seems to have stood still. There are stores selling eggs, *tteok* (rice cakes), chili powder and coffee. You can also buy small items of traditional furniture or shop at an oriental pharmacy and a hardware store packed so full that you can hardly get through the door. At the end of the street are stalls specializing in (very spicy) chicken legs.

▷ *Continue straight ahead. To the right, close to the luxury apartments of the Lotte Castle Tower, are stalls selling tripe cooked in the local style.*

The few traditional houses that remain give an idea of what this area would have been like until fairly recently. On the left, **Hwanghak-dong Flea Market** (see *Cheonggyecheon – Dongdaemun map*) sells second-hand electronic equipment, engines and tools. There's not much to interest the average foreign visitor here, except perhaps for the alley that heads off to the left, before a pharmacy, where a dozen or so dusty antiques stores sometimes do good business.

▶ *In front of Lotte Castle, cross Cheonggyecheon (Cheonggye Stream) via the bridge Yeongdongyo and continue straight toward the shrine Dongmyo and the nearby flea market.*

Dongmyo 동묘 ("Eastern Shrine")

See Cheonggyecheon – Dongdaemun map. Ⓜ *Dongmyo, lines 1/6, exit 3.*

The shrine was built in 1601 in honor of the Chinese General Gwan Yu (also Guang Yu, 160–219) of the late Han dynasty. Deified as a war god soon after his death, he is also the hero of the 14C Korean novel *Romance of the Three Kingdoms*. After the Japanese invasions of 1592–98, the emperor of China, who sent troops to aid Korea, asked for altars to be erected in memory of this illustrious general-god who had played a part in their victory.

Of the five shrines to Gwan Yu that were built in Seoul at public expense, three remain, and Dongmyo is the largest. Sacrifices were made regularly, and today shamans still come here to worship.

The building incorporates elements of Chinese architecture such as the gray brick wall. You can also see various depictions of Gwan Yu—a red statue representing the historical figure and a white statue portraying the general as a divinity—as well as statues of his officers and former cult objects (weapons). ⊙ *On a practical note, the site has Western toilet facilities.*

Dongmyo Flea Market 동묘벼룩시장

See Cheonggyecheon – Dongdaemun map. Near Dongmyo. Ⓜ *Dongmyo, lines 1/6, exit 3.* ⊙ *Open mainly Sat–Sun 10:30am–7pm.*

Shops and bric-a-brac stalls are set up close to the shrine. The charming owner of **Antique Gallery** (*main street,* ⊙ *open daily 10am–7:30pm,* ℘ (02)-2234-9604) may offer you tea. Apart from any bargains you may spot, the main interest here is the general ambience, harking back to times gone by.

▶ *Retrace your steps back to Cheonggye Stream, down the steps at the bridge. Bearing right, walk along the river and enjoy this natural area in the heart of the sprawling city. This urban development project has been a tremendous success (see pp150–151). After this peaceful interlude, climb up the steps of the 3rd bridge you come to (Ogansugyo), and rejoin the hubbub of the city. Dongdaemun is a short distance to the right.*

A Wall of Wishes

Just one of the many points to stop and reflect along Cheonggyecheon, the Wish Wall was created with the help of more than 20,000 people (including oversees Korean nationals and displaced North Koreans), who wrote and painted their hopes on ceramic tiles. The wall is 164ft/49.8m long and found between the two bridges Biudanggyo and Hwanghakgyo.

©KTO

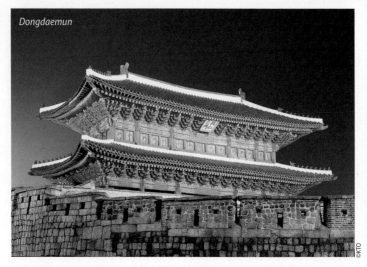

Dongdaemun

©KTO

Dongdaemun 동대문 (Great East Gate)

See Cheonggyecheon – Dongdaemun map. Ⓜ *Dongdaemun, lines 1/4, exits 6/7.*

Built in 1398 during the fortification of the city, it was originally named Heunginjimun but is more usually known as Dongdaemun—the Great East Gate, or the "Gate of Rising Benevolence."

This was the usual exit point for travelers heading to Gangwon-do and the three southern provinces and was also the route regularly taken by the last monarchs, King Gojong and his son King Sunjong, on their way to visit Hongneung, the tomb of Gojong's wife Queen Min. The present gate's wooden construction with a double roof dates from 1869, the original having been destroyed during the Korean War. The gate sits on a massive stone base.

As at **Hwaeseong Fortress** in Suwon, the semicircular structure in front of the gate strengthened the city's defenses by preventing direct access and making it easier to control who passed in and out.

The remains of Seoul's old fortress wall can be seen beside modern church buildings on the hill adjacent to Dongdaemun. A path leads to Naksan Park in Hyehwa (*see p189*).

▶ *End the walk here or, to continue, cross the intersection using the pedestrian crossing in front of the gate and head toward the Dongdaemun Shopping Center.*

Dongdaemun Shopping Center 동대문 쇼핑센터

See Cheonggyecheon – Dongdaemun map.

This part of the shopping district sells fabrics, household linen and notions, with traditional fabrics, ramie and silk *hanbok* in particular on the ground floor. If you walk straight through the center and out the other side, you'll find a **small alley** on the opposite side of the road, to the left of a line of food stalls.

Walk down the alley to find small restaurants selling fish and delicious grilled chicken in the pot (*see Addresses*) typical of a bygone era. This is where local traders from the surrounding markets would come to eat, but today shoppers enjoy the atmosphere too (at its best later in the day), although the result may be waiting in line out into the street for the most popular places.

▶ *Continue straight—the road is crossed by another alley full of lively street stalls—and you will find shops selling tools and other equipment, followed by sporting goods and outdoor activity stores. You will eventually see the famous Gwangjang Market opposite.*

Gwangjang Market
광장시장

🕯️*See Cheonggyecheon – Dongdaemun map. 6-1 Yeji-dong, Jongno-gu.* Ⓜ *Jongno 5-ga, line 1, exit 8.* 🕾*(02)-2267-0291.* 🕐*Open Mon– Sat: shops 9am–7pm, restaurants 10pm.* This **silk** and **traditional clothing** market was founded in 1905 by Korean merchants, when the Japanese occupiers took over Namdaemun Market. Another place that is best explored later in the day to fully enjoy the atmosphere, there's a long line of street restaurants selling delicious *bindaetteok*, local cakes, or *sundae*, famous Korean puddings. You might also catch sight of Baek Yeon-hwa, a local character who wears a black top hat and often plays the saxophone here in the evenings.

ADDITIONAL SIGHTS
Dongdaemun Design Plaza
동대문디자인플라자 and History & Culture Park 역사공원

🕯️*See Cheonggyecheon – Dongdaemun map. Euljiro 7-ga, Jung-gu.* Ⓜ *Dongdaemun History & Culture Park, lines 2/4/5, exit 1.* 🕾*(02)-2266-7330. http://ddp.seoul.go.kr.* 🕐*Open daily 10am–9pm. No charge.* This huge urban redevelopment has transformed the site of the former Dongdaemun baseball and soccer stadium, turning it into a "design-oriented futuristic park" that will make Seoul a leading player in design in Asia. Facilities such as a design museum, exhibition halls and resource and training centers located above and below ground all support South Korea's design industry. Recognizing that culture has a part to play in dynamic economic development in the 21C, the Design Park is a recreational and cultural space with green areas in which to relax as well as venues to enjoy performances. The park was designed by Iraqi-British architect Zaha Hadid and is due to be completed by summer 2012.

ADDRESSES

🛏️ STAY

🍱🍱 Uljiro CO-OP Residence
을지로 코업레지던스 – *32 Uljiro 6-ga, Jung-gu.* Ⓜ *Dongdaemun History & Culture Park, lines 2/4/5, exit 12.* 🕾*(02)-2269-4600. http://residences.co-op.co.kr/. 250 rm. ₩121,000/5,000* 🛏️ ✕. The residence rents out studios, offering all the services expected of a standard hotel. Single rooms, at reasonable prices, with TV and internet and some self-catering facilities. A good location, near the sprawling Dongdaemun Market.

🍴/EAT

🍴 Jinokwa halmae wonjo darkhanmari 진옥화 할매원조 닭한마리 – *265-22 Jongno 5-ga, Jongno-gu.* Ⓜ *Dongdaemun, lines 1/4, exit 9. On leaving the subway walk straight ahead and take the 1st street on the left, then 1st side street on the right.* 🕾*(02)-2275-9666. www.wonjodark.co.kr. Open daily 10am–10:30pm. ₩13,000 for 2–3 people.* A very popular restaurant in an interesting alley in the market district. Sample simple cuisine; the restaurant serves just one type of Korean chicken soup dish with noodles, but it is really delicious. Remember to ask for *guksu* rice noodles once you have eaten the chicken. This is the only renovated building in the alley.

🛍️ SHOPPING

Gyeongdong Oriental Medicine Market 경동약재시장 (Yangnyeong Market 약령시장) –
Ⓜ *Jegi-dong, line 1, exit 2.* 🕾*(02)-969-4793. www.seoulya.com. Open Mon– Sat 9am–7pm (individual store opening times vary). Closed public holidays.* This market has been selling the plants and herbs used in traditional Korean medicine since the 1960s. It is on the site of Bojewon, established by royal decree in the 15C, where the poor came for medicines and medical treatment. Stalls are piled with curious-looking leaves, herbs, roots and dried fungi. Wander around and soak up the atmosphere and exotic smells, and

Seoul Folk Flea Market

©KTO

perhaps buy some gingseng. Next door is the **Jaera Sijang**, a huge fruit and vegetable market, also worth a look if you have time.

Jeilpyeonghwa Market 제일평화 시장 – Ⓜ *Dongdaemun, lines 1/4, exit 7. ℰ(02)-2252-6744. Open daily 10:30am–5am.* Although this is a wholesale market for clothing and fashion items, the traders are generally prepared to make retail sales during the day, so you may be able to grab a bargain.

Janganpyeong Antiques Market 장안평 고미술 상가 – *961-9 Dapsimni 4-dong, Dongdaemun-gu.* Ⓜ *Dapsimni, line 5, exit 4. Go straight on for 650yd/600m. Open Mon–Sat 10am–6:30pm (some shops).* Fifty or so stores (some looking a bit dusty!) in two adjacent buildings. Come here to browse among furniture, paintings, ceramics, clothing and more. There are some fine antique items to be found among the more mundane objects, but the scarcity of Korean antiques means that prices can be quite high and many items come from China or North Korea. Close to the subway station.

Dapsimni Antiques Market 답십 리 고미술상가 – *530 Dapsimni 5-dong, Dongdaemun-gu.* Ⓜ *Dapsipni, line 5, exits 1/2. On the street leading off from between exits 1 and 2. Open 10am–7pm; hours vary by store. Closed Sun.* This market takes up two buildings on either side of the 1st intersection. This market is often confused with the main site and the antiques tend to be of a lesser quality, but it's still worth a visit.

Seoul Folk Flea Market 서울 풍물 벼룩시장 – *109-5 Sinseoldong, Dongdaemun-gu.* Ⓜ *Sinseoldong, line 1, exits 9/10. ℰ(02)-3707-8001. http://pungmul.seoul.go.kr/. Open daily 10am–8pm (Nov–Feb 7pm).* The Seoul Folk Flea Market moved only recently to this two-story building, where all sorts of second-hand goods, from everyday to traditional items, are sold, often at very good prices.

Doota Mall 두타몰 **(Doosan Tower)** 두산 타워) – *18-12 Uliro 6-ga, Jung-gu.* Ⓜ *Dongdaemun, lines 1/4, exit 8. ℰ(02)-3398-3114. www.doota.com. Open Tue–Sat 10:30am–5am, Sun 10:30am–11pm, Mon 7pm–5am.* A shopping center that is popular among young Koreans for its wide range of goods and low prices. Clothing and accessories, shoes and souvenirs are sold on 10 levels. Open until the very early hours.

Hyehwa
혜화

Hyehwa is a university district full of small theaters, live bars and performance venues.
It is sometimes also referred to as Daehangno, which is the name of a nearby road (sometimes also spelled Daehak-ro). The universities of Seonggyungwan and Hansung are here, along with the former campus of Seoul National University, which was moved south of the river by President Park Chung-hee in order to prevent student demonstrations in the city center. It is an interesting area to walk around during the day, and a good place in which to spend a cultural evening. Farther north, the Seongbuk-dong part of the district is less well known but contains many cultural treasures, a number of its historic buildings housing museums, galleries and temples. This district is an absolute must for visitors who are staying a little longer than most and have the time to explore a little farther.

◕◣WALKING TOUR

DAEHANGNO★ 대학로

▶ *Allow 3hr. Departure point:*
Ⓜ *Hyehwa, line 4, exit 3.*

Known for its universities, intimate theaters and many bars, Daehangno also has a few surprises in store, including several reminders of the Joseon era and Korea's tumultuous recent history, and not forgetting the small "mountain" Naksan, one of the four key mountains in Seoul.

Former Daehan Hospital
구 대한의원본관
⏱ *See Hyehwa map. 28-2 Yeonggeon-dong, Jongno-gu, in the Seoul National University Hospital grounds.*
Ⓜ *Hyehwa, line 4, exit 3. No charge.*

- ⏱ **Michelin Map:** Map p188
- ▶ **Location:** North of the historic city. To the east and north of Changdeokgung.
- ⏱ **Timing:** If you don't have time to do the walk in full, we suggest concentrating on Munmyo and Ihwajang (note that reservations are required). You could easily spend a whole day in Seongbuk-dong, and, especially in summer, Kansong Art Museum.
- 👁 **Don't Miss:** Seonggyungwan and Munmyo, the beautiful traditional house Suyeon Sanbang, Syngman Rhee's home Ihwajang and Kansong Art Museum.

Climb the small hill within the Seoul National University Hospital campus to this old neo-Baroque building. When it was built in 1907 by a Japanese architect, it was the largest hospital in Korea. In 1926 it became Keijo Imperial University Hospital and remained a teaching hospital until the new buildings were

Daehangno, University Street ©KTO

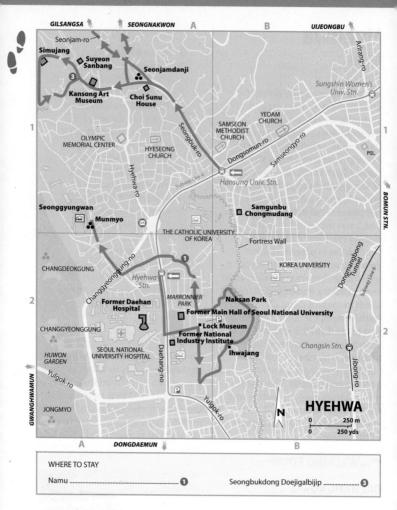

constructed behind it in 1979. The old hospital building now houses a museum of the history of Korean medicine.

◯ *Retrace your steps and cross Daehang-no to Marronnier Park.*

Former Main Hall of Seoul National University
구 서울대학교 본관
◔*See Hyehwa map. 1-130 Dongsung-dong, Jongno-gu.* Ⓜ *Hyehwa, line 4, exit 3. No charge.*

Seoul National University (SNU), the most prestigious higher education institution in Korea, was founded by the Japanese administration in 1924 as part of their new "cultural policy" follow-

ing the Declaration of Independence on 1 March 1919.

In 1972 the university relocated southwest of Seoul, near Mount Gwanak (Gwanaksan), to deter protests from students in the center of the city. The building remaining in Marronier Park was built in 1931 as the administrative center for the Faculty of Humanities and is one of the few buildings from the original campus still standing. The administrative building reflects the Modernist architecture then in vogue in colonial Japan, especially the brick facade introduced to Japan by American architect Frank Lloyd Wright. In 1945 it became the university's administrative center. There is a similar building on the other side of the avenue, opposite the park at the entrance to the hospital. Built in 1936, it is now the administrative center of SNU's Faculty of Medicine (Main Hall of SNU's College of Medicine), the only university faculty to remain at Daehango after the 1972 move.

Former National Industry Institute 구 공업전습소

See Hyehwa map. 199-1 Dongsung-dong, Jongno-gu, on the grounds of Korea National Open University.
Ⓜ *Hyehwa, line 4, exit 2. No charge.*
Just below Marronier Park to the south is the campus of the Korea National Open University (providing distance learning programs), and to the right of the entrance is the former National Industry Institute. Completed in 1908 in neo-Renaissance style, this is the only wooden building still standing from that time. Take note of the German-style shingle facade.

▷ *Take the road from the east between the park and the university to arrive at Lock Museum.*

Lock Museum 쇳대박물관

See Hyehwa map. 187-8 Dongsung-dong, Jongno-gu. Ⓜ *Hyehwa, line 4, exit 2.* ℘ *(02)-766-6494. www.lock museum.org.* Ⓞ *Open Tue–Sun 10am–6pm. ₩3,000. Guided tours in English on request (no charge).*
Located in a beautiful modern building, the Lock Museum has a fascinating collection of antique locks and keys, furniture with locks and key charms (talismanic key rings) from around the world. The pieces are of interest for their aesthetic appeal as well as their intricate mechanisms.

▷ *Keep right and continue to the end of the street. At the crossroads, take the first street on the right and climb up toward Ihwajang.*

Ihwajang 이화장

See Hyehwa map. 1 Hyehwa-dong, Jongno-gu. Ⓜ *Hyehwa, line 4, exit 2.* ℘ *(02)-741-0815/745-0758.*

www.syngmanrhee.or.kr. Ⓞ *Open daily 10am–5pm (closed noon–1pm). Reservations required 24hr in advance. No charge. While you are requested to book your visit in advance by phone (by using the 120 Dasan call center service, for example,* Ⓒ *see p108), if you arrive when other visitors are there, they may let you in.*

This is the home of the first South Korean president **Syngman Rhee** (1875–1965), who lived here from 1947 with his Austrian wife Francesca Donner. Built on a site previously inhabited by a scholar and a 16C prince, the home dates from 1920 and is typical of the architecture of the urban *hanok* of this time. It has a higher ceiling than a traditional house and has been westernized, although it has retained its original furnishings. The small display of the **presidential couple's** personal belongings has a quaint and old-fashioned charm. The tour around the house includes an exhibition of photographs of the president, who was also the leader of the self-proclaimed government in exile in Hawaii and Shanghai during the Japanese occupation. He was forced to resign in 1960 after violent student demonstrations criticizing his authoritarian regime. He died in exile in Hawaii.

To the right of the entrance is a small building, **Jogakdang**, the historic site where the first government was formed in August 1948. Look out for the rock garden, which is particularly pleasing in summer.

▷ *To the right and farther on to the left of Ihwajang are small paths leading to Naksan Park.*

Naksan Park 낙산공원

See Hyehwa map. 9-151 Hyehwa-dong, Jongno-gu. Ⓜ *Hyehwa, line 4, exit 2. No charge.*
Naksan Park is a pleasant place to walk in the fresh air beside Seoul's ancient fortress wall **Seoul Seonggwak** and a great spot to enjoy the beautiful views over the city. There are also sports facilities and an exhibition hall here. On the

far side of the hill, typical neighborhood houses cling to the slopes. Walk through the narrow streets to Hansung University's campus, and then on to Samseon Park. Or return to Daehangno through the park's main entrance. As you do so, look out for the murals and art installations that collectively form the **Naksan Public Art Project**, designed to bring the arts and young artists to the area.

Samgunbu Chongmudang
삼군부총무당

👣 *See Hyehwa map. 512-160 Donam-dong, Seongbuk-gu.* Ⓜ *Hansung University, line 4, exit 3. On leaving the subway, walk straight ahead for 550yd/500m beside the stream until you reach a sign to the monument on the right. Take the 5th street on the right and walk straight on toward Samseon Park. No charge.*

This attractive old building was moved to its current location in the 1930s and, being rather difficult to find, has relatively few visitors. It is one of three buildings that housed government departments during the Joseon era that can still be seen today. First built in 1868 but destroyed by fire two years later and then rebuilt, Originally there were three pavilions; now, only the largest, Chongmudang, has survived. It was part of the Samgunbu, the Department of Military Affairs.

▷ *To continue the walk, head back to Naksan Park, or go to Hansung University subway station (retake the path given above to Samgunbu Chonmudang) and take a taxi to Seonggyungwan. From Naksan Park, after returning to Daehang-no, take the right to Hyehwadong Rotary (intersection). Take the avenue on the left, then the third street on the right.*

Seonggyungwan★
and Munmyo (Confucian
Shrine) 성균관문묘

👣 *See Hyehwa map. 53 Myeongnyun-dong 3 Ga, Jongno-gu.* Ⓜ *Hyehwa, line 4, exit 4.* 🕿 *(02)-765-0501/764-1472. www.skku.edu.* 🔵 *Myeongnyundang*

is open 24hr, Munmyo Mon–Fri 10am–4pm. No charge.

Seonggyungwan is the former Confucian academy situated at the entrance to the present-day Sungkyunkwan University, founded in 1953. Incorporating the national academy of the same name (originally called Gughak or Gukjagam), Seonggyungwan trained the elite of the Goryeo kingdom in Gaeseong (now North Korea) and was one of the first public buildings erected in the new capital Hanyang (Seoul) under the Yi (Joseon) dynasty. Work was completed in 1398, but the academy suffered extensive damage, including total destruction during the Japanese invasion.

Rebuilt in 1601, most of the current buildings date from the 17C and 18C and underwent a major renovation in 1869. They offer insight into the administrative structure of old Korea. Seonggyungwan is where the officials who would go on to assume high public office (having passed the required exams) or become mandarins were educated, but it also nurtured the neo-Confucian ideology, values and rituals adopted by the Joseon dynasty.

Hence the site opens on to a large courtyard and the shrine called **Munmyo**, rather than the actual academic institution. The front gate, Oesammun, was opened only twice a year during the Seokjeondaeje memorial rites because it was reserved for the spirits of the dead, buried in the tombs in the buildings surrounding the courtyard. The building at the back, **Daeseongjeon**, dating from 1602, is dedicated to the five Confucian saints (including Confucius and Mencius), the ten great disciples, the six great sages of Song and, from the post Korean War period, eighteen eminent Korean sages. The side buildings, Dongmu and Seonmu, contained the tombs of 112 Chinese and Korean sages before they were moved to Daeseongjeon.

It is in this sacred place, at 10am on the 1st and 15th day of every lunar month, that the simple **Seokjeondaeje** rituals (music and offerings) are performed, twice a year, in spring and fall (*dates vary according to the lunar calendar*).

Seonggyungwan, the former Confucian academy.

©KTO

The second courtyard contains the large education pavilion **Myeongnyundang** (1606). The buildings at the sides, Seojae and Dongjae, housed the student dormitories, accommodating between 100 and 200 at a time. They are still used by students of the modern university studying classical Chinese, which was originally considered the most prestigious subject.

To the rear, to the east, stands a large building used as a refectory, and administrative buildings, a library (Jongyeonggak) and kitchens for preparing food for the teachers and students and for the many rituals. Look out for the 100-year-old ginkgos, the favorite tree of Confucius, as well as some impressive stelae.

WALKING TOUR

SEONGBUK-DONG★ 성북동

▶ *Allow 2–3hr. Starting point:* Ⓜ *Hyehwa, line 4, exit 6, then green bus no. 1111/2112.*

One of the most beautiful and little-known walks in an area that was originally outside Seoul's fortress wall but which was developed after 1900 as a residential area. The tour takes in several old houses, temples and an important museum.

▶ *Take one of the local green buses at the subway exit toward Hongik Middle and High School, or walk straight ahead for about 15min.*

Choi Sunu House 최순우 옛집

ⓕ*See Hyehwa map. 126-20 Seongbuk-2 dong, Seongbuk-gu.* Ⓜ *Hansung University, line 4, exit 6, then green bus no. 1111/2112. 875yd/800m, 10min walk.* ℘*(02)-3675-3401. http://nt-heritage. org/choisunu.* ◯ *Open Tue–Sat, Apr– Nov 10am–4pm. No charge.*

At the bus stop, on the far side of the avenue, take the lane leading from the corner of Shinhan Bank. Ahead on the left is a small, well-preserved traditional house (1930) that is open to visitors and is a fine example of an urban *hanok* from the early 20C. It was the home of Choi Sunu, a former chief curator of the National Museum and important art historian, who lived here between 1976 and1984.

▶ *Retrace your steps back across the avenue diagonally to the left. Walk back up the lane and, at the intersection, take the steep street on the right.*

Seongnakwon 성낙원

2-22 Seongbuk-dong, Seongbuk-gu. 765yd/700m from Choi Sunu's house, on the far side of the avenue, walking back along the side streets. Ⓜ *Hansung*

University, line 4, exit 6, then green bus no. 1111/2112. Private property. To arrange a visit, contact the office of Seongbuk-dong. ℘(02)-920-34103/ 765-5092.

This little-known gem of a garden is one of the few surviving examples in the traditional Korean style. It was formerly the residence of Sim Sang-eung, a court official in the mid-19C, and then of Prince Ui, who died in 1955 (the fifth son of King Gojong). Unfortunately, the grounds of this once extensive property were subdivided and sold off, and the garden is now wedged between modern buildings, but it is still large enough to contain pavilions, ponds and a lovely natural landscaped area.

▶ *Return to the intersection and take the steep street leading upward. Climb for about 10min to reach Gilsangsa on the right.*

Gilsangsa 길상사 (Gilsang Temple)

323 Seongbuk-2 dong, Seongbuk-gu. Ⓜ Hansung University, line 4, exit 6, then green bus no. 1111/2112, or taxi ₩2,400. ℘(02)-3672-5945. www.kilsangsa.or.kr. No charge.

It may not be the oldest temple in Seoul, but this is one of the most interesting in terms of its history. From the 1960s to the 1980s, this building housed one of the three best-known restaurants in Seoul, **Daewongak**. Famous for being the haunt of politicians from the nearby Blue House (*see p 130*), the restaurant employed the services of *gisaeng* (*see p 311*). The owner retired from business in 1987 to settle in the United States and donated the land to a Buddhist monk to transform the restaurant into a temple. You will see the beautiful main hall, where many "historic" meals took place during its time as a restaurant, but which now houses venerable Buddhist statues. A stream flows across this delightful, peaceful site dotted with trees and shrubs.

At the entrance, information in English is available about weekend Temple Stays. Accommodation is provided in bunga-

lows beside the stream. For more information, email kilsangsa@templestay. com. The *Seon* (Zen) meditation hall is open to everyone *(10am–5pm)*. There is also a tearoom (the Joy of Sharing).

▶ *Return to the same intersection and turn right. Seonjamdanji is on the left at the intersection with the main avenue.*

Seonjamdanji 선잠단지

See Hyehwa map. 64-1 Seongbuk-dong, Seongbuk-gu. Ⓜ Hansung University, line 4, exit 6, then green bus no. 1111/2112. No charge.

Although there is not a great deal to see today the site is nevertheless interesting because, along with Seonnongdan in Jegi-dong and Sajikdan (*see box p 172*), it was one of the altars where the king made offerings once a year to the god of agriculture and where he plowed the first furrow of the season. Seonjamdanji was dedicated to the god of sericulture—the cultivation of silkworms—which was introduced to Korea from China and was a major industry for many years. The rituals, called Seonjamje, began here in 1400 and continued until 1908; they were held on the third day of the third lunar month, although in 1993 the date was changed to 7 May.

▶ *Turn right, then take the next lane on the right to reach Kansong Art Museum, which is poorly signposted.*

Kansong Art Museum 간송미술관

See Hyehwa map. 97-1 Seongbuk-dong, Seongbuk-gu. Ⓜ Hansung University, line 4, exit 6, then green bus no. 1111/2112. ℘(02)-762-0442.
Open to the public for just 2 weeks twice a year, in May and October, 10am–6pm. No charge.

After the National Museum of Korea, this private museum has the best collection of traditional Korean art in the country. It was established in 1938 by Jeon Hyeong-pil, a wealthy collector. Having realized the importance of preserving the national heritage, much of which had been looted during the Japanese colonial period, he assembled a superb collection, consisting mostly of paintings and calligraphy. The building is interesting in its own right. Now slightly dilapidated but still charming, it echoes the Bauhaus architecture of the 1930s. The small museum grounds are also home to some ancient Buddhist statues (Silla, Goryeo).

▶ *Keep right and continue along the avenue to the Seongbuk Museum of Art (a good municipal gallery), then turn right. Suyeon Sanbang is right next door.*

Suyeon Sanbang 수연산방

🐾 *See Hyehwa map.* 248 Seongbuk-dong, Seongbuk-gu. Ⓜ *Hansung University, line 4, exit 6, then green bus no. 1111/2112.* ℘ (02)-764-1736. 🕐*Open daily noon–10:30pm (Sat–Sun 10pm). Closed public holidays.*

This traditional house, dating from the 1930s and set in a charming small garden, was the home of the writer Lee Tae-jun. Her granddaughter has now converted it into a tearoom (🐾*see Addresses*).

▶ *Walk back up to the avenue and, keeping to the right, walk past the restaurants and cross the street. Take the small alley that climbs toward the wall.*

There is a small signpost for Simujang, which is on the right after a flight of steps.

Simujang 시무장

🐾 *See Hyehwa map.* 222-1- 2 Seongbuk-dong, Seongbuk-gu. Ⓜ *Hansung University, line 4, exit 6, then green bus no. 1111/2112. 3min walk from Suyeon Sanbang.* ℘ (02)-920-3412. 🕐*Open daily dawn–dusk. No charge.*

This small old house was the residence of the great poet **Han Yong-un** (pen name Manhae), from 1933 until his death here in 1944. A Buddhist monk, who signed the Declaration of Independence on 1 March 1919, Han Yong-un was a patriot, theoretician and Korean Buddhist reformer. He is best known for his beautiful collection of poems *Nimui Chimmuk (The Silence of My Love)*, where the Nim signifies the beloved, the homeland or the Buddha.

Built in 1933, the house faces north, not south as is usual, because, according to legend, Manhae did not want his home to look toward the seat of the Japanese administration.

▶ *To complete the tour, if you have the time, climb up toward the fortress wall and follow it back down to the starting point of the walk. There is a park with trees and benches, and it has a good view of the whole area.*

Simujang

©KTO

Suyeon Sanbang
©KTO

ADDRESSES

⌘/EAT

⊖ **Seongbukdong Doejigalbijip**
성북동 돼지갈비집 – 114-2
Seongbuk-dong, Seongbuk-gu.
Ⓜ *Hansung University, line 4, exit 6,
then bus no. 1111/03, Seongbuk Cultural
Center stop.* ☎(02)-764-2420. Open daily
9am–9:30pm (last orders 9pm). Closed
1st & 3rd Sun of the month and public
holidays. ₩6,000/7,000. A restaurant
frequented by taxi drivers is usually a
good sign, indicating the likelihood
of generous portions, tasty food and
reasonable prices, which is certainly
the case here. This restaurant has been
specializing in pork barbecued over
charcoal for some 40 years. The portion
of ribs (₩6,000) or ground beef (same
price) arrives cooked to perfection, and
for an additional ₩1,000, you can have
salad, soup, sauce and rice.
⊛ **Note:** *that no alcohol is served here.*

⊖⊜ **Namu** 나무 – *22-1 Dongsung-
dong, Jongno-gu.* Ⓜ *Hyehwa, line 4,
exit 1.* ☎(02)-3675-0003. Open daily
11am–11pm. Closed public holidays.
A la carte ₩9,000/37,000, fixed price
menus: lunch ₩25,000, dinner ₩55,000.
A very reasonable Italian restaurant in
a modern and spacious setting with
a large terrace. Ideal for an aperitif or
dinner before or after a show. Located
just behind the Dongsung Art Center
(walk around it to the right).

⌖ TAKING A BREAK

Suyeon Sanbang 수연산방 –
248 Seongbuk-dong, Seongbuk-gu.
Ⓜ *Hansung University, line 4, exit 6,
then bus no. 1111/3, Seongbuk Cultural
Center stop.* ☎ (02)-764-1736. Open
daily noon–10:30pm (Sat–Sun 10pm).
Closed public holidays. Teas
₩6,500/10,000. This traditional building
(☙ *see description above*) has several
rooms in which you can try teas and
infusions, plus a pavilion in the garden.
It is not very well known, but don't miss
it if you are in the area.

Seodaemun★
서대문

Inwangsan ("Mountain of the Benevolent King") is steeped in history and was once one of the most picturesque locations in Seoul. Some of the most famous painters of the Joseon dynasty came here in search of inspiration while the region was still relatively unspoiled, recording the scenes they saw in a number of paintings. Today Inwangsan is surrounded by rows of apartment buildings. However, in an effort to preserve what is left of the natural surroundings, the area has been designated a "protected landscape," the first of its kind in Seoul. As you leave the many tower blocks behind, following the suggested walk, and climb farther up the mountain, the landscape becomes increasingly rural, and you enter a more spiritual world. Other sites of historical interest are scattered around Seodaemun—the district takes its name from the Great West Gate that was once located here. If you have enough time, the walk can be extended to Buam-dong, on the far side of Inwangsan.

- ⚭ **Michelin Map:** Map p197
- ▷ **Location:** To the west of the historic city, behind Dongnimmun.
- ≗ **Kids:** Visit the Agriculture Museum.
- ⏱ **Timing:** It's easy to spend a few hours learning about the city's traditional culture in Seoul Museum of History, but Seodaemun Prison also provides an interesting, and at times disturbing, insight into Korea's recent past. If you are short on time, try our suggested walk for the atmosphere and the views.
- ⚘ **Don't Miss:** The shamanist shrines, climbing Inwangsan, the Seoul Museum of History

steep set of steps. Continue straight on, with residential buildings on your left. Walk past the entrance arch to the shamanist village in the Muak-dong district, in a road on the left, and continue to climb. You will pass through an area containing a number of what appear to be Buddhist temples but which are in fact shamanist shrines, arriving at the most famous of them all, Guksadang.

🐾 WALKING TOUR

INWANGSAN 인왕산

▷ *Start at Ⓜ Dongnimmun, line 3, exit 2. Allow around 3hr for the entire walk, or 2hr otherwise.*

The walk climbs the **sacred mountain Inwangsan** for a truly superb view of the city, passing shamanist shrines, Seoul's ancient fortress wall (Seong-gwak) and Changuimun (Changui Gate) along the way.

▷ *Leaving the subway, take the 1st alley on the left. At the next intersection, take the 2nd right, leading to a fairly*

Inwangsan city wall

©Chris Stowers/Apa Publications

Guksadang 국사당 (Shamanist Shrine)

See Seodaemun map.
Muak-dong, Jongno-gu.

This important shamanist shrine was originally near the present N Seoul Tower, on Namsan, but was transferred to Inwangsan in 1925 when the Japanese occupiers had a large Shinto (Japan's national religion) temple built below the original location. It was considered inappropriate that Guksadang should overlook a Japanese religious shrine. This colorful building may be small, but it remains an important spiritual center. Offerings are regularly made and many *kut*, shamanist rituals, continue to be held here, particularly in March and October.

The shrine is dedicated to a number of figures and deities: King Taejo (Yi Seonggye), the founder of the Joseon dynasty; Muhak Daesa, a senior religious figure and adviser to Taejo; the Goryeo General Cho Yong; and various deities specific to shamanism, such as the gods of Heaven and the Mountain.

▷ *Just beyond Guksadang, turn left in front of the spring, and you will soon reach the large rocks known as Seonbawi.*

Seonbawi 선바위 (Zen Rocks)

See Seodaemun map.
Muak-dong, Jongno-gu.

The waters at the foot of the rocks are a place of female pilgrimage, as it is believed to increase the chances of giving birth to a boy, considered particularly important in Korea, and in Asia generally.

The rocks themselves are also a place of worship. Some people see in their shape the image of a monk meditating, while others claim to recognize King Taejo and his adviser Muhak. It is said that a quarrel broke out during the construction of Seoul's fortress wall as to whether Seonbawi should be included within its confines or not. Afraid that, even in Seoul, Buddhism would gain ground

at the expense of Confucianism, it was eventually excluded, and the teachings of Confucius remained dominant in the years that followed. One last small pavilion is located a few yards higher up.

▷ *It is not possible to climb any farther at this point, as the wall here is surrounded by a fence erected by the military. Return to the small spring where there is another path that climbs to the right. You will soon reach the path leading to the wall on your left.*

▷ *If you opt for the 3hr walk, go through the small green gate and climb toward the wall, then carry on beside the wall to the top of Inwangsan. If the gate is closed, or if you want to complete the 2hr walk, continue straight ahead along the road that leads downward. To rejoin the 3hr walk, cross over at the next intersection, turn left and you will see the entrance to a path heading upward, which rejoins the wall. For the 2hr option, turn right and the path will bring you to Deunggwajeong, a traditional archery range, then Sajik Park. If you continue straight along the avenue, you will see Ⓜ Gyeongbokgung, line 3.*

Inwangsan's peak 인왕산 정상

See Seodaemun map.

From the top of this mountain (1,109ft /338m) there is a **magnificent view** over Seoul and many of the outlying districts beyond the city. The fortress wall that snakes its way over the mountain was built in 1396, shortly after the capital was moved to its present location, when the city contained some 100,000 inhabitants, unlike the vast, sprawling metropolis that you see today.

▷ *Continue walking beside the wall, heading down to Changuimun. There are regular signposts. To return to the city center, the easiest way is by taxi (approx. 10min), but you can also take green bus no. 212/1020 to Ⓜ Gyeongbokgung, line 3.*

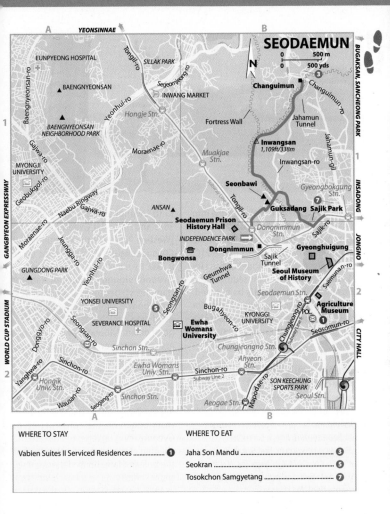

Changeuimun 창의문 (Changeui Gate)

♿See Seodaemun map.
Buam-dong, Jongno-gu.

Changuimun (also known as Jahamun) is one of the four minor gates of the ancient fortified capital. Rebuilt in 1740 and restored in 1958, it remains the only one of the four that is so well preserved. It was a popular crossing point for travelers heading north, following the closure of one of the main gates.

▶ *After Changuimun, you can continue the walk toward Bugaksan (♿see Gyeongbokgung-Bukchon p127).*

ADDITIONAL SIGHTS
Seoul Museum of History★ 서울 역사 박물관

♿See Seodaemun map.
2-1 Sinmuro 1-ga, Jongno-gu.
Ⓜ Seodaemun, line 5, exit 4 or
Ⓜ Gwanghwamun, line 5, exit 7.
☏02-724-0114. http://museum.seoul.kr.
♿ ⏰Open Tue–Fri 9am–9pm, Sat–Sun and public holidays 9am–7pm (Nov–Feb 9am–6pm). No charge.
Free audio guide.

This museum traces the history of the city and its inhabitants (both the ordinary people and the ruling class, as well as the economic life of the people), but concentrates on life under the Joseon

Seoul Museum of History

©KTO

dynasty. Visitors can gain insight into Seoul's culture and how the city grew to its present size, as well as explore the vision for expansion plans in the 21C. Don't miss the scale model of the city (1:1,500) or the touch museum, where ancient tools can actually be handled. There are special educational areas for children, and be sure to check out the program in the temporary exhibitions hall.

Gyeongheuigung 경희궁 (Gyeongheui Palace)

See Seodaemun map.
1-126 Sinmuro 2-ga, Jongno-gu.
Behind the Seoul Museum of History.
Ⓜ *Seodaemun, line 5, exit 4 or*
Ⓜ *Gwanghwamun, line 5, exit 7.*
(02)-724-0274. Ⓞ*Open Tue–Fri 9am–6pm, Sat–Sun and public holidays 10am–6pm. No charge.*

Gyeonghuigung Palace

©KTO

King Gwanghae built this palace in 1616 and named it Gyeongdeokgung (Western Palace) as the counterpart of Changdeokgung *(Eastern Palace, see p 133)*. Its name was later changed to Gyeonghuigung ("Palace of Radiant Happiness") because the original designation was similar to the name of a dead king, which was not felt to be a good omen. Although it was a secondary palace, several kings did take up residence here.

Some of the buildings were destroyed by fire in 1829; others were moved to Sajik Park or simply demolished during the Japanese occupation. In 1907, work began on the construction of Gyeongseong College, to educate the children of the Japanese colonists, but the building later housed the administrative offices of the tobacco industry. In 1988, by which time only the palace foundations remained, a program of restoration was begun. The main gate **Heunghwamun** (original structure) was moved and rebuilt, and the throne hall, **Sungjeongjeon**, was faithfully reconstructed, along with a number of other buildings.

Unfortunately the restoration work has not been able to return the palace to all of its full former splendor, and it is hard to imagine that the palace complex was once so vast that it was connected to Deoksugung, another of Seoul's five great palaces, by a bridge. Today it is a quiet and pleasant place to visit and still has a palpable powerful energy that must have been detected by the mystics of King Gwanghae who chose the site. *Don't miss the demonstrations of taek-*

wondo in the palace courtyard. ☎(02)-724-0150. www.taekwonseoul.org. Wed and Sat, Mar–Nov 2pm–3pm.

Seodaemun Prison History Hall
서대문 형무소 역사관
♿See Seodaemun map.
101 Hyeonjeo-dong, Seodaemun-gu.
Ⓜ *Dongnimmun, line 3, exit 5.* ☎(02)-360-8590. ⏰*Open Tue–Sun, Mar–Oct 9:30am–6pm, Nov–Feb 9:30am–5pm. Closed public holidays. Guided tour in English (reservations required at least one week in advance), ₩1,500.*

Built outside the city wall in 1908 by the Japanese occupiers, this prison is a grim reminder of the suffering endured by the Koreans during the Japanese protectorate and annexation (1905–45). Many who resisted Japanese rule were imprisoned, tortured and killed here. Along with the cellblocks, solitary confinement cells and torture chambers, there was a building to isolate lepers. The exhibits are also rather grim, as you would expect, with video displays and staged chilling reconstructions showing the brutality of the Japanese occupiers. By the post-colonial era, the building was still a place of detention, this time used by the Korean dictatorship, until 1987. It was finally converted into a museum in 1998.

Dongnimmun 독립문 (Independence Gate)
♿See Seodaemun map.
Hyeoneo-dong, Seodaemun-gu.
Ⓜ *Dongnimmun, line 3, exit 4.*

Modeled on the Arc de Triomphe in Paris, the gate was erected in 1896 to replace the old gate (Yeongeunmun) through which envoys from China came to claim their tribute from the Joseon monarchs, who were vassals of the Chinese emperor. When the Japanese army defeated the Chinese army at the end of the Sino–Japanese War of 1895, this monument was built to mark the symbolic ending of vassalage to Beijing and the new independence of Korea. King Gojong subsequently proclaimed himself emperor of Korea in 1897.

👫👤 Agriculture Museum
농업박물관
♿See Seodaemun map.
Chungjeong-no 1-ga, Jung-gu.
Ⓜ *Seodaemun, line 5, exit 5.*
☎(02)-2080-5727. ⏰*Open Tue–Sun, Mar–Oct 9:30am–6pm, Nov–Feb 9:30am–5:30pm. No charge.*

This small museum illustrates different aspects of the history of agriculture in Korea, explaining such practices as the growing of rice and the cultivation of silkworms. It provides a good overview of rural life and is suitable for young children, with displays and interactive games.

Sajik Park 사직공원
♿See Seodaemun map.
1-28 Sajik-dong, Jongno-gu.
Ⓜ *Gyeongbokgung, line 3, exit 1.*
No charge.

A this spot, the Joseon rulers (1392–1910) continued the tradition established by the Goryeo dynasty of performing sacrifices in spring and autumn to Sa, the god of the Earth, and Jik, the god of Harvests. The royal ancestral rituals conducted at Jongmyo, together with the sacrifices carried out at the Temple of Heaven, when Korea became an empire, formed the rites through which the monarchy asserted its power. Built by King Taejo in 1394, little remains of the *Sajikdan* (altar) that was later dismantled by the Japanese occupiers in order to turn the site into a park. The site may seem a little disappointing as a result, but the stone base is still visible, along with parts of the surrounding walls and the main entrance gate, which dates from 1720. The rites have been re-enacted here since 1988, on 3 October, National Foundation Day.

At the end of the park on the left, a flight of steps leads to a small recent shrine dedicated to Tangun, the mythical founder of the Gojoseon kingdom. Farther along the road, behind Sajik Park, is **Hwanghakjeong**, the "Yellow Crane Pavilion," beside one of the traditional archery ranges that the Joseons established in the capital. Built in 1898, it was originally in the Gyeongheui Palace but was moved here in 1923 during the Japanese colonization. Boys of aristocratic families would be taught to shoot a bow here, starting at the age of 13. It was a useful skill for both hunting and war but also contributed to physical training and spiritual development. Archery still takes place here and competitions are held.

▶ *The walk can be continued by following the fortress wall over Inwangsan and down to Changuimun, and the laid-back Baum-dong area.*

ADDRESSES

🏠 STAY

🛏 **Vabien Suites II Serviced Residences** 바비엥스위트 II – *25-10 Uljiro 1-ga, Jung-gu.* Ⓜ *Seodaemun, line 5, exit 6.* ✆*(02)-6399-1188. www.vabienseoul.com. 286 rm, starting from ₩132,000* 🛏 ✕*.* Studios and luxury apartments, some with self-catering facilities but with the same services as you would expect from a high-end hotel. There is a playroom for children, a sauna and fitness room, and an indoor practice area for golfers. Shuttles are provided to the business and shopping districts.

🍴 EAT

🍽 **Tosokchon Samgyetang** 토속촌 삼계탕 – *85-1 Chebu-dong, Jongno-gu.* Ⓜ *Gyeongbokgung, line 3, exit 2.* ✆*(02)-737-7444. Open daily 10am–10pm. ₩13,000.* Try *angyetang*, a one-pot chicken meal, with rice, ginseng and other spices, in the exotic setting of this superb, well-regarded traditional restaurant. The down-to-earth atmosphere has not stopped former presidents from enjoying the excellent food served here.

🍽🍽 **Jaha Son Mandu** 자하 손만두 – *245-2 Buam-dong, Jongno-gu, in a building on the right from Changuimun.* Ⓜ *Gyeongbokgung, line 3, exit 3, then bus no. 0212/1020/ 7022, Jahamun Gogae stop.* ✆*(02)-379-2648. www.sonmandoo.com. Open daily 11am–9:30pm. Closed public holidays. A la carte ₩7,000/48,000, fixed price menu ₩38,000.* This restaurant is so well known for its homemade ravioli *(sonmandu)* that you will probably have to wait in line on the weekend. Enjoy boiled *mandu (₩7,000)*, in soup *(₩10,000)* or in a casserole for three *(₩48,000)*.

🍽🍽 **Seokran** 석란 – *50-5 Daesin-dong, Seodaemun-gu. Next to the Severance Yonsei Hospital, opposite the rear gate of Ewha University.* Ⓜ *Sinchon, line 2, exits 2/3, then bus no. 7024, Ewha University rear gate stop.* ✆*(02)-393-4690. www.sokran.com. Open daily 11:30am–10pm (last orders 9pm). Closed public holidays. Fixed priced menus: lunch ₩22,000, dinner ₩60,000.* This Korean restaurant has been in business since 1981 and sits in a large Western house with a garden. It has maintained its quality despite being able to seat 350 diners. Carefully prepared *hanjeongsik*-type meals with several courses are served.

🍴 A TREAT

Seokparang 석파랑 – *125 Heungji-dong, Jongno-gu.* Ⓜ *Gyeongbokgung, line 3, exit 3, then a taxi or bus no. 1711, Sangmyeong University stop. Bukansan Map p211.* ✆*(02)-395-2500. www.seokparang.co.kr. Open daily noon–3pm, 6pm–10pm. Closed public holidays. Fixed price lunch menus ₩70,000/130,000.* In the 19C the Daewongun (regent) took over Seokpajeong, a beautiful villa (**closed to the public**) in the restaurant grounds built by the statesman Kim Heung-geun. The Daewongun renamed the villa after his pen name, Seokpajeong, and came here to reflect on his political plans. The restaurant Seokparang, in a former *sarangchae* (male quarters), moved here in 1958 by the then owner, serves royal *hanjeongsik* meals with several courses, the finest of traditional Korean cuisine.

Mapo
마포

Originally a small port on the Hangang, Mapo grew to its present size in the latter part of the 20C; the universities that were established here (Yonsei, Ewha, Hongik and Sogang) helped bring the district to life. A reminder of Korea's turbulent 19C history can be found at Jeoldusan, while the area's pleasant parks are proof of how former industrial sites (water treatment plants, landfill sites) can be transformed into green urban spaces (and a cyclist's paradise) with sufficient public investment. Thanks to the Digital Media City (DMC) and the AREX express train station connecting Incheon Airport to Hongik, Mapo is now one of the most fashionable neighborhoods in the capital. Yeouido, the island in the Hangang south of Mapo, was the site of Seoul's first airport before becoming the center of political life (as the headquarters of the National Assembly), as well as of financial and media activity (as the home of the major TV channels).

VISIT
Bongwonsa 봉원사 (Bongwon Temple)

See Seodaemun map.
Bongwon-dong, Seodaemun-gu.
Ⓜ *Sinchon, line 2, exit 3. On leaving the subway take a taxi or bus no. 7024.* ℘*(02)-392-3007. http://bongwonsa. or.kr. No charge.*

The principal temple of the Taego order of Korean Buddhism, Bongwonsa houses some 50 monks led by Kim Gu-hae, a Living National Treasure. Founded in 889 on the site of Yonsei University by Master Do Seon (827–898), the temple complex moved to its present location in 1748. Most of the buildings are fairly recent, dating from the postwar reconstruction of Korea, or even more recently, from the 1990s. However, some attractive old buildings do remain, and

- **Michelin Map:** Map p202
- **Info:** Tourist Office 348-1 Seogyo-dong, Mapo-gu. Ⓜ Hongik Unversity, line 2, exit 5. ℘(02)-323-2240. Open daily noon–10pm.
- **Location:** North of the Hangang, this district is adjacent to the World Cup Park. Yeouido, the large island in the Hangang, is to the southeast.
- **Kids:** Take a cruise on the Hangang, see Seoul from the top of 63 Building, go for a walk in one of the parks.
- **Timing:** The district is best added to your agenda only if you have an extended stay in Seoul. However, Mapo is fun at night, especially given that a number of Seoul's other districts have less to offer by way of evening entertainment.
- **Don't Miss:** Bongwonsa in its rural setting, the Noryangjin Fish Market, Ewha Womans University, a night out in one of Mapo's lively clubs

Bongwonsa ©KTO

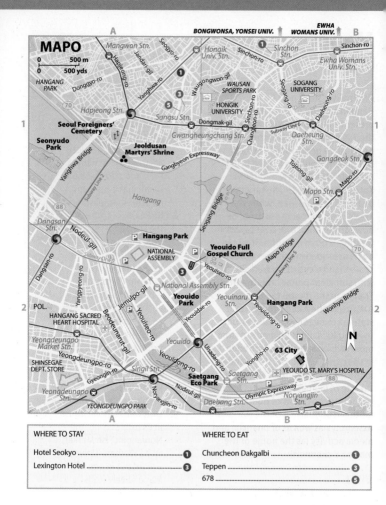

MAPO

0   500 m
0   500 yds

BONGWONSA, YONSEI UNIV.
EWHA WOMANS UNIV.

WHERE TO STAY		WHERE TO EAT	
Hotel Seokyo	**1**	Chuncheon Dakgalbi	**1**
Lexington Hotel	**3**	Teppen	**3**
		678	**5**

the whole site is well worth visiting for its aura of tranquility and lovely natural setting. There are pleasant walks to be had on the trails that lead up the mountain. In summer, the display of lotus flowers, a symbolic plant for Buddhists, is absolutely beautiful. The monastery also holds the *Yeongsanjae* ceremony, through which philosophical and spiritual messages of Buddhism are expressed.

This ritual, a reenactment of the delivery of the Lotus Sutra (sermon) on Vulture Peak in India by Buddha, dates back to the Goryeo period (918-1398) and has been listed as an Intangible Cultural Heritage by UNESCO.

Ewha Womans University
이화 여자 대학교

♿ *See Seodaemun map.*
Daehyeon-dong, Seodaemun-gu.
Ⓜ *Ewha Womans University, line 2, exits 2/3. On leaving the subway walk straight ahead.* ✆ *(02)-3277-3155.*
🕐 *Museum open daily Mon–Sat 10am–4pm. Closed public holidays.*
http://museum.ewha.ac.kr. No charge.
The campus of South Korea's most famous university for women is interesting for several reasons. Firstly, for the layout of the campus itself, with parks and old buildings in a neo-Tudor style in imitation of campuses in Britain and America, while the well-equipped modern buildings also show the wealth of

Seonyudo Park ©KTO

the university. Secondly, for its modern architecture on a monumental scale, with a vast ramp descending toward a flight of steps, between two tall walls faced with glass (lit up at night). French architect Dominique Perrault has succeeded in embedding the modern university buildings in such a way that they do not block the view and yet are not deprived of light. The university also has a very good small **private museum** featuring Korean antiquities.

Seonyudo Park★
선유도 공원

See Mapo map. 700 Nodeulgil, Youngdeungpo-gu. The island is accessed via Yanghwa Bridge.
The best way of reaching the park is to take a taxi from Ⓜ *Hapjeong, lines 2/6, exits 7/8, or from* Ⓜ *Dangsan, line 2, exits 1/4, or* Ⓜ *Seonyudo, line 9, exit 2, approx. 7 min walk.* ℘*(02)-3780-0590.*
Open daily 6am–midnight.

This is surely one of the most inventive and inspiring of the many green areas in Seoul. In 2000 the old water treatment plant on the island of Seonyudo was transformed into an award-winning ecological park. The old industrial structures (basins, conduits) were retained and cleverly adapted to create a labyrinth of water with many aquatic plants and surrounded by greenery, accessed by boardwalks and multilevel walkways. People relax on the grassy areas and bring picnics; toddlers splash about in a specially designed stream.

A pedestrian bridge with a graceful arc links the island to Seoul's south bank.

Jeoldusan Martyrs' Shrine
절두산 천주교 순교성지

See Mapo map. 96-1 Hapjeong-dong, Mapo-gu. Ⓜ *Hapjeong, lines 2/6, exit 7. Follow signs to the river.* ℘*(02)-3242-4434. www.jeoldusan.or.kr.*
Museum open Tue–Sun 9:30am–5pm. No charge.

Looking down over the Hangang, Jeoldusan Martyrs' Shrine is on the former military site known as Saenamto, where many Catholics were martyred, specifically in 1839 and 1866. The site was renamed Jeoldusan ("the hill of decapitated") because of the extensive persecutions carried out at the end of the Joseon dynasty. Many Koreans who had become Catholic were beheaded here, while others were strangled—a round stone with a rope through its central hole for this purpose can still be seen in the garden. A royal edict (1871) by the Daewongun (regent), a fierce enemy of Catholics, carved into stone states ominously: "Anyone who does not fight against the Western invaders is agreeing with them and selling our country to them."

Below the church, a small museum traces the troubled early history of the Catholic Church in Korea. This site, including the small park, its memorials and monuments, is still very important for Korean Catholics, and it was the first stop on John Paul II's papal visit in 1984.

Yeouido Park

© KTO

Seoul Foreigners' Cemetery
양화진 외국인 선교사묘원

⌀See Mapo map. 143 Hapjeong-dong, Mapo-gu. Ⓜ Hapjeong, lines 2/6, exit 7. Follow signs to the river. ℘(02)-332-9174. ⊙Open Mon–Sat 10am–5pm. No charge.

Also overlooking the Hangang, not far from Jeoldusan, this cemetery was founded in the late 19C when Korea first began to open up to the outside world by signing treaties of friendship and commerce with foreign powers. Recently renovated, it is the final resting place for more than 500 Westerners, mostly American or European.

ADDITIONAL SIGHTS
♁♁ Yeouido Park 여의도공원 and Saetgang Eco Park 샛강 생태공원

⌀See Mapo map. Ⓜ Saetgang, line 9, exit 4. http://parks.seoul.go.kr. No charge.

Yeouido Park lies in the center of what was formerly Yeouido Island and was originally covered in black asphalt, retained for so long because it was considered useful as an emergency airstrip in case of conflict.

However, in 1999 the asphalt was ripped up and replaced by a long park divided into themed sections: Korean Traditional Forest, Grass Yard, Culture Grounds and Nature Ecological Forest. Paths for cycling and rollerskating allow the energetic to let off steam, while

others are content to stroll and enjoy the natural scenery. In the southern part of the island, Saetgang Eco Park is a lush wetland full of birds, crossed by walkways and cycle paths.

♁♁ Hangang Park 여의도 한강 시민공원 (on Yeouido)

⌀See Mapo map. North coast of Yeouido Island. Ⓜ Yeouinaru, line 5, exits 2/3. http://hangang.seoul.go.kr/eng/. No charge.

Among the many public parks that line the banks of the Han and collectively make up the Hangang Park, the section on Yeouido is worth a special trip, especially in March and April when the cherry trees are in blossom.

The sight of hundreds of petals drifting down gently onto hordes of walkers below, like a late flurry of snow, is not to be missed. The long line of cherry trees stretches for some way behind the National Assembly building (on Yunjung-no). People also come here to take part in various water sports, and there is an outdoor pool in summer. It is also one of the starting points for riverboat cruises.

♁♁ 63 City 63시티

⌀See Mapo map. Yeouido-dong, Yeongdeungpo-gu. Ⓜ Yeouinaru, line 5, exit 4. ℘(02)-789-5663. www.63city.co.kr. ⊙Open daily 10am–10pm. Sky Art (combining an observatory and an exhibition) ₩12,000, aquarium ₩15,000, IMAX cinema ₩12,000, Pass ₩38,000.

This golden-clad skyscraper, 817ft/249m tall with 63 floors (3 floors underground) was a source of national pride when it was completed in 1985 to become the tallest building in Asia, which it remained until 2002. Although the interior and its facilities (an aquarium, an IMAX cinema and a shopping mall) are now slightly dated, a visit to the observatory at the top is worthwhile for its magnificent view over Seoul, especially at sunset. There is also a panoramic restaurant with an equally fantastic view.

Yeouido Full Gospel Church
여의도 순복음 교회
See Mapo map. 11 Yeouido-dong, Yeongdeungpo-gu. National Assembly, line 9, exit 1. On leaving the subway walk toward the last block on the right. (02)-780-5111. www.fgtv.org. Regular services: Sun 8:30am–2:30pm and Wed 10:30am–1pm.

Built in 1973, this huge Protestant church (*see photo p 83*) is the headquarters of the Pentecostal movement founded by Pastor David Yonggi Cho in 1958, which has approximately 800,000 followers. There are so many worshipers in Seoul that seven services are required on Sundays and, when big events are held, the congregation overspill watches on giant screens in adjacent buildings. Services are subtitled in various languages.

ADDRESSES

STAY

Lexington Hotel
렉싱턴호텔 – *13-3 Yeouido-dong, Youngdeungpo-gu. National Assembly, line 9, exits 1/3. 5min from the National Assembly and the parks bordering the Hangang. Easy access from the airports. (02)-6670-7000. www.thelexington.co.kr. 230 rm. ₩219,000/239,000. ₩19,000 .* This is a New York-style hotel whose aim is to make its customers feel at home and ensure any business travelers have all the facilities they need.

Hotel Seokyo 서교호텔 –
354-5 Seogyo-dong, Mapo-gu. Hongik University, line 2, exit 5. (02)-330-7777. www.hotelseokyo.co.kr. 135 rm. ₩200,000/245,000. ₩22,000 . An international hotel with gym, sauna and restaurant, in a useful position, ideal for those wishing to stay in the fashionable Hongdae area or to be close to Digital Media City. It is also near the new express subway station linking the city to Incheon airport.

EAT

678 육칠팔 – *408-22 Seogyo-dong, Mapo-gu. Sangsu, line 6, exit 2. (02)-326-0678. www.678.co.kr. Open daily 11am–4am. Approximately ₩20,000 per person.* A restaurant chain serving grilled meat run by Korean celebrity Kang Ho-dong, host of TV show *Star King*. The friendly service, delicious meat dishes and quality *banchan* at very affordable prices ensure its popularity. The opening times are perfect for night owls.

Chuncheon Dakgalbi 춘천 닭갈비 – *57-8 Changcheong-dong, Seodaemun-gu. Behind the Hyundai Department Store. Sinchon, line 2, exit 1. (02)-325-2361. Open daily 10am–6am. ₩6,500 per portion of boneless chicken.* A traditional restaurant in a student neighborhood serving chicken fried on a griddle with vegetables and spicy sauce. All the ingredients can then be mixed with rice and fried (for an additional charge). Simple, good and cheap. It's noisy, but there's a fun, student atmosphere.

Teppen 텟펜 – *409-1 Seogyo-dong, Mapo-gu, in the alley where the clubs MI, Joker Red, etc. are located. Sangsu, line 6, exit 2. (02)-336-5578. www.teppenkorea.com. Open Tue–Sun 5pm–1am (Fri–Sat 3am). Dishes approximately ₩12,000.* This famous Japanese restaurant chain is never empty. The reason: the serving staff are trained in Japan in the house style, which involves a loud chorus of welcoming greetings, with the whole restaurant toasting new customers as they arrive. And then there are the dishes, most of which are very

tasty, including an unusual fried beef cartilage salad and *okonomiyaki* cakes. A noisy atmosphere is guaranteed!

🚃 TAKING A BREAK

Café aA aA 까페에이에이 – *Design Museum, 408-11 Seogyo-dong, Mapo-gu. Ⓜ Sangsu, line 6, exit 1. ☎ (02)-3143-7312. www.aAdesign museum.com. Open daily noon–midnight. ₩7,000–15,000.* This café is on the ground floor of the aA Design Museum, whose aims are summed up by the small "a" standing for "architecture," "art" and "alive," and the large "A" representing the highest level of academic assessment. The museum also includes a gallery, bookstore and shop. The café showcases the owner's collection of 19C and 20C Western furniture, so you can sink into the chair or sofa you find most comfortable while sipping your tea.

KT & G Sangsang Madang 케이티앤지상상마당 – *367-5 Seogyo-dong, Mapo-gu. Ⓜ Hongik University, line 2, exit 5 or Ⓜ Sangsu, line 6, exit 2. ☎ (02)-330-6200. www.sangsangmadang.com. Open daily noon–10pm (shop 11pm, café midnight). Closed 1st Mon of the month.* This complex explores different cultural themes on several floors and is shaped like a concrete flower or flame. There is a shop for artists on the ground floor, an arts and experimental cinema, a theater, a gallery and a pleasant café on the sixth floor.

🍸 BARS

Atay Moroccan Bar 아타이 – *19-24 Wausanro 17gil, Mapo-gu, in the same small street as Café aA, opposite the Indian restaurant Diwan-i-am, in the basement. Ⓜ Sangsu, line 6, exit 2. ☎ (02)-336-7760. Open daily 6pm–1am (Sat–Sun 3am). Wine from ₩29,000, drinks from ₩6,000.* Among the dozens of neighborhood bars, this one stands out for its Moroccan theme. Situated in a basement with a high ceiling, the atmosphere is North African – there are alcoves filled with soft cushions and equipped with hookahs. Low-priced wine and an unpretentious snack menu.

Club Day 클럽데이 – *Hongdae district. Ⓜ Hongik University, line 2, exit 5 or Ⓜ Sangsu, line 6, exit 2. www.theclubday.co.kr. Open on last Fri of the month. ₩20,000 (drink included).* There is an excellent scheme for party-goers which has been in operation since 2001: one ticket gives you access to most of the clubs in the area, from the large M2, where MTV Korea is filmed, to the tiny cellar clubs located in the basement of buildings. For information on programs and locations, see the website or the posters on all the walls in the neighborhood. Or simply take your cue from the waves of young people, and music, coming out of every nook and cranny.

🛒 SHOPPING

Hongdae Free & Hope Market 홍대 자유/희망 시장 – *Square, opposite the entrance to Hongik University. Ⓜ Hongik University, line 2, exit 5. ☎ (02)-325-8553. Open Sat–Sun, Mar–Nov 1pm–6pm. No charge for entry.* In the square opposite the university, a small market is held where young students and artists come to sell jewelry and crafts. The Free Market on Saturday is more focused on crafts; the Hope Market on Sunday specializes in accessories. Anyone can take part by registering as a trader in advance. Information is available from Mapo City Hall.

Noryangjin Fish Market 노량진 수산시장 – *Ⓜ Noryangjin, line 1, exit 1, direct entrance to the market. ☎ (02)-814-2211. Open daily 24hr. Closed on public holidays.* This wholesale fish market handles 450 tons of fish per day. From sharks to rays, through crabs and sea cucumbers, all the local species of fresh fish, both live and dried, are sold here. The atmosphere is unique, especially at dawn when the auction is held. You can choose a fish and take it to one of the nearby restaurants to be cooked on the spot, however you like it—fried, poached, grilled….

Southwest of the Han River
한강남서방향

If you are on a quick visit to Seoul with time only for the main sights, this district probably won't be on your itinerary, unless it is to catch a traditional performance at the National Gukak Center, part of the Seoul Arts Center, a huge cultural complex devoted mainly to the performing arts. Most of the area has been developed only fairly recently, since the 1970s. Below the Express Bus Terminal, you'll find a vast shopping mall, along with a department store and facilities such as an international hotel, and if you notice a French feel to the district, it's because the French quarter Bangbae-dong, with its patisseries and cafés, is also located here. In the southwestern part of the district, near Seoul National University, some beautiful walks and hiking trails cross the small mountain called Gwanaksan, also a city park.

- **Michelin Map:** Map p208
- **Location:** Southwest of the Hangang, around the Seoul Arts Center.
- **Kids:** Cool down at Jamwon, one of the outdoor swimming pools along the Hangang.
- **Timing:** A fairly extensive area that is not very pedestrian friendly—the traffic is often congested, so allow plenty of time for journeys by car, or take the subway whenever possible.
- **Don't Miss:** Seoul Arts Center, a free traditional folk art performance at the National Gugak Center.

VISIT
Seoul Arts Center (SAC)
예술의전당
See Southwest of Han River map.
700 Seocho-dong, Seocho-gu.
Nambu Bus Terminal, line 3, exit 5.
(02)-580-1300/1532. www.sac.or.kr.
This enormous cultural complex is dedicated to both Korean and Western art. It includes art galleries (*see below*), the Seoul Calligraphy Art Museum and the

Cycling beside the Hangang

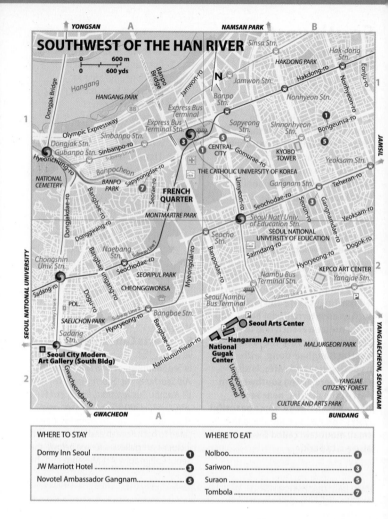

SOUTHWEST OF THE HAN RIVER

WHERE TO STAY		WHERE TO EAT	
Dormy Inn Seoul	❶	Nolboo	❶
JW Marriott Hotel	❸	Sariwon	❸
Novotel Ambassador Gangnam	❺	Suraon	❺
		Tombola	❼

Music Hall (in fact two halls) for classical concerts. Besides the huge central opera-theater (for opera, theater and ballet), shaped like a traditional Korean hat *(gat)*, with its three separate auditoriums, the complex also contains the **National Gugak Center**, where you can see excellent traditional performances, and a museum of traditional Korean instruments and other items associated with music *(www.gugak.go.kr)*.

Hangaram Art Museum
한가람미술관
⌚ *See Southwest of Han River map.*
700 Seocho-dong, Seocho-gu, part of the Seoul Arts Center. Ⓜ *Nambu Bus Terminal, line 3, exit 5.* ☎ *(02)-580-1300. www.sac.or.kr/eng/Space/space_art.jsp.*
⏰*Open daily Mar–Oct 11am–8pm; Nov–Feb 11am–7pm. Closed last Mon of the month.*

On the central square of the Seoul Arts Center, the name of this exhibition center is slightly misleading as it is really a contemporary art gallery with six main rooms for temporary exhibitions. There is also a shop and a café. Similarly, the Hangaram Design Museum (to the right of the main entrance) is also not really a museum but rather a gallery devoted to the theme of "the identity of Korean design." There is a café here too, plus a multimedia center.

Seoul Arts Center

©Chris Stowers/Apa Publications

Seoul City Modern Art Gallery (South Bldg)
서울 시립미술관남서울 분관

See Southwest of Han River map.
1059-13 Namhyeon-dong, Gwanak-gu.
 Sadang, lines 2/4, exit 6. (02)-598-6247. http://seoulmoa.seoul.go.kr.
 Open Tue–Sat 10am–8pm (public holidays –6pm). Closed 1 Jan.
No charge.

This building (1905) is one of the few of its era to be located south of the river, but it was originally in the district of Jung-gu. Built by Japanese architects in the Western style, it housed the Belgian Legation before this was moved to Chungmuro in 1919, at which point the building became the headquarters of a Japanese insurance company. Subsequently used by the Department of the Navy, then by a bank, the building was listed in 1982 and moved to its present location. Its southern annex is now home to the Seoul City Modern Art Gallery and hosts temporary exhibitions.

Jamwon Swimming Pool

See Southwest of Han River map
Near Hannam Bridge (Hannamgyo).
 (02)-536-8263. Open daily July–Aug,
9am–8pm. Adult ₩5,000, children
age 4–12 ₩3,000, age 14–18 ₩4,000.
 Sinsa, line 3, exit 5, 10–15 min walk.
http://hangang.seoul.go.kr/eng

Jamwon is one of several outdoor pools along the Hangang that open in the summer. The pool is complete with water slides and sunbathing areas. The nearby park is a pleasant place to stroll before or after your dip or for a picnic.

Yangjaecheon (Yangjae Stream) 양재천

See Seoul Map I. Hakdong-no,
Gangnam-gu. Dogok, line 3, exit 4
or Daechi, line 3, exits 6/7 or
 Gaepo-dong, line 3, exit 2.
 (02)-2104-2180/1494. http://ypark.
gangnam.go.kr. No charge.

This **stream**, which runs across the city south of Gangnam for 9.7mi/15.6km before emptying into the Han, was among those sacrificed in the 1970s and 1980s in the name of industrialization. Today, however, Yangjaecheon is one of the best examples of the city's recent ecological restoration projects, carried out between 1995 and 2000.

A stroll beside this now clean tributary of the Hangang with the reed banks full of wildlife (frogs, migratory birds) is very pleasant indeed. In the summer, children even come here to swim.

As an oasis of greenery amid the towering buildings, it has become one of the most picturesque natural spaces in Seoul.

ADDRESSES

🏨 STAY

🛏🛏🛏 Dormy Inn Seoul
도미인 서울 – *205-8 Nonhyeon-dong, Gangnam-gu.* Ⓜ *Sinnonhyeon, line 9, exit 3.* ☎*(02)-6474-1515. www.dormy. co.kr. 190rm. ₩121,000/220,000* 🍴.
Located in the heart of Gangnam, Dormy Inn provides studio rooms with kitchenettes. The rooms are quite spacious and comfortable, and the welcome is warm. The best view is from the upper floors. Book by phone if possible, as prices may be lower than those offered on the internet.

🛏🛏🛏 Novotel Ambassador Gangnam 노보텔앰버서더강남 호텔 – *603 Yeoksam-dong, Gangnam-gu.* Ⓜ *Sinnonhyeon, line 9, exit 4.* ☎*(02)-531-6502. http://www. novotel.com. 603rm. ₩200,000/352,000* 🍴✕. From this conveniently located hotel you have access to several different areas south of the Hangang: Garosu-gil, Cheongdam-dong, COEX, and not forgetting lively Gangnam street for an evening drink. The hotel has just been completely renovated and offers luxury accommodation with restaurants, a swimming pool and a fitness club. Book online for the best rates.

🛏🛏🛏🛏 JW Marriott Hotel
제이더블유 매리어트 호텔 – *19-3 Banpo-dong, Seocho-gu.* Ⓜ *Express Bus Terminal, lines 3/7, exits 3/7.* ☎*(02)-6282-6262. www.marriott.com. 497rm. ₩279,000/349,000. ₩20,000* 🍴✕.
This luxury hotel provides top quality service close to the shopping malls of Central City. The most spacious rooms, recently renovated, have views over the river or to the mountains. The Marriott also has a swimming pool and one of the largest spa-fitness clubs in Asia.

🍴 EAT

🍴 Sariwon 사리원 – *1321-7 Seocho-dong, Seocho-gu. A few minutes' walk down the first left after the subway exit.* Ⓜ *Gangnam, line 2, exit 4.* ☎*(02)-3474-5005. www.sariwon.co.kr. 11:30am–10pm. ₩8,000/45,000.*

This Korean restaurant has gained a reputation over three generations for its grilled meat and *bulgogi*, beef marinated in a thin sauce and braised on the barbecue *(₩26,000 per portion).* The cold noodles *(₩8,000)* and beef soup *(₩10,000)* are also tasty.

🍴🍴 Suraon 수라온 – *118-3 Banpo-dong, Seocho-gu. Near the JW Marriott Hotel.* Ⓜ *Express Bus Terminal, lines 3/7, exits 3/7.* ☎*(02)-595-0202. Open daily noon–10pm. A la carte ₩25,000, fixed price menus ₩35,000/110,000.*
Korean court cuisine from the Joseon period and other traditional menus that include an array of dishes with different flavors. The setting is somewhat sedate, but there is a good traditional folk performance *(Thu–Tue 12:30pm, 1:20pm, 6:20pm, 7:20pm and 8:20pm, Wed 6pm, 7pm and 8pm; request seats near the stage).*

🍴🍴 Tombola 톰볼라 – *106-8 Banpo 4-dong, Seocho-gu, on the street next to Paris Croissant.* Ⓜ *Express Bus Terminal, line 7, exit 5.* ☎*(02)-593-4660. www.tombola.co.kr. Open daily noon–3:30pm, 6pm–10:30pm (last orders 9:30pm). Closed public holidays. A la carte ₩16,000/₩35,000, fixed price menus: lunch ₩19,000/25,000, dinner ₩40,000/50,000.* This is a good Italian restaurant serving quality food at moderate prices. All the classics, including excellent pizzas, are served in a simple but friendly atmosphere.

🍴🍴🍴 Nolboo 놀부 – *118-3 Banpo-dong, Seocho-gu. Near the JW Marriott Hotel.* Ⓜ *Express Bus Terminal, lines 3/7, exits 3/7.* ☎*(02)-592-5292. Open daily noon–10pm. ₩55,000 for duck for 3 persons.* A restaurant specializing in duck. Don't miss the *yuhwang ori jinheulk gui*, delicious duck steamed for three hours, stuffed with rice, ginseng and other spices. A real treat! As it takes some time to prepare, you need to order this dish in advance. The restaurant is recognizable by its logo: a traditional Korean black face on a white background.

Songpa-gu-Jamsil
송파구-잠실

Seoul's hosting of the 1988 Olympics provided the impetus for much of the recent building in what appears to be, at first sight, a very modern district. High-rise apartment buildings seem to stretch out to infinity, while the sculpture garden, vast sports arenas of the Olympic Park and the popular Lotte World with its amusement park, shopping malls and restaurants are all resolutely 21C. However, this district also bears traces of the very first human settlements in the city. This is where the kingdom of Baekje established its first capital, as evidenced from the remains of fortifications and burial sites. Nearby, toward the edge of the city, the prehistoric site of Amsa-dong is also a reminder that this area was an important inhabited site from very ancient times. This is where the history of Seoul began, although its modern history is now written in steel and concrete.

VISIT
👪 Lotte World 롯데월드
👁 See Songpa-gu-Jamsil map
40-1 Jamsil-dong, Songpa-gu.

- 👁 **Michelin Map:** Map p212
- ℹ️ **Info:** Tourist Office 27 Jamsil 5-dong, Songpa-gu. Basement of Lotte World, near the Seoul Playground and Lotte Dept. Store. Ⓜ Jamsil, line 2, exit 4. ✆ (02)-2143-7007. Open daily 10am–7pm.
- ▶ **Location:** To the far southeast of the Hangang, near the Olympic Park.
- 👪 **Kids:** Lotte World amusement park and Folk Museum.
- 🕐 **Timing:** More suited to the car than the pedestrian, it's best to use the subway or a taxi to get around this district. A visit to Lotte World can take a good half-day, but beware of endless lines at the weekend!

Ⓜ *Jamsil, lines 2/8, exit 4.* ✆ *(02)-411-2000. www.lotteworld.com.* 🕐 *Open Mon–Thu 9:30am–10pm, Fri–Sun 9:30am–11pm. Day pass ₩37,000.*
This famous amusement park includes an Adventure Park and Magic Island in Seokchon Lake (Seokchonhosu), both packed full of rides, shows and parades (some inside a gigantic dome), restaurants and shops—there are also two Lotte Department Stores, one at either

Lotte World

©KTO

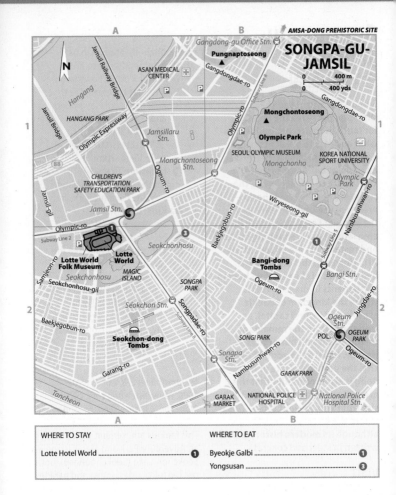

AMSA-DONG PREHISTORIC SITE

SONGPA-GU-JAMSIL

WHERE TO STAY

Lotte Hotel World .... ❶

WHERE TO EAT

Byeokje Galbi .... ❶
Yongsusan .... ❸

end of the complex—and a sports center with a swimming pool.

🚭 *Avoid public holidays and weekends when the crowds are so large that just waiting in line for the rides will eat into your time.*

👥♿ Lotte World Folk Museum
롯데월드 민속 박물관

♿*See Songpa-gu-Jamsil map.*
3F 40-1 Jamsil-dong, Songpa-gu.
3rd floor of the Lotte World building, outside the amusement park.
Ⓜ *Jamsil, lines 2/8, exit 4.* ℘*(02)-411-4761. www.lotteworld.com.* ⏰*Open daily 9:30am–8pm.* ₩*5,000, included in a Lotte World day pass.*

This offers the opportunity to "enjoy and understand" the history and culture of Korea. The exhibition hall traces the main periods in Korea's history, from prehistory to the Goryeo dynasty. The miniature village shows what life was like in the Joseon period with 2,000 figures and buildings. Traditional music and dance shows take place in the performance hall and you can also enjoy the atmosphere and culture of a traditional market. The museum has been designed with children in mind, using reconstructions, models and dioramas.

Amsa-dong Prehistoric Settlement 암사동 선사 수지지

139-2 Amsa-dong, Gangdong-gu.
Ⓜ *Amsa, line 8, exit 4.* ☏ *(02)-3426-3857/67.* Ⓞ*Open Tue–Sun 9:30am–6pm. Reservations required for guided tours one week in advance.* ₩500.

The prehistoric site of Amsa-dong, not far from the Hangang, dates from the Neolithic era and was discovered following the great floods of 1925. A number of pit houses with straw roofs have been reconstructed on the site following the excavations here to give visitors an idea of how the ancient people would have lived. A small museum contains dioramas of the site as well as exhibits of the tools and implements that would have been part of daily life.

Olympic Park 올림픽공원

♿ *See Songpa-gu-Jamsil map.*
426 Olympik-no, Jamsil-dong, Songpa-gu. Ⓜ *Olympic Park, line 5, exit 3 or* Ⓜ *Mongchontoseong, line 8, exit 1.* ☏ *(02)-410-1114.* Ⓞ*Open daily 5am–10pm. No charge.*

This site was built in 1985 for the 1988 Olympic Games and was subsequently transformed into a fine public park with walks, lawns and ponds alongside the various sports arenas. The site also includes **Soma Museum of Art**, incorporating a sculpture park that sometimes hosts cultural events, and **Mongchontoseong**, the remains of a fortress dating from the kingdom of Baekje (18 BC–AD 660) excavated between 1983 and 1989, thought by some experts to be the remains of Hanam (south of the river) Wiryeseong, the first capital of Baekje. However, others believe the ancient city was situated closer to the river, at **Pungnaptoseong** (Pungnap fortress). Of this site, only a section of earthen walls now remain, although some major discoveries from the recent excavations (1997–present) would seem to support the second theory.

With a circumference of 1.4mi/2.2km, Mongchontoseong takes advantage of the natural topography of the site by being built on a hill whose sides were shaved away in places to create ramparts. Thick clay walls that were initially 43-49ft/13-18m high lay at the base, and they were in turn surrounded by a ditch and a wooden fence that has been partially restored. This fortress dates from the 3C.

A small museum (**Mongchon History Exhibition Hall,** Ⓞ *Mon–Fri 9am–9pm; Sat–Sun Mar–Oct 9am–7pm, Nov–Feb 9am–6pm, no charge*) displays objects found during the excavations. On the hill, an ancient settlement with 12 houses from the beginning of the Baekje period has been excavated and preserved under a dome. The site was used throughout the Hanseong Baekje era (until the transfer of the capital farther south) and subsequently by the Goguryeo invaders. It was then largely abandoned for several centuries, although during the Joseon period there were some small villages on the site and several famous scholars, including Kim Gu (17C), whose tomb can be visited, lived here.

Baekje Tombs 백제고분

♿ *See Songpa-gu-Jamsil map.*

If, as some historians believe, this was the site of the ancient Baekje kingdom's capital Hanam Wiryeseong for over 500 years, the presence of burial grounds nearby would be expected. Indeed, a large number of burials took place near here, but only a few sites have been preserved.

Baekje Tombs, Bangi-dong

©KTO

213

Seokchon-dong Tombs

See Songpa-gu-Jamsil map.
248 Seokchon-dong, Songpa-gu.
Ⓜ *Seokchon, line 8, exit 5 or* Ⓜ *Songpa,*
line 8, exit 4. ℘*(02)-410-3662.* Ⓞ*Open*
daily 6am–8pm. No charge.

This is a collection of 89 tumulus or stepped platform graves and 12 earth pits. Four have been completely restored. You can trace the various transitional design stages from the simplest to the more complex style imported by the Goguryeo from the north, characterized by platforms of stones forming low pyramid-style stepped tombs.

Some, like tombs 3, 4 and 5, are a combination of styles. There are also rectangular pits that were almost certainly used to bury the lower social classes, while the large mounds would have been burial places for members of the aristocracy, and perhaps even for kings.

Bangi-dong Tombs

See Songpa-gu-Jamsil map.
47-4 Bangi-dong, Songpa-gu. Ⓜ *Bangi,*
line 5, exit 3. ℘*(02)-2147-2000.* Ⓞ*Open*
daily 6am–8pm. No charge.

Eight tombs can be seen here in the later Baekje style (as also found in Gongju and Buyeo) consisting of a stone burial chamber and an entrance hall beneath a mound of earth. Two styles of megalithic tomb can generally be distinguished in Asia: the northern ("table") style with an above-ground burial chamber and the southern style with underground burial chambers.

The graves of Goguryeo and Silla are in the northern style, as are the graves of Seokchon-dong, while those in Bangi, such as Buyeo and Gongju, are underground, illustrating the transition of the Bangi graves to the southern style. These tombs invariably belong to members of the aristocracy.

ADDRESSES

🛏 STAY

🛏🛏🛏🛏 **Lotte Hotel World**
롯데월드 호텔 – *40-1 Jamsil-dong,*
Songpa-gu. Ⓜ *Jamsil, lines 2/8, exit 3.*
℘*(02)-419-7000. www.lottehotelworld.*
com. 469rm. ₩310,000/360,000. ₩29,000
🛏 ✕. An upscale hotel adjacent to the Olympic Park. If you have children, you can rent a Character Room with magical decorations. In addition to an array of restaurants, bars and shops, a number of clinics offer Oriental medicine, dental treatments and plastic surgery—a reminder of South Korea's relatively recent foray into the medical tourism industry.

🍽 EAT

🍽🍽 **Byeokje Galbi** 벽제갈비 –
205-8 Bangi-dong, Songpa-gu.
Ⓜ *Bangi, line 5, exit 4.* ℘*(02)-415-5522.*
Open daily 11am–10pm. ₩10,000/
75,000. This restaurant is worth visiting for its Korean barbecue. The meat is exceptionally good and melts in the mouth. Fixed price menu for ₩50,000 with plenty of *banchan*. Cold noodles, *sun-myeon*, are available in summer.

🍽🍽 **Yongsusan** 용수산 – *58-17*
Songpa-dong, Songpa-gu. Ⓜ *Jamsil,*
lines 2/8, exit 10. ℘*(02)-425-4674.*
www.yongsusan.com. Open daily 11am
–10:30pm. A la carte ₩20,000/38,000,
fixed price menus ₩38,000/98,000.
Yongsusan serves traditional royal cuisine dishes of the Goryeo dynasty, so expect to experience some quite different tastes. The decor is simple, but the service is good.

🍽🍽🍽🍽 **Pilkyongjae** 필경재 –
739-14 Suseo-dong, Gangnam-gu.
Ⓜ *Suseo, line 3, exit 1.* ℘*(02)-445-2115.*
www.philkyungjae.co.kr. Open daily
noon–3pm, 6pm–10pm. Closed public
holidays. Fixed price menus ₩38,000/
165,000. This restaurant is in an old building that is a fine example of traditional architecture. It serves excellent *hanjeongsik* cuisine consisting of multiple courses. Worth a visit especially for the charm of its small individual rooms and a setting worthy of a period film.

Bukhansan★
북한산

Bukhansan, the highest mountain in the national park named after it, is like the "dragon's tail" of the mountain chain that crosses the Korean Peninsula. The park itself is a fantastic resource for the people of the city who come here to walk and climb and sometimes to take stock and draw strength from this tranquil and spiritual environment. During the weekends, the trails can get quite congested, and overnight shelters need to be booked in advance. However, on weekdays, it really is worth coming here to enjoy this wild place so close to Seoul. As with, it seems, nearly every mountain in Korea, the park is dotted with many ancient Buddhist temples and also has a large fortress, Bukhansanseong, which protected the capital and served as a refuge for the king in the event of invasion.

VISIT
Bukhansan National Park★
북한산 둘레길
Bukhansan National Park Office, see Orient Panel, to the right. http://english.knps.or.kr. ⏱ *Open daily Apr–Oct 9am–3pm, Nov–Mar 10am–3pm. Site closes at 5pm.*

⚓ **Michelin Map:** Seoul Map I pp106–107 and Bukhansan National Park Map p 216

ℹ **Info:** Bukhansan National Park Office San 1-1, Jeongneung-dong, Seongbuk-gu. ✆(02)-909-0497/0498. Bukhansan National Park Northern Office. Uijeongbu-si, Gyeonggi-do. ✆(031)-873-2791/2792.

▶ **Location:** Bukhansan National Park covers an area of 31sq mi/80sq km around the two mountains Dobongsan to the north and Bukhansan to the south. Administratively, it is partly in the city of Seoul and partly in Gyeonggi-do. Choose the entrance closest to the part of the park you wish to explore and based on how much time you have. Most of the main entrances are near subway stations.

☺ **Don't Miss:** The spectacular Bukhansan National Park and its fortress, Hwagyesa in its serene setting.

Bukhansan National Park

©Chris Stowers/Apa Publications

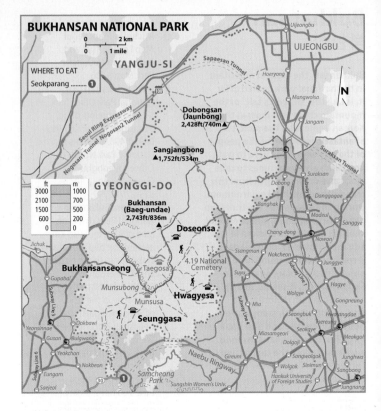

BUKHANSAN NATIONAL PARK

0   2 km
0   1 mile

WHERE TO EAT
Seokparang 1

YANGJU-SI

UIJEONGBU

Uijeongbu

Hoeryong

Sapaesan Tunnel

Seoul Ring Expressway

Nogosan1 Tunnel /Nogosan2 Tunnel

Mangwolsa

Dobongsan
(Jaunbong)
2,428ft/740m ▲

Jangam

Sangjangbong
▲1,752ft/534m

Dobongsan

Suraksan Tunnel

ft   m
3000   1000
2100   700
1500   500
600   200
0   0

GYEONGGI-DO

Suraksan

Dabong

Danggogae

Bukhansan
(Baeg-undae)
2,743ft/836m
▲

Banghak

Madeul

Sanggye

Doseonsa

Chang-dong

Nowon

Jichuk

Ssangmun

Nakcheon

Junggye

Bukhansanseong

Taegosa

4.19 National
Cemetery

Suyu

Gupabal

Hagye

Munsubong

Hwagyesa

Mia

Wolgye

Gongneung

Munsusa

Seongbuk

Hwarangdae

Taereung

Dokbawi

Seunggasa

Miasamgeori

Seokgye

Meokgol

Yeonsinnae

Gusan

Bulgwang

Dolgoji

Sangwolgok

Junghwa

Yeokchon

Nokbeon

Naebu Ringway

Gireum

Wolgok

Sinimun

Sangbong

Eungam

Samcheong
Park

Hankuk University
of Foreign Studies

Jungnang

Saejeol

Sungshin Women's Univ.

Mangwolsa, Dobongsan, Suraksan — Subway Line 1
Subway Line 2, Subway Line 3, Subway Line 4, Subway Line 6

N

Most of the park's hiking trails lead to the peaks, the highest being Baeg-undae (2,743ft/836m) on Bukhansan. There are too many trails to describe in detail, but generally they are well marked and take 1–5hr to complete. The terrain is very steep in places, and many of the trails are quite challenging. You can spend the night in one of the park's shelters (₩5,000, plus blanket ₩1,000/2,000); although it is advisable to take your own sleeping bag.

Accommodations are limited, so be sure to book in advance through the park office.

It is also advisable to take some food on your hike; however, there are normally restaurants located at the various park entrances. It is forbidden to move off the trails and to camp or smoke outside the designated areas. There are some 50 official access points, usually located near a subway or a bus stop. You can buy a map of the park when you purchase your ticket.

With its many gorges, granite peaks, crystal-clear streams and spectacular scenery that changes with the seasons, the park is particularly beautiful. It was established in 1983 and attracts a great many visitors—nearly five million each year—due to its proximity to the city. Before Seoul grew to its current size, Bukhansan, in its location north of the city, was viewed as a natural strategic defense, and **Bukhansanseong**, the mountain fortress that was built here, can still be seen today. However, the park is now completely surrounded by the expanding metropolis.

Under the Joseon dynasty, fortified walls were built to repel invaders, parts of which are still visible at different points along some of the trails; even today, some areas of the park are barred to the public by the military. The area's

---

An Ecological Island

Designated a national park in 1983, Bukhansan National Park is a popular nature escape for those who live in the busy metropolis of Seoul. Being surrounded on all sides by the growing city, the park is easily accessed by road or subway.

Visitors with keen eyes might catch sight of the Great Spotted Woodpecker, a flagship species of the park. The birds are mainly black and white, with red running from the lower part of the stomach to the tail feathers. Along with the more than 1,300 species of flora and fauna, there are also many cultural and historical sights to explore in the park, including the Bukhansan Fortress and over 100 Buddhist temples and the plentiful monks' cells that dot the slopes.

The millions of visitors to the park each year have taken a bit of a toll on the ecosystem, so travellers are encouraged to follow any posted voluntary regulations, such as avoiding restricted areas at all times.

tranquility lends itself to meditation and a number of temples and monasteries can be found along the way.

To climb **Baeg-undae**, the highest point in the park, there are a number of trails, including one that begins at the **Bukhansanseong Hiking Support Center** (Ⓜ *Gupabal, line 3, exit 1, then taxi or bus no. 704/34 to the Bukhansanseong stop*).

To reach **Jaunbong** (*2,428ft/740m*), Dobongsan's highest peak, head for the Dobong entrance (Ⓜ *Dobongsan Station, lines 1/7, then take a taxi or walk for 15–20min along the street lined with outdoor-activity clothing and equipment stalls*).

For a pleasant and normally less crowded trail, start from the southwest at the **Iljimun entrance** or **Jingwan Temple** (Ⓜ *Gupabal, line 3, exit 3, then take a taxi or bus no. 7724 to the temple*).

After the temple, the walk follows an idyllic valley toward the top of Bibong-san (*1,837ft/560m*) and then descends on the other side of the mountain, to the Bibong or Seungga exits, past **Seung-gasa (Seungga Temple)** where there is a famous Buddhist statue.

Finally, to the southeast, the **Hwagye and Naenggol entrances** are also starting points for excellent walks (Ⓖ *see access to Hwagyesa below*).

Bukhansanseong 북한산성 (Bukhansan Fortress)

Bukhan-dong, Deokyang-gu, Goyang-si, Gyeonggi-do. Ⓜ *Gupabal, line 3, exit 1, then taxi or bus no. 704 to the Bukhansanseong stop.* ✆ *(02)-357-9698.* Ⓞ *Open year-round. No charge.*

A fortress was first built on the site in AD 132 during the Three Kingdoms era, but the structure you see today dates from much later. Following the Japanese invasions 1592–98 and the Manchu invasion in 1636, work began on a new fortress that would protect the north of the capital and provide a safe retreat for the king and his family. Construction was completed in 1711 during the reign of King Sukjong.

Fifteen gates and a wall of 6.5mi/10km guarded access to the site, which made the most of the mountainous terrain. The complex included a 120-room palace for the monarch, along with temples (some staffed by warrior monks), military buildings, wells and storehouses. The royal apartments may have been smaller than in the royal palaces of Seoul, but they were adequate in terms of a secondary residence.

Much of the fortress was reconstructed after damage suffered during the Korean War but, thanks to the exceptional setting, it is still worth a visit. This is also the starting point for many walks.

Doseonsa

©KTO

Doseonsa 도선사 (Doseon Temple)

163 Ui-dong, Ganbuk-gu.
Ⓜ *Suyu, line 4, exit 3, then taxi or bus no. 130/170/1217.* ✆ *(02)-993-3261.*
🕐 *Open daily 6am–7pm.*

Founded in 862 b y the famous monk Doseon, this is the largest and best-known temple in the park and gets very crowded at weekends. Behind the main hall is a superb representa-tion of the Avalokitesvara bodhisattva, said to have been carved into the rock by Doseon himself. Buddha's birthday (☾*see p 28*) is the perfect time to visit the temple—not for the peace and tranquility as it will be very busy—but to enjoy the thousands of colorful lanterns and the festive atmosphere. Once you have seen the temple, continue your walk along the trail.

Hwagyesa 화계사 (Hwagye Temple)

487 Suyu 1-dong, Gangbuk-gu.
Ⓜ *Suyu, line 4, exit 3, then bus no. 2 (Maul bus). Get off at Hanshin University, and climb the narrow road leading up the mountain until you reach the temple.* ✆ *(02)-900-4326/902-2663. http://seoulzen.org/information.html.*

Although this temple was founded in 1523, the current buildings date from a reconstruction of 1866. The setting is so serene that it is no surprise to find that the temple is also home to the **Hwa Gye Sa Int'l Zen Center**, which offers a variety of activities for foreigners interested in learning about Zen Buddhism.
🐢 *On Sundays there is a free Dharma talk at 3pm, with instruction for first-time participants at 12:30pm and meditation periods from 1pm. The center also organizes retreats lasting from two days to several months.*

Hwagyesa

©Courtesy Hwa Gye Sa International Zen Center

Wonderful room, W Seoul – Walkerhill

©Starwood Hotels & Resorts

ADDRESSES

🏨 STAY

The Shilla Seoul 신라 서울 호텔 – *202 Jangchung-dong 2-ga, Jung-gu.* Ⓜ *Dongguk University, line 3, exit 5.* ☎*(02)-2233-3131. www.shilla.net/en/seoul. 465rm from ₩230,000.* 🍽 ✕ *₩35,500.* This top-class hotel has a legendary reputation for high-quality service and has played host to many foreign dignitaries. It aims to provide "authentic charm with modern, world-class luxury." There are several renowned restaurants located here, including the famous Parkview buffet. Rooms have views over the city or the national park. Take a dip in the pool, or revitalize yourself by visiting the Guerlain spa.

W Seoul – Walkerhill 더블유 서울 호텔 – *175 Achaseong-gil, Gwangjin-gu.* 🖐*See Seoul Map I, pp102–103.* Ⓜ *Gwangnaru, line 5, exit 2.* ☎*(02)-465-2222. www.wseoul.com. 252rm from ₩220,000.* 🍽 ✕ *₩30,000.* Set away from the city center, this hotel is located amid the lush greenery of Achasan (Mt. Acha) overlooking the Hangang. Fashionable and chic, the rooms are spacious and the design innovative. If it's beyond your budget in terms of accommodation, come for a drink, to have dinner or to play the casino at the Paradise Casino Walkerhill, a sister establishment on the adjacent site. Competitively priced for this level of service.

Hankang Hotel – *188-2 Gwangjang-dong, Gwangjin-gu.* Ⓜ *Gangnam, line 2, Gangbyeon Station exit.* ☎*(02)-453-5131. http:// hankanghotel.co.kr. 116rm from ₩98,000.* 🍽 ✕. Located along the upper banks of the Hangang River, Hankang Hotel offers great views of the natural surroundings. The view outside is the focus for this hotel, so the rooms are understated, but comfortable. Additional on-site facilities include Korean and Western restaurants, a nightclub and a full range of spa services.

🍴 EAT

Gangneung Jip – *Guui 3-dong 212-3 CS Plaza Building 1F, Gwangjin-gu.* Ⓜ *Gangnam, line 2, Gangbyeon Station exit.* ☎*(02)-447-3500. www.kanglungzip.co.kr. Open daily 11am–11pm. From ₩7,000 (lunch), ₩37,000.* From seaweed soup to Korean raw rockfish salad, this restaurant is well-known for its tasty Korean food. A full course meal is typically followed by noodles, a hot and spicy soup, and a cup of herbal tea made with 14 traditional Oriental ingredients.

GYEONGGI-DO

Forming a ring about the glittery metropolis of Seoul, Gyeonggi-do offers fantastic day-trips for anyone based in the city as well as plenty of reasons for an extended visit in this northwestern province. Gourmands will delight in the wealth of culinary treats, ranging from seafood caught in the West Islands to the famed Icheon rice to the east. Hikers can disappear for hours or days in the mountains exploring winding trails and verdant forest so thick that, at times, it's hard to imagine the city just hours away. You can travel back in time by visiting the Korean Folk Village or the many fortresses and ruins that Gyeonggi-do holds.

Highlights

1. Take in the sights, smells and tastes of **local produce** (p225)
2. Go back in time at **Korean Folk Village** (p226)
3. Spend a day soaring to great heights at **Everland** (p227)
4. Watch North Korea watch you on a **DMZ** tour (p229)
5. Spot a Red-crownded crane or other rare **wildlife** (pp231-232)

Seat of Power

Gyeonggi-do's central location to the Korean Peninsula, which includes both North and South Korea, has always been a place of historical significance. Yet it was not until power shifted from the southern provinces of North and South Gyeongsang that Gyeonggi-do assumed its current place of authority.

Fortresses, many made of wood and rebuilt time and again over the centuries, and stone walls echo of ages past when nobles and their armies carved up this mountainous peninsula as if with a jigsaw. In some ways, that is still going on. One trip to the Demilitarized Zone is more than enough of a reminder that, at least on paper, the two halves of the Korean peninsula are still in conflict. Major cities have sprung up in the shadow of Seoul: Suwon and Incheon, along with Seoul, form a triumvirate of urban power that's practically unequaled—the heart of modern South Korea.

Natural World

But travelers don't have to venture far to find that the scenery turns rural quickly beyond the urban centers. Turn a corner to find lush rice fields or thick forests, or a mountain range that seems to reach up and touch the sky. Wander along riversides, hike in national forests or visit temple sites that are hundreds, even thousands, of years old. Head west and discover that island hop by island hop, each isle is renowned for something different and special.

Korean Folk Village, Suwon
©KTO

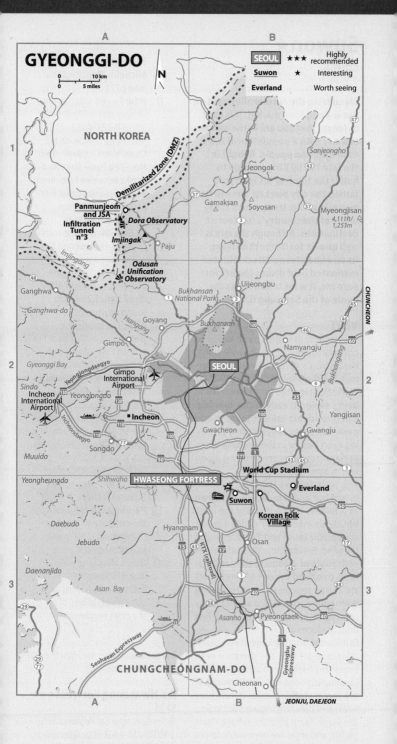

GYEONGGI-DO

SEOUL	★★★	Highly recommended
Suwon	★	Interesting
Everland		Worth seeing

0 ____ 10 km
0 ____ 5 miles

N

NORTH KOREA

Demilitarized Zone (DMZ)

Sanjeongho

47

Jeongok

43

Panmunjeom
and JSA

Dora Observatory

Gamaksan

Soyosan

Myeongjisan
4,111ft/
1,253m

37

Infiltration
Tunnel
n°3

Imjingak

3

37

Paju

Imjingang

Odusan
Unification
Observatory

Uijeongbu

CHUNCHEON

45

Ganghwa

1

*Bukhansan
National Park*

3

47

46

46

Ganghwa-do

Hangang

Goyang

Bukhansan

100

Namyangju

60

Gyeonggi Bay

Gimpo

SEOUL

Yeongjongdaegyo

Gimpo
International
Airport

35

6

Bukhangang

Sindo

130

Yeongjongdo

Yangjisan

Incheon
International
Airport

120

Gwangju

Incheandaegyo

■ Incheon

Gwacheon

3

Muuido

77

100

Songdo

110

50

World Cup Stadium ■

43

45

Yeongheungdo

Shihwaho

HWASEONG FORTRESS

● **Everland**

50

Daebudo

☆
Suwon

○ **Korean Folk
Village**

Jebudo

Hyangnam

15

43

Osan

17

Daenanjido

KTX (railroad)

17

45

Asan Bay

1

38

29

40

29
77

38

Asanho

Pyeongtaek

40

Seohaean Expressway

CHUNGCHEONGNAM-DO

Gyeongbu Expressway

Cheonan

B ↙ *JEONJU, DAEJEON*

Suwon★
수원

Wandering the narrow alleyways of the Ji-dong food market, it is easy to forget that you are in the middle of a city with a population of more than a million people. Rebuilt in the late 18C by King Jeongjo to honor the tomb of his martyred father, the city owes its fame to its magnificent fortress, which today is one of the country's top tourist destinations. Although the city is well known for its football team, its strawberries and its celebrated marinated beef dishes (*galbi*), for Koreans, it is most famous as the home of the Samsung Group.

VISIT

The majority of visitors come to Suwon not only to see, but also to walk along, Hwaseong's fortress wall that surrounded the original city. This UNESCO World Heritage site best lends itself to being explored early in the morning, when residents are out jogging and performing their early morning stretching exercises, or in the evening, when romantic couples are strolling along arm in arm.

The walk follows the wall, winding in and out and dipping up and down as it follows the contours of the land, beside immaculately pruned trees, impeccable lawns and flags flapping in the wind. Behind the wall, small houses with roofs of gleaming tiles and terraces colonized by rows of kimchi pots still cluster together around Hwaseong Haenggung, the palace and its many courtyards, just as when they were first built centuries ago.

Outside the wall, the large city of Suwon stretches off into the distance with imposing high-rise buildings. Other landmarks on the walk are the wings of the soccer stadium's main stand (see p225) and the church towers (including the huge *Jae-il* church), whose exact period and style are impossible to pin down, yet which demonstrate how dif-

- ▶ **Population:** 10,464,051
- **Michelin Map:** Regional map p221.
- **Info:** Tourist office at the railway station (left exit). $\mathscr{C}$(031)-228-4672. http://eng.suwon.ne.kr/. Open Mar–Oct 9am–6pm, Nov–Feb 9am–5pm. Also kiosks between Paldalmun and the market as well as at the railway station.
- **Location:** Suwon is 18.6mi/30km to the south of Seoul. Hwaeseong is 1.2mi/2km northeast of the railway station. The business, hotel and office district are 1.2mi/2km to the southeast.
- **Kids:** The impressive Hwaseong, activities at the Korean Folk Village and Everland amusement park.
- **Timing:** If you just want to see Hwaseong, a day trip from Seoul will be long enough. To explore the area fully, we suggest spending the night. The city is particularly lively in October when it plays host to the Hwaseong Cultural Festival.
- **Parking:** The car park at the entrance to Hwaseong Haenggung is the most practical option.
- **Don't Miss:** The walk along Hwaseong's fortress wall, a meal with *galbi* (beef) in one of the city's restaurants.

ferent Korean cities are from their Western counterparts.

Hwaseong Fortress★★★
화성

 See Gyeonggi-Do Regional map. $\mathscr{C}$(031)-228-4410. http://ehs.suwon.ne.kr/. Open daily 24hr. ₩1,000.

GETTING THERE

BY TRAIN/SUBWAY – The rail and subway **station** is 1.2mi/2km southeast of Paldalmun (fortress gate). Get there on bus no. 11 or by taxi. Suwon is on line 1 of the Seoul subway (*1hr*, ₩*1,500*) and has frequent departures for Seoul. The trains are faster (*30min*) but depart less frequently.

BY BUS – Numerous buses link Suwon train station with Incheon (*1hr30min,* ₩*12,000*) and Gimpo (*1hr*, ₩*6,000*) airports. Departures for Korea's major cities leave from the **bus station** (*0.9mi/1.5km S of the station, bus no. 5*).

Entrances at various points on the path along the total 3.5mi/5.7km length. Buy tickets at Seojangdae and Janganmun (⏰open 9am–6pm). A leaflet in English details the different construction stages. One of the most beautiful military constructions in Asia, the fortress was **completed in 1796** when King Jeongjo (1776–1800), 22nd ruler of the Joseon dynasty, decided to move the tomb of his father Sado Seja from Yangju to the Suwon region. Jeongjo crowned his father king posthumously. As a result, in addition to its commercial and political roles, Hwaseong is seen as a tribute by a son to his ancestor, an important act of virtue in Eastern philosophy.

Despite its obvious high-rise, high-tech modernity, Suwon could never be a threat to Seoul's status as "top city." But as a historical monument, the fortress is quite breathtaking, in spite of its functional role as a military construction. Solid enough to withstand arrows and firearms alike, its defensive role ultimately became a secondary one. The sophisticated building techniques, the combined use of brick and stone and the imposing size of the gates are all remarkable for the period, as is the speed with which the work was completed (within three years) and the level of preservation of the whole structure. Thanks to the existence of precise records, we know that much of the fortress was renovated and largely rebuilt in the 1970s to repair damage incurred during the Korean War. This accounts for its almost new appearance in places, which may detract slightly from the whole effect for Westerner travelers, who tend to look for the patina of age.

Hwaseong Fortress

©Chris Stowers/Apa Publications

Four gates and several command posts are situated at various points along the wall; 41 of the original 50 structures are still visible today. **Paldalmun**, the southern gate near to the market, and **Janganmun**, the northern gate, mark the ends of an axis running parallel to the Suwon River (Suwoncheon) that divides the city in two. At a height of 64ft/19.5m, Paldalmun houses a water reservoir that was designed to put out any fires set by attacking forces. Leave Paldalmun (*follow the arrows*) in a clockwise direction, and climb the steps up the side of the hill called **Paldalsan** (469.2ft/143m). The route passes various defensive structures, including Namporu, a brick stronghold designed to withstand cannon fire; Seonam Ammun, with a secret door allowing people and goods to come and go during periods of conflict; and finally Seonodae, an octagonal tower from which archers could protect the western side of the city. Don't forget to ring the 12-ton Hyowon bell three times (₩1,000) for good luck.

If you have the time, take a quick detour to the new part of the city outside the wall to view the wall from below and see just how intimidating it would have looked to potential attackers.

From the highest point, **Seojangdae**, the view★ is superb. Joggers like to stop here to stretch their muscles while looking out over the city with its wide variety of architectural styles. It is a perfect location for a lookout, with an excellent view of the city and a suitable point from which to signal across to other strategic points—signal flags would have been raised here. Passing Hwaseomun, the western gate with a double roof perched over a solid wall pierced by an arch, the route begins to descend gently toward Jangamun. Note the area immediately in front of the gate, enclosed by crescent-shaped walls, which served as a protective buffer zone.

At the point where the wall meets the river is the north water gate Hwahong-mun, installed to allow the river to flow

through the wall (its southern counterpart has disappeared). It consists of seven arches crowned with an elegant pavilion. Farther on, **Banghwasuryu-jeong**, a beautiful and ornate pavilion made of brick, stone and wood, is reflected in the picturesque Dragon pond.

Next, at the northern tip of the fortress, is the busy area (boutiques, parking, cafés, tourist offices) around **Yeonmu-dae** (Dongjangdae), which was originally a military training area. Arms training is still practiced here, although in a more peaceful fashion. Tourists are invited to try out their **archery** skills at the foot of the wall (*open 9:30am–5:30pm Mar–Oct, 9:30am–4:30pm Nov–Feb, ₩2,000*). Don't expect to be able to beat the schoolchildren who may gather around to watch; archery has earned Korea a number of Olympic medals. The arrows are fired in the direction of **Dongbuk Gongsimdon**, an unusual oval-shaped brick tower on a stone base. Finally, heading down toward the south and the market (*see below*), the walk passes **Bongdon, the signaling tower**, which is easily identifiable by its five brick chimneys. The flames (at night) or smoke (during the day) from the chimney made it possible to send signals as far as Yong-in, to the southeast. One lit chimney signaled danger, two a "hostile enemy," while three, four, and five indicated how far the enemy had progressed.

The **Hwaseong Trolley** (Hwaseong tourist train) drawn by a locomotive with a dragon's head takes tourists from Paldalsan (behind Hwaseong Haeng-gung) to Yeonmudae (*open 10.00am–5:30pm, ₩1,500*).

Hwaseong Haenggung★ 화성행궁 (Hwaseong Palace)

Open Tue–Sun 9:30am–5pm. ₩1,000. Heralded by a large square, this building is one of just a few historical buildings still standing in Suwon, aside from the fortress wall and its pavilions and gates.

Severely damaged during the Japanese occupation, this **former palace**—also used as a government headquarters—has recently been renovated. Completed in 1796 by King Jeongjo in memory of his deceased father, the palace contained a total of 576 rooms. Hwaseong Haenggung, meaning "temporary palace," was a place for Jeongjo to stay when he was away from his palace in Seoul.

A tour of the building takes in large and small courtyards and a number of different rooms, ranging from simple alcoves to royal chambers. Green and ochre are the dominant colors here. There are displays of uniforms, offerings, and musical instruments shaped like animals (*bang hyang, ulla*). During the weekends between March and November (🕐 *10am–5pm*), the palace comes to life with various activities, including changing of the guard (🕐 *Sun 2–3pm*) and a variety of entertaining demonstrations in which visitors can take part, such as the Tago (beating-the-drum) ceremony and firing an arquebus (muzzle-loaded firearm). There is also an opportunity to have a photo taken with King Jeongjo (actually the actor portraying the king in the guarding ceremony).

For more information on the palace, its history and its reconstruction, visit the interesting **Suwon Hwaseong Promotional Hall** (*in the modern building to the south, 🕿 (031)-228-4410,* 🕐*open 9am–6pm, no charge, signs in English*).

ADDITIONAL SIGHTS

From the top of the fortress wall, Suwon's skyline and the varied parts of the city are clearly visible. Within the area encircled by the wall, where the streets still follow their original layout, Suwon looks like a large provincial village, whereas around the station and farther east, in the administrative and commercial district frequented by a young consumer-driven generation, it "wears" its million inhabitants well.

Following the wall in a clockwise direction, you reach the edge of the Suwon River, where both banks are now occupied by **Paldalmun Market★**. Like all Korean markets, Paldalmun is full of different smells, tastes and colors. Ji-dong, the food market, sells seasonal produce such as the famous Suwon strawberries that appear in late spring. The smells of boiling and frying dishes mingle in the air, and cross-legged *ajumma* sell all kinds of roots and herbs. Enjoy a meal in the thick of the market at one of the cafés found behind the windows of butcher's shops. If you're not sure what to do, just watch what other people are ordering and point to the dish that you would like. Across the bridge are piles of bowls and miles of fabric for sale. You may even surprise a bride-to-be hesitating over a beautifully colored *hanbok* (traditional costume).

Hwaseong Palace

©KTO

Just over a mile/2km farther east is the **World Cup Stadium** (⚲*See Gyeonggi-Do Regional map. 228 Uman 1-don, ℘ (031)-259-2070*), which looks as though it is ready to take to the skies. The fruit of Franco-Korean cooperation, the stadium was built to accommodate the 2002 Soccer World Cup matches, and the South Koreans are tremendously proud of it. Capable of seating more than 42,000 people, fans still watch soccer games here, although smaller numbers now gather to view the matches played by local team Suwon Bluewings (*www.fcbluewings.com*), one of the better teams in Asia.

EXCURSIONS

▷ *Travel about 12mi/20km E of Suwon to Korean Folk Village. Leave Suwon following Rte 42 toward Yong-in. Free bus service is available between Suwon Tourist Office (in the railway station) and the Folk Village. Departs every hour between 10:30am and 2:30pm, last return departs 5pm (journey 30min). Bus no. 37 takes the same route (1hr, ₩1,000) but departs every 20min.*

🏃‍👥 **Korean Folk Village★** 한국민속촌

⚲ *See Gyeonggi-Do Regional map. 107 Bora-dong, Giheung-gu, Yong-in. ℘ (031)-288-0000. www.koreanfolk. co.kr.* 🕐*Open daily summer 9am–6:30pm (Sat–Sun and public holidays 7pm), winter 9am–5pm (Sat–Sun and public holidays 5:30pm). Adults ₩15,000, combined ticket including museums ₩18,000. Tickets may be bought from the Suwon Tourist Office.*

The first sight of the car park, with buses lined up in neat rows according to color, may put some people off as some type of the fairground-style attraction. The Korean Folk Village may seem more like an amusement park than a re-creation of Korean village life, but for visitors seeking to gain an impression of what **rural Korea** looked like in times gone by, it serves its purpose. The village is often overrun by hordes of students with huge picnics having a good (and noisy) time.

Surrounded by wooded hills that offer splendid foliage displays in the fall and situated around a lake, the "village" is made up of just over 250 buildings from the late Joseon period (14–19C), which have been reconstructed here and positioned according to their function or region of origin. At first glance, the general construction of thatched roofs, cob walls, multiple courtyards and low protective walls seems common to all the buildings, but closer inspection reveals numerous differences in the shape of the buildings and their layout. For example, the thatch on the roofs of buildings from Jeju Island are secured with ropes to withstand the elements,

Performance at the Korean Folk Village

©KTO

Everland

©TOPIC PHOTO AGENCY IN/age fotostock

while wooden tiles protect the houses from Ulleung-do. The houses from the south consist of two parallel buildings. The social hierarchy is clearly mirrored in Korea's architecture: nobles and rulers slept and officiated protected by the stone walls of huge mansions, topped by roofs of gleaming tiles, such as the provincial governor's house (used for filming period dramas), where an enormous drum was employed to summon the people.

Tour the gardens, and wander from courtyard to courtyard, glancing in at the reconstructed interiors and imagining the daily life of the peasants and nobles, or the pupils at the Confucian school. The wooden totem poles carved with strange, grinning male and female figures are known as *jangseungs* and supposedly drive away evil spirits, a tradition dating from the 10C.

There are numerous demonstrations, including reconstructions of ceremonies (weddings with offerings, shamanism) and demonstrations of local traditions (dances, music, New Year). Craft demonstrations and workshops include **producing mulberry paper and straw sandals**, and there's also a forge, a woodcutter and a herbalist. Silk weaving and the preparation of bean paste or soy sauce are also demonstrated, and children gasp in awe at the exploits of tightrope walkers and acrobats on

horseback (*see the timetable for shows at the entrance*).

At the far end, beyond a sort of pseudo craft bazaar, there are various open-air kitchens offering a variety of specialties and regional dishes: soups (*seolleongtang*), acorn jelly (*dotorimuk*), grilled fish, rice cakes (*injeolmi*), green onion pancakes (*pajeon*) and more. You can taste the dishes while watching them being prepared. Alongside a family amusement park and the World Folk Museum, which is a little lackluster, there is also a small Korean Folk Museum.

Korea has a number of folk villages, in Jeju-do in particular. The most authentic are: **Hahoe** (⌖*p275*) and **Yangdong** (⌖*p292*).

👥 Everland 에버랜드

⌖*See Gyeonggi-Do Regional map. From Seoul,* Ⓜ *Gangnam, line 2, exit 10, then bus no. 5002. From Suwon or Yong-in, bus no. 66. From Yong-in bus terminal, take bus no. 5002 or 5800.* ☎*(031)-320-5000 or 822-759-1940. www.everland.com.* ⏰*Open daily from 9:30am–10pm (Sun and public holidays 9am).*

This is the ideal place to entertain children, but parents not wanting to spend their entire vacation in an amusement park should be aware that this is the **fourth largest theme park in the world,** and it would be quite easy to spend several days here. There are five themed areas with thrill rides and mammoth roller coasters (₩29,000–38,000 per day depending on age): Global Fair, American Adventure, Magic Land, European Adventure and Zootopia, which includes a safari with animals roaming freely. **Caribbean Bay** (₩30,000–65,000 depending on the season) is a separate, huge water park, and, on a less frenetic note, **Hoam Art Museum** (🖉 (031)-320-1801, www.hoammuseum.org, 🕐 open daily Tue–Sun 10am–6pm, ₩4,000) offers visitors gardens to walk through and a collection of Korean art and craftwork to view.

ADDRESSES

🏠 STAY

🛏 **Hotel Central** 센트럴호텔 – 1-2 Gyo-dong. 🖉 (031)-246-0011. 40rm. ₩75,000. A stone's throw from Paldalmun on a street with little traffic but teeming with small businesses. The rooms are a little outdated but good.

🛏 **Suwon Hwaseong Sarangchae Youth Hostel** 수원화성사랑 채유스호스텔 – 14 Namchang-dong, Paldal-gu. 🖉 (031)-254-5555. www.sarangchae.org/. 31rm. Korean or Western rooms, doubles from ₩30,000. An extremely welcoming and well-situated youth hostel (next to Haenggung). There are private bathrooms in all rooms except the dormitories.

🛏🛏🛏 **Hotel Ibis** 이비스호텔 – 1132–12 Ingye-dong. 🖉 (031)-252-110. www.ibishotel.com 🅿. 240rm. ₩170,000. Amid the malls of the new part of the city, this charcoal-colored modern building contains reassuringly comfortable rooms. There is a direct bus to Incheon.

🛏🛏🛏🛏 **Hotel Castle** 캐슬호텔 – 144-4 Uman-dong. 🖉 (031)-211-6666. www.hcastle.co.kr. 🅿. 81rm. ₩250,000. Not in a particularly good location but very comfortable. There are direct limousine bus links to Gimpo and Incheon.

🛏🛏🛏🛏 **Hotel Ramada** 라마다호텔 – 940 Ingye-dong. 🖉 (031)-230-0001. 🅿. 150rm. ₩250,000. 0.9mi/1.5km east of Paldalmun. A 5-star hotel inside a huge glass tower, with comfortable rooms, a gym and a restaurant.

🍴 EAT

The pedestrian street opposite the station is lined with restaurants serving the city's specialty, galbi (beef). Even more popular are the market cafés (🕯 p225).

🛏 **Compad'or** 꽁빠도르 – 797-2 Jeongjo-ro. Open 8am–6pm. Close to Paldalmun, offering delicious sweet and savory dishes. Eat in or take away.

🛏🛏🛏 **Yeonpo Galbi** 연포갈비 – 25-4 Buksu-dong. 🖉 (031)-255-1337. Open noon–10pm. Behind the green facade of this restaurant near Hwahongmun lies a large dining room with an open kitchen. Don't miss the famous galbitang. The lunch menus are less expensive but just as delicious.

🛏🛏🛏 **Buguk Garden** 부국가든 – 572-4 Jeongja-dong, Jangan-gu. 🖉 (031)-271-3996. Open 11am–10pm. To the northeast of the city (short taxi ride), a restaurant famous for its galbi (₩30,000), beef marinated for 24 hours in ginseng, best served with wild mushroom liquor.

TOURS

Take a city bus tour with Suwon City Tours: departing Tue–Sun, 10am and 2pm from the station tourist office. ₩11,000. Duration 2hr30min. Info 🖉 (031)-256-83000 or www.suwoncitytour.co.kr.

🎭 EVENTS AND FESTIVALS

Hwaseong Cultural Festival (October) – Processions, parades, craft demonstrations and a culinary festival all bring the fortress area to life. Information: http://eng.suwon.ne.kr/.

DMZ★
(Demilitarized Zone)
비무장지대

The DMZ—the demilitarized zone 2.5mi/4km wide, with 1.2mi/2km each side of the demarcation line—was put in place at the end of the Korean War. In the travel agency brochures displayed in Seoul hotels, the letters "DMZ" are rendered dramatically in iron and fire, ringed with barbed wire, playing on the threat of the North and the sometimes slightly macabre curiosity that attracts visitors to this area. People in search of the ghoulish will be disappointed, but instead will learn about the reality of a country split in two and how a desire both for conflict and for dialogue can coexist at the same time. In this somewhat surreal environment there is one winner, however: nature has thrived unmolested in this protected zone for nearly sixty years.

A BIT OF HISTORY
History and Organization

After three years of conflict (*see The Korean War, In Context, p60*), an **armistice** was signed on 27 July 1951 at Panmunjeom and Munsan by the military commanders of the two forces. This

- **Michelin Map:** Regional map p 221 and below.
- **Info:** www.tourdmz.com; www.koreadmztour.com
- **Location:** The DMZ extends west to east for 149.1mi/240km along the demarcation line between North and South Korea. The part of the zone described here lies just to the north of Seoul.
- **Timing:** Most agencies offer day trips.
- **Don't Miss:** Panmunjeom, a symbol both of the division and dialogue between North and South; catch a glimpse of the North from Dora Observatory.

called a halt to hostilities on the front line and implemented a way of separating the opposing sides by establishing a demarcation line with a **demilitarized zone** (*2.5mi/4km wide*), which stretched across the entire width of the peninsula. The zone is the responsibility of the **Military Armistice Commission** (MAC). Meetings between MAC representatives from the **United Nations Command** (UNC) and the **Korean People's Army** (KPA) take place in the **Joint Security Area** (JSA) within the DMZ.

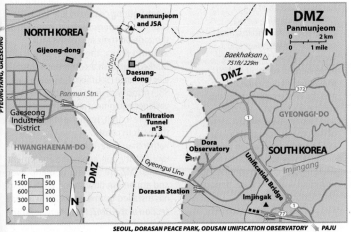

SEOUL, DORASAN PEACE PARK, ODUSAN UNIFICATION OBSERVATORY ↘ *PAJU*

TOURS

As organized tours are the only possible way of visiting Panmunjeom, most tourists choose to visit the DMZ from Seoul.

TOURS DEPARTING FROM SEOUL

Several agencies offer tours of the DMZ. Compare prices and tour programs (*1/2 to 1 day*); you may prefer to avoid those that focus too heavily on stops for shopping.

United Service Organization (USO) – *Yongsan, Seoul.* ℘*(02)-724-7003.* Ⓜ *Namyeong, line 1, exit 2. www.uso.org/korea.* Ⓒ *Open Mon–Sat 8am–3pm.* This US Army association offers by far the cheapest and most complete excursion (*Tue, Thu & Sat 7:30am–3pm. $70, or you can pay in Won*) to Panmunjeom, Dora and Infiltration Tunnel no. 3. Book at the USO office or by telephone at least four days in advance.

The advantages of the **other agencies** offering a variety of tour options (Panmujeom alone or with Dora and Infiltration Tunnel no. 3) are that you can book on the day before at the latest, and that they leave from the city center. Several are based on the 6th floor of the Lotte Hotel, including **Tour DMZ** (*Myeong-dong,* ℘*(02)-755-007, www.tourdmz.com,* Ⓒ *tours Tue–Sat,* ₩*77,000*). Also: **Global Tours** (*Golden Tower 6F, 191 Chungjeongno 2-ga,* ℘*(02)-330-4036,* ₩*77,000/*₩*120,000*).

Tours departing from Imjingak
Buses leave here for Dora and Infiltration Tunnel no. 3 (*Tue–Sun, duration 3hr,* ₩*9,000*). Advance ticket registration required at DMZ ticket office in Imjingak parking lot.

ENTRY REQUIREMENTS

Citizens of some African, Middle Eastern and communist countries are not permitted to enter the DMZ (*for a list, visit www.uso.org/korea*), and **children** under the age of 10 may not enter Panmunjeom. For citizens of other countries, **passports** are required. You must also be dressed appropriately (meaning modestly) to enter, i.e. no shorts, sleeveless tops, jeans, T-shirts, sandals, etc., and you must behave appropriately (do not try to speak to the guards, etc.). **Note:** tours may be cut short or even cancelled at short notice depending on the situation.

DMZ Wildlife

Because the area of the DMZ contains such varied geography—mountains, tidal marshes, prairies, lakes and swamps—great biodiversity exists here. In addition to the threatened Red-crowned crane and the White-naped crane, the wild bear, Chinese water deer and Amur leopard are just a few of the other species that call the DMZ home. Conservation efforts are underway to protect the area, while officials are also considering offsetting economic costs through conscientious ecotourism.

The **military demarcation line** (MDL) is marked by a series of signposts installed along what was the front line when fighting ceased in July 1953. Each country is responsible for 1.2mi/2km of the zone on their side of the MDL.

In South Korea, the DMZ is physically marked out with a continuous double electric fence (Southern Boundary Line/ SBL) fitted with various alarms and surveillance equipment and patrolled along its entire length, from the Imjin River to the eastern coast.

Rather than being banned outright, military activity, operations and equipment in the DMZ are subject to manpower and armament limitations. Each camp has installed **guard posts** in their own section of the DMZ. From here, infantry units watch each other at regular points along the MDL.

The MDL extends into the Han River estuary (the Han River from the confluence with the Imjin River) and a short maritime demarcation line at the river's mouth (A–B Line). There is also a **maritime boundary** (👆see p62).

Since 1951, the military camp at **Panmunjeom** has been granted the special status of a neutral zone divided by the demarcation line and contains barracks that are used for meetings of the Armistice Commission and the **Neutral Nations Supervisory Commission** (NNSC). It is open to visitors under certain conditions.

Protected Countryside

For nearly sixty years, there has been virtually no human activity within the DMZ, with the exception of two villages near Panmunjom, one on the south side and one on the north side (👆see p235). Due to the quietness of the area, nature has been allowed to run wild, and the DMZ is now a precious natural site for Korea—in fact, for the whole of Northeast Asia. Some 3,000 rare species of plants and animals, some almost extinct, are able to survive and even thrive in peace. For example, Siberian Cranes, a critically endangered species, stop off here in the winter during their migration toward southern Japan.

Siberian cranes stop in the DMZ

©A. Nass/Michelin

With both preservation and ecotourism in mind, the South Korean government has stepped up projects to enhance the zone, and access restrictions across it have been relaxed.

Specialist agencies offer themed trips, and local authorities have begun to establish permanent trails for hiking, cycle touring, green tourism and educational activities.

EXCURSION

DMZ (Demilitarized Zone), JSA (Joint Security Area), observatories… Organized visits from Seoul are the most popular way of visiting what is in fact,

Freedom Bridge, Imjingak

©Wendy Connett/age fotostock

despite its name, one of the most "militarized" places in the world (&see Tours p230). Visiting the area by tour is also strongly recommended for purely practical reasons, as the agencies take care of all necessary formalities and will ensure that you see all there is to see.

Imjingak 임진각

&See Gyeonggi-Do Regional map and DMZ map. Imjingak-ro, Paju-si. Tourist office. &(031)-953-4744. http://en.paju. go.kr. Hourly commuter trains travel directly from Seoul station to Imjingak.

This **tourist area** or **"resort"** includes amenities such as a station, tourist office, shops, restaurants, fairground attractions and also several monuments on the themes of unification and reconciliation. Some of the shops and restaurants even offer North Korean goods and food. Looking toward North Korea using the telescopes mounted on the platform, you can see the railway and the bridge straddling the Imjin River (Imjingang), whose waters flow into South Korea from the North and so are subject to intense scrutiny.

A steam train bombed during the Korean War has pride of place next to the remains of the **Freedom Bridge**, hastily built in 1953 to facilitate the transfer of some 130,000 South Koreans and Allied prisoners of war.

Note: every October the Imjingak resort's huge car park plays host to a large agricultural fair where the farmers living in the DMZ sell their produce. The rice, maize and especially soy have a reputation for high quality since they are grown in an area with little pollution. Some tours cross into Tongilchon where local produce is also sold.

The Gyeongui rail line stops at Imjingak before continuing to the ultramodern **Dorasan Station** (& (031)-953-3334) and then across the DMZ to the North. Apart from some test runs in 2007, trains do not actually cross the border. The Dorasan Station is just 98.5ft/30m from the zone that is off-limits to civilians; it symbolizes South Korea's hope that their railway network will one day be reconnected with Pyongyang (capital of North Korea), China and Russia.

The peace park (**Dorasan Peace Park** – & (031)-953-4854. ©Open Tue–Sun) is also worth a visit: sculptures, walks….

Dora Observatory★ 도라전망대

&See Gyeonggi-Do Regional map and DMZ map. &(031)-954-0303. http://en.paju.go.kr © Open Tue–Sun 10am–5pm. Closed public holidays. Visited as part of an organized tour from Seoul or Imjingak.

Located in the DMZ, the observatory has the "best" possible view of South

Dorasan Station

©KTO

Infiltration Tunnel No. 3

©Chris Stowers/Apa Publications

Korea's northern neighbors, either with the naked eye or binoculars (₩500). Beyond the wild landscape of the DMZ, magnificent mountains are visible, as well as the North Korean model village of Gijeong-dong with its huge flag on top of a tall metal mast and the industrial city of Gaeseong (where many North Koreans work for South Korean companies) and a statue of Kim Il-sung.

Infiltration Tunnel No. 3
제3땅굴

🖝 See Gyeonggi-Do Regional map and DMZ map. Jeomwon-ri, Gunnae-myeon. 𝒫 (031)-940-8345. http://en.paju.go.kr 🕐 Open Tue–Sun 9am–5pm. Visited as part of an organized tour from Seoul or Imjingak.

Discovered in 1978, this invasion tunnel dug by the North Koreans is 5,364ft/1,635m long, 6.6ft/2m wide and 6.6ft/2m high and located just 32mi/52km from Seoul.

Other tunnels have since been discovered (the most recent in 1990). Infiltration Tunnel No. 3 penetrates 1,427ft/435m beyond the demarcation line, reaching a maximum depth of 239.5ft/73m. The tunnel could accommodate 30,000 soldiers moving through it in 1hr. Visitors who don't suffer from claustrophobia will be able to see where the North Koreans painted the rock black, in the hope of disguising the tunnel as a coal mine.

Joint Security Area★ (JSA)
공동경비구역 and
Panmunjeom 판문점

🖝 See Gyeonggi-Do Regional map and DMZ map. http://en.paju.go.kr. May only be visited as part of an organized tour from Seoul. Children under 10 years of age are not permitted to enter.

From Imjingak, the tour buses cross the Imjin River and weave between the concrete blocks of the **Unification Bridge**, built by the president of Hyundai, originally from the North. The road then passes various anti-tank devices and serene rice fields before reaching the entrance of the American Base Camp Bonifas (the name commemorates one

JSA

Released in 2000, the movie *Joint Security Area, JSA,* from director Park Chan-wook, remains one of Korean cinema's greatest successes. Set within the unique Joint Security Area, the film tells the story of a cross-border friendship against the backdrop of the events of the time and the efforts at diplomacy.
JSA is renowned for its high level of artistic quality as well as for its mass appeal to varied audiences. The film drew more than 5 million viewers.

Joint Security Area

of the two US officers killed in a 1976 border incident). The flags of the countries that helped South Korea during the War fly here, and the slogan "in front of them all" is displayed. After a presentation about the zone, security regulations (*notably covering when and where to take or not take photos*) and the handing out of badges, you will be transferred to a military bus that will take you into the JSA (Joint Security Area) and to Panmunjeom, which, as a tourist destination, is rather surreal.

Inside the JSA, controlled by the UN and North Korea, **Panmunjeom** with its sky-blue barracks (a color known as "UN blue") must be one of the most famous places in Korea. Also known as the "truce" or "peace village," peace talks began here on 25 October 1951 and the armistice was signed on 27 July 1953. Until then, it had been just a modest rural hamlet.

Symbolizing the North–South talks and confrontation, **Panmunjeom** is where the famous photos were taken of North and South Korean soldiers standing motionless on either side of a line, facing each other yet not looking at each other. The JSA is split down the middle by the MDL. Inside the MAC (Military Armistice Commission) conference room, where

Panmunjeom Truce Village

bilateral meetings take place, you can be photographed a few centimeters in front of the border. On the other side of the line within the compund stands the North Korean building. Sometimes it is deserted, but at others, when Chinese and North Korean tourists are present, it is well guarded.

Apart from the odd squirrel skipping about in blissful ignorance of the human tensions at the border, the silence is particularly striking here.

Farther on, the **Bridge of No Return** spanning the Sachon River looks rather mundane and uninteresting (near an egret nest), but it is highly symbolic. This is the place where the exchange of prisoners of war took place in 1953, after they had been given the choice of remaining in the country where they were captured. The crossing of the bridge on foot has since been played out in numerous films set during the Cold War.

Daesung-dong 대성동 and Gijeong-dong 기정동
See DMZ map.

Both these villages are out-of-bounds to tourists. Situated just 2,625ft/800m apart, the huge flags flying over them make it easy to tell which belongs to which country. In the South Korean village of Daesung, the farmers are envied for their financial advantages and for the equipment at their disposal, while North Korean Gijeong has been nicknamed the "Propaganda Village" by Americans and South Koreans.

Intended to present an idealized image of a North Korean village to tourists and the South, it was originally planned as a show village, inhabited only by actors during the day. In fact, it is used as a dormitory village for the workforce of the nearby Gaeseong collaborative industrial park.

You can't miss the flags that dominate the two villages, the result of many years of manic competition in the spirit of "anything you can do, I can do better." The huge 47.2st/300kg North Korean flag with a red star flies atop a 524.9ft/160m-high mast!

Farther west, farther east...
The part of the DMZ described above is the most popular with visitors due to its proximity to Seoul, but the DMZ runs the entire length (149.8mi/241km) of the demarcation line. You can peer into the forbidden territory of North Korea from several points along it and also see some of the flora and fauna of this protected zone.

One such location is the **Odusan Unification Observatory** (*See Gyeonggi-Do Regional map. (031)-945-2390. www.jmd.co.kr, open Nov–Feb 9am–4:30pm, Mar and Oct 5pm, Apr–Sep 5:30pm, ₩3,000*) at the confluence of the Han and Imjin rivers, accessible by bus from Seoul via Geumchon.

The observatory opened in 1992 as an educational facility, a reminder of the conflict and a symbol of hope for a unifed Korea in the future. Historical materials are on display to help educate generations who have not lived through the conflict that led to the difficult division of the peninsula.

The northern areas of the Cheorwon and Yanggu regions, severely affected by the Korean conflict, are also worth a detour. In addition to war memorials, tunnels (the fourth infiltration tunnel was discovered here in 1990), former battlegrounds and observatories, the area boasts a botanical garden, man-made lakes and art and historical museums, among other interesting stops.

For regional tourist information, visit *http://ygtour.kr*.

Finally, **Peace and Life Hill**, in the northeast of the country (*Seohwa-myeong, www.inje.go.kr/home/english, open Tue–Sun 9am–5pm, ₩1,000*), is a park dedicated to restoring and preserving the region's ecosystem. For the easternmost observatory at **Goseong**, *see p252.*

Visit Gangwon-do for a host of amazing things to see and do along the northeastern side of South Korea. While the province doesn't have any big cities that compare to Seoul or Incheon, it does boast some spectacular coastline, and in the summer, these beaches can be packed with bright umbrellas. The more adventurous explorers will seek out the river rafting or parachuting or delve underground into giant limestone grottoes. Less adventurous travelers may opt for a quiet meander in the town where *Winter Sonata* was filmed. The lucky wanderer will visit at a time when relations between the two Koreas are strong, making it possible to visit the Geumgang Mountain range in North Korea on a guided sightseeing tour, although these visits do require advance notice and navigating lots and lots of red tape. Known as the prettiest range in the whole peninsula, the Geumgang can be seen without setting foot in North Korea either by boat or by a visit to the northern border near Hwajinpo.

Highlights

1 Enjoy a view of the valley at **Sangwonsa** (p254)

2 Enjoy fresh powder at **Yongpyong Ski Resort** (p254)

3 Eat warm, fresh, homemade tofu in **Chodang** village (p255)

4 Go underground in **Hwanseon** and **Daegeum** caves (p259)

5 Explore a former **gold mine** or the healing waters of a **spring** (p260)

Mountain Life

If the Geumgang range is inaccessible, consider a visit to Seorksan National Park, which contains the mountain range that is widely considered the most stunning in South Korea. You could spend a day or a week here. Giant time-worn granite formations project out from the treeline, evocative of mountain gods. Keep an eye out for wild goats, deer, birds and other native wildlife. Nearby are several of Korea's top ski resorts, with all that skiers have come to expect: lifts and gondolas, lodges, downhill and cross-country trails, snow-making, and excellent food. Chiaksan National Park is another top Gangwon-do attraction.

Beach Life

Summer visitors will find the Gangwon-do coastline well worth exploring. Swimmers can enjoy numerous beaches, fishing is possible for those with rods and equipment, and there are a number of historic sites to fill up rainy days. Gangneung, on the East Sea, has one of Korea's most extensive Dano festivals (see p29)—expect crowds and a carnival type atmosphere, with all sorts of activities, demonstrations, food and performances.

Sinheungsa Temple, Ulsan

Discover
Korea's Delicious Secret

Taste the harmony of Hansik

Hansik - for harmony of taste and nutrition.

Through a delicate integration of various

ingredients that deftly balance taste, smell,

texture, temperature, and form.

Hansik achieves a harmonious symmetry

to satisfy the five senses.

GUJEOLPAN
A dish combining nine flavors for
a taste of harmony.

THE TASTE OF KOREA
HANSIK

GANGWON-DO

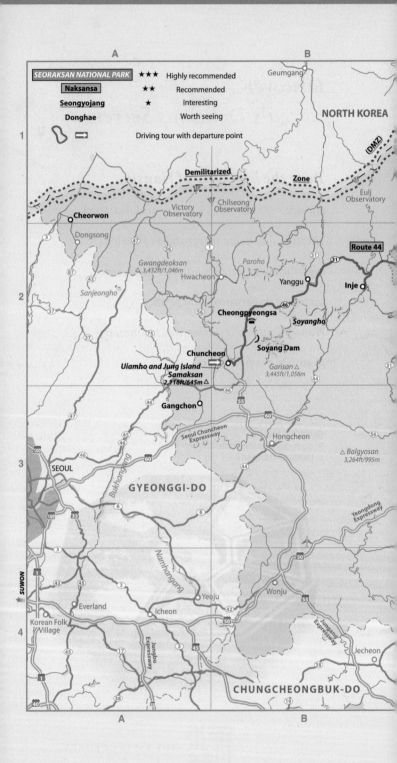

SEORAKSAN NATIONAL PARK ★★★ Highly recommended
Naksansa ★★ Recommended
Seongyojang ★ Interesting
Donghae Worth seeing

Driving tour with departure point

NORTH KOREA

(DMZ)

Demilitarized Zone

Geumgang

Victory Observatory
Chilseong Observatory
Eulj Observatory

Cheorwon

Dongsong

Route 44

Gwangdeoksan
△ 3,432ft/1,046m

Paroho

Hwacheon

Yanggu

Inje

Sanjeongho

Cheongpyeongsa

Soyangho

Chuncheon

Soyang Dam

Uiamho and Jung Island
Samaksan
2,116ft/645m △

Garisan △
3,445ft/1,056m

Gangchon

Seoul Chuncheon
Expressway

Hongcheon

△ Balgyosan
3,264ft/995m

SEOUL

GYEONGGI-DO

Bukhangang

Namhangang

Yeongdong
Expressway

SUWON

Everland

Icheon

Yeoju

Wonju

Korean Folk
Village

Jungbu
Expressway

Jungang
Expressway

Jecheon

CHUNGCHEONGBUK-DO

238

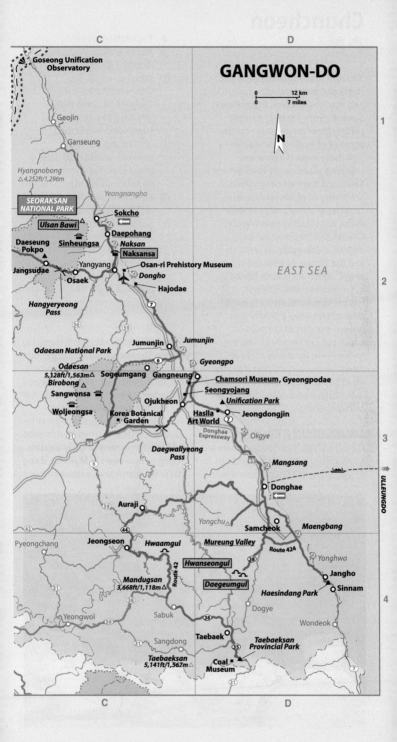

GANGWON-DO

0   12 km
0   7 miles

N

Goseong Unification Observatory

Geojin

Ganseung

Hyangnobong
△ 4,252ft/1,296m

Yeongnangho

SEORAKSAN NATIONAL PARK

Ulsan Bawi

Sokcho

Daeseung Pokpo

Sinheungsa

Daepohang

Naksan

Naksansa

EAST SEA

Jangsudae

Yangyang

Osan-ri Prehistory Museum

Osaek

Dongho

Hajodae

Hangyeryeong Pass

7

56   59

Odaesan National Park

Jumunjin

Jumunjin

6

Gyeongpo

Oddaesan
5,128ft/1,563m△

Sogeumgang

Gangneung

Chamsori Museum, Gyeongpodae

Birobong △

Seongyojang

Sangwonsa

Ojukheon

△ Unification Park

Woljeongsa

Korea Botanical Garden

Haslla Art World

Jeongdongjin

7

Donghae Expressway

Okgye

31   50

Daegwallyeong Pass

6

35

65   Mangsang

Auraji

59

Yongchu△

Donghae

ULLEUNGDO

42

Pyeongchang

Jeongseon

44

Hwaamgul

Mureung Valley

Samcheok

Maengbang

Route 42A

Hwanseongul

38

Yonghwa

Mandugsan
3,668ft/1,118m△

Route 42

Daegeumgul

Jangho

Sinnam

31

Yeongwol

38

Sabuk

Dogye

Haesindang Park

Wondeok

59

Sangdong

38

Taebaek

35

Taebaeksan
Provincial Park

Taebaeksan
5,141ft/1,567m△

Coal Museum

7

31

239

Chuncheon
춘천

Situated at the confluence of two rivers and surrounded by mountains and man-made lakes, Chuncheon benefits from a serene natural setting that compensates for the absence of historical buildings. This lively town is a pleasant stopping place on the road between Seoul and the east coast. There are plenty of restaurants, leisure facilities and fine places to walk in the surrounding countryside. Chuncheon is known for its delicious *dak-galbi*, its festivals and the *Winter Sonata* television series, which was partly filmed in Chuncheon and on Nami Island (Namisum) and is famous throughout Asia. The hilly area toward the east of Chuncheon, which suffered much during the Korean War, gives way to more mountainous terrain that is perfect for extreme sports and culminates in the high peaks of the Seoraksan mountain range.

CHUNCHEON ATMOSPHERE

From the visitor's perspective there are no significant historical buildings to be explored, but Chuncheon is worth

▶ **Population:** 267,514
◔ **Michelin Map:** Regional map pp238–239
▤ **Info:** Tourist Offices–Gangwon Drama Gallery/Folk Crafts Hall, ✆(033)-244-0088; Namchuncheon Station, ✆(033)-250-3322; bus terminal, ✆(033)-250-3896. http://tour.chuncheon.go.kr/eng/index.asp.
▶ **Location:** Chuncheon is 55mi/89km east of Seoul and 106mi/170km east of Sokcho.
⬡ **Don't Miss:** Tasting Chuncheon's delicious *dak-galbi*, wild and beautiful Route 44 south of Seoraksan.

visiting for its markets and shopping streets. The intersection of five avenues (including Jungang-no and Geumgang-no), surrounded by buildings plastered with advertisements and billboards, is at the heart of the downtown area.

An underground shopping mall, virtually undetectable at street level, is good for browsing in rainy or chilly weather. Young people meet in **Myeong-dong** *(SW of the intersection)*, a smaller version

Fall landscape, Osaek
©KNTO

GETTING THERE

BY BUS – The **Intercity** and **Express Bus** terminals are adjacent to each other, on the south side of the town, near an E-Mart store. ℘*(033)-256-1571/251-3205, www.chterminal.co.kr.* There are departures for Dong Seoul Bus Terminal *(1hr50min, ₩8,500)*, Daegu *(4hr, ₩16,500)*, Sokcho *(2hr, ₩13,500)* and to the airports in Seoul and other major towns.

BY TRAIN – The city has two stations: **Chuncheon** to the west and **Namchuncheon** to the south. Trains leave for Seoul's Cheongnyangni Station *(2hr, ₩5,500)* and the popular resort Gangchon *(20min, ₩1,100)*. ℘*(02)-917-7445. http://info.korail.com* .The KTX express train is scheduled to begin serving Chuncheon in 2013–14.

of the same area in Seoul with an array of shops, cinemas and fast-food outlets. Part of the hit series *Winter Sonata (see box p242)* was filmed here.

You may notice a distinct military presence in the city—there are several Korean bases nearby, although the US military base Camp Page that was once here was shut in 2005. On Saturdays, soldiers in uniform are out and about to have fun and join the throng, in groups or arm in arm with their girlfriends. This fashionable world of colorful shop displays contrasts with a very different Korea in the form of a traditional market. While the Lotte Department Store and E-Mart discount stores on the outskirts are massively popular with families, the traditional market fortunately continues to exist and sells clothes for the older generation and foodstuffs such as herbs, fish and offal. You can also find all the ingredients for kimchi among the mingling smells of spices, cooking and roasting.

In the heart of Myeong-dong is a pedestrian street called **Dakgalbi Geori** *(which starts near Benetton on Geumgang-no)*, famous for its twenty or so numbered restaurants emblazoned with an image of a smiling rooster, all serving the city's specialty, **dak-galbi**. You have to stand in line to eat in the most popular restaurants. The ingredients (marinated chicken, cabbage, spices, etc.) are stacked on a large griddle in the center of the table, watched over and turned by the waitresses. Seated on the floor, diners watch with anticipation as their food is cooked. Be patient—it will be delicious. (See Addresses).

VISIT

Chuncheon National Museum

Seoksa-dong, ℘ *(033)-260-1500, http://chuncheon.museum.go.kr/html/en/* Open Tue–Sun 9am–6pm, ₩1,000 Located east of the city, this museum is worth a detour, but more for the building than its displays of jewelry, weapons and various implements divided into themed rooms (prehistory, Joseon dynasty, etc.).

Euiamho (Lake Euiam) 의암호 and Jung Island 중도

At the southern end of Chuncheon's Jungang-no, eye-catching sculptures seem to float on the surface of the water, attracting the attention of people on the pleasant walking and cycle path at the edge of the lake. You can rent bikes *(open 9am–7pm, ₩3,000/15,000)* or swan-shaped pedal boats and have a bite to eat. The unusual building near Gongjicheon Stream in the form of three linked conical domes is the **Memorial Hall for Ethiopian Veterans in the Korean War** *(℘(033)-254-518, www.ethiopian-mh.or.kr,* open Tue–Sun 9am–5pm). Inspired by the Ethiopian huts of Africa, the building houses a small exhibition *(in Korean)* about the involvement of Ethiopian soldiers in the war and the relationship between Chuncheon and Addis Ababa, its twin city since 2004 (see box p243).

Beside Lake Uiam, **Peace Park** commemorates the Battle of Chuncheon fought at the outbreak of the Korean War, during which the outnumbered South Koreans fought off the invading forces from North Korea.

Winter Sonata – **Summer Scent**

Winter Sonata *(Gyeoul yeonga)* has been Korea's most successful television series in recent years. Written by Oh Su Yeon and aired in 2002, much of it was filmed in the area around Chuncheon. The plot begins with a love story between two high-school students who are tragically separated as a result of a car accident. Ten years pass and the heroine meets a married man with a strange resemblance to her student sweetheart. He is a famous architect who lives in the United States and has no recollection of his Korean past.

This 20-episode romance was extremely popular throughout Asia. It made international stars of the leading actors, Choi Ji-woo, **Bae Yong-jun** and Park Yong-ha, who also became a pop star in Japan. His suicide at the age of 32, in June 2010, was a great shock to his fans, who had already begun visiting locations used in the series, such as the romantic cedar-lined path on Nami Island and the ski resort in Yongpyong.

Most of the leisure amenities can be found on beautiful **Jungdo (the island)**. Recreational options such as swimming pools, sports facilities, restaurants, camping and bicycle-, boat- and jet-ski-rentals keep families and tourists busy in the summer. Take a ferry *(bus no. 74)* from a landing stage in the south of the city. The crossing only takes five minutes (🕙 *9am–6pm, return ₩5,400; ₩1,000 supplement for bikes)*.

To the north of Chuncheon, the pretty regions of Cheorwon *(www.cwg.go.kr)* and Yanggu *(http://ygtour.kr)* border the **DMZ**. Less popular with tourists than Panmunjeom (👣 *see p 234)* but just as interesting, you can visit the infiltration tunnels, memorials and look-out posts. This hilly region was severely affected by the Korean War, and it holds the remains of many battle sites.

🚗 **DRIVING TOUR**

From Chuncheon to Sokcho

▶ *112mi/180km drive to be completed in one day. Leave the city in the direction of Soyang Dam.*

Soyangho (Soyang Lake) 소양호
👣 *See Gangwon-do regional map.*

▶ *Access by bus no.11 from the city center (Jungang-no, next to the KB tower). The bus terminates at Soyang Dam.*

The road climbs to **Soyang Dam** and the various parking areas for the large number of cars bringing weekend visitors. From the parking area, there is a panoramic view of the country's longest man-made lake (40mi/65km), surrounded by forested slopes. The beauty of the scenery is determined by the light and the water level in the lake, so you may be delighted or disappointed, depending on the day. The road continues down to the pier and is lined with stalls selling boiled corn and potatoes. Various trips are available: a 1hr cruise around the lake (🕙*9:30am–5pm, ₩10,000)*, a speed-boat ride *(₩30,000 for 2.5mi/4km)* or, best of all, a 15min cruise toward the peaceful Cheonpyeong Temple area (🕙*9:30am–5pm, ₩5,000; then 30min walk to the temple)* offers a pleasant boat trip and walk. The temple is also accessible by car via the route given below.

Soyang Dam to Inje 인제
👣*See Gangwon-do regional map.*

▶ *Take Rte 46 toward Yanggu. Continue upward through the hills to a pass where, on the weekends, buses drop hikers ready to climb Majeoksan (1,985ft/605m). At the bottom of the descent, turn right at the traffic lights toward Cheongpyeongsa. If you are in a hurry or have already visited the temple by boat (👣see above), continue on Rte 46.*

The winding road climbs again before dropping down to Soyang Lake and **Cheongpyeongsa** (₩2,000), popular with locals for its forest walks, waterfalls, restaurants and the modest temple in the Joseon style (although it was originally built in the 10C). Take the road that leaves from the far end of car park no. 3. Little used, this road meanders up and down, leading you through stunning scenery before reaching a remote valley where a few scattered farms and cultivated areas create a delightful rural landscape.

▶ *At Ohang, turn left onto Route 46, toward Inje.*

The road takes you through dark mountain tunnels, forested landscapes and farmland, passing close to the very center of the Korean Peninsula. Farther south, the town of **Inje** offers a variety of outdoor sports: climbing, bungee jumping, rafting, mountain biking, etc.

▶ *Before Inje, take the Yangyang direction (Rte 44).*

South of Seoraksan National Park★★ (Nam-Seorak) 남설악
ⓖ *See Gangwon-do regional map.*
Route 44 skirts the southern side of the magnificent Seoraksan National Park (Nam-Seorak/South Seorak) before reaching the coast. It is wilder and more beautiful than the alternative Routes 46 and 56 to the north, although the latter follows the steep-sided Hangyeryeong

Cheongpyeongsa ©KTO

valley and gives you an excellent view of the unique Seoraksan landscape. Depending on the season, the wooded slopes of Route 44 blaze with gold or are scattered with blossoming trees. Above the vegetation, spectacular bare peaks rise up, streaked with mountain streams whose vigor varies with the time of year.

🚶 In **Jangsudae**, a small cottage marks the start of the hiking trails *(summer only)*. One of them leads to Daeseungnyeong *(3,970ft/1,210m, round-trip 2hr)*. A 0.6mi/1km walk toward **Daeseung Pokpo** culminates in this dramatic 289ft/88m waterfall tumbling down a rocky cliff. The road reaches the **Hangyeryeong Pass** at an altitude of almost 3,619ft/1,103m.

Ethiopia and Korea

When the UN decided to form a coalition army to repel attacks from North Korea (ⓖ *see p 60*), the Ethiopian emperor Haile Selassie (a staunch defender of a collective security force) sent the 1st Kagnew infantry battalion. These elite soldiers belonging to the imperial army landed in Pusan (Busan) on 7 May 1951. Attached to the 32nd US Infantry Regiment, they took part in numerous battles, including the victories of Sam-Hyon, Tokan-ni and Pork Chop Hill. None of the 3,518 soldiers were taken prisoner, but 121 were killed during the conflict. Their courage was recognized and praised by the US and Korean authorities. Some of the troops stayed behind after the armistice as part of the peacekeeping force. The last soldier left the peninsula on 3 January 1965.

Behind the car park and shop is a superb backdrop of jagged peaks that look like the crest of a sleeping dragon. As proof of the region's wealth of tourist attractions, a sign announces that the sea is only 21mi/34km away. The tightly winding road leads directly down to the sea, but you may wish to stop off at **Osaek** ("five colors"), a small spa town nestled on a slope, which is covered with blossoming trees during spring. In addition to the hot springs (86°F/30°C), there is a temple and a number of restaurants and motels.

The trail leading up the south side of Mt. Seorak (*Daecheongbong, 5,604ft/1,708m, 3hr 10min*) begins here.

After Yangyang, Rte 7 heads north to Naksan, Sokcho (see p251) and the central and northern parts of Seoraksan Park (see p245), or south to Donghae and Samcheok.

ADDRESSES

🛏 STAY

CHUNCHEON

IMT 아이엠티 호텔 – *Jungang-dong.* (033)-257-6111. www.imthotel.co.kr. ₩55,000. This motel is well positioned on the hill leading to the Provincial Office. The modern rooms are in the chic "love hotel" category.

Sejong Chuncheon 세종 춘천 호텔 – *Bongeui-dong.* (033)-252-1191. 80rm. ₩85,000/98,000. *At the intersection, follow signs to the Provincial Office and then to the hotel.* Pleasant, large rooms with views. The hotel has a waterfall (stops at night) and is a popular venue for local family celebrations.

The resort village of **Gangchon** (*See Gangwon-do regional map*), 13mi/21km south of Chuncheon, with B&Bs and a youth hostel ((033)-262-1204), is another possible stopping place.

OSAEK

Green Yard Hotel 그린야드 호텔 – *Osaek.* www.greenyardhotel.com. (033)-670-1000. ₩75,000. Hotel complex and spa offering family accommodations at affordable rates.

🍴 EAT

There are around 20 restaurants in **Dakgalbi Geori 닭갈비거리** (see p241), serving the specialty of the town—*dak-galbi*—all day. Nos. 9, 14 and, particularly, 7 (*at the intersection,* (033)-256-6448) are so popular that you often have to wait in line. *Allow ₩9,000.*

🏃 SPORTS AND ACTIVITIES

AROUND CHUNCHEON

Walkers climb **Mount Samak** (Samaksan, 2,116ft/645m) to see the view of Chuncheon and its lakes (*bus no. 3, ₩1,600, 2hr walk to the top*). Benefitting from a superb location, the tourist **resort of Gangchon** (*http://tour.chuncheon.go.kr/*) attracts families and students for hiking, **skiing**, climbing, etc.

Water sports in the region

In summer, the rivers are popular with seasoned water-sports enthusiasts for **rafting** and **kayaking**. Services and departure points are located in Inje and Cheolwon. www.paddler.co.kr, www.injetour.net and www.hanleisure.com.

🎉 EVENTS AND FESTIVALS

International Mime Festival – www.mimefestival.com. During May in the town center.
Puppet Festival – www.cocobau.com. August, in the north of the town.
Dak-galbi Festival – Eng August/beginning September, celebrating Chuncheon's very own stir-fried marinated chicken dish.

Seoraksan National Park★★★
설악산국립공원

Often hailed as Korea's most beautiful national park, Seoraksan —"snow peak mountain"— is a UNESCO Biosphere Preservation Reserve. A network of paths enables everyone, from the casual Sunday walker to the seasoned hiker, to explore the many granite peaks, mountain streams, verdant valleys and temples.

The forests of pine, birch, wild cherry, ash and oak are also a paradise for birdwatchers, harboring numerous birds, including rare woodpeckers. Covered with flowers in the spring or the vivid colors of falling leaves in the autumn, the park draws great crowds also during the July and August holiday season. The unusual rock formations and jagged peaks that make up the landscape provide a challenge for climbers and inspiration to artists and poets.

EXPLORING THE PARK

The national park is divided into three areas: Oe-Seorak (Outer Seorak) to the east, Nae-Seorak (Inner Seorak) to the west and Nam-Seorak to the south. The first two areas are separated by the jagged line of Madeungryeong's north–south ridge.

Oe-Seorak (Outer Seorak)
외설악

▶ By car from Sokcho, take Rte 7 toward Naksan and then turn right at the signs to "Seoraksan/Seorak-dong." Alternatively, follow the state highway signposted from the center of Sokcho, via Cheoksan Spa. There's a bus service to Seorak-dong from the Express and Intercity Bus terminals in Sokcho, no. 7/7-1 (20min, ₩1,000).

- **Michelin Map:** Regional map pp238–239
- **Info:** ☎(033)-635-2003. http://english.knps.or.kr/Knp/Seoraksan.
- **Location:** In the northeast of the country, the national park covers an area of 137sq mi/354sq km, across a 25mi/40km stretch, between Sokcho and Inje.
- **Kids:** The cable car ride to Gwongeum.
- **Timing:** The best time to visit Seoraksan is in the fall when the leaves are a blaze of colors, although spring is also lovely, when the trees are in blossom. During the freezing winter, roads can be closed because of heavy rain, while dry-season drought may create a risk of fire. The roads in the park open 2 hours before sunrise and close up to 2 hours after sundown. It can be quite crowded at weekends.
- **Parking:** Car parks are located at each entrance to the park (charges apply).
- **Don't Miss:** The spectacular walking trail to Ulsan Bawi, the colors of the trees in the fall.

GETTING THERE

Sokcho is the closest town to Seoraksan, and is served by buses to various locations in the park. ▶See Getting There for Sokcho, p252. In the height of the season, buses run from Seoul to Osaek.

USEFUL INFORMATION

Information is available from the **tourist office** (▶see above) and the **rangers** (☎(033)-636-7700).

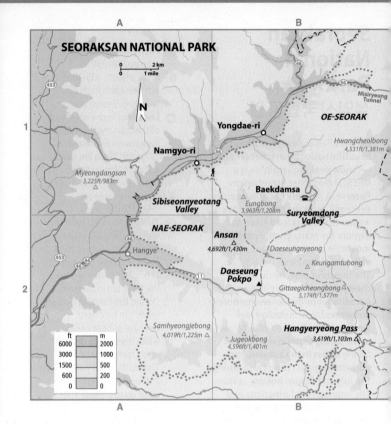

SEORAKSAN NATIONAL PARK

The park has trails for Sunday walkers and seasoned hikers alike. Make sure you have good shoes, water and a water-/windproof jacket if you plan to go beyond the Sinheung Temple area. The "outer" region of Seoraksan, to the east of the park, offers spectacular landscapes, cliffs, peaks and waterfalls, and is by far the most popular.

Seorak-dong 설악동

See Seoraksan National Park map.
This is the main entrance to Seoraksan, 7.5mi/12km southwest of Sokcho.
Before you arrive at the park entrance, there are a few miles of hotels, restaurants, car parks and services, among which you will also find the pleasant modern wooden building that houses the **Visitor Center** (*(033)-635-2003, open Tue–Sun 10am–5pm*), providing information, an exhibition and guides. The magnificent scenery from the smooth asphalt road, shaded by flowering trees, leading to the park entrance gives a hint of what awaits. The road terminates at a large car park (*₩5,000*), which is also the end of the line for bus no. 7 and 7-1.

After paying to **enter the park** (*₩2,500*), you will pass a small tourist office and the rangers' office (*(033)-636-7700, 9am–5pm*), where you can buy maps (*₩1,500*) and leave your bags. This is also the beginning of a large esplanade from which the footpaths depart.

The restaurants, souvenir shops and stands offering boiled corn and silkworm larvae create an amusement-park atmosphere a bit out of place in the natural setting, but this is soon dispelled by the superb landscape. Providing you are not visiting the park in the high season, you can quickly find yourself alone with the wildlife and the murmur of a river.

From the park entrance, one of the shortest walks (1.2mi/2km) leads to the **Yukdam waterfall (Yukdam Pokpo)**.

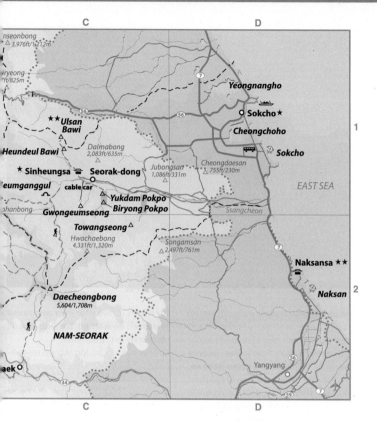

From the cable car station (ⓒ*see below*), the path follows a beautiful mountain stream. This walk is particularly pleasant at daybreak, just as the birds begin to stir. Farther down, the breathtaking waterfalls of **Biryong** and **Towangseong** are also spectacular.

Among the other interesting sights near the park entrance is **Geumganggul (Geumgang Cave)**, whose mouth opens on to the slopes of Mireukbong's dramatic triangular peak at an altitude of 1,970ft/600m. It used to serve as a retreat for Buddhist monks, and you can see why when you glimpse the superb view of the Cheonbuldong Valley. The cave is 1.8mi/2.9km from Sinheung Temple (ⓒ*see below*). From here, keen walkers can continue to Daecheongbong.

♣♣ Gwongeumseong★ 권금성

ⓒ*See Seoraksan National Park map.*
The quickest and easiest way up this mountain to the south of Seorak-dong

is by **cable car** (ⓒ *open summer 7am–6pm, winter 8:30am–5pm, ₩8,500).*
The 0.68mi/1.1km ride is fast and well organized but may be cancelled if it is too windy. At the top, after the inevitable café, there is a short climb to an open rocky area with a marvelous panoramic view of the western side of the park. A Korean flag flies on a small hill that marks the summit. Nearby are the remains of a fort (**Gwongeumseong**) that was built in 1253 and served as a refuge during the Mongol invasions.

Sinheungsa★ 신흥사 and Ulsan Bawi★★ 울산바위

ⓒ*See Seoraksan National Park map.*
Sinheungsa lies in a peaceful setting beside a stream, 547yd/500m from the park entrance. Established in 652 by the monk Jijang, the temple of "divine inspiration" is one of the oldest in the country but has only occupied its current site since 1642. The bell is more than 1,400

Ulsan Bawi

years old. On the outer walls of the main hall is a series of 10 pictures, the *Allegory of the Herdsman* (the path to wisdom). From here, paths lead to **Daecheongbong** (see below) and **Ulsan Bawi★★**. This spectacular cliff is one of the most popular destinations; its six peaks rise to an altitude of 2,864ft/873m and majestically overlook the surrounding area. The stunning 2.7mi/4.3km walk takes about 2hr and passes the photogenic **Heundeul Bawi**, or "unsteady rock." *Be warned, the last section to Ulsan Bawi involves a steep flight of steps (more than 800) that can be difficult to climb in strong winds.* But the effort is worth it: from the top the **view**★★ of the coast is extraordinary.

Daecheongbong 대청봉

See Seoraksan National Park map.
The highest point in Seoraksan and the third highest in the country, the complex, jagged peaks of this majestic mountain rise to a height of 5,604ft/1,708m. There are two possible routes to the summit: 3.3mi/5.3km *(3hr 10min)* and 9.9mi/16km *(11hr 20min)*.
The most popular and direct path goes up the south side, from the Osaek Ranger Station, and takes hikers through Seorak Pokpo. You may wish to stay a night in one of the four **huts** available

for hikers *(bring your own equipment and food)*. Be warned, the huts can fill up quickly in the summer.
The hut in Jungcheong accepts reservations *(℘(033)-672-1708, http://english. knps.or.kr/Knp/Seoraksan).*
The longer hike travels from the ticket office at the main entrance. Along the way to the peak, visitors pass a Buddhist temple, waterfalls and a hot spring before heading down the other side of the mountain to Osaek.
Returning from Seorak-dong to Sokcho, turn at the brown sign on the right to "Hangmujeong" and you will pass a little house, before reaching a hamlet in which every house is surrounded by walls of round stones.

Nae-Seorak (Inner Seorak) 내설악

By car from Sokcho, travel Rtes 46 and 56 toward Chuncheon and Seoul. From Sokcho, buses stop at the entrance to Yongdae-ri/Baekdam (₩6,500) then Namgyo-ri (₩7,000), 5 times daily.

Routes 46 and 56 to the north of Seoraksan are faster, but busier. Although less spectacular than Route 44 to the south (see p243), they lead through Nae-Seorak, a part of the park that is spectacular in the autumn, with ridges, valleys and splendid forests.

Yongdae-ri 용대리

See Seoraksan National Park map.

A pretty village of windmills and farms, some of which offer *minbak* (bed and breakfast), Yongdae-ri is popular with tourists, so it can be packed on the weekends—and when the road to Baekdamsa is closed. Park (or get off the bus) in the car park *(₩5,000)* where there are restaurants and souvenir shops. You can try *pajeon* (pancakes) here and other dishes made of trout and mushrooms. The trout, which can be enormous, are also sold "dried" in the shops alongside delicious pots of honey. A **shuttle** from the car park *(15min, single ₩1,800)* will take you to the temple and to the departure point for the walking trails (another 4.35mi/7km).

Baekdamsa 백담사 and Suryeomdong Valley 수렴동계곡

See Seoraksan National Park map. Yongdae 2-ri. (033)-462-6969. www.baekdamsa.org. Open daily dawn–dusk.

The Temple of a Hundred Pools (Baekdamsa) was founded in the 7C but has been rebuilt many times. Its name comes from the number of pools between the temple and Daecheongbong, which, according to legend, were counted by a monk in the 16C. The temple is also known as the retreat of the poet and reformer Han Yong-un (1879–1944), who wrote some of his most beautiful texts there.

Set out for the short walk from the temple to the beautiful **Suryeomdong Valley**. A trail (8.7mi/14km) from the refuge ((033)-462-2576) in the valley returns to Nam-Seorak at Jangsudae. *A good 7hr walk. Another trail leads to Seorak-dong (6–7hr walk).*

Farther west, leaving from **Namgyo-ri** *(accessible by Rte 46)*, there is a trail to the superb and little-visited **Sibiseonnyeotang Valley** (which follows a beautiful stream) and reaches the waterfall Dumun Pokpo *(2hr 30min walk)* and, after another 2hr walk, finally the peak of **Ansan** at an altitude of 4,692ft/1,430m. Seasoned walkers may choose to continue to Nam-Seorak at Jangsudae.

Local Specialities

The ancient cuisine of the temples and farming communities can now be sampled in some of the fashionable restaurants in Seoul. Colorful, healthy and vegetarian, it is known for its subtle flavors and recipes based on **seasonal ingredients**: herbs, mushrooms and vegetables, or flowers picked in the mountains. Some specialties are derived from **local traditions**, like *megeun namul*, which consists of 12 dishes made from vegetables, such as bellflower root, gingko nuts and chestnuts, and is eaten on the first full moon in the lunar year. For **Chuseok** (a harvest festival and Korean thanksgiving day), taro soup is served with rice cakes made with chrysanthemums or stuffed with sesame seeds and cooked over pine needles.

Koreans love to eat seasonal foods whenever they are on holiday, such as *sanchae bibimbap* (rice with herbs and local vegetables), pancakes made with scallions and other spring vegetables or, in the summer, *boyangcha* tea (jujube and chestnut). In Seoraksan, they are proud of their **songi mushrooms** known as "diamonds of the forest." Yangyang is the songi mushroom "capital," and holds a festival in their honor. An important ingredient in cooking and medicine, the mushrooms were offered as a gift to kings and are often sold in their dried form in markets. The best ones grow under 30-year-old pine trees and have a strong pine fragrance.

Nam-Seorak

▶ *The southern part of the national park is served by Rte 44, which connects Inje to Naksan. There is a bus to Osaek (₩4,000) and Jangsudae (₩5,500) from the Intercity Bus Terminal in Sokcho.*

Among other attractions, there are hot springs in **Osaek**, the waterfall **Daeseung Pokpo** and the **Hangyeryeong Pass**. These are described in the driving tour *From Chuncheon to Sokcho* (see p 238).

ADDRESSES

STAY

IN SEORAK-DONG

This area has many hotels and *yeogwan*.

Mt. Sorak Youth Hostel 설악 유스호스텔 – (033)-636-7116. www.sorakyhostel.com. Mon–Fri ₩25,000/50,000, Sat–Sun ₩30,000/75,000. This youth hostel, offering dormitories and rooms, is 1.2mi/2km from the park entrance. The no. 7 bus stops here.

Kensington Stars Hotel 켄싱톤 스타 호텔 – *106-1 Seorak-dong* (033)-635-4001. www.kensington. co.kr. 109rm. ₩169,000/249,000; out-of-season reductions. The red double-decker buses, wooden paneling and thick carpets might make visitors wonder for a fleeting moment whether they have taken a wrong turn and ended up in the UK! Some of the very comfortable rooms have Zen or "celebrity" decor. Located a short walk from the park entrance with panoramic views, shops and restaurants.

Seoraksan Tourist Hotel 설악산 관광호텔 – *151 Seork-dong* (033)-636-7101. www.seorakhotel.com. 45rm. Sat–Sun ₩120,000. The only hotel inside the park, it has small and fairly comfortable rooms with mountain views. Friendly, but prices are high.

ELSEWHERE IN THE PARK

There are numerous *minbak* in **Yongdae-ri** (allow ₩20,000 per person). **Osaek** has a hotel (see p238) and several *yeogwan* (₩35,000/65,000) with access to the hot springs. For the huts in the park see p243 and *http://english.knps.or.kr/Knp/Seoraksan*.

EAT

There are many restaurants close to the park entrances (Seorak-dong, Yongdae-ri, Osaek). They offer menus usefully illustrated with photos. The pancakes *(pajeon)*, freshwater fish and dishes with **mountain herbs** and **mushrooms** are the most popular choices. Alternatively, brace yourself to try some silkworm larvae.

SPORTS AND ACTIVITIES

Besides the **walking trails**, the **hot springs** are also popular in Seoraksan. There are spa resorts in Osaek (see p240) and **Seorak Waterpia** *(Jangsadong, www.seorakwaterpia.com, 6am–8:30pm, ₩65,000 per day)* with a spa and water park built around a hot spring (120°F/49°C), between Sokcho and Seorak-dong. see also p241.

EVENTS AND FESTIVALS

Songi Festival – In Yangyang *(SE of the park)* at the end of Sept, celebrating their famous mushrooms.

Salmon Festival – *www.yangyang.go.kr* Between late Sept and mid-Oct, see the salmon returning to Namdaecheon (river), Yangyang.

Sokcho★
속초

Sokcho lies in the far northeast corner of the country, bordered by the sea, two lakes and the mountains. You can sunbathe on the beach, enjoy super-fresh seafood or stretch your legs hiking on the slopes of Seoraksan. There is plenty to keep you busy! Although this delightful little town, rich with the salty aroma of sea spray, does not have any significant historical buildings to explore, the vibrant markets and inexpensive restaurants in town and around the port create a lively atmosphere. From here, ferries depart northward to Vladivostok, the "end of the earth," or follow the coast south and you'll find busy fishing villages, temples and old houses. Miles of coiled barbed wire along the beaches indicate how close the town is to North Korea.

VISIT
The Town
See Gangwon-do regional map.
The town includes two lakes, **Yeong-nangho** in the northern part and the more centrally located **Cheongcho**. The small downtown district lies to the east of Cheongcho Lake, which connects to the port. The main street, **Jungang-no**, has

▶ **Population:** 84,568

Michelin Map: Regional map pp 238–239

Info: Sunrise Park, 3.1mi/5km S of the town on Rte 7. ℘(033)-635-2003. www.sokcho.gangwon.kr. 9am–5pm. Gangneung Bus Terminal, ℘(033)-640-4414. www.gangneung.gangwon.kr. 9am–5pm.

Location: Sokcho is in the northeast, 109mi/175km from Chuncheon and 149mi/239km from Seoul. The town is built around a lake, with the town center to its north and the beach to the south.

Kids: The beaches at Sokcho and Naksan, the warship in Unification Park.

Don't Miss: The local squid specialty in Sokcho, the superbly situated Naksansa, the Dano Festival in Gangneung.

sidewalks lined with shops and services *(banks, post office)*. At its northern end there is a small **Museum of Ceramics** *(℘(033)-638-7711, 9am–6pm. Closed Mon. ₩3,500)* with an exhibition of vases and plates from various parts of Asia.

Sokcho port and town
©Chris Stowers/Apa Publications

The main attraction is **Jungang Market★**. To reach it, turn left opposite the statue of some children carrying a fish. From here you will find yourself immersed in a maze of streets and alleyways full of stalls selling huge fish, vegetables, and spices. Colorful parasols and arcades provide shelter for the sellers, some of whom simply sit on the ground next to bunches of herbs.

A short walk from Jungang-no (walk down to the statue of the bull), boats bob alongside the **Gaetbae quays** and old women chat as they patch fishing nets. The seafront is lined with simple but very popular seafood restaurants. Many offer grilled seafood and numerous accompaniments. Try no. 88 (📞 (033)-633-8892) or the restaurant with the terrace (📞 (033)-631-4279).

From the quayside, a small hand-pulled **ferry** (🕐 4:30am–11pm, ₩200) takes you to the **Abai** district (Cheongho-dong). This area has kept its fishing village atmosphere despite the construction of a large bridge and a passenger port. Locals queue here for the famous stuffed squid (*ojing-eo sundae*); no. 15 has the best reputation. "Abai" means "grandfather" in the dialect of the northern region of Hamgyong-do, a clue that the district grew as a result of the influx of North Korean refugees in 1951.

Keep exploring and you will pass Cheongcho-dong's low houses, captivating old-style grocery stores and alleyways leading to the beach.

Dongmyeong port, to the north of Jungang-no, is a popular spot with families for big Sunday lunches; unfortunately, the fish stalls have now been moved indoors, but the postprandial stroll along the pier to the lighthouse where couples carve their names remains a tradition.

At another nearby lighthouse perched on the hillside, you can gain a view over the town. For an alternative view of the town and the mountains, south of **Cheongcho Lake** and Abai, visit the curious spiraling **Expo Tower** (243ft/74m), built in 1999 for an international exhibition (🕐 9am–9:30pm, ₩1,500). The slightly eccentric architectural theme continues in the motels as you approach the **beach**. The edge of the lake is also a good place to spot migratory birds resting.

North of Sokcho
🔍 *See Gangwon-do regional map*

Route 7 heads north along the closely monitored beaches strewn with rolls of barbed wire. After 34mi/55km, at the **Goseong Unification Observatory** (📞 (033)-682-0088, www.tongiltour.co.kr, 🕐 daily 9am–4pm, ₩1,500, passport required), you can hire binoculars (₩500) with which to peer into North Korea and Geumgangsan, the revered Diamond Mountains (5,377ft/1,639m).

DRIVING TOUR

BETWEEN SOKCHO AND DONGHAE
A 118mi/190km drive to be completed in a day and a half, spending the night in Gangneung. The buses keep to Rte 7, but

Soothing the Spirits

Dano, also known as Surit-nal, is a festival that takes place on the fifth day of the fifth month of the lunar year. A public holiday in both North and South Korea, the day has, for centuries, been associated with sacred folk rituals that combine dancing, chanting and alcohol. These mark the end of the sowing period and are supposed to chase away evil spirits during the year to come. The remarkable **Dano-je Festival in Gangneung** (which is on UNESCO's Intangible Cultural Heritage list) is the perfect place to see these rituals come alive again. The greatest shamans in the country communicate with spirits during the *kut* ritual and enter into a trance to the sound of rattles and the beat of drums. People dress in blue and red, and the women wash their hair in iris water to make it gleam, while men wear belts made of iris rhizomes. Colorful flags fly from the masts of traditional small boats and everyone eats rice cakes. There are masked dances, a lantern parade, Korean wrestling *(ssireum)* for the men, and competitions on swings for the women. All in all, it is an astonishing spectacle.

you can also take the scenic coastal train between Gangneung and Samcheok (⌚see p 255).

▶ *Leave Sokcho heading south on Rte 7 toward Naksan.*

After a few miles, you reach the little port of **Daepohang★**, famous for its lines of seafood stalls with all kinds of fish displayed in colorful plastic bowls. The market is run by an army of *ajumma* (female stallholders), often sporting dyed hair. Sit on one of the stools and try the squid stuffed with rice and vegetables (₩4,000), fish stews or shellfish thrown live on to the grill—all with a dash of *soju*. Unfortunately, the stalls at Daepohang may soon be transferred to a vast sterile hall, which may be less intimidating but will also be infinitely less picturesque.

👤👤 The Beach and Naksansa 낙산해수욕장과 낙산사
⌚*See Gangwon-do regional map.*
This is one of South Korea's most well-known beaches—the strip of white sand is lined with legions of motels and fish restaurants. There is a distinct seaside resort atmosphere and a wide variety of recreational activities are available. In the evening the sea glitters with hundreds of lights: the fishing boats use lamps to attract and hypnotize the

squid. A large hill to the north constitutes Naksan Provincial Park (✆(033)-670-2518). A pretty pine forest, which unfortunately caught fire in 2005, surrounds the temple, **Naksansa★★** (✆(033)-672-2447/8, www.naksansa. or.kr, ⌚5am–7pm).
The temple was founded in 671 and features a tall white statue of Avalokitesvara (the bodhisattva of compassion) standing on a lotus blossom looking over the temple. Several buildings were damaged by the fire but have since been renovated. Look out for the oldest building, **Wondongpo**, and the seven-tier pagoda that dates from 1468. For a temple to be so close to the sea is extremely unusual in Korea. The view is superb, not only over the sea but also of Seoraksan's summit.
From Naksan, before setting off again on Route 7, visit the **Osan-ri Prehistory Museum** (http://osm.go.kr, ⌚daily 9am–6pm, ₩1,000), where you will find exhibits of some of the oldest traces of prehistory in Korea. The road continues to the south and offers a brief panorama over **Dongho Beach** before rejoining Route 7 and passing near **Hajodae**, a pavilion perched high above the waves. If Routes 418 and 59 are open, you can make for Odaesan National Park directly. Otherwise, continue along the coast to the working fishing port of **Jumunjin**, which has a colorful **market★** and some popular restaurants.

▷ *Continue on Rte 7; then turn right on Rte 6 toward Odaesan.*

Odaesan National Park
오대산 국립공원
See Gangwon-do regional map.
The road follows the Yeongokcheon (Yeongok Stream) before plunging into the scented forests and lush scenery of the **national park** (*℘(033)-332-6417, http://english.knps.or.kr).* On turning left to **Sogeumgang**, the road reaches a village from where there are trails to some wonderful waterfalls. Information is available from the rangers, near the blue bridge. Foodies may also like to try the mountain mushroom specialties in one of the local restaurants.

▷ *Continue on the road, which climbs steeply to a pass and then drops down to a junction. Turn left on Rte 44 toward* **Woljeongsa**.

After passing through the park entrance (🕘 *9am–7pm, no charge; ₩7,500 with a car, map of the park ₩1,000),* you reach **Woljeongsa** (*℘ (033)-332-6661, 🕘 open dawn–dusk)*—or the "Temple of the Watchful Moon"—a vast complex surrounded by cypress trees that lies in a bend in the river, reached by two stone bridges. When the crowds are small, the birdsong is so loud that it drowns out the sound of the tumbling water. Founded in 643 by the monk Jajang, the temple complex includes a beautiful nine-tier **octagonal pagoda** that dates from the Goryeo period (10C) and a rare kneeling bodhisattva from the 11C. Exhibits on Buddhist culture from the Goryeo and Joseon periods are presented in a small **museum** (🕘 *open Wed–Mon 9:30am–4:30pm, lunch break at noon; ₩1,000).*
The road becomes a track and continues for 5.6mi/9km to another temple, **Sangwonsa** (*℘ (033)-332-6666, 🕘 open dawn–dusk, no charge).*
The valley is superb, with its mountain stream strewn with smooth, marbled rocks, friendly squirrels and the fragrance of pine resin. Perched on the hillside, the small temple complex is famous for its enormous carved bronze bell, said to be the oldest in the country (A.D. 725). 🚶 Various paths leave from the temple, including a round-trip *(3hr, 4mi/6.5km)* to **Birobong** (5,128ft/1,563m), the highest point in the region.

▷ *Return to Rte 6.*

In the summer, flower enthusiasts should make a detour to the **Korea Botanical Garden** (*℘(033)-332-7069, 🕘 open Apr–Oct 9am–6pm, ₩5,000).*
After the Kensington Hotel (which you can't miss), turn left on to Route 456. This is a popular winter sports region near the ski resort in Yongpyong. The neighboring town of Pyeongchang has even applied to host the 2018 Winter Olympic Games. Windmills signal the proximity of the **Daegwallyeong Pass** where the panoramic view reveals that you are much higher than you may have realized. In the past, villagers would climb up here to be closer to the gods. The winding descent offers magnificent views of the surrounding landscape and the sea.

▷ *At the outskirts of Gangneung, turn left onto Rte 7 (toward Sokcho) and then quickly right toward Ojukheon.*

Gangneung★ 강릉
See Gangwon-do regional map.
Known as the "city of pines," this town has 220,000 inhabitants and is 47mi/75km south of Sokcho. It is known for its *yangban*-style houses, beaches and the **Dano-je Festival★★**. Based on secular traditions, the folk festival commemorates the "double five" (fifth day of the fifth lunar month) and pays homage to *Daegwallyeong sansin* (a protecting deity) with spectacular masked dances and various rituals (*see box p253).*
The no. 202 bus leaves from the bus station *(toward Gyeongpo)* and goes to **Ojukheon House** (*℘ (033)-640-4457, 🕘 open 9am–5:30pm, ₩3,000),* which is surrounded by a small, carefully tended garden and groves of black bamboo. The house is a fine example of architecture from the Joseon period; the stone fireplaces are part of an under-

Chamsori Museum

©KTO

floor heating system, *ondol*. It was here that the female artist Shin Saimdang (1501–1554), a model mother in the neo-Confucian tradition, gave birth to the politician and philosopher Yi I, known as Lee Yulgok(1536–84). Her face is on ₩50,000 bills, while her son appears on ₩5,000 bills.

▷ *Go back the way you came and follow signs to Gyeongpo/Seongyojang.*

Don't miss **Seongyojang**★ (✆(033)-640-4799, ◷ open 9am–6pm, ₩3,000), a vast *yanban* residence that was home to the Confucian elite in the Joseon period (15–19C). With its delightful courtyards, white walls, wooden beams and grey tiles, it is often used to film historical dramas. The road then arrives at Gyeongpoho, a lake that is ideal for cycling around. It is overlooked by the elegant **Gyeongpodae** (1326), a pavilion perched discreetly on a slope among pine trees.
The nearby **Chamsori Museum**★ (✆ (033)-655-1130, www.edison.kr, ◷open 9am–5pm, ₩7,000) contains an amazing international collection, which began as one man's passion, of gramophones, musical boxes and objects connected to the life of Thomas Edison.
Venture to the long white sandy **beach** of **Gyeongpo**, lined with restaurants and motels that are noticeable for their romantic names; this is a popular desti-

nation for families, friends and couples. Not far away, **"Chodang village"** consists of a few restaurants *(follow signs from the lake)* that serve specialties made with *chodang sundubu*, a creamy tofu prepared using sea water (₩5,000/8,000), available at To Dam (✆(033)-652-0336) and Halmeoni (✆033-652-2058).

A special **Sea Train** travels along the coast three times a day between Gangneung and Samcheok (✆(033)-573-5473, www.seatrain.co.kr, 1hr20min, ₩10,000/15,000) via Donghae, Jeongdongjin and several beaches.
With seats positioned to face the extra-large widows, the views of the sea through the specially adapted railcars are lovely.

TOWARD JEONGDONGJIN
정동진 가는길

⌖*See Gangwon-do regional map.*

▷ *Leave Gangneung heading first toward the town center (City Hall), then toward Jeongdongjin. Follow the signs to "Unification Park" as soon as you are able.*

The coastline here is uneven and protected with wire netting; eventually you come to a large warship that has been permanently immobilized on dry land in **Unification Park**★ (✆(033)-640-4469, ◷ open 9am–5pm, ₩3,000 with car park).

255

👥👤 A **tour** of the American ship, which was built in 1945, takes you around the galley, cabins and the bridge. The **submarine** lying next to it became stranded on this coastline on 8 September 1996 with 25 North Korean agents aboard. It took several weeks for the South Korean authorities to find them all. The interior of the sub is not for the claustrophobic, but it is fascinating to see how 25 people managed to live in such cramped conditions. As for the wooden boat also here, it carried 11 North Korean refugees to these shores in 2009.

The coast road continues, passing below **Haslla Art World★** (☏ (033)-644-9411, www.haslla.kr, 🕐 summer 8am–10pm, winter 8:30am–7:30pm, ₩5,000), a collection of open-air sculptures, situated on the hillside with a panoramic view of the sea. There is also an interesting designer hotel on site (👜see Addresses). The next stop is the tourist resort of **Jeongdongjin**, dominated by a hotel in the shape of an ocean liner (the Sun Cruise Resort) perched on a hill.

▶ In Jeongdongjin, follow the signs to Sun Cruise Resort but without going all the way there. The road then follows the coast along a jagged stretch. Finally you reach Donghae and Samcheok (👜see following chapter).

ADDRESSES

🛏 STAY

IN SOKCHO

🛏 **House Hostel** 하우스호스텔 – 452-5 Dongmyeong-dong. ☏(033)-633 -3477. www.thehouse-hostel.com. ₩20,000/50,000. A quiet hostel with a wooden facade run by a friendly manager. Single or double rooms, with a laundry service, internet, kitchen and bikes.

🛏🛏 **Hotel Good Morning** 굿모닝호텔 – Haeorum-gil. ☏(033)-637-9900. 70rm. ₩60,000–80,000. A seaside hotel; rooms with kitchens and balconies.

ON THE COAST

🛏🛏💳 **Naksan Beach Hotel** 낙산비치호텔 – Naksan. ☏(033)-672-4000. www.naksanbeach.co.kr. 126rm. ₩80,000/135,000. This luxury hotel is a short walk from the beach near the entrance to the temple.

🛏🛏💳 **Hyundai** 현대호텔 – Gyeongpodae, Gangneung. ☏(033)-651-2233. www.hyundaihotel.com. 92rm. ₩150,000. On the landscaped hill south of the beach in Gyeongpo, this is the most comfortable option.

🛏🛏💳💳 **Haslla Art World Museum Hotel** 하슬라 호텔 – Jeongdongjin-ri San 33-1. ☏(033)-644-9414. www.haslla.kr. 20rm. From ₩185,000. Reservations necessary. Something of a UFO in the hotel world, this colorful metal building contains ultramodern designer rooms (shell-beds, works of art) and has a restaurant and sea views.

IN ODAESAN

🛏🛏💳💳 **Kensington Flora Hotel** 켄싱톤 플로라 호텔 – Dongsan-ri, Odaesan. ☏(033)-330-5000. www.kensingtonflorahotel.co.kr. From ₩180,000, but significant discounts are available. A large concrete building that sits incongruously among the small fruit and vegetable farms in the valley. Kitschy but comfortable.

🍽 EAT

Between the seafood in **Sokcho, Daepohang** and **Jumunjin** and the chodang sundubu in **Gangneung**, there is plenty of choice.

🎭 EVENTS AND FESTIVALS

Dano-je Festival in Gangneung – Late May to early June, an exceptional festival classified by UNESCO (👜see box p253).

Sokcho Maritime Festival – July and August, games and rock concerts on the beach.

From Donghae to Samcheok★
동해 *to* 삼척

These two coastal towns have a somewhat urban appearance and are characterized by their ports, beaches and lively streets. Samcheok is the more pleasant of the two and is known mainly for its fresh seafood. Both towns are best considered as useful bases from which to explore the east coast. While the delightful Mureung Valley provides a trip into the countryside, the region's main attraction is the extensive Hwanseongul mountain cave system, which is always a hit with young children. There are also some pretty and peaceful rural roads in the surrounding area.

🚗 DRIVING TOURS

FROM VALLEY TO MOUNTAIN

⬤ *68–87mi/110–140km drive to be completed in a short day.*

Donghae 동해
⬤*See Gangwon-do regional map.*
This town, meaning "eastern sea," is well known to Koreans because it is men-

▶ **Population:** 95,850 Donghae and 72,431 Samcheok.
⬤ **Michelin Map:** Regional map pp238–239
ℹ **Info:** Tourist Offices Samcheok Bus Station. 📞(033)-575-1330. http://eng.samcheok.go.kr. 9am–6pm; Donghae, Cheongok Donggul. 📞(033)-532-7303. www.donghae.gangwon.kr. 9am–6pm.
▶ **Location:** Donghae and Samcheok, the two main towns, are 62mi/100km south of Sokcho and 9.3mi/15km from each other.
👥 **Kids:** Hwanseongul with its stalactites and cascades of water.
😊 **Don't Miss:** The spectacular caves of Hwanseongul, the Mureung Valley.

tioned at the beginning of the national anthem. However, the sprawling blocks of housing and shopping centers offer little to charm visitors. Instead, walk along Mangsang Beach to the north of town, stroll through the vast market in

Mureung Valley
©KTO

GETTING THERE

IN DONGHAE

BY BUS – The bus station is on Route 7 between the town center and Mukho. There are buses to Dong Seoul Bus Terminal; bus no.12/4 serves the Mureung Valley.

BY TRAIN – Donghae Station is south of the town center (℘(033)-521-7789). There are trains to Seoul Cheongnyangni Station (6hr, ₩18,700), Taebaek, Gangneung and Samcheok. Mukho Station is north of downtown, in the port area.

BY FERRY – Mukhohang Terminal is near Mukho Station, 1.9mi/3km to the north (℘(033)-531-5891). In the summer a ferry departs every morning for Ulleungdo (3hr, one-way ₩51,000).

IN SAMCHEOK

BY BUS – The **Intercity** and **Express Bus** terminals are adjacent to each other, near the market in Chunamno (℘(033)-572-7444). Buses serve Seoul (3hr30min, ₩16,000), Sokcho (2hr30min, ₩12,000), Taebaek (2hr, ₩5,600), Donghae (20min, ₩1,500) and Hwanseongul (50min, ₩2,800).

BY TRAIN – From Samcheok Station – The Sea Train (● see p255) serves Donghae and Gangneung.

USEFUL INFORMATION

In **Donghae**, the post office, banks and shops are located at the intersection of Cheongok-no and Jungang-no. There are similar facilties in **Samcheok** on Osipcheon-no.

Bukpyeong and explore the cave system of **Cheongok Donggul** (℘(033)-532-7303, ●9am–6pm, ₩3,000) before taking the ferry to Ulleungdo (● see box, p 259).

▷ Take Rte 42 out of town signposted Mureung Valley. Bus no. 12/4, 6:30am–9pm.

Mureung Valley★ 무릉계곡

● See Gangwon-do regional map.
Known as the "grand canyon" of Korea, which is a bit of an exaggeration, Mureung welcomes visitors with a huge cement works.
But once you have passed through the entrance (₩1,500, parking ₩2,000), a delightful valley is revealed with a choice of flower-lined paths and more serious walking trails leading to waterfalls (Ssangpok and Yongchu Pokpo) and unusual rock formations. Most visitors are happy to picnic on the vast flat rock of Mureung (5,382sq yd/4,500sq m), overlooked by the pavilion called Geumnanjeong.
However, beyond Samhwa Temple (built on the site of a 7C retreat) the valley becomes narrower and crosses a pleasant forest of broad-leaved trees and prickly shrubs. In the spring the perma-

nent dark green foliage is lightened with tender new leaves, which turn to brilliant shades of red and gold in the fall. There are about 20 restaurants near the car park serving sanchaebaekban (rice with fragrant mountain vegetables).

▷ Return to Rte 42, then take Rte 7 toward Samcheok.

Samcheok 삼척

● See Gangwon-do regional map.
More compact than neighboring Donghae, this town is split into two separate areas. The center, 0.6mi/1km inland, has long shaded shopping streets that are always busy, a central covered market and **Jukseoru** (Seongnae-dong, 8am–7pm, ₩1,000), a pavilion that has been a source of inspiration to poets since 1402.
The other part of town stretches along the very jagged coastline, from the **beach** to the north (bus no. 10 from the bus station, 30min, ₩1,100) down to the picturesque **fishing port** (short taxi ride), and is lined with numerous restaurants.

▷ 17mi/27km SW of Samcheok, follow Rte 38 toward Taebaek and

Hwanseongul. On-site car park ₩1,000. Bus from Samcheok, 6 times daily, 50min, ₩2,900.

🚶🚶 Hwanseongul 환선굴 and Daegeumgul★★ 대금굴 (caves)

🚗 *See Gangwon-do regional map.*

The pretty road is surveyed by an army of radars as it snakes between beautiful hills and hamlets surrounded by crops. After you turn right toward Hwanseongul, the landscape becomes wilder around Deokhangsan. The picturesque rocky peak towering above the forest is a beacon for climbing enthusiasts.

The two cave systems of Hwanseongul and Daegeumgul penetrate deep into the mountain. The path to **Hwanseongul** (📞(033)-541-9266, 🕐 Mar–Oct 8am–5pm (Nov–Feb 8:30am–5:30pm), ₩4,000, allow 2hr for full viewing) is very steep but well maintained (0.8mi/1.3km), or you can take a slow trip on a monorail (single ₩3,000, return ₩5,000). One of the largest in Asia, this **cave** system extends for 3.9mi/6.2km into the mountain. The spectacular rock formations that emerge along the 1.2mi/2km path evoke fantastical animals, and the largest cavern (109yd by 32yd/100m by 33m) is like a cathedral. The lighting of the pools and waterfalls is perhaps a little garish and overdone, however.

Opened in 2007, **Daegeumgul** (same times, guided tours every 30min, ₩12,000

Ulleungdo – 울릉도

Situated 84mi/135km off the east coast, Ulleungdo offers tourists (numerous in the summer but rare during the rest of the year) beautiful sea landscapes of cliffs, creeks, fishing ports and rocks with strange silhouettes. The summit of Seonginbong (3,228ft/984m) towers over this **volcanic island,** which is also well suited to walks through the colorful vegetation. Accommodation is on sleeping mats in traditional rooms with *ondol* (heated floors). Gourmet specialties include squid and a famous pumpkin caramel.

🚢 3hr by ferry from Donghae (🚗 see Addresses) in the summer and from Pohang year-round. *www.ulleung.go.kr.*

including entry to Hwanseongul) takes its name from a traditional flute.

Visits have to be booked in advance (see tourist office or http://eng.samcheok. go.kr). This cave system is narrower and less extensive than its neighbor, but no less spectacular with waterfalls, enormous stalagmites, a cave lake and rock in varied colors.

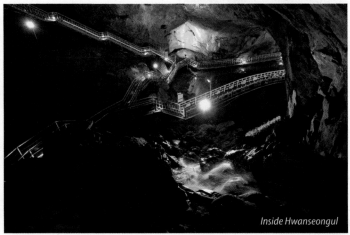

Inside Hwanseongul

©KTO

▷ *Back on Route 38, continue to Taebaek (24mi/38km) or return to the coast following* **Route 424**.

You can then follow the coast, either returning to Samcheok with a stop at the beautiful **Maengbang Beach**, or head south via the little port of **Jangho**, known for its seafood, and **Haesin-dang Park** (📞 *(033)-572-4429*, 🕐 *open Tue–Sun 9am–5pm, ₩3,000)* in **Sinnam**, famous for its phallic sculptures.

Maengbang Beach

©KTO

EXPLORING INLAND

▷ *90mi/145km drive. Need not take a full day, depending on stops.*

This drive may not include any exceptional sites, but it is pleasant and continues the journey south at a leisurely pace.

▷ *From Donghae, follow Rte 42 toward Jeongseon. Then make a detour to the beautiful Mureung Valley (🕐 see p258).*

Route 42 climbs upward, offering **panoramas** of the flooded valley and the distant coastline. After reaching a pass at 2,559ft/780m, you will see **crops** in the farmland around the village of Imgye. Neatly trimmed around the base and then slightly layered to leave room for the crops, the groups of trees look almost as though they have been given bowl haircuts. While the rural scenery in this part of Korea may not be spectacular, it makes a welcome change from the barbed wire along the coast. Take the opportunity to savor the simple pleasure of traveling at your own pace, stopping by the roadside to look at the work in the fields, a passing tractor or the mosaic of crops.

The next valley is occupied by the peaceful village of **Auraji**. As you leave, on the right after the large bridge, follow the "Rail Bike" sign. After 4.3mi/7km, there is a small leisure center with bikes for rent (*₩20,000*). Use these to follow the old railway line. Kids love it, but sometimes you have to ride in single file.

▷ *Continue along Route 42.*

Jeongseon, in the heart of a hilly rural region, is famous for its version of *Arirang*, a traditional 600-year-old chant that describes the journey of some travelers through a pass.

▷ *From here, follow Route 59 then 421.*

Rural villages follow one after the other in a beautiful landscape streaked with strips of black sheeting protecting cultivated areas. If desired, make a short stop at another cave, **Hwaam Cave** (🕐 *See Gangwon-do regional map*, 📞 *(033)-562-2578, www.jeongseon.go.kr*, 🕐 *open 9am–5pm, ₩5,000)*, a former gold mine, where there is a 1.1mi/1.8km trail. Farther on, in the village of Hwaam, there is a mineral spring with healing waters among flowering trees.

◗ *On leaving Hwaam, take Route 424 past the dramatic cliffs plunging down to the river.*

You may notice the villages here appear to have more greenhouses than houses for people.

◗ *Return to Route 421 on the right, alongside the pretty Mandugsan, then take Route 38 (toward Taebaek).*

This route follows a valley bristling with condominiums as the ski resorts come within range.

◗ *Continue on Route 35 which crosses the basin containing the town of Taebaek.*

Sitting at the gates to the provincial park *(http://tour.taebaek.go.kr)* **Taebaek** protects Taebaeksan (5,141ft/1,567m), a sacred shaman mountain that is surrounded by valleys full of forsythias and azaleas. Follow signs to "Taebaeksan Provincial Park/Coal Museum" (or take bus no. 7 from the town) to reach the park entrance and the interesting **Coal Museum** (℘(033)-552-7720, ○ *open 9am–5pm, ₩2,000 for entry to the park and car park),* whose bland building does little to suggest its purpose. Mines are still in operation in the region.

Route 35★ *(described on p 278)* continues southward to the Andong region in Gyeongsang-do (see p273).

ADDRESSES

☞ STAY

IN DONGHAE
New Donghae Hotel 뉴동해관광호텔 – *484 Chongkok-dong.* ℘*(033)-533-9215. www.hotelnd.com. ₩75,000/130,000, breakfast included. At the intersection between the main street Cheongongno and Rte 7.* Don't be put off by the hall, the tastefully decorated rooms are fine except for the opaque windows. A friendly welcome.

IN SAMCHEOK
There are numerous motels near the bus station and the beach.

Hotel Palace 삼척팰리스호텔 – *Jung Ha Dong, Samcheok.* ℘*(033)-570-1353/575-7000. www.palace-hotel.co.kr. 100rm. ₩70,000/150,000 depending on the season.* Situated on a hill overlooking the coast between the port and the beach, this is a "family celebration"- style hotel with comfortable rooms and fine views.

☜/EAT

IN DONGHAE
Koryeo Jeong 고려정 – *5-1 Hangol 1-gil..* ℘*(033)-531-4800. 11am–10pm. ₩10,000/25,000.* Away from the upper part of Cheongongno, this is a good traditional restaurant.

Look out for the fish restaurants in the market in the port and between Eodal Beach and Mukho.

IN SAMCHEOK
Bonjuk 본죽 – *Daekah-ro 32-9.* ℘*(033)-572-6281. 8am–9pm. ₩10,000.* A restaurant chain specializing in the various savory Korean rice porridges *(juk),* on the corner opposite the post office.

For seafood, head for the restaurants on the beach and in the port.

☷ EVENTS AND FESTIVALS

Many Koreans come to celebrate the New Year on Mangsang Beach at Donghae. At the end of January, Taebaek celebrates the winter season with the **Taebaeksan Snow Festival** and its famous ice sculpture competition.

GYEONGSANG-DO

Gyeongsang-do was once the seat of Korean royal power. Everything in the mountainous peninsula happened here, and thus, Gyeongsang, which is now split into north, Gyeongsangbuk, and south, Gyeongsannam, offers some of the country's most rewarding historical finds. Proud Koreans will say that these lands have been invaded over 1,000 times—probably more—so history buffs will have interesting stops in almost every town.

Highlights

1 See the UNESCO World Heritage site **Haeinsa**, the Tripitaka Koreana Buddhist scripture library (p270)

2 Deight your tasetebuds in **Andong** (p273)

3 Enjoy a place of **calm and serenity** (p276)

4 See the relics in the **Gyeongju National Museum** (p286)

5 Visit the uçnderwater tomb of **King Munmu** (p294)

Ancient Kings and Capitals

The largest cities in this region, Busan, Daegu and Ilsan are actually separate non-provincial governments, but Gyeongju is not to be missed. Travelers often compare Seoul to Tokyo and Gyeongju to Kyoto. Indeed, like Kyoto, Gyeongju was once the Korean capital, and as well, many of the temples, shrines, pagodas and other historic structures were spared aerial bombing. Even visitors who aren't history buffs will enjoy meandering past the lotus ponds, museums, galleries, and stores. Of par-

ticular interest are the curious funeral mounds, known as tumuli—large earthen tombs containing the body of a Korean king, queen, or other royalty, who were often buried with scepters, crowns, and other priceless items of gold or jewels. Many have been excavated and their contents put on display in the Gyeongju National Museum. Likewise, visitors will encounter the Silla, Korea's first unifying power. Silla artifacts fill Korean museums, and Gyeongsang provinces have preserved or restored many of the Silla palaces and ruins.

A visit to the coastline of the East Sea offers religious curiosities both ancient and modern day, including Korea's only underwater tomb. King Munmu requested to be buried beneath the sea along the mild coastline so that he could return in the form of a dragon and protect his beloved homeland. Shamanists of all kinds gather here to perform unique ceremonial rites, often chanting, praying, drinking soju or presenting offerings of dried codfish.

No other area of Korea offers the traveler more culture, history, art and archeology. Gyeongju is a must-visit for anyone wanting to explore beyond the city limits of Seoul.

Andong Town

©Chris Stowers/Apa Publications

Daegu★
대구

First documented in 261 as Dalgubeol, Daegu acquired its present name in 757. It has been the regional capital since 1601 and, over the course of the centuries, has become a major communications hub on the Seoul–Busan and Gyeongju–Jinju routes. Extensive markets, first established at the end of the Joseon period, are still held regularly in the city. Now famed for its textiles, traditional medicine and the Samsung Lions, its baseball team, Korea's third city is emerging from the shadows of Seoul and Busan to make its name as a regional center, having hosted the World Athletics Championships in 2011. With a reputation as a dynamic city and quite hot during the summer season, Daegu has invested in fountains and sculptures to smarten up its center and is launching more and more initiatives to improve facilities for foreign visitors. At first sight, shopping appears to be the main activity, as can be seen from the countless stalls, boutiques, markets and malls, which seem to be open 24/7. To avoid this frenzy of commercialism, visitors can escape on foot along the trails of Palgongsan Provincial Park or by car to Jikjisa and Haeinsa, two of the most interesting temples in Korea.

A BIT OF GEOGRAPHY

Daegu is located on a fertile plain that gets too hot for comfort in summer. The city center is spread out along both sides of Jungang-no, which runs north to south between the central station and Banwoldang Junction. The junction is served by Daegu subway line 1, which connects with line 2 at Banwoldang. The markets at Seomun and Yangnyeongsi lie to the west, and to the east there are the shops, restaurants and cafés of Dongseong-no and Yasigolmok. The

▸ **Population:** 2,512,604
▸ **Michelin Map:** Map p 263
▸ **Info:** Daegu Tourist Offices ✆(053)-1330. www.daegutour.or.kr. Open 9am–5pm. At Duryu Park, Daegu Airport, Dongdaegu Station, Seomun Market, Daegu Station, Dongseongno, Palgongsan, EXCO Daegu, Yangnyeongsi Market
▸ **Location:** 174mi/280km from Seoul and 78mi/125km from Busan.
▸ **Timing:** A day should be sufficient if you are not traveling beyond Daegu.
▸ **Parking:** Your hotel car park is by far the best option.
▸ **Don't Miss:** Daegu's fascinating markets, the superb Jikjisa, the treasures of Haeinsa.

bus terminal and the KTX station are at Dongdaegu, 2mi/3km to the east.

VISIT
Jung-gu, the Central District
중구시내

With the exception of the reconstructed buildings Seonhwadang (office of the provincial governor) and Jingcheonggak (residence of provincial governor), in the heart of **Gyeongsang-gamyeong Park** (Ⓜ Jungangno, line 1, exit 3), Daegu's city center boasts few historic buildings, but it was here that a power base was established 400 years ago and from which the entire province was ruled.

The lack of ancient architecture is made up for by the impressive amounts of **goods for sale**, and as you stroll through the roads of the central Jung-gu district, you may well find yourself wondering who buys it all. Luxury boutiques, markets, international retailers and tiny stalls run by locals dot the labyrinthine streets, all vying for customers. And that's just at ground level—you'll

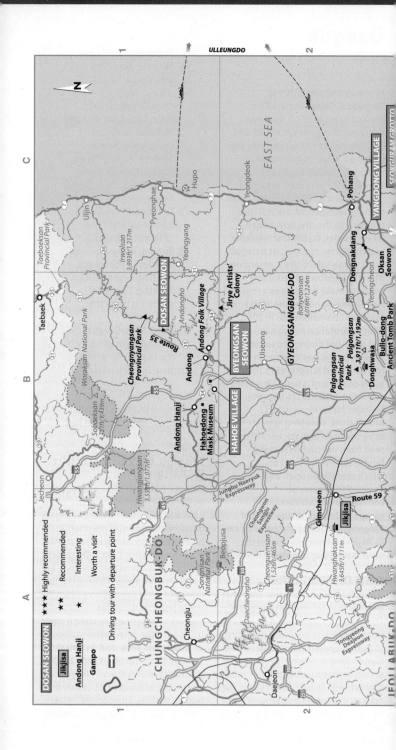

ULLEUNGDO

EAST SEA

DOSAN SEOWON
Jikjisa
Andong Hanji
Gampo
Driving tour with departure point

★★★ Highly recommended
★★ Recommended
★ Interesting
Worth a visit

CHUNGCHEONG-DO

Taebaek

Taebaeksan
Provincial Park

Uljin

Pyeonghae

Hupo

Yeongdeok

Irwolsan
3,993ft/1,217m

Yeongyang

Woraksan National Park

Soebaeksan
4,271ft/1,439m

Cheongnyangsan
Provincial Park

DOSAN SEOWON

Andongho

Andong Folk Village

Jirye Artists'
Colony

Route 35

Jecheon

Hwangjangsan
3.53ft/1,077m

BYEONGSAN
SEOWON

Andong

Uiseong

GYEONGSANGBUK-DO

Bohyeonsan
4,016ft/1,224m

Andong Hanji

Hahoe Village

HAHOE VILLAGE

Hahoedong
Mask Museum

Palgongsan
Provincial
Park

Palgongsan
3,911ft/1,192m

Donghwasa

Bullo-dong
Ancient Tomb Park

Oksan
Seowon

Yeongcheon

Dongnakdang

YANGDONG VILLAGE

Pohang

SEOKGURAM GROTTO

Jungbu Naeryuk
Expressway

Cheongwon
Sangju
Expressway

Beopjusa

Songnisan National Park

Cheongjeomsan
1,526ft/465m

Gimcheon

Route 59

Jikjisa

Hwanghaksan
3,645ft/1,111m

Hwanghaksan
1,111m

Cheongju

Songnisan National Park

Daecheongho

Daejeon

Tongyeong
Daejeon
Expressway

JEOLLABUK-DO

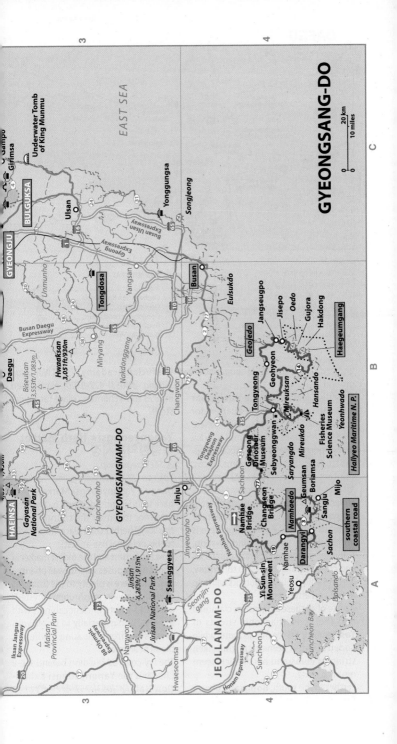

GYEONGSANG-DO

EAST SEA

BULGUKSA

GYEONGJU

HAEINSA

Daegu

GYEONGSANGNAM-DO

GYEONGSANGNAM-DO

JEOLLANAM-DO

Tongdosa

Underwater Tomb
of King Munmu

Gampo

Girimsa

Ulsan

Yonggungsa

Songjeong

Busan

Eulsukdo

Jangseungpo

Jisepo

Oedo

Gujora

Hakdong

Geojedo

Haegeumgang

Geohyeon

Mireuksan

Tongyeong

Hansando

Yeonhwado

Fisheries
Science Museum

Hallyeo Maritime N. P.

Geoseong
Dinosaur
Museum

Seobyeonggwan

Saryangdo

Mireukdo

Geumsan

Boriamsa

Mijo

Sangju

southern
coastal road

Namhaedo

Changseon
Bridge

Namhae
Bridge

Darangyi

Sacheon

Namhae

Yi Sun-sin
Monument

Yeosu

Dolsando

Suncheon Bay

Suncheon

Hwaeseomsa

Jirisan National Park

Jirisan
6,283ft/1,915m

Ssanggyesa

Jinju

Hapcheonho

Gayasan
National Park

Hwaaksan
3,051ft/930m

Biseulsan
3,553ft/1,083m

Unmunho

Yangsan

Miryang

Nakdonggang

Changwon

Jinyeongho

Jirisan

Iksan Jangsu
Expressway

Maisan
Provincial Park

Namwon

Seomjin-
gang

Bulguksa Expressway

Gyeong Expressway

Busan Ulsan Expressway

Busan Daegu
Expressway

Tongyeong
Daejeon
Expressway

Namhae Expressway

Honam Expressway

88 Olympic
Expressway

0   20 km
0   10 miles

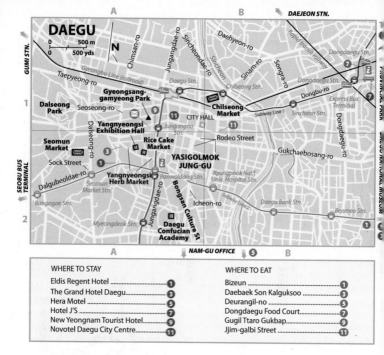

WHERE TO STAY

Eldis Regent Hotel	❶
The Grand Hotel Daegu	❸
Hera Motel	❺
Hotel J'S	❼
New Yeongnam Tourist Hotel	❾
Novotel Daegu City Centre	⓫

WHERE TO EAT

Bizeun	❶
Daebaek Son Kalguksoo	❸
Deurangil-no	❺
Dongdaegu Food Court	❼
Gugil Ttaro Gukbap	❾
Jjim-galbi Street	⓫

find several more levels of shops underground.

The city is laid out like a **great bazaar** with themed streets and quarters for jewelry, medicines and fashion—where mini-skirted sales girls attempt to draw in shoppers—as well as restaurants, tattoo studios, scooter showrooms, discos, printers and even socks (Ⓜ *Seomun Market, line 2, follow directions for Sock Street*). Festooned in bright, eye-catching signs, the buildings all but disappear beneath them, yet the energy here is unmistakable: you can window-shop, compare, try things on, make purchases and consume like there's no tomorrow, and the ubiquitous restaurants will help revive you afterward.

A taste of all these elements is crammed into the pedestrian-only streets of **Yasigolmok** (💷 *see Daegu map*), while Rodeo Street is home to an unbroken string of clubs and bars which seem never to close.

Farther to the south, **Bongsan Culture Street** (Ⓜ *Banwoldang, line 1, exit 9*) has a bohemian feel with cafés and galleries. Turn right at the end to find the **Daegu**

Confucian Academy (*753-4 Namasan 3-dong, ℰ(053)-422-8700*), established in 1398 and a charming place for a quiet stroll.

Yangnyeongsi★ Herb Market
약령한약재시장

💷 *See Daegu map.*

Yakjeon. Ⓜ *Banwoldang, line 1, exit 4.*

Daegu's Yangnyeongsi Market dates back to 1658 and a decision by the local governor to gather the country's best medicinal herbs in one place (admittedly for his personal use at first).

Now the largest and the oldest market in Korea, it comprises wall-to-wall pharmacies, and there is plenty to see (bundles of strange twigs, mushrooms, mysterious little sachets, ancient cabinets with drawers) and especially to smell, with every store front releasing a different blend of aromas.

The ivy-covered building behind Jae-il Church is the **Yangnyeongsi Exhibition Hall** (*ℰ(053)-257-4729*, 🕐 *open Mon-Fri 9am–6pm; Sat, public holidays and in winter 9am-5pm; no charge*), full of information about Oriental medi-

GETTING THERE
Arrival/departure
BY TRAIN – Dongdaegu Station to the east of the city is served by express trains, including the KTX: Busan *(1hr, ₩11,000)*, Seoul *(1hr50min, ₩35,000)*. **Daegu Station** is served by tonggeun and mugunghwa local trains.

BY BUS – There are a number of bus terminals from where you can reach all the cities in the country, including two at Dongdaegu (Ⓜ *Dongdaegu, line 1, exit 4)*: Intercity Bus Terminal *(℘(053)-756-0017)* for Seoul *(4hr)*, Gyeongju *(55min)*, Busan *(2hr)*, Jinju *(2hr)*, Andong *(1hr30min)*; and Express Bus Terminal *(℘(053)-743-3701)* for Gyeongju. In the south of the city is **Seobu Terminal** (Ⓜ *Seongdangmot, line 1, exit 3. ℘(053)-656-2825)* for Tongyeong, Jinju and Haeinsa.

BY PLANE – Daegu International Airport is northwest of the city, and there is a connection to Daegu's Ayanggyo subway station via bus no. 401/104. Flights to Seoul, Jeju and China *(℘(053)-980-5290, www.airport. co.kr/doc/daegu_eng/index.jsp)*.

Car rental – Kumho Rent a Car (Ⓜ *Dongdaegu, line 1, exit 1, ℘(053)-611-8000). www.kumhorent.com*

GETTING AROUND
Daegu's two subway lines (three by 2015) make it easy to get around the city, and there's a good bus network *(tickets ₩1,100/1,500). http://businfo.daegu.go.kr/ba/index/index.do Directions in English.*

USEFUL INFORMATION
Post office – The main post office is near Gyeongsang-gamyeong Park (Ⓜ *Jungangno, line 1, exit 3.* ◷ *Open Mon–Fri 9am–8pm, Sat 6pm)*.
Health – Kyung buk University Hospital, *50 Samdeok 2-ga. ℘(053)-422-1141.*

SIGHTSEEING
A vast range of trips and excursions is available: a *hop-on, hop-off* bus does a round-trip through the city *(Tue–Sun 10am–6pm, ₩5,000)*, and there are six other themed routes *(Tue–Sun, ₩5,000)* including one to Palgongsan. Information: tourist offices *℘(053)-627-8900. www.daegucitytour.com.* If you are short of time, take the **Daegu Vicinity Tour** *(Sat–Sun 9am–6pm from Dongdaegu, ₩26,000)* to see various local places of interest, including Andong, **Hahoe**, Gyeongju, Haeinsa and industrial **Ulsan**. Information from the tourist offices, bookings at *℘(053)-746-6407 and www.daegutravel.or.kr.*

---

cine, its history, the use of plants and animal parts, and the human body and its care. These last topics are presented in English on touch screens—perhaps you'll find a cure for any ailments you may have.
Don't miss the little **Rice Cake Market** (ⓒ *see Daegu map)* at the beginning of the street on the left (approaching from Jungang-no).
The rice cakes are laid out in colorful displays, sometimes forming pictures of elaborate dishes (seafood platters, vegetables) that are eaten on Buddha's birthday and other occasions.

Seomun Market★ 서문시장
ⓒ *See Daegu map.*
Ⓜ *Seomun Market, line 1, exit 1.*
◷ *Nov–Feb 9am–5pm (closed 2nd & 4th Sun of the month), Mar–Oct 9am–6pm.*
While there is nothing left of the original Joseon dynasty market established in 1669, you will find, in a **maze of alleyways** and extending into several large buildings, open-air stalls and stores with miles and miles of shelves laden with pretty much everything possible to sell. This city within a city is the place to find blankets by the ton, giant seaweed, trestle tables of dried anchovies, strange-

looking roots, live fish, dead fish (and some that look distinctly unwell), traditional robes and silly trinkets in bright colors, while the ubiquitous small diners offer an opportunity to regain your strength. Despite the crowds and the continual dance of scooters and delivery porters, Western ears will notice something missing—there is little noise from the traders themselves. Few call out incitements to buy; in fact, the market is almost entirely silent.

A little farther to the north, the oldest fortress in Korea once stood in **Dalseong Park** (ⓖ *see Daegu map*), but now there are just some pleasant walks and a rather sorry-looking zoo.

Daegu's Other Highlights

Two subway stops north of the fashionable boutiques of Jung-gu, **Chilseong Market** (Ⓜ *Chilseong, line 1, any exit*) is a very traditional Korean market. There is a fairly innocent-looking DIY section, but for the full Korean market experience, don't miss the rows of market gardeners and fishmongers, with their bowls of writhing eels and turtles, or the stalls where every part of a pig from snout to tail seems to be boiling merrily. The colors and smells are impossible to sum up in a few words.

A little farther to the east, the ultra-modern **Dongdaegu Station** (Ⓜ *Dongdaegu, line 1*) is a constant hive of activity; surrounded by local facilities, it is bound to feature in your travels at some point during your stay.

Located a little way out, to the south of the city center, the **Daegu National Museum** (ℰ *(053)-768-6051, http://daegu.museum.go.kr/english/index.htm,* Ⓒ *open Tue–Sun 9am–6pm (Sat, Sun and public holidays 7pm), no charge; bus no. 242 from the city center, or bus no. 514/814 from Dongdaegu Station*) preserves the memory of the Silla dynasty (ⓖ *see p288*).

The southeast of the city is also home to **Daegu Stadium** (Ⓜ *Daegongwon (Grand Park), line 2, then take the shuttle bus*). A vast open shell with a capacity of 65,857, the stadium was built for the 2002 soccer World Cup, and was used again for a major sporting event in 2011 when the world's athletes, the sports media and spectators flocked here during the IAAF World Championships in Athletics.

NEARBY SIGHTS
Palgongsan Provincial Park
팔공산도립공원

▶ *12mi/20km N of Daegu. From Dodong Junction, follow signs for Palgongsan. From the center of town, follow signs for the airport, then Palgongsan. Bus no. 401 follows a circular route from the exit to Dongdaegu train station and serves the entrance to the Gatbawi site, Donghwa Temple and the cable car station.*

ⓖ *See Daegu map .*
Allow for a 2hr round-trip on foot.

Escape the frenetic activity of Daegu to find a calm setting and magnificent views of the surrounding hills and valleys from the top of **Palgongsan** (Palgong Mountain, 3,911ft/1,192m). Situated to the north of the city, Palongsan has been sacred since the Silla era. The mountain's name is a reminder of the "eight worthy officers" who saved the life of Wang Geon, the founder of the kingdom of Goryeo, in a battle near here—*pal* means "eight."

Other places of worship can be found in the neighboring valleys. **Donghwasa (Donghwa Temple)**, founded in 493 *(Dohak-dong, ℰ(053)-982-0101, www.donghwasa.net,* Ⓒ *open 8am–6pm, ₩2,500, parking ₩2,000)*, lies in a steep valley lined with trees. It is in two parts, with an imposing bright white Reunification Buddha looking out over the most impressive buildings in the complex. For a fine view with the minimum of effort take the **cable car** (ℰ *(053)-982-8801,* Ⓒ *open 10am–dusk, ₩6,000)*, which will whisk you to a height of 2,690ft/820m for a memorable panorama of Daegu.

At **Gatbawi★** rock (2,789ft/850m) the Buddha of Medicine, a statue dating from 638, serenely awaits visitors *(Daehan-dong, Wachon-myeon, ℰ (053)*

Bullo-dong Ancient Tomb Park
©KTO

-983-8586, www.seonbonsa.org), imperturbable beneath his stone hat. You'll find a superb view, this time of the park, from here too.

Bullo-dong Ancient Tomb Park★
sits between Daegu and Palgongsan (*N of the airport near Dodong Junction, ℰ (053)-940-1224/984-3506, ⏰open 9am–6pm, no charge*). This vast burial ground is easily accessible by car. Some 211 burial mounds, the graves of nobles dating from the 2C to the 6C, are scattered about the park's low hills.

EXCURSIONS
Jikjisa★★ (Jikji Temple)
직지사

▶ *43mi/70km W of Daegu. By car: take Rte 1 toward Daejeon, exit 23 Gimcheon, then follow signs for Jikjisa. Or: Rte 4 toward Gumi/Gimcheon, then follow signs for Jikjisa (Rte 903) on the left after this last town. Otherwise, bus or train to Gimcheon (55min), then bus no. 11/111 from Daegu Intercity Bus Terminal (20min).*

⏰*See Daegu map. ℰ (053)-436-6084. http://www.jikjisa.or.kr/. ⏰Open Mar–Oct 7am–6:30pm, Nov–Feb 7am–5:30pm. ₩2,500. Guided tour in English.*
After **Gimcheon**, the road leads through vineyards—a somewhat unexpected sight in Korea—and a village full of restaurants serving grilled grasshop-

pers (*mettugi*) before finally reaching this **superb temple**. The best time to visit is early in the morning before the buses have arrived and when the paths are still pristine, neatly swept and with the marks of the broom still upon them. At this hour, with just the squirrels for company and the sounds of a breeze through the trees and lapping water nearby, the natural oasis of peace lends itself to quiet contemplation. The surrounding forest is magnificent all year round, with flaming colors in the fall and a magical quality during winter.

"The directly pointed temple" was founded by the monk Ado in 418 in the foothills of Hwanghaksan (3,645ft/1,111m) just as the kingdom of Silla was beginning to accept Buddhism.

Of the 20 or so buildings that remain (of the original 40), the one to see is the 15C **Hall of One Thousand Buddhas** (*Birojeon*), where the statuettes in white jade (which were then gilded) cover an entire wall.

It is said that the first person present to pick out the one representing a naked baby will have a son.

Opposite Birojeon is a small stone pagoda from the 9C. Look out for three paintings in the main hall (*Daeungjong*) behind the three Buddhas (*Sakyamuni* in the center, *Bhaisajyaguru* to the east and *Amitabha* to the west). This **triad of enormous paintings** on silk, created by 16 monks in 1744, is remarkable for

Jikjisa

©KTO

the detail in the facial expressions and the use of color.

To drive from Jikjisa to Haeinsa, take **Route 59** (*Rte 4 toward Daegu, then turn right onto Rte 59*), a quiet road that passes through small farming communities and valleys strewn with greenhouses shielding crops, and orchards, before reaching the glorious uplands and forests of Gayasan National Park.

Haeinsa★★★
(Haein Temple) 해인사

37mi/60km SW of Daegu. By car: take branch Rte 451 then arterial Rte 12 toward Gwangju; take exit 24 for Haeinsa, then follow Rte 1033. By bus: journey of 1hr30min from Seobu Intercity to Daegu, 1 departure per hr during the day, ₩6,200; 20–30min walk from car park.

See Daegu map.
Gaya-myeon. (055)-931-1001.
www.haeinsa.or.kr. Open Wed–Mon 8:30am–6:30pm. ₩3,500 (₩6,000 including parking).

After the toll, the route follows a delightful stream overhung with pines. The "Temple of Reflection on a Smooth Sea" was founded in 802 among the magnificent wooded slopes of **Gayasan** (Mt. Gaya, 4,691ft/1,430m), which saw both the birth and growth of Buddhism in

Korea and whose name echoes Bodh Gaya in India, the place of the Buddha's enlightenment. It is now one of the most visited mountains in the country and has come to symbolize "religious teaching." After an enchanting 20min walk through trees and past waterfalls, and girls selling products from the forest, you reach **Iljumun** (Ilju Gate), the threshold to the world of the Buddha. Very steep steps lead to various buildings supported on solid wooden pillars, once the dwelling place of many renowned monks. As you climb between Iljumun and Janggyeong Panjeon, each of the 108 steps symbolizes the renunciation of one of the 108 desires that plague humans.

Daegwangjeon, the **main hall**, dates from 1817 and is dedicated to Vairocana, the Buddha of Wisdom. The mural behind the figure of Vairocana (1769) and its six attendant statuettes recounts the **legend of the wooden fish**. According to the legend, a lazy monk who is transformed into a fish upon his death and cursed to carry a trunk on his back until the end of time helps a passing Buddhist cross the river by taking him on the trunk. At this point the monk is freed from the curse and relieved of his burden. Subsequently a *moktak* was carved from the trunk—a wooden percussion instrument decorated with a fish head—and similar instruments have been kept in temples ever since; they are played by being struck with a small stick and accompany recitations of the sutras.

The main reason to visit **Haeinsa**, however, is to see a treasure that, despite its UNESCO classification, is almost hidden away: the **Tripitaka Koreana★★★** (*Palman Daejanggyeong* in Korean). "Tripitaka" can be traced back to a Sanskrit word meaning "the three baskets," such as those said to contain the teachings of the Buddhist religion. Assembled in Southeast Asia in the 10C, the texts were first carved in woodblocks in the 11C. They were destroyed by the Mongols and then re-carved between 1237 and 1251 onto both sides of 81,256 woodblocks of identical dimensions and weight (7.7lb/3.5kg). King Gojong assigned this laborious task to the monks of the temple at Jeondeung (Ganghwa Island). Not a single mistake has yet been discovered among the 50 million engraved Chinese characters.

The Tripitaka became a model for later collections. The act of re-carving the blocks, like a monumental act of prayer to Buddha, was intended to protect the country against the Mongol invasions. The woodblocks of this, the oldest intact collection of Buddhist texts in Chinese characters, have been stored since 1488 in **Janggyeong Panjeon** (8am–5pm, *summer 6pm),* a well ventilated pavilion through which the dry, fresh mountain breezes are allowed to waft. Built with the sole purpose of protecting the woodblocks (*see cover photo),* it represents a considerable technical feat for the period. Glimpsing these thousands of woodblocks lined up on their shelves through the slatted windows really is an extraordinary sight.

The **Haeinsa Museum** (*(055)-934-3150,*   *open Wed–Mon 10am–5:30pm,* ₩*2,000),* near the car park, houses the temple's treasures, a modern art exhibition and a cafeteria.

  The main complex is surrounded by various retreats, statues and religious sites, which are spread out across the valleys and accessible via numerous paths. The most remarkable has to be the hermitage perched high up at

Haeinsa

©KTO

Heuirang-dae, where Hirang, a great monk of the Silla period, attained enlightenment.

ADDRESSES

STAY

  Hera Motel 헤라모텔 – *Sinam 4-dong*   *(053)-958-2200.*   *Dongdaegu, line 1, exit 1.*   – *47rm.* ₩*70,000.* A recently built motel of superior quality.

  New Yeongnam Tourist Hotel 뉴영남관광모텔 – *177-7 Beomeo-dong, Susung-gu.*   *Beomeo, line 2, exit 4.*   *(053)-752-1001. 45rm.* ₩*65,000/95,000.* A little antiquated when set against the high-rise buildings of Beomeo, with basic rooms and a lackluster welcome.

  Hotel J'S 제이스호텔 – *326-1 Shinchun 4 Dong, Dong-gu*   *Dongdaegu, line 1, exit 3.*   *(053)-756-6601. www.hotel-js.com.*   – *60rm.* ₩*160,000, discounts possible.* Located near Dongdaegu, this comfortable business hotel has pleasant rooms and impeccable service.

⊖⊜🖳🖳 **Eldis Regent Hotel**
엘디스리젠트 호텔 – 380 Dongsang
-dong. Ⓜ Seomun Market, line 2, exit 5.
✆(053)-250-7711. www.eldishotel.com.
60rm. ₩250,000. The Eldis has something of a European feel to it. The air
is scented with herbs from Mt. Seorak,
the rooms are modern, and there's a
spa and much more.

⊖⊜🖳🖳 **The Grand Hotel Daegu**
그랜드 호텔 – 563-1 Beomeo-dong,
Susung-gu. Ⓜ Beomeo, line 2, exit 3.
✆(053)-742-0001. www.daegugrand.
co.kr. 150rm. ₩215,000. South of an
intersection bristling with high-rise
buildings, the Grand offers US standards
of comfort (thick fitted carpets and a
abundance of soft furnishings). Not to
mention a spa and four restaurants.

⊖⊜🖳🖳 **Hotel Novotel Daegu City
Centre** 노보텔 – 11-1 Munwha-dong,
Jung-gu. Ⓜ Jungangno, line 1. ✆(053)-
664-1101. www.noveldaegu.com.
203rm. ₩200,000. A glass tower in a very
central location, with enormous rooms
that are modern and comfortable. Ask
for the highest room available to get
the best view.

JIKJISA

Try the *Temple Stay* program (✆(054)-
436-6084, www.jikhisa.or.kr, ₩50,000) or
the **Park Hotel** 파크호텔 (Daehang-
Myun, ✆(054)-437-8000, ₩66,000) with
its enormous, old-fashioned rooms.

HAEINSA

Try the *Temple Stay* program (✆(055)-
934-3105, www.haeinsa.or.kr, ₩30,000–
50,000), the yeogwan at Chiinli and
Haeinsa ist Hotel 해인사관광호텔
(Chiinli, ✆(055)-933-2000, ₩90,000), a
comfortable hotel in the mountains.

✟ EAT

Dongdaegu Food Court (on the same
level as the station) is a good place for
travelers changing trains to grab a bite;
try the excellent *bibimbap* at the **Go
Gung** restaurant. In the evenings, the
locals flock to the south side of town
to visit the dozens of restaurants in the
Deurangil-no area (bus no. 401 from
the center or from Dongdaegu).

⊖ **Bizeun** 빚은 – Suseong Junction.
Ⓜ Beomeo, line 2, exit 3. ✆(053)-
741-3386. www.bizeun.co.kr. Open
7am–10pm. Discover just what can be
done with sugar and rice! The biscuits,
mochi and *manjoo* are all as tasty as
they look, and you can try before
you buy.

⊖ **Gugil Ttaro Gukbap** 국일따
로국밥 – Jungang Intersection.
Ⓜ Jungangno, line 1, exit 3. ✆(053)-
253-7623. Open 24hr. This restaurant,
which is often packed, has been serving
ttaro gukbap (₩6,000), a local soup
based on beef, liver, onions and radish,
since 1946. The service is incredibly
efficient.

🖳 **Daebaek Son Kalguksoo** 대
백손칼국수 – 2-1 Namseong-ro,
Jung-gu. Ⓜ Seomun Market, line 2.
✆(053)-255-1517. Open 11am–10pm.
Located at the end of the street
with the herb market, this simple
establishment offers about a dozen
dishes. Agreeable service.

⊖🖳 **Jjim-galbi Street** 찜갈비거리
– Ⓜ Chilseong, line 1. Around 220yd/
200m to the east of City Hall, this street
has its roots in a cheap and cheerful
eatery run by a local grandmother
for the workers of the district. It now
includes a number of restaurants
specializing in dishes featuring boiled
beef, including the locally very popular
Dongindong galbi. **Bongsan Jjim-
galbi**, with its wooden facade (✆(053)
-425-4203, open 10am–10pm) is the
best known.

🎭 ENTERTAINMENT

The clubs and bars are clustered
around Yasigolmok and **Rodeo
Street** (Ⓜ Banwoldang, line 1, exit 3):
Bubblebar, MK, G2.

🎭 EVENTS AND FESTIVALS

Daegu's **Herb Medicine Festival** is
held at Yangnyeongsi Market in May
(*http://english.daegu.go.kr*).

Around Andong★★

안동

Andong, in the north of Gyeongsangbuk-do, is an essential stop-off, not only so that you can experience its lively market and try some of its famous salted mackerel, but also for the scenery of the surrounding area, which is among the most serene and beautiful in the entire country. The wooded hills and meadows crossed by winding rivers have been home to scholars, artists and noble families, many of whom were responsible for establishing various schools, retreats and delightful villages in the region between the 16C and 19C. With two Confucian academies nearby, Andong is often promoted as the cradle of Confucian culture in tourist brochures. The area has some important cultural heritage sites too. UNESCO recognized its historic associations by inscribing the village of Hahoe as a World Heritage Site in 2010.

▸ **Population:** 167,432
🖐 **Michelin Map:** Regional map pp 264–265
▯ **Info:** Tourist Office Rail station forecourt. ☎(054)-852-6800. www.andong.go.kr. Open 9am–6pm. Helpful staff and a very practical map in English with bus timetables for the tourist sites.
◗ **Location:** Andong is located 50mi/80km north of Daegu on Rte 55. Hahoe Village is 15.5mi/25km to the east of Andong. The local tourist sites are well served by public transport.
🕐 **Timing:** Expect to spend at least two days exploring the Andong area.
👁 **Don't Miss:** The delightful alleyways of Hahoe Village, the tranquil Confucian schools at Byeongsan Seowon and Dosan Seowon, tasting Andong mackerel.

⟣WALKING TOUR

OF ANDONG
Andong City Center
🖐 *See Gyeongsang-do Map*
The rather compact city center is laid out along the northern banks of the Nakdong River between the railway station and the avenue called Dongmun-no. Most visitors simply make Andong their base from which to explore the surrounding area, since the city itself doesn't offer much in the way of exploration, although it is pleasant enough and has good facilities (banks, post office, stores). With its rail station and inevitable attendant motels, the area's pedestrian-only streets are lined with any number of stores and restaurants and are often filled with children eating multicolored donuts after school hours. Andong is much like any other South Korean city.

The covered market attracts browsers, and the ranks of food stands in the narrow streets tempt customers of all ages who cluster around large containers of *tteokbokki* (rice noodles and vegetables in a red spicy sauce). A number of restaurants offer **culinary specialties,** and there is great local pride in the regional dishes associated with the city's name. Although the coast is 43mi/70km away, Andong serves the best mackerel in the country. The locals salt the catch to preserve it, giving the fish a typically strong taste, with tender flesh and a golden, crunchy skin.

Jjimdak, a stewed chicken dish marinated in spices and soy sauce, is another must, but only the local *soju* (a strong, rice-based drink) has a **museum** devoted to it (**Andong Soju Museum**, *Gyeonsangbukdo, Andongsi, Susan-dong 280,* ☎(054)-858-4541, 🕐*open Mon–Sat 9am–5pm).* It may only be of real interest

GETTING THERE

Andong Train Station (℘(054)-857-8951) and **Andong Intercity Bus Terminal** (℘(054)-857-8296) are close by on Hwarang-no on the south side of the city center. **Trains** for Daegu (2hr), Seoul (4hr30min) and Gyeongju (2hr) are much less frequent than the **buses**: Daegu (1hr30min, ₩15,000), Daejeon (3hr, ₩13,600), Gyeongju (1hr50min, ₩12,000) and Seoul (3hr, ₩17,500).

USEFUL INFORMATION

The **post office** and the **banks** are all concentrated on Jungang-no, the main road. KB and Shinhan banks both have *Global ATMs*.

to fans of the drink who have learned to distinguish the subtle differences between the various regional brews. The museum is on the south side of the city (*in the direction of Rte 5, or take bus no. 34/36, ₩1,000*), and there is a restaurant.

Sinse-dong 신세동 and Andong Folk Village 안동민속촌

▷ *2mi/3km NE of Andong, follow signs for Andong Folk Village. By taxi, approx. ₩4,000–5,000, or bus no. 3 (14 departures daily, ₩1,000) from Hwarang-no; turn left out of the station.*

⌚*See Gyeongsang-do map.*
A discreet sign at the exit to Andong reads "7 storeys brick pagoda" and, sure enough, tucked away behind the railway bridge you will find **Sinse-dong**, the tallest ancient **brick pagoda** in the country and the only remaining relic from the temple Beopeungsa. Built during the period of the Unified Silla (668–918) and 55ft/16.8m high, its base is decorated with bas-reliefs of the 12 terrestrial divinities and eight guardians of Buddhism.

▷ *From here, the road continues to Andong Lake (Andongho).*

A footbridge from the car park leads to the folk village. (If you drive to the village, continue past the bridge.) In a clearing on a hillside, **Andong Folk Village** contains a number of houses that were threatened with submersion when the nearby reservoir was created in 1976. They were moved here to higher ground along with other buildings, including peasant shacks and the houses of aristocrats.
The overall look is authentic but lacks something and the effect is rather like a **film set**, which indeed it is—a number

Sinse-dong, Andong

©KTO

Traditional houses, Hahoe Village ©KTO

of KBS (Korean Broadcasting System) dramas have been shot here and their soundtracks boom out from a series of loudspeakers.

The small **museum** on the site (*(054)-821-0649, *open 9am–5pm, ₩1,000) has a collection of local folk objects: masks, dioramas of ceremonies, etc.

EXCURSIONS
AROUND HAHOE VILLAGE

See Gyeongsang-do map.
Hahoe is 15mi/24km W of Andong.
By car: from Andong, take Rte 34 toward Yecheon and turn left onto Rte 916 toward Hahoemaeul.
By bus: no. 46 (8 departures daily, 50min, ₩1,100) from Hwarang-no; exit the station to the left and the stop is on the other side of the road.

▷ *At the Rte 916 junction, look for the sign on the right for Andong Hanji Exhibition Hall. The exhibition and the ... are housed in the building ... pink walls.*

...★ 안동 한지
...-do map. *(054)-858-7007. www.and...onghanji.co.kr.
Open Mon–Sat 9a...m–6pm.
... store, but really a Part museum, part ... ch the traditional factory, you can wat... of han...ji, Korean paper manufacture of han...ji, Korean paper (... see box p276) and... see examples of how it is used.

Britain's Queen Elizabeth II visited the factory in 1999, still evidently a source of local pride.

A walk through the various rooms will mark a change in temperature and even odor, according to the stage of manufacture. The friendly staff work in silence, but you can join in various activities for a small fee, and decorate paper boxes, notebooks, etc.

Hahoe Village★★★
하회마을

See Gyeongsang-do map.
Located 3mi/5km S of Andong Hanji.
(054)-854-3669/852-3588.
*www.hahoe.or.kr *Open 9am–6pm in summer (dusk in winter). ₩2,000 (parking ₩2,000). A map is available at the entrance, and there are English information panels in front of the main houses.*

After passing through an agricultural area and the usual complex of restaurants and shops selling souvenirs, nip into the interesting **mask museum★ (Hahoedong Mask Museum,** *(054)-853-2288, www.maskmuseum.com, *Open 9:30am–6pm, ₩2,000), which was partially renovated recently.

Local masks, celebrated in the **International Mask Dance Festival (** *see p279)* and masks from all over the world—smiling, thoughtful, grimacing, frightening—are all displayed to great and sometimes unnerving effect.

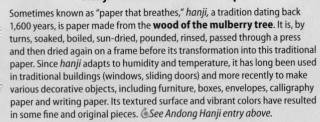

Hanji - Traditional Korean Paper

Sometimes known as "paper that breathes," *hanji,* a tradition dating back 1,600 years, is paper made from the **wood of the mulberry tree**. It is, by turns, soaked, boiled, sun-dried, pounded, rinsed, passed through a press and then dried again on a frame before its transformation into this traditional paper. Since *hanji* adapts to humidity and temperature, it has long been used in traditional buildings (windows, sliding doors) and more recently to make various decorative objects, including furniture, boxes, envelopes, calligraphy paper and writing paper. Its textured surface and vibrant colors have resulted in some fine and original pieces. *See Andong Hanji entry above.*

As you walk back to the village along the river, any sneaking suspicion that it is really just an amusement park is allayed by the knowledge that in 2010 the area was designated a UNESCO World Heritage Site. The Nakdong River forms a loop here, as if to protect Hahoe and its paddy fields, a feature evoked in the village's name, which means "encircled (*hoe*) by water (*ha*)." The village has been **preserved and restored**, but unlike folk villages populated by actors in costumes, Hahoe is a real village going about its daily business, although its architectural uniformity might lead you to question its authenticity. You might be tempted to imagine its 250 or so quiet and discreet inhabitants—who are used to being stared at—letting their hair down as soon as all the cars have departed at 6pm.

Nevertheless, the village is beautiful, with houses of cob, brick and stone surrounded by low walls, flower beds and well-tended kitchen gardens through which cats slink. There are one or two stores, a pocket-size clinic and a church. The air is rich with the scent of lilacs, and the beautiful natural soundtrack is provided by songbirds. Strolling along the Nakdong River and exploring the few streets will take up to half a day; you can even choose to stay here in a *minbak* (B&B) (*see Addresses).*

The village was probably founded at the end of the Goryeo period (14C) by the Ryu family on a site which had been selected for its auspicious position. The modest thatched peasant houses and the residences of the noble families (*yangban*) with their roofs of broad

tiles are typical of the **Joseon period**. In among these remarkable buildings don't miss Yangjin Manor, the oldest house in the village and the ancestral seat of the Pungsan branch of the Ryu clan. The Bukchon residence (1862) is organized into different quarters for men, women and servants. Yeongmogak Exhibition Hall houses the personal effects of Ryu Seong-yong, a prime minister of the Joseon dynasty.

You can see the village from above from **Buyongdae Cliff**. Take the path from the far side of the river when the small ferryboat is operating, or follow the road along the river for 2.5mi/4km as far as Byeongsan Seowon (*see below*).

To head west from Hahoe, take **Route 916** (*toward Sangju), a quiet road that passes through busy little market towns as it snakes between fields and burial mounds topped with pine trees.*

Byeongsan Seowon★★★
병산 서원

See Gyeongsang-do map. 2.5mi/4km E of Hahoe. Well-signed unpaved road. By bus: no. 46 to Byeongsan Seowon (2 departures daily, timetable at the tourist office). On foot: a 2.5mi/4km walk along the river between Hahoe and Byeongsan Seowon. 𝄞 (054)-853-2172. www.byeongsan.net Open 9am–5pm (summer 6pm). No charge. Detailed information in English. Make a detour to visit this small **Confucian academy**, a place of calm and serenity on the sandy banks of

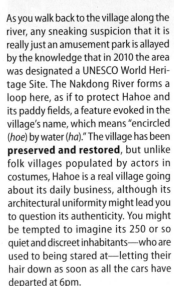

Byeongsan Seowon ©KTO

the Nakdong River. Located opposite a rock and surrounded by flowers, it was founded in 1572 by Ryu Seong-yong (1542–1607), the chief minister of King Sonjo. When he died, his successors preserved his funeral tablet here before teaching began in 1614. The complex construction and unusual dimensions (100ft/30m long) of the lecture hall (*Mandaeru*) alone make the trip worthwhile—200 people can meditate in here at one time. Supported on wooden pillars, the building seems to float among the gentle tree-lined landscape. The rest of the academy complex includes reading carrels, dormitories and *Jondeoksa*, the ceremonial hall, with its striking bright colors.

NORTH AND EAST OF ANDONG
Dosan Seowon★★★
도산 서원

♿ *See Gyeongsang-do map.*
21mi/34km N of Andong on Rte 35 toward Taebaek. Bus no. 67 from Hwarang-no, leaving the station on the left. (4 departures daily, 40min, ₩1,100). ℘*(054)-856-1073. www.dosanseowon. com.* ⏱*Open 9am–5pm (summer 6pm). ₩1,500* 🅿 *₩2,000. Brochure in English.*
This renowned Confucian academy is set in a superb wooded landscape, seen to its best advantage when the waters of the lake are high enough to

lap at the base of the pine trees. To reach the academy, follow a well-kept path between neatly trimmed hedges leading to an esplanade that looks out over the far northern end of Andongho, an enormous man-made lake. Look out for Sisadan (established in 1796; rebuilt in 1824), a monument and shelter on a stone mound; when the water is high enough the mound becomes an island. Close by is the academy itself. It was established in 1574 in honor of **Yi Hwang** (1501–70), known as **Toegye**, the scion of a noble family who, after much study and refinement of his own theories, introduced neo-Confucianism

Dosan Seowon Confucian Academy ©KTO

to Korea. Having held a number of high offices in the government at Seoul, from minister of royal works to adviser to the prime minister, he is considered one of the most famous and influential thinkers in Korean history and was also a poet. You can see his portrait on the ₩1,000 bill. Over the centuries, "his" school has become a famous place of Confucian learning and the venue for important functions and ceremonies.

Once through the main gate of the complex, which was renovated in the 1970s, there is a network of paths leading to buildings entered through low doors between finely carved portals. Some bear the marks of the centuries, while others, freshly painted, seem almost new.

Beautiful in its simplicity, **Dosanseodang**, the school where Toegye taught before the complex was founded, is immediately to the right after the entrance. The students slept in the neighboring dormitories, which are arranged in an H-shape. In the upper reaches of the complex, a courtyard is surrounded by three lecture halls, including **Jeongyodang**, the main hall, indicated by a tablet that was a gift from King Sonjo (1552–1608). Note the fine floral decoration. The printing house (*Jangpangak*), in a small courtyard on the right, once housed 2,790 woodcuts, which are now stored in Seoul. Finally, **Sangdeoksa** contains Yi Hwang's memorial tablets, and there is also an exhibition hall recounting his life story.

Route 35★ 35번도로

See Gyeongsang-do map.

If you wish to continue north from Dosan Seowon, take **Route 35★** (*toward Taebaek*), a pleasant stretch of road allowing periodic glimpses of the twists and turns of the Nakdong River. The wooded hills (which burst into flaming colors in the fall) end in cliffs that plunge down into the river in **Cheongnyangsan Provincial Park** (open 8:30am–6pm).

From the park's well signposted entrance, a number of forest paths radiate out in different directions toward high peaks, grottos and mountain retreats. Passing through cultivated valleys (with beautiful panoramic views), the road emerges into a lively agricultural area where enormous "caterpillars" of black sheeting snake across the fields, protecting market garden produce. Pickup trucks and tractors set the pace of the traffic in the villages along the way, amid blossoming trees and indefatigable elderly women almost bent in two by their labors. The journey ends at the mining valley just outside Taebaek (see p257).

Take Rte 34 toward Yeongdeok and turn right after 15.5mi/25km at a brown sign (that pops up unexpectedly, immediately after a bridge on the lake) indicating a distance of 7mi/12km to your destination.

Behind the Mask

Originating during the Goryeo period, **mask dances** grew in popularity when Confucianism began to supplant Buddhism. They allowed performers to parody the injustices of everyday life, making fun of the powerful and calling for fruitful harvests. Each region developed its own style of dance, and performances marked the turning points in the year, including the lunar New Year and the arrival of spring. Shamanist ceremonies of this kind were often accompanied by rhythmic percussion music (*nong-ak*) and featured **stock characters,** such as the seductress, the servant, the aristocrat, the lecherous monk and the butcher. The wide variety of expressions carved into the wooden masks left no doubt as to the stories that were being told through the dances. See International Masked Dance Festival (p279) and Mask Museum (p275).

Jirye Artists' Colony
지례예술촌

🐾 *See Gyeongsang-do map.*
22.5mi/37km E of Andong. Bakgok-ri,
Imdong-myeon. 📞*(054)-822-2590.*
www.jirye.com.

The road slowly doubles back on itself
and seems to go on forever, but after
passing through superb forests and a
small farming village, it drops down to
this remote and enchanting cultural village. The former residences of the *yangban* (aristocrats) from the 18C and 19C,
with their black tile roofs, have been
welcoming artists and writers since
1988. Artists who work here do so in a
beautiful natural environment among
birds and flowers, with the heady scent
of resin in the air and the lake spread
out below.

The village is not really geared up for
visitors, but you can try one of the
monthly cultural workshops (cooking,
calligraphy) or perhaps spend a couple
of nights in this peaceful haven, staying in one of the traditional rooms with
*ondol (14rm, from ₩50,000/night; transfer
from Andong station on request).*

ADDRESSES

🛏 STAY

There are a hotel and a number of
motels around the rail station; they offer
mostly modest accommodations.

🍴 **Andong Hotel** 안동 호텔 –
103-3 Samsan-dong. 📞*(054)-854-0622.*
37rm. ₩40,000–50,000. A decent motel
in the restaurant quarter.

🍴 **Andong Park Tourist Hotel**
안동파크호텔 – *324 Unheung-dong.*
📞*(054)- 853-1501/859-1500. 44rm.*
₩50,000/60,000. A practical and easy-
to-reach solution for accommodation.
Floral decor and rather average rooms,
but with refrigerator and internet.

AROUND ANDONG

Why not stay in a **traditional Korean
house**? The easiest way is to arrange
a reservation at the tourist office in
Andong. As in Hahoe, the *minbak* offer
a variety of levels of comfort, from

the simplicity of **Bunnam** (📞*(054)-
852-8550,* ₩*50,000/90,000)* to the
luxurious surroundings of **Rak Ko Jae
Andong** (📞*(054)-857-3410, www.rkj.
co.kr,* ₩*150,000)* and **Hwa Kyung Dang**
(📞*19-228-1786, from* ₩*200,000).*
Or try one of the peaceful rooms
provided by the artists' colony at
Jirye (🐾*see above).*

🍽 EAT

There is no shortage of restaurants
in the city center, with a whole street
devoted to *galbi* and *pojangmacha*
just waiting for you.

🥐 **Mammoth Bakery** – *164 Nambu-
dong, Andong-si,* 📞*(054)-857-6000.*
Open 8am–11pm. This upmarket bakery
in the pedestrian-only zone (beside
Dunkin Donuts) has been serving
pastries adapted to local tastes and
excellent sandwiches since 1974.

🍜 **Yangban Bapsang** – *513-2
Sanga-dong.* 📞*(054)-855-9900.*
Open 10:30am–9pm. ₩*7,000–15,000.*
This well-known restaurant near the *Folk
Village* (a thatched building opposite
the footbridge) specializes in mackerel,
served baked, grilled or in a variety of
sauces; the beautifully golden mackerel
(₩*8,000)* is served with eight side dishes.

🎭 EVENTS AND FESTIVALS

Byeolsingut Talnori – An impressive
mask dance, performed at Hahoe
Village *(near the car park, May–Oct,
Sat–Sun, 3pm).*

International Mask Dance Festival –
Andong and Hahoe each host a week
(end Sept/beginning Oct) of folk mask
dances from Korea and farther afield;
www.maskdance.com.

Seonyu Julbulnori – A festival of
fireworks with illuminated boats held in
Hahoe during the same period.

Gyeongju★★★
경주

It would be impossible to come to South Korea and not visit the open-air museum that is the city of Gyeongju. Capital of the kingdom of Silla for 992 years (from 57 BC until AD 935) and then the jewel in the crown of Korea's cultural tourist industry, this serene city boasts a number of UNESCO World Heritage Sites, often tucked away amid superb scenery in areas that are now national parks. Gyeongju's star reached its zenith after the southern part of the Korean Peninsula was unified in 668. The arts continued to develop here despite civil war and invasion, as can be seen from the superb exhibits in the Gyeongju National Museum, which include exquisite items of great finesse and subtlety, from jewels and golden crowns to ornamental tiles and everyday objects. The city also has a number of imposing Buddhist temples and Buddhas carved in rock. Fifty-six kings ruled from here in succession, each laid to rest beneath a grass-covered tumulus. The unusual landscape that these burial mounds have created is quite unique and stands in testament to six centuries of Korean history.

▶ **Population:** 267,466
⚇ **Michelin Map:** Regional map pp264–265.
🗊 **Info:** City Tourist Offices http://guide.gyeongju.go.kr. Open 9am–6pm. English-speaking staff on hand. There are offices at the rail station, ✆(054)-772-3843/(054)-1544-7788; the bus terminal, ✆(054)-772-9289; Bomun Lake, ✆(054)-745-0750; and small offices or touch screens at the main sites.
▷ **Location:** Gyeongju is located 21.5mi/35km from Korea's east coast, 40mi/65km east of Daegu and 43mi/70km north of Busan; both cities are reached by expressway.
🚹 **Kids:** Amusement park at Bomun Lake, cycling.
🕓 **Timing:** Allow at least three days to see all the main sights.
☺ **Don't Miss:** Daereung-won Tumuli Park (by day or night), the treasures of Gyeongju National Museum, the superb Bulguksa, the fascinating Yangdong Folk Village, trying Gyeongju cake (Gyeongju bbang).

VISIT

The **center** of Gyeongju is typical of an average city—on the South Korean scale, that is (it has a population of more than 250,000!). **Hwarang-ro**, the avenue that heads west from the rail station, is lined with banks and offices. Two markets at its extremities add a dash of color and flavor as the beguiling aromas of fresh herbs and simmering thick soups waft through the air. The bowls and baskets of fruit expertly set out by smiling ajumma generally overflow onto the sidewalks.

The streets and alleys of **Nodong-dong**, south of Hwarang-ro, boast a fine collection of restaurants, fashion boutiques, cafés and movie theaters and are flooded with young people as soon as the schools close for the day. A couple of café terraces round off the provincial atmosphere. The buildings come to an abrupt halt at the tombs of Nodong-ri and Noseo-ri along Daejong-no, where you can catch the enticing scent of Gyeongju bbang, a local pastry stuffed with bean paste. The city's main cultural sites are grouped together south of Daejong-no.

GETTING THERE

BY PLANE – There are 12 daily bus connections from Gyeongju Intercity Bus Terminal to **Busan-Gimhae International Airport** *(1hr15min, ₩9,000)*. http://www.airport.co.kr/doc/gimhae_eng/index.jsp.

BY TRAIN – The high-speed **KTX** now serves Gyeongju, arriving at the brand-new **Singyeongju Station** to the west of the city (15min by bus to downtown, bus no. 50/700). From the pretty, **central Gyeongju Station** (*℘(054)-743-4114*) you can catch the Saemaul to Seoul *(4hr30min)*, trains for Dongdaegu *(1hr10min, numerous connections)* and Ulsan *(35–50min)*.

BY BUS – Helpfully, the two terminals are side by side: **Express Bus Terminal** (*℘(054)-741-4000*) and **Intercity Bus Terminal** (*℘(054)-743-5599*) provide connections to Busan *(1hr, ₩4,000)*, Andong *(3hr, ₩17,000)*, Daegu *(1hr, ₩4,000)*, Seoul *(4hr30min, ₩27,600)*, Daejeon *(3hr, ₩18,000)*, Ulsan *(1hr, ₩3,800)*, Pohang *(1hr, ₩3,000)*, Jinju *(2hr30min, ₩15,000)* as well as Gwangju, Donghae and Cheongju, etc.

BY CAR – Turn left out of Gyeongju Station, and you will find branches of **Avis** and **Kumho Rent a Car**. The hotels at Bomun Lake Resort provide a similar service.

GETTING AROUND

There are **taxis** everywhere, thoughtfully sounding their horns to remind you that there is an alternative to walking, and easy-to-use buses serving all the major sites. **Bus no. 10** *(clockwise)* and **11** *(counterclockwise)* make a circuit of the city every 20min for ₩1500, taking in the rail and bus terminals, the Gyeongju National Museum, Namsan (Tongiljeon), Bulguksa, Bomun Lake Resort and back to the rail and bus terminal. You can also hire **bicycles** *(₩12,000/day)* and **scooters** *(₩40,000/6hr)* near the various stations and at Bomun Lake Resort.

USEFUL INFORMATION

Bank – There are several banks and the main post office on Hwarang-ro, the avenue leading to Gyeongju Station. *℘(054)-740-0114.* ◑ *Open Mon–Fri 9am–5pm.*

SIGHTSEEING

If you have only a day, you might join one of the bus tours organized by **Hanatours/Gyeongju Tours** *(Daejong-ro 685 Beon-gil, ℘(054)-743-6001/2, ₩8,000/12,000, plus entrance fees)*, departing from the tourist office at the Intercity Bus Terminal. The commentary is in Korean, but you will at least have the advantage of being whisked rapidly from location to location.

Ask at the tourist offices for details of the **many themed events**: night walks through the sites, a stay on a farm or rice plantation, pottery-making, or a class in *Seonmoodo* (a combination of meditation and martial art) at Golgul Temple *(http://golgulsa.com/)*… the choice is yours!

Nodong-ri 노동리 and Noseo-ri 노서리 Tombs★

◔*See Gyeongju map II.*

The areas containing the tombs are not fenced off, so people wander through them on their way to and from the office or school, or even picnic among them on the well-kept grass. Fairly uniform in shape and size for the most part, the burial mounds date from between the 4C and 6C. To the east, by Noseo-ri, is **Bonghwangdae** ("Hill of the Phoenix"), the tallest of the tombs, with a couple of trees growing on top of it.

At a height of 73ft/22m and a circumference of 820ft/250m, it is the second-largest known tomb from the Silla period. The neighboring tombs of Singnichong and Geumnyeongchong were undoubtedly those of princes—

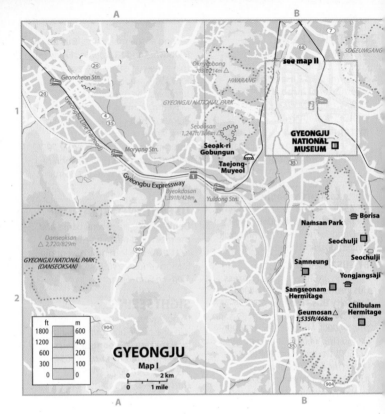

GYEONGJU

Map I

ft / m
1800 / 600
1200 / 400
600 / 200
300 / 100
0 / 0

0 — 2 km
0 — 1 mile

numerous jewels, drinking vessels and grave goods (mainly in gold and silver) were discovered in them and their interior structures are identical to that of Bonghwangdae, suggesting a strong link between the occupants of these three tumuli. To the west, by Nodong-ri, tombs with wooden burial chambers are ranged alongside others with stone chambers accessed through a tunnel, indicating a gradual change in construction methods.

View of the heart of Gyeongju with its royal tombs

©KNTO

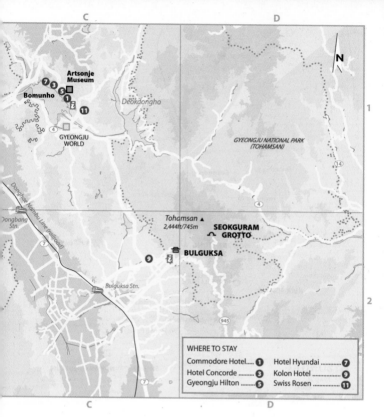

WHERE TO STAY

Commodore Hotel..... ❶	Hotel Hyundai .... ❼
Hotel Concorde .... ❸	Kolon Hotel .... ❾
Gyeongju Hilton .... ❺	Swiss Rosen .... ⓫

Daereung-won Tumuli Park★★★ 대릉원

♿See Gyeongju map II.
℘(054)-779-6061. http://eguide.
gyeongju.go.kr. ◷Open 9am–10pm.
₩1,500. Two entrances: on Daejong-no
to the north (no parking) and at the
end of Gyerim-no to the south, near the
entrance to Wolseong Park opposite
(large car park, ₩2,000). A guided tour
in English is available, departing from
the ticket office near the entrance to
Cheonmachong's tomb.

Twenty-three of Gyeongju's 200 tombs
are to be found at Daereung-won and
date back to the Silla dynasty, pre-
unification. They contain the graves of
kings and court officials. The aerial photos of these remarkable **tumuli**, which
feature on the postcards sold around the
site, provide a good overall view of this
complex, which is quite **unique in the
world**. Walk between the mounds and
amid the trees and shrubs that grow in

the hollows between the tombs, which
add to the appeal of the site, especially
in spring and fall. If you have the chance,
don't miss out on a nighttime stroll here,
which is a completely different experience.

During the excavation of the tombs,
which began in the 1970s and entailed
the demolition of a number of buildings, many thousands of objects were
unearthed by the Korean and Japanese
archaeological teams, and some of the
finds are on display in the city's National
Museum (♿see below).

Entering the site from the north, the first
tomb of interest is **Hwangnamdae-
chong** to the left—more than 50,000
objects were discovered here, some
of which provide compelling evidence
of significant interaction between the
Korean Peninsula and Central Asia. It is
a double tomb of either a father and son
or a husband and wife. A little farther
on is **Michu-wangneung** (the tomb

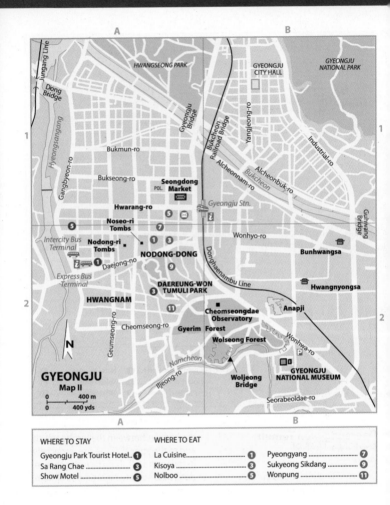

GYEONGJU
Map II

WHERE TO STAY		WHERE TO EAT			
Gyeongju Park Tourist Hotel..	❶	La Cuisine	❶	Pyeongyang	❼
Sa Rang Chae	❸	Kisoya	❸	Sukyeong Sikdang	❾
Show Motel	❺	Nolboo	❺	Wonpung	⓫

of King Michu), the 13th king of Silla, who reigned from 262 until 284 and who is known to have fought repeated campaigns against the rival dynasty of Baekje.

From the interior of the tomb of **Cheonmachong** ("Heavenly Horse Tomb"), the grave of an unknown 5C or 6C king, it is clear that the tumuli are skillfully constructed with chambers of interlocked stones covered by earth and then planted with grass. The body of the deceased and his or her most precious possessions were laid to rest in the center of the chamber, the whole mound being surrounded by a low log fence (◔see illustration p65). Original pieces from the tomb on show at the

National Museum include the famous golden crown of Cheonmachong. The tomb's name is taken from a painting of a flying white horse that was found inside, painted on a birch bark saddle flap used to protect a saddle blanket from mud splashes.

◔ The peaceful district of **Hwangnam** to the immediate west of Daereung-won is surrounded by pleasant streets and alleys lined with picturesque low-rise houses. Cars are rare here, allowing pedestrians to wander about freely among the interior courtyards, small workshops, restaurants, grocery stores and small market.

Gyerim Forest★ 계림숲

See Gyeongju map II.
Located immediately to the south of Daereung-won, opposite the row of *ssambap* restaurants, the Banwolseong and Gyerim Forest areas boast a number of historic sites.

The first building you will see is **Cheomseongdae Observatory★** (*(054)-772-5134, http://eguide.gyeongju.go.kr ⏰ open 9am–9pm (summer 10pm), ₩500*), built during the reign of Queen Seondeok in the 7C and acknowledged as one of the oldest in Asia. Barely 30ft/9.17m high, its dimensions are less impressive than its silhouette, which is a rather particular bottle or kiln shape, a great technical achievement for the period. The 362 stones used in its construction correspond to the number of days in the lunar calendar and the squares at the base and the platform at the top indicate the cardinal points of the compass. The 27 interposed layers of stones gradually taper toward the top, lending the structure a sinuous curve. Access was via an opening facing south, halfway up the tower (using a ladder). Astronomers would observe the sky and forecast the weather and seasons.

At the edge of the ancient **Gyerim Forest** of willow and pines ("rooster forest," *see p288*) are a number of tumuli, tastefully illuminated at night, among which is the tomb of King Naemul, the 17th king of Silla. According to legend, some of the centuries-old trees in what is now a rather modestly-sized wooded area would have witnessed the birth of Kim Alji, the founder of the Kim clan (*see p288*).

Wolseong Forest, with its beautiful cherry trees, is on a hill where ramparts protecting the royal palace once stood. Nothing remains of the palace-fortress of Banwolseong apart from an 18C storehouse (*Seokbinggo*, an icehouse) and some embankments which once supported walls.

Close by, a reconstruction of **Woljeong-gyo, the great covered bridge**, is being built and is due to be completed by the end of 2012. Erected in 760, the original was the first and largest stone bridge in the entire Korean Peninsula. Its size is a good indication of the amount of human and goods traffic that there would have been during the era.

Anapji 안압지

See Gyeongju map II.
(054)-772-4041. ⏰ Open 8am–7pm (winter until dusk). ₩1,000.
Despite the war between the dynasties of Silla, Goguryeo and Baekje which dominated the era, in 674 **King Munmu** ordered the construction of a pleasure garden first known as Wolji ("park of the moon") and then renamed Anapji ("the park of geese and ducks"). The 26 build-

Cheomseongdae Observatory

©KTO

ings that burned to the ground here in 935 and the site, which included various ponds and a reserve for rare birds and flowers, werer not rediscovered until 1974 when the pond was drained. Most of the objects recovered from the bottom of the lake are displayed in a separate room in the Gyeongju National Museum along with a diorama of the site.

Three pavilions have been reconstructed and the park attracts crowds of locals who are drawn here by its romantic associations. Unfortunately, the rather saccharine-sweet music that blasts from the loudspeakers is hardly conducive to contemplation of the beautiful lotus flowers (Jun–Jul) or the birds. You could always try a game of *juryeonggju*, discovered during excavations, involving a 14-sided wooden die inscribed with forfeits; you can buy a replica *(inscribed in Korean only)* at one of the souvenir stalls. A little to the north you will find the site of the 6C **Hwangnyongsa**, the largest temple ever constructed in Korea.

Before being razed to the ground by the Mongols in the 13C, it had been dominated by an immense 230ft/70m, nine-tier pagoda. Although only the foundations of the complex now remain, you can see a model of the site inside the National Museum.

Gyeongju National Museum★★★ 국립경주박물관

See Gyeongju map II.
Bus no. 11/600/601/603/604/605/607/608/609 from the city center, 118 Iljeongno. ℘ (054)-740-7518. http://gyeongju.museum.go.kr/eng/. Open daily 9am–6pm (Mar–Dec, Sat and public holidays 7pm). No charge. English audio guide ₩3,000.

The museum, which has occupied this site since 1975, houses a collection of objects found at various locations around the ancient royal capital. While the presentation of the finds is a little underwhelming, the crowds of school-children and tourists can be quite the opposite, but the museum has **some outstanding exhibits**.

Thanks to information panels in English, you will learn much about the wealth and refinement of the kingdom of Silla. The museum contains three main halls, a section for children and a temporary exhibition space.

A series of monuments, statues and assorted stone lanterns discovered on sites nearby, such as the pagoda from the Goseon Temple complex and the Sacred Bell of the Great King Seongdeok (see p288), can be found on the museum grounds and lining the path leading up to the museum building.

Anapji pond

Gyeongju National Museum ©KTO

Archaeology Hall

The chronologically arranged exhibits begin with a display of pieces predating the Silla period, when stone, bronze and then iron were used to make plowshares, arrowheads and ornamental buttons. Note the beautiful carved stone dagger and zoomorphic objects such as lion buckles and a jug shaped like a duck. The two rooms dedicated to the Silla period include pottery and jewelry in gold, silver and bronze, much of which was found during the excavation of great tombs such as Hwangnamdae-chong and Cheonmachong, which have become stars in their own right in the Tumuli Park (see p283).

The centerpiece of the museum—and now a symbol of the Silla kingdom—is the splendid and exquisitely executed **gold crown**★ (*Cheonmachong Geumgwan*, 6C) discovered in the Cheonmachong tomb (Daereung-won Tumuli Park). Made of gold and decorated with jade dragons and pearls, its unique shape is reminiscent of a trident or even a stag's antlers. The "prongs" once formed a Chinese character.

See also the **gold sword** (*Geumjegamjangbogeom*) found in the tomb of King Michu, whose Western-influenced ornamentation suggests exchanges with Europe via Central Asia.

You will also find many weapons, equestrian equipment, funerary urns and very expressive clay figures representing the signs of the zodiac—half-man

Silla gold crown, Gyeongju National Museum ©KTO

and half-animal—which guarded royal tombs. The last room houses objects from the collection of Dr. "Gugeun" Lee Yang-seon, covering a period from prehistory to the Goryeo dynasty. The best-known piece is an earthenware sculpture from the kingdom of Gaya (*Gimainmulhyeongtogi*) depicting an armored horse bearing an armed rider, which has provided valuable information about the equipment used by warriors of the period.

Anapji Hall

This extended hall houses various objects collected from the bottom of Anapji (see p285) when it was drained in the 1970s. These principally include

The Kingdom of Silla

Its History

Gyeongju, the capital of Silla from 57 BC, can look back on 10 centuries of Korean history. Its story begins with the rise of three clans that gradually took control of the surrounding fertile valley: the Kim, Sok and Park clans. At the end of the 4C, the clan chiefs adopted the title of king, and the custom of their sons inheriting upon the sovereign's death. When they died, they were buried and enshrined in tumuli.

The southern part of the Korean Peninsula was unified in 668 after the defeat of the kingdoms of Baekje and Goryeo by King Munmu, and Gyeongju became a powerful capital with a population of 200,000, ruled over by an elite group of young men known as Hwarang. The arts flourished during the reigns of kings such as Gyeongdeok, magnificent temples were built and Buddhism, the state religion, left its mark on education and military organization. As the decades passed, however, internal strife and invasions weakened Silla's influence.

... and Some Legends

The **Divine Bell of King Seongdeok**, which can be seen in the courtyard of Gyeongju National Museum, was commissioned by his son Gyeongdeok in his honor. Famed as one of the heaviest (18.9 tons) and oldest (completed in 771) bells in the world, it was originally installed at Bongdeok Temple in Gyeongju.

Exceptionally clear, its sound would carry over 2mi/3km. Its nickname, "Emille," derives from a chilling story. According to the legend, the first attempt at casting the bell produced no sound at all and the body of a young girl had to be added to the metal before it would deign to ring. Just before her death, the little child is said to have cried "em-ee-leh" ("mommy" in the Silla dialect), and this desperate cry is still heard every time the bell is struck.

A Vital Letter

Soji, the 21st king of Silla, was journeying through his kingdom when a mouse advised him to follow a crow. The bird led him to the edge of a pond, from the middle of which an old man covered in weeds and grasses rose up out of the water and handed the king a letter on which were written the words: "If you open the letter, two people will die, if you fail to open the letter, one person will die."

A valet suggested that the single person to die might be the king, so he opened the letter and read an order to shoot at his wife's harp case. The king obeyed, and inside the case they found the body of a monk who had been plotting against the king... with the complicity of the queen, who was executed immediately. The pond was named **Seochulji**; *seo* means "letter," like the one that saved the king.

...and a Rooster on a Golden Chest

One night in the year 65, King Talhae heard a rooster crowing. Intrigued, the sovereign sent a valet into the forest from which the rather early dawn cry was emanating. The servant found the animal perched on a small golden casket hanging from a branch. Opening the casket, he discovered a baby boy. The king, delighted at the incongruity of the situation, took the child under his wing, naming him Kim Alji ("Kim" being the written Chinese character for gold) and renaming the forest **Gyerim** ("the forest of the rooster"). The forest still lies south of the Tumuli Park, while the child went on to found the Kim clan.

everyday objects (a small boat, lacquered bowls, door handles and masks, mostly dating from the 7C), which certainly give a better idea of life at court than do the royal jewels. Look out for pottery decorated with recurring, simple motifs—circles, birds, clouds—and superb tiles and other decorative architectural features, some depicting lotus flowers or fabulous animals.

Arts Hall

The ground floor is dedicated to various **Buddhist arts** (triads, Medicine Buddha, etc.) and outlines the evolution of depictions of the Buddha during the Silla period. Looking at the serene face of the Buddha, it is fascinating to note the tiny, virtually imperceptible details that barely alter his expression yet make each sculpture unique.

The influence of religion on architecture is demonstrated by a number of roof ornaments, including tiles decorated with symbols such as lotus flowers or *apsara* (nymphs) and other features collected from nearby temples. These ornamental tiles seem to date predominantly from the Silla period. **Dioramas** of the city provide an idea of its historical size and layout. Hwangnyong Temple and its nine-tier pagoda have also been re-created. Finally, there is a room dedicated to **inscriptions** such as those on gravestones and commemorative monuments.

Bunhwangsa (Bunhwang Temple) 분황사

See Gyeongju map II.
1mi/1.5km NE of Anapji and the Gyeongju National Museum. ℘(054)-742-9922. http://eguide.gyeongju.go.kr
Open dawn–dusk. ₩1,300.

Little remains of what was once one of the seven large tombs of the kingdom of Silla. Although there is nothing spectacular to see, there are always large crowds. The temple was probably built under Queen Seondeok in 634. The small pagoda with three remaining tiers (of an original nine) in the middle of the courtyard is probably the biggest attraction. It was the first of its kind to

be built by the Silla dynasty, and two Buddhist guardians and four beautiful lions flank its base.

EXCURSIONS
Bomunho (Bomun Lake) 보문호

See Gyeongju map I.
3mi/5km E of the city center. Bus no. 10 from the bus and rail stations.

A typically **Korean tourist resort** has been built around this modest man-made lake, including giant hotels, amusement parks, restaurants and plenty of other facilities. It looks its best when the cherry trees are in blossom, and you will no doubt stay here if you are on a group tour. The resort area may be far removed in cultural terms from the treasures of Gyeongju, but the hotels are of a high standard.

Many families come here, and delegates from the numerous conference centers and honeymooning couples rub shoulders with students on the Korean equivalent of spring break. Stroll along the waterside, work on your swing on the golf course, pedal tandems or giant floating swans on the lake—where you can also scoot about on jet-skis—all with food available round the clock.

The structures in the various nearby amusement parks create a strange landscape, with Gyeongju World Resort (gigantic roller coasters), California Beach water park and the Shilla Millennium Park, an amusement park dedicated to the Silla dynasty. South of the lake, a 270ft/82m pagoda-style tower looks out over the World Culture Expo complex.

For art lovers, the permanent and temporary exhibitions at the **Artsonje Museum** (℘(054)-745-7075, www.art-sonje.org, open Tue–Sun 10am–6pm, ₩3,000), next door to, and almost adjoining, the Hilton, might be a better option.

AROUND BULGUKSA
Bulguksa★★★ (Bulguk Temple) 불국사

See Gyeongju map I.
9mi/15km SE of Gyeongju. By car:
Rte 7 toward Ulsan, then turn left at

Double-sectioned staircase, Bulguksa
©KTO

Bulguksa junction. By bus: no. 11 from the bus terminal or the Gyeongju National Museum (20–30min, ₩1,500). ✆ (054)-746-9913. ⏱ Open summer 6:30am–6pm, winter 7am–5pm. ₩4,000.
The **temple** was founded on the slopes of the sacred mountain of Toham (Tohamsan, 2,444ft/745m) in 535 when King Beopheung adopted Buddhism as the state religion. Its current appearance dates back to its reconstruction between 751 and 774. Spread out over a series of terraces, the temple originally comprised some 24 buildings, which were destroyed in the 16C by the invading Japanese in a battle against resistance fighters. The partial reconstruction attempted in the 1970s has been a resounding success, and the temple attracts more visitors than almost any other in the country.

There are endless school groups, and it gets very crowded on the anniversary of the Buddha's birth. You will also find what amounts virtually to a small town of restaurants, hotels and stores clustered around the site, but these are soon forgotten as you enter the temple grounds, especially when the cherry trees are in bloom. Bulguksa is a masterpiece of **Korean Buddhist architecture** and an indication both of the skill of the local artisans and the religious devotion of the Silla period. Built according to the Lotus sutra, it was intended to recreate

the Buddhist ideal on earth as an eternal palace for the Buddha, hence its name **Temple of the Buddha Land**.

The temple was designated a UNESCO World Heritage Site in 1995. A **double-section staircase** *(closed to the public)* leads up to the temple entrance, symbolizing the passage between the terrestrial world and the divine. On the western side of the temple, Bridge of Lotus Flowers *(Yeonhwagyo)*—not actually a bridge but a flight of 10 steps—and the Bridge of Seven Treasures *(Chilbogyo,* seven steps, representing seven hoards of gold or silver) lead to the Hall of Paradise *(Geuknakjeon).*

On the eastern side, Blue Cloud Bridge *(Cheongungyo)* and White Cloud Bridge *(Baegungyo)* with 33 steps each (just as there are 33 heavenly bodies and 33 steps to enlightenment) lead to Jahamun (Mauve Mist Gate), which opens on to the main hall *(Daeungjeon,* 1765). The less decorative **galleries** connecting the various buildings delineate the spaces, inviting visitors to stroll and meditate. In a spectacular setting, the temple buildings seem to float in the air, their gray tiles contrasting attractively with the blue-violet painted detail of the paneling.

Two **pagodas** stand on either side of the central courtyard, symbolizing yin and yang. **Dabotap** (the Pagoda of Many Treasures) to the right is in the ornate style associated with the kingdom of Baekje; the central platform was once guarded by four lions.

The *sarira*, or sacred zone (♿ *see box p 397*), is topped with a ring of water lilies and the tip of the pagoda (34ft/10.4m) bears a lotus flower. **Seokgatap** (Sakyamuni Pagoda), which stands opposite, has three tiers and is 27ft/8.2m high. Its more sober style is typical of the period of unification (668–935). The statues surrounding the *Sakyamuni* Buddha in the main hall represent the past and the future, and there are also some fine paintings to be seen both inside and outside.

The Hall of Paradise itself is located in the western courtyard and houses a bronze gilt Buddha Amitabha. The Gwaneumjeon in the far northeastern corner of the complex is dedicated to the bodhisattva Avalokitesvara, who is depicted standing on a lotus. From the raised platform supporting the shrine there is a good view over the tiled roofs and courtyards of the temple.

Among all these riches, don't miss the Hwanghak-budo stupa in pink granite, shaped like a carved lantern decorated with Buddhas.

Seokguram Grotto★★★ 석굴암

♿ *See Gyeongju map I.*
4mi/6km from Bulguksa, well signposted. By bus: no. 12 toward Seokguram from the Bulguksa car park (every hour, 20min). On foot: follow the 2mi/3km hilly path between the ticket offices of the two sites. 📞 *(054)-746-9933.* ⏰ *Open summer 6:30am–6pm, winter 7am–5pm. ₩4,000, parking ₩2,000. A .3mi/600m path leads from the entrance to the site.*

Now a UNESCO World Heritage Site, this superb **shrine** was commissioned in 751 during the reign of King Gyeongdeok and completed in 774 under King Hyeong. Rather than being carved out of the hillside, the grotto is in fact an artificial chapel made of huge white granite blocks housing an imposing (and exquisite) **statue of the Buddha** (*Bonjonbul*).

Generally considered the greatest masterpiece of Korean Buddhist art, the monumental statue sits on a white-granite lotus flower pedestal and seems to be in deep contemplation of the distant horizon. The whole shrine, which recounts the story of Sakyamuni's enlightenment, may also

Seokguram Grotto

©TOPIC PHOTO AGENCY IN/age fotostock

have been intended to protect the peninsula against Japanese invasion, as the Buddha looks out toward the East Sea. The 11.5ft/3.5m statue is surrounded by statues of 42 divinities and bodhisattva, as well as heavenly guardians sculpted in bas-relief, which watch over the antechamber and the cardinal points of the compass.

The **rotunda** and the **dome** beneath which the Buddha sits are an astonishing **architectural achievement**. The rotunda symbolizes Buddhist paradise, where living beings are guided to nirvana; its lower section is occupied by the Buddha's 10 disciples, while the upper alcoves contain bodhisattva. The dome above *Bonjonbul* is made up of 360 stones that fit together perfectly without the aid of mortar—further evidence of the skill of the builders.

The grotto was designed so that the Buddha would be bathed in direct sunlight on only one day in the year, the spring solstice. Sadly, the whole shrine is now protected by a sheet of glass, which spoils the magic a little.

Outside, from the area in front of the grotto, there is a fantastic view of wooded hills that erupt in color during the fall as they descend in waves of red and gold toward the coast. There is a beautiful panoramic view from the car park, too, this time of a mosaic of rice fields and Namsan (South Mountain).

Namsan Park 남산공원
See Gyeongju map I.

The groups of royal tombs radiating from the south and west of Gyeongju include **Taejong-Muyeol**, the burial place of the last Silla ruler before the unification in 668. Although the tombs of his successors have gradually been covered in ornamentation, his retains its simplicity. The tumuli in nearby **Seoak-ri Gobungun Tombs Park** mark the graves of his ancestors. But it is, above all, the attractive paths and trails of Namsan Park that draw visitors to the south of Gyeongju.

Namsan★★ (South Mountain) 남산
See Gyeongju map I.
Bus no. 11 from the city center toward the eastern entrance to the park (1.5–2mi/2–3km south of the Gyeongju National Museum), including Seochulji. Bus no. 500–508 for the eastern slopes of the mountain.

Gyeongju's Namsan (1,529ft/466m, not to be confused with Namsan in Seoul), is situated just to the south of the city. Namsan Park owes its fame to the mountain retreats, temples, pagodas (64), tombs and pavilions that are scattered across its superb scenery, and to the 57 Buddhas that have been carved into the rock *(maaebul)* of its 35 valleys since the 7C. There are several entrances and numerous paths, which are generally well signposted. Although the park is not vast and the highest points are not that high, take a good map or a Korean friend if you don't have a good sense of direction as it's easy to get lost. Peaceful cycle paths cut across the lower slopes.

Samneung, the most popular entrance, is on the western side and is the departure point for various trails to the center of the mountain *(3hr–7hr walk)*. Sights not to miss include the hermitage of **Sangseonam** with its beautiful panoramas, the summit of Geumosan (1,535ft/468m), **Yongjangsaji** (the site of Yongjang Temple with its seated Buddha) in the deep valley at Yongjanggol, and **Chilbulam**, the Hermitage of the Seven Buddhas, including *Samjonbul*, a triad carved into the cliff face. In the northeast corner of the park you will also find the reconstructed convent of **Borisa** and **Seochulji** (*see also p288*), a pond with a pavilion "floating" on lotus flowers.

EXCURSIONS
Yangdong Village★★★ 양동마을
See Gyeongsang-do map.
12mi/20km N of Gyeongju. By car: take Rte 68 toward Angang or Rte 7 toward Pohang, then follow the brown signs for the village. By bus: from

The Giants of the Sea

Today South Korea, a small country that 60 years ago was on its economic deathbed, is a world leader in producing microchips and flat-screen televisions, as well as in shipbuilding, steel and automobile manufacture. The heavy industries have had the effect of flattening the countryside around cities such as Pohang and Ulsan (including islands such as Geoje, 🔊 *see p317*) and tourists have deserted these areas in droves, but perhaps too quickly. These cities are part of the country's landscape, its daily reality and its prosperity, and for this reason alone, they are worthy of interest.

South Korea produces the world's largest supertankers at a rate and a quality that leaves their competitors standing, and **50 percent of all the ships built in the world** are *Made in Korea* (35 percent are Chinese, 5.5 percent made in the European Union). Given the relatively high cost of local labor, this is a real achievement and its explanation lies in the extremely high standards of Korean technology and its work culture. The world's largest shipyard, in Ulsan, is owned by Hyundai and employs a workforce of 25,000 people who churn out a giant ship every four days. Other companies, including Samsung, STX and Hanjin, maintain several other sites and have even been acquiring existing shipyards abroad. That said, China, whose output is currently lower and of a lower quality, is hard on Korea's heels· 🚌 Guided tours of Ulsan (🔊 *see p294*), Geoje Museum of Shipbuilding (🔊 *see p317*).

Gyeongju rail station. Turn right out of the station to the bus stop in front of a pharmacy. From there, take bus no. 200/201/202. A 40min journey will take you to within 1mi/1.3km of the village entrance. Gyeongju Tourist Office has a comprehensive guide to Yangdong in English. No charge.

Designated a **UNESCO World Heritage Site** in 2010, the origins of the village have been dated to around 1400. Surrounded by trees and flowers, it is situated partly in a fertile valley and partly on the lower slopes of Seolchangsan (Mt. Seolchang). There are more than 170 houses, most of which are still inhabited, containing many culturally valuable items ranging from local folk art to national treasures.

The whole site is a fine example of an **aristocratic village** of the Joseon period, during which time it was also an important Confucian cultural center, and is a chance to see a little of a Korea that has now all but disappeared. The scholar Yi Eonjeok (1491–1533) lived here for a time, linking his name and that of his family to many of the buildings in the village. The level of conservation of the various houses is fairly unique. Of

the more notable, **Hyangdan** (1543), with its elegant roof, is a highlight; it originally contained 99 rooms! All the houses in the village are surrounded by stone walls and immaculate gardens. The thatched houses, home to the servants who worked for the aristocracy, are particularly numerous around Gwangajeong, where the governor lived at the beginning of the 16C. Beyond these houses you will see a pavilion, some pri-

Yangdong village

©KTO

vate *(seowon)* and public schools, and there are several teahouses in which to take a break.

If you are traveling by car, you will be able to make a detour to two sites relating to the scholar Yi Eonjeok: the Confucian school at **Oksan Seowon**, built in his honor in 1572, and **Dongnakdang**, a beautiful house from 1532 where he lived for a time—it can be visited by request at the tourist office. These two sites are a short distance along Route 28 to the west of Yangdong Folk Village.

Toward the Coast

See Gyeongsang-do Map.
Gyeongju is just 19-25mi/30-40km from the southeast coast, so if you have the time to extend your trip, here are a few minor sights of interest.

Follow Route 7 to the dynamic port town of **Pohang** (population 500,000), whose principal claims to fame include POSCO (the Pohang Steel Company, the second largest steel factory in the world) and POSTECH (Pohang University of Science and Technology), Korea's top-rated university. Ironically, POSTECH is bankrolled by POSCO. Take a ferry from here to the island of Ulleongdo (*see box p259*) or head for the beach at Bukbu to the north of the city. The restaurants along this long and very popular stretch of sand serve excellent seafood.

Route 4 leads past various sights as it winds its way to the coast. A sign at the junction with Route 14 invites you to head a little farther north to **Girimsa** *(Girim Temple, (054)-744-2292, open 8am–8pm, ₩3,000)*. This vast complex on the slopes of Hamwolsan was founded in 643 under the name of **Imjeongsa**. You will find one of the smallest stone pagodas in the country here.

Make a U-turn and take Route 14 *(then 929)* to the coast, where an "annex" of the Gyeongju National Park contains the **Underwater Tomb of King Munmu**, which does not quite live up to its name—it is not much more than a few rocks in the surf. The king's ashes were scattered here at his request, in the hope that he might become a sea dragon to protect the peninsula from

invasion; for this reason, shamanist ceremonies are occasionally held here. The nearby stone pagodas of the temple at Gameun (44ft/13.4m high) are a rather more satisfying sight.

The many seafood restaurants of the small port of **Gampo** lie another 6mi/10km to the north *(Rte 31 toward Pohang)*.

Ulsan★ 울산

See Gyeongsang-do map.
25mi/40km SE of Gyeongju, Ulsan is 50min away by road and rail. It is also easily reached as a day trip from Busan (1hr by bus) and Daegu. Note: visits to the industrial sites are only possible on one or two occasions per week, with prior booking; checking ahead is advised.

Ulsan is not the most beautiful city in South Korea, or even in the region. Sandwiched between the Beonyeong and Sageori intersections, the city center with a Lotte "mini-city" (a hotel, mall and amusement park run by the Korean-Japanese Lotte conglomerate), restaurants and stores is of little interest. In the shadow of the skyscrapers that seem to have sprung up as far as the eye can see, a wholesale market is a hive of activity and trucks piled with pallets trundle to and fro. There is nothing in Ulsan that you won't have seen already if you have visited other cities on the peninsula.

Ulsan's main claim to fame is as the South Korean capital of heavy industry and the home city of the Hyundai Group, which altogether employs the best part of a million people. **Ulsan City Tour** *((052)-275-0295, www.ulsancitytour.com, duration 6hr, ₩5,000/10,000)* periodically organizes guided tours of the impressive industrial complexes, including SK Petrochemical Company's factory, which supplies the entire country with gasoline; the **Hyundai Motor Company plant**, where 34,000 workers manufacture 5,600 cars per day; and Hyundai Heavy Industries, which employs a workforce of 25,000 in the **world's largest shipyard**. The gigantic cranes of this city churn out the world's largest supertankers at an impressive rate (🕯️*see box p293*). 🕯️*See p267 for industrial tours leaving from Daegu.*

ADDRESSES

🛏️ STAY

GYEONGJU CITY CENTER MAP II

🛏️ **Gyeongju Park Tourist Hotel** 경주파크 관광호텔 – *170-1 Noseo-dong.* 📞*777-7744. 40rm.* ₩*50,000–85,000.* The advantages of this accomodation include its proximity to the bus terminal and its status as a classic hotel, although the rooms are a little uninspiring and the bathrooms can be basic.

🛏️ **Sa Rang Chae** 사랑채민박 – *23 Paseok-ro 1068 Beon-gil.* 📞*(054)-773-4868. www.kjstay.com.* ₩*30,000.* Located in a traditional building in the pleasant Hwangnam district, Sa Rang Chae will provide a comfortable and charming stay despite being at the budget end of the market. Korean *ondol* rooms or Western bedrooms around a multi-purpose courtyard.

🛏️ **Show Motel** 쇼 모텔 – *Noseo-dong.* 📞*(054)-771-7878. 35rm.* ₩*50,000–80,000.* The most comfortable and novel of the motels near the bus terminal. Part of a chain, the rooms are huge with decor as colorful as it is daring. Note the interesting bathrooms, among other surprises.

BOMUN LAKE RESORT (BOMUNHO)
If you are on a group tour, you will stay at one of the hotels at this resort. Good deals during the week and during the off season.

🛏️ **Swissrosen Hotel & Pension** 스위스로젠호텔 – 📞*(054)-748-4848. www.swissrosen.co.kr. 40rm.* ₩*60,000 (during the week).* Somewhat off the beaten track in the hills, a hotel providing three-star comfort and good value for the money.

🛏️ **Commodore Hotel** 코모도 호텔 – 📞*(054)-745-7701. www.commodore.co.kr. 262rm.* ₩*150,000.* A beautiful hotel with very pleasant rooms.

🛏️ **Hotel Concorde** 콩코드 호텔 – 📞*(054)-745-7000. www.concorde.co.kr. 250rm.* ₩*140,000.* The cruise liner lobby is a little dated, but the rooms, each with a view of the lake, are good value out of season.

🛏️ **Gyeongju Hilton** 힐튼 호텔 – 📞*(054)-745-7788. www.gyeongjuhilton.co.kr. 324rm.* ₩*255,000.* A retro lobby, adorned with a Miró, and predictably comfortable rooms. Beautiful swimming pool and contemporary sculpture on the grounds.

🛏️ **Hotel Hyundai** 현대호텔 – 📞*(054)-748-2233. www.hyundaihotel.com. 449rm.* ₩*240,000.* Industrial-sized but comfortable with a clientele that is a mixture of tourists and conference delegates. Several restaurants, a good swimming pool and charming flower gardens.

BULGUKSA

🛏️ **Kolon Hotel** 코오롱 호텔 – *Ma-dong* 📞*(054)-746-9001. www.kolonhotel.co.kr. 160rm.* ₩*160,000.* A peaceful and comfortable hotel surrounded by greenery (woodland and a golf course).

POHANG

🛏️ **Commodore** 코모도 호텔 – *311-2 Songdo-dong, Pohang Regional Map C2.* 📞*(054)-241-1400. 50rm.* ₩*160,000.* Located 21.5mi/35km from Gyeongju in the port city of Pohang, with "Zen"-style renovated rooms and a view of the bay.

ULSAN

🛏️ **Lotte Hotel** 롯데호텔 – 📞*(052)-960-1000. www.hotellotte.co.kr. 211rm.* ₩*250,000* The largest luxury chain in the country, Lotte hotels provide all the convenience you expect, including several restaurants and an on-site business center and a fitness center.

🍽️ EAT

GYEONGJU CITY CENTER MAP II.
You will find several **ssambap** restaurants at the southern entrance to the Tumuli Park, offering various rice and meat packages wrapped in lettuce leaves. Hotel restaurants dominate in Bomun Lake Resort.

🍽🍽 **Nolboo** 놀부 부대찌개 – *1 Wonhyo-ro 105 Beon-gil.* 📞*(054)-773 -7892. Open 10am–10pm.* A lively restaurant situated among the stores popular with young people, and a good place to try Korean specialties.

🍽🍽 **Pyeongyang** 평양냉면 – *109-2 Wanghyo-ro.* 📞*(054)-772-2448. Open 11am–9pm.* Just off the road with all the cinemas, a basic restaurant at the end of a courtyard.

🍽🍽 **Sukyeong Sikdang** 숙영식당 – *60 Gyerim-ro.* 📞*(054)-772-3369. Open 11am–9pm. From ₩15,000.* Pass through a courtyard—not to mention the kitchen—to reach a tranquil, rustic-looking dining room where they serve unforgettable *pajeon.*

🍽🍽🍽 **Kisoya** 기소야 – *90 Wanghyo-ro.* 📞 *(054)-746-6020. Open 11am–9pm ₩8,000/15,000.* A pleasant place with hints of Japanese influence about the decor and the menu, and a terrace at the back. Eat classic Japanese food (tempura, *unagi*) augmented with a dash of Korean (*udon kimchi, kimchi katsudon*).

🍽🍽🍽 **La Cuisine** 라퀴진레스토랑 – *88-1 Gyerim-ro.* 📞*(054)-743-5000. Open noon–10pm (Sat–Sun 11:30pm). ₩10,000/20,000.* Recently opened by a young and charming French speaker, the interior is simply decorated. For a change from kimchi, try their salads, pasta, pizza and steaks, accompanied by a wine list.

🍽🍽🍽🍽 **Wonpung** 원풍식당 – *105 Cheonmseo dong.* 📞*(054)-772-8630. Open 11am–2pm, 6pm–10pm.* A beautiful building in a traditional style on the edge of Hwangnam district, with large kitchens and intimate dining rooms packed in around a courtyard. It is renowned for its extraordinary *hanjeongsik* (table banquet).

🍸 BARS

Cafe Esmeralda 에스메랄다 커 피숍 – *Nodong-dong.* 📞*(054)-749-9449. Open 11am–11pm.* A modern-looking café with pleasant decor.

Le Tango du Chat 르탱고뒤샤 커피숍 – *Gyerim-ro/Dongseong-ro. Open 10:30am–10:30pm.* Situated at a strategic intersection in a shopping district, there's a café with a terrace or a quieter room upstairs.

🛒 SHOPPING

FOOD

The picturesque **market** at Seong-dong is opposite Gyeongju Station. South of Hwarang-ro the district of Nodong-dong is a mass of stores and you will find a **supermarket** at the intersection between the bus terminal and the tumuli. The streets of the city center are lined with any number of stands and stores selling **Gyeongju bbang** (little cakes filled with bean paste).

Hwangnam Bread 황남빵 – *Near the tumuli.* 📞*(054)-749-7000. www.hwangnam.co.kr.* The best-known store. The confectioners behind the counter have been filling their cakes here since 1939. Fantastic packaging.

CRAFTS

There are plenty of craft items to buy in the stores in the city center, near Bulguksa or at the Folk Craft Village (*Hadong,* 📞*(054)-746-7270*) between Bomun Lake Resort and Bulguksa, including objects inspired by the Silla period: ceramics, lace, amethyst, violet quartz, replica silver bowls, etc. In some instances, you can watch them being made before you buy.

🎭 EVENTS AND FESTIVALS

There are performances in **dance and traditional music** at Bomun Lake's open-air theater and at Anapji from May to October *(full programs from the tourist office).* Don't miss the **Traditional Drink and Rice Cake Festival** *(end Mar–beginning Apr)* or the dancing and music at the wonderfully colorful three-day **Silla Cultural Festival** in October.

Busan★★
부산

Busan may lack the buzz of Rio de Janeiro or Sydney, but it enjoys a similarly superb location among bays and headlands, mountains and valleys. South Korea's second-largest city profits from its coastal location with its busy port and beaches. A far cry from the "living museums" that typify many of South Koreas urban spaces, it is Busan's ambience and panaoramic views that charm the visitor. Once your ear is sufficiently attuned, you may detect the local accent and snatches of Japanese, Tagalog and Russian, as people barter and make deals in the business districts and markets. Busan is a city with ambition—the largest port in the country, it is keen to dismiss its inferiority complex in relation to Seoul with a series of architectural and cultural projects. The inhabitants are proud of the fact that there are many different kinds of things to do here, from jogging on the beach and a rural stroll in the heart of the city, to shopping, watching a Lotte Giants baseball game, or having dinner while watching ships make their way out to sea from the port.

VISIT

Only a few of Busan's districts are featured here. If you have time, there are plenty of beaches and creeks to explore, accessible via subway and bus.

The list of possibilities is endless: Dadaepo Beach—with its famous sunsets and rock festival—Songjeong, Songdo, and Ilgwang Beach, as well as Eulsukdo, an island in the Nakdong River estuary that is a paradise for ornithologists.

In fact, the city is **changing constantly** and new attractions appear practically every day.

Immense skyscrapers punctuate the horizon, a light rail line is being constructed to the airport and hugely ambitious building projects are under-

▶ **Population:** 3,574,340

⏱ **Michelin Map:** Regional map pp264–265.

ℹ **Info:** Tourist Offices Busan Station, ℘(051)-441-6565, open 9am–8pm; Haeundae, ℘(051)-749-5700, open 9am–6pm; International Ferry Terminal, ℘(051)-465-3471, open 9am–6pm; Gimhae Airport, ℘(051)-973-2800, open 7am–9pm. http://etour.busan.go.kr/index.jsp.

▶ **Location:** Busan is located in the southeast of the peninsula, 240mi/385km from Seoul. The city covers a large area, from the markets of Nampo-dong, the "historic" quarter in the south, to the shopping and business district Seomyeon in the north.

👥 **Kids:** The beaches, Haeundae aquarium and the cable car ride at Dongnae, Jagalchi Fish Market for a lesson in identifying creatures of the deep.

🕐 **Timing:** Allow at least two days to fully soak up Busan's atmosphere. Note: hotel rates can shoot up at the weekend, especially near the beaches. There are festivals in June and October.

◉ **Don't Miss:** Jagalchi Fish Market and Beomeosa, *Dongnae pajeon* (seafood waffles) and walks on the beach, panoramic views, beaches and bays, the cliffs at Taejongdae.

way in the northern port, with marinas, a "green city" project, an attractive esplanade and all kinds of businesses opening up. Dynamic Busan is very much a case of "to be continued."

NAMPO-DONG, JUNG-GU AND TAEJONGDAE
👥👤 Jagalchi Market★★
자갈치시장
ⓘ *See Busan map II.*
Ⓜ *Jagalchi, line 1, exit 10.* ☏*(051)-245-2594/713-8000.* 🕐 *Open 8am–10pm.*

The famous **Jagalchi Fish Market** (the name means "pebble") lost some of its authenticity when a modern building with a roof in sections shaped like the wings of an albatross was built to shelter part of it, but it is still a fascinating place for the visitor. Women in gumboots are very much in charge in this colorful world, where fish are piled high in row upon row of containers kept fresh by hoses constantly trickling water. Just about everything the sea has to offer passes through this market (you might almost expect to come across the giant mutant creature from the Korean monster movie *The Host*), all freshly unloaded from the boats that bob up and down in the port.

The aisles of the modern Jagalchi Market are well organized, while the stands overflowing into the nearby streets form the picturesque **Sindonga Market (more fish!)**, just to the west. If browsing is not enough, you can pick out your choice of fish and have it cooked on the spot. You can also try the freshest possible fish (the seafood is consumed live)

in the upstairs eateries and diners above Sindonga Market and in the back streets. The **Dried Fish Market**, a little farther to the east, is housed in diminutive buildings that have managed to survive the advance of the glass giants. The fish here are arranged by size, lined up in neat rows alongside mountains of mussels and clumps or strands (some of which can be up to 6ft/2m long) of seaweed. Stalls selling fishing nets, buoys and plants all add to the riot of colors and scents.

BIFF Square 스퀘어 (formerly PIFF) and Gukje Market 국제시장
ⓘ *See Busan map II.*
Ⓜ *Nampo-dong, line 1, exit 1, or*
Ⓜ *Jagalchi, line 1, exit 7.*

PIFF is the former name of the famous film gala, now known as **BIFF** (Busan International Film Festival, www.biff.kr). It was founded in 1996 when Busan was still spelled Pusan (ⓘ *see Romanization p33*). A pedestrian-only area, the square has been home to a number of movie theaters, playhouses and 24-hour restaurants since the 1960s, as well as some inviting ranks of *pojangmacha*, typical Korean street stalls (some with long queues, some practically deserted). Try a hot *hotteok*, a delicious little pancake stuffed with sugar syrup and crushed nuts.

Drawn by the nearby shopping streets, local young people and tourists flock to BIFF Square, especially at the end of the afternoon. Fashion boutiques and street cafés appear along **Gwangbok-ro** as you get closer to the gigantic **Gukje Market** (🕐 *open daily except 1st & 3rd Sun of the month*), a checkerboard of alleys where you can buy just about anything you can imagine: pink hair bows, toilet brushes, dried persimmons, globes, bowls of every color, craft items, bedding, engagement rings.

There are no time restrictions here—you can shop at just about any time of the day or night in this typically Korean labyrinthine market.

Jagalchi Market

© Pietro Scozzari/age fotostock

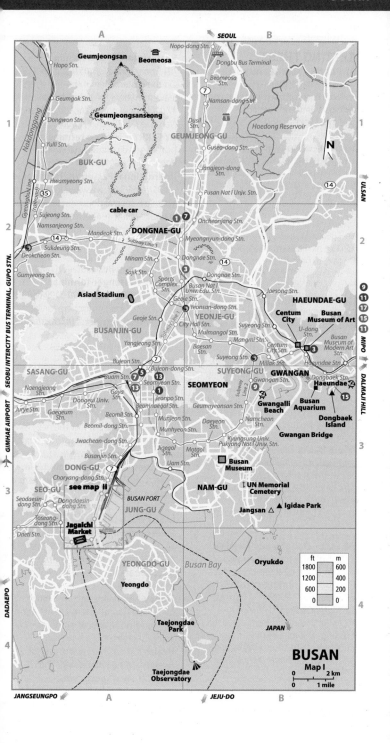

BUK-GU

Geumjeongsan
Beomeosa

Geumjeongsanseong

Hopo Stn.
Geumgok Stn.
Dongwon Stn.
Yulli Stn.
Hwamyeong Stn.

Nakdonggang

Gyeongbu Line (railroad)

35

Nopo-dong Stn.
SEOUL

Dongbu Bus Terminal
Beomeosa Stn.
Namsan-dong Stn.
7

Dusil Stn.
GEUMJEONG-GU
Gusea-dong Stn.
Jangjeon-dong Stn.
Pusan Nat'l Univ. Stn.

Hoedong Reservoir

N

ULSAN

14

cable car
Sujeong Stn.
Namsanjeong Stn.
14
Sukdeung Stn.
Mandeok Stn.   Subway Line 3
Minam Stn.
Deokcheon Stn.
Sajik Stn.
Gumyeong Stn.

DONGNAE-GU
1 7
Oncheonjang Stn.
Myeongnyun-dong Stn.
Dongnae Stn.
14
3

Asiad Stadium

Busan Nat'l
Univ. Edu. Stn.
Sports
Complex
Stn.
Geoje Stn.

Yeonsan-dong Stn.
YEONJE-GU
City Hall Stn.

Jaesong Stn.
HAEUNDAE-GU
9
11
17
11
15

BUSANJIN-GU

Geoje Stn.
Yangjeong Stn.

Suyeong Stn.
Mulmangol Stn.
Baesan
Stn.
Suyeong Stn.

Centum
City
Busan
Museum of Art
U-dong
Stn.
Centum
City Stn.
Busan
Museum of
Modern Art
Stn.

MIPO

7
Bujeon Stn.
SASANG-GU
Bujeon-dong Stn.

Naengjeong Stn.
Jurye Stn.

Buam Stn.
7 5
Seomyeon Stn.
13
Gaya Stn.
Dongeui Univ.
Stn.
Gaegeum Stn.

Jeonpo Stn.
1
SEOMYEON
Jeonpo Stn.
Beomnaegol Stn.
Beomil Stn.
Beomil-dong Stn.

Geumnyeonsan Stn.
Daeyeon
Stn.

Millak Stn.
Haeundae Stn.
GWANGAN
Gwangan Stn.
9
Suyeong
Line 2
Namcheon
Stn.
Gwangalli
Beach
Dongbaek Stn.
Haeundae
15

Busan Aquarium

Dongbaek
Island

Gwangan Bridge

DALMAJI HILL

GIMHAE AIRPORT
SEOBU INTERCITY BUS TERMINAL, GUPO STN.

Jwacheon-dong Stn.
Busanjin Stn.
Munjeon Stn.
Munhyeon Stn.
Jigegol Stn.
Motgol Stn.
Uam Stn.

Kyungsung Univ.
Pukyong Nat'l Univ. Stn.

Busan Museum

DONG-GU
Choryang-dong Stn.
7
SEO-GU
Dongdaesin-
dong Stn.
Seodaesin-
dong Stn.
Toseong-dong Stn.
Daeti Stn.

see map II
Dongdaesin-
dong Stn.

Jagalchi
Market

BUSAN PORT
JUNG-GU

NAM-GU

UN Memorial
Cemetery

Jangsan
Igidae Park

DADAEPO

YEONGDO-GU

Yeongdo

Busan Bay

Oryukdo

ft	m
1800	600
1200	400
600	200
0	0

Taejongdae
Park

JAPAN

BUSAN
Map I

0   2 km
0   1 mile

Taejongdae
Observatory

JANGSEUNGPO

A

JEJU-DO

B

GETTING THERE

BY PLANE – Gimhae Airport –
*(051)-974-3115/1666-2676.
www.airport.co.kr/doc/gimhae_eng/
index.jsp. 9mi/15km west of the city.*
The international and domestic
terminals are 550yd/500m apart and
both are easy to negotiate and well
equipped. There are flights to Seoul
and Jeju as well as Japan, China and
Southeast Asia. A light rail line will
soon link the airport with Busan
subway, or you can take the limousine
bus to Haeundae *(every 20min, ₩6,000)*
and Busan Station *(every 40min,
₩5,000)*, all via Seomyeon.
By taxi, expect to pay around ₩25,000
to Seomyeon. There are also direct
buses to Ulsan, Daegu and Gyeongju
(12 departures daily, 1hr10min). Please
check the opening time of the
extension and that it is a light rail line

BY TRAIN – Busan Station –
Ⓜ *Busan Station, line 1. In Jung-gu.
www.korail.go.kr.* The KTX trains
from Seoul terminate here at Busan's
downtown station, as do trains from
most other parts of the country.
There are frequent high-speed train
connections from Busan: to Seoul *(3hr,
from ₩49,200)*, Daegu *(1hr, from ₩6,100)*
and Daejeon *(1hr50min, from ₩29,000)*.
Seoul is also served by *saemaul*
(4hr30min, ₩39,300) and *mugunghwa*
(5hr30min, ₩26,500) trains. A second
station (Gupo) is in the western part
of the city.

BY BUS – Dongbu Bus Terminal –
In **Dongbu**, *at the northern end of
subway line 1.* Ⓜ *Nopo-dong, line 1.*
It includes the **Intercity** *(*(051)-
508-9966/1577-9969)* and **Express**
((051)-508-9955/1577-9956)*
terminals. Frequent departures for
Gyeongju *(50min, ₩4,000)*, Tongdosa
(25min, ₩2,000), Ulsan *(1hr, ₩4,000)*
and Seoul *(4hr30min, ₩31,000)*.

Seobu Intercity Bus Terminal –
(Ⓜ *Sasang, line 2, *(051)-322-8301)*.
On the eastern side of the city. Buses
leave from here for Jinju *(1hr30min,
₩7,000)*, Tongyeong *(2hr, ₩10,500)* and
Namhae *(2hr30min, ₩11,000)*.
BY FERRY – The **two terminals** are
both located centrally *(*Ⓜ *Jungang-
dong, line 1, exit 12)*.
International Passenger Terminal –
(051)-465-3471. www.busanferry.co.kr.
There are several departures for Japan:
Fukuoka *(daily, 3–6hr crossing, ₩90,000/
115,000)*, Shimonoseki *(daily, 9hr
crossing)* and Osaka *(3 departures
per week, 6hr crossing)*. There is a bus
connection to Busan Station *(₩800)*.
**Coastal Passenger Terminal
(domestic) –** *(051)-400-3399/660-
0117.* Ferries leave from here for Jeju
*(6 departures per week, 11hr crossing,
from ₩32,000)* and there are daily
sailings to Gohyun, Okpo and
Jangsengpo.

GETTING AROUND

Busan has a good bus network and an
excellent **subway** with upgrades and
extensions planned over the next few
years *(4 lines, easy to use with automatic
gates; tickets: each journey is ₩1,100–
1,300 according to destination, a 24hr
ticket costs ₩3,500. Info: www.humetro.
busan.kr/english/main/)*.

USEFUL INFORMATION

Main post office – *Jungang-no.*
Ⓜ *Jungang-dong, line 1, exit 9.* Open
Mon–Fri 9am–8pm (Sat–Sun 1pm).
There are also local post offices in
the individual districts.
Money – Exchange service centers,
banks and Global ATM branches can
be found at the airport, station and
in tourist areas.
Health – Pusan National University
Hospital, *10 1-ga Ami-dong.* *(051)-
254-0171. www1.pnuh.co.kr.*

SIGHTSEEING

In addition to the pleasure boats departing from Haeundae (*see p304*), **Busan City Tour** runs several different circular tours a day—Haeundae, Taejongdae, Downtown and Eulsukdo Eco course— ℘(051)-464-9898.

www.citytourbusan.com. Open Tue–Sun. ₩10,000 (20 percent discount with a KTX ticket). 12 departures daily from 9:20am–4:40pm. The tours depart from Busan Station (*Arirang Hotel*) or at various stops on the way; there is also an evening tour (*summer 7:30pm, winter 7pm*).

Yongdusan Park 용두산공원 and Busan Tower 부산타워

See Busan map II. Ⓜ *Nampo-dong, line 1, exit 3, then first right.*

This small urban park is a favorite with older folks for morning callisthenics and evening strolls. The slender **Busan Tower** (℘(051)-245-1066, www.busan-tower.org, ⏰ open 9am–9pm, ₩4,000), built in 1973 as a rival to the N Seoul Tower, looks almost old-fashioned, and the images of the Eiffel Tower and the Toronto Tower adorning its corridors are almost like family photos.

At just 226ft/69m in height, it can't compete with its French and Canadian cousins, but a trip to the top is still highly recommended; the **view★★** of the city is fantastic, and gives you a chance to see just what an exceptional place Busan is. Spend some time taking in the deep bays set among mountains trailing plumes of cloud, green expanses contrasting with azure skies, valleys bristling with meticulously planned high-rise buildings, green-painted roofs and terraces, an armada of fishing boats, departing ferries and tankers—not to mention the new construction sites, including the immense Lotte World Tower, that are transforming the area. You will also find a range of exhibitions and souvenir shops at the tower.

Farther on from the park, **Donggwang-ro**, with its restaurants and antiques shops, is a peaceful and pleasant place for a stroll.

The nearby **Modern History Museum** (*see Busan map II, Daecheong-no, ℘(051)-253-3845, ⏰open Tue–Sun 9am–6pm, no charge*) traces the city's roots.

Cliff views along Taejongdae Park

©Sehee Kim/Michelin

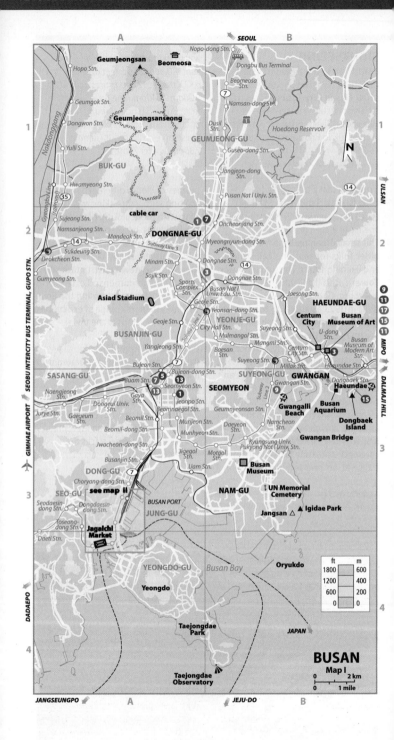

BUSAN
Map I

WHERE TO STAY		WHERE TO EAT	
Hotel Angel	①	Dongnae Byeljang	①
Arpina Youth Hostel	③	Dongnae Halmae Pajeon	③
Lotte Hotel	⑤	Lotte Department Store	⑦
Nongshim Hotel	⑦	Millak	⑨
Novotel	⑨	Mipo	⑪
Sunset Business Hotel	⑪	Shintobuli	⑬
Toyoko Inn Seomyeon	⑬	Tebuhang	⑮
Westin Chosun	⑮	Yeyije	⑰

Busan Station 부산역

👣 See Busan map II. N of Nampo-dong along Jungangdae-ro.
Ⓜ Busan Station, line 1.

To the north of Jung-gu and its office blocks, this old brick station has been transformed into a vast, modern glass building at the end of the high-speed KTX rail line from Seoul. Inside you'll find a tourist office, restaurants and stores. Outside, the vast concourse in front of the station is often the scene of demonstrations.

Across the street to the west are Chinatown and the Texas Street (also known as Russian Street) area—many Russian ships dock at the port. Although popular with tourists (who run the risk of being mistaken for Russians), the souvenir stores, shops selling vodka and pickles, and seedy bars with signs in Cyrillic are ultimately rather unappealing.

Taejongdae Park★ 태종대공원

👣 See Busan map I. Yeong Island (Yeongdo-gu). Bus no. 30 from Nampo-dong (Jagalchi Market side).

To escape the hustle and bustle of Busan for a time and enjoy a more relaxing atmosphere, don't miss out on the short trip to Taejongdae Park at the far end of Yeongdo (Yeong Island). A small tourist **train** (🕐 Apr–Oct 9am–8pm, Nov–Mar 9:30am–7pm, ₩1,500) makes a number of stops on its 2.4mi/4km round-trip, during which you will see fine views of the steep **cliffs**, the sea, the rocky beach and the tall pines and camellias that grow on the slopes of Mt. Taejongsan (820ft/250m).

On a clear day, from the **Taejongdae Observatory** at the southernmost tip, there are fantastic views out over the East Sea and to **Oryukdo Island** and Japan's Daema Island. Or you can make the journey around the Yeongdo on foot.

SEOMYEON AND NAM-GU
Seomyeon 서면

👣 See Busan map I.

Radiating out from around an immense traffic circle (roundabout), Seomyeon never sleeps. Whatever your interests and at whatever time of day, there is something to keep you occupied here. In addition to the large Lotte Department Store, there are hundreds of places where you can spend your money, on every avenue and in every alleyway, at street level or underground, not to mention in cafés, restaurants and *pojangmacha* (temporary street stalls). It's a real mix of old and new, blending seamlessly, as pretty wannabe models sip bowls of thick soup that cost 20 times less than the hair accessory they have just bought. Stroll past fashion store windows, gingseng stalls at Bujeon Market and Starbucks coffeeshops; watch the locals knead dough and boil up pork in kitchens opening onto the road. Billboards, neon signs and radios blaring out advertisements all compete for attention and, when evening comes, the clubs and bars take over.

UN Memorial Cemetery
유엔기념공원

👣 See Busan map I. Nam-gu district, not far from Jangsan. Ⓜ Daeyeon, line 2, exit 5. ✆ (051)-625-1608. www.unmck.or.kr. 🕐 Open daily 9am–5pm (summer 6pm). No charge.

The flags of the 22 countries that took part in the Korean War under UN command flutter above the graves of 2,300 soldiers who fell in combat between 1951 and 1954. The remains of 11,000 others were repatriated to the four corners of the world (including Europe, the US, Australia, Turkey, South America, Ethiopia and North Africa).

There are plenty of trails and paths on Jangsan (Mt. Jang, 740ft/225m) and in **Igidae Park**, from where there are also good views of the city and the sea. **Busan Museum** (℘(051)-610-7111, http://museum.busan.go.kr/english/01busan/index.jsp, ⏰open 9am–6pm, ₩1,000) is here, too, recounting the history of the city from Neolithic times to the present day.

Asiad Stadium★
아시아드 스타디움

🕯See Busan map I. Ⓜ Sports Complex, line 3, exit 9.

This stadium built between 1993 and 2001 has an amazing structure. From the air, it could be the shell of a giant mollusk clinging to a rock, or a space-ship. Its translucent Teflon roof allows sunlight through onto the 53,769 seats arranged in waves of different colors. The 2002 Asian Games, the Peace Cup and soccer matches in the 2002 FIFA World Cup all took place here. On that occasion, Korea made it to the semifinals by beating Poland 2–0. The stadium is now the home ground of Busan I'Park Football Club, the local team.

THE BEACHES OF HAEUNDAE AND GWANGALLI
👥**Haeundae** 해운대

🕯See Busan map I.
E of the city. Ⓜ Haeundae, line 2.
http://eng.haeundae.go.kr.

Of all Busan's beaches, cosmopolitan Haeundae is the star. The best-known 1mi/1.8km strip of golden sand in the country, Haeundae offers scores of luxury hotels, restaurants and crowds of visitors who descend at weekends. The resort has attracted more wide-spread attention, too, because of its role in Yun Je-gyun's disaster movie *Haeundae* (2009)—released in English as *Tidal Wave*—which dramatizes its

destruction in a tsunami and was seen by 10 million Korean cinemagoers.

The area between the station and the beach is a mass of motels beside a well-stocked market.

The pleasant promenade is lined with pine trees behind which there is a row of hotels and apartment buildings. The mornings here have a Californian feel, with joggers working up a sweat before going to the office. The terraces attract both expats and locals, who are gradually learning to love coffee (often with as much sugar as possible). Recreational activites range from swimming and playing volleyball on the sand to dancing in one of the fashionable clubs before watching the sunrise.

For a family outing, visit **Busan Aquarium** (℘(051)-740-1700, www.busanaquarium.com, ⏰open Mon–Thu 10am–7pm, Fri–Sun and holidays 9am-9pm; Jul 17–Aug 22 9am–9pm, ₩18,000). The exotic fish, sharks, otters and penguins should help pass a rainy afternoon; there are more than 35,000 creatures in total!

Small yellow and blue **cruise boats** set off from the eastern end of the beach to take tourists to neighboring bays, and the view of Busan from the sea is magical at any time of the day or night (℘(051)-742-2525, www.coveacruise.com, about ₩15,000). The boats also serve Oryukdo (Oryuk Island, or Islands—depending on the tide, there may appear to be several islands) and Jalgachi (3 departures daily). **Mipo**, the area near the pier from where the boat trips leave, is famed for its seafood restaurants.

They are already busy in the mornings, and eating in the Haeundae Seafood Hall feels rather like dining in an aquarium. The **Dalmaji Hill** district is home to a number of the city's art galleries and is also known as the Art District. There are cafés here too.

The **Sand Festival**, celebrated in Haeundae at the beginning of June, is a three-day burst of activity—concerts, sport, dancing and sand sculpture.

⛩The temple buildings of **Yonggungsa** are in a spectacular location (Ⓜ Haeun-

From Waegwan to Busan, and the Olympics

With records of its existence dating back to the period of the Gaya kingdom (and annexed by Silla in the 6C), Busan is gradually renouncing its historical status as a small fishing port. The **proximity to Japan promoted trade**, which was regulated in the 15C with a treaty combating piracy, but this very proximity made Waegwan (as Busan was known at the time) the first town to be invaded by its neighbor.

Admiral Yi Sun-sin statue, Busan

©Chris Stowers/Apa Publications

After being attacked several times (most notably in 1592), the town was razed to the ground despite strong resistance organized by Admiral Yi Sun-sin (*see box p336*). Further attacks ensued over the centuries, until the Japanese empire annexed the Korean Peninsula in 1910 (until 1945) and Pusan (as it was by now named) was confirmed in its strategic position close to the Japanese archipelago.

When the Korean War broke out, Pusan briefly became the only zone controlled by the Allies (the Pusan Perimeter area) during North Korea's great offensive, and more than four million refugees flocked here. Since the 1960s, Pusan has been the country's principal economic motor and its main international port. With the adoption of the new system of romanization (Korean words written using the Roman alphabet, *see Romanization p 37*) in 2000, the city's name is now spelled Busan, although it is still pronounced "Pooh-san." Today this hive of commercial and cultural activity has a population of nearly four million and has become the fifth-largest port in the world. With its sights set on even greater recognition, Busan was bidding for the 2020 **Olympic Games** until Pyeonchang won the honor of hosting the 2018 Winter Olympics.

Busan skyline, Korea's largest port

©KTO

dae, line 2, exit 7, then bus no. 181), straggling across wave-battered rocks right at the edge of the sea.

Dongbaek Island 동백섬

See Busan map I.
Dongbaek, line 2.

This rocky headland (it is no longer an island, but is attached to the mainland) dotted with pines and camellias forms the westernmost extremity of Haeundae Beach. An attractive wooded coastal path leads around it, starting (and finishing) at the Westin Chosun hotel. As you reach the tip of the headland, a beautiful panoramic view opens up of nearby Gwangan Bay (*see below*) with its impressive bridge and high-rise buildings surrounding the marina. In addition to a small lighthouse, you will see a circular modern building called **APEC House**, a venue for prestigious international conferences (*(051)-743-1974, open 10am–5pm, no charge*), in another spectacular location, right by the sea.

Busan Museum of Art 부산 시립미술관

See Busan map I. *Busan Museum of Modern Art, line 2, exit 5.* *(051)-744 -2602. www.busanmoma.org/main/.*
Open Tue–Sun 10am–8pm. Entrance fees for major exhibitions.

Located opposite the enormous Bexco trade fair complex, the museum hosts a wide variety of interesting temporary exhibitions, from Picasso to modern Vietnamese art.

Close by is **Centum City** (*see Busan Map I*, *Centum City*), the largest shopping complex in the world and a city within a city: besides the Shinsegae Department Store, there are restaurants of every kind, as well as a skating rink, movie theaters and **Spa Land** (*open 6am–midnight, ₩12,000–14,000*), a health facility which ranks among the largest in the world (22 spas, 13 *jjimjilbangs*).

Gwangan 광안

See Busan map I.
E of the city center. *Gwangan, line 1, or Geumnyeonsan, line 2.*

The gentle curve of the long beach at **Gwangalli** is no poor relation of its neighbor at Haeundae; there are fewer luxury hotels but the shady promenade with its pines and palm trees, enlivened every so often with a sculpture, is extremely pleasant. An unbroken rank of café terraces lines the boulevard leading north to **Millak Raw Fish Town**, a compact district entirely given over to restaurants serving fresh (or, indeed, raw) fish. You will be spoiled for choice here (including the Four Seasons on the second floor). The bay is closed off by an **immense bridge** that is especially impressive at night when illuminated, although it somewhat spoils the view. The bridge takes center stage during the fireworks display for the **Eobang Festival** (named after an ancient fisherman's tradition), which is held every year at the beginning of June. Experienced sailboarders can take a closer look at it by hiring a board at **Blue Wave** (*(051) -622-9999*) to the south of the bay.

NORTH OF THE CITY

Subway line 1 toward Dongbu serves all the sites in these areas to the north.

Dongnae-gu 동래 and Geumjeongsanseong 금정산성

See Busan map I.

Located in a long valley to the north of the city, the district of Dongnae is famed principally for its *pajeon* (a green onion and seafood pancake) and a spa that attracts a mixture of locals and Japanese tourists. The Japanese were also responsible for the development of Dongnae's **"Spa City"** district around Oncheonjang subway station (*oncheon* means hot springs), where there are plenty of restaurants (notably Japanese *izakaya*) and all the features you might expect of a spa resort.

To take advantage of the waters of Dongnae, try the **Heosimcheong** spa complex (*(051)-550-2200, open 5:30am–10pm, ₩8,000*), in Hotel Nongshim, where you will find a choice of saunas, outdoor and indoor baths, oak hot tubs, a *hammam* and more to soothe the body.

Small roads climb up toward Geum-gang Park, where an old-fashioned-looking but rapid ♿🚶**cable car** *(one way ₩3,000, round-trip ₩5,000)* will whisk you up to the top of the park and to **Geumjeongsan Fortress** *(Geumjeong-sanseong)*. The **view of the city★★** during the five-minute ascent is fabulous: office blocks, 50-story apartment bulidings, the Asiad Stadium, the sea and the mountains, Gwangan Bridge. Once at the top, you can admire the view unimpeded by the windows of the cable car and then just ride it back down over the beautiful forest.

🥾 Or, if you follow one of the paths through the woods, you may eventually come across the remains of the fortress walls. Built in the 18C and 19C, the walls were originally 11mi/18.8km long, but only about 2.5mi/4km remain today, and the local natural beauty outweighs any historical significance. The southern (*Nammun*) and northern (*Bungmun*) gates bring your walk to a close. From the former there is a 5.5mi/9km path leading to Beomeo Temple on the far side of the mountain.

Beomeosa★★ 범어사

ⓘ*See Busan map I.* Ⓜ *Beomeosa, line 1, exit 7. Make a U-turn as you leave the subway and walk up the road immediately to the right to reach the small bus terminal. Bus no. 90 (₩1,000) follows a circular route that passes the temple entrance and various hiking trails.* ✆*(051)-508-3122. www.beomeosa.co.kr.*
🕐*Open 7am–7pm. ₩1,000.*

Immerse yourself in a beautiful **natural setting** with a stream, swaying bamboo, the scent of pine trees and tumbling wisteria flowers. Although you are still in Busan, the busy activity of Seomyeon seems far away. Despite having been burned and pillaged in the past, the "Temple of the Nirvana Fish" is still one of the most beautiful in Korea. Founded in 678 by the monk Uisang, the complex now extends over three terraces. The first structure you see is **Iljumun** (1614), or "One Pillar Gate"—when viewed from the side it looks as though it is standing on just a solitary pillar, though in reality it is supported by four sturdy, squat pillars. The ceiling of **Daewoongjeon** (the main hall) is decorated with flowers, symbolizing the word of the Buddha falling from the heavens. A stone pagoda from the Silla period (9C) lies opposite, and to the right you will see the shrine of **Gwaneumjeon**. Behind, water from a sacred fountain flows from the spring where legend tells us Beomeo, the golden fish after which the temple is named, lived. Beomeo is said to have descended from Nirvana on a colored cloud to live in a golden pool in a rock on Geumjeongsan ("Golden Mountain"), where a spring still flows. Before leaving, look at the ancient stone lantern near the vast reading room—it is believed to date from the time of the temple's founding. The bus back down to the city passes a number of restaurants serving excellent *pajeon,* among other dishes.

🛏 Foreign visitors can immerse themselves in the environemnt with a stay at **Beomeosa** through the *Temple Stay* program. Info: www.beomeosa.co.kr.

EXCURSIONS
Tongdosa★★
통도사

ⓘ*See Busan map II. 21.5mi/35km N of Busan, not far from Sinpyeong. Access via Rte 1, exit for Tongdosa. By bus: from Busan Dongbu every 30min (25min, ₩2,000).* ✆*(055)-382-7182.* 🕐*Open 4am–8pm. ₩2,000, car admission ₩3,000. Otherwise, there is a free car park in front of the entrance to the complex and then a 1mi/1.2km walk.*

You reach the **largest temple in the country**, known as "Salvation of the World Through the Mastery of Truth," along a pleasant path beside a river and through a pine forest where the trees seem to dance in the sunlight. Come here early in the morning, when the silence is disturbed only by birdsong, and the city's motels, restaurants and bars seem far away. Cuckoos make their inimitable cry, woodpeckers hammer frenetically on tree trunks and the stream burbles along its course.

The first building you see is the **temple museum** (🕐*open Wed–Mon 9am–5pm (summer 6pm), ₩2,000*), renowned for its superb collection of Buddhist art, including a magnificent *tanka*—a giant portrait of the Buddha, dated to 1792. Walking farther into the temple complex reveals its compactness, with some of its dense group of buildings freshly painted and others looking a bit more worn. Like many Korean temples, Tong-dosa has had its share of troubles, suffering damage during foreign invasion and from fire. However, it is said that its **Beopdeung** (temple candle) has never gone out.

The complex was **founded in 646** as a shrine to hold relics of the Buddha: a habit, a bowl, a fragment of skull and *sari*, the substance said to develop inside the body of a person who leads a pure life, which had been brought back from China by the **monk Jajang**. The absence of any statue in the **main hall** (*Daeungjeon*, 1641) is unique among Korean temples, the monks considering the relics *(kept in a pagoda outside the hall)* sufficient for worship.

🚶In order to reach the temple entrance, you will have to pass through the small town of **Sinpyeong**, with its motels, pocket-sized market and narrow streets. The pleasant town center becomes quite lively at night, as you will discover if you decide to spend the night here.

The facilities are all concentrated around the new bus terminal (at the junction of Sonpyeong-ro and Tongdo-ro), where a small supermarket and several cafés are located.

The **Nature Tourist Hotel** near the site entrance has functional rooms *(618- 2 Sunji-ri, ☎(055)-381-8180, 45rm, up to ₩70,000)*. If you are eating out, try the **Tongdo Do** restaurant *(77 Tongdo-ro, ☎(055)-382-7070, 🕐open 10am–10pm)*, an unpretentious place just before the toll booths with an open kitchen preparing classic Korean dishes at reasonable prices.

ADDRESSES

🛏 STAY

🛈 *Beware, prices rise at the weekend.*

NAMPO-DONG AND SEOMYEON

🛏 **Hotel Angel** 엔젤호텔 – 223-2 Bujeong-dong. Ⓜ *Seomyeon, lines 1/2, follow Judies Taewha exit.* ☎*(051)-802-8223. www.angelhotel. co.kr. 45rm. ₩44,000/60,000.* If you like being in the thick of the action (bars, restaurants and stores), this is the place for you. Once past the rather incongruous facade and the fake "Olde English" lobby, you will find some nice small rooms.

🛏🍴 **Tower Hotel** 타워호텔 – 20-3-ga, Donggwang-dong. Ⓜ *Nampo-dong, line 1. ☎(051)-243-1005. 75rm. From ₩60,000.* Good if you are on a tight budget. The rooms are modest, but the standard of comfort is acceptable, and the welcome is agreeable in this green building near Yongdusan Park.

🛏🛏 **Toyoko Inn Busan Station** 토요코인호텔 – 2-1 Gwangjang. Ⓜ *Busan Station, line 1. ☎(051)-466-1045. www.toyoko-inn.com. 250rm. ₩55,000/75,000.* An extremely good value hotel owned by a Japanese chain and located right next to the station. The price includes breakfast, laundry, internet access and the efficient service. There is a sister hotel in Seomyeon: **Toyoko Inn Seomyeon**, 666-8 Jeonpo-dong. Ⓜ *Seomyeon, lines 1/2, exit 8, then straight on for 550yd/500m. ☎(051)-638-1045. ₩63,000/73,000.*

🛏🛏🛏🛏 **Lotte Hotel** 롯데호텔 – 503-15 Bujeodong. Ⓜ *Seomyeon, lines 1/2, exit 7. ☎(052)-810-1000. www.lottehotel busan.com. 760rm. ₩320,000.* Eleven restaurants, a fitness studio, spa, swimming pool, casino and, of course, rooms with fine views from the hotel's tall towers.

HAEUNDAE

🛏 **Motels** – There are plenty of choices between the station and Haeundae Beach, with very reasonable prices during the week.

☺ **Arpina Youth Hostel** 아르피나 유스호스텔 – *45 Haeundae Haebyeon-no.* Ⓜ *Busan Museum of Modern Art, line 2, exit 3.* ☎(051)-731-9800. *www.arpina.co.kr. 103rm. ₩29,000 for a dormitory bed, also rooms and studios.* A very good youth hostel located near the marina.

☺☺ **Sunset Hotel** 선셋 호텔 – *1391-66 Jung-dong, Haeundae-gu.* Ⓜ *Haeundae, line 2, exit 5.* ☎(051)-730-9900. *www.sunsethotel.co.kr. 72rm. ₩77,000–99,000. Set back from the beach, reception on the 9th floor.* The recently refurbished modern rooms are tastefully decorated, and the staff is obliging.

☺☺☺☺ **Novotel** 노보텔 – *1405-16 Chung-dong.* Ⓜ *Haeundae, line 2, exit 3.* ☎ (051)-743-1234. *www.novotelbusan.com. 325rm. ₩190,000.* A good level of comfort and a superb view of the beach—if you are on the right side of the hotel.

☺☺☺☺ **Westin Chosun** 웨스틴 조선 호텔 – *737 Woo 1-dong.* Ⓜ *Dongbaek, line 2, exit 3.* ☎(051)-749-7000. *www.westin.com/busan. 290rm. ₩200,000.* Situated at the western end of Haeundae Beach with the hills of Dongbaek spread out to the rear. The lobby has wood and leather decor and modern frescos, and the rooms are tasteful. A haunt of presidents and visitors from overseas, this is the best there is in Busan.

DONGNAE

☺☺☺☺ **Hotel Nongshim** 농심호텔 – *137-7 Onchun-dong, Dongnae-gu.* Ⓜ *Oncheonjang, line 1, exit 1.* ☎(051)-550-2100. *www.hotel nongshim.com. 242rm. ₩230,000 at weekends.* A comfortable hotel in the heart of Dongnae-gu's *Spa City.* Pleasant rooms and old-school service with direct access to the spa.

♀/EAT

NAMPO-DONG
Around BIFF Square you will find an endless supply of restaurants that are open 24hr, as well as a number of *pojangmacha.*

☺☺ **Nampo Samgyetang** 남포 삼계탕 – *BIFF Square.* ☎(051)-245-5075. *Open 9am–11pm.* The muted interior makes a change from the neon lights in the street. Nampo Samgyetang has been serving its famous *samgyetang (chicken soup with gingseng,* ₩12,000) since 1962.

☺☺ **Seoul Kakdugi** 서울깍두기 – *Nampo-dong.* ☎(051)-245-3950. *Open 8am–10pm.* Hundreds of diners of all ages pass through this large canteen on a daily basis, fortifying themselves with a portion of *seolleongtang* (milky beef and rice soup for ₩7,500).

☺☺☺ **Myeongseong Chobap** 명성초밥 – *Donggwang-dong.* ☎(051)-246-1225. *Open noon–9pm. ₩12,000/60,000.* A simple storefront on a quiet street, with a "sushi" signboard outside. An excellent sushi restaurant with table or counter service.

JAGALCHI MARKET
☺ **Chung Mu** 충무 – *Sindong.* ☎(051)-246-8563. *Open 10am–10pm.* Rustic decor and a down-to-earth atmosphere. Their seafood is excellent.

☺☺☺☺ **Oase** 오아제 뷔페 – *Jalgachi Market (5th floor).* ☎(051)-248-7777. *www.oasebusan.co.kr. Open noon–3pm, 6pm–11pm (Sat–Sun all day).* A luxury version of a seafood buffet, with fashionable decor and a view of the port.

SEOMYEON
☺☺ **Lotte Deparment Store** 롯데백화점 – *503-15 Bujeon-dong.* Ⓜ *Seomyeon, line 1, exit 2.* ☎(051)-810-2500. The assorted fast-food counters on the first basement floor (including sweet and savory, Korean, Japanese, Turkish), or the restaurants on the ninth floor, provide a number of easy dining options, including **The Hôme** (☎(051)-810-3963), serving omelets of every kind, and **Sumisan** (☎(051)-810-3927), specializing in octopus with every imaginable sauce.

☺☺ **Shintobuli** 신토불이 – *Bujeon 2-dong.* ☎(051)-817-8877. *Open 10am–11pm. ₩7,000–25,000.* The decor is pleasant (flagstones, wood, tiles) and they serve steamed pork specialties (*bossam*).

Haeundae and Gwangan – There are plenty of seafood eateries to explore around the markets at **Mipo** (Haeundae) and **Millak** (Gwangan). *See p306.*

🍲 **Tebuhang** 테부항 – *Mipo, Haeundae. Open 24 hr. From ₩6,000–8,000.* People stand in line here from early morning for the excellent fish soup with all the trimmings.

🍲🍶🍽 **Dongnae-gu** – There are plenty of Japanese restaurants around the Spa City area, subway Oncheonjan. *See p306).*

🍲🍶🍽 **Dongnae Halmae Pajeon** 동래할매파전 – *367-2 Bokcheon-dong.* Ⓜ *Dongnae, line 1, exit 2.* ℘*(051)-552-0791. www.dongraehalmaepajun.co.kr. Open noon–10pm, closed every other Mon.* Where *pajeon* becomes an art form. The seafood and green onion pancake (*₩20,000*) is served in a setting that is traditional with a modern flare.

🍲🍶🍽 **Yeyije** 예이제한정식 – *Pale de CZ (2nd floor), 1124-2 Jung-dong.* ℘*(051)-746-9933. Open noon–11pm. From ₩7,000/25,000.* Beautiful panelled rooms with private areas in which to try a fine choice of Korean dishes washed down with local brews. The lunch menu is a good deal.

🍲🍶🍽🍽 **Dongnae Byeljang** 동래별장 – *Oncheon-dong.* ℘*(051)-552-0157. Open noon–3pm, 6pm–10pm.* Housed in a 1940s building set among trees, this Korean restaurant is famed for dishes whose visual appeal is rivalled only by their tastiness.

🍷 BARS

The café terraces of Haeundae and Gwangalli are not short of custom; for a more peaceful and "artsy" atmosphere, try the **Dalmaji district** (*p304*). With the presence of sailors from the port and a large student population, Busan nights tend to be lively. The bars and clubs are concentrated at **Seomyeon** (mega-clubs), **Haeundae** (upmarket and cosmopolitan) and around the **universities** (Ⓜ *Kyungsung-Pukyong;* students).

🎭 ENTERTAINMENT

CINEMAS
The movie theaters on BIFF Square and in the malls show all the latest blockbusters.

MUSIC
Busan Cultural Center 부산시시민회관 – *(848-4 Daeyeon 4-dong Nam-gu.* ℘*(051)-625-8130,* Ⓜ *Daeyeon, exit 3).* Busan Philharmonic Orchestra's home base. Concert and events listings at *http://culture.busan.go.kr/english/main.*

🛍 SHOPPING

Between Gukje Market and the various shopping areas, there is ample opportunity to shop for Busan's **star buys**: clothes, leather goods and jewelry.

🎭 EVENTS AND FESTIVALS

Busan International Film Festival – Held in October, around Haeundae and BIFF Square (*www.biff.kr*).

Busan International Rock Festival – Held in August, a free music festival on Dadaepo Beach. *www.rockfestival.co.kr*

Gwangalli Eobang Festival and Haeundae Sand Festival – held in June (*http://festival-eobang.suyeong.go.kr/eng/index.asp and http://sandfestival.haeundae.go.kr).*

Jagalchi Festival – A large seafood festival held in October at the fish market and in the surrounding area: prize-giving, competitions, tastings, etc. (*www.ijagalchi.co.kr*).

🔎 *For complete festival listings: http://etour.busan.go.kr/index.jsp.*

Jinju and Hallyeo Maritime National Park★★

진주 and
한려 해상국립공원

The city of Jinju, known for its bullfighting (home of the National Bullfighting Contest) and silk manufacture (famed for its softness and vibrant colors), is the gateway to a region of enormous variety. After making a circuit of Jinju Castle's walls, visit the beautiful Ssanggye Temple, set in a lush forest and surrounded by tea plantations. Venture farther afield and set off to discover the islands and islets of the southern coast by boat and by car. Lovely coastal roads wind their way around bays and between hills, passing charming fishing villages where the rhythm of life is determined by the tides, and the sparsely populated, unspoiled islands will show you another— rather different—Korea from that of the great, bustling cities and wide, fertile plains.

VISIT

The city center fans out from the base of the fortress on the northern bank of the broad **Nam River**. The heart of the city offers an abundance of motels, stores, restaurants and the main market.

Jinjuseong★ 진주성

Bonseong-dong, Namseong-dong. www.jinju.go.kr. Open 9am–6pm (Sat 7pm). ₩1,000. starting at ₩1,000
Jinju Castle (fortress) has stood, perched on its fortified hill, since 1379. In 1592 and 1593 it was the site of three great and bloody battles against the Japanese, which resulted in its virtual destruction. Another event took place here that is well known to every Korean child: the story of **Nongae**, a *gisaeng* (courtesan) who, when summoned to a banquet with the Japanese invaders, threw herself from the cliff above the Nam River,

▶ **Population:** 432,903
◔ **Michelin Map:** Regional map pp 264–265
ℹ **Info:** Tourist offices at the entrance to Jinju Castle, ℘(055)-749-2055, www.jinju.go.kr, open 9am–6pm; Tongyeong, various offices, including at the city entrance; Chungmu Bridge and the pleasure boat terminal, ℘(055)-650-4681; Namhaedo, ℘(055)-863-4025 (1588-3415), S of Namhae Bridge, 9am-6pm
▶ **Location:** Jinju is located 53mi/85km west of Busan; Jirisan National Park and Hallyeo Maritime National Park are an additional 37-43mi/60-70km away— Tongyeong is the most practical option from which to explore both of these.
👥 **Kids:** A boat trip to the islands of Hallyeo Maritime National Park, the cable car ride to the top of Mireuksan.
🕐 **Timing:** To see the coastal roads at their best, avoid the weekends, when they are clogged with traffic.
👀 **Don't Miss:** The coastal roads of Namhaedo and Geojedo, the beautiful Ssanggyesa, trying Jinju eels and Tongyeong *chungmu gimbap*.

taking a senior Japanese general with her. The pavilion near where this took place, **Chokseongnu**, has been adopted as Jinju's emblem.
Built in 1241, the fortress was used as a military headquarters in times of war, and as a place of rest and study in times of peace. Re-enactments of the battles

311

Chokseongnu pavilion, Jinjuseong

©Chris Stowers/Apa Publications

that raged on this very spot are held at weekends near the two main gates of the fortress (*Chokseokmun to the east and Gongbungmun to the north*). The cliff area is now a peaceful green oasis in the middle of the city. People come here to sit on the grass and enjoy the sunset or just to watch the river flow by below them. To the west of the castle grounds, a modern building houses Jinju National Museum.

GETTING THERE

BY PLANE – **Sacheon Airport** is located 12mi/20km to the west of Jinju (*bus transfer, 30min, www.airport. co.kr/doc/sacheon_eng/index.jsp, ₩1,600*). There are flights from here to Seoul-Gimpo and Jeju-do.

BY BUS – **Jinju Cross-Country (Intercity) Bus Terminal** (℘(055)-741-6039) in the center of the city, **north of the Nam River.** From here there are bus connections to Busan (*1hr30min, ₩8,500*), Namhae (*1hr30min, ₩5,200*), Tongyeong (*1hr30min, ₩6,500*) and Ssanggyesa (*1hr30min, ₩6,600*). The **Jinju Express Bus Terminal** (℘(055)-758-3111/752-1001) is south of the river, near the train station.

BY TRAIN – **Jinju Station**, south of the Nam River, (℘(055)-752-7788). Trains leave for Seoul (*7hr*), Busan (*2hr50min*), Mokpo (*4hr30min*).

GETTING AROUND

BY ROAD – Buses from the towns of Namhae, Geoje and Tongyeong serve large towns, and there are connections from Tongyeong to Busan. Although there are bus connections from Namhae to Sanju and Mijo, renting a car is the best option if you want to make the most of the coastal roads.

BY BOAT – Aside from pleasure cruises (℘*see Sports and Activities in addresses*), there are ferry connections from Tongyeong port (℘(055)-641-6181) at the northern end of the bay to many of the islands.

USEFUL INFORMATION

Most of the services at Jinju (post office, police, banks) are clustered around the Jungang-no traffic circle.

Jinju National Museum★
진주 국립박물관

169-14 Namseong-dong. ℘(055)-742-5951. http://jinju.museum.go.kr/html/en. ⏱Open Tue–Sun 9am–6pm (Sat and holidays –7pm; Apr–Oct: Sat –9pm). No charge.

A comprehensive exhibition deals with the **Imjin War** (the Japanese invasion of 1592), telling the story with engravings, maps, dioramas and weaponry, as well as a number of different objects taken from nearby temples, including bronzes from the Goryeo period (13C), white porcelain from the Joseon period and a variety of objects from the Gaya Confederacy (42–532).

A row of restaurants leading down to the river near the main bridge serves various dishes involving eel—a Jinju specialty—and *bibimbap*. **Jungang-no**, the road that leads off into the city from the bridge, cuts the **city center** in two, with the "young" district and its fashion stores and fast food to the west, and the lively district of the **covered market** (in fact, somewhat open to the elements) to the east. The clientele on the eastern side may be a bit older but is no less dynamic—toward the end of the day, you will often see women dancing in the streets to the strains of dance mixes of traditional music. People from both sides of the city congregate around food stands that appeal to all generations. The far banks of the Nam River have been laid out as a long promenade.

EXCURSION
Ssanggyesa★ 쌍계사

♿ *See Gyeongsang-do Map 47mi/ 75km W of Jinju. By car: Rte 10 (turn off at exit 17, Hadong) or Rte 2 toward Hadong. Then Rtes 19 and 1023 following signs for "Ssanggyesa." By bus: several direct bus connections from Jinju (1hr30min, ₩7,000). Otherwise, take bus toward Hadong (1hr30min, ₩4,500) then one of the frequent connections to the temple. ⏱Open dawn–dusk. ₩2,500. Signs in English. 🅿 ₩2,000–4,000 ♿ See also Jirisan National Park, p330.*

The road follows first the Seomjin River, then a stream whose banks gradually disappear beneath a succession of **green tea plantations**. The vast swathes of tea bushes soften the relief of the terrain, creating a more regular landscape. Before visiting the temple, you might stop off at the **Green Tea Culture Center**, a building topped with a giant bowl, where you can sample and buy the local produce. **Ssanggyesa** (originally named Okchenosa) was

Ssanggyesa

©KTO

founded in 722 and acquired its present name, meaning "Twin Streams," in the 9C, although some of the current buildings date back only to the 17C.

Of interest more for its setting than its history, the temple is spread out over a number of terraces among flowers (magnolias and camellias), trees (Japanese cedars) and bamboo. After a flight of steps, the temple compound is entered through three gates. A high, nine-tier pagoda towers over the main courtyard.

The **reading room** (Pallyeong-ru) with its characteristic Silla features (840) is where the priest **Master Jingam** (774–850) created the Korean-style Buddhist music and dance (Beompae). He was influenced not by the ji-ji bae-bae ("tweet-tweet") of the countless birds in the area, but by fish swimming in a nearby stream, which inspired him to compose Eosan ("Fish Mountain").

From the highest point of the temple, there is a path leading to Guksaam Hermitage (1,640ft/500m) and the pretty waterfall **Buril Pokpo** (1.5mi/2.3km).

🚗 DRIVING TOUR

HALLYEO MARITIME NATIONAL PARK AND SURROUNDING AREA

See Gyeongsang-do map.

👥 Hallyeo Maritime National Park

This park lies on the southern coast of the Korean Peninsula, extending from the outskirts of Busan in the east to Yeosu in the west and taking in **400 or so islands and islets**. The park can be reached by road or sea. Boats depart from Yeosu and the larger islands **Namhaedo** or **Geojedo**. The round-trips generally head west–east, unless you leave from Busan. If you don't have the time for an entire round-trip, you can explore just one of the two large islands featured here.

Namhae★★ 남해

See Gyeongsang-do map.

This is the third-largest island in the country, and South Korea's "Treasure Island," with a population of 51,000. As soon as you cross **Namhae Bridge,** it is as though you have been transported to another world in another time. The island's cliffs plunge abruptly into the sea, and its valleys and hillsides are full of the scent of the **wild garlic** that grows everywhere, mixed with the smell of sea air. You'll find no shortage of picture-perfect panoramas of paddy fields, fishing villages and the sea, of course, where supertankers and smaller boats zigzag between the islands. Most of the roads are quiet, and you will pass women carrying bundles of garlic on their heads, laying them out to dry or perhaps selling them on the sidewalk.

Two miles (three kilometers) beyond Namhae Bridge along Route 19 is the **Admiral Yi Sun-sin Monument** (*see box p 336)*, a memorial to the admiral who died at this very spot in November 1598 when he was hit by a stray bullet. A modern building with a curved roof reminiscent of his famous turtle boats houses an exhibition and a film recounting the story of his naval battles (Yi Sun-sin Movie Theater, 4–6 showings daily, ₩3,000). Namhae Tourist Office (open 9am–6pm) is located behind the car park.

There isn't a great deal to see in the town of **Namhae** (*see Gyeongsang-do Map*) beyond its rather dour central market smelling strongly of garlic. A few minutes farther down Route 19 you will find the **Garlic Museum** (open Tue–Sun 9am–6pm, no charge), dedicated to the essential ingredient for making kimchi.

▷ *To return to the coast from town, take a right toward Seo-Myeon, then turn left after 3mi/5km toward Nam-Myeon.*

This is the beginning of the **coast road★★** that winds to the southernmost point of the island (take Rte 1024 toward Sachon). As you pass Sachon

Beach, the green slopes of the mountains above it seem to plunge down into the sea. Soon a panoramic view of the gardens and blue-painted roofs of **Darangyi**★★ open up, beneath tiers of terraced paddy fields.

◗ *Take Rte 19 toward Sanju.*

The **eastern side of the island** is more rugged, with unspoiled forests. Look out for **Geumsan** ("Silk Mountain," 2,234ft/681m) among the rather worn-looking rocky peaks emerging from the vegetation. As you climb higher, you approach **Boriam,** where King Taejo prayed for 100 days. The panoramic view from the temple site down to the sea is simply unforgettable and many people come here just to watch the sunrise. Return to sea level to see the beautiful white sand at **Sangju Beach**, hidden behind pine trees and lined with restaurants and motels.
Or, when hunger strikes, you may prefer to choose from the restaurants strung along the quay of the small port of **Mijo**.

◗ *Follow the eastern coast along Rte 3 toward Changseon.*

You will find more fantastic views along the way, this time a succession of sweeping vistas of the islands and, in the narrow Jijok Strait, just before the bridge, Jukbangryeom, a reconstruction of an ancient fixed-net fishing site made of oak pillars (33ft/10m) driven into the seabed.

◗ *Go straight on at Changseon or continue your coastal journey along Route 1024 to the left after the bridge. For Tongyeong, take routes 77 and 1010, an attractive drive that follows the coast.*

Many dinosaur fossils have been found near here and a themed museum is dedicated to these vanished giants: **Goseong Dinosaur Museum**, beside a dinosaur footprint fossil site (*see Gyeongsang-do Map,* ☏*(055)-832-9021,* ⏱ *open 9am–5pm,* ₩*5,000).*

Tongyeong★ 통영
♿ *See Gyeongsang-do map.*
With a population of 135,000, Admiral Yi Sun-sin's old base is now a charming and lively port city, catering to both the fishing and tourist industries, and has a ferry terminal and a shipyard to boot. If you are pushed for time, head directly for **Gangguan**, the busy port area with its atmospheric restaurants, fishing vessels and reconstructed turtle boat.
This is also where you will find **Jungang Live Fish Market**★. Very much a work-

Tongyeong ©KNTO

ing market, animated discussions take place among the onlookers as sharp knives slice the fish expertly amid the aroma of frying fish. Sample the *chungmu gimbap*—seaweed rolls stuffed with rice and served with pickled radishes and spicy but sweet strips of squid.

Not far from here is **Sebyeonggwan**, a pavilion that is said to be the oldest and most beautiful wooden structure to survive from the Joseon period (1605), with rows of columns supporting its ornate roof. It was used as the general headquarters for the military fleet.

▶ *The trip around Mireukdo, the island to the south of Tongyeong, begins as you cross Chungmu Bridge, followed by an immediate left turn.*

A road opposite the pleasure boat port (follow signs to Ropeway Station) leads to the **cable car** station (ⓞ *open 9:30am–5pm (summer 6pm), ₩9,000).* You can take a cable car from here to the top of **Mireuksan** and take in the **panoramic view** of Hallyeo Maritime National Park.

Back at sea level, the coastal road Route 1021 heads around the island, past fishing villages with boats constantly chug-ging in and out of their small harbors. To discover more facts about fishing, follow the signs to the interesting **Fisheries Science Museum** (℘ *(055)-646-5704,* ⓞ *open Tue–Sun 9am–5pm, ₩1,500).* Housed in a large concrete blockhouse perched on top of a hill, it commands yet another magnificent **panoramic view★** of part of the national park.

A number of the islands in the national park are accessible from Tongyeong's port (♿ *see Getting There, and Sports and Activities in Addresses).* If you have time to spare, of the many things to see these are recommended: the rock formations at Deungdaeseom; the beach at Bijindo (Bijin Island); Saryangdo (comprising several islets rather than just one island); Hansando, the scene of Yi Sun-sin's naval triumph; or Yeonhwado, without doubt the most beautiful and isolated of the islands and a paradise for walkers.

▶ *For a quick route to Geojedo, take Exprwy 14 (toward Geoje). After 7mi/12km, turn right just before the large bridge onto Rte 1018 (toward Dondeok), to reach Geojedo by the "back door."*

Haegeumgang

©KTO

Geojedo★★ (Geoje Island)
거제도

See Gyeongsang-do map.

After the urban city blocks of Tongyeong, **Route 1018★★** follows the south coast of South Korea's second-largest island, skirting cliffs that drop sharply into the sea as it passes bay after bay. The road carries on through a succession of sleepy fishing villages amid rural scenery, with the view changing constantly at the whim of the tides and time, from bays lapped by calm water to stretches of glistening rock and sand among which people search for crustaceans and mollusks. The changeable weather adds its own variations, alternating between mist and bright sunlight. The fish farms visible off the coast look like floating cities.

Bridge linking Geojedo and Busan
©Sehee Kim/Michelin

▶ *At Seoyang, take Rte 14 toward Haegeumgang/Myeongsa.*

Enjoy views of the inland areas and especially the sweeping panorama of **Yulpoman** (Yulpo Bay), before rejoining Route 1018.

Haegeumgang★ is a tourist magnet, famed for its rugged coast and its creeks of clear water, lined with centuries-old pine trees, although parts of this rocky island have been somewhat marred by the tourist infrastructure. Since it is best seen from the sea, boat tours are run during holidays and busy periods *(departing either from Hakdong or Tongyeong)*. Alternatively, if there are no trips available, you can see it from the viewing platform.

A little farther on, at the bottom of steep mountain slopes, is the pebbly expanse of **Hakdong Beach**, bordered by a line of seafood restaurants that are highly recommended. Hakdong is followed by the sinuous sandy curves of the beaches at Gujora and Wahyeon, where the large Hotel C Palace marks the beginning of town. Offshore, **Oe Island (Oedo) Marine Botanical Garden** *(www.oedobotania.com,* ◷ *open 8am–5pm,* ₩*8,000),* with its 740 plant species, is a big draw for Koreans. Crowds flock here in April when the azaleas are in bloom.

The garden is accessible from Hakdong or Haegeumgang *(3hr return journey,* ₩*17,000, admission included).*

The bay at **Jisepo** is dominated by two buildings that are hard to miss: the **Fishing Village Folk Museum** and the **Shipbuilding Marine Museum** *(* ☏ *(055)-639-3410,* ◷ *open 9am–5pm,* ₩*3,000 admission to both sites).*

Both house well-presented exhibitions *(although with little information in English)* about the island's two principal industries: fishing and shipbuilding.

Follow the road round to the north to reach the port of **Jangseugpo**. Once past the enormous Geoje Art Center (complete with its own hotel), the road passes between two hills, and you are suddenly confronted with the giant gantries of the DSME shipyard where supertankers are assembled. Farther on, at **Geohyeon** (Geoje), there is a terminal belonging to Samsung. The island's principal town is also known for being the location of one of the largest POW camps to be built during the Korean War.

⊙ The **new bridge** linking the island directly to Busan opened in December 2010 and provides a direct route between Tongyeong and South Korea's second city in an hour.

ADDRESSES

🛏 STAY

JINJU

🖥 **Motel Movie 37°2 무비모텔** –
*Behind Bonsongno Hospital, turn left
out of the bus terminal. ☎(055)-743-
4114. 35rm. ₩50,000.* A very
comfortable motel.

🖥🛏🍴 **Dong Bang 동방호텔** –
*Okbong-dong. ☎(055)-743-0131.
www.hoteldongbang.com. 100rm.
₩130,000.* On the waterside about
a 10min walk east of the castle, the
most comfortable option in town has
disappointingly average rooms, but
the car park, friendly service and lovely
views go some way toward making
up for this.

NAMHAE

There are plenty of **motels** around
Sachon, Sanju and Mijo; the tourist
office has a list of accommodations.

🖥🛏🍴 **Hilton Namhae남해
힐튼호텔** – *Nam Deokwol. ☎(055)-
860-0100. www.hiltonnamhae.com.
170rm. ₩200,000.* Studios and villas
with balconies, on a hill surrounded by
an 18-hole championship golf course.
Luxurious rooms with sea views.

TONGYEONG AND GEOJE

🖥🛏 **Hansan 한산호텔** – *Hangnam-
dong, Tongyeong. ☎(055)-642-3384.
40rm. ₩45,000/90,000, depending on
the season.* The refurbished rooms of
this hotel (near the ferry terminals and
the port) are simple, but very clean and
well equipped. The welcome is friendly.
There are plenty of B&Bs around
Haegeumgang, Hakdong and Gujora
Beach—choose from the latter two
locations out of preference.

🖥🛏🍴 **Hotel C Palace 팰리스 C 호텔**
– *Wahyeon-ri. ☎(055)-730-1000. 170rm.
₩220,000/250,000.* Opened in 2009,
this hotel looks out over Wahyeon Bay.
The rooms are luxurious and tastefully
decorated. There are also restaurants
and a spa.

🍽 EAT

JINJU

The **eel** restaurants, including **Youjung
Jangeo** *(25-1 Nongae-gil, ☎(055)-
746-9235, open 10am–11pm)*, are
concentrated around Jinju Castle and
the bridge. The diners and eateries of
the market, where you can sample the
local *bibimbap*, are good if you are in a
hurry or on a tight budget. If you can't
stand the thought of any more kimchi,
try the elaborate omelets at **Omu Sweet**
*(15-1 Jinnyngho-ro, ☎(055)-742-5995,
open 11am–10:30pm, ₩9,000)*.

TONGYEONG AND THE ISLANDS

🖥 **Ddungbo Halmae Gimbap
뚱보할매김밥** – *Gangguan,
Tongyeong. ☎(055)-645-2619. Open
7am–2am. ₩4,000.* A sign depicting a
venerable Korean grandmother draws
tourists and locals to this famous diner
serving spicy and nourishing *chungmu
gimbap*. If you like seafood, try the port
restaurants at Mijo and Hakdong.

🏃 SPORTS AND ACTIVITIES

The **pleasure boat** terminal at
Tongyeong *(☎(055)-645-2307)* is
located at the south end of the bay.
To see the islands from the sea, such
as Haegeumgang, Maemuldo or
Jeseungdang on Hansando, a round-
trip takes anywhere from 1hr 30min to
4hr *(₩9,000/25,000)*. On **Namhae** boats
departing from Sangju and Mijohang
Port head for the beautiful rock
formations at the southeastern end
of the island *(₩12,000)*.

📅 EVENTS AND FESTIVALS

Hadong Wild Tea Cultural Festival –
Held at the end of May; tea picking,
tastings and other events *(☎(055)-
880-2375)*.

Hansan Daecheop Festival – Held in
August and celebrating **Yi Sun-sin's
victory** over the Japanese in the 16C,
with a re-enactment of the naval battle
in Tongyeong port.

Namgang Yudeung Festival –
Huge lanterns are set afloat on the Nam
River at Jinju. The main **bullfighting**
tournament takes place during the
same month, October.

Head to South Korea's southernmost region for scenic wonders, landscapes so picturesque they seem cut from a silk scroll and rural life that hasn't changed in centuries. Gourmands will want to visit the birthplace of *bibimbap*—one of the few Korean foods to gain fame outside the country.

South Sea

Until 1946, the island of Jeju was part of the Jeolla kingdom, but now these two are separated both geographically and politically. However, the southern coast of Jeolla, a province known as Jeollanam, holds one of the peninsula's best-kept secrets: the 10,000 Isles, a vast area peppered with islands just offshore. In Mokpo, a quiet city on the southwest coast, several hill hikes give glimpses of beautiful shoals if the weather isn't foggy. Another option, especially for those planning to keep going to Jeju, is a ferry ride, which offers spectacular views of the many, often mist-shrouded islands. Some are tiny, mere pincushions sticking out of the sea. Others are large enough to support small fishing and industrial communities.

Seafood is abundant, fresh and tasty here along the coast. Try the popular *haemul guksu* (seafood soup), a seafood pancake with fish, shrimp, or squid, or order fresh grouper cooked whole. To the north in the province is Jeonju, the birthplace of *bibimbap*—a mix of rice, vegetables and spicy hot sauce that is often served in a steel bowl or a sizzling stone pot. This extremely popular dish has spread throughout Korea, but many

Highlights

1 Visit the **Damyang Bamboo Crafts Museum** (p328)

2 View the 10,000 Isles on a ferry trip to **Jeju** (p335)

3 Sample great seafood in quaint **Mokpo** (p337)

4 Travel through traditional Korea in **Hanok Village** (p351)

5 Delight in a bowl of Jeonju-style **bibimbap** (p357)

restaurants pride themselves on making *bibimbap* in "Jeonju-style." A trip to this region wouldn't be the same without a sample. Try washing it down with a cup of the area's pine-tree wine if traditional *soju* gets humdrum.

Other reasons to earmark trip time for this part of the country include Buddhist temples that haven't changed in centuries, exquisite national parks and hiking trails, and even—despite the southern clime—skiing in the winter. The high-speed KTX line makes Mokpo, which is the region's southernmost tip, only a six-hour sojourn from Seoul.

Gochang Dolmen Park

©KTO

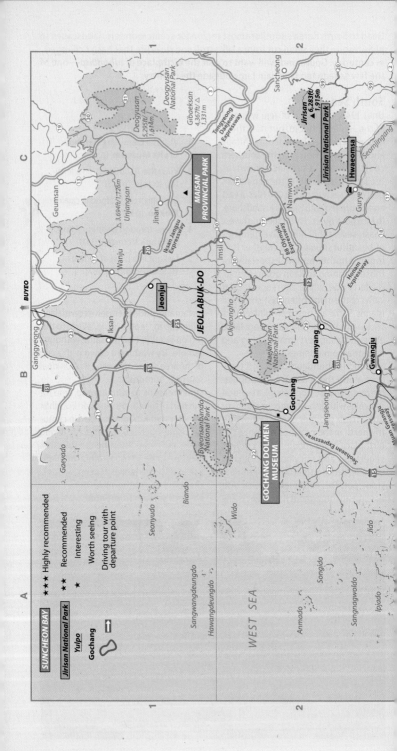

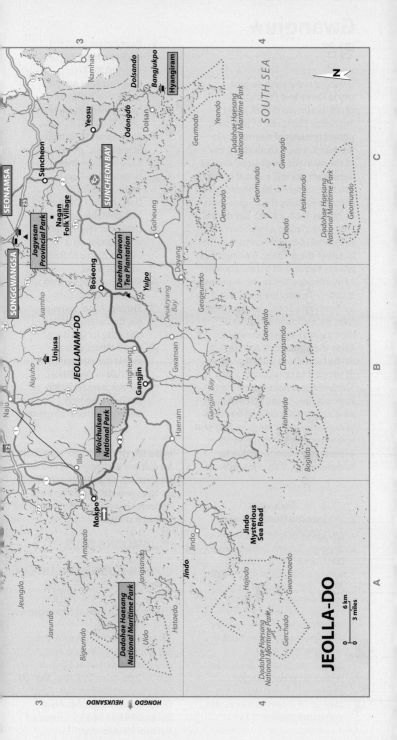

JEOLLA-DO

SOUTH SEA

SUNCHEON BAY

SEONAMSA

SONGGWANGSA

Jogyesan
Provincial Park

Nagan
Folk Village

Daehan Dawon
Tea Plantation

Wolchulsan
National Park

Dadohae Haesang
National Maritime Park

Dadohae Haesang
National Maritime Park

Dadohae Haesang
National Maritime Park

Jindo
Mysterious
Sea Road

Bangjukpo

Hyangiram

Namhae
Suncheon
Yeosu
Odongdo
Dolsando
Dolsan
Boseong
Goheung
Doyang
Yulpo
Unjusa
JEOLLANAM-DO
Juamho
Jangheung
Gwansan
Haenam
Gangjin
Naju
Illo
Mokpo
Amtaedo
Najuho
Jindo
Jindo
Jeungdo
Jaeundo
Bigeumdo
Uido
Hataedo
Jangsando
Hajodo
Gerchado
Gwanmaedo
Bogildo
Nohwado
Cheongsando
Saengildo
Geogeumdo
Deukryang
Bay
Gangjin Bay
Geomundo
Jeokmando
Chodo
Gwangdo
Geomundo
Oenarodo
Yeonado
Geumodo

Geomundo

HONGDO ▓ HEUKSANDO

0 ___ 6 km
0 ___ 3 miles

N

Gwangju★
광주

Gwangju is the sixth-largest city in Korea and the capital of Jeollanam-do (South Jeolla Province). The is one of the most potent symbols of democracy in modern Korea. A stroll along any of the main thoroughfares, such as Geumnam-no, will inevitably bring you face-to-face with a monument commemorating the tragic events of 18 May 1980, a black day during which the civilian population was subjected to brutal reprisals at the hands of the military. Gwangju has always had an anti-establishment bent, perhaps due to the deprivation it suffered under the centralized authorities in Seoul, and its citizens have no wish to brush difficult, dark periods under the carpet. Quite the opposite is true, in fact, as the locals have used the scars of the past to pursue new paths. The Gwangju contemporary arts biennale, one of the first in Asia, is now a powerful cradle of freedom of expression that is expanding year upon year; the immense National Asian Culture Complex, due for completion in 2012, is intended to

- ▶ **Population:** 1,439,031
- **Michelin Map:** Regional map pp320–321
- **Info:** Gwangju Airport, ℘(062)-942-6160; in Gwangcheon Bus Terminal, ℘(062)-360-8733, open 9am–6pm; at Gwangju Station (rail), ℘(062)-522-5147; ⓜ subway Geumnamno 5-ga, ℘(062)-233-9370. Don't forget 1330, the indispensable hotline.
- **Location:** The capital of Jeollanam-do is located 205mi/330km south of Seoul.
- **Kids:** Gochang Dolmen Museum and its park.
- **Timing:** Allow a whole day for Gwangju and half a day for Gochang.
- **Don't Miss:** Cultural events during Gwangju Biennale in September, the poignant May 18th National Cemetery, Gwangju National Museum.

make the city Asia's new crossroads for cultural exchange and mutual understanding. With its gaze fixed on an ever-widening democratic horizon, Gwangju is rebuilding itself stone by stone.

WALKING TOUR

BUK-GU MUSEUM QUARTER★
See Gwangju map.

Gwangju National Museum★★
광주국립박물관
114 Bakmulgwan-ro, Maegok-dong, Buk-gu. ℘(062)-570-7000. http://gwangju.museum.go.kr. Open Tue–Fri 9am–6pm; Saturdays Mar–Dec 9pm; (Sun and holidays 9am–7pm). Closed Mon and 1 Jan. No charge. Bus no. 29/48/63/84/85/95, Gwangju National Museum stop.

Gwangju International Center

509 Jeon-il Bldg F5, Geumnam-no, Dong-gu. Subway Culture Complex, line 1, exit 1. ℘(062)-226-2733. www.gic.or.kr. Open Mon–Sat 10am–6pm. A useful place to pick up the *Gwangju News*, a daily newspaper written by English-speaking expats that has its finger on the pulse of the various events taking place in the city.

See also the *Gwangju Guidebook*, published by the Gwangju International Center in 2007. For more up-to-date information, visit www.gwangjuguide.or.kr.

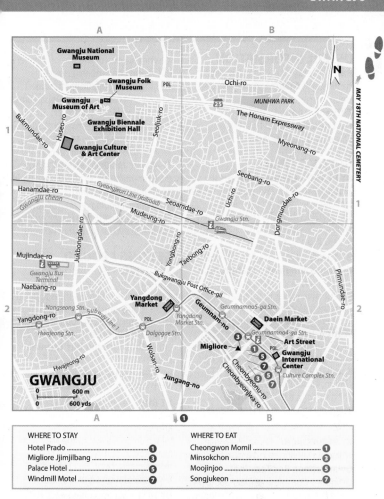

MAY 18TH NATIONAL CEMETERY

GWANGJU

0 ─────── 600 m
0 ─────── 600 yds

WHERE TO STAY		WHERE TO EAT	
Hotel Prado	1	Cheongwon Momil	1
Migliore Jjimjilbang	3	Minsokchon	3
Palace Hotel	5	Moojinjoo	5
Windmill Motel	7	Songjukeon	7

Gwangju National Museum

©KTO

USEFUL INFORMATION

Bank – Plenty of exchange service centers and **ATM** machines on Geumnam-no.
Citibank – *Jukbong-no*
Post office – Central Post Office, *Chungjang-no. Free internet access.*

GETTING THERE

BY PLANE – Gwangju Airport – ℘*(062)-940-0214.* The airport is served by Korean Air and Asiana Airlines (*see p20*), who offer dozens of daily flights to Seoul (7:30am–7:30pm) and to Jeju (8am–7:30pm).

BY TRAIN – There are two rail stations: **Gwangju Songjeong Station**, from which the KTX departs, is to the east of Gwangju and some distance from the city center *(15min by taxi, depending on traffic)*; **Gwangju Station**, for all Korail departures, is more centrally located.
There are departures to **Mokpo** by Korail *(1hr30min, ₩4,800)* or by KTX *(35min, ₩8,100)*, to Seoul *(2hr40min, 11 times daily, ₩36,000)* by KTX and to Mugunghwa by Korail *(4hr, 4 times daily, ₩21,500).*

BY BUS/COACH – This is the most efficient way of getting around town.
Gwangcheon Bus Terminal – U-Square Complex. ℘*(062)-360-8114. www.kobus.co.kr.* An excellent modern station with information displayed clearly in English and equipped with a good bookshop, a couple of great cafés and an array of computers with internet access for the use of travelers. Buses and coaches are constantly coming and going from stops all around this vast terminal. Departures for Daejeon *(6am–9pm, every 30min, 2hr30min, ₩9,300)*, Damyang *(5:50am–10:45pm, every 15min, 40min, ₩2,000)*, Jeonju *(6:05am–10:20pm, every 15–40min, 1hr20min, ₩5,800)*, Mokpo *(5:20am–midnight, every 20min, 50min, ₩4,300)* and Seoul *(almost 24/7, every 5–30min depending on time of day, 3hr30min, from ₩15,000 for the ordinary bus to ₩22,000 for the luxury version).*

GETTING AROUND

BY SUBWAY – As in most traffic-saturated large cities, the subway is a very practical means of transport, but there is only one line, with 22 stations *(5:30am–midnight, ₩1,000)*. Although it serves the airport, it does not stop at either **Gwangcheon Bus Terminal** or the rail stations (Gwangju Station and Gwangju Songjeong). *www.gwangjusubway.co.kr.*

BY BUS – More than 80 lines crisscross the city. One of the best known is no. 518, the "18 May" route, which crosses town to the May 18th National Cemetery. Bus no. 17 runs from Gwangcheon Bus Terminal to Gwangju Station *(20min, ₩900).*

BY TAXI – Minimum fare ₩3,200. Expect to pay ₩8,000 to Dong-gu district from Gwangcheon Bus Terminal.

With more than 50,000 exhibits, the museum is noted in particular for its collection of celadon porcelain from the Goryeo era (*see box p339*).
The Buddhist art that flourished during the Later Silla period has left a rich treasury of *sarira* reliquaries (*see box p397*).

▷ *Take the right-hand exit from the museum and follow the tunnel under the expressway. About 15min walk.*

Gwangju Municipal Folk Museum★
광주시립민속박물관
Yongbong-dong Buk-gu. ℘*(062)-613-5337.* 🕐 *9am–6pm. ₩600. Comprehensive information panels in English.*
In spite of its rather old-fashioned style of presentation, which is based on a series of diorama scenes illustrated with figures, this ethnographic museum is of great interest for the insight it affords into the various folk costumes worn by

5-18 The Bloody Tragedy of 18 May 1980

The year 2010 marked the 30th anniversary of one of the darkest chapters in recent Korean history. The first step toward the uprising that was so brutally crushed had occurred on 26 October 1979 with the assassination of President Park Chung-hee by the director of the Korean Central Intelligence Agency (KCIA). While many Koreans saw in his removal a spark of democratic hope, it was to be short-lived; on 12 December 1979, a military junta led by General Chun Doohwan seized power. Martial law was declared on 17 May 1980, with paramilitary troops taking control of all the big cities. Universities were closed, although students in Gwangju, a political bastion of the opposition, took to the streets on 18 May, demanding the reopening of Chonnam National University.

The democratic movement spread like wildfire, despite brutal reprisals by the army, and 100,000 people joined the marches. Troops finally resorted to firing live rounds on 21 May and, faced with such extremes of violence, the townspeople formed a citizens' army of Gwangju. The might of five military divisions was unleashed on the city on 27 May and just 90 minutes later, the democratic uprising had been crushed in a bloodbath. Of a total of 4,369 people who sustained wounds or were arrested, 154 died and 74 simply disappeared. With the establishment of a democracy in 1987, the uprising was re-evaluated and the event was officially renamed the Gwangju Democratization Movement. Former president Chun was tried and sentenced to death, but after receiving a pardon, lived under house arrest until 2007. The story of this tragic episode in history has been recounted in two works of art: *There a Petal Silently Falls*, a novel by Choe Yun, and the film *May 18* by Kim ji-Hoon (2007).

the Korean people. The rituals marking every chapter of Korean life are documented and demonstrated with almost military precision and the remaining exhibits are a reminder that Jeolla-do was not only the "rice bowl" of Korea but also that off its shores lie the country's most important fishing grounds. Fishing and cereal agriculture therefore feature in a number of the museum's windows on the past.

▷ *Head SW for 220yd/200m.*

Gwangju Museum of Art
광주시립미술관

52 Haseo-ro Buk-Gu, 48 Bangmulgwanro Buk-gu. ☎*(062)-613-7100. www.artmuse.gwangju.go.kr.* ◷*Open Tue–Sun 9am–6pm. ₩500.* Although this building has a modern and somewhat industrial look outside, the space inside is used for temporary exhibitions devoted to local artists.

▷ *Head for Buk-gu district, about 3mi/5km N of Gwangju.*

May 18th National Cemetery★★ 5-18 국립 묘지
San 34beonji, Unjeong-dong, Buk-gu Bus no. 518 from along Geumnam-no (every 30min, allow approx. 45min, ₩1,000) or from Gwangcheon Bus Terminal. http://kdu518.mpva.go.kr, ◷ *daily Mar–Oct 8am–7pm, Nov–Feb 8am–5pm, no charge.*

Memorial Tower, May 18 National Cemetery

©TOPIC PHOTO AGENCY IN/age fotostock

Gwangju Contemporary Art Biennale

Founded in 1995 to mark the 50th anniversary of Korean independence and the 15th anniversary of 5/18 (see box p325), the Gwangju Biennale was the first to be established in Asia and has since become one of the most important contemporary art events on the entire continent. Here more than anywhere else, artistic freedom is primarily thought of as freedom of expression, one of the liberties that now flourishes in the democratic soil that Gwangju sees itself as having fertilized. The eighth biennale in 2010 brought together more than 100 artists from 25 different countries under the aegis of its Italian director, Massimiliano Gioni. *Info: www.gb.or.kr.*

This is one of the most moving places in Gwangju and a must for anyone wishing to understand the history and the soul of this city. The site is dominated by a 130ft/40m commemorative tower shaped like two hands cradling an egg, the symbol of new life. Among the various buildings is a **museum** (photos, film, multimedia) and the **Photographic Memorial House**, a hall of remembrance dedicated to the memory of all those who lost their lives during the uprising for democracy that took place in May 1980.

The new cemetery was built in 1997, in part to provide a more fitting resting place for the victims, who had been carted away in garbage trucks by the army and buried in a mass grave in the old Mangwol-Dong cemetery, which has been left intact by the city. It is located on the other side of the National Cemetery.

DOWNTOWN
Chungjang-no 충장로 and Geumnam-no 금남로
See Gwangju map.
Geumnamno 5-ga.
The great Geumnam-no arterial road is to finance what Gwangju's Chungjang-

Daennamu Tongbap

This typical Damyang dish consists of steamed rice cooked inside hollowed-out bamboo and topped with ginkgo nuts, dates and chestnuts.

no road, and indeed the whole Chungjang district, is to fashion. Although the former has impenetrable-looking offices with smoked-glass windows, high-decibel music blares out from the wide-open doors of the buildings in the latter.

The point where these two universes collide, at the great **Migliore** department store on the **Jungang-no** road, is a very popular meeting place for Koreans. As night falls across the cheap food stalls, with their stacks of *soondae* (sausages), *twigim* (fried food) and *tteokbokki* dripping with *gochugang* (rice cake in red pepper sauce), clairvoyants and manicurists compete for the hearts, minds, wallets and hands of passers-by.

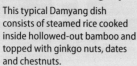

Rejoin Geumnam-no heading east (toward the tourist office), and as you reach May 18 Democratic Plaza, you will see that great works of outsized dimensions are under way.

Some 700 million US dollars have been invested into what is described by some as the greatest cultural project in Korean history, the **National Asian Culture Complex**.

Designed by the Korean architect Kyu Sung Woo, the key aim of the architectural complex after its inauguration in 2012 is to become one of the principal sites for the exposition, exploration and understanding of Southeast Asian cultures.

5min walk NE from Democratic Plaza.

Gucheung Seoktap, Unjusa ©KTO

Art Street (Yesuleui Geori)
예술의거리

51-6 Gung-dong, Dong-gu. Located between Dongbu police station and Jungang-no. ⊙ *10am–7:30pm.*

Art Street, with its many brightly lit arcades, is a 1,000ft/300m succession of art galleries, teashops, antiques stores, bookstores, clothes outlets as well as traditional clothing and paper *(hanbok, hanji)* merchants. This lively street has retained its popularity over the years and is visited by both foreign tourists and those from other areas of the country. The bookshops are well stocked and the traditional papermakers sell the famous Jindari bamboo brushes (which have been designated items of Intangible Cultural Heritage).

There is a little flea market *(Gaemi Market)* at weekends.

▷ *Continue north to explore the raw fish market quarter at Daein. Ideal for sushi lovers (⊙see Addresses).*

EXCURSIONS
Unjusa★ (Unju Temple) 운주사
⊙*See Gwangju map. Located 25mi/ 40km S of Gwangju. Allow half a day. Bus no. 218/318 from the stop opposite Gwangcheon Bus Terminal. Allow 90min for the journey (₩3,000) and 10min walk to the temple. The last bus departs Unjusa at 7:50pm. www.unjusa.org.*

⊙*Mar–Oct 7am–7pm, Nov–Feb 8am–5pm. ₩2,500.*

Although it is the source of numerous historical legends, very little is actually known about this site, which was probably built during the Silla kingdom (57 BC-AD 668). The first of these legends recounts how more than a thousand pagodas and statues of the Buddha once stood here, their weight providing a counterbalance to the poorly distributed mountains of the region (there are not enough to the southwest, according to some geomancers); a rather less poetic explanation suggests that the site was once a training school for masons.

Moyang Festival

Every year around 9 September, depending on the lunar calendar, a number of events are held to celebrate the fortress wall, which the locals believe provides protection and also restores health. The story goes that just walking the length of it is enough to ensure healthy legs. The torch-light procession reveals a cheerful crowd of participants in brightly colored finery parading along the ramparts in single file.

More information is available at the local tourist office.

There now remain just under 100 statues and around 20 pagodas, of which the most remarkable is the nine-tier **Gucheung Seoktap★★**, a National Treasure located near the entrance. Equally famed for the complexity of their execution are two recumbent statues of the **Buddha★**—known as *Wabul*—located a little farther along the path.

Damyang 담양

🌀*See Gwangju map. Damyang is accessible from Gwangju by regional bus (🌀see Useful Information) or by local bus no. 311/322 (6am–9:50pm, every 10min). Allow half a day.*

A region with little industry (not something that strikes you at first sight), Damyang grew up on the strength of its bamboo, an originally Asian plant of which there are about 1,300 different species. While the town is not a tourist destination in the strictest sense, the region tends to attract visitors with an interest in ecology.

The community of **Samjicheon**, a little to the south of Damyang *(easily reached by taxi)*, was labeled Asia's first "slow city" in 2007, an appellation that refers to preserving cultural legacies and promoting slower lifestyles; encouraging tradition over technology. The fame of the small town of Damyang is due largely to its annual **Bamboo Festival** held in May. Apart from this event two main features attract Koreans to Damyang—a museum and a bamboo park, located at opposite ends of the town. There are also pleasant walks to be had beside the river.

The **Korean Bamboo Museum** *(401-1, Cheonbyeon-ri, Damyang-eup, 15min walk west from Damyang Public Terminal, ☎(061)-380-3484, www.damyang.go.kr/ museum/ 🕐 open 9am–6pm. ₩1,000)* contains a large exhibition of bamboo products through the ages and the different uses to which the plant is put. That said, there is no way of judging how well modern artisans have reproduced the traditional forms.

If you are on a tight schedule, save your time for the **Bamboo Park** *(Juknokwon,*

San 37-6 Hyanggyo-ri, ☎ (063)-380-3245, 🕐 open 9am–7pm, ₩2,000)*, ideally visiting on the 2nd, 7th, 12th, 17th, 22nd or 27th of the month, when the 300-year-old **bamboo market★**, one of the largest and oldest in Korea, is held. The bamboo garden, which is laid out on a hillside *(about 15min walk NE of Damyang Bus Terminal)*, features eight interlinking themed paths that allow you to stroll through fresh greenery that is particularly welcome in summer. The average temperature is considerably lower here than elsewhere because of the anions (ions with a negative charge) released by the bamboo. With a great capacity for retaining water, when carbonized, bamboo charcoal also possesses strong deodorizing properties, a quality that has made its modern fortune. You can see a range of the products obtained from the plant, including tea, wine, vinegar, etc.

Damyang, the cradle of **Gasa literature**, now promotes this form of narrative poetry through its annual festival in July *(Gasa Poetry Hall, ☎ 061-380-3141)*.

GOCHANG 고창

🌀*See Gwangju map. Buses depart from Gwangcheon Bus Terminal (6:45am–8:30pm, every 30min, 1hr10min, ₩4,500).*

The town of Gochang, undergoing reconstruction, is gambling on a future as a tourist destination based on the elements of its cultural and religious heritage that have made its modern reputation: *pansori* (Korean opera) and *goindol* (dolmens).

Moyangseong (Gochang-eup Fortress) 고창읍성 (모양성)

15min walk from Gochang Bus Terminal. ☎(063)-560-2714. www.gochang.go.kr. 🕐 open 9am–6pm. ₩1,000.

The Moyangseong fortress, perched on a hillside overlooking the little town of Gochang, was built in 1453 during the reign of King Danjong (1452–55), the sixth monarch of the Joseon dynasty, to defend Jeolla Province against an impending Japanese invasion. From about 1mi/1.6km of curtain wall there are some good views of the town. The various pavilions and houses and the prison that the wall encloses are all reconstructions, so they lack significant historical interest, but they do serve to break up the pleasant walk alongside the wall.

▶ *Head to your left as you leave the fortress.*

Gochang Pansori Museum
고창 판소리 박물관
☎ (063)-564-8425.
www.pansorimuseum.com.
🕐 open 9am–6pm. ₩800.
Established in 2001 in a house once belonging to **Dongri, Shin Jae-hyo** (1812–44), the museum is dedicated to this native son of Gochang. Rocked in his cradle from an early age to the husky strains of *pansori*, he decided to devote himself body and soul to this art form. Both a theorist and a performing musician, Dongri (his stage name) went on to write a major work on *pansori*. For the first time in its history, this polyphonic art form, whose oral tradition is based on popular, anonymous song and recitation, was stripped down and codified in a form that went beyond the simple notation of a musical composition. The structure of *pansori* simultaneously includes song, dance, narration and improvisation by the performer.

Dongri began his mission of reviewing the entire *pansori* repertoire (the topics and the narratives of its stories), from which he selected only a certain number: of 12 pieces, he retained only six, essentially stories which chimed with the Confucianist beliefs that were popular at the time. Once he had established the repertoire, he divided and codified the structure of each of the *pansori* into separate units: song, narration and gestures, without prescribing the improvisation, of course, which was to be provided by the performer to form the very essence of *pansori*.

Alongside various personal effects belonging to Shin Jae-hyo, there are numerous multimedia displays presenting performances by the greatest sing-

Pansori: A Multiple Art Form

The roots of *pansori* date back to the 17C and are to be found in shamanic chants from Jeolla Province. *Pan* is the word for a place where something happens and *sori* describes all the natural sounds one might hear (water, wind, animals). While *pansori* was at first primarily social satire aimed at the dominant class of the *yangban* (aristocrats and landowners), by the 19C it had acquired a wider audience and become less serious, thanks to an artistic maturity that owed much to cultural borrowings from classical Chinese narratives and poetry in particular.

ers, including Jin Chae-seon and Kim So-hei. There are many signs in English to inform visitors at greater length about this art form.

👥 Gochang Dolmen Museum★★★
고창 고인돌박물관
Access is complicated by bus, so a taxi is a better option; to arrange the return journey, ask the help of the museum staff, some of whom speak English. 676, Dosan-ri, Gochang-eub. ☎ (063)-560-2576. www.gcdolmen.go.kr. 🕐 Open 9am–6pm (Nov–Feb 5pm). ₩3,000.
People are often unaware that while most of the 80,000 dolmens recorded around the world are concentrated in Europe (in the UK, Ireland and France), more than 36,000 are to be found on the Korean Peninsula, with the great majority of these concentrated on three southern sites: Hwasun, Ganghwa and Gochang, which were recognized as UNESCO World Heritage Sites in 2000. The Gochang region alone boasts more than 2,000 dolmens, of which 447 are to be found in the square mile/2.5sq km of grounds surrounding the museum. As the greatest concentration of megalithic remains in the world, it was only natural that in 2008 it should become the site

Kim Young-Sung

Born in Gwangju in 1965, Kim Young-sung is one of a generation of photographers investigating Korea's ancient history. His photographic series *Dolmen* (2005), shot in black and white, is one of the most beautiful homages to megalithic culture. American museums have their fingers on the pulse as they acquire more of his work into their collections.

ied; and the gravestone style, with an upright stone set in the ground. In the last case, the deceased was actually buried, whereas the body may only have been placed on the ground in the three other forms.

The museum gives an idea of how the dolmens were built and for what purposes: as grave monuments, fertility stones, astronomical instruments and the first intimations of an indigenous cosmology (one that was not Chinese in origin). Such notions are important: archaeological research was halted during the Japanese colonial period since, as far as the Japanese occupiers were concerned, a colonized country should have no roots, especially if those roots should happen to be even older than those of the colonizer.

Outside the museum buildings there is a **large park**, scattered with dolmens, where you can take a walk in magnificent surroundings and convert the theories you have learned in the exhibition halls into practice.

of the first Korean museum to be dedicated in its entirety to these monuments dating back to the first millennium BC. The three-level museum *(information in English)* offers infromation about these strange stones. Weighing between 10 and 300 tons, they are known as *goindol* in Korean (literally "the stone which is supported by other stones") and are found in a wide variety of forms. Those in Gochang are in four styles: the table type, with a large flat stone placed on two large, vertical stones; in the form of a sarcophagus, where the main stone covers a series of vertical stones; the *baduk* checkerboard style (the Korean version of the Chinese game of Go), where a single stone is supported by four or eight stones which have been arranged vertically and almost bur-

JIRISAN NATIONAL PARK
지리산 국립공원 AND HWAEOMSA★★ 화엄사
🕭 *See Gwangju map.*
The park, which straddles three separate regions (Jeonbuk, Jeonnam and Gyeongnam), also has three main entrances, each with a temple. Two of these, Ssanggyesa (🕭 see p313) and

Jirisan National Park

©KTO

Daewonsa, are located in Gyeongsang Province and the third, Hwaeomsa—the one of principal interest to us here—lies at the western entrance to the park in Jeollanam-do (South Jeolla).

▷ *Take a bus from Gwangcheon Bus Terminal for Jirisan National Park and Hwaeomsa (every 90min, 90min, ₩6,400). Parking no charge. For the temple, see: www.hwaeomsa.org. Open dawn–dusk. ₩3,800.*

Jirisan, meaning "the mountain of the wise and strange," refers to the hermits who have roamed its vast reaches in search of absolute truth. The largest of Korea's mountainous parks (181sq mi/470sq km) was also the first area in the country to be designated a national park (in 1967). The park boasts about a dozen peaks, of which the majority are over 3,300ft/1,000m high (at 6,283ft/1,915m, **Cheonwangbong** is the second-tallest mountain in Korea). The peaks form a picturesque **ridge line★★** that runs from east to west for a distance of nearly 28mi/45km, along which is a challenging hiking trail for fit walkers. Unsurprisingly, such geographical and climatic diversity has allowed a wide range of species to flourish in the park, including corylopsis (witch hazel), with its beautiful sprigs of pale yellow flowers, and impressive animals like the Asian black bear.

Hwaeomsa★★
(Hwaeom Temple) 화엄사
The temple is located 0.6mi/1km from the park entrance.
Hwaeomsa was constructed in 544 by Yeongi Josa during the reign of King Seong (523–54) of the Silla dynasty (57 BC–AD 668) and extended during the Later Silla period (668–918). Although a number of features have survived to the present day (stone lanterns, five-tier stupas decorated with representations of the 12 divinities of the zodiac), most of the temple is a reconstruction dating back to the 16C and 17C and the aftermath of the destruction caused by war with Japan (1592–98). Having passed

Hwaeomsa
©IDREAMSTOCK / age fotostock

through the gates of **Geumgangmun★** and **Cheonwangmun★** and their representations of the celestial guardians of the four points of the compass, you will soon find **Gakhwangjeon★★**, the largest wooden Buddhist structure in Korea. This two-story building, now a National Treasure, was reconstructed in 1703 on stone foundations that date back to the Silla period. As you walk between the buildings, look out for a pagoda to the west where each of its five tiers bears images of the 12 gods of the zodiac.

The next pagoda with four lions dates back to the 9C, and there is also a small museum in the Bojeru pavilion.
Behind the temple a path leads to a number of hermitages. It is also possible to walk up to Nogodan, a plateau at 4,944ft/1,507m.

⊘*Allow around 3hr30min for the 4.5mi/7km walk. The small information office near the bus stop may be able to give you some tips and a local map.*

From Hwaeomsa, you can also walk along the ridgeline to Daewonsa, the temple at the far eastern end of the park *(allow 3 days on average for approx. 25mi/40km; overnight stays possible in converted climbers' refuges).*

ADDRESSES

🏠 STAY

Apart from the traditional range of hotels and motels, you can also stay with a host family organized by **Gwangju International Homestay** 광주 외국인홈스테이 – Jeon-il Bldg. F, Geunmanam-no. ℘ (062)-226-2734. www.gwangjuguide.or.kr/2011/06/gwangju-international-homestay. Fifty-five Korean families have been selected for this accommodation program to date, and requests for reservations should be made a minimum of two weeks in advance, specifying the district where you would like to stay. *Expect to pay ₩35,000 per person; no charge for infants up to age three; 50 percent reduction for children under 10.*

DONG-GU DISTRICT

🛏 **Migliore Jjimjilbang** 밀리오레 찜질방 – 29-2 Chungjang-no 4. Top floor of the Migliore department store. ℘(062)-616-7081. *Open 24hr.* One of the most popular saunas in Gwangju. At a rate of ₩5,000 and with a level of comfort to match, this is perennially popular with students as a place to spend the night. An experience!

🛏 **Palace Hotel** 팔라스호텔 – 11-4- Hwanggeum-dong. ℘(062)-222-2525. 🖥 41rm. ₩50,000. Prices can double in July and August, depending on demand. Lying as it does in the heart of the pulsating Chungjang-no district (with its restaurants, cafés, clothes stores), the Palace Hotel is ideally situated for those who wish to explore this lively neighborhood. The spacious and comfortable rooms are immaculate and boast all the conveniences of a motel (TV, computer, water boiler). There's a sauna at reception, a nightclub in the basement and a café on the ground floor called the **WaBar**, which closes at 4am, the perfect place for a beer. Note that the reception is on the third floor.

🛏 **Windmill Motel** 윈드밀모텔 – 42-6 Honam-dong. ℘ (062)-223-5333. www.windmillmotel.co.kr. 🖥 60rm. ₩35,000. Like every establishment in the love motel category, this too offers all the facilities likely to lead to sleepless

nights: giant TV screens, computers, hot and cold water dispensers and plenty of soap and toothpaste, all in a baroque setting.

NAM-GU DISTRICT

🛏🛏 **Hotel Prado** 프라도관광호텔 – 638-1 Baegun-dong. ℘ (062)-654-9999. 🖥 - 🍴. 111rm. ₩80,000–120,000. Located 20min by taxi from Gwangju rail station, this hotel is part of the famous Benikea chain (*Best night in Korea*) and one of the most luxurious in town, with a vast range of services (sauna, massage, sports hall, Chinese and Japanese restaurants, a business center). Don't forget to visit the **Sky Lounge** to relax with a cocktail while gazing at the illuminated city below.

🍽 EAT

DONG-GU

🍴 **Cheongwon Momil** 청원모밀 – 31-7 Chungjang-no 3. Opposite Migliore department store. ℘(062)-222-2210. 10am–9:30pm.-🍴. This restaurant has been serving competitively priced noodles (*about ₩3,500*) since 1960 and has become an institution. The house specialty is *momil guksu*, buckwheat noodles.

🍴🍴 **Minsokchon** 민속촌 – 69 Gwangsan-dong. ℘(062)-224-4577. *Open 1:30am–midnight.* ₩8,000–13,000 -🍴. A popular restaurant and a good place to try delicious *dwaeji galbi* (marinated pork ribs), among other dishes.

🍴🍴🍴 **Moojinjoo** 무진주 – 1-4 Bullo-dong. ℘ (062)-224 8074. *Open 11:30am–midnight. ₩15,000–25,000. Menu in English.* The house specialty is roast pork, served, for example, with Boseong green tea. Try the signature dish, *bossam*, which is boiled pork cut into fine slices, wrapped in blanched Chinese cabbage leaves and topped with kimchi.

🍴🍴🍴 **Songjukeon** 송죽헌 – 128-1 Nam-dong. ℘(062)-222-5919/4234. Open noon–2pm, 6pm–10pm. Expect to pay about ₩160,000 for a filling *hanjeongsik*, a traditional set meal for 4 persons, served with a host of *banchan*, little side dishes. A unique dining experience in a superb *hanok* house, although it might be wise to book ahead.

🛒 SHOPPING

Daein Market – *Gyerim-dong-Daien Market, behind Art Street. Bus no. 6/37/52/54/56/58/70/81/170/180/184/518, Daein Sijang stop.* You'll find about a dozen restaurants clustered here; recommended for fans of raw fish (sashimi).

Geumnam Underground Market 금남로 지하상가 – This enormous subway mall runs between Democratic Plaza and Geumnamno 4-ga stations. Traditional clothes and the latest fashions.

Yangdong Market – *Yang-dong, Seo-gu.* Ⓜ *Yangdong Market, exit 1. Bus no. 19/30/36/37/39/48/52/59/61/65/71/72/77/89/177, Yangdong Sijang stop.* The biggest market in the city has been open since 1975 and is considered the best traditional market in the country, with row upon row of stalls, arranged by type of product for sale.

🤸 SPORT AND ACTIVITIES

BASEBALL
Mudeung Stadium 무등야구장 – *Bus no. 16/38/51/53/58/89/95/98/151, Mudeung Stadium stop.* Come and cheer on the **Kia Tigers** *(www.tigers.co.kr)* professional baseball team in the magnificent Mudeung Stadium. Games usually start at 5pm or 6:30pm. For advance tickets, check *www.ticketlink.co.kr (from ₩6,000).*

🎭 EVENTS AND FESTIVALS

World Kimchi Culture Festival 김치축제 – Held in the World Cup Stadium Area or Jungoe Park Area *(📞(062)-613-3642)* in October, the timing of this festival is a reminder that kimchi was traditionally made in this month with the aim of preserving vegetables and also to ensure a greater variety of food during the long winter months. You'll be able not only to sample all sorts of kimchi but also to vote for the best kimchi in the festival, while watching games, traditional events and performances, or enjoying such highlights as *samulnori* concerts (Korean percussion music) and *nongak* (rural music).

Gwangju Biennale – An international contemporary art fair, held Sept–Nov every two years, *(counting even years)* at the Gwangju Biennale Hall and around the city. *(📞(062)-608-4114. http://gb.or.kr)*

Gwangju Design Biennale – Started in 2004 to promote the design industry in Gwangju. The biennale celebration features exhibitions and fairs spotlighting unique techiniques in design. Every two years, Sept–Oct. *(📞(062)-608-4114. http://gb.or.kr)*

Im Bang-Ul's Korean Traditional Music Festival – Named after the famous Korean vocalist Bang-Ul and held in September at the Gwangju Culture and Art Center *(📞(062)-521-0731, www.imbangul.or.kr).*

Moyang Fortress Festival – Held around 9 Sept each year. Lantern parade, ancient government office tour and a walk around the fortress. *(📞(063)-560-2710).*

Kimchi Festival, Gwangju

©Chris Stowers/Apa Publications

Mokpo
목포

On the sea route between China and Japan, Mokpo has made its mark on history, although few architectural traces of this have survived. At first sight, this city seems a little unprepossessing, but its shoreline has plenty of variety no matter what you are looking for: to the west are the peaks of Yudalsan Park, while the areas around the ferry terminal and the port at Naehang are more industrial; heading east there's a cluster of museums around Gatbawi and, farther east again, beaches near Pyeonghwa Square. As a busy port city with industries and activities associated with shipping and the sea, the streets of downtown Mokpo seem far removed from the beach resorts where the aroma of sunscreen hangs in the air. Mokpo serves as the entrance both to the Korean Peninsula's southern coast and to the many islands that make up the Dadohae Maritime National Park.

VISIT
Yudalsan Park★ 유달산 공원
20min walk from the rail station, the park entrance is watched over by a statue of Admiral Yi. ◷ *Open 8am–6pm. ₩700.*

There is a magnificent **view★** from **Ildeung-bawi**, the highest point (748ft/228m) of this mountainous park with trails, surrounded by rugged cliffs and pavilions. There is a **sculpture park** and a number of commemorative monuments (more of interest for the events they record than for their structures) including the statue of Admiral Yi on **Nojeokbong**, a reminder of the admiral's cunning deception (◷*see box p336*) and another, more vocal, monument nicknamed "the Tears of Mokpo," as every hour it strikes up this famous 1930s song recounting the suffering of the Korean people during the Japanese

- ▶ **Population:** 247,207
- ◷ **Michelin Map:** Regional map pp320–321
- ℹ **Info:** There is one tourist office located in the middle of the rail station, ☎(061)-270-8599, http://tour.mokpo.go.kr, open 9am–6pm and another at Gatbawi, close to Mokpo Natural History Museum, 9am–6pm.
- ◑ **Location:** Mokpo is situated along the southern coast of the peninsula, 255mi/410km from Seoul.
- ♟ **Kids:** The dinosaur models at the Natural History Museum, islands of Dadohae Maritime National Park.
- ◷ **Timing:** Allow half a day to explore Yudalsan Park. Allow a further half-day for the museum quarter (note: closed on Mondays) and a whole day to explore Dadohae National Maritime Park.
- ◔ **Don't Miss:** The fascinating National Maritime Museum.

occupation. There is also a view point at the top of another peak, **Ideung-bawi**, which is impossible to miss if you follow the small ridge.

From between Ildeung-bawi and Ideung-bawi, a small path heads west and down to a modest beach. ◔ **Note:** *this beach is not suitable for swimming.*

GATBAWI DISTRICT★:
The Museum District
2.5mi/4km E of Mokpo city center. Take bus no. 7/15/111. A taxi from the center will cost around ₩3,500. Note: due to the various maritime industries located along the shoreline, it is not possible to access the district by walking along the seafront.

The district of Gatbawi derives its name from a pair of rocks that resemble two

GETTING THERE

BY BUS/COACH – From the bus terminal *(2mi/3km from the city center)*, there are departures for **Boseong** *(6:50am–8:30pm, every hour, 1hr45min, ₩8,700)*; Mokpo–Yeosu *(every hour, 3hr30min, ₩17,000)*.

BY TRAIN – From Mokpo Station there are departures for Gwangju *(1hr30min, ₩4,800)* and Seoul (by KTX).

GETTING AROUND

BY BUS/COACH – From the bus terminal *(2mi/3km from the city center)*, bus no. 1 goes to the rail station and the ferry terminal *(every 20min, 10min, ₩1,000)*. Bus no. 2/3/101/112 serve the city center and Yudalsan.

BY TAXI – As with everywhere else in Korea, you will have no problem in finding a taxi. Expect to pay an average of ₩3,000 for 2.5mi/4km, the distance between the center of Mokpo and the Maritime Museum.

FERRIES – There are departures from the **International Ferry Terminal** for **Jeju** *(9am and 2:30pm for car ferries, 4hr30min crossing covering 53mi/85km)*. The rather faster *Pink Dolphin* departs daily at 2pm *(3hr crossing, expect to pay ₩25,800 round-trip)*.

There are departures from the **New Coastal Ferry Terminal** for many destinations, including Heuksando *(3 times daily, 56mi/90km, 1hr30min, ₩26,700)* and Hongdo *(68mi/110km, 2hr15min, Return ₩32,600)*.

---

people standing side by side wearing *satgat* (traditional hats). There are about a dozen museums here, some of which are not very fascinating, either because the exhibits on display are rather mediocre (**Mokpo Ceramic Livingware Museum, Namnong Memorial Hall**), or because the absence of information in English makes a visit rather uninformative (**Mokpo Museum of Literature**). In some cases, the museum's chosen topic (dinosaurs, for example, in the **Mokpo Natural History Museum**) may be interesting but has little to do with the local flora and fauna. The attractive and fascinating National Maritime Museum is an exception, however, and is worth the trip to Gatbawi on its own.

National Maritime Museum★★
국립해양문화재연구소
138 Namnongro. ℘*(061)-270-2000. www.seamuse.go.kr.* ○*Open Tue–Sun 9am–6pm. No charge.*
The museum is divided into four sections; the first two exhibition halls display objects retrieved from vessels that have come to grief off the Mokpo coast.
The first ship on exhibit is the *Wando*, which was discovered in 1984. The vessel was carrying no fewer than 30,000

National Maritime Museum ©KTO

celadon ceramic objects manufactured in and around Gangjin, Buan and Haenam and seems in all probability to date from the late 11C or early 12C. The *Wando* was lost while delivering its cargo to Gaegyeong, the capital of the Goryeo dynasty. Among the articles recovered, there are a number of navigational instruments and various everyday objects providing a wealth of

Admiral Yi Sun-Sin (1545–98)

A fearless aristocrat, who showed no pity toward the enemy yet was totally devoted to his men, Yi Sun-sin is a national hero who liberated Korea from the yoke of Japanese oppression during the gruelling Imjin War which took place between 1592 and 1598. A masterful tactician, he also invented the turtle boat (*Geobukseon* or *Kobukson*), the first armored ocean-going vessel in Korean naval history, and defeated the Japanese fleet in a number of engagements. Yi Sun-sin proved his cunning again at Mokpo, where he succeeded in repulsing the enemy fleet by stockpiling enormous heaps of wooden stakes on the summit of Yudalsan, guarded by civilians dressed as soldiers. The Japanese concluded that this was a colossal arms dump, hardly propitious for the siege that they had intended to begin. The admiral was killed in the course of the victorious battle at No-Ryang, which put a conclusive end to the Imjin War.

There are several places where the admiral's life is recalled: Jinju (National Museum), Namhae (monument, museum), Yeosu (battlefield, general headquarters), Tongyeong (reproduction of a turtle boat) and Seoul (Gwanghwamun Square).

information about the Goryeo period. The model of the ship is a re-creation, about half the size of the original.

The second ship exhibit, the **Sinan**, explores a Chinese vessel that foundered off the Sinan coast in 1323 en route to Japan. Her hull, a length measuring 113ft/34m of which has been recovered, is presented in an excellent display. The objects found on board have provided valuable insights into the nature of the items that were transported between Korea, China and Japan: ceramics, silk, tea and incense from China; and *insam* (ginseng, see box p385), fans, gold and silver from Korea. Japan exported swords and screens in exchange for sandalwood, spices and medicine from China, or cotton, hemp and tiger pelts, which, while often of Indian origin, were sold by the Koreans.

The third room is an exhibition titled "The Life of a Korean Village," with special emphasis on the Joseon period. Thanks to such exhibits as an encyclopedia of maritime life written in 1814 by Jeong Yak-jeon, we learn that raw octopus or abalone (*jeonbok-juk*) served with rice porridge was already a well-established dish. Traditional fishing techniques, tools and the living condi-

tions of the times are explored in-depth in this hall.

The fourth and final room demonstrates the evolution of Korean shipbuilding over the course of history. Many models are on display, including rabbit- and turtle-shaped ships.

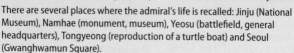 Natural History Museum
자연사박물관

From the Maritime Museum, cross over the main road. (061)-274-3655, *Open Tue–Sun 9am–6pm. http:// museum.mokpo.go.kr/eng/index.htm. ₩3,000 combination ticket with the Mokpo Ceramic Livingware Museum.*

If you have the time to also visit this museum, the diplodocus and allosaurus models will delight the kids, and you will learn much about the local plant and animal life. The presentation on butterflies is particularly original.

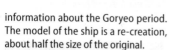 Upon leaving the museum, return to the seafront; in about 10min you will reach the two rocks at Gatbawi and a walkway which allows you to walk around them without getting your feet wet. You can continue from here along the seafront to the part of Mokpo that is more like a seaside resort.

👥 Dadohae Maritime National Park★★ 다도해 해상국립공원

See Jeolla-Do map.

The national park contains some 1,700 islands. A number of these are virtually no larger than rocky outcrops protruding from the sea, but **Hongdo★★** is one of the more beautiful and more popular islands. *Ferries dock at Hongdo at the village of Ilgu, which has several min-bak (family B&Bs) and yeogwan (inns). http://english.knps.or.kr. Expect to pay ₩30,000–50,000 per night. Hongdo visitor fee: ₩2,600.*

Red Island, as Hongdo is nicknamed because of its unusal reddish-brown color, is 4mi/6km long, 1.5mi/2.5km wide and has a large number of very bizarre rock formations that are only really visible from the circular boat tour *(2hr, 2 sailings daily, ₩15,000)*. With the exception of the villages and the small beach known as "Ppadol" with its quartzite pebbles, the island is a protected nature reserve, so exploring on foot remains largely forbidden.

🚶 The trip to Hongdo will also take you past the island of **Heuksando★**, which is larger and more populated and also has the advantage of being accessible to walkers. Climbing to Heuksando's summit, **Sangnabong★** (679ft/207m), is one of the undisputed highlights of a visit to the national park. Otherwise allow 9hr to walk around the island.

Visitors disembark at Yeri, the main village on the island. Accommodations should be readily available.

Jindo loses its island status for just a few days each year during the great spring tides. The phenomenon, christened a "Moses miracle," has become a very popular attraction, with crowds of people following the mysterious "sea road" which appears as the waters retreat leaving a long sandbar connecting Jindo with Modo, a small island to the south. An amazing spectacle.

ADDRESSES

🛏 STAY

🛏 **Chosun Beach Motel** 조선비치모텔 – *Haean-ro 167-dong.* 📞*(061)-242-0485.* 🛏 *₩30,000.* Located 200ft/60m from the New Coastal Ferry Terminal, the hotel offers basic rooms (with no internet access) that are among the cheapest in Mokpo.

🛏 **Daeyang Park Motel** 대양파크모텔 – *Chukbok-dong.* 📞 *(061)-243-4540.* 🛏- 🖥. With its location right next to the rail station, this is a good place to stay. Clean and well-appointed rooms offer TV, computers and a range of products in the bathroom.

🛏🛏🛏 **Shangria Beach Hotel** 샹그리아비치관광호텔 – *1144-7 Sang-Dong-4.* 📞 *(061)-285-0100. www.shangriahotel.co.kr.* 🖥. *71rm. ₩129,000 (expect to pay 40 percent more in summer). ₩12,000 for breakfast.* Located on Mokpo's shoreline, this recently built hotel (which opened in 2004) is one of the best in town.

🍴 EAT

Mokpo specializes in fish restaurants, and there are any number of these opposite the port on the quay facing the New Coastal Ferry Terminal. If you find it hard to choose between them, pick one for its atmosphere. With guaranteed freshness and reasonable prices, these are the most typical restaurants in Mokpo.

🍴🍴🍴 **Yeongnan Raw Fish** 영란횟집 – *5 Jungang-dong.* 📞*(061)-243-7311. Open 11am–9pm.* The food served in this restaurant's small rooms with rather old-fashioned wallpaper comes from one of the best kitchens in Mokpo, specializing in seasonal raw fish in all its incarnations: sole, bass, crab, not to mention the renowned local specialty of raw croaker, a fish known to science as *Pseudosciaena crocea. Expect to pay* ₩45,000 *for sole sashimi.*

From Mokpo to Yulpo★

목포 to 여수
Jeollanam-do

The route between the two large cities of Mokpo and Yulpo is pleasant and lined with places that are particularly unique to Korea. Wolchulsan National Park is worth a detour for its unusual landscape of granite rocks (something it has in common with a number of South Korea's national parks) and Gangjin Celadon Museum will satisfy even the most ardent and experienced fan of porcelain and ceramics. Some of the most beautiful scenery is man-made, however—you are unlikely ever to forget your first sight of the tea plantations at Daehan Dawon, a short distance from Boseong.

- **Michelin Map:** Regional map pp320–321
- **Info:** Boseong Cultural Tourism Office, ℰ(061)-850-5224. www.boseong.go.kr
- **Location:** The city of Mokpo is located 255mi/ 410km south of Seoul and 112mi/180km from Yeosu.
- **Kids:** Explore Wolchulsan National Park, Boseong tea plantation, enjoy Yulpo Beach.
- **Timing:** A whole day could be spent at Wolchulsan National Park or two days at Yulpo, alternating between visits to the green tea plantation and the beach, but allow three days for the complete circuit.
- **Don't Miss:** Daehan Dawon tea plantation, Wolchulsan's "Cloud Bridge."

🚗 DRIVING TOUR

👥 Wolchulsan National Park★ 월출산국립공원

⏱See Jeolla-Do map. Take a bus for Yeongam from Mokpo Bus Terminal (every hour, 20min, ₩3,200). From Yeongam Bus Terminal there is a bus (every 15min, 10min, ₩850) to the park's main entrance, which lies to the east. ℰ(061)-473-5210. ⏱Open 8am–6pm. ₩2,000.

Visitors generally cross the park from east to west or vice versa, moving between **Cheonhwangsa** and the temple **Dogapsa** (which is less interesting)

GETTING THERE
BY BUS/COACH – Mokpo–Gangjin (30mi/48km) (every hour, 1hr, ₩4,500); Gangjin–Boseong (every 30min, 45min, ₩3,600); Mokpo–Boseong (6.50am–8:30pm, every hour, 1hr45min, ₩8,700); Gangjin–Yeosu (every 30min, 2hr, ₩13,200).

near the eastern entrance. Allow around 6hr for the 5mi/8km walk. There are restaurants and *minbak* adjacent to the two entrances to the park.

Covering an area of just 16sq mi/42sq km, this park called "the Mountain Where the Moon Rises" (the translation of "Wolchulsan") is the smallest national park in Korea. Bristling with odd-looking hills, of which **Cheonhwangbong** is the highest point (2,654ft/809m), the park has plenty of interesting places to explore, despite its restricted size, and is ideal for a day's walking. Besides a delightful 26ft/8m high statue of the seated **Buddha** cut into the rock, there is also a fantastic **panorama★★** for hikers to enjoy from a steel bridge (the "Cloud Bridge") suspended at a height of 164ft/50m between two ridges.

Gangjin 강진
⏱See Jeolla-Do map.
Gangjin was an important center for the manufacture of **celadon porcelain** between the 10C and 14C, a period

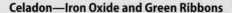

Celadon—Iron Oxide and Green Ribbons

Celadon, known as *cheongja* in Korean, is stoneware with a monochrome glaze that varies between green and a kind of transparent blue-gray color, achieved by firing at high temperatures (2,190°F–2,336 °F/1,200°C–1,280°C) in an oxygen-reduced atmosphere within the kiln, which results in the production of carbon monoxide and carbon. When these are deprived of oxygen they seek it in the iron oxide in the clay, which then takes on blue or green hues, depending on its iron content. Interestingly, the European name dates back to the 17C and the ladies at the court of the French king Louis XIII; in Honoré d'Urfé's novel *L'Astrée*, the shepherd Celadon was never seen without a costume decorated with green ribbons, and the name stuck.

known as the Goryeo (918–1392) and the golden age of ceramics in Korea. A visit to the **Celadon Festival** held every year at Gangjin (⚓*see Addresses*) soon makes it clear just how much interest there still is in celadon ware among Koreans today. Gangjin was responsible for 80 percent of the most beautiful celadon pieces made in Korea, and of the 400 kilns across the country, 188 were to be found here (about 15 are still in operation).

There are two reasons for this concentration: situated so close to Mokpo, Gangjin was ideally placed for the trade routes between China and Japan, and contrary to what might be assumed today, celadon ware was intended for everyday use and was mass-produced and exported in great numbers. Secondly, the conditions in Gangjin are perfect for the production of such porcelain: a good climate, supplies of water, plenty of high-quality wood (the kiln had to reach 2,336°F/1,280°C) and clay, the key ingredient, rich in iron oxide and vital for the coloration (⚓*see box above*).

This was much prized for its resemblance to jade and was in great demand from Korea's northern neighbors; tradition had it that jade was the stone that prevents the vital energy of the dead from escaping, and the Chinese, who invented celadon and manufactured it from the 5C, adopted it as a much less expensive replacement for the precious stone.

▷ *Travel 11mi/18km S of Gangjin on the local bus (every 30min, 25min, ₩1,600) from Gangjin Bus Terminal (platform 13) to Maryang and get off at Cheongju dayoji. This is the stop for the Celadon Museum.*

View from Wolchulsan National Park

©KTO

Gangjin Celadon Museum

©KTO

Gangjin Celadon Museum★
강진청자박물관
(061)-430-3524.
Open 9am–6pm. ₩2,000.
Fortunately the quality of the universally renowned pieces dating from the Goryeo period speaks for itself, as the information in English is rather limited. A pottery workshop and a kiln dating back to the 12C (discovered in the 1960s) are just part of the range of exhibits and there are various outlets selling quality ceramics.

▷ *Allow 45min from Gangjin Bus Terminal to Boseong.*

Boseong 보성
See Jeolla-Do map.
Boseong is the gateway to exploring the famous green tea plantations that are immaculately maintained. Of these, **Boseong Daehan Dawon** is the oldest (1939) and, by far, the most beautiful, with five million tea plants that appear to wrap themselves around the side of the hill like a turban. Not only does the region account for 40 percent of Korea's modern green tea production, Boseong is also the originator of *Seopyeonje*, a variant of *pansori*.

▷ *Take the bus for Yulpo Beach from Boseong Bus Terminal (15min, ₩1,000). Spend the night at Yulpo and leave early in the morning to stroll among the dew-drenched tea plants.*

Yulpo Beach★ 율포해수욕장
See Jeolla-Do map.
The tiny seaside resort of Yulpo stretches out along a seafront lined with seafood restaurants, and the beach is located beyond the road that runs along to your left as you enter the village. Lying between the sea and a pine forest, this 200ft/60m strip of sand is about 1mi/1.5 km long and is open during July and August, when it is usually packed with visitors.

As you go down to the beach, you will notice a strange yellow building on your right. This is the **Yulpo Nokchatang** (*(061)-853-4566, www.visitkorea.or.kr/, open 6am–8pm ₩5,000*), a thermal spa in which you can take green tea baths (seawater and green tea combined), a specialty unique to Boseong!

A little farther along on your left you will find the Condominium, the most luxurious hotel in the resort town (*see Addresses*).

▷ *From Yulpo, catch the bus opposite the Family Mart located at the entrance to the village (5.15am–9pm, every 40min, ₩1,000) and ask the driver to drop you at the stop for Daehan Dawon. The plantation is 220yd/200m to your left, coming from Yulpo (go under the bridge, cross the car park and follow the magnificent avenue of cypress trees).*

👥 **Daehan Dawon Tea Plantation**★★ 대한다원농장

🕑 *See Jeolla-Do map.*
1288-1 Bongsan-ri, Boseong-eup, Boseong-gun. 📞*(010)-3780-3455 (ask for Mr. Jang Yeongseop). www.dhdawon.com.*
🕐*Open summer 8am–7pm (winter 6pm).* ₩*2,000.*

The cultivation of green tea in Korea is documented in sources dating back to the Silla period. Green tea grew in popularity during the Goryeo period (918–1392) under the influence of Buddhist monks who found the drink helped both to refresh them and improve their concentration. However, tea plants were not cultivated in Boseong until 1939 after tests had established that the region provided perfect conditions for planting tea, with 60in/1,500mm of annual precipitation, porous and permeable soil, and cool air with a wide range of daytime temperatures, combined with beneficial humidity brought by spindrift from the sea. There are now 5.8 million tea plants at Daehan Dawon planted on more than a fifth of the 1,408 acres/5.7 million square meters of land owned by the plantation, which is the largest in Korea.

In the plantation restaurant, you will be able to sample *jajangmyeon*, noodles with black bean sauce and green tea, as well as excellent *bibimbap*, also prepared with green tea *(expect to pay* ₩*4,000–7,000).*

ADDRESSES

🏨 STAY

Since **Boseong** itself is not very interesting, we suggest staying overnight at **Yulpo Beach**.

YULPO BEACH

🛏 **Pension Golf** 골프펜션 – *406 Yulpo-li Hwacheon-myeon, Boseong. Beside the main post office in Yulpo.* 📞*(010)-6253-4300. 9rm.* 📺. ₩*30,000. No breakfast but there is a Family Mart 220yd/200m away.*
This little B&B facing the seafront is run by the postmaster and offers simple, well appointed rooms looking out over a small garden and a golf course.

BOSEONG

🛏🛏🛏 **Dabeach Condominium** 보성다비치콘도 – *Adjacent to Yulpo Beach.* 📞*(061)-850-1100.* 📺. *61rm.* ₩*108,000/180,000 during high season (Jul–Aug).* At prices like these you can hire a sumptuous apartment intended for four. Spa, thermal baths—a complex dedicated entirely to rest. Book well in advance.

🍴 EAT

There are plenty of seafood restaurants looking out over the sea at **Yulpo Beach**.

🎉 FESTIVAL

Gangjin Celadon Festival 강진청자축제 – 📞*(062)-222-4234. www.eng.gangjinfes.or.kr.* A different way to learn about celadon. The festival is usually held between 7 and 15 August.

Daehan Dawon Tea Plantation ©KTO

Yeosu★
여수

A small industrial town in the heart of Korea's south coast and an international maritime crossroads—with Northeast Asia on one side and the Pacific Ocean on the other—Yeosu and seafaring are inextricably linked. With a total surface area of 193sq mi/500sq km spread over 300 islands, Yeosu is not lacking in either hills or character. Having been chosen to organize Expo 2012, the city is trying to broaden its horizons and is currently a vast building site. The theme of the Expo for which Yeosu—"Beautiful Waters" in Korean—has been selected is "The Preservation and Sustainable Development of the Ocean and Coast."

- **Population:** 296,479
- **Michelin Map:** Regional map pp320–321
- **Info:** Tourist office at the entrance to the Odongdo pedestrian zone. ℘(061)-664-8978. www.yeosu.go.kr. Open 8am–6pm.
- **Location:** Yeosu is a port city along Korea's southern coast, 231mi/372km from Seoul.
- **Kids:** The walk to Hyangiram, bustling Yeosu Fish Market.
- **Timing:** Allow a morning to explore Hyangiram and an afternoon for Yeosu.
- **Don't Miss:** The hermitage Hyangiram in its spectacular coastal location.

VISIT
Odongdo 오동도
See Jeolla-Do map.
Bus no. 2/8/9/10/13/15/17/107.

This tiny island attached to the mainland by a 2,470ft/750m-long causeway (*or you can take a little train,* Mar–Nov, ₩500) is a very popular holiday destination for Koreans, and foreign visitors will enjoy its restaurants, cafés, souvenir shops and fountains too. Odongdo is, in effect, a **botanical garden** full of camellias (blooming from November until April) and offers a chance to exchange the highway for a network of interesting trails and paths.

In the midst of the greenery stands a **lighthouse-observatory** (*elevator, open 9:30am–5:30pm, no charge*) from which you can **look out★** over the surrounding port and the ships sailing to and fro.

If you have time, just as you leave Odongdo (*to your right*), visit the **Expo 2012 Information Center** (*open 9am–6pm, no charge*) where the ecosystem of the vast Yeosu archipelago is explained. The city is also the venue for the 2012 World Expo. (*http://eng.expo2012.or.kr see box, p344*).

Jinnamgwan 진남관
10min walk NE of Yeosu Ferry Terminal.
The largest wooden building in Korea is to be found in Yeosu city center, a pavilion 250ft/75m long, 45ft/14m high and with a roof supported by 68 columns. Built in 1717, the pavilion was used as a guesthouse by the Korean Navy.

With its relatively favorable location on one of the city's hills, the site also served as Admiral Yi Sun-sin's (1545–98) general headquarters during his struggle against the Japanese invasion a century earlier (*see box p336*).

Upon the admiral's death, which also brought the Imjin War (1592–98) to a close, the site found a new use and an immense pavilion was built in 1599. After burning down, it was rebuilt in 1717. The stone statue facing the pavilion (there are seven of these in the city) was a ruse intended to deceive the enemy, a strategy in which Admiral Yi was well versed.

Just below the pavilion (*to your left as you walk back down*) there is a small **museum** (*open 10am–5pm, no charge*) explaining the naval tactics adopted by Yi to outwit the Japanese

GETTING THERE

BY BUS/COACH – **Yeosu Express** and **Intercity Bus Terminal** is located 2.5mi/4km north of the port area. There are departures for Mokpo (*5:45am–7:30pm, every hour, 3hr30min, ₩17,000*), Gwangju (*every 30min, 2hr15min, ₩9,400*), Busan (*every hour, 3hr, ₩18,700*) and Seoul (*every hour, 5hr, ₩31,000*).

BY TRAIN – From **Yeosu Station** (the main station) there are departures for Suncheon (*45min, ₩2,500*). There is an additional smaller station called **Yeocheon Station**. The KTX is due to be extended to Yeosu to coincide with Expo 2012 Yeosu Korea.

BY BOAT – ☏(*61)-663-0117*) **Yeosu Ferry Terminal** is at the western end of the harbor. There are ferries available to many of the nearby islands.

troops; there is little information in English, unfortunately.

From Jinnamgwan, follow **Jungang-ro**, the main road, down toward the port. You will have to negotiate the central intersection **Jungang-dong Rotary** but can then stop off to browse Market Alley before reaching Yeosu Ferry Terminal. The fish market is not too far away, in the direction of **Dolsan Bridge** (&see below, allow 30min for the walk).

👥 **Yeosu Fish Market** 여수수산시장

The wide range of produce on sale is a reflection of the wealth of fish in the surrounding waters. Among the raw fish consumed here you will find: the delicate flesh of parrotfish, dorado, sole—seasoned with *makgeolli* vinegar—and sea eel either raw, grilled or boiled as in the famous *hamo yubiki,* which is very popular in summer, not to mention tautog, bass, *mya japonica, pleuronichthys cornutus,* red scorpion fish, crab marinated in soy sauce and served with white rice, blue crab soup, traditional grilled oysters or *hapalogenys mucronatus,* a bottom-feeder.

Dolsando★ 돌산도

&See Jeolla-Do map.

The island of Dolsan is accessed along **Dolsandaegyo★★**, the "Great Bridge at Dolsan," the largest cable-stayed crossing in the country.

The bridge carries traffic to and from the mainland 200ft/60m above the sea below. Once across its 1,480ft/450m span, you will soon see Admiral Yi's turtle boat to your right (&see box p336).

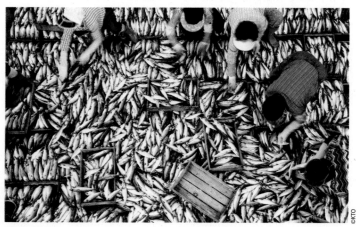

Yeosu Fish Market

The Living Ocean and Coast

Expo 2012 Yeosu will devote three months (12 May–12 August) to expert debate on the sustainable use of the world's oceans and coastlines, as well as the preservation of natural resources—all with an eye toward future global climate changes, green industries and cooperation between nations. The Expo will be open to everyone. Many new facilities are being constructed for the Expo, including a floating stage, an ocean playground, a new pedestrian bridge and an observatory deck, all of which are expected to be available to visitors for years to come.

Admiral Yi Sun-sin's Turtle Boat
이순신장군 거북선

Bus no. 102/105/106/109/111/113/114/115/116. ◷*open 8am–6pm. ₩1,200.*
This replica (◷*see photo p50*) is a reproduction of the first armored boat to set sail under the flag of the Korean Navy. With no keel and a flat bottom, the *Geobukseon* (or *Kobukson*) replica is approximately 100ft/30m long with a beam approaching 40ft/12m and a deck shrouded in planks covered with closely-fitting metal plates like a turtle shell. These plates bristle with row upon row of spikes to discourage any attempt at boarding. The boat was equipped with large hatches (about 20 on each side) topped with firing ports. Cannons and other firearms could take turns firing without interruption, and every point of the boat from stem to stern was equally well armed. The interior of the vessel is deceptively large.

The bridge, which was protected by curved armor plating covered with spikes, prevented boarding but allowed the firing of projectiles. The dragon head adorning the prow was not just intended to give a face to the "beast;" it was also

able to emit sulfurous smoke to choke the enemy.

The flotilla was completed with *panok-seon*, nimble craft that were ideal for maneuvering between the little islands. Admiral Yi Sun-sin fought a decisive battle at Yeosu, repelling the invading Japanese and forcing them to abandon all hope of conquering the Korean Peninsula for the moment.

☺ From here it is possible to take a cruise around Daegyeongdo (*1hr, ₩15,000*), and you will find a string of raw fish restaurants in Dolsan Seafood Town, just beside the landing stage.

Approximately 5mi/7.5km before Hyangiram, the bus passes the beautiful beach at **Bangjukpo,** and on the way, you can also explore **Dolsan Leaf Mustard Farming Union**, one of the places where the renowned Dolsan mustard leaves are produced.

The crop is endemic to the island—a result of the alcalifying properties of the soil—and is an essential ingredient in all Yeosu kimchi.

☺ *To arrange a visit to the center, call the Daeyul Village Association ☏ (061)-644 8722.*

♟♟ Hyangiram★★ 향일암

◷*See Jeolla-Do map. Located 16mi/26km from Dolsan Bridge. Bus no. 111 from the Express Bus Terminal, Jinnamgwan or Dolsan Bridge (4:30am–10pm). For the return journey, bus no. 15 (9:22am – 5:42pm, allow about 1hr, ₩1,000).* ◷ *Open Mar–Oct 6am–10pm, Nov–Feb 9pm. ₩2,000.*
Hyangiram is a Buddhist hermitage and one of four Korean religious sites dedicated to the deity Gwaneum, one of the most important divinities in the Mahayana Buddhist pantheon. Known as Guanyin in China and Kannon in Japan, she also bears the Sanskrit name Avalokitesvara, "She Who Brings Solace to the Anxious." As the goddess of mercy, Gwaneum is also the personification of compassion and a bodhisattva.

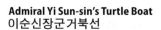

The geography of the temple, which was built by a Buddhist monk named Won-Hyo in the eighth year of the reign of Queen Seondeok of the Silla dynasty (659), was not chosen at random. If you look closely at the peak of Geumsan, you will see that it resembles a turtle about to leap into the sea, and its rocks also seem to overlap like the scales of a turtle's shell.

Building a hermitage on such a rock was associated with a divinatory art, cheloniomancy, which involved the sacrifice of a turtle and the burning of its shell so that the cracks that resulted could be interpreted. Since turtles shared a long life with the universe, it was of the universe itself that the Chinese were thereby asking questions, a custom soon to be adopted by the Silla kingdom. The most unsettling detail is that the buildings making up the hermitage (the Buddha Hall, bell tower and hermitage office) all burnt down in their entirety in 2009. Rather than attempting to interpret the cracks in the rocks, visitors follow a winding narrow path through a magnificent chaos of rocks to an elevation of about 330ft/100m above this place of worship dedicated to the goddess of compassion.

As the jumble of rocks finally stops at a dead end, return to the main walkway before heading left, passing to the right of the Buddha Hall location and following the marked footpath leading to the summit (1,378ft/420m, *allow 30min*). From here, there is a fine **panoramic view★★**, the most impressive part of the site, taking in the headland of the isthmus, which is particularly popular with Koreans at dawn and dusk. To the east you will see Yeosuman (Yeosu Bay) and to the west the archipelago of Dadohae Maritime National Park.

ADDRESSES

🛏STAY

🛏 **Suite Motel** – *504-8 Dundeok-dong.* 𝄐 *(061)-654-3002, (061)-1330 for English. 21rm. ₩30,000.* Choose from six Korean-style rooms or one of the 15 Western-style rooms in this motel, located about 15min (by car) from Odongdo Island.

🛏🛏 **Hotel Eastern Jewelry** 이스턴쥬얼리호텔 – *Chungmu-dong 346.* 𝄐*(061)-664-7070.* 🖥 ✕. *58rm. ₩80,000.* An impeccable business hotel right next to Yeosu's main shopping street, and the hotel of choice for those on business trips.

ⵏ/EAT

Yeosu is an ideal place in which to try **raw fish**. The main districts for this are Jonghwa-dong, Manseongni, Soho-dong and Dolsan Bridge.

🛏🛏 **Hemingway** 헤밍웨이 – *Located to the left of the entrance to Dolsan Bridge.* 𝄐*(061)-662-9912.* It's not so much the food—which is fine—but the excellent view of the bay and bridge that makes this establishment unmissable. *Expect to pay ₩9,000 for a cutlet and ₩11,000 for a steak.*

Hyangiram Temple, Dolsando Island

©TOPIC PHOTO AGENCY IN / age fotostock

Suncheon
순천

As a large agricultural and industrial city, Suncheon is emerging as the ecological capital of South Korea. The city and surrounding area comprise a natural—relatively untouched—ecosystem. The city itself provides a good base from which to explore the region, which includes some magnificent temples in Jogyesan Provincial Park and fine natural sites such as Suncheon Bay.

VISIT

Jogyesan Provincial Park★★
조계산도립공원

See Jeolla-Do map. Allow around 6hr for the 5.5mi/8.5km walk between the park's two temples. There is a collection of small restaurants beside the entrance.

Janggunbong, the principal peak of the mountain Jogyesan, is 549ft/884m high, but the main attractions in this small park are the two magnificent temples. A number of paths lead from one to the other, and one of the most spectacular of these will also take you across Janggunbong.

Seonamsa★★★
(Seonam Temple) 선암사

See Jeolla-Do map. Located 17mi/28km W of Suncheon. Bus no. 1 from the bus terminal or the rail station (5:50am–8:20pm, every 30min, 50min). www.seonamsa.net. Open 4am–10pm. ₩1,500.

Nestled at the foot of Jogyesan, on the eastern slopes of its peak Janggunbong, Seonamsa was built in the 9C by a priest called Doseon. Its name—which means "the Rock of the Heavens"—was inspired by a summit on which the mountain god was said to have played the game Go (*baduk*). The temple has been the headquarters of the Taego Buddhist order since 1985.

To reach the temple you first have to cross running water; for Buddhists, a natural boundary such as this separates

- ▶ **Population:** 270,274
- **Michelin Map:** Regional map pp320–321
- **Info:** Rail station, ✆(061)-749-3107, open Mon–Sat 9am–6pm; bus terminal, ✆(061)-749-3839, open Mon–Sat 9am–6pm. Excellent tourist maps. http://english.suncheon. go.kr/home/english/
- ▶ **Location:** Suncheon is located 45mi/73km southeast of Gwangju; 90mi/145km northeast of Mokpo; 132mi/213km west of Busan and 28mi/45km northeast of Yeosu. Seonamsa and Songgwangsa are 17mi/28km and 30mi/48km west of Suncheon, respectively.
- **Kids:** Go birdwatching in Suncheon Bay, see how Koreans used to live at Nagan Folk Village, explore Suncheon Open Film Set.
- **Timing:** Allow a whole day for Jogyesan Provincial Park. The Suncheon City Tour will enable you to visit all the main sites in a day.
- **Don't Miss:** Songgwangsa (one of the Korean Buddhist "Jewel Temples") and Seonamsa.

the sacred from the secular. As you cross **Seungseongyo★★★** (1707), the stone bridge with a perfect semicircular arch, you enter a different world and a different mood.

The temple is in perfect harmony with its surroundings in this tranquil setting. The mirror image of the bridge reflected in the water makes a perfect circle, perhaps prompting visitors to pause for reflection. This helps ensure that they approach the entrance to the temple in the correct frame of mind, an aesthetic sense being, for many, a religious one.

The dragon head adorning the central section of the arc was intended to drive away evil spirits; as its eyes are lowered, it is possible to imagine that these dark forces were perceived in the swirling waters below.

Among the other curiosities, there are the temple bathrooms (*haeuso*), much prized for their communion with nature, and four great stone basins, **seokjo★**, with interlinking bamboo pipes that allowed the temple to transport water to the kitchen in the absence of modern plumbing.

A number of films and television series have been made at Seonamsa. The producer Joo Kyung-jung, for example, used Seungseon Bridge and the stone basins for his film *A Little Monk* (2002), and several locations in the temple are identifiable in Im Kwon-taek's very beautiful film, *Drunk on Women and Poetry* (2002).

Songgwangsa★★★
(Songgwang Temple) 송광사
See Jeolla-Do map. Located 30mi/ 48km W of Suncheon. Bus no. 111 from the bus terminal or the rail station (6am–8:40pm, every 30min, 70min, ₩1,000). Buses leave the temple every 40min (first bus 7am, last bus 8:55pm). www.songgwangsa.org.
Open 4am–10pm. ₩2,500.
The rise of Songgwangsa is bound up with the influence of the great *Seon*

GETTING THERE
BY TRAIN – There are departures for Jeonju from the centrally located Suncheon Station. (*1hr30min, ₩7,200*).
BY BUS/COACH – There are departures from Suncheon Jon-Hab Bus Terminal complex (*in the city center, 1mi/1.5km from the train station*) for **Songgwangsa** (*buses at 8:45am/9:55 am/10:45am/2:55pm/3:45pm, 90min, ₩6,500*).

SIGHTSEEING
City Tour – The city organizes a number of outings and these represent ideal and economical excursions for visitors on a tight schedule; tours leave from the rail station. The route takes in the Open Film Set followed by Seonamsa, Nagan Folk Village and Suncheon Bay. *Tour begins at 9:50am on Tue and Fri, returning at 5:30pm, ₩7,000. Same route on Mon and Wed with the addition of Songgwangsa, which is farther away: departs 8am, returning 5:30pm, ₩9,000. Reservations are required in advance.*

(Korean Zen Buddhism) master Jinul (1158–1210), who had brought together the two dominant schools of Buddhist thought of the time; the nine mountain schools imported by the Chinese Tang dynasty had favored meditation,

Seungseondngyo, Seonamsa
©KTO

Songgwangsa

©KTO

while the studious nature of the Gyo doctrine schools inclined toward the study of Buddhist texts. By synthesizing these two approaches, Jinul opened a new path to enlightenment that also awakened hope of national unity in the kingdom of Goryeo (918–1392).

As this sense of unity matured, a new location for its teaching was required,

The Third Jewel?

Songgwangsa is the Third Korean Jewel Temple—there are three Jewel Temples in all, each one representing one of the three jewels of Buddhism (the Buddha, dharma and sangha). The two other temples are both in Gyeongsang Province: Tongdosa, associated with the Buddha (*Bul* in Korean) for its Sakyamuni relics (see p304), and Haeinsa, associated with *dharma* (Buddhist teachings, *beob* in Korean) for the 80,000 carved tablets of its *Tripitaka Koreana* (see p267). Songgwangsa, known for its many *guksa* or national masters, is associated with *sangha* (community of Buddhist monks, or *seung* in Korean).

and in 1200 the master relocated to the little hermitage of Gilsangsa at the foot of Songgwangsan, which he renamed Jogye in honor of the mountain in southern China where the man who had inspired him, Huineng (638–713)—the sixth patriarch of the Dhyana school of Buddhism and the founder of Chan (Japanese Zen)—had once taught. Gilsansa became Songgwangsa, "the Monastery of the Great Pine Tree," Jinul was awarded the title **Bojo-guksa**, "the Master of Universal Enlightenment," and the order he founded was named Jogye. Since the death of its founder (the 800th anniversary of which was in 2010), the Jogye order has been the largest Buddhist order in the country. After Jinul Bojo, 15 other Koreans have attained the rank of master (*guksa*), an exceptional number, which has earned the temple the title of the third jewel of Buddhism (see box above).

Although the temple was founded in the 9C, most of the religious buildings are 17C reconstructions. Among the most remarkable works is the National Treasure **Guksajeon★★★** (1369), which houses portraits of 16 national masters. **Seongbo Museum★** in the middle of the temple complex (open 9am–11am, noon–6pm) has a fine collection of pieces, including in particular a

bulgam★★, a portable wooden triptych of Buddhist statues. The other buildings, which include dormitories for the monks and rooms for teaching, study and meditation, are closed to the public.

ADDITIONAL SIGHTS
🏛🧍 Nagan Folk Village★
낙안민속촌
🚻 *See Jeolla-Do map. Bus no. 1/111 from Suncheon (every hour, 40min, ₩2,000). Naganeupseong.*
☎️ *(061)-749-3347. www.nagan.or.kr.*
🕐 *Open 9am–6pm. ₩2,000.*
Nagan Folk Village (*Naganeupseong*) is in a league of its own. Surrounded by 1,500yd/1,400m of fortress wall dating back to a Joseon-era stronghold, it is one of the few fortified villages to have survived intact. The earthworks built in the 14C were replaced in the 17C on the orders of General Im Gyeong-eop (1594–1646), resulting in this small curtain wall, dressed with stone and punctuated by four gates and six watchtowers.
Now designated a folk village, this is a perfect place to discover how Koreans lived in the past—with wickerwork demonstrations, changing of the guard, singing and folk dancing, there is everything you would expect, right down to the small ethnographic museum.

🏛🧍 Suncheon Bay★★★ 순천만
🚻 *See Jeolla-Do map.*
Suncheon City Daedae-dong 162-2.
☎️ *(061)-749-3107, (061)-749-3328.*
www.suncheonbay.go.kr. 🕐 *Open Apr–Sep: Tue–Sun 10am–9pm. ₩2,000.*
Bus no. 67/81/82 from Cheil High School and bus no. 91/92 from Samsam-dong every 40min. Suncheon City Tour ecotourism tours depart daily 9:50am, return 6:30pm.
Recognized in 2006 by the Ramsar Convention (the international convention whose mission is "the conservation and wise use of all wetlands through local and national actions and international cooperation, as a contribution toward achieving sustainable development throughout the world"), Suncheon Bay (*Suncheonman*) is a protected wetland that has been preserved as closely as possible to its original state as a coastal estuary ecosystem.

Autumn, Suncheon Bay

©KTO

Ecotourist activities revolve around watching the migratory birds that find refuge in this coastal marsh and its magnificent beds of golden reeds (21sq mi/54sq km), which can be crossed in part via a splendid **walkway★★★**; you may be lucky enough to catch sight of birds such as the hooded crane, the black-faced spoonbill, Saunders' gull, wild duck and snipe (a close relative of the woodcock).

From the **Yongsan Observatory** (*open Apr–Sep 10am–9pm, ₩2,000*) there is a very beautiful view, especially at dusk, of the S-shaped channel leading out to Suncheon Bay.

👥 Suncheon Open Film Set★
순천드라마세트장

Jorye-dong. About 10min by bus no. 777. *Open 9am–6pm. ₩3,000.* Suncheon boasts one of the largest film sets in Korea (with some 200 buildings). Numerous television series have been made here and the studio area of some 60,000sq yd/5ha includes three whole suburbs, each representing a different era from the 1960s to the 1980s. You might stumble across a Seoul neighborhood from the 1980s or a 1970s shanty-town spread over a hillside. The set can be rented for ₩800,000 a day.

ADDRESSES

🏠 STAY

SUNCHEON

🛏 **Motel Romeo** 로미오모텔 – *290-7 Pungdeok-dong.* *(061)-745-6060.* 📠. *35rm. ₩35,000. Close to the rail station (5min by taxi).* A little characterless but very comfortable (internet access, TV and toothbrushes).

SONGGWANGSA

🛏 **Songgwangsa Temple Stay** 송광사 템플스테이 – *12 Seojeong-ri, Songji-myeon.* *(061)-755-0108. www.songgwangsa.org.* 📠. *₩40,000.* During the summer, the temple organizes meditation retreats in English. These generally start at 6pm on a Saturday and run until 9pm before resuming at 3am on Sunday until 10am, during which time participants are fully involved in the spiritual and physical life of the temple, with compulsory daily chores. The *beopgo*, the ritual drum that calls monks to prayer, soon becomes a familiar sound.

🍽 EAT

SUNCHEON

🍴🍴🍴 **Cheonghae Japanese Food** 청해한일정식 – *Deokwol-dong 2-11.* *(011)-603-0000/(061)-742-1717. Open 11am–midnight. ₩30,000. A taxi is recommended; expect to pay ₩3,500 from the rail station.* This sophisticated restaurant is an agreeable surprise, and the freshness of the raw fish is as impeccable as the service. Expect to pay ₩20,000 for a set menu. A treat indeed.

🎭 EVENTS AND FESTIVALS

Southern Province Food Cultural Festival 남도음식문화축제 – *Nagan Folk Village.* *(61)-749-4221. www.namdofood.or.kr* . Representatives of more than 22 towns and cities gather here over five days at the end of October to show off their cooking skills, an annual event which attracts huge crowds to the many stalls.

Reed Festival 갈대축제 – *Suncheon Bay.* *(61)-749-3328/3742.* For several days each November the focus is on exploring the amazing reed beds of Suncheon Bay.

Jeonju★★
전주

Jeonju, the capital city of North Jeolla Province and South Korea's "rice bowl," also saw the rise of one of the greatest royal dynasties the country has ever known—the Joseon dynasty, which was to rule Korea for more than five centuries. Although only a few great buildings have survived from this period, a unique traditional village has been preserved: Jeonju Hanok Maeul. The Hanok Village is the largest in the country and is certainly worth seeing. As the most celebrated tourist site in Jeonju, it is also a showcase for the city's traditional activities such as making paper and fans and brewing alcohol, as well as its gastronomy and delicious "*bibimbap*," which can be sampled here within the walls of a traditional *hanok*. However, Jeonju does not live solely on past glories; the city also plays host to the most eclectic film festivals in Korea, and one of its districts boasts the greatest concentration of movie theaters in the country.

⚓WALKING TOUR

Hanok Village

▶ *From the bus terminal, take the bus for Nambu Market and get off at Jeondong Cathedral; from the rail station, take bus no. 163/111 and get off at the same stop. Expect to pay ₩3,200 by taxi and ask to be dropped off in front of Pungnammun, 55yd/50m from the village entrance which is located on the other side of the Paldal-ro road, opposite the cathedral.*

Jeonju Hanok Maeul★★★
전주한옥마을
The useful mini-map of the area available from tourist offices makes it very easy to get around. No charge.

▶ **Population:** 41,549

⌖ **Michelin Map:** Regional map pp320–321

▤ **Info:** Of the three tourist offices in the Hanok Village, the easiest to find is situated to the right of Gyeonggijeon Shrine: ☏(063)-287-1330, http://tour-eng.jeonju. go.kr/, open 9am–6pm. The second is on Taejo-ro road, and the third is tucked away near the Jeonju Traditional Culture Center. www.chf.or.kr/chf/eng/

▶ **Location:** Jeollabuk-do's (North Jeolla Province) capital city is located 145mi/233km south of Seoul.

▲▲ **Kids:** The trails of Maisan Provincial Park.

◷ **Timing:** Allow a whole day for the Hanok Maeul and half a day or even a whole day for Maisan Provincial Park.

✿ **Don't Miss:** The traditional houses of Hanok Maeul, beautiful Maisan Provincial Park.

Kimchi jars, Jeonju Hanok Maeul

©KTO

GETTING THERE

BY TRAIN – Jeonju Station – Situated east of the city center. Frequent departures for Seoul, including by KTX (but change at Iksan) and south to Jeollanam-do.

BY BUS/COACH – Express Bus Terminal – There are departures for Gwangju (*every 30min, 1hr15min, ₩6,000*) and Seoul (*every 10min, 3hr, ₩11,000*).

Intercity Bus Terminal – There are departures for Gochang (*every 30min, 1hr30min, ₩5,400*). The Intercity terminal is located a few blocks south of the Express Terminal.

GETTING AROUND

BY BUS/COACH – The Intercity and Express Bus terminals are in the city center, located a few blocks from each other.

BY TAXI – The minimum fare is ₩2,200; expect to pay ₩3,800 for a 2mi/3.5km journey *(10min)*.

USEFUL INFORMATION

Banks – If you experience difficulty withdrawing money using a Visa card, the **City Bank** ATM at the corner of Paldal-ro and Daedong-ro is one of the few that allows transactions.

http://tour-eng.jeonju.go.kr/ (click on "Hanok Village" banner).

The Hanok Village, which lies to the south of the modern city of Jeonju, contains 700 traditional houses (*hanok*), of which about a dozen have been converted into guesthouses (⊙ *see Addresses*). The others accommodate stores, restaurants, cafés and museums, while some are still occupied as dwellings. Having been restored over the years—in a sometimes overly fastidious manner—the village has an attractive architectural cohesiveness with its sea of roofs and rows of *hanok* neatly divided by alleyways, but as the majority of the village is now a visitor attraction, it can get extremely busy, with large numbers of visitors particularly at weekends.

The many and varied sites of interest are located on either side of **Taejo-ro**, the main road through the village which is also the place to sample delicious *pondegi*, boiled silkworm larvae, among other delicacies.

Of the usual four gates that classical Chinese geomancy dictates must be present, only the southern gate, **Pungnammun★★ (풍남문)**, has survived, with the other three having fallen victim to town planning initiatives since 1905. Restored in 1978 and now listed as a National Treasure, this 18C gate has its roots in a 14C structure from the beginning of the Joseon period, and is the pride of Jeonju.

Just opposite the Paldal-ro expressway, at the entrance to the village on Taejo-ro

Traditional *Hanok*

Traditional *hanok* are based on an architectural principle known as *baesanimsu*, literally meaning that the ideal house should be built facing a river with its back to a mountain. The layout should respect the demands of the seasons—in a closed square form in colder regions, more open in warmer regions—with a spatial partition to divide the sexes. The *sarangchae*, the room where the men live and work, is the most visible part of the house and also most closely linked to the exterior; the *anchae*, the space reserved for the women, is located in the farthest reaches at the back of the house. While men and women live apart, they share the same underfloor heating system, the *ondol*. By contrast, the *maru* is a room with a wooden floor that is largely open to the elements. The *hanok* represents a successful union and synthesis of two architectural approaches that initially had been intended for two entirely dissimilar areas and climates.

Jeonju *Bibimbap*

Jeonju, one of the gastronomic capitals of Korea, is famous for its *bibimbap*, largely thanks to the surrounding region of Honam, one of the most fertile in Korea. The richness of the soil allows the locals to make increasingly complex *bibimbap*, using some 30 or more ingredients, according to the recipe. Every cook jealously guards his or her own recipe, but here is one version to try: to rice that has been cooked in the skimmed stock obtained from simmering a calf's head add sesame oil, soy sauce, liquid honey, *mung* bean sprouts, soya beans, cress, edible fern stems, spinach, carrots, leeks, zucchini, a few Chinese bellflower roots, some *pyogo* mushrooms, herbs from the chrysanthemum family known as *ssuk* in Korean, an egg and, of course, some beef. All seasoned with red pepper sauce…

is the charming redbrick facade of **Jeon-dong Cathedral★**. The work of Xavier Baudounet (1859–1915), a French missionary, this was one of the first cathedrals to be constructed in Korea (1914). The Romano-Byzantine building is a commemoration of Korea's first Catholic martyrs, who were put to death in Jeonju; six Catholics were decapitated here in 1801 and their heads put on display in front of **Pungnammun** in an attempt to dissuade others from taking up the faith; the cathedral's stained-glass windows are dedicated to these first victims of persecution.

▷ *Cross over Taejo-ro.*

Gyeonggijeon★ (🕐 *9am–6pm*) is an impressive architectural illustration of the ancestor worship that was an essential part of the Confucianism espoused by the Joseon dynasty (1392–1910), under whom the first national Confucianist academy (*Seonggyungwan*) was founded. **Gyeonggijeon Hall★** (1410) provides an opportunity to pay homage to the royal portrait of Taejo (Yi Seong-gye before his coronation), a native of Hamheung (North Korea) and the founder of the Joseon dynasty (🝰*see p57*). The memorial tablets of the king and his wife are held at **Jogyeong Shrine★** (1771).

▷ *For a good view of the village and to maintain the historical theme, keep walking to the end of Taejo-ro to reach Omokdae.*

Pungnammun

© Manfred Gottschalk/age fotostock

Celebrating the Silver Screen

A number of film festivals are now held in South Korea. The **Jeonju International Film Festival** (*www.jiff.or.kr*) held at the end of April is very accessible and a must for fans of art house and experimental cinema. It also promotes and finances original productions.

Summer is punctuated by two equally original festivals: **Pifan — or the Puchon International Film Festival** (*www.pifan.com*)—is held in mid-July and is dedicated to fantasy films from all over the world, while at the beginning of August it is the turn of the **Jecheon International Music and Film Festival** (*www.jimff.org*).

Finally, 1 October each year signals the start of the **Busan International Film Festival** (*www.piff.org*) on Haeundae Beach, one of the most important film festivals in Asia (see also p298 and p310).

Omokdae is the pavilion where Yi Seong-gye (before he became king) gave a banquet to celebrate a victory over Japanese corsairs in 1380.

You may find the places listed below more of interest for the buildings than for the exhibits they house.

Jeonju Oriental Medicine Culture Center (전주한방문화센터 *open 10am–6pm*). The only museum dedicated to Korean medicine explains the use of medicinal herbs. Visitors can try various tests intended to establish that the causes of sickness lie in an imbalance of vital forces weakening the immune system, rather than any organic pathology. The more interesting **Jeonju Hanji**

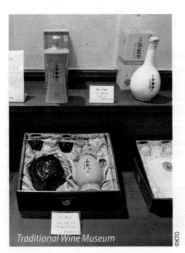
Traditional Wine Museum
©KTO

Center (전주한지박물관 *open Tue–Sun 9am–5pm*), located in a very beautiful *hanok*, exports to Japan 80 percent of the traditional paper that it makes from mulberry bark.

The **Traditional Wine Museum** (전주전통술박물관 *open Tue–Sun 9am–7pm (winter 6pm)*), also housed in a fine *hanok*, has a stock of traditional wines from the Honam region. Five types of alcoholic drink are generally broadly recognized: *yakju*, a pure spirit refined from fermented rice, much like *cheongju*, also known as "clear liquor," which is rather similar to sake; *takju*, an unrefined, thick drink made from fermented grains—a classic example of this is *makgeolli*. There is distilled liquor, such as *soju*, which can be made from rice, potatoes, wheat, barley, sweet potatoes or tapioca (known as *dangmil* in Korean); and last but not least, wine, either fruit-based, such as *igangju*, a liqueur made from pears and ginger, or medicinal concoctions made from cereals and roots.

The temporary exhibitions in the **Traditional Craftwork Exhibition Hall** (*open Tue–Sun 10am–7pm (winter 6pm)* on Taejo-ro are often of quite good quality. (*You can also try your hand at making porcelain or hanji, 20min–1hr, ₩2,000–10,000 per person*).

Beyond the Hanok Village, the main streets of interest in Jeonju are concentrated in the Gosa Dong district, about 20min walk NE of Pungnammun.

Gosa Dong and Around 고사동

Of the many themed streets running through the district of **Gosa Dong**, Street of Film is by far the most interesting. There are numerous movie theaters, in which you can see the latest releases (*in the original version, average admission ₩7,000*). Some of the sidewalks, which are thronged with people in the evenings, are imprinted with the names of Korean actors just like the world-famous but rather more understated *Walk of Fame* on Hollywood Boulevard.

▷ *Head due east from the Street of Film, and you will come to the Street of Youth*

Also known as the "*street that is desired to walk,*" the **Street of Youth** is a partially roofed-over pedestrian street dedicated to committed shoppers. Walk farther north along this gallery of stores to reach **Tools Street**, which meets the appropriately named Consumerism Street at an angle. Heading in the other direction (*due south*), the Street of Youth leads to **Jeonju Gaeksa** (*92 Chunggyeong-ro*), a largely restored 15C house used to accommodate important visitors.

Once a symbol of the authority and might of the Joseon dynasty, it is now a place for trendy young people to meet before making for the consumerist delights of the Street of Youth.

▷ *Head west to the other side of Chunggyeong-ro to see a pleasant Chinese gate.*

The gate is the entrance to **Chinatown**, Jeonju's rather disappointing and small Chinese quarter. Its main street, which has a number of (good) Chinese restaurants, crosses Jungang-dong district before turning into **Wedding Street**, where couples with marriage plans and deep pockets can enjoy a spending spree (*the best time to visit is Saturday*).

EXCURSIONS

👥 Maisan Provincial Park★★★ 마이산 도립공원

🕐 *See Jeolla-Do map. Allow at least half a day. Take the bus to Jinan (25mi/40km E of Jeonju, every 30min, 50min, ₩4,000) from the Intercity Bus terminal. At Jinan Bus Terminal, take another bus to the northern entrance of Maisan Park (every 40min, 10min, ₩1,000).* 🕐*Open Mar–Oct 9am–6pm, Nov–Feb 9am–5pm. Once past the usual assembly of assorted stores at the entrance, a flight of steps leads to the first temple.*

Maisan means a mountain "shaped like a horse's ear," referring to two magnificent peaks composed of conglomerate rocks (rare in Korea) around the foot of which visitors must skirt to reach the temples **Eunsusa★** and **Tapsa★★**. **Sutmaisan** (Male Maisan) is the eastern peak at 2,231ft/680m, while **Ammaisan**

Mt. Maisan
©KTO

(Female Maisan) is slightly higher at 2,251ft/686m. The "female" mountain being larger than the male might seem a little unusual, but the smaller mountain is in a position to watch the sun rise while the larger is only illuminated as it sets.

The most striking feature within the grounds of the first temple, **Eunsusa**, is a magnificent **pear tree**★★, 59ft/18m high and 10ft/3m around. The **path**★★ leading down to **Tapsa**, which lies at the foot of Ammaisan, is lovely.

Tapsa (Pagoda Temple) is surrounded by tall piles of stones forming towers, astonishingly remaining intact despite a lack of mortar. This strange sight is the work of one lay Buddhist monk called Yi Kab-ryong (1860–1957), who built it on the principles of *um* and *yang*—the Korean equivalent of the Chinese *yin* and *yang*—and *Paljindo*, a deployment plan for troops favored by the Chinese strategist Zhu Geliang (181–234). The result is a world of shapes as "auspicious" as the small cairns that his followers pile up here as tokens of a wish that has been granted or is yet to be fulfilled.

From here you may like to continue on to **Tapyeongje Lake**★, which is particularly popular when the cherry trees are in blossom.

ADDRESSES

🏨 STAY

Although value for money may sometimes be sacrificed in the interests of profit, spending one night in a *hanok* really is a must if you can manage it. The rooms may be handkerchief-sized and some may not necessarily give you much of a sense of cultural dislocation when they come equipped with a television, a mini-fridge and a tiny bathroom with modern facilities, so try to check out the rooms before committing yourself, and avoid the weekends. Booking at busy times is essential.

IN THE HANOK VILLAGE

🛏 **Seunggwangjae** 승광재 – *20 Todam-gil.* ℘ *(063)-283-0071. www.royalcity.or.kr. 7rm. From ₩60,000.* 🛏 *₩5,000.* This B&B is run by Lee Seok, an English-speaking descendant of King Gojong, the 26th king of the Joseon dynasty. An interesting place to stay.

🛏 **Yangsajae** 양사재 – *35 Ssangsaem 1-gil.* ℘ *(063)-282-4959. www.jeonju tour.co.kr. Open Mon–Sat. 6rm. From ₩40,000.* Tiny but comfortable rooms in a delightful building that has the advantage of a convenient location at the end of Omokdae-gil in the southwest corner of the village, well clear of the area overrun by tourists. English spoken.

🛏🛏 **Hakindang** 학인당 – *65 Hyanggyo-ro.* ℘ *(063)-284-9929. 7rm. ₩60,000–100,000.* While the rooms are small, the rest of the site, which was completed at the end of the Joseon dynasty and is laid out around a pleasant Japanese-style garden, is one of the most beautiful *hanok* houses in Jeonju. You can also take part in a tea ceremony in one of the magnificent rooms in a house that once played host to such personalities as Kim Gu (1876–1949), one of the great historical figures in the Korean independence movement.

🛏🛏 **Jeonju Hanok Living Experience Center** 전주한옥생활체험관 – *33-43-ga Pungnam-dong, Wansan-gu.* ℘*(063)-287-6300. www.jjhanok.com. 7rm. ₩60,000–120,000 depending on room size.* This recently refurbished building has the feel of a youth hostel, and breakfast and bicycle hire are included in the price. Plenty of activities offered.

🛏🛏🛏 **Jeonju Core Riviera Hotel** 코아리베라호텔 – *480 Girin-ro, Wansan-gu, Hanok Village.* ℘*(063)-232-7000. www.core-riviera.co.kr.* 🍽 *166rm. ₩150,000.* 🛏 *₩10,000.* With its lofty location above the traditional roofs (make sure you get a room with a view of the village), this large hotel is the most luxurious in the city. An excellent location right next to the traditional district.

GOSA DONG DISTRICT

🛏 **Hall in One** 홀인원 모텔 –
5 Jungangdong-gil, Wansan-gu.
✆*(063)-232-7123.* 📠 . *28rm. ₩40,000.*
Branded under the Koreanized name
of *Horiwon*, this hotel offers some
bargain rates. Internet available.

🛏 **Jeonju Tourist Hotel** 전주관
광호텔 – *28, Daga-dong 3 (sam)-ga,
Wansan-gu.* ✆*(063)-280-7700.*
www.jjhotel.co.kr. 📠 – 🍴. *42rm.*
₩60,000. This very good hotel offers
excellent value for the money.
Although a little way from the Hanok
Village (*20min walk*), it compensates
by lying right in the heart of the Gosa
Dong district, just around the corner
from the Street of Film and its many
multiplexes. Ideal for anyone hoping to
escape the tourist frenzy in the Hanok
Village. Internet available.

🍴/**EAT**

🍴 Most of the **restaurants** are open
between *11am and 9pm*; you can
book a table via the tourist office.

🍴 **Damun** 다문 – *Located in a lane
running parallel with Eunhaeng-ro.*
✆*(063)-288-8607. Around ₩30,000.
Reservation recommended.* The
signature dish of this restaurant
occupying an extremely old *hanok*
building is *hanjeongsik*, a traditional
Korean banquet meal using the best
local produce.

🍴 **Hangookjib** 한국집 – *At the corner
of Paldal-ro and Chunggyeong-no.*
✆*(063)-284-2224.* Pass on the first
room and head for the delightful
pavilion at the back, which looks out
over a little Japanese garden. A very
popular place with families. *Delicious
bibimbap for less than ₩10,000.*

🍴 **Pungnamjeong** 풍남정 – *Not
far from the cathedral.* ✆*(063)-285-
7782.* Uncomplicated, tasty and good
value for the money; an ideal place to
sample Jeonju's specialties, such as
kongnamulgukbap, rice served in a
broth with bean sprouts, or excellent
bibimbap (*₩8,000*). No charge for
coffee or water.

Jeonju International Film Festival

©Jeonju International Film Festival

🎭**EVENTS AND FESTIVALS**

Jeonju Bibimbap Festival
전주비빔밥축제 – Held at the end
of **October,** an ideal opportunity to
try the best *bibimbap* in Korea.
www.bibimbapfest.com.

Jeonju Hanji Culture Festival
전주한지문화축제 – Held every year
in the Hanok Village at the beginning
of May. *www.jhanji.or.kr*

Jeonju International Film Festival
전주국제영화제 – One of the most
dynamic festivals in Korea takes place
every year from the end of April to
the beginning of May in the Sori Art
Center and on the Street of Film
(*www.jiff.or.kr*).

CULTURAL EVENTS
Jeonju Traditional Culture Center
전주전통문화센터 – *7-1 Gyo-Dong,
in the southeast corner of the Hanok
Village, beside Hanbyeokgyo Bridge.*
✆*(063)-280-7000. www.jt.or.kr. Tue–
Sat 7:30pm. ₩5,000.* This theater
presents evening performances of
Korean culture (*pansori*, dance and
other art forms). You can also take part
in various workshops, including a tea
ceremony, Korean cookery and more.

JEJU-DO

Jeju Island, off the peninsula's southern tip, has long been the "Hawaii" of South Korea and, as such, was for decades the most popular Korean honeymoon spot. But as newlyweds these days often splurge for a trip to the real Hawaii, Jeju has lost a bit of popularity while remaining just as beautiful as ever. For the tourist, this means reasonable prices in even the higher-end hotels, plus smaller crowds than you might expect elsewhere.

Highlights

1 Spot pheasants or deer on a hike up **Mt. Halla** (p364)
2 Walk the **Manjanggul Lava Tube** (p365)
3 Discover the mermaids of **Jeju-do** (p366)
4 Watch sunrise from the peak at **Seongsan Ilchulbong** (p367)
5 **Golf** at one of the many world-class courses (p375)

Natural Playground

More than anything else, people visit Jeju for its host of rare natural wonders, some found nowhere else in the world. Manjanggul, one of the numerous lava tube caves, is one of the longest in the world and is part of a larger system that has UNESCO World Heritage status. A popular hike is the sunrise visit to Seongsan Ilchulbong Peak, a cinder cone that projects into the ocean and offers an unparalleled view.

Equally impressive is Mt. Halla, which rises from the center of Jeju, the tallest volcanic crater in a "sea" of smaller ones. Hiking here is varied—the woods and grasslands gradually give way to alpine-like tundra. Look back over your shoulder to see the smaller cinder cones. Many have eroded to gentle mounds, but together they make up a fascinating portrait of volcanoes long gone.

Most of the big tourist hotels and golf courses lie on the southern side of the island, but Jeju City, the capital, is on the north. The city offers nightlife and entertainment, along with a host of excellent Korean and international restaurants.

On arrival on Jeju-Do, visitors will notice almost immediately curious stone totems, some large, some small, resembling a happy gnome carved out of the black basalt. Known as dol hareubang ("stone grandfathers"), these curious idols grin out at passersby everywhere. Their origins are unknown, but they are a picturesque Jeju symbol that is not easily forgotten. Also ubiquitous are Jeju's clementine orange farms. Many offer tourists the chance to grab a box and pick their own, which are then charged by the kilo. It's fun and usually reasonably priced.

Dol hareubang – "stone grandfathers" of Jeju-do

©TOPIC PHOTO AGENCY IN/age fotostock

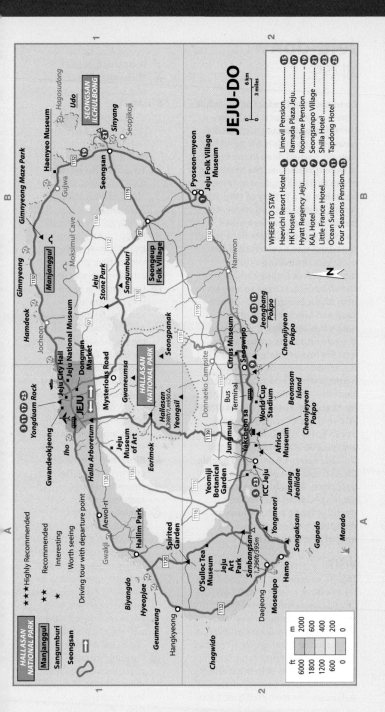

JEJU-DO

HALLASAN NATIONAL PARK
- ★★★ Highly Recommended
- ★★ Recommended
- ★ Interesting
- ● Worth seeing
- → Driving tour with departure point

WHERE TO STAY
Haevichi Resort Hotel......	❶
HK Hostel................	❸
Hyatt Regency Jeju.......	❺
KAL Hotel..............	❼
Little France Hotel......	❾
Ocean Suites...........	⓫
Four Seasons Pension....	⓭
Limevil Pension........	⓯
Ramada Plaza Jeju......	⓱
Roomine Pension.......	⓳
Seongsanpo Village.....	㉑
Shilla Hotel...........	㉓
Tapdong Hotel.........	㉕

ft / m
6000 / 2000
1800 / 600
1200 / 400
600 / 200
0 / 0

0 ————— 6 km
0 ——— 3 miles

N

Jeju-do★★
제주도

An island paradise for some—while others despair that it has been turned into an amusement park—nowhere else in Korea is quite like Jeju-do. Forged deep in the furnace of raging volcanoes, the black land of the ancient kingdom of Tamna has taken on a variety of surprising forms, from cones and craters to basalt columns and lava tubes. The subtropical climate has turned the island into a colorful garden of forests containing a riot of mandarin trees, palms and azaleas. Luxurious hotels have sprung up near idyllic beaches where white sand and black rocks contrast with turquoise seas. A variety of themed museums are breathing new life into an island culture founded on legends, while the hiking paths are popular with eco-tourists—Jeju-do has something for everyone. There are restaurants all over South Korea—compare South Korea's 12.2 restaurants for every 1,000 inhabitants with the United States' 1.8 per 1,000 people, for example—and Jeju is no exception. A wealth of restaurants serve specialties that include porridge made with abalone or pumpkin, barbecued black pig and, of course, fresh fish.

VISIT

Jeju-si, or Jeju City, the island's capital, is a busy, sizable town of 400,000 inhabitants with the normal Korean city sights you would expect: small vans selling vegetables dawdle down residential streets in the evenings, local temples are hung with lanterns for the Buddha's birthday, scooters deliver advertising leaflets and traffic queues jam the central streets. The town itself is not a tourist destination, but with all its facilities, transport links, hotels and restaurants, you are almost certain to pass through at some point. Life here revolves around

▶ **Population:** 565,519

Michelin Map: Regional map p359

Info: Tourist offices at Jeju airport, open daily 6:30am–8pm; the ferry terminal, open daily 6:30am–8pm; Yongduam Rock, open daily 9am–8pm; Jungmun, at the resort entrance, open daily 9am–6pm; and Seogwipo, Cheonjiyeon Pokpo car park, open daily 10am–6pm. General information: ℘(064)-1330. http://english.tour2jeju.net/

Location: Jeju Island is 45mi/73km long and 19mi/31km wide, and lies 53mi/85km off the south coast of the peninsula. There are two main conurbations, Jeju-si on the north coast and Seogwipo on the south coast; the island's interior is dominated by Hallasan, an extinct volcano (6,398ft/1,950m).

Kids: There are plenty of activities, including amusement parks and water parks.

Timing: The island is accessible all year and takes at least two days to explore, although four days would be better. Jeju is crowded in the summer months as well as during holidays and on long weekends, when prices are higher. Booking well ahead is essential during these times.

Parking: There are car parks, for which there is often a charge, at most tourist attractions.

Don't Miss: Walking on Hallasan, tasting abalone porridge.

GETTING THERE

BY PLANE – Jeju International Airport, 2.5mi/4km W from center of Jeju-si. *(064)-742-3011. www.airport.co.kr/jeju.* For flights to/from the major towns in South Korea, and Japan, China and Taiwan. Compare prices (*from ₩50,000*) at the airport or on the internet and choose between mainstream companies such as Asiana (*1588-8000, www.flyasiana.com*) and Korean Air (*1558-2001, www.koreanair.co.kr*) or *budget airlines* like Jeju Air (*1599-1500, www.jejuair.net*), Air Busan (*1588-8009, www.flyairbusan.com*) and Jin Air (*1600-6200, www.jinair. com*). **Note:** occasional delays due to thick fog are possible.

In the arrivals hall there is a **tourist office**, a left-luggage office and ticket machines. To reach **Tap-dong** (*Dongmun traffic circle, between the river and the market*), take bus nos. 100/500 (*toward University, ₩1,000*); bus no. 200 is best for the return journey. The Limousine 600 bus serves the big hotels at Jungmun and Seogwipo.

BY BOAT – Jeju Ferry Terminal and the **International Ferry Terminal** are both located in Jeju-si, a few miles east of Tap-dong and are reached by taxi or bus no. 92. There are daily sailings to/from **Mokpo** (*(064)-758-4234/(061)-243-1927, 3am–4:30am, from ₩27,000*) and crossings several times a week to/from **Busan** (*(064)-751-1901/(051)-463-0605, 11am, from ₩35,000*) and **Incheon** (*(064)-721-2173/(032)-889-7800, 1pm, from ₩67,000*). First-, second- and third-class tickets available.

GETTING AROUND

BY BUS – Buses serving the whole island depart from **bus stations** at Jeju-si (*Seogwangno, *(064)-753-1153*) and Seogwipo (*near the stadium, *(064)-762-9369*). The **1100 Road** bus (*from Jeju-si to Jungmun, via Eorimok and Yeongsil*) runs nine times a day in both directions. The **5.16 Road** bus (*along Rte 1131*) links Jeju-si to Seogwipo (*two or three buses an hour*), via Jeju-si City Hall and Seongpanak, the eastern entrance to Hallasan National Park. The **West Ilju Road** (*from Jeju-si to Seogwipo via Hallim and Jungmun*) and **East Ilju Road** (*from Jeju-si to Seogwipo via Seongsan*) buses go right around the island. *Bus timetable available at the airport.*

On two wheels

The island is ideal for both cycling and motorcycling, but beware: hills beyond the coast road (*155mi/250km*) can be steep. Hotels often offer a rental service; otherwise go to **Tourbike** (*Tapdong-ro 4-gil, Jeju-si, *(064)-758-9888*) behind the Ocean Hotel or **Rent a Scooter** (*Sanji-ro 27, *(064)-711-4979*), between the market and the harbor, to rent a scooter in Jeju-si.

Car rental

The agencies at the airport are used to renting out cars to visitors arriving fresh off the plane. You can rent a car from **Avis** (*(064)-749-3322, www.avis.co.kr/eng*); **Kumho/Hertz** (*(064)-751-8000, www.kumhorent.com*) or **Jeju Rent a Car** (*(064)-742-3307*), from ₩45,000 per day (+ insurance). Driving is more relaxed than on the mainland, and there are signs in English everywhere.

USEFUL INFORMATION

Post office – The main post office is in Jeju-si town center (*Gwandongno, open Mon–Fri 9am–6pm, Sat 1pm–6pm*). There are local post offices in every town on the island.
Bank – ATMs and exchange counters at the airport. Most banks are located along Jungang-no in Jeju-si and on Jungjeong-no in Seogwipo. The majority of the island's luxury hotels have a Global ATM.

three districts, of which **Tap-dong**, beside the sea, is the nicest, with restaurants, a colorful market and a boardwalk lined with hotels and stores to which the young flock in droves. Away from the seafront, the offices around City Hall rub shoulders with the bars, clubs and eateries of **Shi-Cheong's** nightlife district and to the west, not far from the airport, **Sinjeju** (New Jeju) is a grid of streets mixing residential areas, malls, smart restaurants and grand hotels.

The Seafront and Town Center

Despite its seaside-style decor, you can't actually access the beach from the **boardwalk** at **Tap-dong**, but it is still a pleasant place to stroll close to the sea. On weekends the area turns into a children's playground while the adults linger over their seafood suppers in the jetty restaurants. The incessant air traffic—the planes are so near it feels as though you could reach out and touch them—seems to disturb few people. Photographers gather early in the morning to snap picturesque scenes as the locals set off on fishing trips. The hotels and motels are slightly set back from the promenade and cater primarily to families. Traditional performances are held in the open-air amphitheater (*mainly in summer*) at the **Seaside Art Center**.

From the boardwalk, the most popular walk is along the seafront to the Ramada Hotel and then on toward **Yongduam Rock** (*well signposted, across the Yongyeon reservoir*). This craggy rocky outcrop features in countless travel brochures and has been adopted as the symbol of the town because it resembles the head of a dragon.

As you walk down Jungang-no from Tapdong-no, the main tourist area near the boardwalk, the stores gradually multiply until you reach **Chilseongno** shopping precinct and the intersection with Gwandeong-no, complete with underground mall.

Follow Gwangdeong-no in a westerly direction to reach **Jeju-Mok Gwana** (*also known as Mokgwanaji, Gwandeong-no; ☎(064)-702-3081, ⊙ open daily 7am–7pm, ₩1,500*). The administrative center for the Joseon dynasty from the 15C, it was finally rebuilt in 2002 after its destruction by the occupying Japanese. The site includes Hongwhagak, a military command center; Yeonhuigak, the governor's office; and Gyullimdang, a leisure area where people played "Go" (*baduk*) and recited poetry. **Gwandeokjeong**, a large pavilion built in 1448 at the entrance to Mok Gwana, was used as a training ground for soldiers.

For **Dongmun Market** and the Sanji River, at the Jungang-no/Gwandeong-no intersection, head east along Gwandeong-no. At the market look out for *okdom-gu-i* (a local pink fish that is semi-dried then fried), and piles of mandarin oranges and *hallabong* (large Korean oranges).

Continue along Jungang-no (walking away from the sea) past the KAL Hotel until, on the left, you reach **Samseonghyeol** (*Samseongno, ☎(064)-722-3315, www.samsunghyeol.or.kr, ⊙ open daily 8am–6pm, ₩2,500, brochure in English*), a sacred shrine shaded by beautiful pines, camellias and camphor trees, in which birds perch and sing. Samseonghyeol owes its existence to a curious **legend** involving three holes that appeared in the middle of a glade, from which three demigods emerged to found the kingdom of Tamna (⊙ *see box p363*). According to another legend, three mysterious young women who later arrived by boat, bringing with them livestock and five types of grain, sparked the first farming activity on Jeju-do. A temple was built on this very spot in the 16C around the stone tablets honoring Jeju-do's ancestors. Next to Samseonghyeol is **Jeju Folklore and Natural History Museum** (*Samseong-ro 46, http://museum.jeju.go.kr, ☎(064)-722-2465, ⊙ open daily 8:30am–6pm, ₩1,200, information in English*), which is divided into three sections. The museum contains extensive information about Jeju's volcanic origins (rock formation, lava tubes, etc.) and the island's wildlife. The folklore section, which is rather static but still interesting, displays typical costumes and reconstructions of ceremonies, and also explains the unusual local headgear.

The History of the Black Island

Jeju-do emerged 2 million years ago as a result of volcanic eruptions that have continued to shape its topography over the centuries. Legend has it that the island's population is the product of unions between Yang, Go and Bu, three demigods, and three young maidens who arrived by sea (*see Samseonghyeol p 362*), creating the **kingdom of Tamna**. Very little is known about the island before it was annexed to the peninsula under the Goryeo dynasty (10–14C). Along with Taiwan and Okinawa, the land mass was part of the vast Austronesian ethno-cultural region that stretched from Asia to Oceania. This is confirmed by the mythology of the kingdom of Tamna which, like all Oceanian mythologies, refers to a white paradise in the east. The protective **dol hareubang** "grandfather" figures must therefore be related to Polynesian *tiki* figures. There is a marked difference between the local dialect and standard Korean. The island was renamed Jeju in 1121 and in 1273 the **Mongols** invaded, introducing horse breeding. Their departure opened up the coast to **Japanese pirates**, forcing the islanders to settle inland permanently. The Joseon era (from the 14C) saw an influx of political refugees and intellectuals from the peninsula, which had the effect of improving education on the island. The occupying Japanese built the coast road in 1917 to draw the locals back down from the hills to where they would be easier to control. Communist uprisings after independence (1946–53) were quashed by a pro-government militia (allegedly with the help of America) in a persecution that claimed 30,000 lives, an episode now often passed over in silence. The modern island enjoys the status of a **special autonomous province**. Island culture, which combines legends, a close relationship with stone and a matriarchal society, has largely been preserved, and Jeju's two traditional activities of agriculture and fishing are both thriving. The last 30 years have seen **tourism** pepper the coast with hotels and golf courses.

Lastly, the maritime room features an impressive oarfish suspended in formaldehyde. Outside in the museum grounds, you will have the chance to study some of the rare and original **dol hareubang**, and volcanic-stone sculptures (*see Jeju Stone Park p 369*).

On the Outskirts of the City
Jeju National Museum
Junction of Rte 1132 and Rte 97. (064)-720-8000. www.jeju.museum.go.kr. Open Tue–Sun 9am–6pm (Sat 9pm March–October). Bus no. 26.
Housed on the east side of town in a building with a central, shallow dome, the museum's historical collection is eclectic but not unmissable, with prints, old books, celadon ceramics, furniture and a small outdoor display.

Halla Arboretum
Follow directions on Rte 1139. Jungmun. (064)-746-4423. www.sumokwon. jeju.go.kr. Open daily 9am–6pm,

(winter and for hothouses 9am–5pm). No charge.
Created in 1993 and spread out across a hillside in the south of the city, this is a perfect place for a tranquil walk among trees and bamboo, hibiscus and roses; the locals go jogging here in the morning, before the paths get crowded.

Jeju Museum of Art
Follow directions on Rte 1139, Jungmun. (064)-710-4300. www.jmoa.jeju.go.kr. Open Tue–Sun 9am–6pm (summer 8pm). ₩1,000.
This angular glass and concrete building not far from the Halla Aboretum often holds temporary exhibitions by the painter Chang Ree-suok.

EXPLORING HALLASAN NATIONAL PARK
Hallasan National Park★★★
한라산 국립공원
See Jeju-Do map. (064)-713-9950. www.hallasan.go.kr/english/.

View of Hallasan
©KNTO

The park has four entrances that are accessible by car and a number that are served by bus routes (⚫ *see Jeju-do info p 361*). The western entrances, Eorimok (*10.5mi/17km from Jeju-si and 12mi/20km from Seogwipo*) and Yeongsil (*3.7mi/6km farther south*), lie on the scenic Rte 1139 (*Rte 1100*), and Seongpanak, which lies farther to the east (*10mi/16km from Jeju-si and Seogwipo*), is accessed from Rte 1131.

For **Gwaneumsa** (Gwaneum Temple), which lies 4mi/7km S of Jeju-si, take Rte 1131 or 1139 toward Seogwipo and follow Rte 1117 toward Gwaneumsa.

😊 A Bit of Advice 😊

Negotiating Hallasan on foot may not be too much of a physical challenge, but it is advisable to call ahead (📞 *(064)-713-9950 or (064)-1330*) to find out what times the paths are open. On rare occasions, admission is refused after 10am to ensure that walkers can return in good time. Some paths may be closed when weather conditions are bad. The humid climate and random heavy rainfall can make walking difficult. Take plenty of drinking water and good rain boots, even when the weather is fine.

At 6,397.5ft/1,950m, Hallasan (Mt. Halla), with its crater Baeknokdam, is the country's highest point and looks out over all of Jeju-do. The sharply defined outline is the very image of the perfect **volcano**, and in its shadow are some 360 volcanic vents (*oreums* in the local dialect), or secondary cones.

The mile after mile of lava tubes, grottos and strange mineral formations were accorded **UNESCO World Natural Heritage** status in 2007. With nearly 2,000 plant species (including azalea and *Abies koreana*, an endemic conifer) thriving in its hills and valleys, the landscape changes color with the seasons, from snow white in winter to russet and gold in the fall.

It will be no surprise to learn that the area's geology and plantlife routinely attract crowds of walkers. Paths and trails crisscross the park, from which you can glimpse some of its wide range of flora and fauna (5,000 varieties, including 4,361 insect species).

😊 **Note**: it is not possible to stay overnight in the park.

The most popular path, the **Eorimok** trail that lies to the northwest, has a visitor center (🕘 *open 9am–5pm, car park ₩1,800*). The silhouette of Korea's highest peak towers over the car park, from which there is a marked trail (*4.2mi/6.8km, 3hr one way*) through a verdant oak forest and—in April and May—flower-filled rhododendron meadows. The trail leads to the crater and the **Witse-oreum shelter** at 5,577ft/1,700m (*no accommodation*) and then continues on to the south cliff junction, although the last .8mi/1.3km of the trail are closed off for preservation efforts.

The other trail up the western flank runs from the **Yeongsil** management office and also ends at the Witse-oreum shelter (*3.6mi/5.8km, 2hr30min one way*) at the base of the summit area. This trail passes even more spectacular landscapes of semitropical forests and rock formations on the way. In fact, the Yeongsil trial is considered one of the ten most beautiful scenic views on Jeju-do. You will be able to access these two routes on the 1100 Road bus that runs between Jeju-si and Seogwipo, and it is possible to ascend via one trail and descend via the other. On the north flank, the **Gwaneumsa** trail (*5.4mi/8.7km, 5hr one way*) across the steep slopes of the Tamna Valley is the most arduous and least popular, with no bus access. The view of the lake from the summit in the middle of the crater is superb, however.

The **Seongpanak** trail (*5.9mi/9.6km, 4hr30min one way*) is less challenging and well laid out. Hikers are lead through fields of azalea to the eastern side of the summit.

This route offers a spectacular panorama of the gently sloping volcanic cones scattered across the eastern side of the island and opportunities to local spot wildlife such as roe deer, badgers and white-backed woodpeckers.

🚗 DRIVING TOURS

EAST OF THE ISLAND★★

♿ *See Jeju-Do map. Driving tour of 62mi–81mi/100km–130km starting from Jeju-si.*

▶ *Take Rte 1132 toward Seongsan. This tour, which zigzags between beaches and the volcanic formations of the UNESCO World Natural Heritage Site, takes one or potentially two days, with an overnight stay possible near Seongsan.*

Your first stop could be **Hamdeok Beach** (*turn left at the sign*), with its beautiful golden sand in the lee of a hill plunging straight down to the turquoise sea. You are now far enough out of town for the first cultivated fields to appear, surrounded by small walls of black lava rock and, a little farther on, the smaller **Gimnyeong Beach** is divided in two by a cascade of black rocks that seem to float on the crystal-clear water.

▶ *Return to Rte 1132 and exit at Manjanggul.*

Manjanggul★★ (Manjang Cave) 만장굴

♿ *See Jeju-Do map. The bus between Jeju-si and Seongsan stops 1.3mi/2km from the entrance.* ☎ *(064)-783-4818.* 🕐 *Open daily 9am–5pm (summer 6pm). ₩2,000. Parking no charge.*

🚫 **Note:** it is dark and cool inside the caves and often wet underfoot. The uneven ground (especially after rain) makes it unsuitable for those wearing heels or with weak ankles.

The trees lining the road that leads to this **long lava tube** seem to draw back to allow you through as you approach the very **bowels of the earth**: the round-trip walk (*40min*) is a unique experience. The **tube** is a tunnel 8.4mi/13.5km long (of which 0.6mi/1km is negotiable) with a diameter ranging from just 6.5ft/2m to more than 65ft/20m. Its twists and turns reach depths of 98ft/30m below ground level in places.

The tube was created some 200,000 to 300,000 years ago during an eruption of the secondary volcano Geomunoreum (a vent known as a "parasitic" volcano). Information panels in English highlight and explain various volcanic features (stalactites, blisters, etc.) as well as the different textures and colors of the walls. The return journey begins at an impressive 26ft/8m-high solidified **lava tube★★** that is a perfect example of these strange structures.

The Mermaids of Jeju-Do

Arrive early in the morning and you will still see matronly *haenyeo* ("women of the sea") diving to a depth of 66ft/20m, holding their breath for two minutes as they search for shells. This practice seems to have originated in the 19C, when their husbands persuaded them to dive in place of their menfolk to avoid a punitive tax system. Despite using only very basic equipment, the women proved to excel at the diving, and set up a cooperative taking control of their households (no mean feat in a Confucian country!). Some of the women migrated during the off-season, making money from their expertise on the Korean mainland and even in Japan and Russia.

This difficult work has little appeal for the modern generation of women however, and while there were 30,000 *haenyeo* on the island in the 1940s, only 2,800 women are still diving today. Nonetheless, they remain a symbol of the island and a source of pride for its inhabitants. ♿*Haenyeo Museum, see entry below.*

Gimnyeong Maze Park
(김녕미로공원 *ℰ*(064)-782-9266, ⏱*open daily 8:30am–6pm, ₩3,500),* 0.6mi/1km before Manjanggul, is a labyrinth of cypresses in which visitors of all ages will have fun getting lost.

▷ *Return to Rte 1132 and turn left toward Shore Road to follow the coast as closely as possible.*

Along the succession of beaches, rocks and harbors, you will see people searching with expert fingers in the mud, sand and rocks at low tide for what may well be the ingredients for your next meal.

▷ *Turn left at the sign for Haenyeo Museum.*

Haenyeo Museum★ 해녀박물관
♿*See Jeju-Do map. Sehwa, ℰ(064)-782-9898.* ⏱*Open daily 9am–6pm. ₩1,000.*

This museum tells the story of the *haenyeo*, female divers who have come to symbolize the island (♿*see box above).* After watching an introductory film, visitors have four exhibition halls to investigate, with explanatory information in English on the divers' origins, their work, the way they function as a cooperative and their very basic equipment (nets, buoys and hooks).

▷ *Rejoin the coast road, still heading toward Seongsan.*

Haenyeo Museum

©KTO

Seongsan Ilchulbong dominating the landscape

© Vincent Prevost/hemis.fr

The houses in the villages huddle behind **low black walls**, sheltering from the wind and sea spray. The stunning coastal vista is a palette of black, turquoise and gold, the last being the color of both the sand and the tall grasses that undulate in the wind. Once you are past a vast beach, a volcanic cone covered in vegetation suddenly appears on the horizon and the imposing form of Seongsan Ilchulbong comes into view, towering over the lagoon and the village's colorful houses.

▷ *At the intersection, take the road for Seongsan.*

Seongsan Ilchulbong★★★
일출봉

♨*See Jeju-Do map. Seongsan.* ℘*(064)-784-0959.* ◷*Open daily 1hr before dawn until dusk.* ₩*2,000.*

🚶This **legendary extinct volcano**, a natural fortress whose sheer black flanks drop away into the sea, has withstood the combined might of wind and waves for thousands of years and is an impressive sight from any angle.

To the west, it spreads out in a cascade of rock, strange mineral formations that are covered in lush vegetation. A flight of wooden steps *(a climb of about 20min)* leads to a point towering 597ft/182m over the crater; the forest that has filled the crater is now protected. The view of the surrounding area from the edge of the crater is magnificent, taking in the

colorful roofs of the village, the lagoon, the hills in the middle of Jeju-do and the uplands of Udo, the neighboring island. Watching the sunrise from Sunrise Peak is a must for visitors, ideally on New Year's Day, but you are unlikely to be disappointed whenever you visit the volcano. You are also unlikely to be alone at the peak, as Seongsan Ilchulbong is so spectacular.

The village of Seongsan empties of day-trippers in the evenings, but accommodation, usually modest, is available and there are numerous seafood restaurants, so staying the night is an option if desired.

The small island of **Udo★** (population 1,700) off Jeju-do's northeast coast has a rugged coastline and a lovely beach. It can be reached by boat from Seongsan harbor *(every hour, 15min, ₩4,500 round-trip ticket)* and can be explored on foot or by bicycle. It is best avoided, however, on busy weekends.

▷ *Leave Seongsan and take the coast road toward Sinyang Beach. If you have a tight schedule, head straight for Seongeup Folk Village (♨see below) without making the optional detour to Jeju Folk Village Museum.*

Sinyang Beach is known for its great waves and gusty winds, and so, inevitably, also for its windsurfers. From here, the coast road snakes between fish farms.

▷ *Back on Rte 1132, follow signs for Pyoseon-myeon then Jeju Folk Village Museum.*

The fishing village of **Pyoseon-myeon**, with its hills, market and restaurants, surrounds a beach, a vast stretch of sand at low tide, that remains fairly unspoiled. This is also where you will find **Jeju Folk Village Museum**, (Pyoseon, ℰ (064)-787-4501, www.jejufolk.com, ○ open 8:30am–5pm, ₩8,000), which is worth visiting mainly for the 200- to 300-year-old houses that have been moved and rebuilt here to give visitors an idea of the architectural differences between coastal and mountain villages, with buildings ranging from aristocratic houses to peasant hovels. There are also some decent restaurants.

▷ *Return to the crossroads and take Rte 97 toward Seongeup.*

👤👤 Seongeup Folk Village★★
성읍민속마을

🐾 *See Jeju-Do map. Accessible by bus from Jeju-si and Pyoseon-myeon.*

If Jeju Folk Village Museum did not quite live up to expectations, Seongeup, an **authentic village**, should make up for it. Unlike Jeju Folk Village Museum, Seongeup is inhabited by people who sleep, work and generally go about their business here, which is all the more amazing when you consider that the dwellings (of which there are nearly 500) were mostly built in the 19C in the style of an era now long gone. Made of black stone and topped with rounded thatched roofs secured by a woven mesh, the houses crouch behind small stone walls (which are also black, of course). All of these characteristic architectural details serve just one purpose: protection from wind and rain.

Despite some concessions to mass tourism, strolling along these few streets is rather enjoyable. You will notice the *jeongnang* at the entrance to the houses. This device, comprising three pegs and a board with holes, tells a caller whether a person is home, out or due back soon, depending on the arrangement of the pegs in the holes. These houses once had *dotongsi*, open-air toilets, on an adjacent plot of land enclosed by a low wall and guarded by a pig. The entire village huddles beneath the shelter of huge elm trees that are hundreds of years old; the oldest has apparently been here for 1,000 years.

▷ *Take Rte 1112, on the left, toward Sangumburi Crater.*

The landscape changes as you follow this stretch of road past large stud farms with their immaculate pastures. Small *Jorangmal* horses have been grazing here since the time of the Mongols; you can see them sheltering in copses when it rains. Soon there is the occasional glimpse of black rock

Seongeup Folk Village

©KTO

and a succession of secondary volcanic cones appears in the distance. Around 1,312ft–1,640ft/400m–500m high, one of these, **Sangumburi★**, is open to visitors (*Rte 112, ☏(064)-783-9900, ⏰open daily 9am–6pm, ₩3,000*). Look out for its landscaped car park. A walk of just a few minutes through rich vegetation (more than 400 plant species) leads to Sangumburi's crater, which has a circumference of 1.2mi/2km.

Situated not far from the secondary volcano Geomunoreum, the **Jeju World Heritage Site Center** is expected to open in 2012. Housed in a very modern-looking glass building, the center will celebrate the volcanic features that have earned the island recognition by UNESCO.

Make a round trip via Highway 1118 to **Jeju Stone Park★** (☏(064)-710-7731, www.jejustonepark.com, ⏰open daily 9am–6pm except 1st Mon of the month, ₩5,000), a chance to enjoy fine volcanic scenery swathed in elegant forests. Here and there you will also encounter sculptures, blending harmoniously with their outdoor setting, including the "grandfathers," or **dol hareubang**, the protective figures and fertility symbols that have become the island's emblem. Inside the exhibition hall there is a display exploring the close relationship between the islanders and stone in a celebration not only of Jeju-do's volcanic landscape and rocks—its sculptures both natural and man-made—but also of the important role played by stonemasonry in Korea through the ages. Return to Route 1112 and then take Route 1131, brushing the flanks of Hallasan as you cross pastureland scattered with solitary trees or enclosed by woodland.

After ranks of pines and shrubs you eventually catch sight of Jeju-si and the sea, far below. On your way back to Jeju-si, make a short detour down **Mysterious Road** (round trip on Rte 1117, A1), where an optical illusion makes it look as though everything that is traveling up is actually travelling down.

WEST OF THE ISLAND★

🚗See Jeju-Do map. The round-trip of about 81mi/130km can be done in a day.

▶ Leave Jeju-si on Rte 1139 (Rte 1100) heading toward Jungmun.

The road climbs a hill before quickly disappearing into the forest. If you wish to stop off to climb Hallasan or just walk around its base, follow signs for *Eorimok* to the left or *Yeongsil*, a little farther on. After negotiating the volcano, the road crosses a pass at 3,281ft/1,000m before descending toward the south coast, with a great panoramic view of the hills with their citrus orchards and the sea.

Exit at the sign for Route 1136 (*toward Seogwipo*) just after the intersection with Route 1115 and follow signs for the **World Cup Stadium**. The highly controversial presence of this large **stadium** in a peaceful citrus fruit-growing region is certainly unexpected; a host of administrative relocations and housing projects were planned in 2002 to regenerate the town, but all were subsequently abandoned. Since the 2002 FIFA World Cup, when the stadium played host to national soccer teams from Germany, Paraguay and Brazil among others, the impressive stadium's masts have pointed resolutely skyward but the terraces, which were pretty empty even then, are deserted when Jeju United takes to the field. The Seogwipo bus station is right beside the stadium.

Seogwipo 서귀포

🚗See Jeju-Do map.

If all those citrus orchards have whetted your appetite to find out more about how they are tended, follow Route 1132 (toward *Seongsan*) to visit the **Citrus Museum** (*Sinhyo dong, ☏(064)-767-3010, ⏰open daily 9am–6pm, ₩1,500*), which you will soon see signposted on the left. Once past the rather old-fashioned exhibition, you enter a greenhouse containing all the citrus fruits of Asia (over 100 types); the variety in size and shape of the fruit is astonishing, not least the "hands of Buddha," a type of lemon with "fingers."

▷ *Return toward Seogwipo along the coast.*

Cascading straight into the ocean from a 75ft/23m-high black cliff, **Jeongbang Pokpo★** is one of the most impressive waterfalls on the island, but you may have to stand in line to snap the perfect photo. (✆*(064)-733-153, 🕐open daily 7:30am–6pm, ₩2,000).*

The elevated **town center of Seogwipo** (population 155,042) includes a covered market and streets lined with stores offering goods and services.

A pedestrian-only avenue descending to the harbor has been decorated with characters created by **Lee Jung Seop** (1916–56), and there is a **museum** (*87 Lee Seob-ro,* ✆ *(064)-760-2484, www. seogwipo.go.kr,* 🕐*open Tue–Sun 9am–6pm, ₩1,000)* dedicated to the work of this nationally celebrated artist, who settled here in 1951. On display you will find drawings, watercolors and oil paintings, Although his style is eclectic, the works display certain recurring themes, including female divers, archers and crabs. Outside, there are reconstructions of traditional houses to be explored.

The main attractions are to be found at the lower end of town, where a huge car park near the harbor eateries is surrounded by souvenir stores and an informative tourist office.

The path to another waterfall, **Cheonji-yeon Pokpo** (✆ *(064)-733-1528,* 🕐*open daily 7am–10pm, ₩2,000),* starts here. The lovely 547yd/500m walk through lush vegetation beside a steeply banked river is almost worth the detour more than the waterfall itself, even if the latter is said to be inhabited by angels. **Seog-wipo Submarine** (*✆(064)-732-6060, www.submarine.co.kr,* 🕐 *open daily 7:20am–6:40pm, 18 trips daily, ₩51,000 plus ₩1,500 entrance to maritime park)* offers fascinating tours beneath the waves. Passengers first board a ferry at Seogwipo Port to travel to Munseom, where the submarine is then boarded for underwater tours. The descent to a depth of 130ft/40m lasts 30min, ample time in which to admire the underwater volcanic formations, fish and coral.

▷ *To rejoin Jungmun, walk up Taepyeong-no, the Sun Beach Hotel road, and turn left at Oedolgae.*

The prize at the end of a pleasant 273yd/250m walk among the pines is the strange rock formation of **Oedolgae**. This vertical rock rising out of the surf resembles a large boot, abandoned beside the cliff by some giant. It is a lovely spot early in the morning, when there is no one else around. The path that leads here from Seogwipo (*1.1mi/1.8km)* continues for a short distance past the rock. Out to sea, you can just make out the outline of **Beomsom Island** and its smaller twin.

Follow the same road, briefly rejoining Route 1132 before turning sharp left toward **Beobhwan-dong**, and turn left again to pass the base of **Yakcheonsa**, a huge temple built in the 1990s, famed for its giant Buddha and the healing water that is reputed to flow there. Look out for garlic drying on the sidewalks as you pass through the villages.

As you continue on toward Jungmun you may be surprised to see a rather poor copy of the Djenné Mosque in Mali, which houses the **Africa Museum** (✆*(064)-738-6565,* 🕐*open daily 10am–7pm (summer 9pm), ₩6,500),* just before a sign for **Jusang Jeollidae** (🕐*open daily 8am–6pm, ₩2,000, parking ₩1,000),* a cliff with great basalt pillars braced against the relentless assault of the sea.

Jungmun 중문
🕐*See Jeju-Do map.*

With its wide palm-lined avenues, vast luxury hotels and myriad attractions heralded by the enormous glass edifice of **ICC Jeju** (a conference center), Jungmun is the **official honeymooners' paradise**. The **Pacific Land** complex is principally a venue for dolphin and sea lion shows (*✆(064)-738-2888, ₩12,000; schedule varies according to season)* but it is also the departure point for catamaran, jet boats and yacht pleasure cruises. Farther on, a futuristic-style building houses the **Yeomiji Botanical Garden** (✆*(064)-735-1100. www.yeomiji.or.kr/ eng.jsp.* 🕐*Open daily Apr–Oct 9am–*

6:30pm, Nov–Mar 9am–7:30pm. ₩6,000). Of the five themed sections (water, cacti, flowers, jungle and **exotic fruit★**) the last is the most interesting as it contains exotic fruits such as papaya, mango, guava and breadfruit, with the bread-fruit tree's distinctive orange trunk, as well as cacao and the macadamia nut. The nearby **Cheonjeyeon Pokpo** (☎(064)-738-1529, ⏰ open daily dawn–dusk, ₩2,500) is a three-tier waterfall (not to be confused with Cheonjiyeon Water-fall near Seogwipo), which visitors can admire from a red bridge as the water cascades into a deep and verdant valley of great beauty.

But where is the **beach** that gave rise to all these tourist attractions? The strip in question, with its four colors of sand, is in fact rather difficult to reach, despite its beautiful setting at the foot of the cliff. The lush, fragrant gardens of the grand hotels end abruptly here, but a stroll nearby will at least give you a view of the jagged coastline.

▷ *Leaving Jungmun, turn left toward Daejeong.*

TOWARD HALLIM 한림가는길, COASTAL ROUTE

▷ *Continue left toward Sanbangsan.*

👁 *See Jeju-Do map.*
The imposing, rocky outline of **San-bangsan** (1,296ft/395m), with its rounded but steep vertical surfaces, soon creeps into view.
According to legend, it is a piece of Hallasan that was blown away by a typhoon. The peak towers over Hwasun Beach and a splendidly rugged stretch of coast called **Yongmeori**, but, sadly, the site is spoiled by an amusement park of sorts built around a replica of a Dutch vessel (the *Sperweer*) that ran aground at **Gapado** in 1653 (👁 *see below*). Hendrik Hamel, one of the sailors to survive the wreck, was taken prisoner by the Kore-ans, and on his release, he wrote one of the first descriptions of the country from a European perspective. Get closer to the rocky coast via a path leading from

Sanbanggulsa (☎ (064)-794-2940, ⏰ open daily 8:30am–7pm, ₩2,500), or by traversing another path farther down, 437yd/400m away. The temple is built around a Buddhist grotto looking out over the sea.

From here you can either cut directly across to **Hamo Beach** or make for **Songaksan** crater (341ft/104m), the southernmost point of the island and a location popular with Korean visitors, as it is where the TV series *All In* is filmed. Seasoned walkers will soon shake off the competition to enjoy a 360° panoramic view of the surrounding area. Along the coast are 19 caves where weapons were hidden, dug out by hand by the occupy-ing Japanese in the 1940s.

The road toward **Hamo** and its beach continues down to the harbor at **Moseulpo** (market, restaurants), where boats depart for the **small islands of Gapa and Mara**, Jeju-do's two south-ernmost satellite islands. Their location alone has turned these two rather flat pieces of land into something of a tourist destination (☎(064)-794-5490, 10 ferry sailings daily, 8:30am–2pm; 30min round trip to Marado ₩15,500, 15min round-trip to Gapado ₩8,000).

Return to Route 1132, which passes through fields of garlic and wheat sepa-rated by low walls. The combination of black earth and fresh rainwater creates beautiful wisps of mist that float in the wind.

▷ *Turn left toward Chagwido.*

Enjoy a minor detour to a tiny fishing port that was once the site of a Neolithic settlement and from where there are views across to **Chagwido**, another small offshore island. There is an irregu-lar boat service to this sparsely inhabited rock, where fishing is the main activity.

▷ *Return to Route 1132, and exit at the sign for Hyeopjae.*

From here you will see **Geumneung Beach**, a fine fringe of white sand that brings out the clarity of the water and the blackness of the rocks; there is a view of **Biyangdo**, an inhabited crater island covered with a mosaic of cultivated plots of land.

The next stop is **Hallim Park★** (*(064)-796-0001, www.hallimpark.co.kr, open daily 8:30am–6pm (summer 7:30pm), ₩8,000*), an amusement park claiming to represent Jeju-do in miniature, with palm-lined walks, flowers (cherry blossom, lotus, tulips), a little folklore village, traditional restaurants, a subtropical garden, and in particular two real lava tubes some 550yd/500m long (known as Hyeopjae and Ssangyong caves), which can be explored. Farther on is the sparkling white sand of the lovely **Hyeopjae Beach**.

TOWARD HALLIM 한림, INLAND ROUTE

See Jeju-Do map.

From Route 1132, head toward **Jeju Art Park** (*(064)-794-9680, open daily 8:30am–6pm (summer 7:30pm), ₩4,500*), a vast garden housing some 200 contemporary sculptures by various international artists.

Turn onto Route 1120 and continue until you reach **O'Sulloc Tea Museum** (*(064)-794-5312, open daily 10am–6pm (–5pm Oct–Mar), no charge*). The tea bags provided in your hotel room are highly likely to have been made by Sulloc, the foremost producer of *nokcha* (green tea) in Korea, and here you can learn about the history of tea, admire an exquisite collection of antique teacups and take a stroll through the plantations. Next, make for the **Spirited Garden** (*Hankyeong myeon*, *(064)-772-3701, www.spiritedgarden.com, open daily 8am–6pm (summer 7:30pm), ₩9,000*), a well-tended park that's worth the detour just for its magnificent outdoor **bonsai collection★**; each tree is a (mini) masterpiece. The garden, created by Bum Young-sung on difficult terrain, also features some wonderful landscaping with splendid, full-size trees.

Note: a Korean buffet is available (*10:30am–3:30pm, ₩7,500*).

The surrounding area is an odd combination of forests, cultivated fields (of garlic, citrus fruit, sweet potatoes) enclosed by low walls, lush vegetation, solitary trees and wooded volcanic cones; here and there you may see horses grazing. The trees thin out as you near the sea, leaving more space for crops that extend to the wave-pounded black rocks of the coast.

▷ *Take a left toward Geumneung (4.3mi/7km farther) to return to Hallim.*

White sand of Hyeopjae Beach

©Chris Stowers/Apa Publications

Return to Jeju-si

▶ *From Hallim, take Route 1132 toward Jeju-si. After a few miles, turn left toward **Aewol-ri** and follow the coast road to the outskirts of Jeju-si.*

The pleasantly rugged seaboard here is enlivened by some interesting rock formations, and this is the most popular part of the coast for vacations, as can be seen from the many small hotels. Once past the small port of Hagwi-ri, far below, you will know you are getting close to the capital when the traffic jams start. If you are returning to Tap-dong, follow the signs for **Iho Beach** and from there to Yongduam Rock the road passes one restaurant after another.

ADDRESSES

🏠 STAY

JEJU-SI

🛏 **HK Hostel** HK 호스텔 – *29 Tap-dong.* 📞*(064)-703-6775.* ₩*30,000.* Guarded by two statues, this modern youth hostel opposite the E-Mart is a stone's throw from the good restaurants along the boardwalk. Every room has a bathroom.

🛏 **Tapdong Hotel** 탑동 호텔 – *Haejing-no.* 📞*(064)-723-3600. 40rm.* ₩*40,000.* Service with a smile in a motel minutes from the boardwalk. Good value for the money, and huge rooms.

🛏🛏🛏 **Ocean Suites** 오션스위트 – *Tap-dong.* 📞*(064)-720-6000. www.oceansuites.kr. 200rm. From* ₩*130,000.* Situated on the boardwalk itself. Decorated in restful tones, each of the impeccable rooms boasts a work of Korean art. Good breakfast and a bar with a panoramic view.

🛏🛏🛏 **Ramada Plaza Jeju** 라마다 호텔 – *Tap-dong.* 📞*(064)-729-8100. www.ramadajeju.co.kr. 25rm.* ₩*200,000.* This luxurious floating hotel at the end of the boardwalk combines comfortable rooms with restaurants, boutiques, a patisserie, a swimming pool, a casino, and plenty more.

ON THE EAST COAST

🛏 **Seongsanpo Village** 성산포 빌리지 – *Seongsan.* 📞*(064)-782-2373. 20rm.* ₩*40,000.* The facilities are fairly basic, but will be unimportant when you see the view of Ilchulbong through the bay windows.

🛏🛏🛏 **Haevichi Resort Hotel** 해비치호텔 – *About 10mi/16km S of Pyoseon.* 📞*(064)-780-8000. From* ₩*150,000.* A large and comfortable complex that's a stone's throw from the sea with a great all-weather swimming pool.

🛏🛏🛏 **Roomine at Shell Beach** 루마인팬션 – *Jongdal-li.* 📞*(064)-722-5233 or 010-6482-0332. www.roomine.com. 7rm. From* ₩*170,000.* Lying about 1mi/2km north of Seongsan along the coast road, this rather isolated establishment facing the beach combines a café with splendid suites. Contemporary decor with all the modern comforts, vast bay windows, terraces and more.

IN SEOGWIPO AND JUNGMUN

East of Seogwipo (Topyeong-dong) there are numerous little hotels between the sea and the orange groves.

🛏🛏 **Four Seasons Pension** 포시즌팬션 – *636 Topyeong-dong, Seogwipo.* 📞*(064)-732-5222 or 019-214-0329.* ₩*80,000.* A small group of rooms, each with *ondol* heating, a kitchenette, balcony and parking. Sea view.

🛏🛏 **Little France Hotel** 리틀프랑스 호텔 – *486-1 Seogwi-dong, Seogwipo.* 📞*(064)-732-4552. www.littlefrance hotel.co.kr.* ₩*60,000/90,000.* Comfortable rooms with either classic or Asian decor. Roomy showers and firm beds.

🛏🛏🛏🛏 **Hyatt Regency Jeju** 하야트 호텔 – *Jungmun.* 📞*(064)-733-1234. www.jeju.regency.hyatt. com. 224rm. From* ₩*200,000.* With its stunning views, the first of the resort's luxury hotels has maintained its leading position. The building somehow seems to be on the point of diving into the ocean.

🛏🛏🛏🛏 **KAL Hotel** KAL 호텔 –
*Topyeong-dong, Seogwipo. ✆(064)-
733-2001. www.kalhotel.co.kr. 225rm.
From ₩200,000.* Surrounded by lush
vegetation with a view of gardens
running down to the sea. Marble lobby
and bellboys in white uniforms set
the tone for the old-fashioned but
very comfortable rooms. A choice of
swimming pools.

🛏🛏🛏🛏 **Shilla Hotel** 신라 호텔 –
*Jungmun. ✆(064)-735-5114.
www.shilla.net. 429rm. ₩300,000.*
Modern, Zen and luxurious, the
Shilla is in a league of its own among
Korean hotels. Fabulous gardens.

🍴/EAT

JEJU-SI

There is an entire street between the
market and the boardwalk dedicated
to the island's renowned barbecued
black pig (called "mud pig" by
Koreans). **Abalone porridge,** another
specialty, is available in the Tapdong-
ro eateries opposite E-Mart. Seafood
lovers should head to the end of the
boardwalk, and of course **Shi-Cheong**
district, around City Hall boasts many
restaurants, bars and clubs.

🍴 **Curry House** 커리 하우스 –
*31 Gwandeok-ro 11-gil. ✆(070)-4038-
4649. Open daily 11am–10pm. ₩6,000/
8,000.* Tuck into generous servings
of Japanese curry in a contemporary
setting.

🍴🍴 **Dombedon** 돔베돈 식당 –
*Ildo 1-Dong. ✆(064)-753-0008. Open
daily noon–2am. ₩10,000/30,000.* The
best-known place to sample the famed
black pig. A dark wood interior that is
modern and welcoming.

🍴🍴 **Haejin** 해진식당 – *Tap-dong
boardwalk. ✆(064)-722-4584. Open
daily noon–10pm. From ₩10,000.*
For seafood fans.

🍴🍴 **Man-O** 만오식당 – *1 Jungangno
2-gil. ✆(064)-751-1443. Open daily 11am
–2pm, 6pm–11pm. From ₩12,000.* This
restaurant, which opened behind Jeju-
Seoul Hotel 25 years ago, is renowned
for its eel dishes (₩16,000). Cooked to
a beautiful caramel color, the fish is

served in pleasant surroundings that
have been tiled with lava stone.

🍴🍴🍴 **The Island/Seom** 섬식당
– *271-41 Yeon-dong, New Jeju. ✆(064)-
742-2929. Open daily noon–11pm.
₩60,000 for two people.* Located
near the Juwon Intersection, "the
island" specializes in seafood with a
fusion twist; Korean, Japanese and
Mediterranean ingredients meld
together in well-presented dishes.

ON THE EAST COAST

The restaurants around **Ilchulbong
car park** mainly serve fish dishes and
abalone porridge, and one such
is **Gombawi** (*open daily 7am–3am.
₩8,000/25,000*), above the LG 45 store.

IN SEOGWIPO

🍴🍴🍴 **Lime Orange** 라임오렌지 –
*Topyeong-dong. ✆(064)-767-4888.
Open daily noon–10pm.* Lying on
the east side of town beyond the
KAL Hotel, this is a charming place to
enjoy salads, pasta and steaks—not
to mention citrus-based cocktails—
as you relax around their sturdy
wooden tables.

🍴🍴🍴 **Saeseom Galbi** 서섬 갈비 –
*On the cliff overlooking the Cheonjiyeon
car park. ✆(064)-732-4001/763-2552.
Open daily 10am–11pm. From ₩15,000.*
The best-known place on the island to
serve its specialty, barbecued black pig.

🍴🍴🍴 **Su-Hee** 수희식당 – *Seogwi-
dong, Seogwipo. ✆(064)-762-0777.
Open daily 11am–9pm. ₩10,000/25,000.*
Perfectly decent traditional cooking,
sadly served in a school canteen
setting. On the menu you will find
sea urchin porridge and fresh fish,
either grilled or stewed.

IN JUNGMUN

In addition to the restaurants in the
luxury hotels there are reasonably
priced eateries around the tourist office.

🍴🍴🍴 **Shillawon** 신라원 – *No 107.
✆(064)-739-3395. Open daily 8:30am–
10:30pm.* Specializing in copious "table
for two" servings of the great Korean
classics, as well as dishes that are as
cheap as they are excellent. For a
slightly more refined setting but higher

prices, try **Jeju Mawon** 제주마원식당 (℘ *(064)-738-2000, open daily 11am–11pm*), between the Shilla and Hyatt hotels.

🚋 TAKING A BREAK

BAKERY

Jeju Chocoart 제주 초코아트 – *Donggwang-ro, Jeju-si. ℘(064)-756-2253. www.jejuchocoart.com Open daily 10am–11pm.* Located near City Hall, this is a place to enjoy cakes that really taste of chocolate in a European setting; fruit juices, coffees and delicious milkshakes, ciabatta, crusty loaf or bagel sandwiches and more, all served by charming waitresses.

🛒 SHOPPING

As tourism and shopping are inextricably linked in Korea, there are countless opportunities for retail therapy in Jeju. The **best buys** are citrus fruits (especially the large and sweet *hallabong*), millet liqueur, peanuts, cactus-flower jam, honey, reproductions of *dol hareubang* (volcanic stone statues), and traditional garments dyed with persimmon juice.

🎣 SPORTS AND ACTIVITIES

The **tourist offices** will point you in the direction of agencies offering **watersports** (in Seogwipo and Jungmun), **mazes, hiking, diving, climbing, fishing, citrus-fruit picking, shell collecting, go-karting, baseball, concerts, horseback riding** and much more.

Golf is particularly popular among holidaymakers, who come to practice their game on one of the island's 18 courses. The Jungmun golf course (℘*(064)-738-1201, www.jungmun beachgolfclub.com*), which hosts a PGA tournament, is known for its demanding standards and equally challenging winds. The island also boasts a vast network of **hiking** trails. *www.jejuolle.org:8080/eng/.*

📅 EVENTS AND FESTIVALS

Jeju hosts a cornucopia of festivals, often linked to nature and horticulture (azaleas in May, mandarin oranges in December…). On 1 January, the first sunrise of the year simply has to be seen from Seongsan Ilchulbong.

Chilshimni Festival – Held in Seogwipo at the end of September, with parades, dancing and fireworks.

Tamna Cultural Festival – The traditions of the ancient kingdom of Tamna are brought back to life in Jeju-si's Shisan Park in October.

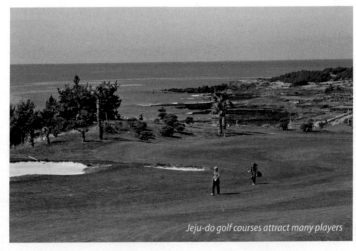

Jeju-do golf courses attract many players

©KNTO

CHUNGCHEONG-DO

While many visitors travel through this region heading specifically to Daejeon in Chungcheongnam-do (South Chungcheong province), this landlocked area is often overlooked by the Western traveler. However, there are many scenic, historical and religious treasures that are often just a weekend or even a day-trip from Seoul. This is a mountainous, heavily forested region with less farming per capita than neighboring provinces such as Jeolla. Those who take the time to explore Chungcheong-do will find a lot more than meets the eye.

Highlights

1 Enjoy **hot springs** in relaxed atmopshere (p384)

2 Glimpse the heavens at the country's largest **planetarium** (p384)

3 Marvel at the serene face of the **Maitreya Buddha** (p388)

4 Get dirty at the **Boryeong Mud Festival** (p399)

5 **Gaze** at 1,500-year-old earrings, diadems, silver bracelets and a bronze mirror (p400)

Down to Earth

Beopjusa is one of the area's most visited historical and religious attractions. Although many of the buildings have burned down and been rebuilt, the area was founded about 1500 years ago. Some of the structures are unique and worth exploration. The five-story pagoda, for instance, is built of wood, not stone, as are most other pagodas throughout South Korea. A large (108.3ft/33m-high) golden statue of the Maitreya Buddha is another popular tourist draw.

Two national parks draw visitors to this region. Gyeryongsan National Park encompasses 15 valleys between 20 peaks and is a hot spot for visitos year-round. The main mountain for which the park is named—Gyeryongsan—has remarkable feng shui characteristics and was once a location for many holy festivities. Songnisan National Park, located a bit farther inland, boasts many native wildlife species that are protected by the Ministry of Environment. The main peaks of the park are connected along the Baekdudaegan mountain range, also known as the Backbone of Korea.

Koreans and international travelers alike often make a yearly "pilgrimage" to Boryeong, a small city in Chungcheongnam-do that hosts the annual Boryeong Mud Festival. Touted as a way to increase awareness that Korean mud is good for the skin's pores, the festival has become much more than just an advertisement and has made Boryeong as synonymous with mud as Sapporo is with beer. With parades, fireworks, marching bands, and all kinds of mud-related revelry, the mud festival offers something for almost anyone. Mud races, mud soccer, mud volleyball, and of course, mud wrestling are all sports that people will be playing. Be prepared, though: the chances of getting dirty are high even for those not planning to participate in any of the festivities.

Boryeong Mud Festival

© Jeon Heon-Kyun/EPA/Photoshot

Discover
Korea's Delicious Secret

Taste the *health* of Hansik

With a four to one ratio of vegetables to meat,

Hansik is slow food, gaining global recognition

for its outstanding nutritional value.

Hansik's balance of essential nutrients makes

it an ideal health food for effectively fighting

various diseases and obesity.

BIBIMBAP
Keeping the nutrients
'alive' for a taste of heath.

THE TASTE OF KOREA
H A N S I K

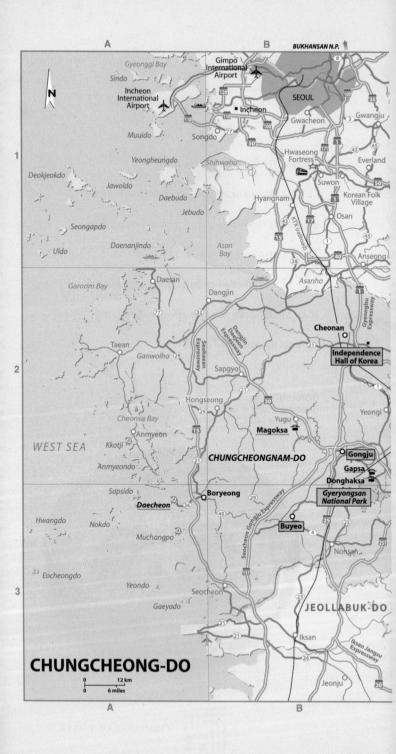

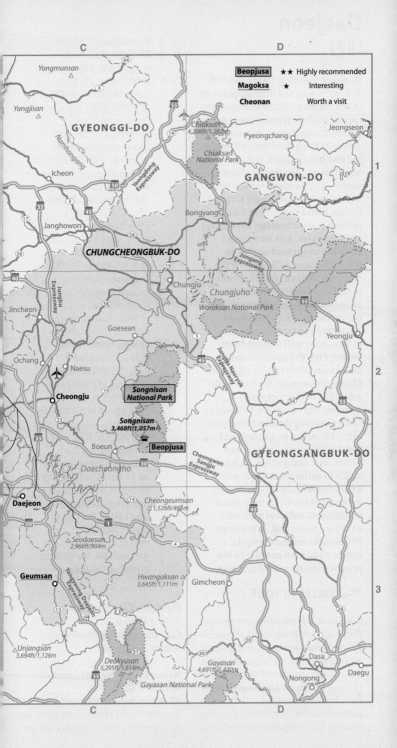

Beopjusa ★★ Highly recommended
Magoksa ★ Interesting
Cheonan Worth a visit

Yongmunsan △

Yangjisan △

GYEONGGI-DO

Namhangang

Icheon

Janghowon

CHUNGCHEONGBUK-DO

Jincheon

Goesean

Ochang

Naesu

Cheongju

Boeun

Daecheongho

Daejeon

Geumsan

Seodaesan
2,966ft/904m △

Unjangsan
3,694ft/1,126m △

Deokyusan
5,295ft/1,614m △

Chiaksan
4,206ft/1,282m △

Chiaksan
National Park

Pyeongchang

Jeongseon

GANGWON-DO

Bongyang

Chungju

Chungjuho

Woraksan National Park

Yeongju

Songnisan
National Park

Songnisan
3,468ft/1,057m △

Beopjusa

Cheongwon
Sangju
Expressway

GYEONGSANGBUK-DO

Cheongeumsan
△ 1,526ft/465m

Hwangaksan △
3,645ft/1,111m

Gimcheon

Gayasan
4,691ft/1,430m △

Gayasan National Park

Nongong

Dasa

Daegu

Yeongdong Expressway

Jungbu Expressway

Jungang Expressway

Jungbu Naenuk Expressway

Tongyeong Daejeon Expressway

C   D

Daejeon
대전

Daejeon, meaning "large field" in Korean, is now the fifth-largest city in the country. The administrative capital of Chungcheongnam-do (South Chungcheong Province) serves as the hub of South Korea's rail and bus network. It is also the scientific and technical suburb of Seoul—the Daedeok Innopolis district is Asia's very own Silicon Valley, with a concentration of science and technology businesses and institutes. Just 50 minutes from the congested capital by the high-speed KTX rail link, the city's future looks full of promise. In fact, Daejeon is already home to several large administrative departments which have been decentralized from Seoul and, in time, may well compete with Sejong City, the government's planned administrative capital in Chungcheongnam. Such constant additions to this incredibly dynamic city owe more to frenzied town planning than architectural inspiration, but this should not blind visitors to its attractions as a tourist destination. Daejeon is rich in cultural heritage, with exceptional museums, as well as being a spa town. There is also a magnificent national park with excellent walks and, in the town of Geumsan on the outskirts, a center dedicated entirely to the production and sale of ginseng.

- **Population:** 1,502,579
- **Michelin Map:** Regional map pp 378–379
- **Info:** Tourist offices at Daejeon Station, ℘(042)-221-1905, open 9am–6pm; Seodaejeon Station, ℘(042)-523-1338, open 9am–6pm; Express Bus Terminal, ℘(042)-632-1338, www.daejeon.go.kr, open 9am–6pm; Daejeon City Tour Information Center, ℘(042)-253-0005, www.baekjetour.com/djcity, city tour Tue–Sun: 9am, noon, 2:30pm and 5pm (1hr40min, ₩2,000).
- **Location:** Daejeon is located 104mi/167.3km south of Seoul, in the heart of South Korea (*allow for a journey time of 50min by KTX*); 105mi/169km north of Gwangju; 84mi/135km northeast of Daegu; 182.7mi/294km west of Busan.
- **Kids:** Splash in the Yuseong hot springs, explore Gyeryongsan National Park.
- **Timing:** Allow a day for Daejeon, a late afternoon for Yuseong, half a day for Geumsan, a whole day for Gyeryongsan National Park.
- **Don't Miss:** The Ungno Lee Museum of Art, the trails in Gyeryongsan National Park, the ginseng markets at Geumsan.

⚞⚟ WALKING TOUR

If you have only limited time to spend in Daejeon, the following walk will enable you to explore museums and gardens, and see a little of the city's way of life. You will also see some of the new architectural and town-planning projects, including the first-class but distinctly austere National Government Complex housing the new government offices.

Daejeon City Center★
Allow a whole day.
▷ *Head north from the station. Approx. 15min walk.*

National Government Complex
대전정부청사
Ⓜ *Government Complex, exit 3. ₩1,000.*
Aligned in cool, pristine symmetry, the four towers of the complex are evi-

dence of the relocation that is being undertaken in some sectors of the Seoul administration. The aim of the project is to reduce the concentration of people and economic activity in the capital, which is one of the most densely populated metropolitan areas on earth (11 million inhabitants live within the city limits, although this rises to almost 50 percent of the population of Korea if Greater Seoul is also included; ⓖ *see p103*). Daejeon Government Complex, which has been under construction since 1997, now houses the Korean customs services, intellectual property office, office of national statistics and the national archives, among other departments. The whole relocation project will reach its zenith in the much-disputed Sejong City (ⓖ *see box p384*).

▷ *Walk to the north about 15min. Cross Dunsandae-ro and walk past the Daejeon Culture and Arts Center (ask for a concert schedule if you are a music lover) before reaching the museum on the right.*

Daejeon Municipal Museum of Art★ 대전시립미술관

396 Mannyeon-dong, Seo-gu. ℘(042)-602-3200. http://dmma.metro. daejeon.kr/ENG. ⓞ*Open Tue–Sat, Mar– Oct 10am–7pm (Fri 9pm), Nov–Feb 10am–6pm (Fri 9pm). Closed public holidays. ₩500.*

The city's museum of fine art opened the doors to its 86,000sq ft/8,000sq m of exhibition space in 1998. The contemporary art on show is primarily the work of Korean artists; its generally high-quality temporary exhibitions often addresses challenging topics that push the envelope of conventional museum exhibits.

No sooner are visitors through the door than their attention is seized by **Fractal Turtle Ship** ★★★, one of the museum's few permanent holdings. The work of Paik Nam-june (1932–2006), the doyen of video art, the installation is a large assembly of television sets, radios, record players, electric toasters and other bric-a-brac (there are just short

of 350 components). With its flashing lights and crackling sounds, this enormous three-dimensional structure of all the modern technological equipment that serves to alienate us is in fact an homage to Yi Sun-sin (ⓖ *see box p336*), the 16C admiral who repulsed the invading Japanese using turtle-shaped boats, their armor plating represented by a black carapace of television screens.

▷ *The Ungno Lee Museum of Art is almost immediately on the left upon leaving the Daejeon Museum of Art.*

Ungno Lee Museum of Art★★ 대전이응노미술관

99 Dunsandae-ro, Seo-gu. ℘(042)-602- 3275. http://ungnolee.daejeon.go.kr. ⓞ*Open Tue–Sat Mar–Oct 10am–7pm (Fri 9pm), Nov–Feb 10am–6pm (Fri 9pm). ₩500. Bus no. 606/618/911.*

Opened in 2007, this magnificent museum was designed with pristine exhibition spaces and a roof formed—as Laurent Beaudoin, its French architect, explains—"from a horizontal array of large concrete beams over a facade of natural wooden slats that filter the light." The concept was envisioned as a walk through the natural light and shadows cast by the gardens surrounding this collection of works by the Korean painter **Lee Ung-no** (1904–89). After an apprenticeship with several revered Korean masters of calligraphy, Lee fled the ruling dictatorship in Korea to discover non-figurative art while a political exile in Europe. Settling in Paris in 1958, he soon became familiar with "informal art," a creative movement which embraced the gamut of artistic and gestural abstraction of the postwar period (1945–60), including lyrical abstraction, abstract impressionism, materialism, tachisme, drip painting and much more; the behavior of the materials and the "happy accident" were as important in determining artistic creation as representational techniques or the artist's hand. Lee himself endeavored to deconstruct Asiatic signifiers in order to reappropriate them in a gestural art which is profoundly interiorized. As an exponent

USEFUL INFORMATION

Bank – There are plenty of places to withdraw or exchange money in the city, particularly in the expatriate district (Ⓜ *Jungangno*). **Post office –** On Inhyoro, behind Daejeon Station.

GETTING THERE

BY PLANE – The nearest airport is at Cheongju, 25mi/40km north of Daejeon.
Cheongju International Airport. ℘*(043)-210-6616/6114*. There are seven shuttle transfers daily from the airport between 7am and 9:30pm, and six limousine buses daily to the airport from Dongbu Bus Terminal (*6:50am–4:30pm, 45min, ₩3,400*).
BY TRAIN – There are two stations in the city: **Daejeon Station** on the Gyeongbu Korean Train Express (KTX) line, which goes to Busan in the southeast of the Korean Peninsula; and **Seodaejeon Station**, on the Honam line (the second KTX line), which serves the southwest (Gwangju, Mokpo).

Daejeon Station – *Jeong-dong, Dong-gu.* ℘*(042)-253-7150 or 1588 7788*. There are KTX connections to Seoul (*104mi/167km, 58min, 50 trains daily, ₩21,400*) and Busan (*171mi/276km, 1hr50min, 50 trains daily*). There are also Saemaeul connections to **Seoul** (*1hr40min, ₩14,900*) and **Busan** (*3hr, ₩28,300*) and Mugunghwa connections to Seoul (*allow 2hr*).
Seodaejeon Station – *74 Oryu-dong, Jung-gu.* ℘*(042)-524-0988 or 1588 7788*. KTX connections to Gwangju (*119mi/192km, 2hr, 20 trains daily*) and Mokpo (*153mi/247km, 2hr20min, 8 trains daily*). Allow 1hr 40min to Seoul and 3hr to Mokpo by Saemaeul train.

BY COACH/BUS – Daejeon has three bus terminals; two of these lie to the east and north of Daejeon Station and the third is to the south. In addition to these three terminals there are two terminals at Yuseong that serve destinations to the west of Daejeon.

East of Daejeon:
Dongbu Intercity Bus Terminal – *Yongjeon-dong.* ℘*(042)-624-4451.* Departures for Cheongju (*every 10min, 50min, ₩3,400*) and Beopjusa (*6:50am–7pm, bus no.11, 1hr40min, ₩6,900*), as well as for Incheon airport, Cheongju airport and other destinations.
Express Bus Terminal – *Not far from the Intercity Terminal.* ℘*(042)-625 8792.* Departures for Busan (*176mi/283km, every 2hr, 3hr15min, ₩14,400*), Daegu (*93mi/149km, every 40min, 2hr10min, ₩8,400*), Gwangju (*111mi/179km, every 30min, 2hr30min, ₩10,100*) and Seoul (*98mi/157km, every 15min, 2hr, ₩8,700*).
To the south:
Seobu Intercity Bus Terminal – *Yucheon-dong.* ℘*(042)-584-1616.* Departures for Buyeo (*every 20min, 1hr20min, ₩6,100*), Boryeong (*hourly, 3hr, ₩10,500*) and Jeonju (*hourly, 90min, ₩5,100*). Other destinations include Gongju, Nonsan and Geumsan.
To the east:
Yuseong Intercity Bus Terminal – *Bongmyeong-dong, (110yd/100m from the Riviera Hotel in the direction of Guam subway station).* ℘*(042)-823-2240.* Departures for Gongju (*every 40min, 1hr, ₩3,800*) and Geumsan (*every 10min, 50min, ₩3,600*). Also Gapsa (*40min, ₩1,200*) and Gyeryongsan (*bus no. 107, 15min, ₩1,400*).
Yuseong Express Bus Terminal – *Jangdae-dong.* ℘*(042)-822-0386.* 110yd/100m north of Yuseong Intercity Bus Terminal. For Seoul destinations only.
General transport information and online map: *www.daejeon.go.kr/language/english*

GETTING AROUND

BY SUBWAY – Daejeon Express Transit Corporation (*www.djet.co.kr*). Like most large Korean cities, Daejeon is extremely spread out and most of the time very congested. User-friendly and inexpensive, the subway is decidedly the preferable option.

The only downside is that there is only one line, running from east to west, with 14mi/23km of track serving 22 stations between Panam and Banseok. *Trains run 5:30am–12:15am. ₩1,000 or ₩1,100 depending on journey.*
BY BUS – Inexpensive (*around ₩1,000*), but not quite so easy to use as the subway. Bus no. 2, 201, 501 or 701 for Daejeon Station, no. 106 for Yuseong

(*allow at least 40min*), no. 102 for Gyeryongsan (*approx. 1hr*). Bus no. 841 connects Daejeon Station with the three bus terminals. Red buses are express buses stopping at major stops only.
BY TAXI – There should be no problem finding a taxi. Fares start at ₩2,500.

of calligraphic writing and drawing, he fused materialist painting and line drawing with the three-dimensional inventiveness of a Picasso anchored in the deep abstraction of a Zen master, producing an oeuvre whose artistic roots could be traced in the works of Hartung, Soulages, Fautrier, Michaux, Pollock, Rothko, Tàpies and Klein, to name but a few. A chance to explore a great artist in a setting that does him justice.

▷ *Walk northward for a few hundred yards.*

Hanbat Arboretum★
대전 한밭수목원
111 Dunsandae-ro Seo-gu. ☏(042)-472-4973. www.daejeon.go.kr/treegarden. ⏰Open Jun–Sept 5am–11pm, Oct–May 7am–9pm. No charge.
Scented paths, small groves for meditation and reflection, a little pond, a stony slope dotted with cacti, water features

for the kids and experimental planting combine to make this man-made garden of more than 99 acres/400,000sq m a popular spot among the locals. There is a good panoramic view of the city from the pretty pavilion.
North of the arboretum is **Gapcheon,** a river that provides a haven for migratory birds and is a very popular picnic area for Koreans. Cross the pedestrian **Expo Bridge** which straddles the river to discover around 30 pavilions and buildings that were erected for the 1993 international fair held in Daejeon which attracted 14 million visitors.
The pavilions in **Expo Park** (⏰*open Tue–Sun 9am–6pm, ₩4,000*) feature different treatments of the exhibition's theme "The Challenge of a New Road of Development," with contributions from international artists. Now, nearly 20 years later, you can stroll around the empty buildings (*an evening visit is ideal to see the illuminations*).

Daedeok Innopolis—Asia's Silicon Valley

Asia's "Silicon Valley" occupies an area of 12sq mi/30sq km to the north of Daejeon; the moniker is a little reductive in respect of the great variety of research that has been conducted here since the 1970s, in fields as diverse as telecommunications, nanotechnology, biotechnology, nuclear fusion, aeronautics, robotics, biology and chemistry. More than 8,000 researchers, five scientific universities (including KAIST, the prestigious Korea Advanced Institute of Science and Technology), some 60 public and private national research institutes, a dozen or so public bodies (such as KIAT, the Korean Institute of Aerospace Technology) and more than a thousand companies dealing with high-tech business form the heart of Korea's scientific and technological community. The *Boston Consulting Group*, a prestigious international consultancy and strategic think tank, recently ranked the country at a global second place for the quality of its research, just below Singapore.

Sejong—A New Capital

The idea of creating an entirely new capital city in order to relieve pressure on a Seoul that had become overpopulated and industrially saturated was first proposed by Roh Moo-hyun, president of South Korea from 2003 to 2008, but the project was rejected by the Constitutional Court in October 2004 and Roh was obliged to seek an alternative. The southern province of Chungcheong was finally selected to reap the benefits of what would be a less radical solution, and while the new city—named Sejong after the king who invented the *Hangeul* alphabet—might never be the capital, it was to become the default center for the government's administrative departments. Roh anticipated transferring nine ministries and most of the executive offices to Sejong City. In 2007, Lee Myung-bak, the outgoing conservative mayor of Seoul, was himself elected to the presidency of the republic and, having supported the Sejong City project to win the hearts of Chungcheong voters, promptly made a U-turn, effectively quashing his predecessor's scheme. As work had already begun, the new president was faced with pressure from all sides, including from within his own camp, and his compromise solution was to turn Sejong City into a new economic hub promoting research, education and industry (Lee had also been head of the Hyundai Construction group). After a poor showing in local elections in June 2010 (and despite retaining an overall majority in parliament), Lee was finally obliged to reconcile himself to Roh Moo-hyun's brainchild. Sejong City was to become a center for the state executive after all, which was ratified by the national assembly… until the next elections, at least.

Daejeon's two amusement parks can be found right behind Expo Park: **Kumdo-riland** (*℘(042)-862-4000*, ○*open summer 10am–6pm, ₩22,000*) and **O World** (*www.oworld.kr*, ○*open daily 9:30am–6pm (Sat–Sun 10pm), ₩25,000*). O World is a slightly more sophisticated affair than the former, with Flower Land, Joy Land (rides) and Zooland—a zoo and a safari area of nearly 148 acres/600,000sq m.

A short distance to the east of Kumdori is the enormous **National Science Museum** (*www.sciences.go.kr*, ○*open Tue–Sun 9:30am–5:50pm, ₩1,000*), the home of Korea's largest planetarium, where the night sky is projected onto a 76ft/23m dome in the Astronomical Hall.

If you would rather see magnificent heavenly bodies moving in real time and are prepared to take a chance on the whims of the weather, head for the **Daejeon Observatory** (*7-13 Sinseong-dong, http://star.metro.daejeon.kr, ℘(042)-863-8763* ○*open Tue–Sun 2pm–10pm; 15min walk, heading north from the National Science Museum*), one of the few observatories in Korea that is open to the general public (*telescope with an 88in/2,250mm focal length, and planetarium*). Farther to the north is the technological research and development district of **Daedeok Innopolis** (*◖see box p383*).

Eunhaeng-dong 은행동

Allow an evening. Ⓜ *Jungangno.*

This district is popular with the fashionable young of Daejeon and an ideal place to spot style trends amid deafening music. From the tourist's point of view, there is nothing of great note to see here, but globalization is hard at work providing consumer choice.

In the mall beneath the Milano 21 and Galleria department stores there is the celebrated **Sung Sim Dang** bakery (established 1956) and some inviting and excellent foreign restaurants (*◖see Addresses*).

♨ Yuseong Spa 유성온천

Ⓜ *Yuseong Spa.*

Koreans have been enjoying the hot springs of Yuseong for over a thousand years. Today this spa resort looks slightly out of place on the outskirts (*6.5mi/11km W of Daejeon center*) of the city which

Insam—Korean Ginseng

Medicinal Properties?

Ginseng is known as *insam* in Korea (meaning "man-root," a reference to its anthropomorphic appearance) and the Koreans consider it a veritable panacea for all ills. Cultivated since the Baekje dynasty and the reign of King Muryeong, the plant was exported to the Chinese court at Jian Kuan (modern Nanking), then under the control of Emperor Wu of the Liang dynasty, before being imported to the West by Dutch merchants several centuries later. Korean insam was even tried by Louis XIV, the king of France, before eventually going on to acquire the reputation it enjoys today. How can a plant that is 75 percent water be so successful? The answer is its high saponin content (5.2 percent), a glycoside with effervescent properties that may help combat tiredness, stress, arteriosclerosis and diabetes, among other conditions.

The Different Types of Insam

It is often assumed that red ginseng (*hongsam*) and white ginseng (*susam*) are two different varieties, but this is not the case; red ginseng is nothing more than white ginseng that has been steamed and dried, a process intended to kill off the parasitic infections to which white ginseng is subject. It is known as *baeksam* when it has been dried only. *Hongsam* (dried and steamed) is therefore always obtained from a selection of the best roots: the rhizomes must be straight, well developed, solidly attached to the main stem, unblemished, not too smooth-skinned and at least four years old. *Hongsam* is itself divided into several categories (*cheonsam*, *jisam* and *yangsam*) according to its quality, age and origin, and these are indicated on the certificate provided by reputable dealers; this is all the more important when prices can reach several million won. Of the very best brands, Cheong-Kwanjang, the national supplier, had an exclusive monopoly for decades, from 1899 until 1996.

Insam in Cooking

Don't forget to try the local specialty: **samgyetang** is a young chicken, about the size of a cockerel, stuffed with glutinous rice, garlic, dried jujube fruits, chestnuts and fresh ginseng, and then boiled. This very popular dish is served up during the heat of summer.

Insam (ginseng)—the specialty of the town of Geumsan, near Daejeon ©KTO

Pungsujiri

Pungsujiri, translated as "the natural laws of the wind (*pung*) and water (*su*)," is the equivalent of China's famous feng shui, the science of geomancy. According to this art of positioning man in context with Mother Earth, Gyeryongsan (Mt. Gyeryong) is one of the three most important mountains in Korea. It was here that the ruling dynasties would conduct rituals intended to bring peace and prosperity to the country during the Later Silla (668–935) and Joseon (1392–1910) periods. Geomantic principles are even incorporated into the Korean flag (*see box p58*).

refuses to stop spreading into the surrounding countryside, and the springs are now a stop on the subway network. Yuseong Spa has a relaxed atmosphere despite its growing popularity with tourists, having become fashionable in the 1930s with the extension of the rail network. Yuseong owes its reputation to its spa waters, which bubble up from a granite fault in the oldest volcanic rocks in the Korean Peninsula, and to the min-

Ginseng for sale
© Chris Stowers/Apa Publications

erals (potassium and sodium) that lend the springs the much desired alkaline properties which soothe skin conditions. If you want to visit a spa in South Korea, you don't need to find a hotel with spa facilities. There are now nearly 150 dedicated spas in the country, each of which is built around a hot spring. Stroll past shaded flower beds and dip a toe (*for free*) in the small channel of bubbling thermal spring water which begins at the Hongin Hotel (*see Addresses*).

EXCURSIONS
Allow half a day.

Geumsan★ 금산
 See Chungcheong-do map.

▷ *Take the bus to Yuseong Intercity Bus Terminal (no number, but the destination is indicated). Every 10min, 6am–8pm. 50min. ₩3,600. Note that the markets are closed on the 10th, 20th & 30th of each month.*

Lying 25mi/40km south of Daejeon, there is not a great deal to recommend this small town of 57,000 inhabitants other than its involvement in the production of *insam* (ginseng, *see box p383*)—some 80 percent of all ginseng produced in Korea passes through the town. No sooner have you crossed Geumsan Bridge (*15min walk from the bus terminal, heading southeast*) than you are in the middle of the famed **Insam Yakcho-ro**, a street with more than a thousand stores offering every kind of root and a great variety of medicinal plants. You won't be able to escape the innumerable bottles of *Insamju*, a rice-based medicinal wine that also contains the precious herb and is one of the most popular souvenirs on sale here. Various markets have their entrances up and down the street, each selling its own ginseng specialty and targeting a different customer base.
Geumsan Ginseng & Medicinal Herb Market handles 70 percent of the national output of white ginseng, some 6 tons daily, and **Geumsan Raw Insam Center**, which handles 80 percent of the

domestic market, has a daily throughput in excess of 130 tons. **Geumsan Insam and Drug Market** stocks more than 300 varieties of plants on a daily basis. A total of between 50,000 and 60,000 tons of *insam* are bought and sold here every day, amounting to an industry worth an annual 45 billion won (approximately 42 million US dollars/26 million pounds sterling/30 million euros).

To find out more, visit **Geumsan Insam Exhibition Hall** (*110yd/100m farther on the right, at the end of Insam Yakcho-ro, ☏(041)-754-9444 ⏰open Wed–Sun 9am –6pm (winter 5pm)*).

It has an excellent permanent exhibition explaining all about ginseng and its benefits from a medical, historical and economic perspective, and celebrating the plant that has also made Geumsan's fortune.

👥 Gyeryongsan National Park★★ 계룡산 국립공원

⚐ *See Chungcheong-do map.*
Situated W of Daejeon and best accessed from Yuseong (Ⓜ Yuseong Spa). Take Inner City bus no. 107 from the subway station, (approx. every 20min), 15min, ₩1,400 (taxi fare approx. ₩20,000). There is a tourist office (9am– 6pm) at the park entrance. ⏰ The park opens 2hr before sunrise and closes 2hr after sunset. ₩2,000. Leaflets showing trails are available in English.

🥾 The path to the park entrance (*766yd/700m from the car park where the bus drops off visitors*) follows the river, along which are a dozen or so restaurants with terraces (⏰ *open 10am–midnight*), where you may wish to stop for refreshment on the way back. (*Simple and traditional Korean food, around ₩5,000 for bibimbap.*)

First opened in 1968, the 25sq mi/64sq km Gyeryongsan National Park is bordered by the cities of Hongju to the north, Daejeon to the east and Nonsan to the south—you can access the park from them all. Ideal for a day's hiking (*Gapsa, near Gongju, is easily accessible from Daejeon, for example*), Chungcheong-do's smallest park is also its most popular, with nearly 1.5 million

visitors who come to walk the trails of **Gyeryongsan**, named after the ridge of the small mountain chain which resembles a dragon (*ryong*) with a rooster's coxcomb (*gye*) on its head—the peak called Gwaneumbong, 2,677ft/816m high. As you pass through the entrance, you will see to your left the **Tam Bang Visitor Center** (⏰*open 9am–6pm*) with information boards describing the park's 2,500 species of flora and fauna, including sparrowhawks, kestrels and cuckoos. The walk to **Donghaksa** (Donghak Temple) takes around 30min. It was built in 724 by a Buddhist priest during the reign of King Seongdeok of Silla.

Destroyed in the 18C and rebuilt over the years (with little regard for elegance by the time concrete had come to replace wood), Donghaksa is now one of the best-known centers for Buddhist study in the country, as it is reserved for female monks of the great Jogye order, with 150 studying here at any given time.

After leaving the temple, continue to Eunseon Pokpo (*1mi/1.2km further on*), where the **Eunseon Waterfall** marks the start of the return journey for some visitors.

"Jikji"

Published in 1377, a good 78 years before Gutenberg's 42-line Bible (the first book to be printed in Europe using movable type), *Jikji* was a Korean Buddhist document and printed in two volumes. The first of these is now lost and the second, after having been sold to a French traveler in the 19C and subsequently making its way to the Bibliothèque Nationale in Paris via a donation, was finally repatriated to the National Museum of Korea in Seoul in April 2011. Instituted in 2004, UNESCO's Jikji Memory of the World Prize is awarded every two years to "individuals who have made a significant contribution to the preservation and promotion of access to humanity's documentary heritage."

Sambulbong, Gyeryongsan National Park
©KTO

Continue for another 0.6mi/1km or so until you reach a point where three paths meet. Take the path to the left and the next junction leads to two temples: head west for **Sinwonsa** (*approx. 0.6mi/1km*) or east (*the right-hand path*) for Gapsa (*about 1.5mi/2.5km*).

If you turn right, however, you will find yourself on the **magnificent ridge path** which runs for around 1mi/1.6km between **Gwaneumbong** (*2,677ft/816m*) and **Sambulbong** (*2,543ft/775m*).

At another junction in the path around 200 yards beyond Sambulbong, there is another choice: either head left to Gapsa (*about 2.5mi/4km*) via Geumjandi Hill before reaching the **Shinheung-am Hermitage** (*approx. 4.5mi/7km from Donghaksa to Gapsa*), or turn right to make your way back, past the pagoda **Nammaetap** (*550yd/500m*) to Mupoong Bridge in front of the park entrance (*1.5mi/2.7km*).

Allow between a half and one full day to make a circuit of approx. 5–9mi/7–14km.

Cheongju 청주

See Chungcheong-do map.
Allow half a day.

There are two main reasons for visiting this rather ordinary town of 650,000 inhabitants. The first is because of its geographical location—it is in effect the main entrance to **Songnisan National Park** and so the access point for **Beopjusa** (*see below*).

The second is that Cheongju is where the first use of movable metal type took place, with the printing of the *Buljo jikji simche yojeol*, an anthology of Buddhist teachings, also known simply as *Jikji*, the world's oldest printed book (*see box p 387*).

You can learn more about this book and details of its printing at **Cheongju Early Printing Museum** (*866 Uncheong-dong, Sangdang-gu, (043)-269-0556, open Tue–Sun 9am–6pm, ₩800; bus no. 831 from stop opposite the Express Bus Terminal*). The museum also has a large selection of materials and information (*in English*) relating to the history of printing around the world.

Songnisan National Park★★
속리산국립공원 **Beopjusa**★
법주사

See Chungcheong-do map.
Allow a whole day to visit the temple and walk through the park.
From Cheongju Intercity Bus Terminal, take the bus to the national park (6:40am–8:30pm, 1hr30min, ₩7,500). The last bus back to Cheongju departs from Beopjusa at 7:50pm.
Leaflets and admission tickets can be obtained from the tourist office on the sidewalk, diagonally opposite the bus terminal exit.

To reach one of the most popular national parks in South Korea—also home to the ancient Beopju temple—follow the road lined with restaurants and shops for about 0.6/1km. On your left is the Lake Hills Songnisan Hotel, situated at the foot of a craggy mountain (&see Addresses), identifiable by the incongruous Greek-style Ionic capitals on its columns.

Founded in 553 during the reign of the Silla king Jinheung, **Beopjusa★** (☉open 6am–7pm, ₩3,000) initially comprised some 60 buildings, a dozen or so stone monuments and 70 hermitages. Along with many other Korean shrines, it was razed to the ground by invading Japanese troops in 1592, lying in ruins until the 17C when the monk Byeokam breathed new life into the complex. The temple has undergone several reconstructions, and none of the original buildings are still standing.

As you approach the temple in its magnificent **natural setting★★** surrounded by mountain peaks and pine trees, you will notice an immense golden statue of **Maitreya**, the Buddha of the Future. The 108.3ft/33m statue was cast in 1990, requiring 160 tons of bronze and costing $4 million, to replace a cement version which had begun to crack. The statue was later covered in gold leaf and powder.

The elegant five-tier pagoda **Palsangjeon★★**, built in 1624 and now a national treasure, is the last surviving example of this period of architecture in Korea. Built around a central pillar 69ft/21m high, the pagoda, also known as the Hall of Eight Pictures, contains around a thousand representations of the Buddha, whose life is recounted on eight suspended panels (pal means eight in Korean).

The **beomjonggak**, or bell pavilion, stands nearby. Inside is the enormous drum (**beopgo**) whose job it is to rouse people from their morning slumbers. Beside this is the **beomjong**, an enormous bell. It is regularly struck three times with what looks like a battering ram, a large piece of wood suspended from the ceiling, in order to free mortals from hell. A wooden percussion instrument in the shape of a carp (**mogeo**) is played with sticks to save creatures in water, and the **unpan**, a gong in the shape of a cloud, is struck to save flying creatures and spirits in heaven.

Note the three beautiful **stone lanterns★** nearby, which date from the Silla period (720). The first is supported by two lions and the second is guarded by the four heavenly kings, who can also be seen on **Cheonwangmun**, the imposing entrance gate. The god of the east carries a sword; that of the west, a

View from Songnisan National Park

©Esther Arnett/Michelin

Maitreya, the Buddha of the Future, Beopjusa

©Chris Stowers/Apa Publications

pagoda; that of the south, a dragon; and that of the north, a Korean lute.

As you make your way into the courtyard, look out for **Daeungbojeon★★**. This split-level, 66ft/20m-high pavilion supported by 300 pillars was rebuilt in the 17C to house immense statues of the Buddha, including the central **Birojanabul**, the Vairocana Buddha or "Omniscient Lord," and to the right, **Seokgamoni**, the Shakyamuni or historical Buddha. There is also an immense iron bowl—**Cheolhwak★**—(from the Silla period), a little over 3ft/1m high and nearly 10ft/3m in diameter, in which it is said soup was prepared for more than 30,000 believers.

Beyond the temple a series of paths wind their way to various peaks in the park. The most popular—and the

easiest to reach—is **Munjangdae** (3,389ft/1,033m); around a 3hr walk over about 4mi/6km (*allow another 2hr for the descent*).

The park boasts eight peaks stretched out like a bow and is home to various wildlife, including flying squirrels and otters as well as endangered animals such as the marten.

ADDRESSES

STAY

If you are going to be in Daejeon for a few days, the **Yuseong Spa** area is a good place to stay. It is pleasant and has the advantage of being in the west of Daejeon, close to Gyeryongsan National Park.

YUSEONG SPA

🛏 **Carib Motel 카리브 모텔** – *Bongmyeong-dong.* 📞 *(042)-823-8700.* 🛏. *28rm.* ₩*40,000.* A good motel just 110yd/100m from the Legend Hotel (*from the Legend, turn right into the first turning*). A warm welcome and well-appointed rooms with a computer, TV, fridge, hot water and all the home comforts provided by other motels, without the sometimes rather gloomy surroundings.

🛏🛏 **Hotel Hongin 홍인호텔** – *536-8 Bongmyeong-dong.* 📞 *(042)-822-2000. www.honginhotel.co.kr.* 🛏 🍴. *49rm.* ₩*77,000.* One of the oldest hotels in Yuseong. The rooms are not terribly imaginative in decoration, but they are comfortable and well appointed (no internet access). The spa is very popular with the locals (*5am–9pm, ₩5,000, massage ₩10,000*).

🛏🛏 **Legend Hotel 베스트 웨스턴 레전드 호텔** – *547-5, Bongmyeong-dong.* 📞 *(042)-822 4000. www.legend hotel.co.kr.* 🛏 🍴. *75rm.* ₩*100,000.* This recently renovated but rather soulless business hotel (part of the Best Western chain) is nonetheless extremely comfortable and offers some of the best value for the money at this price point.

🛏🛏🛏 **Hotel Riviera 리베라 호텔** – *444-5 Bongmyeong-dong.* 📞 *(042)-823-2111. www.hotelriviera.co.kr.* 🛏 - 🍴. *174rm.* Expect to pay ₩*180,000 for a standard room, plus 20 percent for taxes and service.* This top-of-the-range international hotel located 5min from Yuseong Intercity Bus Terminal boasts one of Yuseong's finest spas (*6am–9:30pm, ₩20,000, ₩6,000 for residents*). Maps and newspapers in English are available (*Korea Times*). The upstairs restaurants are a little on the expensive side.

DAEJEON

🛏 **Family Tourist Hotel 훼밀리관 광호텔** – *460-3, Daehung-dong.* 📞 *(042)-256-1717.* 🛏. *30rm. Approx.* ₩*50,000. 5min from Jungangno subway station.* This charming hotel with its slightly old-fashioned but comfortable rooms is located in Eunhaeng, Daejeon's most fashionable district. **Note**: no internet access or breakfast.

🛏🛏 **Cosmos Tourist Hotel 코스모스관광호텔** – *68-20, Yongjeon-dong.* 📞 *(042)-628-3400.* 🛏. *41rm.* ₩*45,000/ 150,000.* Only 5min walk from the Express Bus Terminal, this hotel cannot claim to have the most understated facade or the least kitschy rooms, but it does offer a good value. Internet access. The best option for anyone with an early bus to catch.

🛏🛏 **Daelim Tourist Hotel 대림관광호텔** – *230-6 Seonhwa-dong, Joong-gu.* Ⓜ *Jungangno.* 📞 *(042)-251-9500.* 🛏. *44rm.* ₩*45,000/88,000.* 🚭. The excellent rooms in this brand-new hotel are stylish, clean and comfortable. Only 0.6mi/1km from the rail station. As it is often booked up, it is best to reserve in advance if possible. Internet access.

CHEONGJU

🛏 **Hotel Newvera 뉴베라관 광호텔** – *1027 Gagyeong-dong, Heungdeok-gu.* 📞 *(043)-235-8181. www.newvera.co.kr.* 🛏. *45rm. Approx.* ₩*50,000* 🚭. An excellent hotel just around the corner from the Express Bus Terminal. The beautiful rooms on the first three floors have been completely renovated. Free internet access at the business center. English language newspapers.

BEOPJUSA

🛏🛏🛏 **Lake Hills Songnisan Hotel 속리산 레이크힐스 호텔** – *98 Sanae-ri Naesongni-myeon. On the road to Beopjusa, 10min walk from the Express Bus Terminal.* 📞 *(043)-542-5281. www.lakehills.co.kr.* 🛏 - 🍴 *132rm. From* ₩*150,000* 🚭. First opened in 1968, this is Songnisan's luxury hotel. The good-sized rooms are clean and enjoy lovely views of the countryside, and while they should assure guests of a good and restful night's sleep, it is easy to feel a little lost in this vast building. It is just around the corner from a tourist village which is deserted by nightfall, despite its location at the foot of a magnificent mountain. The best rates are offered midweek, avoiding holidays—the prices drop to ₩*80,000.*

♀/EAT

DAEJEON

🍽🍽 **Flying Pan** 플라잉팬 –
*153 Eunhaeng-dong. ℘(042)-223-3004.
www.sungsimdang.co.kr. Open 11:30am
–10pm. Expect to pay ₩15,000 for a full
meal.* This is the place to sample fine
Italian cooking in stylish surroundings
while accompanied by Chopin. Pizza,
pasta and meat dishes are served with
panache and there is wine by the
glass (*₩5,000*). The tiramisù is delicious
(*₩3,000*), which comes as no surprise as
it is sourced from the patisserie run by
Sung Sim Dang (🕯*see below*), who also
owns this trattoria.

🍽🍽 **Joseanok** 조선옥 – *462-11
Daehung-dong. ℘(042)-252-5678.
Open 24hr.* 🍴. Ⓜ *Jungangno.*
☺ **Note** *that a number of dishes
are prepared for a minimum of four
persons. Expect to pay ₩19,000–39,000
(i.e. ₩5,000–10,000 per person,
depending on choice of dishes).* This
restaurant is open 24hr (a husband and
wife team work shifts) and has been for
20 years. Renowned both for the quality
of its cooking and the great conviviality
of its owners, the restaurant specializes
in octopus in its every incarnation
(although you can also try fermented
chicken or spicy beef) and the kitchen
often looks to medicinal texts for
inspiration for its recipes.

🍽🍽🍽🍽 **Rainbow Korean
Restaurant** 무지개한정식 – *498-2
Daeheng-dong.* Ⓜ *Jungangno.* ℘(042)-
255 8881. www.rainbow-food.com.
Open 11:30am–10pm. ₩20,000–50,000.*
This restaurant serves only *hanjeongsik*,
a series of lavish gourmet dishes
presented in the style of the great
houses of the aristocracy. The ₩30,000
menu includes around 20 dishes,
starting with beef accompanied by
seasonal vegetables.

BEOPJUSA

🍽🍽 **Lake Hills Hotel** 레이크 힐스
레스토랑 (🕯*see Stay*). *₩10,000/20,000.*
Come here for a quick, simple meal
(Chinese and Western), including an all-
day breakfast complete with eggs and
toast. There's also a pleasant terrace.

GOURMET TREATS

Sung Sim Dang 성심당 –
*153 Eunhaeng-dong. www.sungsim
dang.co.kr. Open 8am–10pm.* People
come from far and wide to sample
the pastries in this store, which has
been open since 1956. The cookies are
divine, the bread magnificent, and the
restaurant upstairs serves salads and a
high-quality range of fresh snacks.

♀ BARS

Try **makgeolli**, also known as "the
people's alcohol," the oldest alcoholic
drink in Korea, originally consumed
by the peasants. Made partly
from fermented rice, it has a milky
appearance and a bittersweet taste.
It is low in alcohol and rich in nutrients.
Eunhaeng-dong, Daejeon's lively
bar district, is on the doorstep of
Jungangno subway station (*exit 4*),
right next to the *J&J Fitness Club.*
Le club J-Rock (℘(042)-223-6515)
might be a good starting point to
bump into expatriates and track down
the latest smart places. It holds regular
themed evenings with a dress code
(*open 9pm–5am*).

🎏EVENTS AND FESTIVALS

Kumdori Science Festival –
This great five-day science festival
is held in April at the **Expo Park** in
Daejeon.

**Daejeon International Balloon
Fiesta** – The sky over Daejeon is
filled with hot-air balloons in October.
Enquire at the tourist office or see
www.djibf.org.

Geumsan Insam Festival –
Explore ginseng (*insam*) varieties, enjoy
performances, cooking demonstrations
and more, each autumn.

Buyeo★★
부여

Despite being much smaller than Gongju, Buyeo shares the distinction of having been one of the capitals of the celebrated kingdom of Baekje, when, in 538, King Seong decided to transfer the Baekje seat of power from Ungjin (modern-day Gongju) to Sabi (modern-day Buyeo). Six kings in succession ruled the Baekje kingdom from Sabi over a period of 123 years until 660, when the kingdom finally collapsed, giving rise to a number of legends including the tragic tale of Nakhwa Cliff, which has since become a place of pilgrimage for all Koreans. Fact and fiction have merged in the desire to revive the significance of the Baekje civilization, whose influence spread as far as Japan, and Buyeo sees itself as the standard bearer in this quest for identity.

🐾 WALKING TOUR

The most interesting tourist sites in this compact city are within easy reach of one another, the two principal sites being at either end of Sabi-ro, the main road through the city. At the northern end there is a statue of King Seong and Mt. Buso (Busosan) and its fortress, while a statue of General Gyebaek stands at the southern end, a short distance away from the Buyeo National Museum.

NORTH OF THE CITY
Allow half a day, ideally an afternoon, so that you can enjoy a sunset from Busosan before spending the evening in Buyeo's liveliest district.

Buso Sanseong★ (Buso Fortress)
부소산성
About 15min walk from the statue of King Seong. The main entrance (Busosanmun) is at the end of the car park, just behind the tourist office. Open Mar–Oct 7am–7pm, Nov–Feb 8am–5pm. ₩2,000.

▶ **Population:** 81, 850
Michelin Map: Regional map pp378–379
Info: Tourist office at the foot of Busosan (Mt. Buso) not far from the main entrance to the fortress (Busosanmun/Busosan Gate), ✆(041)-830-2523. www.buyeo.go.kr/eng/html/main.html. Open 9am–6pm. Very efficient, English-speaking staff; brochures and city maps.
Location: 121mi/195km south of Seoul, 21.5mi/35km west of Daejeon.
Kids: Beautiful Daecheon Beach; Boryeong Mud Festival, one of the most popular summer events in South Korea.
Timing: Allow a whole day for Buyeo and another one or two for Daecheon.
Don't Miss: The incense burner (Daejeon's emblem) in the Buyeo National Museum.

GETTING THERE
BY COACH/BUS – Intercity Bus Terminal (old Moh Chit Station), *324-1 Gua-ri, in the center of town.* ✆*02-936-2841–8.* Buses leave from here for Daejeon (*6.55am–9:30pm, every 20min, 1hr, ₩6,100*) and Gongju (*every 30min, 45min, ₩3,400*). For Jeonju, first take a bus for Nonsan (*every 15min, 40min, ₩2,100*) then for Jeonju (*8am–7:35pm (am every 1hr, pm every 2hr), 1hr30min, ₩5,100*).

Koreans say that an ill wind blows from the north, and it was from the kingdom of Goguryeo, now North Korea, that enemy forces came to plague the Baekje. In an effort to combat this threat, the fortress on **Busosan (Mt. Buso)** was built, looking out over the southern banks of the Baengma River (Baeng-

Korean Architecture in Japan

The architecture of Baekje palaces and temples has been preserved for posterity in Horyu-ji, the "Temple of the Flourishing Law," in Japan's Nara prefecture. This architectural masterpiece from the Japanese Asuka period includes the oldest wooden buildings in the world and was constructed by Korean carpenters in 607 on the orders of the Japanese prince regent Shotoku.

magang), which provided an additional, natural defense. The river protected the rear of the palace garden which was laid out at the foot of the mountain as dictated by Korean feng shui principles. At one time the fortress complex included a number of pavilions arranged along an axis pointing toward the southeast.

🏃 A number of paths weave their way across Buso Sanseong's wooded park with its scattering of pavilions, temples and shrines. The buildings themselves have little architectural merit; their interest lies instead in their historical value, as places where Koreans come to pay their respects to those who were involved in the creation of a collective history that is now a source of great pride. **Samchungsa**, the first and the most imposing building you pass after entering the park, is a shrine dedicated to the memory of local Baekje court officials, including **General Gyebaek**, the subject of considerable national pride. It was under his command that in 660 Baekje forces, with the 31st and last monarch, King Euija (641–60), at their head, confronted their arch enemy one more time. The brilliant general was under no illusions however: the kingdom of Silla was supported by the extremely powerful Chinese Tang dynasty (618–907) and Gyebaek knew that his cause was doomed to failure from the sheer strength of the opposing armies (5,000 Baekje against 50,000 Silla). Fearful of what would happen to

his wife and children at the hands of his enemies, he killed them before leading his men into the last battle at Hwangsanbeol (near Nonsan). The Baekje bravely fought off several attacks but were eventually overrun. Soon it was the Goguryeo's turn to be conquered (668), and the Unified Silla (668–935) became the rulers of the entire Korean Peninsula. There are few traces remaining today of the fortress that was built here 1,500 years ago. However, as the place where, according to legend, 3,000 women of the court threw themselves into the river to certain death rather than fall into the hands of the Baekje's enemies, **Nakhwaam (Nakhwa Cliff,** "the Rock of Falling Flowers") occupies a poignant place in the collective consciousness. All schoolchildren learn about this legendary episode, which has been re-enacted countless times on television. From the small belvedere **Baekhwajeon,** the highest point on the mountain (348ft/106m), there is a beautiful **panoramic view★** of the river and the opposite bank, where a large museum dedicated to the renowned Baekje dynasty has recently been built (**Baekje History & Culture Museum,** (041)-830-3400, 🕐 *open Tue–Sun, Mar–Oct 9am–6pm, Nov–Feb 9am–5pm, ₩1,500*).

The best way to see the cliff is from the river. A stony path winds past **Goransa,** a temple that was probably built to honor the souls of the women who sacrificed themselves and also houses an ancient cult site that is still very popular. The spring water rising up from a gaping gorge behind the temple is said to rejuvenate all those who drink it.

A flight of steps leads down to a small landing stage, from where you can catch a **ferry** (🕐 *9am–6pm, approx. 20min, one-way ₩3,500, round-trip ₩5,500*) to the site of the ancient port of **Gudeurae**, on the western side of Busosan. The ferry passes the foot of **Nakhwaam**, at which point the captain may tell you in hushed tones that its red earth is stained with the blood of the 3,000 women who killed themselves.

From **Gudeurae port**, you can walk to **Gudeurae Sculpture Park**, where a

Baekhwajeon pavilion ©KTO

hundred or so sculptures (of only average artistic merit) are scattered about the landscape. From here the road into the center of town is lined with restaurants (🍴*see Addresses*).

Instead of taking the ferry for the return journey, or if it is later than 6pm, you can make your way back down Busosan by the farthest path to the west from the fortress (*turn right at the site of Seobok Temple*) and leave via Seomun, the gate which is next to the car park close to the Samjeong Youth Hostel.

South of the City

▶ *Allow half a day. Make an early morning start at Gungnamji Pond.*

Among the sculptures at **Seodong Park**, a short distance from the statue of General Gyebaek at the end of Sabi-

Korean Buddhism

Although it originated in India, Buddhism first found its way to Korea in the 4C via China. While it became the state religion in the northernmost kingdom of the Korean Peninsula in 372 (the royal family of Goguryeo was highly susceptible to Chinese influence), it would be another 12 years before it was accepted in Baekje, which had links to Nanjing, the capital of southern China. Buddhism was strongly in the ascendant during the reign of King Seong (523–54), who established his capital at Sabi (modern-day Buyeo) in 538, benefitting from the cultural renaissance that was flourishing in Baekje at the time and whose iconography was to influence artists as far away as Japan. The statue of Amida (one of the most popular Buddhas in Great Vehicle Buddhism) that was given in 552 by the kingdom of Baekje to the Japanese emperor Kimmei (*now preserved in the temple of Zenko-ji in Nagano*) is the oldest representation of the Buddha known to exist in Japan. The figure of the Buddha in the temple of Koryu-ji in Kyoto was copied almost exactly from the celebrated sculpture of the Maitreya (the Buddha of the Future) in meditation (late 6C–early 7C), a masterpiece of Korean heritage which can now be seen in the National Museum at Seoul. While the original is in gilt-bronze, the copy is carved from red pine wood. Some experts maintain that it was carved in Korea before being transported to Japan during the Asuka period (592–710), perhaps by one of the numerous refugees who migrated to Japan after the collapse of Baekje rule.

ro, is the first artificial pond to be created in Korea, **Gungnamji** (○*open 24hr, no charge*). Literally, "the pond to the south of the palace," Gungnamji was excavated in 634 on the orders of King Mu (600–641), the 30th and penultimate monarch of the Baekje dynasty. Its simplicity (compared with many such ponds in Korea), with only some willow trees on its banks and a small island at its center, should not detract from the sophistication of its planning, with irrigation, overflow and drainage all provided for (the water has been channeled here from more than 5mi/8km away).

Why take such pains to achieve something that necessarily will be so hidden from view? Koreans consider a pool dug from the earth to be a receptacle for the beauty of heaven, for this reason, in contrast with Chinese or Japanese gardens, the desired effect is not the creation of artificial landscapes but rather of the greatest possible space, where any form can exist. Nothing is more potent with meaning than a body of water reflecting the beauty of the sky, as long as the surface is calm and the water is clear, hence the sophisticated methods for admitting and draining the water.

The same Taoist-influenced considerations dictate that the pavilion is never beside the pond but always at the heart of a small island (which here represents Bangjangseonsan, one of the heavenly

The Lotus and Purity

Just as it chose to follow Buddhism, the Baekje dynasty chose for its emblem one of Buddhism's most potent symbols: the lotus flower. A representation of the utmost purity, the lotus takes root in the earth before climbing toward the light in a burst of immaculate whiteness. The lotus flower is also the throne on which the Buddha is generally seated, an association of ideas which suggests that the greatest of humans is also without fault… just like the royal families that adopted it as their symbol.

mountains in Chinese cosmology), lost not in the middle of a pond but floating in the immensity of the skies. Hundreds of lotus flowers are cultivated in the surrounding small pools and these take center stage every year in July for the Seodong Lotus Festival, which celebrates their blossoming (*for further information ask at the tourist office*).

Buyeo National Museum★★
국립부여박물관
Head east, 15min walk from Gungnamji. 16-1 Dongnam-ri. ☎*(041)-833-8562. http://buyeo.museum.go.kr/.* ○*Open Tue–Fri and public holidays 9am–6pm, Sat–Sun 9am–7pm (Apr–Oct 9pm). No charge. Information in English.*

The thousand or so exhibits on display provide an excellent introduction to the culture of the Baekje kingdom (18 BC–AD 660), known as the "Lost Kingdom" because of the paucity of surviving historical documents and works of art. In its sophistication, Baekje culture surpassed every artifact attributable to the Silla and Goguryeo kingdoms with which it co-existed, reaching its zenith during the Sabi period (538–660). This explosion of creativity was inspired under royal patronage by the new artistic forms required by Great Vehicle (or Mahayana) Buddhism, in which the bodhisattva are recurring images. Of these, Avalokitesvara and Maitreya, the Buddhas of compassion and of the future respectively, are most frequently depicted in the decoration of **sarira reliquaries**, created to enshrine relics of the Buddha or, in the absence of these, the remains of great Buddhist masters (○*see box, opposite page*).

Daggers, halberds and bronze mirrors vie for space in the display cabinets of **Exhibition Room 1**, which is dedicated to the Bronze Age and the early Iron Age preceding the Baekje period. **Exhibition Room 2**, devoted to the Sabi period, contains a **urinal★** (*hoja*) in the rather unusual form of a headless animal. The star exhibit is nonetheless the gilt-bronze **incense burner★★★** (6C), which was cast in bronze and then gold-plated. Weighing 26.4 pounds/12kg

(*24.5in/62cm high and 7.5in/19cm in diameter*), it consists of three pieces: the pedestal in the form of a dragon; the body of the burner itself shaped like an opening lotus flower decorated with the figures of animals and birds, some of which are between the lotus petals; and the lid decorated with 17 human figures, more animals and 74 mountain peaks, crowned with a *Bonghwang*, a phoenix with outstretched wings. Adopted by Buyeo as the city's emblem, the whole piece has an undeniable energy and harmony. This harmony is also to be found in the religious philosophies shared by the Sabi, and their two cosmological visions of the world, represented on the incense burner: the container's lotus petals are tokens of the Buddhist universe, while the Taoist understanding of the world is inherent in the lid's sculpted mountain peaks populated with immortal beings who live among the gods in the Kunlun Mountains, a paradise through which incense smoke wafts when the burner is used.

Room 3 contains several fine statues of **bodhisattva** in gilt-bronze. Note in particular the bodhisattva (*National Treasure no. 330*) bearing what has come to be known as the distinctive **Baekje smile★★★**. The figure's subtle, enigmatic smile and meditative air of

great tranquility are emblematic of the genial enlightenment which features in the iconography of most of the Baekje statues. Originating in India, the style reached China along the Silk Road via Central Asia. The folds of cloth, known as "damp fold drapery," are characteristic of Gandhara (an ancient kingdom in Afghanistan) and Greco-Buddhist art, a syncretization of Greco-Roman and Indian Buddhist influences.

▷ *On your way back, don't forget to stop off at the Baekje Hyang restaurant (⚹see Addresses).*

The City Center
Jeongnimsa-ji 정림사지
36 Jeongnimsaji-gil, Dongnam ri. ✆*(042)-602-3200. www.jeongnimsaji. or.kr.* ⊙*Open Oct–Mar 10am–5pm, Apr–Sept 9am–7pm. ₩1,500.*
This mid-6C, five-tier stone pagoda is one of the oldest Baekje pagodas to survive more or less intact (*the pagoda at Mireuk Temple, Iksan, has six tiers remaining*). The 1/12-scale model of Jeongnim Temple in the adjoining museum shows the religious architecture of the period. Pagodas such as these were always erected in front of a wooden temple in the center of a courtyard which linked

6C incense burner, Buyeo National Museum

©Chris Stowers/Apa Publications

the priests' room with the entrance portal, while a rectangular covered gallery marked the perimeter of the temple. Studies of the Shitenno-ji Temple at Osaka in Japan, which was built by Korean craftsmen, have helped historians further their knowledge of the buildings of the period. Although Shitenno-ji is largely a modern reconstruction in concrete *(after bomb damage in 1945)*, it gives an idea of how Korean Buddhist temples were designed and built.

EXCURSIONS
Baekje Royal Tombs
백제왕릉
See Chungcheong-do map.
2mi/3km E of Buyeo. Take the bus from Wangungno (opposite Busosanseong) which goes to Nonsan (every 30min, 5min, ₩1,000), or take a taxi (approx. ₩3,500). (042)-602-3200.
Open Mar–Oct 8am–6pm, Nov–Feb 8am–5pm. ₩1,000.

Seven royal tombs dating back to the Sabi period have been discovered at this site. Unfortunately, they had all been broken into and robbed, so there were few finds uncovered and little information could be gleaned about who had been buried here.

Only Tomb 1 revealed something of note. When it was restored, four heavenly beasts (a dragon, tiger, phoenix and tortoise) were discovered guarding the four points of the compass. It was in one of these tombs that the exquisite incense burner that can now be seen in the Buyeo National Museum (*see pp 396-397*) was unearthed in 1993.

👥 Daecheon Beach★
대천해수욕장
See Chungcheong-do map.
Allow a whole day. Take a bus to Boryeong from the bus terminal (7:25am–7:45pm, every hr, 1hr, ₩4,500), then a city bus from Boryeong Bus Terminal to Daecheon Beach, approx. 2mi/3km (every 10min, 15min, ₩1,200, or take a taxi (approx. ₩10,000). Get out at Boryeong Mud Skincare Center,

Daecheon Beach

where you will also find the tourist office ((041)-931-4022, 8am–8pm).

The most beautiful beach on the west coast is almost 2.5mi/4km long and, at low tide, 110yd/100m wide. This stretch of glorious white sand is flanked by hotels, cafés and two-tier restaurants with glass walls that make them look like immense aquariums. Of the local gastronomic specialties, try *kkotgejjim*, steamed blue crab, baby octopus or roasted oysters.

Boryeong Mud Skincare Center
(041) 931-4022. Open 8:30am–6pm. ₩5,000 for a mud bath, ₩45,000 for a full-body mud massage.

Mud reigns supreme behind the walls of this building (unfortunately with all the stylistic charm of a concrete blockhouse), just a stone's throw from the ocean. Thanks to its germanium mineral content, the mud is reputed to have some beneficial properties. You can wallow in a mud bath here before plunging into an aromatic hot tub or sweat it out in the sauna. The sexes are separated, with men on the first floor and women on the second; the whole establishment lies just seconds away from the bracing spray of the ocean.

ADDRESSES

🛏 STAY

BUYEO

🏠 **Samjeong Buyeo Youth Hostel** 삼정부여유스호스텔 – *105-1 Gugyo-ri.* 📞 *(041)-835-3102.* 📠. *65rm. ₩13,000/bed, ₩39,000 for members, ₩44,000/77,000 for non-members.* This modern building in a green setting right beside the river is indeed the youth hostel. The rooms are functional but quite comfortable for the price range.

🛏 **Motel VIP VIP 모텔** – *At the corner of Sabi-ro and 71 Beon-gil, near the Boganso Rotary. Leaving the Intercity Bus Terminal, follow Sabi-ro for approx. 330yd/300m heading toward the statue of General Gyebaek (₩2,500 taxi fare).* 📞*(041)-832-3700.* 📠. *30rm. ₩40,000/60,000 for a room with a computer.* This has to be the most hospitable hotel in Buyeo, with nice rooms decorated in understated and refined tones and a level of comfort comparable with the motels (fridge, TV). The owner will do his utmost to accommodate your wishes.

🛏🛏 **Baekje Tourist Hotel** 백제 관광호텔 – *433 Ssangbuk-li.* 📞*(041)-835-0870.* 📠. *30rm. ₩70,000(₩10,000:).* The best hotel in town is a little *out* of town, opposite the Baengma River near Busosan. The light and airy rooms are extremely comfortable.

DAECHEON

🛏 **Motel If** If 모텔 – *Next to the tourist office.* 📞*(041)-931-5353. Approx. ₩50,000.* A functional motel with an excellent location close to the beach and seafood restaurants. The rooms are a little characterless but come equipped with a computer. Bear in mind that prices jump quite a bit during the Mud Festival in July.

🍴/EAT

BUYEO

🍽🍽 **Gudeurae Dolssambap** 구드래 돌쌈밥 – *96-2 Gua-ri.* 📞 *(041)-836-9259. Open 10am–9pm. Expect to pay ₩10,000 for dolssam jeongshik (a traditional gratin of meat, rice and red beans cooked in an earthenware pot).* This restaurant is much admired for its delicious *dolssambap* (hot rice with different accompaniments, depending on the dish chosen, wrapped in lettuce leaves) with a generous selection of *banchan* (little dishes of dressed vegetables, kimchi, noodles, etc., which you can pick at until the main course arrives) and *suyuk* (sliced boiled meat). *Menu in English.*

🍽🍽🍽 **Baekje Hyang** 백제향 – *Next door to the Forestry Association, in the first road on the right after the statue of General Gyebaek.* 📞*(041)-837-0110. Open 10am–9pm. ₩10,000/20,000.* Try Baekje Hyang's simple but refined dishes of nutritious lotus leaves, tofu and fish served in soothing surroundings hung with beautiful black and white photography.

🍽🍽🍽 **Baengmagang Shikdang** 백마강 식당 – *On your right as you leave Baekjaedaegyo bridge.* 📞*(041)-835-2752. Open 10am–9pm. ₩10,000/ 20,000.* A specialist seafood restaurant famed for its *maeuntang* (seafood soup with chillies) and grilled eel fresh from the river.

🎉 EVENTS AND FESTIVALS

👥 **Boryeong Mud Festival** – Nine glorious days of muddy celebrations in July. Some 1.5 million people (of whom half are expat British) arrive at this popular tourist spot to wallow in the mud, while maintaining their dignity at all times, of course. The mud here is the best kind for the skin and is sold as shampoo and soap etc. See also *www.mudfestival.or.kr.*

Gongju★★
공주

It's hard to imagine that this sleepy little town bisected by the Geum River—with the older, tourist-oriented sites to the south and the modern facilities found to the north—was once one of the great capitals of the Baekje dynasty. Known at the time as Ungjin, it was at the height of its prosperity during the reign of King Muryeong (501–23). Now, 1,500 years later, this king has roused the city from its torpor once again, thanks to the excavations carried out at the royal burial site. The tomb of the 25th monarch of the Baekje dynasty was discovered here undisturbed in 1971 and has proven to be a treasure trove of artifacts—no fewer than 2,900 items have been discovered, benefitting hugely the museums of Gongju. The town can now hold its head high on the strength of a past of which every Korean is proud, attracting even Japanese tourists curious to learn how the kingdom of Baekje created a culture that was to influence their own civilization.

VISIT
THE SOUTH BANK★

▷ *Allowing for a whole day, start for the south bank of the Geum River, just to the left of the bridge, and from here enter Gongsangseong through Geumseoru, the western gate.*

Gongsanseong★
(Gongsan Fortress) 공산성
(041)-856 0333. Open Mar–Oct 9am–6pm, Nov–Feb 9am–5pm. ₩1,200. The long fortress wall of Gongsanseong looks out over the southern banks of the Geum River (Geumgang), which is the third-longest river in Korea. Its natural defenses and strategic location were enough to prompt King Munju, who ruled from 475 to 477, to move his capi-

▶ **Population:** 130,595
Michelin Map: Regional map pp378–379
Info: Tourist office at 65-3 Sanseong-dong, south bank of the Geum River, next to the entrance to Gongsanseong, *(041)-856-7700. Open 9am–6pm. 57 Ungjin-dong, Tomb of King Muryeong. *(041)-840-2548. Information: *1330. www.gongju.go.kr.
Location: Gongju is located 84mi/135km south of Seoul, 25mi/40km from Cheonan and 25mi/40km northeast of Daejeon.
Kids: See a *pansori* performance, watch the changing of the guard at the fortress, attend the Baekje Cultural Festival in October.
Timing: Allow two or three days—one day for exploring Gongju and two for Magoksa and Gapsa.
Don't Miss: A walk at sundown along Gongsanseong's wall, the royal tombs at Songsan-ri, the Baekje treasures at the Gongju National Museum, a delicious dinner at Gomanaru.

tal farther south from Hanseong (*the approximate site of modern-day Seoul*) when faced with the marauding Goguryeo armies of the north. The kingdom of Baekje's new seat of power was established at Ungjin (*the site of modern-day Gongju*) in 475. The fortress defended Munju's capital against the Goguryeo dynasty for the next 60 years or so, until 538, when King Seong (523–54), the new ruler and one of the sons of King Muryeong, decided to move the court to Sabi, present-day Buyeo (*see p393*). Originally made of earth, the wall (now restored) was rebuilt in stone during the

GETTING THERE

BY COACH/BUS – The **Gongju Inter-city Bus Terminal** (*☏(041)-854-3136*) and **Kumho Express Bus Terminal** (*☏(041)-855-2319*) are both located north of the river in the modern part of Gongju. Departures for Boryeong (*every 30min, 1hr45min, ₩6,700*), Buyeo (*every 30min, 45min, ₩3,400*), Cheonan (*every 20min, 1hr, ₩4,700*), Daejeon (*6:40am–10pm, every 40min, 1hr, ₩3,800*) and Seoul (*6am–23.05pm, every 20–30min, 1hr45min, ₩7,300*). The **Local Bus Terminal**, located on the south bank, serves Magoksa, Gapsa, Tancheon (youth hostel), etc.

GETTING AROUND

Most of the sites both north and south of the river can be reached on foot. Allow 15min to walk across the bridge or expect to pay ₩2,000 by taxi.

SIGHTSEEING

Gongju & Buyeo Tour – *Gongju Tourist Office. Tours Mid-Mar–mid-Dec, every 2nd & 4th Sun. No charge.*
Gongju City Tour – *Gongju Tourist Office. Tours Apr–Nov, on the 1st, 3rd & 5th Sun or the 2nd & 4th Sat of the month. No charge.*

Joseon period (1392–1910) under the reigns of King Seonjo and King Injo. It follows the contours of the mountainous terrain for almost 2mi/3km.

Numerous pavilions, also comprehensively restored, occur at intervals, although their principal interest today is as **viewpoints** over Gongju and the river. Various paths crisscross the area enclosed by the wall, including a circular walk through the woods that is very popular. 👥 See the **changing of the royal guard** as they parade in period costume in front of the Geumseoru pavilion and gate (🕐 *Apr–Oct, excluding Jul and Aug, Sat–Sun every hour between 2pm and 8pm, approx. 10min*).

The Songsan-ri Tumuli 송산리 고분 and the Tomb of King Muryeong★ 무령왕릉

Muryeongwangneung.
☏(041)-856-0331. 🕐 Open 9am–6pm.
₩1,500. Audio guide in English (no charge). Bus no. 1/25 (every 15min, 5min, ₩1,100) or 20min walk. Expect to pay ₩2,000 by taxi.

Gongju's fortress wall is nearly 2mi/3km long

©KTO

Supernatural Creatures

In the Baekje kingdom, when a person died their relatives sought to secure for them a long, peaceful afterlife. It was also important to keep evil spirits away from the dead—a belief that was imported from China. In order to ward off the evil spirits, supernatural creatures in the form of drawn images or objects were placed beside the dead. More than equal to this task were the *dokkaebi*, identifiable by their arms stretched out beneath large gaping mouths bristling with sharp teeth, or the *girin*, a cousin of China's *qilin*, a mythological beast known in the West as the unicorn. Linked with the dragon, the phoenix, the tiger and the tortoise, the interplay between this group of symbolic creatures was essential to achieving peace, longevity and happiness.

The visit begins with the museum where there are life-sized replicas of several of the Baekje dynasty royal tombs. The sixth and seventh tombs each comprise a tunnel leading to a brick-lined grave chamber with lotus flower markings (ⓒ *see box p396*). In the sixth tomb, a wall painting depicts the guardian divinities (ⓒ *see box above*) of the four points of the compass: *Cheongnyong*, the blue dragon of the east; *Baekho*, the white tiger of the west; *Jujak,* the phoenix of the south; and *Hyunmu*, the black tortoise of the north. The seventh tomb is that of King Muryeong.

Behind the museum building lie the green burial mounds, man-made tumuli concealing the tombs (*closed to visitors*). Of the dozen or so on the site, a total of seven have so far been excavated, and the last to be discovered was the most important by far, the tomb of King Muryeong (461–523). According to the inscriptions on the gravestone, the king was buried on 12 August 525, two years after his death. His wife, who lay by his

right side with her head facing south (toward the kingdom of the dead in Hinduism), joined the king in 529, some three years after her demise. No fewer than 2,906 finds have been recorded, of which around a dozen have been designated National Treasures (earrings, necklaces, bronze mirrors, head and foot pillows) and reproductions of these finds can be seen in the display cases adjoining the tombs. The originals are held at the Gongju National Museum (ⓒ *see below*).

Turn right out of the museum (*or bus no. 8 from the foot of Gongsanseong*) and continue for around 0.6mi/1km to reach **Geumgang Spa** (*299-3 Ungjin-dong, ℘(041)-856-0033*), whose hot spring water is a particularly good treatment for skin rashes.

Gongju National Museum★
공주국립박물관

Jeongjisa-gil 30. ℘(041)-850-6300. http://gongju.museum.go.kr. ⓄOpen Mon–Fri 9am–6pm, Sat–Sun 9am–7pm (Sat Apr–Oct 9pm). No charge. Audio guide in English (no charge). Bus no. 8; the stop is in front of the museum entrance.

This enormous and rather austere building was opened in 2004 in order to accommodate a reorganization of exhibits from the Baekje dynasty, prompted by the discovery of the tomb of King Muryeong. More than 20,000 objects, including 19 National Treasures, are now on display in the museum.

The rooms of the first gallery are dedicated exclusively to objects found in the royal tomb, and among these there are 1,500-year-old earrings, diadems, **silver bracelets and a bronze mirror★★★**, illustrating the splendor of the kingdom and the great virtuosity of its artists, who were initially influenced by the Northern Wei (386–535), a Turco-Mongol dynasty from northern China. These influences can be seen in the extremely strange stone beast known as **Seoksu★★★**, designated a National Treasure by the Korean government. In its presumed role as guardian of King

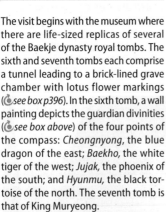

Gongju National Museum ©KTO

Muryeong's tomb, Seoksu is also evidence of funerary traditions imported from China.

The five rooms of the second gallery comprehensively outline successive stages in the history and culture of Chungcheongnam (South Chungcheong) Province, from the Paleolithic to the unification of the Three Kingdoms. Among the most remarkable pieces are three National Treasures, including an **Avalokitesvara★★★** in gilt-bronze ("Avalokitesvara" means "Lord who looks down on the world" in Sanskrit and personifies the bodhisattva of compassion in Mahayana Buddhism) and a **seated stone Buddha★★**, created during the Later Silla period (668–935), at a time when the Buddhism that had been spreading through Korea since the 4C began to take ever firmer hold.

👁 *Expect to pay ₩3,800 for a taxi back to the Intercity Bus Terminal.*

The North Bank★

As it is difficult to reach by public transport, the easiest way to visit the Birthplace of Park Dong-jin—situated 4.5mi/7km to the east of Gongju city center—is on the Gongju City Tour organized by the tourist office (🕐Apr–Nov: 1st, 3rd & 5th Sun and 2nd & 4th Sat of the month). The program is frequently subject to change, so it is essential to enquire first at the tourist office. ₩7,000 by taxi.

King Muryeong

In 501, by the time he ascended the throne of his assassinated father, King Dongseong (479–501), King Muryeong (461–523) was 40 years of age. Known also by the name of Buyeo, the 25th king of the Baekje dynasty was to reign for 23 years, a testament to his skills as a tactician. He formed an alliance with the rival Silla dynasty to neutralize the threat of the great third Kingdom of the North, ruled by the Goguryeo. This stability allowed the Baekje kingdom to flourish and, thanks to its geographical position beside the Yellow Sea, it adopted a mediating role between China and Japan. However, the kingdom was more than just a simple conduit for Chinese culture on its journey to Japan; it also passed on an Indo-Chinese culture that had been transformed by the various geographical and cultural environments through which it had traveled.

The kingdom of Baekje was the final crucible from which new artistic inspiration was drawn, an inspiration which was to leave its mark on Japan in the Asuka period (538–710).

♨♨ Birthplace of Park Dong-jin★
박동진 판소리 전수관

℘ (041)-856-5811/7770.
www.parkdongjin.com. ⏰ Open Tue–
Sun 9am–6pm. No charge. To get the
most out of your visit, include a pansori
performance: generally Tue at 11am
and Sat–Sun at 3pm as part of the
Gongju City Tour.

This small museum is next to the house
(not open to the public) in which Park
Dong-jin (1916–2003) was born. One
of the most famous pansori singers,
the museum traces the life and work of
this celebrated balladeer, who radically
rewrote the history of modern pansori
(unfortunately, little information is given
in English). Park Dong-jin's popularity is
essentially due to two things: firstly his
extraordinary stamina—he was capable
of remaining on stage for more than
eight hours at a time to sing the entirety
of the pansori piece selected. A great
deal of physical effort is involved—bear
in mind that the gwangdae, the singer
and actor who performs pansori, has to
sing and narrate the story and mime
the gestures of all the characters he is
playing, with only a fan as a prop, and
that passages alternate between singing and speech to the accompaniment
of a drum (buk), beaten by the gosu
who provides the rhythm. There are no
intervals in pansori, with only brief and
impromptu verbal sounds uttered by
the gosu to emphasize the performance
and allow the singer to catch his breath.
The second reason for Park Dong-jin's
popularity is related to the fact that,
despite his highbrow background, he
had no compunction in recounting
comic stories that were sometimes quite
racy or even downright salacious. While
he played down the pomp, his singing
technique was beyond reproach, and
he was able to popularize his art by
improvising jokes, getting closer to his
public while making constant use of
breathing and vocal techniques in his
performance. Park Dong-jin belonged
to the category of Aniri Gwangdae (dialogue performers), pansori performers
who specalize in fluent narration (aniri)
with flashes of wit (jaedam), rather than
in singing (sori) (⏳ see also box p329).

EXCURSIONS
The Outskirts of Gongju★
Allow half a day or even a full day if you
plan to walk some of the forest paths.

Magoksa★
(Magok Temple)
마곡사
⏳ See Chungcheong-do map.
Take bus no. 7 (7am–8:50pm, 45min,
round-trip ₩2,400) from the Local
Bus Terminal, in the south of Gongju.

Magoksa

©KTO

Gapsa ©KTO

(041)-481-6221. www.magoksa.or.kr.
Open 6am–6:30pm. ₩2,000.
Magok Temple was built on the eastern slopes of Taehwasan in 643 during the reign of King Euija (641–60), the last ruler of the Baekje dynasty. The complex has since been extensively restored and is surrounded by a wonderful natural setting. The location has also often been described as symbolic of the *taegueuk*, the initial state of the universe, when yin and yang were in perfect harmony. Magoksa belongs to the Jogye order, to which 90 percent of Korean Buddhists belong.

Three paths lead from the temple to the surrounding peaks; the longest of these (*4.5mi/7km, 3hr30min*) leads to Nabalbong (1,368ft/417m) and then on to Hwarinbong (1,388ft/423m).

Gapsa★ (Gap Temple) 갑사
See Chungcheong-do map.
Take the bus (7am–10pm, 30min, Return ₩2,200) for Gapsa (11.5mi/19km) from the Local Bus Terminal, in the south of Gongju. (041)-857-8981.
Open 8am–6pm. ₩2,000.
Although this Buddhist temple is primarily famous for its mountainous surroundings (*15min walk from the entrance*), it was nonetheless one of the greatest buildings of the Later Silla period. A magnificent 16C bronze bell (*dongjong*) is housed in the lecture hall

Dongjonggak. Echoes of the shamanic divinities (Chilseong, Sansin and Dokseong), which are celebrated in the relatively modest ancillary temple, are to be found in the Buddhist divinities worshiped in the main temple.

It is possible to climb Sambulbong in Gyeryongsan National Park directly from Gapsa, on a trail that passes the Yongmun Waterfall (*Yongmun Pokpo*) and the small hermitage at Sinheungam (*2mi/3km, 2hr45min*).
For the temple at Donghaksa, see Gyeryongsan National Park p387.

Cheonan 천안
See Chungcheong-do map.
Situated some 62mi/100km south of Seoul and accessible from Gongju in just 30min by KTX (Gyeongbu Line or Honam Line, Cheonan Station) or 2 hours by subway from Seoul, www.cheonan.go.kr.
Cheonan is a city whose star is ascending. Although something of a temple of consumerism where the streets are quite animated at night, the city also possesses an excellent contemporary art gallery and the largest museum in the country dedicated to Korean independence. The first stirrings of the independence movement were indeed felt here on 1 March 1919, in a demonstration that was met with terrible reprisals claiming more than 7,000 victims.

Arario Gallery★ 아라리오 갤러리

354-1 Shinbu-dong, Dongnam-gu.
By the Express Bus Terminal exit. 🖉*(041)-620-7259. www.arariogallery.co.kr.*
🕐 *Open noon–7pm. ₩3,000.*

This international gallery (*with additional branches in Seoul, Beijing and New York*) is on the busiest street corner in Cheonan. An immense male head and torso, like a cutaway model of the body for medical students, by Damien Hirst stands in splendid isolation in a glass cube a few paces from an amusing sculpture by the French artist Arman (*Un million de miles*, 1989). Look up to see a man seated on a bench while a woman climbs a ladder several feet above the road.

In addition to all this slick packaging, the gallery shows top-rate Korean artists such as Lee Hyungkoo and Won Seoungwon. There is a café-restaurant on the ground floor.

▶ *In front of Cheonan Express Bus Terminal, take City Bus no. 400 (approx. 35min, ₩1,200). By taxi: 20min, ₩13,000.*

Independence Hall of Korea★★
독립기념관

230 Namhwa-ri, Mokcheon-eup.
🖉*(041)-560-0356. www.i815.or.kr/html/en.* 🕐*Open Tue–Sun: Mar–Oct 9:30am–6pm, Nov–Feb 9:30am–5pm. No charge.*

This immense museum was built as a testament to one of the most traumatic periods ever endured by Korea: the Japanese occupation of 1910–45. The country suffered 35 years of colonization and cultural expropriation during which the Korean people were obliged to forget their language, their nationality and their identity, while the occupying Japanese saw the land as no more than an economic resource to be exploited to the full.

It is estimated that more than 200,000 Korean women were kidnapped to serve as "comfort women," in other words sex slaves, for the Japanese army. This entire story is narrated (*in English*) and presented in a way that is at times gratuitous (torture scenes) and unexpected (*visitors are invited to stand on a firing range and shoot at Japanese soldiers*). This multimedia journey leads through seven buildings, each of which deals with a specific moment in history; the periods covered in Buildings 4 (*The March First Independence Movement*) and 5 (*Patriotic Struggle for National Independence*) are particularly well documented.

Although Seoul and Tokyo resumed diplomatic relations in 1965, they remain strained, with the Japanese authorities refusing to offer an official apology for the tragedy of the "comfort women" until 2010.

ADDRESSES

🛏 STAY

GONGJU

🛏 **Gongju Youth Hostel** 공주 유스호스텔 – *Bus no. 20 from the Gongju Bus Terminal, toward Tancheon (7am–7pm); the youth hostel is 5min walk from the stop.* 🖉*(041)-852-1212. www.gongjuyh.com.* 📺 - 📠. *12rm. ₩66,000 for a family of 5, ₩13,000 per adult and ₩10,000 per child.* Some way out of town, about 9mi/15km south of the Geum River.

🛏 **Motel Gangseojang** 강 서장여관 – *597-8 Shinkwan-dong.* 🖉*(041)-852-8323.* 📺 - 📠🛏 *12rm. ₩35,000. No breakfast.* Beside a little canal south of the river, this modest motel with its faded wallpaper has an array of perfunctory but clean and comfortable rooms (some of which have a TV and a computer). For breakfast, make for the market (*approx. 330yd/300m*) next to the Local Bus Terminal. There is a bus from here to Magok Temple. A warm welcome despite speaking no English.

🛏🛏 **Kum-Kang Hotel Tourist** 금 강관광호텔 – *597-8 Shinkwan-dong.* 🖉*(041)-852-1071. www.hotel-kumkang.com.* 📺. *49rm. ₩40,000/110,000.* On the north bank of the

Geum River about 330yd/300m west of the Intercity Bus Terminal, this modern hotel is the best place to stay in Gongju. Clean and well-equipped rooms (fridge, internet, TV). A snack breakfast is included in the price.

MAGOKSA

▱ **Magok Motel** 마곡모텔 – ✆(041)-841-0047. http://magokmotel.com. ▤ 12rm. From ₩40,000 (expect to pay 10 percent more at weekends) ⌕ This inescapable motel (you pass it on the way to the temple) has well-appointed rooms, a spa and a hotline in English.

CHEONAN

▱ **Western Hotel** 웨스턴 호텔 – 468-7 Shinbu-dong. ✆(041)-551-0606. ▤ ✕ ⌕. 8rm. ₩30,000/80,000 breakfast included. Expect to pay ₩2,300 by taxi from the station. Located 220yd/200m from the Intercity Bus Terminal among the cheaper motels, this hotel offers well appointed rooms of medium size with all the amenities.

▱▱▱ **Metro Hotel** 메트로 호텔 – 7-9 Daeheung-dong. ✆(041)-6220-8211. www.hotelmetro.co.kr. ▤ - ✕ -. 50rm. ₩130,000/210,000. Visible to your left as you come out of the station, the hotel is usually overrun by business travelers. Comfortable rooms (with internet access), limousine service to the airport, English-speaking staff.

♀/EAT

GONGJU

▱▱▱ **Gomanaru** 고마나루 쌈밥집 – Opposite Gongsanseong. ✆(041)-857-9999. Open 10am–10pm. ₩10,000/30,000. Sit cross-legged in a rustic setting (a dining room groaning with agricultural implements) to sample the cuisine of one of the best kitchens in Gongju. Their specialties feature local traditional cooking including *ssambap* (rice and meat wrapped in lettuce leaves), *dolsot bibimbap* (rice, vegetables and eggs served in a cast-iron pot), smoked duck or perhaps even *bulgogi*, grilled marinated beef with side orders of vegetables and wildflowers.

MAGOKSA

▱▱ **Tae Hwa** 태화 식당 – At Magoksa (Magok Temple). ✆(041)-841-8020. 9am–8:30pm. Around ₩10,000. This is where most visitors to the temple eat; a good atmosphere on Sundays. Generous portions of fine Korean cooking at reasonable prices.

🎭 EVENTS AND FESTIVALS

👥 **Baekje Cultural Festival** – Korea's oldest festival (1955), co-organized by Buyeo and Gongju, the two former Baekje capitals, is an annual celebration of the glories of the **Baekje period**, with re-enactments of historic scenes such as the Battle of Hwangsanbeol (featuring a thousand professional actors), parades illustrating the splendor of the dynasty and games from the period, etc., held on a number of sites throughout Chungcheongnam Province from 17 September to 17 October. www.baekje.org/html/en/index.html.

Chestnut Festival – Gongju is the country's premier producer of chestnuts, providing 12 percent of the total national output. The festival is very popular with Koreans, who take part in the harvest (**end Sept–beginning Oct**; *approx. ₩10,000 for every 6.5 pounds/3kg collected*). The many dishes cooked include: *bammukchaebap* (mixed rice and vegetables served with a chestnut preserve) and *bampajeon* (chestnut cake), washed down with a glass of *bammakgeoli* (chestnut liqueur).

Pansori Contest – Gongju organizes the largest annual *pansori* competition in the country (*check the tourist office for precise dates*). The winner is generally assured of a promising start in the business. www.parkdongjin.com.

Discover
Korea's Delicious Secret

Taste the beauty of Hansik

Celebrated around the world for its splendid

cornucopia of colors and for its unique character

and exquisite taste. Hansik stimulates your sense

of sight as it pleases the palate.

So come sample these veritable works of art,

these delectable dishes.

SINSEOLLO
A dish of fish and vegetables that strikes
a delicious harmony for a taste of beauty.

THE TASTE OF KOREA
H A N S I K

INDEX

INDEX

INDEX

INDEX

INDEX

MAPS AND PLANS

MAP LEGEND

	Sight	Seaside resort	Winter sports resort	Spa
Highly recommended	★★★	�	✳✳✳	‡‡‡
Recommended	★★	☐☐	✳✳	‡‡
Interesting	★	☐	✳	‡

Selected monuments and sights

◉ ⟶	Tour - Departure point
⛪ ✝	Catholic church
⛪ ✝	Protestant church, other temple
✡ ☪ ᠵ	Synagogue - Mosque
▭	Building
▪	Statue, small building
✝	Calvary, wayside cross
◎	Fountain
━●━■━	Rampart - Tower - Gate
✕	Château, castle, historic house
∴	Ruins
∪	Dam
✿	Factory, power plant
✩	Fort
∩	Cave
▣	Troglodyte dwelling
⛏	Prehistoric site
⊤	Viewing table
ᴪ	Viewpoint
▲	Other place of interest

Sports and recreation

🏇	Racecourse
⛸	Skating rink
🏊 🏊	Outdoor, indoor swimming pool
🎬	Multiplex Cinema
⛵	Marina, sailing centre
⛺	Trail refuge hut
□━■━□	Cable cars, gondolas
□━┼┼┼┼━□	Funicular, rack railway
🚂	Tourist train
◆	Recreation area, park
🎭	Theme, amusement park
ᴪ	Wildlife park, zoo
⊛	Gardens, park, arboretum
◉	Bird sanctuary, aviary
🚶	Walking tour, footpath
🎃	Of special interest to children

Abbreviations

G, POL	Police (Federale Politie)	**P**	Local government offices (Gouvernement provincial)
H	Town hall (Hôtel de ville ou maison communale)	**P**	Provincial capital (Chef-lieu de provincial)
J	Law courts (Palais de justice)	**T**	Theatre (Théâtre)
M	Museum (Musée)	**U**	University (Université)

Additional symbols

🛈	Tourist information	✉	Post office
═══ ═══	Motorway or other primary route	☎	Telephone
❶ ❶	Junction: complete, limited	▭	Covered market
⇌ ⇌	Pedestrian street	⋅✕⋅	Barracks
⌶⌶⌶⌶⌶⌶	Unsuitable for traffic, street subject to restrictions	△	Drawbridge
ᴑᴑᴑᴑᴑ ----	Steps – Footpath	∪	Quarry
� 🖥	Train station – Auto-train station	✕	Mine
🚌 sncf	Coach (bus) station	Ⓑ Ⓕ	Car ferry (river or lake)
━•━•━	Tram	⛴	Ferry service: cars and passengers
Ⓜ	Metro, underground	⛵	Foot passengers only
P Ⓡ	Park-and-Ride	③	Access route number common to Michelin maps and town plans
♿	Access for the disabled	Bert (R.)...	Main shopping street
		AZ B	Map co-ordinates

419

The Michelin Adventure

It all started with rubber balls! This was the product made by a small company based in Clermont-Ferrand that André and Edouard Michelin inherited, back in 1880. The brothers quickly saw the potential for a new means of transport and their first success was the invention of detachable pneumatic tires for bicycles. However, the automobile was to provide the greatest scope for their creative talents. Throughout the 20th century, Michelin never ceased developing and creating ever more reliable and high-performance tires, not only for vehicles ranging from trucks to F1 but also for underground transit systems and airplanes.

From early on, Michelin provided its customers with tools and services to facilitate mobility and make traveling a more pleasurable and more frequent experience. As early as 1900, the Michelin Guide supplied motorists with a host of useful information related to vehicle maintenance, accommodation and restaurants, and was to become a benchmark for good food. At the same time, the Travel Information Bureau offered travelers personalised tips and itineraries.

The publication of the first collection of roadmaps, in 1910, was an instant hit! In 1926, the first regional guide to France was published, devoted to the principal sites of Brittany, and before long each region of France had its own Green Guide. The collection was later extended to more far-flung destinations, including New York in 1968 and Taiwan in 2011.

In the 21st century, with the growth of digital technology, the challenge for Michelin maps and guides is to continue to develop alongside the company's tire activities. Now, as before, Michelin is committed to improving the mobility of travelers.

MICHELIN TODAY

WORLD NUMBER ONE TIRE MANUFACTURER
- 70 production sites in 18 countries
- 111,000 employees from all cultures and on every continent
- 6,000 people employed in research and development

Moving
for a world

Moving forward means
developing tires with better
road grip and shorter braking
distances, whatever the state
of the road.

CORRECT TIRE PRESSURE

RIGHT PRESSURE

• Safety

• Longevity

• Optimum fuel consumption

-0,5 bar

• Durability reduced by 20% (- 8,000 km)

-1 bar

• Risk of blowouts

• Increased fuel consumption

• Longer braking distances on wet surfaces

forward together
where mobility is safer

It also involves helping motorists take care of their safety and their tires. To do so, Michelin organises "Fill Up With Air" campaigns all over the world to remind us that correct tire pressure is vital.

WEAR

DETECTING TIRE WEAR

The legal minimum depth of tire tread is 1.6mm. Tire manufacturers equip their tires with tread wear indicators, which are small blocks of rubber moulded into the base of the main grooves at a depth of 1.6mm.

Tires are the only point of contact between the vehicle and road.

The photo below shows the actual contact zone.

NEW TIRE

WORN TIRE
(1,6 mm tread)

If the tread depth is less than 1.6mm, tires are considered to be worn and dangerous on wet surfaces.

Moving forward
means sustainable mobility

INNOVATION AND THE ENVIRONMENT

By 2050, Michelin aims to cut the quantity of raw materials used in its tire manufacturing process by half and to have developed renewable energy in its facilities. The design of MICHELIN tires has already saved billions of litres of fuel and, by extension, billions of tons of CO2.

Similarly, Michelin prints its maps and guides on paper produced from sustainably managed forests and is diversifying its publishing media by offering digital solutions to make traveling easier, more fuel efficient and more enjoyable!

The group's whole-hearted commitment to eco-design on a daily basis is demonstrated by ISO 14001 certification.

Like you, Michelin is committed to preserving our planet.

Chat with Bibendum

Go to
www.michelin.com/corporate/en
Find out more about
Michelin's history and the
latest news.

QUIZ

Michelin develops tires for all types of vehicles.
See if you can match the right tire with the right vehicle…